THE MIDDLE ENGLISH BIBLE

The Book of Judges

THE HOLY SCOTTISH BIBLE

The Book of Judges

THE MIDDLE ENGLISH BIBLE

The Book of Judges

BY

CONRAD LINDBERG

NORWEGIAN UNIVERSITY PRESS

Norwegian University Press (Universitetsforlaget AS), 0608 Oslo 6
Distributed world-wide excluding Scandinavia by
Oxford University Press, Walton Street, Oxford OX2 6DP

London   New York   Toronto
Delhi   Bombay   Calcutta   Madras   Karachi
Kuala Lumpur   Singapore   Hong Kong   Tokyo
Nairobi   Dar es Salaam   Cape Town
Melbourne   Auckland

and associated companies in

Beirut   Berlin   Ibadan   Mexico City   Nicosia

This book is published with a grant from the Norwegian Research Council for Science
and the Humanities

British Library Cataloguing in Publication Data
The Middle English Bible.
   Vol. 3: The book of Judges
   1. Bible — Critical studies
   I. Lindberg, Conrad, 1934- II. Bible. O. T. Judges.
   English (Middle English), 1989
   220.6

ISBN 82-00-02811-9

Printed in the German Democratic Republic
by Druckhaus Köthen

Preface

This is the third and last of my Norwegian re-editions of books of the Middle English Bible. The previous volumes of the trilogy were the *Prefatory Epistles of St. Jerome* (Oslo 1978) and the *Book of Baruch* (Oslo 1985). Together they form a construction of the crucial part of this translation of the Bible: the beginning, a middle section, and the end of the first part of the Early Version (called EV I) with the corresponding portions of the Later Version and the Latin Vulgate text for comparison. More work on the complete material of Bible MSS can be done, but I must leave it to other researchers. The picture emerging from my three volumes will, I hope, be clear enough for a proper understanding of the making of these versions. I wish to express my thanks to the British Library and Corpus Christi College Oxford for permission to use their manuscripts for the texts, and to my colleagues at Trondheim for facilitating my work in every possible way.

Linköping 1987

Conrad Lindberg

Table of Contents

I. Introduction

Like the previous volume in this trilogy, the Book of Baruch, the Book of Judges was chosen for re-editing for special reasons. In the first part of the Early Version (EV I) it forms a much more substantial part of the Bible text than either the Prefatory Epistles of St. Jerome or the Book of Baruch, which give perhaps one per cent each of the entire text; together the three books represent about five per cent of the Bible. Apart from this numerical consideration, the Book of Judges is remarkable for the break at 7.13 in the earliest manuscript, MS Bodley 959 (*E*), where the writing and idiom suddenly changes from Western to Eastern. I wanted to find out whether this change is reflected in other MSS of the Early Version and possibly in the Later Version.

In the course of my work on Judges I tried to reconstruct the work of the translators with the help of the Latin source and the two Middle English versions. This attempt resulted in an article, 'Reconstructing the Lollard Versions of the Bible' accepted for publication in Neuphilologische Mitteilungen. The material is here utilised and expanded in section 5 of this introduction, The translational evidence.

1. The Manuscripts

There are thirty-three manuscripts extant containing the Book of Judges in this Middle English Bible, nine in the earlier version, twenty-four in the later. They are, in the order of Forshall & Madden's and my own lists, the following:

(London MSS)

A	6	B. M. Royal I. C. VIII (text MS of LV)
B	7	B. M. Royal I. C. IX
C	9	B. M. Cotton Claudius E. II
Ha	17	B. M. Harley 2249 (in FM called b)
D	27	B. M. Lansdowne 454
E	29	B. M. Arundel 104
F	42	Sion College ARC L 40.2/E.1
U	46	Archiepiscopal Libr. Lambeth 25; (also called D)

(Oxford MSS)

I	60	Bodl. 277
L	61	Bodl. 296
E	65	Bodl. 959
K	71	Bodl. Fairfax 2; (also called I)
C	87	Bodl. Douce 369 (1st part), def. 1.21—4.4; (2nd part K)
B	88	Bodl. Douce 370
X	91	Christ Church 145
A	94	Corpus Christi College 4 (text MS of EV)
G	96	Lincoln College Latin 119
O	97	New College 66
M	101	Queen's College 388
N	103	St. John's College 7

(Cambridge MSS)

R	106	Univ. Libr. Dd. 1. 27
Q	112	Univ. Libr. Mm. 2. 15
S	116	Corpus Christi College 147
P	118	Emmanuel College 21
Ma	123	Magdalene College 1603 (in FM called d)

2. The Versions

In the list of MSS above the letters assigned to them by Forshall & Madden and myself are of two types: *A* etc. for MSS in the Early Version, A etc. for MSS in the Later Version. These two versions were established by Forshall and Madden in 1850 and all the MSS attributed to one version or the other. Some MSS were found by them to be partly in EV and partly in LV. This fact explains the use of different types for MS Lambeth 25 (called U and *D*). As for alleged 'intermediate' versions we shall discuss these in section 6 of this introduction.

The MSS of the Early Version are the following:

A	(94)	Corpus Christi College 4 Oxford (ONT in EV)
B	(88)	Bodl. Douce 370 Oxford (Gen.-II Par. in EV)
C	(87)	Bodl. Douce 369 Oxford (1st part: Num.-Bar. in EV)
E	(65)	Bodl. 959 Oxford (Gen.-Bar. in EV)
F	(150)	Trinity College Dublin A.I.9 (Gen.-Job in EV)
H	(155)	Cambr. Univ. Libr. Addnl 6681 (OT in EV)
Lo	(178)	Longleat 3 (ONT in EV)
Wo	(153)	Ducal Libr. Wolfenbüttel Aug.A.2 (ONT in EV)
X	(91)	Christ Church E.4 (now 145) Oxford (ONT in EV)

The MSS of the Later Version are the following:

A	(6)	B. M. Royal I.C.VIII London (ONT in LV)
Ac	(154)	earlier Acland, now Scheide 12, Princeton (ONT in LV)
B	(7)	B. M. Royal I.C.IX London (Gen.-Job in LV)
C	(9)	B. M. Cotton Claudius E.II (ONT in ELV)
Ca	(191)	Univ. Libr. Addnl 6680 Cambridge (ONT in LV
D	(27)	B. M. Lansdowne 454 London (Gen.-Ps. in LV)
E	(29)	B. M. Arundel 104 London (ONT in LV)
F	(42)	Sion College London ARC L 40.2/E.1 (OT in LV)
G	(96)	Lincoln College Oxford Latin 119 (ONT in LV)
Ha	(17)	B. M. Harley 2249 London (Jos.-Ps. in LV)
I	(60)	Bodl. 277 Oxford (ONT in ELV)
K	(71)	Bodl. Fairfax 2 Oxford (ONT in ELV)
L	(61)	Bodl. 296 Oxford (Gen.-Ps. in LV)
Ma	(123)	Magdalene College (Pepys) 1603 Cambridge (Gen.-Ruth in LV)
M	(101)	Queen's College Oxford 388 (ONT in LV)

N	(103)	St. John's College 7 Oxford (OT-exc. Ps.- in LV)
O	(97)	New College 66 Oxford (Gen.-Ps. in ELV)
P	(118)	Emmanuel College 21 Cambridge (ONT in LV)
Q	(112)	U.L. Cambridge Mm.2.15 (ONT in LV)
R	(106)	U.L. Cambridge Dd.1.27 (ONT in ELV)
S	(116)	Corpus Christi College Cambr. 147 (ONT in LV)
U	(46)	Archiepiscopal Libr. Lambeth 25 (ONT in ELV)
W	(144)	City Libr. Norwich Ih 20 (Gen.-Pr. in LV)
X	(137)	Hereford Cathedral Libr. O.VII.1 (ONT in LV)

3. The Latin Original

When this translation of the Bible was started, or even before it was started, a Latin text of the Vulgate version had to be established which was accurate enough to serve as original. This appears from the prologue to copies of the Later Version, where the author complains of the state of Latin bibles current at the time. But even after establishing a 'true' Latin text to work from, various or variant readings must have been considered, as is seen from variations between the two versions and within the versions themselves. On the whole, however, these deviations from a common norm (the best Vulgate text) are not considerable, and with the help of parentheses (slanting strokes) some of these have been incorporated in the Latin text appended here. Again I have used the Heyse-Tischendorf text as base with modifications from the Vatican edition.

The guiding principle for selecting Latin variants to be incorporated here was to harmonize the versions and the Vulgate Latin as far as technically possible. One branch of the Vulgate MSS, the Omega in the Vatican edition, more particularly the Ω^s, proved to be the clue for many variant readings in WB.

A check against an ordinary Vulgate edition (Biblia Sacra juxta Vulgatam Clementinam, Desclée & Co., Paris, 1956) showed an over-all agreement between the two texts, exceptions made for punctuation and spelling.

4. The linguistic evidence

In this section, the forms and spellings used in the thirty-three MSS will be listed and briefly commented on, as in my previous volumes, to form a basis for localization and dating of the MSS. The arrangement follows the manuals of Jordan and Brunner.

OE *a*

In stressed positions it is written *a*, e.g. *asse* EV & LV. A special case is EV *nouel* 'navel' (OE nafela), where the vowel is influenced by the following sound (Jordan § 29, Anm. 1: EM).

In unstressed positions it is written *e* as in *asse* above, or in *tyme* EV & LV. Besides *name* EV & LV there is Ø (zero) ending in *nam* E.

ON gata shows lengthening in *gaat A* besides *gate cet.* (exc. *H*: weye).

OE *å*

This symbol is used for OE a/o in front of a nasal. It is written *a* in most cases except before lenghtening groups (mb, nd etc.). Examples are *answere* EV & LV (also *onswer/-/* BE), *man* EV & LV, *many* EV & LV (also *moni* L); (ON) *same* EV & LV, but *naame* P beside *name* EV & LV in open syllables.

In front of mb there is *o* or *oo* in *co/o/mbe* EV (also *comb CEX*) and *co/o/mb* LV (also *combe* DIR) and in *wo/o/mbe* EV & LV (also *wom/b/* E). In front of nd we find *o* or *oo* in (ON) *bo/o/nd* EV & LV (also *bo/o/nde BHLoWo* & EIR), *bro/o/ndis* etc., *ho/o/nd* or *ho/o/nde* EV & LV beside *a* in *hand/e/ CEFLo* & KLMaP (in compounds also *AX* & AHaS), *lo/o/nd* & *londe* EV & LV (*loonde F*) beside *a* in *hand* E, and in *strond/e* LV. In front of ng there is *o* in *among/e* EV & LV, *long/e* EV & LV (also *loong A*), *song/e* EV & LV, *strong/e* EV & LV (also *stroong/e A* & *stroong* S), *wonge* EV beside *woong A* & I and *wang/e* EV & LV (in compounds).

In unstressed positions it is *a* or *o* in *an* (*on* E) *hiʒ* A, *anon* etc. EV & LV beside *onon* E; in a final syllable it is *e* as in *byhynden* FHaO.

OE *æ*

It is normally written *a*, e.g. *glad* EV & LV. From lengthening in open syllables (pl. *glade* C) there is *aa* in *glaad* O, and conversely pl. *gladde*

K beside sg. *glade* Lo; the adverb is *glaadly A* & S beside normal *gladly* EV & LV (*gladdly* O). Other irregularities can be variously explained: *gres X* is N (Jordan § 32, Anm. 3) from ON influence (EV *gras/se*), *heruest/e* LV (OE hærfest) is from the mutated form, and so is *steppis* EV & LV (beside *stappis* EV).

OE *e*

It is normally written *e*, e.g. *helle* EV & LV & *hell BF* (*hil X* is mixed with 'hill' with OE y); *weest* Ha beside *west* EV & LV (also *weste Lo*) may be influenced by 'east'. Other cases of lengthening occur in open syllables such as *me/e/te* EV & LV (also *meet A* and *mede?* Ha) and *spe/e/re* LV & *spere* EV (also *speer A* beside *sper E* & NX), and in front of lengthening groups in *e/e/nde* EV & LV (also *eend A* & R beside *end* E) and *feeld* EV & LV (also *fe/e/lde* EV & *felde* EHaR beside *feld CX* & HaSU; *fild E* & U has *i* from OE).

Unaccented it is *e* or *i/y* in initial syllables as in *bifor/e* LV & EV and *befor/e* EV, *besides* LV and *bisidis* EV & LV. In final syllables there is variation of *e*, *i/y*, and *u*, as in *anentis* EV & I, *anuntys E* (with unexplained *-u-*), *anentes B*, *anentus C* (also *anent X*); examples with final *d*: see verbs; with final *l*: *mydil* EV (*myddil* IMa), *mydel Lo* (*myddel CEWoX*), *myddul E*; with final *r*: *fader* EV & LV, *fadir* LV & EV, *fadur* E (also *fadre BF LoWo*); *fynger* EV & FKRU, *fyngir* LV (*fyngyr E*), *fyngur* LV (also *fyngre Lo* & I); and *vndur A* & LV, *vnder* EV & LV, *vndir A BEFHWo* & LV (also *vndre BLo*).

As for final *-e* it may be retained, dropped, or added. It is retained in e.g. *herte* EV & LV (beside *hert BFHWo* & E), retained or dropped in e.g. *neuer/e* EV & LV, dropped in e.g. *metship A* beside *meteschip/e cet.*, added in e.g. *efte LoWo* & BDEHaLR (beside *eft* EV & LV).

OE *i*

The vowel is spelt *i* or *y*, which are graphic variants only. Examples are *smith* EV & *smythe Lo*; for variation *i/y* in front of a nasal see strong verbs (endings). Besides *i/y* we find cases of *e*-spellings to be variously explained: *þeder E* & *þedir* PU (besides *þider* etc. EV & LV) from OE variant, *cherche* CaFLM beside *chirch Wo* (*chirche* EV & LV) from SE lowering, *kede E* & U from (perhaps) lengthening in the open syllable (besides *kide* etc. EV & LV). In front of lengthening groups there is *ij* in *chijld* K beside *child/e* EV & LV, *i* + *-e* in *þinge BFHLoWo* (*þing* EV & LV).

OE o

This vowel is normally written *o*, e.g. *lot/t* EV & LV (also *lotte Lo*); *Wo lote* & *loot* indicate lengthening from open syllables. Other cases of lengthening are: in front of lengthening groups in *boord CE* & LV (also *borde BFHLoWo* beside *bord* EV & LV), *woord CE* & P (beside *worde LoWo* & E and *word* EV & LV), probably in *corne EHaR* (beside *corn* LV), *golde Lo* (beside *gold* EV & LV), possibly in *forþe HLoX* & ER in view of *foorþ F* & DP (beside *forþ* EV & LV); in open syllables in e.g. *smook A* & AP (also *smo/o/ke* EV & LV beside *smok* E & N smeke *Lo*), *throot A* & *þrote cet.*

In unaccented syllables it is written *e*, *i/y*, or *u* (*o*); examples are *brother* & *broþir* EV & LV, *broþur* E, *hamer* EV & LV, *hamir* EPQ, & *hamor Lo*, *moder* & *modir* EV & LV, *modur* O beside *modre Lo*.

OE u

The spelling is mostly *u* or *o*, initially also *v-*, all graphic variants like *i/y*. Examples are *ful* EV & LV, *fol E*, *sunne* & *sonne* EV & LV (also *son* E), *vp* EV & LV beside *up Wo* & I and *op/p ELo*. Lengthening is indicated in e.g. *hoony* O beside *hony* EV & LV (in an open syllable); in front of lengthening groups in *houndis* etc. EV, *pound* & *pownde* EV, *wound/e* EV & LV, and in *tounge E* (beside *tonge/tunge* & *tong* E), *ȝoung/e* I (beside *ȝong/e* & *ȝung/e* EV & LV); *ou* in *bourȝ ABFH* or *bourgh/e BFHLo* is probably a French spelling.

Unaccented it is *a* in *apon BFHWo* (beside *up-* etc.), and *o/u* in the suffix (*litil*) *melom/e* EV, *-melum CX*.

OE y

The spellings reflect three developments: either unrounding (*i/y*-spelling), or unrounding with subsequent lowering (*e*-spelling), or again preservation of rounding (*u*-spelling). Examples of this variation are *hipe* EV & LV (also *hipp/e* & *hip E*), *hepe E* & U, *hupe E*; variation *i/y-e* is seen in e.g. *yuel* EV & LV, *euel CWoX* & *euel ELPQ* (also *euyl/e E* & *EFGLPQ*), *left* EV & LV, *lift* EV & LV, *myrye* EV (*myre Lo*) & *merie X*; variation *i/y-u* is seen in e.g. *hil* EV & LV (also *hill/e* EV & LV), *hul E* & E (E also *hulle*), *mych/e* EV & LV, *much/e* EL & *moche ELo* CaEFNUX, *sich/e* EV & LV, *such/e* CELoX & LV.

OE $\bar{a}$

This long vowel is mostly written *o* or *oo*, with or without a final *-e*. Examples are *bo/o/n* EV & LV, also *bone Lo* & G, *boone Lo*, *sto/o/n* EV & LV beside *sto/o/ne BFHLoWo* & EHa. Besides *o* or *oo* we find *oe* in *X anoen*, *coepe*, *loef*, *oi* in *loif E* and in *cloiþ* & *wroiþ* K; *a* occurs in *spatil Lo* (besides *spotel* & *spotle* etc. EV & LV), probably short.

In compounds there is *o* in *lijflod/e* EV & LV (also *-loode* X), *o* or *e* in *childhod/e* EV & *childhed CX*, *princehod/e* etc. EV & LV and *princehed* X, from OE variants.

OE $\bar{æ}^1$

The long mutated $\bar{æ}$ is spelt *e* or *ee* in e.g. *de/e/l* LV, *see* EV & LV beside *se CX*, *vnclene* EV & *vncle/e/ne* LV, *whete* EV & *whe/e/te* LV. From shortening there is *a* in *lasse* EV & CaEK beside *lesse LoX* & LV, *ladde* K & *ladden* EV etc., *spradden IK* & *sprad HaKO*, beside *e*-forms EV & LV; there is variation *a-e-o* from OE variants in *any CEX* & KLPUX, *eny* EV & EHaL, *ony E* & LV.

OE $\bar{æ}^2$

The continuation of Germanic $\bar{æ}$ is normally *e* or *ee* in e.g. *deed A* & R beside *de/e/de* EV & LV, *drede* EV & LV beside *dreede FH* & BG and *dreed B* (*e* also in pt.sg. *dredde* EV & LV etc.). In *ridels Wo* (beside *redels* etc. EV) the *i* is from shortening of Anglian $\bar{e}$. For *there* EV & LV, *þeire Lo* is doubtful and *þare E* from OE variant.

OE $\bar{e}$

This is either the unrounding of OE $\bar{æ}$ or the continuation of Germanic $\bar{e}$. Examples of the regular *e* or *ee*-spelling are: *demyde* EV & LV or *deemede* LV (*dymyde* O looks like an early sign of the vowel-shift), *swete* EV (shortened in *swettnesse BFH* etc. beside *sweetnesse* K), *we/e/ry* LV (*wirinesse* E is ambiguous); *me/e/de* EV & LV beside *meed A* etc.

OE $\bar{i}$

The long vowel is spelt *i/y* or *ij/iy* in e.g. *lijf* or *lyf* EV & LV beside *life ELo* & E, and *wyn/e* EV & LV beside *wijn* & *wiyn* LV. Cases of shortening are the *e*-spelling in prep. *be E* & RS beside *bi* (or *by*) EV & LV, and the plural *wymmen* EV & LV (also *wymen C*) beside *wommen BDGQ* from rounding as in sg. *womman* EV & LV (also *woman ALo* & EHaP) beside *wumman CaFMW*.

OE $\bar{o}$

The spelling is regularly *o* or *oo*, e.g. *blod* EV & U and *blood* LV beside *blode* BFHLoWo & ER, *doom* EV & LV & *dom* CX & AU beside *dome* BFHLoWo & EHaR (as suffix it is *-dam* in *kingdam CEX* beside *-dom/e* cet.), *flood A* & *flod CX* beside *flode BFHLoWo*, *roof* EV & LV beside *rof* U and *roofe BFHLo*.

OE $\bar{u}$

The spelling is regularly *ou* or *ow*, which are graphic variants only. Examples are *down* EV & *doun* LV (also *a/-doune* E), *mouth* EV & LV beside *mouþe* EU or *mowþe BLoWo*. The letter *ȝ* is added to the digraph in *H*, e.g. *abouȝte* (also LU), *ouȝt/e* (also *Lo*); *u* alone is used in *suþ* S (beside *south* EV & LV & *southe LoWo* & D). When shortened it is *u* or *o* in *but* EV & LV and *bot* BFH & E, also *bute F, bote E* & *butt X* (*b'* D is ambiguous).

OE $\bar{y}$

As with the short OE *y*, there is a three-fold variation in the spelling of the continuation of the long OE $\bar{y}$ as exemplified in pt. sg. *hiride* etc. EV & LV, *herede E* & *heride G*, ptc. *huyred Wo*. Similar variation occurs in *fier* EV & LV beside *fijr CE* & CaIMWX, *fire ABHLo* & DEILP (also *fyr X* & EFLP) and *fuyr/e ELoWo*.

OE *ea*

This OE diphthong has various origins; it arose from front or back mutation or breaking; after a palatal it is *a* in *schar* LV (also *schare* BN & *schaar* Ca) and *ȝate* EV & LV (also *ȝat* N); in front of an *r* + cons. also *a* in *swarm* EV, *toward* I, and *warp* EV (also *warpe Lo*); in front of an *l* + *d* (a lengthening group) it is mostly *o* or *oo* (from Anglian *a*) in e.g. *bo/o/ldly* etc. LV, *housho/o/ld* LV (also *-holde* CE), and *o/old* & *olde* EV & LV beside *e* or *ee* (from West Saxon *ea*) in *e/eld* or *e/elde* LV.

OE *eo*

Like OE *ea*, this diphthong arose out of breaking or mutations; it is mostly *e* or *ee* in front of *r* + cons. as in *hert/e* EV & LV, *lern/e* EV & LV (also *leerne FWo*), *sterris* etc. EV & LV, *swerd/e* EV & LV (also *sweerd E* & DFLPR), *ee* also in *eerþe* CaIRS (beside *erþ/e*); when mutated it is *e* in *bynethe* etc. EV & LV (also *-neeþe* R), *senewy* EV & *senewis* etc. LV (*sin-/syn-* DELMaNP from OE) and *o* after palatal ʒ *in biʒonde* etc. EV & LV (also *-ʒunde CX* & *-ʒounde* S) beside *-ʒende* etc. *E* & AEFRU, and *ʒok* EV & LV (also *ʒock/e Lo* & R).

OE *ie*

This is either West Saxon mutation of *ea* or palatal influence on *e*. The spellings are *e* and *ee*. Examples: *e/elde* LV (also *eeld* HaR), imp. *he/e/lde* EV beside *he/e/ld* (also *hellid A*), *sche/e/ld* LV (also *scheelde* C; *i* occurs in *schiltrun A* & *shiltron A* beside *s/c/hel-*etc.), *ʒerde* EV & LV beside *ʒeerd/e A* & R (also *ʒerd E* & HaN and *ʒarde* K).

OE *ēa*

Whether an original diphthong or developed from palatal influence, it is spelt *e* or *ee*. Examples are: *breed* EV & LV, also *bre/e/de* EV & *bred CEX* & EHaIL, *deeth* EV & LV beside *deþ* EV & LV & *deþe* E, *eere* EV & LV beside *eer* AI & *ere* EV & LV (*er BCEX*), *e/est* EV & LV beside *este A* & BF, *hepe* EV & E and *heep* LV & *EF* (also *hep CX*), *le/e/p* or *le/e/pe* EV, *reed* or *rede* EV & LV (*reede* GKQ), *streem* or *strem/e/* EV; (after palatals) *cheek/e* or *chek/e* EV & LV, pt. *s/c/hedde* EV & LV (*shadde* C with *a* from shortening beside *sched* D), *ʒeer* EV & LV beside *ʒer/e* & *ʒeere* HLo. Occasional spellings are *ea* in pl. *cleas A* beside *cle/e/s CELoX* and *dead BCEX* & GQ beside *deed* etc., *ei* in *heid X* beside *heed* etc.

OE *ēo*

This long diphthong is spelt *e* or *ee* in e.g. *kne/e* EV, *freend* EV & LV *ffreende BF*) beside *frend/e*, *pre/e/st* EV & LV & *preste* E, *tre/e* EV & LV, (*re/e* EV & LV. The spelling *eu* in *fleus* 'fleece' K indicates rounding from OE flēos beside *flees/e* & *fles/e* EV & LV; for *uy* in *fluys E* see OE *īe* below.

OE *īe*

Like the short *ie*-diphthong, this is either the West Saxon mutation, in this case of *ēa*, or palatal influence on *ē*. In the former case the spelling is *e* or *ee*, e.g. *ne/e/de* EV & LV (also *ned-* LPSU), *þeefte* O beside *þeft/e* LV (possibly shortened). In *fluys E* beside *flees/e* etc. (cf. OE *ēo* above) there is an indication of SW rounding, as in *fleus* K from OE flēos. In the latter case we find *i* in *ʒit/t* EV & LV beside *e* in *ʒet* E and *u* in *ʒut* E.

OF *a*

The normal spelling is *a* or, to mark length, *aa*, e.g. *char/e* or *chaar/e* EV & LV, *gra/a/pe* EV, *pla/a/ce* LV, *staat* or *state* EV & LV; the prefix is *par-* or *per-* in e.g. *perfit* A & *parfit* F. In front of a nasal there is *a* or *au* in e.g. *a/u/ngel* EV & LV, *la/u/mp-* EV & LV, *serua/u/nt* EV & LV.

OF *e*

The normal spelling is *e* or, to mark length, *ee*, e.g. *beest/e* EV (also *best* Wo), *feest/e* or *feste* EV & LV, *feble* EV & LV (also *feeble* GX), *tent/e* EV & LV, *terme* EV & *teerme* LV. Differing accent may be reflected by *ee-e*(-Ø) in e.g. *auter* EV & LV beside *auteer* E & GQ, *autere* Lo and *autre* B, *deseert* EV & LV beside *desert/e* (also *deseerte* R).

In unaccented positions it is either *e* or Ø, e.g. *generacio/u/n* EV & LV and *gneracioun* Lo, *experiens* A & *experience* EX, *flawme* EV & LV beside *flawm* A, *maner/e* EV & LV; *ei* in *graueil* E & X (beside *grauel* etc.) may be an inverted spelling after *counse/i/l* etc. As for OF *-é* it is *e* or *ee* in e.g. *cite/e* EV & LV, *entre/e* EV. Like other cases of ME *-e* it may be added as in e.g. *panyere* A beside *panyer* LV, *squyer/e* etc.

OF *i*

The spelling is *i/y* or, to mark length, *ij/iy*, e.g. *prince* or *prynce* EV & LV, *stri/j/f* EV & LV beside *stryf/e* EV, *v/i/yn* or *vyne* EV (also *vyn* A). Variation with *e* in an open syllable occurs in *dyte* A and *detee* E & *deete* Lo, *presoun* PQSU beside *prisoun* etc., *preue/i/* etc. beside *pryue/i/* etc. EV & LV, *sperit* X beside *spirit* etc.

In unaccented syllables it is *i/y* or *e* in e.g. *peryl/e* EV & EHaU and *perel/e* E & LV (for *pereyl* GQ compare *graueil* under OF *e* above). A secondary accent may perhaps be indicated by the spelling *iʒ* in *profiʒte* H and *spiriʒt/e* H & L (compare *fugitijf* LV).

OF *o*

The spelling is *o* or, to mark length, *oo*, e.g. *bro/o/ch-* EV & LV, *co/o/st* EV & LV (also *cost/e* E & *cooste* Lo & X) beside occasional *oe* in *coest* X and *oi* in *coist* E, *coot* or *co/o/te* EV & I (also *coete* X), *foly/e* EV & LV beside *fooly* B; *perso/o/ne* EV & LV, and *-io/u/n* passim, may represent secondary stress, compare OF *u* below.

OF *u*

The spelling is either the digraph *ou* (*ow*) or simple *u* (*o*). Examples are *dowble* EV & *double* LV and *dubble* E, *do/w/tous* EV (also *dotouȝs H*), *dou/ȝ/teful* LV, *frount/e* (also *front* DO) EV & LV, *iourney* beside *iurney* & *iorney* LV, *mount/e* EV, *noumbre* EV & LV beside *numbre* E, *sotil* & *sutel* I. The stress may vary in e.g. *lioun* EV & LV (*leoun CX*) and *lion* EK (also *lione* E).

OF *ü*

The spelling is *u* (*o*) or, to mark length, *uy*, also *ew* (*eu*). Examples are *du/y/k* EV & LV, also *du/y/ke* and *duik* A, *du/w/e* LV beside *deu* E & *dewe* I, *studie* and *stodye* EV & LV (*stody F*). Unaccented it is variously spelt, e.g. *armer/i/s* LV beside *armuris* Ma.

OF *ie*

This OF diphthong was reduced to an AN monophthong, in ME spelt *e* or *ee*, e.g. *cheef* I, *che/e/re* EV & LV beside *cher/e* LV, *fe/e/rs* & *fers/e* EV & LV; with or without stress in *pile/e/r* and *sole/e/r* EV & LV (also *solere Lo* & E); *e* alone in *ryuer* LV, *e* or *i* in *relef BEFX* & *relif/e cet*.

OF *ue*

This is represented by *u* in *puple* EV & LV but also (unrounded) by *e* in *peple BEFHLoWo* & LV MSS. From alternating stress in OF there is *co/o/uer-* EV but *keuer-* E, *meue* EV beside *moue CX* (also *moeue E*), also *mooued* SX, *preue* EV & LV beside *proue* C.

OF *ai*

This is either a monophthong in ME (in front of dentals) as shown by *e* or *ee* in *pees* or *pes/e* EV & LV, or kept as a diphthong spelt *ai/ay* or *ei/ey* as in *sai/say* or *sei* LV, in unaccented syllables also spelt *a, e,* or *i/y* as in *batal* N, *batel* AEI (*batele* K), *batil* E, beside *batail/bateil* etc. (also *batle* K).

OF *ei*

This is mostly spelt *ei/ey*, less often *ai/ay*, as in *h/eyre* or *h/eir* EV & LV, *prey* or *pray/e* EV & LV (also *prey/ʒ/e* or *pray/ʒ/e* BEFHW*o*) whereas *pry* D is an exceptional spelling perhaps related to the vowelshift. In unaccented syllables there is also *e* as in *counsel* A beside *counseil* etc., and in -eie from -ée as in *cuntre/i* etc. LV and *monee* beside *money* EV.

OF *oi* & *ui*

The spellings are *oi* (*oy*) and *ui* (*uy*). Examples: *soile* & *soyle* EV & LV; *spoil-* & *spuyl-* EV & LV (also *spul-* E); *distruye* & *distroie* EV & LV (also *destroʒe* CX & *destrue* E) besides *destrie* LV & H; *fruytis* EV & LV (also *fruyʒtis* KMa), *froites* E, & *frutis* etc. CX & LP; *pursu/w/e* EV & LV etc.; besides *buyschel* A (also *buyʒscheel* K) & *boischel* N there is *buschel* EV & LV.

OF *au* etc.

Examples of OF u-diphthongs are: *cause* EV & LV, *defau/ʒ/ten* EV; *rewme* LV; *vow/e* EV & LV, also *vouʒ* IR.

OE *labials*

The bilabial *b* occurs written double after a short vowel in e.g. *webbis* EV & LV, but single in the consonant cluster in *websters* Lo.

The corresponding voiceless *p* is single when final in e.g. *cop* EV & LV beside *coppe* Lo*Wo* & I but double also in *copp* BFHW*o*.

The nasal bilabial *m* is single when final in e.g. *welsum* EV but double in *welsomme* Lo beside *welsome* Wo. *Fro*, beside *from* — both EV & LV —, is from ON.

The bilabial half-vowel *w* is normally written *w* (*u*) as in *s/c/hadewe* EV & LV beside *schadowe* (also *shadwe* ELOP), pl. *shadues* ELP. It forms diphthongs with preceding vowels, as in *soule* EV & LV, *rewthe* & *ruþe* LV, *trewþ/e* & *truþe* EV & LV. The voiceless variant, OE hw, is normally *wh* as in *what* EV & LV (also *wat* E) and *whelp/e* EV & LV beside *welp* OU.

The labiodental *f* (also = /v/) is spelt *f* or *ff* and, when voiced, *u* (*w*), e.g. *fyue* EV & LV (also *fyfe* K), *chaf/f* EV (also *chaffe* Lo), *of* EV & LV beside *off* BEFX; variation is seen in e.g. *aboue* EV & LV, *abowen* BFHW*o*, *a-boof* R; Ø occurs in *hed/i* CELo*X* beside *heued/i* A, assimilation in *unbilef/f/ul* LV beside *vnbileueful* etc.

The voiced dental *d* is written *d* or *dd* in e.g. *bed/de* EV & *bed* LV, *fod/d/re* etc. EV; beside *and* EV & LV it is omitted in *an/d/* E. Variation *d/þ* occurs in words like *hider* etc. EV & LV & *hiþer* etc. *BFX* & R; from ON influence in *forþ*- EV & *fo/o/rþ*- LV beside *fo/o/rd*-EV & LV. There is assimilation in *sheltron* etc. EV & LV from OE scieldtruma.

The voiceless dental *t* is written *t* or *tt* after a short vowel as in *fat/t* EV & LV (*fatte Lo*), *pot/t* EV & LV (*potte Lo*), *at* EV & LV (also *att E, atte Lo*). Simplification is seen in *out/t/aken* etc. LV.

The nasal dental *n* is single or double *n* in e.g. *den or denn/e* EV & LV, *syn* E & *synn* B beside *synne* EV & LV, *þan* & *þann/e* etc. EV & LV, *whan* & *whann/e* etc. EV & LV. Final *-n* is dropped or preserved in e.g. *kynrede* EV & LV and *kynreden Lo*, *wiþoute/n* etc. EV & LV. Assimilation (or omission) occurs in *myl/n/stoon H.*

The lateral *l* is written single or double in e.g. *al* & *all/e* EV & LV, *stil/le* EV & *styll* BF, *welle* EV & LV beside *well* BFH & *wel* D, *wil/le* EV & LV beside *wyll* BFH. It has disappeared in *ech/e* beside *vch/e* E & E (E also *ich*) from OE ælc etc.

The letter *r* occurs single and double in e.g. *fer* EV & LV, *ferr* CLoWoX, & *ferre* ABF (also *feer* GS), *war* EV & LV beside *warre* BF (also *ware* D). Metathesis has taken place in *þrist/e* EV & HaU & *threst A* beside *þirst* Wo & LV & *þurst* (= OE) DF, and in *thrillynge A* beside *thirllyng Lo*, *thirlende CX*, & *þurlynge E* (OE þyrlian etc.)

The sibilant *s* is *s* or *ss* in e.g. *gras* CE & *grasse A* etc. (*gres X*), always *asse* EV & LV, *los/s* LV (also *losse* I); the suffix -ness is *nes/se* EV & LV. Besides the interjection *whist A* etc. there is *whisht* in *CELoX.*

The interdental lisping sound *þ* is spelt *þ* or *th*, e.g. *broth* or *broþ* EV & LV, also *brothe Lo* & *broþe* E, *broþþe* (text *broththe*) *A*, beside *brooþ E* & AcMaR, *wraþ* or *wrath* beside *wraþþe E* & LV (also *wrathe LoX* & *wreþ BHWo*). For various reasons there is *t* instead of *th* (*þ*) in *droȝte CX* beside *drouȝth/e cet.* (dissimilation), *tou* E for *þou* after a dental (assimilation); simple *t*-spellings in E for *th* etc. are dubious, such as *wit* or *nort.* The dental is dropped in *wher/e* for *whether* etc. in *HLo* & LV (compare *or* & *oþer* etc. EV & LV), and in *worship* etc. EV & LV from OE weorþscipe etc.

OE *palatals*

OE palatal ȝ (=/j/) is written ȝ in e.g. *aȝen/s* etc. EV & LV (*agens* E from Scand. influence), *ȝ/if* EV & LV (also *ȝife LoWo*). It forms diph-

thongs with preceding vowels in e.g.: (with OE æ) *brayn/e* EV & LV
(also *breyn* BFHWo), *day* EV & LV, *fair/e* CELoWoX & LV beside
feyr A; (with OE e) *wey/e* EV & LV beside *way Lo* & *E* & *away* EHINO
and *aʒeyn/s* EV & LV beside *aʒen/s* above etc. (also *aʒa/i/ns* E); (with
OE *ǣ¹) either* etc. EV & LV beside *eþer* CD, and *key/e* EV & LV (also
keʒe X). It is dropped in *bodi* EV & LV.

OE palatal *h* (=/ç/) is spelt *ʒ* in e.g. *nyʒt/e* EV & LV (E also *niʒth* &
night), *riʒt* EV & LV (E also *ri/ʒ/th*), *siʒt/e* EV & LV (E also *shiʒt*);
weiʒt/e EV & LV is influenced by the verb, *wiʒt/e E* & BO = OE *wiht*.
It forms diphthongs with preceding vowels in e.g.: (with OE ēa etc.)
heiʒ- CaFMW beside *hiʒ-* LV, *ne/e/iʒ* CWo beside *nyʒ* EV & LV (I)
and *neeʒ CE* (*E* also *neegh*); (with OE ēo) *þeiʒ* CaFMW beside *thiʒ/h/*
LV (*þi/ʒ/e* EI); (with OE ïe etc.) *heiʒt/e* EV (*heghet Lo*).

OE palatal *g* (=/dʒ/) occurred in the groups *cg* & *ng*; the latter is
instanced in the text in the group *ngþ*: *leyngþ BF* beside *lengthe* EV & LV
(also *lenkþe* Ma) and *streyngþ BEF* beside *strength/e* EV & LV (also
strenkþ/e MaR).

OE palatal *c* (=/tʃ/) is normally spelt *ch*, e.g. *cheek* etc. EV & LV,
which etc. EV & LV (also *whic* E). Variation *ch/k* occurs in *dich/e* LV
(also *dijch* X) & *dijk* K, with *k* from ON, and *wrech- AB* beside *wrek-
cet*. The spelling is *cch* or *tch* in *wacch-* or *watch-* EV & LV (also *waiʒcch-*
K). It is dropped in ptc. *queynt/e* EV and in *barly* LV (also *barlei* K)
beside *barli/ch* EV.

OE palatal *sc* (=/ʃ/) is usually spelt *s/c/h*, e.g. in *s/c/hal* etc. Its palatal
nature is seen in *fleisch* EV & LV (also *fleiʒssh* K) beside *flesch/e* EV &
LV, and *thre/i/sch-* LV (also *þreiʒssh-* K & *þrisch-* C) beside *þresch-*
etc. EV.

OE *velars*

OE velar *c* (=/k/) is written *c* or *k*, doubled *ck* or *kk*. Examples are *bak*
EV & LV, *back* RU, & *backe* Lo, *chec* CE beside *che/e/k* etc. EV & LV,
kno/c/ke EV & LV (also *knoc* E), *lok* EV & LV beside *lock/e* (also *loke*
Lo); OE *cw-* is *qu* or *qw* as in *quyk* LV & *qwyke* R. An intrusive *c* occurs
in *sclepe Wo* beside *slepe* etc. EV & LV.

OE velar *g* (=/g/) is *g* or *gg* in e.g. (ON) *leg* EV & I, *legg* BFHLo,
legge Wo, pl. *doggis* & *dogges* LV (also *dogghis* E), *gesside* etc. LV (E
also *ghessid*). For the group *ng* see OE palatal *g* above.

OE velar *ʒ* (=/γ/) is regularly *w* in e.g. *morwe/n* EV & LV (also contracted *morn CX* & B). It forms diphthongs with preceding vowels in

e.g.: (with OE a) *lawe* EV; (with OE ā) *low/e* EV & LV beside *low3* LV (also *law* E).

OE velar *h* (=/χ/) is normally spelt *3*, with or without a u-glide after a preceding vowel, as in *sla/u/3ter* EV (also *slawtyr* E), *thou3* LV & *þau3* E; it is omitted in *douter* EL beside *dou3ter* EV & LV and *do3ter CX* + *do3tyr E*, from lack of stress in *not* EV & LV (also *nott X*) beside *no/u/3t Lo* & L, and *nat* I beside *nau3t* S. From variation with inflected forms there is *holwe* E (*holu* C) beside *holw3* EV (also *holow3/e HLoWo*) & *hol3* X, and *bo/o/w* LV (*bowe* D) beside *bo/o/w3* LV (*bouw3* W).

OE initial *h-* (=/h/) is retained or dropped in *hit EHWo* beside *it* EV & LV; an *h* is added in *his* O beside *is* (*ys*) EV & LV.

OF *labials*

OF *b* is single or double in e.g. *glob A* & *globb BFHWo* (also *globbe ELo* & *glubbe CX*), *stobil* EV & LV beside *stubbil* etc. LV.

OF *m* is single or double in e.g. *co/m/maundement* LV.

OF *p* is single or double in e.g. *ap/p/eride* etc. EV & LV. It is expressed or suppressed initially in *p/salm* or *psalme* EV, medially in *solem/p/nyte* LV and *ram/p/ne* LV.

OF *f* is single or double in e.g. *ef/f/ect* etc. EV. It varies with *v* (*u*) in e.g. *saaf* EV & LV (also *saufe Lo*) and *saue BFWo* & E. It is *v* only in *viol/e* EV & LV.

OF *v* is normally *u* (*v*) as in *enuyroun* EV (*A* also *in* + *viroun*), *plenteuous* etc. EV & LV. There is variation with *f* in *olyif* K beside *olyue* EV & LV, with *w* in *eschewide* LV beside *escheuede* ELP.

OF *dentals*

OF *d* varies with *þ* (*th*) in *sider* etc. *Wo* & LV and *siþer* etc. EV & LV.

OF *t* is single or double in e.g. *closet/t* LV, *gobet/t* LV. Final *-d* for *-t* occurs in *deserd* NSWX beside *desert* etc. EV & LV.

OF *n* is single or double in e.g. *pyn/n/aclis* EV. It varies with *m* in *co/u/nfort* & *comfort* etc. EV & LV. It is added in *messa/n/ger-* etc. EV & LV, dropped in *vendage* etc. EV & LV. The n "mouillé" is *gn* in *signe* LV (also *sing* E), *n/gn* in *enpu/n/gn-* LV, *yn* in *matrimoyne* E beside *matrimonye* LV.

OF *l* is single or double in e.g. *al/l/as* LV, *botel* EV & LV beside *botell BF* & *botele* K, *pomel* EV & LV beside *pomell BF*, *vesel/l* EV.

OF *r* is double in e.g. *werr/e* EV. Final (syllabic) *r* varies in combinations and positions, e.g. *lettre* EV & LV beside *letter Wo* & EHa and *lettir* D, *propre* EV & CMa beside *proper* X & EF and *propyr* E & *propir* LV, also *propur* HaL; *l* for *r* in *purpul* ELP beside *purpur* EV & LV and *purpre* CEX & W.

OF *s* is spelt *s* or *c*, also *ss* or *sc*, e.g. *grees* A & *grece cet.*, *silence* EV & LV beside *scilence* C & *s/c/ilens* D, *trespas* EV & LV (also *trispas* Lo & D) beside *trespasse* EV, *vois* EV & LV beside *voice* EV & LV. It is dropped (dissimilation?) in *scar/s/nesse* EV and *dise/se/ful* etc. LV. It varies with *s/c/h* in *angwish* etc. EV & LV and *angwis-* EK, *vanys/c/h-* etc. EV & LV and *uanis-* E.

OF *palatals*

OF palatal *g* or *j* (both $=$/dʒ/), e.g. *veniaunce* EV & LV and *vengeaunce* ELo & CGIKRU (also *vengheaunce* E), *iugis* EV & LV and *juges* LoX (also *iughes* E), *iow* or *jouwe* EV. When doubled it is *gg* or *dg* as in *ag/g/-reggid* EV beside *agredgyd* BF.

OF palatal *ch* ($=$/tʃ/) is *c/ch* or *tch*, e.g. *letcherie* LV & *lecherie* CaFLM *catchynge* EV & *cacchende* CX. Besides *charis* etc. LV there is *scharis* CQU (*sharris* N). For variation *ch/c*, see OF velar *c* below.

OF *velars*

OF velar *g* ($=$/g/) is single or double in *ag/g/reggid Lo* (EV & LV *agreggid*). There is variation *g/k* in *fige* (E *fike*) tree.

OF velar *c* ($=$/k/) is *c* or *cc* in e.g. *ac/c/ordyngli* LV, *c* or *k* in *couer-* EV & *keuer-* E, *duc* or *duk* CX beside *duke* etc. EV & LV. Variation *c* (*k*) & *ch* occurs in *ascape* etc. EV & LV and *aschape* BF, *caitiues* CWoX (*caytifes* Lo) and *chaytyues* EV (*chaytyfs* E), *camels* EV & LV beside *chamels* EV, also *kameylys* E & *kamelis* Lo.

OF initial *h-* ($=$/h/) is unstable in e.g. *h/eritage* LV, *h/oost* etc. EV & LV; hence inverted spellings like *abhomynable* LV beside *abomynable* A, and *haboundedyn* E beside *aboundiden* A etc.

Nouns

The inflexions are almost entirely confined to the genitive and plural endings, both mostly in *-s* with or without a preceding vowel. Examples: gen. sg. *mannes* I, *Goddis* LV (*goddes* F); Ø-ending occurs with 'family' names in *-r*: *fader* etc. EV & LV beside *fadris* etc. EV & LV, *modir* I (*modr?* X) beside *modris* etc. LV, *douȝter* LV beside *douȝters* etc. I;

gen. pl. *mennus* A & I, *mens* BH, *mennys* ELo, *mennes* F; with plurals in -s, this s serves for the gen. as well;

plurals in -s like *backis* EV & LV (*backes* EWoX & ER), *colours* A & LV (*colouris* C & A, *coloures* LoWoX & W), *frendus* CX (*fre/e/ndis* EV & LV, *frendes* LoWo & EFO), *names* EV & LV (*namys* BEFHWo & G);

plurals in -n are *asshen* A (*asken* BCFHWoX, *askyn* E beside *a/i/schis* etc. LV), *brither/e/n* EV & LV (also *bryþryn* E & *briþren* KG beside *breþ/e/ren* EV & LV and *breþern* CEX & EK, *breþerin* E; for *breþer/e* BFWo compare mutated plurals below), *children* EV & LV (also *childryn* E & *childrin* EP; for *childer* BCX & *childre* EHWo compare plurals in -r below), *douȝtren* BFHLoWo (also *dowȝtryn* E, beside *douȝtris* etc. EV & LV), *ey/ȝ/en* EV & *e/i/ȝen* LV (also *eȝyn* & *yȝyn* E), *oxen* LV & C (also *oxun* A & *oxyn* E, whereas *oxe* A is dubious);

plurals in -r are only *childer* BCX and *childre* EHWo beside *children* etc. EV & LV (above);

plurals in Ø are either mutated as *feet* EV & LV (also *fe/e/te* BLoWo & ER), *geet* EV & LV (also *get* CX & HaQ, *gete* DR, *gett* E, beside *geyt/e* BFHLoWo & *geytt* K, whereas *got* CX is dubious), *men* EV & LV (the weak form *me/n/* used as indef. pron. is from sg. &/or pl.), *wymmen* EV & LV (also *wymen* C beside *wommen* BDGQ); or they are OE long-stemmed neuters as *hors/e* EV, *hous* X & BEIKMaX (beside *housis* etc. EV & LV), *pound/e* EV, *scheep/e* or *shep/e* EV & LV, *ȝeer* etc. EV & LV (also *ȝeris* DI & *wynter* B).

Adjectives

The *positive* form appears uninflected or with a final -e after defining words and as a mark of the plural, e. g. *alien* EV & LV and *aliene* CEX & BCaEHaKMRW, *euene* LV & *euen* DEIR, *fe/e/le* & *fewe* EV, *other/e* etc. EV & LV (also *oþre* FPR).

The *comparative* form regularly adds -er etc. to the positive form as in *fairer* LV (also *fairere* EV & LV); irregular are comparatives from a different stem:

bet/t/er etc. EV & LV (also *bet/t/ir* F & DR), *lasse* EV & CaEK and *lesse* LoX & LV, *more* etc. EV & LV; and mutated forms: *elder/e* etc. EV & LV (also *eldur* E) & sb. pl. *eldren* A (*eldryn* E, *elderes* X), *lenger* & *leng/e/re* EV, *strenger/e* EV & LV besides *stronger/e* A & LV (E also *strong/h/ar*).

The *superlative* form regularly adds -est etc. to the positive form as in *fairest/e* LV (also *fairist/e* BDI & *fairste* X); irregular are superlatives from a different stem: *first/e* EV & LV, *last/e* EV & LV, *leest/e* & *lest/e* EV & LV, *mo/o/st* & *mo/o/ste* EV & LV, *worst/e* EV & LV (also *wurste* CaFMW beside *werst/e* BCEFHWoX & P and *wherst* E); and mutated forms: *strengest* IMa (also *strengeste* CaLWX and *strengist* IMa) beside *strongest* etc. EV & LV.

Adverbs

The *positive* form adds *-li/-ly* or *-lich/e* to the adjectival form, e.g. *bisily* EV & I and *bisilich* A (also *bysylyche* B & *bysileche* E), *gre/e/tli* etc. EV & LV and *gretlich/e* etc. ABEFHWo, *strongly* etc. EV & LV beside *stronglich/e* EV. OE adverbs in *-e* are reflected in e.g. *faire* AI, *faste* I (*fastly A*), *hiȝe* I.

The *comparative* form adds *-lier/e* or *-loker* (I) to the positive form of the adjective, as in *bisilier/e* LV & *bisiloker* I, *stronglier/e* LV (or periphrastic *more strongli* HaI); irregular is the addition of *-li/-ly* to the mutated comparative form of the adjective in EV *strengerly* etc.

The *superlative* form adds *-liest/e* to the positive form of the adjective: *strongliest/e* LV.

Numerals

Cardinal numbers: 1 *oon* etc. EV & LV (*oone* HLoWo, *one* HWo & E, *oen* CX, *on* Wo & ESUW, and *oo* EV & LV, *o* A & AIX) and weak (indef. art.) *a/n* EV & LV; 2 *two* EV & LV (also *to* L) and *tweyne* etc. EV & LV (*tweyn* EFLPU, *twene* N, *tweye* LV, *twei* EV & LV, *twie* Ca); 3 *þre/e* EV & LV; 4 *four/e* EV & LV; 5 *fyue* EV & LV (*fife* K); 6 *six/e* EV & LV and *sex/e* ABFLo & E; 7 *seuen/e* EV & LV (*seuenn* X, *sefne* EF, *seue* O); 8 *eiȝt/e* EV & LV (*eghte* E); 9 *nyn/e* EV & LV; 10 *ten* EV & LV (*tenn* BFH); 11 no inst.; 12 *twelue* EV & LV (*twelfe* K); 13—14 no inst.; 15 *fifteen* & *fyftene* EV, *fiftene* LV; 16—17 no inst.; 18 *eiȝtene* EV & LV (*eiȝtetene* CEX & N, *eiȝteene* F & N) and *eiȝteen* A (*eiȝten* I, *eyten* E); 19 no inst.; 20 *twenti* EV & LV; 30 *thretti* & *þritty* EV & LV (*thirty* E); 40 *fourti* EV & LV; 50 no inst.; 60 no inst.; 70 *seuenti* EV & LV (*seuynty* E); 80 *eiȝti* KM & *eiȝteti* NSX beside *foure score* etc. EV & LV; 90 no inst.; 100 *hundred* & *hundrid* etc. EV & LV (*hundret* E & E) and *hundreþ* & *hundriþ* BFLoWo & E; 1000 *þousand* etc. EV & LV (*þousant* B & N), *þousend* CEX & LV, *þousynd/e* LV, *þousont* E (also *þousount* & *þousondys*).

Ordinal numbers: 1st *first/e* EV & LV; 2nd *secounde* etc. EV & LV; 3rd *thridde* EV & LV (*þredde* E, *þirdde* E); 4th *ferthe* EV & E (*ferþ* BF) and *fourthe* LV; 5th—6th no inst.; 7th *seuenþ/e* EV & LV (*seueþe* BE, *seuent* E); 8th etc. no inst.

The numerical *adverbs* 'once' & 'twice' are *o/o/nes* & *o/o/nys* etc. EV & LV (*oons ABH* & I), and *twies* etc. EV & LV (*twei/e/s* FHaO, *twyse BF*).

Pronouns

Personal pronouns: sg.1 *I* or *Y* (*y*) EV & LV, obl. *me* EV & LV; sg.2 *thou* etc. EV & LV (*þu B*, and /—/*tou* etc. E after dentals), obl. *thee* & *þe* EV & LV; sg.3 masc. *he* EV & LV (*hee* S), obl. *him* & *hym* EV & LV (dubious are *hem A* & AcENMaR, *hum* X); fem. *s/c/he* EV & LV (also *schee E* & S, *ʒhe* S, *sho* E) and dubious *he* HaL, obl. *hir/e* EV & LV, *here ELo* & EF, *her* BCaEMUW, *hur* E; neutr. *it* EV & LV (*hit EHWo*); pl.1 *we* EV & LV (also *wee BCELoX*), obl. *vs* EV & LV; pl.2 *ʒe/e* EV & LV, obl. *ʒou* etc. EV & LV; pl.3 *thei* EV & LV (also *þai* E and *þe* HX & ACaE) and dubious *he* NOU, *tey* E after a dental, obl. *hem* EV & LV (dubious *him A* & AcCDELRUX) and *them* EI & *CEFLoX* (*þeym BF*).

Possessive pronouns: sg.1 *my* & *myn/e* EV & LV (*mijn* K); sg.2 *þi* & *þin/e* EV & LV (*þijn* K, dubious *þe BEFHLoWo* & OLX); sg.3 masc. *his/e* EV & LV (ES also *hijs* & E *is*); fem. *hir/e* EV & LV and *her* HLo & LV, *here* FGHaQ; neutr. = masc.; pl.1 *our/e* EV & LV; pl.2 *ʒour/e* EV & LV (*ʒore* S); pl.3 *her/e* EV & LV and *hir/e* ELOP beside *þeir BCEFWoX* & *þer BCELoX* + EK (*þere E* + *A*?).

Reflexive pronouns: sg.1 no inst.; sg.2 *thi self* (or *silf*) EV; sg.3 masc. *hym silf* (or *self*) EV, also *h. selue E* & *h. seluen Lo*; fem. no inst.; neutr. = masc.; pl.1 no inst.; pl.2 no inst.; pl.3 *hem self* (or *seluen*) EV beside *þem s. CEX*. — The various forms of 'self' are: *silf AWo* & LV (*sif* Ma), *self* EV & LV, *selue BEFHWo* & CaES, *seluen ACFHLoWoX*, *selfen B*, *seluyn E*.

Demonstrative pronouns: sg. *this* & *that* EV & LV; pl. *thes/e* (also *þeis BFWo*, *þise* EU, & *þis* E) and *tho* EV & LV (also *þoo ACELo* & IRX) beside *þos/e BFWo* (B also *þase*) and *þat BEFHLoWo*. The definite article *the* EV & LV (also *þee FLo* & X, *te* E after a dental, dubious *þi WoX* & L) varies with *þo* CEIMa; similarly *þo* varies with *þe AFLoWoX* & GHaQRS. Demonstrative is also *thilk/e* EV & LV (also *þulke E* & *tho* (*þoo* C, *þoe* E) *ilk/e* EV), which again varies with *þat X* & I & *þo CLoX*.

Interrogative pronouns: *who* EV & LV (E also *wo*), gen. *whos/e* EV & LV (also *whas AE*), obl. *whom* EV & LV (also *whome BFLoWo* & *wham/*

wam E); *what* EV & LV (E also *wat*); for *which* (no interrogative inst.) see below.

Relative pronouns: for *who* (no relative inst.) see above; gen. *whos/e* EV & LV (also *whois* E & K, *whoos* K, *wos/e* E); obl. *whom* EV & LV (EV also *whome* BFHLoWo, LV also *w/h/am* E & *wom* EHa; dubious are *whomee* B, *whomm* H, & *whon* H + L); /EV *the/* which & *whiche* LV (*þe wh.* also I) besides *wheche* E & *wich/e* CaEKLN & *H*; neutr. *what* EV & LV (also *wat* E); *that* EV & LV (also *at* E after a dental), varying with *which* etc. in *CX* & BGHaI.

Indefinite pronouns: sg. & pl. *al, all,* & *alle* EV & LV (adv. *al/le* EV); *a/n,* the indefinite article, reduced form of 'one', with which it varies in *CELo* & LV; *any CEX* & KULPX with variants *eny* & *ony* EV & LV, for which see OE $\bar{æ}^1$; *another* EV & LV (also *anoþir* LV, *an oþur* E, & *an oþere* Ac); *both A* & *boþe* EV & LV (also *booþ* R); *ech/e* EV & LV (E also *ich* & *vch/e*), no inst. of 'every'; *fe/e/le* & *fewe* EV; *many/e* EV & LV (also *moni* L); *me/n* LV 'one' /from/ sg. or pl.; *mych/e* EV & LV (also *moche ELo* & CaFNUX, *much* E, & *muche* L) and comp. *more* EV & LV (*mo/o* EV & LV is the adv.); *n/eiþer* LV (*either* EV) beside *noþer* EU; *n/oon* etc. EV & LV (also *n/oen* X) beside *n/o* etc. EV & LV; *no/u/ʒt* EV (also used as negation *Lo* = *not* EV & LV); *other/e* etc. EV & LV besides *toþer/e* etc. EV & LV after *the* (= *that*); *same* EV & LV; *sum/me* LV beside *som-E* & *somme LoWo* (EV also *sum-*); *sich/e* & *such/e* EV & LV (dubious is *shuc* E); *whether* etc. EV & LV (*wheþere Lo*) beside *wher/e HLo* & LV (conj.).

Verbs

The endings of the various tenses, numbers, persons, and moods are as follows:

Present singular 1st person indicative ends in *-e* or Ø, e.g. *biseche* etc. EV & LV (*bisiche* S) besides *bisech Wo* & EN; 2nd person ends in *-est* or *-ist,* also *-este* or *-iste,* and, less often, in *-es* or *-is,* e.g. *askist* & *askest* EV (*askis BFWo*) and *axist* & *axest* LV, *bryngist/e* & *bryngeste* LV (also *brinkst* S); 3rd person ends in *-eþ* or *-iþ* etc. EV & LV, less often in *-es* etc., e.g. *bigynneþ* & *biginniþ* ELV besides *bygynnes Lo* (*bigynneʒ* E), *stondiþ* etc. & *stont BFHWo, stant CEX;* plural (all persons) ends in *-en* or *-yn* etc. ELV, e.g. *dwellen* & *dwellyn,* also in *-e* as *kepe* X, besides a few instances of *-eþ/-iþ* as *comaundeþ Wo* and *-es/-is* as *sittes Lo.*

Subjunctive singular ends in *-e* or, less often, in Ø, e.g. *rest/e* EV & LV or *mak/e* ELV; the plural ends in *-e* or *-en/-yn* etc. ELV, e.g. *bere/n, delyuere/n.*

Imperative singular ends in -*e* or Ø, e.g. *dwel/l* EV or *dwelle* /*thou*/ EV & LV; the plural ends in -*eþ/-iþ* or -*e* /*ʒe*/ EV & LV, e.g. *blesseþ* etc. EV (also *blessis Lo*) & *blesse* /*ʒe*/ LV (also *bles* E).

Participle present ends in -*ing/e* etc. or, less often, in -*ende* etc., e.g. *criyng/e* EV & LV (*crienge* E) and *criende CX*, *seying/e* ELV & *seiende CX* besides *seyand/e* EV. (Compare the verbal noun in -*ing/e* with erroneous -*ende* in *CX* 2x).

Infinitive ends in -*e* predominantly or in -*en* etc. or again in Ø, e.g. *adde* EV & LV (*addyn E*), *answere* ELV (*onswer* B), *dwell/e* ELV & *dwellen* EV (*dwellyn E*).

Past forms of *weak* verbs (for *strong* verbs see below): 1st & 3rd persons singular end in -*ede/-ide* or -*ed/-id*, e.g. *appered/e* or *apperid/e* etc. EV & LV (also *apeerd B*), or in -*d/e* & -*t/e* as in *herd/e* & *brouʒt/e* etc. EV & LV; 2 person singular ends in -*edest/-edist* or -*idist/-idest*, e.g. *passedest* & *passedist* ELV or *passidist* & *passidest* ELV (also *passideste* B), or in -*dest/-test* etc. as in *sendest Lo* & *sentest* etc. LV & EV (R also *sentiste*); plural (all persons) ends in -*eden* or -*iden* with many variants, e.g. *answereden* & *answeriden* ELV beside *answerden* LV & A (*answerdyn E* & *answerdin* P), *answered* P & *answeridin* B; past participles end in -*id* or -*ed*, e.g. *s/c/hewid* or *shewed* EV & LV (also *schewide* HaR; final -*e* is frequent in ELV with or without inflectional value), with variants like the simple past.

Strong verbs

Class I: *abide* ELV — *abood* etc. ELV (*aboid* E) — *abiden* etc. ELV (*abedin* PU, *abo/o/den* I) beside *abideden* etc. LV; *ris-* etc. ELV — *roos* etc. ELV (*roes X*) — *risen* etc. ELV (*resin* EILP, *ros* E) beside *risiden* etc. LV (*reisiden* MaOSU?) — *risen* etc. ELV (also *rise* ELV & *rese* U); *smyte/n* ELV (*smyʒte* U) — *smoot* etc. ELV (*smoit* E) — *smyten* etc. ELV (*smite CLo*, *smetyn E* & EILPU, *smoten* I) beside *smytiden* etc. LV — *smyte/n* etc. ELV (*smetyn E* & ELP); *stryue* A — *stroue* A and *stro/o/f* EV (*stroif* E & *stroffe Lo*) beside *stryuede* etc. LV.

Class II: (*chesen*) — *chees* LV (*chese* E) — *chosen* etc. EV (*chose* C) — *chosen* etc. LV (*chose* ELP); *fle/e* ELV & *flee/ʒe/n* EV — *fleiʒ* & *fliʒ* EV (*fleeʒ Lo*) beside *flewe Lo* (*flewʒ H*) & *flow/e* BEFWo (*flowʒ A*) — *flowen* A (*floun CX* & *flowyn E*) beside *flewen Lo* — LV pt. *fledde/n* etc., no inst. of pt. ptc. ELV; *forbe/e/de* LV (C *forbed*) — *forbeed* etc. LV (*forbed* EGQ) — no inst. of pt. pl. or ptc.

Class III: *bigynne* etc. ELV — *bigan* etc. ELV — *bigunnen* etc. ELV beside *bigunne* etc. ELV (*bygunn* B) — *bigunnen* etc. ELV (also *bigunne*

ACX & CIN and *bygun* B); *bynden* etc. ELV — *bo/o/nd* etc. ELV beside
bound/e *ALo* & EHa — *bounden* etc. ELV (*bounde* X & *boonden* X) —
bounde/n etc. ELV (*bound* E, *boundon* E, & *bonden* Wo & Ha); *drynk/e*
ELV — *drank/e* ELV (*dronke* A) — *drunken* ELV etc. (*dranken* N) —
drunken etc. ELV; *fynd-* ELV — *fond/e* & *foond/e* ELV — *founden* etc.
ELV (also *fo/o/nden* ELV & *fonde* E) — *founden* etc. ELV (also *found/e*
ELV, *fonden* B & *funden* E); *fiʒten* etc. ELV — *fauʒt/e* ELV (*faʒt* CX &
fowʒt E) — *fouʒten* etc. ELV (*foʒten* CX & X, *fouten* E) and *fauʒten*
GHaIQ — *fouʒten* ELV (*fauʒtyn* E) & *fo/u/ʒte* EV; *help/e* LV — no
inst. of pt. sg. — *holpen* CX beside *helpeden* etc. LV — *holpe/n* LV beside
helpid A etc.; *ren/ne* LV (*rynn-* BF) — *ran* etc. ELV (*ron* E) — *runnen*
etc. ELV — *runne* etc. LV; *synge* ELV — *song/e* LV — *songen* or *sungen*
ELV — no inst. of pt. ptc.; *sprynge* (subj.) EV — *sprong/e* EV — no
inst. of pt. pl. — *sprongen* or *sprungen* etc. EV.

Class IV: *bere/n* etc. ELV (*beire* R) — *bar/e* (also *baar* EKNLPX)
EV & LV beside *beer/e* EV — *baren* etc. *Lo* & LV beside *beren* etc.
EV — *born/e* etc. ELV (also *bore* EV); *come/n* etc. ELV (*cum* E) — *cam/e*
ELV (*caam* HaNS) beside *co/o/me* EV & *co/o/m* EV & E — *camen* etc.
ELV beside *co/o/men* etc. ELV (*commen* Lo, *cum* or *com* E) — *come/n*
ELV etc. (*com* CE or *cum* E).

Class V: *breke/n* etc. ELV — *brak/e* ELV (*braak* K) — *bre/e/ken* etc.
EV beside *braken* etc. *Lo* & LV — *broke/n* etc. ELV; *e/ete* ELV etc. —
e/ete & *eet* ELV (*e/ett* *ELo*) — *e/eten* etc. ELV — *e/ete* LV (*eet* R);
gete/n LV (*ghete* E, *geete* G) — *gat/t* ELV & *gate Lo* & IR (*gaatt* K &
bigaate I) — no inst. of pt. pl. — *goten* etc. ELV (*gote* X) beside *geten*
LoWo; *ligg-* & *li-* etc. ELV — *lay* ELV (*ley Lo, laiʒ* K) — *lay/ʒ/en* etc.
ELV beside *leʒen CX* — no inst. of pt. ptc.; *se/e* ELV (*seen CEX*) —
sawʒ/e EV & I (also *saw/e BEFHLoWo* & *saʒ CX*) beside *siʒ/e* & *sei/ʒ*
etc. LV (*seie* E, *saiʒ* X) — *se/e/yʒen* etc. EV & LV (also *seen* A & Ha &
syʒyn E) and *si/ʒ/en* etc. LV beside *saw/ʒ/en Lo* & I — *seen* etc. ELV &
sey/ʒ/en etc. ELV (also *sei/e* ELGQS); *sitt-* ELV — *sat/t* & *sat/t/e* ELV —
se/e/ten etc. EV and *sa/a/ten* etc. LV — no inst. of pt. ptc.; *speke/n* etc.
ELV — *spak/e* ELV (*spaac* K; pt. sg.2 *speke* etc. EV) — *spe/e/ken* etc.
EV (*spoken Lo*) & *spaken* etc. LV — *spoken* etc. ELV (also *spok/e* ELV);
ʒeue ELV (*ʒefyn* E) & *ʒyue* etc. ELV (*ʒifen* E, *ʒif/e* EK) — *ʒaf* & *ʒaue*
ELV (*ʒafe Lo* & R, *ʒaaf* I) — *ʒauen* ELV (also *ʒafen Lo* & KM, *ʒaf* E,
and *ʒouen* A) beside *ʒeuen* etc. EV (*ʒefyn* E, *ʒeue* C, & *ʒeeuen* X) and
ʒyuen ALoWo — *ʒeue/n* EV & Ma, *ʒiue* etc. EV & E (*ʒifyn* E), & *ʒoue/n*
etc. X & LV (*ʒof* E, *ʒofe/n* K).

Class VI: *drawe* etc. EV & LV (imp.) — *drowʒ* ELV (also *drow/e*
LV & *LoX*, *droʒ CX* &X) beside *drew/e* EV & ILP (also *drewʒ* F) —

drowen EV (*droowyn* E) and *drewen* A — no inst. of pt. ptc.; *forsake* etc. ELV — no inst. of pt. sg. — *forso/o/ken* etc. (also *forsoke* EV) — *forsake/n* etc. ELV; (shave) — *shoof/e* EV (*schofe* Lo, *shooue* Wo) beside *schauede* etc. LV — no inst. of pt. pl. — *s/c/hauen* etc. ELV (*shaue* C); *sle/e* ELV & *sle/e/n* EV (*slea* B, *scle/e* Lo) — *slowʒ/e* EV (also *slow/e* EWo, *slo/o/ʒ* CX, & *sloo* C) beside *slewʒ* & *slew/e* EV — *slowen* etc. (also *sloowe/n* C) — *slawen* etc. EV & IK (also *slawʒen* Lo and *slan* C & A) beside *slayn/e* & *sleyn* ELV (*sclayne* Lo); *stonde/n* etc. ELV (also *stoond-* EV and *-stande* Lo) — *stood* etc. ELV — *sto/o/den* etc. ELV (*stode* FWo & E) — no inst. of pt. ptc.; *swer-* EV — *swoor* etc. ELV + sg.2 *swo/o/re* EV — *sworen* etc. LV — *sworn* ELV (*swore* X); *take/n* etc. ELV (*taak/e* A, *tak* E) — *took* etc. ELV — *token* etc. ELV (also *toke* FWo, *tok* E) — *take/n* etc. ELV (also *taak-* EV & *tak* E).

Class VII: *falle* etc. ELV — *fell* etc. ELV (*ful* E¹, *fil* CE²Wo & *fylle* Wo) beside *felde* LV (*fild/e* D) — *fellen* etc. ELV (*fullen* A, *fullyn* E, *follen* Lo, *fillen* BFWo) beside *felden* etc. LV (*filde/n* D) — *falle* I; *hew-* EV — *he/e/wʒ* EV (also *hewe* LoWo & *heew* X) — no inst. of pt. pl. — *hewe/n* etc. EV; *holde/n* etc. ELV — *he/e/ld* etc. ELV (*heuld* K, *hilde* OU) — *he/e/lden* etc. ELV (*heulden* K, *hilden* U) — *holden* etc. ELV; *know-* ELV — *knew/e* ELV (*kneew* Ma, *knewʒ* E & I, *kneʒ* X) — *knewen* etc. ELV — *knowen* etc. ELV (*knowe* C & I, *know* E); *þrowen* etc. EV — *þrew/e* EV (*þrewʒ* E, *þreʒ* X) — *threwen* etc. EV — *throwen* etc. EV (*þrou* BF, *þrouʒ* H); *waxe* CELoX & *wexe* A etc. (subj.) — *wex/e* EV (*wax* E?) — *wexen* etc. (also *woxen* A & *woxyn* E) — *waxen* EV (*wexyn* E).

Weak verbs

Class 1: e.g. *de/e/me* ELV (imp. & subj.) — *demede* or *demyde* etc. ELV (*dymede* & *dymyde* O) — *demed* I; *he/e/re* etc. ELV (*hire* U) — *herd/e* ELV — *herd/e* ELV; *bilde* A etc. (*bulde* E, *beelde* R) — *bild/e* EV (*bulde* E) beside *bildide* etc. LV (*beeldide* R, *bilde* E) — *bild* & *bylde* EV (*buld* E) beside *bildid* etc. LV (*beldid* R); *leyn* etc. EV has generalized the *lei-* stem (cf. *legge* E in Joshua 6.26 sec.m.). The stem-vowel is shortened in e.g. *kept-* ELV from *ke/e/p-* etc. The *-t* is extended to cases like *dwelt-* ELV (also *twelte* E) beside *dwelled-* etc. ELV, *sent-* ELV beside *send-* etc. Change of stem occurs in verbs like *bring-* & *brouʒt* ELV, *tell-* & *told-* etc. ELV beside *teld-* etc. LV.

Class 2: e.g. *answere* ELV (*onswer* B) — *answer/i/de* etc. ELV (*onswerd* E) — *answer/i/d* etc. EV; *aske/n/* EV & *axe* ELV — *axid/e* & *axed/e* LV — *askid* etc. EV & *axid* etc. LV; *clepe* ELV (*Lo kalle*) —

clepide etc. ELV beside (strong) *cleep/e BEF* (*clepe Lo*) — *clepid* etc. ELV.; *make* etc. ELV (also *maak A*) — *ma/a/de* etc. ELV (*mad* DE) — *maad* etc. ELV (*y-maad* I).

Class 3: only three verbs remain of this OE class of verbs, modern 'have', 'live', and 'say', as follows.

'have': sg.1 *haue* ELV (also *ha C, hafe E*), sg.2 *hast* ELV (also *haste Lo* & R, *haast R, has Lo; haxstow* E), sg.3 *hath* ELV (also *h/aþe E, hat* E, *has Lo*), pl. *han* ELV (also *haue LoX* & IR, *ha X*); subj. *haue* ELV; inf. *haue* ELV (also *han* ELV, *ha BC, a G*); ptc. *hauyng/e* ELV (also *hafynge E, hauende CX*); pt. sg. *had/de* ELV (also *hade* GO), sg.2 *haddist* & *haddest* ELV, pl. *hadden* etc. ELV (also *had BFHLoWo* & EI, *haadyn C* & P, *hedden* L), ptc. *had* ELV — imp.sg. *haue* ELV (also *hafe E*), pl. *haue* (*ʒe!* LV and *hath!* EV (also *hafeþ E* & *haueþ Lo*).

'live': sg.3 *lyueth* ELV, *lyuiþ F, liueþe E, lyfiþ BH, lifeþ K, lyues Lo*; pt.pl. *lyueden* ELV, *lyuyden GQ, lyuedyn E, lifeden K.*

'say': sg.2 *seist* ELV (also *seyest Lo* & R, *saist E*), sg.3 *seith* ELV (also *saiþ* & *seit/sayt E, seys Lo*), pl. *seyn* ELV (also *seien A* & *Lo, sayen E, seyne Lo*); subj. *seye* ELV (also *sey FWo* & I, *say E*); inf. *seye* ELV etc. (also *say EV* & EI, *saye E*) beside *seyn* EV (also *seyen HLo* & *seyne Lo*); ptc. *seiynge* etc. ELV (also *saying/e BEH* & E, *seiende CX*, and *seyand/e BCEFLoWo*); pt.sg. *seide* ELV (also *seid E* & *BWo*) & *said/e* E, pl. *seiden* etc. ELV (also *saidyn* etc. *E* & E), ptc. *seid/e* ELV (also *said/e* E) — imp.sg. *seye /thou/* ELV (also *sey EV* & EIU and *say BFHWo*), pl. *seie* (*ʒe!* LV.

Preterite-presents

Can: no inst. of either 'can', 'could', or 'cunning'.

May: sg.1 & 3 *may* ELV, sg.2 *mayst* ELV (also *may E, maiste R, maiʒt ELP, mayʒte Lo, myʒt E*), pl. *mowen* etc. ELV beside *moun* ELV (also *mow ELPX* & *may BFHLoWo*); inf. *mowe/n* EV & *mow/e* LV (also *mouwe F, mowʒ R*, and *moun BCEFX*); pt.sg. *myʒt/e* ELV, pl. *myʒten* etc.

Must: no inst. of either present or past forms.

Shall: sg.1 & 3 *s/c/hal* ELV (*shall L, schalle Lo*), sg.2 *schalt* ELV (also *schal* AEHaMS, *shult E*), pl. *schul/l/en* etc. ELV (also *sholyn E, schal BFH* & I); pt.sg. *shuld/e* or *shold/e* etc. ELV, pl. *shulde/n* or *sholde/n* etc. ELV, sg.2 *s/c/huldist* or *s/c/huldest* (*schuldiste R*), *scholdest Lo* & *scholdist* CaMW.

Wit: sg.1 & 3 *woot* or *wot/e* ELV (*wott* K), sg.2 *wo/o/st* ELV (*woste Lo, wotiste R*), pl. no inst.; pt.sg. *wist/e* ELV, pl. *wiste/n* ELV; inf.

wite/n etc. ELV & *wete/n Wo* & U; imp. *wite* (*thou!* ELV (*witte Lo*) & *wete Wo* & U.

Anomalous verbs

Be: sg.1 *am* ELV, sg.2 *art* ELV (*arte* E) & *ert BFHWo*, sg.3 *is* etc. ELV, pl. *ben* etc. ELV (also *be* DEMaW & *beth* E; sbj. *be* (*bi* U) ELV and (pl.) *be/n* ELV; imp.sg. & pl. *be* /etc./ ELV; inf. *be/n* ELV (*been* E); ptc. *be/n* EV; pt.sg.1 & 3 *was* ELV (*waas* A), sg.2 *were* EV & I (*wer* B), pl. *were/n* etc. ELV (also *wern* B, *wer* C & E, *wher-* E); subj. *were* A

Do: sg.1 *do* A (*doo* K), sg.2 *do/o/st* ELV (*doste* E, *dust* O) beside *doist* LV & E (*doest Lo*), sg.3 *do/o/þ* LV (also *doþe* E) beside *doith* A, pl. *doon* etc. ELV (*doen* A, *done* ER); subj. *do* (also *doo* A) and (pl.) *do/n* ELV; imp.sg. *do* /*thou*/ ELV (*doo* BFH), pl. *do/o/* (*ʒe!* ELV; inf. *do/o/n* etc. ELV (also *do/o* & *do/o/ne BHLoWo*); ptc. *doynge* ELV (*doing* ELP, *doende* X); pt.sg. *dide* ELV (*did* E, *dydde* BFH, *dede* CE & F, *dode* E, *dud* E), pl. *diden* etc. ELV (*dydden* BF, *dide* MaO, *ded-* CE & EFLPU, *dode* E), ptc. *do/o/n* & *do/o* ELV (also *do/o/ne* EV & ER, *y-do* E).

Go: sg.1 *go* ELV (also *goo* EV), sg.2 *go/o/st* ELV (also *goist* A & *gooste* I), sg.3 *go/o/þ* ELV (also *goiþ* LV & *goþe* E), pl. *go/o/n* ELV (also *goen* BDNORS, *gone* ER, *go* C & E); subj.sg. *go/o* ELV, pl. *go/o* ELV & *go/o/n* LV (also *goen* A & *gone* E); imp.sg. *go/o* (*thou!* ELV, pl. *go/o/þ* EV & *go* (*ʒe!* LV (also *goo* P & B, *goos Lo*); inf. *go/o* ELV beside *go/o/n* (also *go/o/ne BLo* & *gan Lo*), ptc. *goyng/e* etc. ELV (*goende CX*); pt.sg. *ʒede* etc. ELV (also *ʒide CX*, *ʒeod/e* EK, *ʒode Lo*), sg.2 *ʒedist* & *ʒedest* LV (also *-e* R), pl. *ʒeden* etc. ELV (also *ʒiden* etc. *CEX*, *ʒeoden* K), ptc. *go/o/n* or *go/o* ELV (also *goen* BDOR, *gone* BFLoWo & GKR, *goone* B).

Will: sg.1 & 3 *wile* CEX (*wil EFX* & LP, *wylle* B) and *wole HLo* & A (*wol* A & BEL, *woll* B, *wolle* F), sg.2 *wilt* BCEFHWoX & EILPUW and *wolt ALo* & A (*wolte* BDI), pl. *wiln* BCFWoX (*wilyn* E, *wille Lo*, *wyll* BF, *wyl Wo*) and *wolen* A & A (*wole HLo*, *wolyn* E); inf. *wiln/e* ELV (E *willen*); ptc. *willynge AEHLo* (*willende CX*) beside *wilnynge ABFHWo* (*wilnende CX*, *wolnynge A*); imp. pl. *wil/l/eþ CELoX* and *wol/l/eþ AFHWo* (*wol/l/iþ* BFH); pt.sg. *wold/e* ELV, sg.2. *woldest* etc. ELV, pl. *wolden* etc. ELV.

The date

The linguistic evidence presented above shows a well known type of late Middle English from about 1400. Some elements may be earlier relics, some may be later developments. We shall return to details below in connection with a survey of the MSS.

Forshall & Madden dated these MSS as follows: *A* perhaps written before 1420, *B* before 1400, *C* before 1390, *E* certainly before 1390, *F* before 1400, *H* early in the xv. century, *Lo* probably about 1400—1410 (pencilled note in Madden's copy of the preface of FM, kept in the Bodleian library), *Wo* written at the beginning of the xv. century, *X* not much after 1400; A probably before 1420, Ac about 1410 or perhaps earlier, B not later than 1410, C probably before 1420, Ca (not known to the editors) early xv. cent. (acc. to catalogue), D perhaps about 1420, E probably in the middle of the xv. cent., F about 1420, G about 1420, Ha perhaps about 1420, I perhaps of the date of 1440, K written in 1408, L about 1420, M about 1420, Ma about 1430, N about 1420, O perhaps about 1430, P about 1420, Q about 1430, R perhaps about 1430—1440, S perhaps before 1430, U about the year 1400, W probably before 1420, X about 1420.

If FM's dating of the MSS is correct, *E* is the earliest MS of EV and E the latest MS of LV giving a range from before 1390 to the middle of the 15th century. The only dated MS is K, written in 1408, which date places it in the middle of the time-span. The date of the versions themselves will be discussed later.

The dialect

The type of language illustrated above is clearly in the main standard Midland (East or Central) late Middle English with comparatively few features from outlying areas. Again we shall return to details in the linguistic survey of MSS below.

Forshall & Madden did not concern themselves much with specifications of the language of the MSS but contented themselves by giving scattered instances of linguistic features in a few of the most important MSS only, besides adducing variant forms in foot-notes and in the glossary. We have now, besides the earlier ME dialect maps drawn by Meech, Moore, & Whitehall, a comprehensive linguistic atlas of late medieval English (which I shall refer to as the Atlas) compiled by Professors McIntosh, Samuels, and Benskin. A few of the MSS involved here, i.e. containing the book of Judges, are represented in the Atlas, where they (or the language of the scribes rather) are localized as follows: for A (text MS of LV) Bucks.; for C and E (earliest MSS of EV) N Midland and Soke respectively in the parts concerned, for E also connexions with Hereford; for Ac (containing GP) Bucks. (if hand of GP = MS); for G (also containing GP) Hunts. (again if hand of GP = MS); for Q (again containing GP) Beds. (same proviso).

If the localizations given in the Atlas are correct, and I have no serious doubts on the matter, we can see a clustering of WB MSS in a fairly central and limited area with the notable exception of *E* before 7.13 where Western influence comes in.

The MSS of EV offer greater variation in linguistic forms than those of LV, which are remarkably uniform. Still, as appears from what was said about date and dialect above, both versions agree in presenting a text from about 1400 in a roughly CM dialect. Below will be taken up features in the various MSS that may shed light on the age and place of the MS in question.

A (text MS of EV) is fairly representative of the version. It has some late spellings such as the doubling of vowel signs in e.g. *gaat* and Ø-ending in *maak* inf., mixing of *ai/ei* in *feyr* & *hay*, *tch* for the affricate in e.g. *pitchinge*, loss of ʒ in *broute* and *gh* in e.g. *burgh/is*; on the other hand it has some early forms such as pl. *eldren*, *asshen*, gen. *fader*, ptc. *liggynge*. Dialect features are pt.pl. *fullen* 'fell' (W), *threst* 'thirst' (SE), pl. *sittith* (S); other forms of interest are *eny*, *fleisch*, *old*, *puple*, *siche*, *fier*, *silf.* — On the whole a somewhat mixed MS.

B shows some late developments such as *þ* for *d* in e.g. *geþer-* & *to-giþer*, *dg* for the affricate in *agredgyd*, *ea* in *dead* & *slea*, Ø-ending in e.g. *erþ* & *synn*; early forms are *strengrely*, *feiʒt*, *wirchen*, pt. *cleepe*, pl. *breþer* & *childer*, also *wynter* 'years', *asken* 'ashes'. Dialect features are *hundreþ* (N), *þousant* (W), sg.2 *askis* (N), sg.3 *stont* (S) & *weeldis* (N), *rynn-* (N), ptc. *seyand* (N), pron. *þeym* & *þeir* (N), *þase* & *þeis* (N), pl. *geyt/e* (N), sg.2 *ert* (N); other forms of interest are *woll* 'well' adv., *leyngþ* & *streyngþ*, *peple*, *ʒifiþ!*, pl. *douʒtren.* — Also somewhat mixed but with strong N (NM) influence.

C has some early characteristics such as the lack of a glide in e.g. *slaʒter, doʒter,* & *neʒhebore*, retention of -te- in *eiʒtetene*, pt. *steiʒ*, pl. *childer* and *asken*, ptc. *holpen* and *aʒt*; late forms are *dead*, *litle* and *þreshold*. Dialect features are *besili* & *besinesse* (SE), sg.3 *stant* (S), ptc. in *-ende* (EM), pron. *þem* & *þe/i/r* (N), pt. *dede/n* (SE); other forms of interest are *hand*, *any*, *anentus* etc. (abbreviated *-us* frequent in pl.), *beʒunde*, *seluer*, *oen* 'one', *such*, *fijr*, *werche*, *loouen*, ptc. *seande* etc. (*-ande* used after a vowel), ptc. *slan*, sg.1 & inf. *ha.* — Less mixed Midland (the Atlas says: N Midland) text of an early type.

E is the crucial MS of Judges changing scribes and idioms at 7.13. Early forms are *eghte* '8', *neʒhebore*, *hit* 'it', *wiʒt* 'weight', *eiʒtetene*, *whenne* 'whence', *doȝtyr* etc. (cf. *C*), *eldryn* pl., pt. *cleep*, pl. *childre* & *askyn* 'ashes'; late forms are *dead, slawtyr* (beside *slaȝtyr*), *litle* (beside *litul*), *þreshold*. Dialect forms are *anuntys* (W), *fluys* (SW), *besinesse* (SE), *hul* 'hill' (W), *hupe* & *hepe* 'hip' (W & SE), *fuyr* & *fijr* (W & E), imp. *stont!* (W), *hundret* & *þouso/u/nt* (pl. *þousondys*; both W), sg.2 *comys* (N), sg.3 *stant* (S), *seyande* (NM), pt. *bulde* (W), *twelte* 'dwelt' (W), *folfullede* (W), *herede* 'hired' (SE), *buryeden* (W) & *beried* (SE) 'buried', pron. *þem* & *þe/i/r* (N), *þulke* (W), pt.sg. *ful* (W) & *fyl* (E) 'fell', pl. *fullyn* (W), *dede* 'did' (SE), *vch/e* (W), ptc. *seyand/e* (NM); other forms of interest are *hand* & *land, loif* 'loaf', *any* & *ony, fild* 'field', *beȝende, wol* 'well' adv., *streyngþ, moche, such*, pt. *dode*. — The mixture is mainly of W forms before 7.13 ('Hereford') and E forms after 7.13 ('Soke').

F is very like *B*: late forms are *to-giþer/s* etc., *agredgyd, erþ*; early forms are *strengrely, feiȝt!, wirchen*, pt. *cleep*, pl. *breþere, asken* 'ashes'; dialect features are *hundreþ* (N), sg.2 *askis* (N), sg.3 *stont* (S) & *weeldis* (N), *rynn-* (N), ptc. *seyand/e* (N & NM), pron. *þe/y/m* & *þeir* (N), *þeis* 'these' (N), pl. *geyt/e* (N), sg.2 *ert* (N); other forms of interest are *hand, noȝt, woll* 'well' adv., *leyngþ* & *streyn/g/þ, foorþ, peple, sich, fier*, imp. *ȝifiþ*, pl. *douȝtren*. — Like *B* somewhat mixed but with strong N (NM) influence.

H resembles both *B* & *F*. Late forms are *wiche* 'which', *wher/e* 'whether', *profiȝte* etc. & *wiþ-ouȝte/n* etc. in which *ȝ* is a mute sign; early forms are *hit* 'it', pt. *cleep*, pl. *childre* & *asken* 'ashes'. Dialect features are *stont* sg.3 (S), *ert* sg.2 (N), *owiþ* pl. (S); other forms of interest are *peple, a-fier* & *fire*, imp. pl. *ȝifiþ*, pl. *douȝtren* & *geyt/e* (N), ptc. *þrouȝ* 'thrown'. — Less individual than the previous MSS of EV but of the same general type as most of the EV MSS.

Lo is less standardized than most EV MSS. Early forms are *erende* 'errand', *wreccheful, saufe* 'safe', *noȝt, kynreden*, pt.sg.2 *speke* & pt. *clepe*; late forms are *way, soundynge, doutres* (beside *douȝtren*), pt.pl. *spoken*. Dialect features are *sustre* (S), *fuyre* (W, beside *fire*), imp. *late* (N) & pl. *occupies!, blessis!* etc. (N), *hundrith/e* (N), sg.2 *comes* (N), sg.3 *bygynnes, descendis* etc. (N), pl. *sittes* (N), ptc. *seyande* (NM), pron. *þem* & *þer* (N), pl. *geyte* (N), pt.pl. *follen* (W) 'fell', inf. *gyue* (N), sg.2 & 3 *has* (N), inf. *gan* 'go' (N); other forms of interest are *hande, spatil* 'spittle', *gneracioun, waley* 'valley', *ȝife* 'if', *sclauȝter* etc., *deete* 'ditty', *hamor* 'hammer', *smeke* 'smoke', *peple, moche, suche*, inf. *kalle* etc., sg.3 *liggeþ, þat* pl., *-stande*, pt. *ȝode*, sg.2 *mayȝte*. — The mixture of forms is apparent, but the N additions to the Midland idiom are striking.

Wo is more standard EV. Early forms are *hit* 'it', adv. *strengrely*, pt. *clepe*, pl. *breþer* & *childre, dawes* 'days', *asken* 'ashes'; late forms are *ridels, throne, vncircumcisid.* Dialect features are *fuyr/e* (W), *hundreþ* (N), sg.2 *askis* (N), sg.3 *stont* (S) & *weeldis* (N), pl. *comaundeþ* & *sitteþ* (S), ptc. *seyand/e* (NM), *buryed* (W), *kallid* (N), *huyred* (W), pron. *þeir* & *þeis* (N), pl. *geyt/e* (N), sg.2 *ert* (N); other forms of interest are *sclepe* 'sleep', *ȝife* 'if', *peple, sich, wirchen, silf* & *selue/n, douȝtren,* pt. *fil* etc. 'fell', *wete/n* 'wit'. — Again a mixed type of language with fairly strong N influence.

X resembles *C.* Early forms are *erende* 'errand', *neȝhebore, keȝe* 'key', *holȝ* 'hollow', *noȝt* & *slaȝter, eiȝtetene,* pt. *sleep,* pl. *childer* & *asken* 'ashes', imp. *draȝ,* ptc. *holpen;* late forms are *hiþer* & *togiþere, dead, litle, þreshold.* Dialect features are *merie* (SE), sg.3 *stant* (S), ptc. in *-ende* (EM), pron. *þem* & *þe/i/r* (N); other forms of interest are *anoen* etc., *gres* 'grass', *any, hil* for 'hell', *flex* 'flax', *heid* 'head', *beȝunde, wrþi* 'worthy' etc., *such, fier* etc., *werche,* pl. *buschemens* etc., *findingus* etc. (abbreviated *-us* frequent in pl.), *hendes* 'hands' (beside *hond-/hand-*), pt. *kneȝ* 'knew' & *þreȝ* 'threw' (with *ȝ* = voiceless w?) — Like *C* less mixed (NE?) Midland text.

A (text MS of LV) is a serviceable copy of the version. It has some late forms such as *tch* for the affricate in *letcherie* etc., the otiose use of *ȝ* in e.g. *douȝteful,* the weak past in *lippide* 'leapt', *felde* 'fell', *smytiden* 'smote' etc.; there are also some early forms such as imp. pl. *perceyueth!*, the stem *ligg-* 'lie', gen. *douȝter* & *fadir.* Of dialect forms there are such as *eld* etc. 'old' (S), *axe* etc. 'ask' (S), pt.pl. *seelden* 'sold' (S); other forms of interest are e.g. *ony, fleisch, puple, sich/e, fier, silf, aischis* pl., ptc. *sla/y/n, beȝende.* — The S influence on the Midland language is conspicuous (the Atlas says Bucks.).

Ac (formerly Acland) is very like *A* and offers very few variations from it. It has the obsolete form *þreisfold* for 'threshold'; a late form is *streiȝte* for 'strait'. A dialect form is *þerstide* 'thirsted' (SE); other forms of interest are *aȝenus* 'against' (*-us* abbreviated), *brooþ* 'broth', *sich* 'such', and *vpbroididen* 'upbraided'. — For GP in Ac the Atlas says Bucks. as for *A.*

B is also similar to *A.* Early forms are *wiȝt* 'weight', *seueþe* '7th', and *hows* pl. Dialect features are *onswer* 'answer' (W) and *þerstide* 'thirsted' (SE). Of late form there are *perfiȝt,* inf. *pay,* and pl. *wommen.* Other forms of interest are *ony, lift* 'left', *sich* 'such', *firþer* 'further', ptc. *rynnynge* & *doen.* — *B* seems to be an ordinary MS of LV as to age and dialect with a somewhat mixed type of Midland language.

C is another MS of the same type as *A.* Of the few peculiarities there is the old forms *þresfold* for 'threshold' and pt. *broȝte* for 'brought' and the late form *secoundari* with no final *-e.* A dialect form is pt. *þer-*

stide 'thirsted' (SE); other forms of interest are *aȝenus* 'against' (*-us* abbreviated), *sich* 'such', *þrischide* 'threshed', *hirtid* 'hurt', *hirdis* 'hards', and *wecchis* 'watches'. — Slightly mixed SM dialect.

Ca (a former Ashburnham MS) also differs little from A. Early forms are *lowȝ* 'low' and *þreschfold*, later forms *wich* for 'which' and *such*. Dialect features are *cherche* 'church' (SE), *sustir* 'sister' (S), *þurste* & *þerst-* 'thirst' (W & SE), ptc. *y-do* (S), sg.2 *nelt* 'wilt not' (SE); other forms of interest are *aȝenus* 'against' (*-us* abbreviated), *peple, moche, fijr, werrely* 'verily'. — Again somewhat mixed SM dialect.

D is fairly like A. There are some late forms such as *perfiȝt* (mute ȝ-sign), *pry* 'prey' & pl. *pries* (vowelshift) cf. *abstyne* & *pertynynge*, inf. *waast*. pl. *wommen* and *ȝeris*. Dialect features are *þurst/e* 'thirst' (W), *ȝilde* (SW); other forms of interest are *ony, trispas, suche, fire*, pt. *fild/e* 'fell'. — A later form of somewhat mixed SM type.

E is the most varied MS of this part of LV. It has a great number of forms differing from A (and the bulk of LV MSS). Late forms abound, such as *wich* 'which', adj. *new, away*, sb. *syn. douter* beside *douȝtur, fornication, purpul, þreshold, son* (also 'sun'), inf. *bring* etc., *þirdde* & *thirty*, ptc. *saying*, ptc. *girt, vncircumcised*, pl. *batles, remainants*; early forms are sparse, e.g. *a-doun/e* 'down', *seueþe* '7th' (beside *seuent*), ptc. *a-gone*. Dialect forms are various, e.g. *onswerd* (W), *vch/e* (W) beside *ich*, *ȝut* (W), *hul* etc. 'hill' (W), *suster* (S), *bulde* 'build' (W), *hundreþe* (N) & *hundret* (W) beside *hondred* etc., sg.2 *comes* & *cries* (N), sg.3 *bigynneȝ* etc. & *dwellis* (N) beside e.g. *axet* & *comyt*, ptc. *liggind* (S), *y-entred* (S), pron. *hur* 'her' (W), *þem* (N) & *þer* (N) beside *hir*, pl. *beth* (S), *dedin* (SE), sg. *dud* 'did' (W); other forms of interest are *anghel* 'angel', *law* 'low', *eny, þar* & *whar-, to-ghedre* etc., *fadur* etc. (*-ur* frequently abbreviated & hence ambiguous), *wherk* 'work' etc., *þauȝ* 'though', *tou* for *þou* after dentals (likewise *at* for *þat*), *deu* 'due', *peple, moche* etc., *such, fire* etc., *wirche, ligg-* 'lie', *felleden* 'filled' (SE), *sho* 'she', *w/h/am* 'whom', pl. *hendis* beside *hondus, stringþe* & *strinȝt*, pt. *ȝeod, beȝende, agens* & *aȝa/i/ns*. — An extremely mixed type of language with strong W influence.

F is an ordinary LV MS, rather like A. Early forms are *oþer* 'or', *þreschfold, doȝtres*; late forms are rare. Dialect features are *cherche* 'church' (SE), *þurst/e* 'thirst' (W), *burþe* 'birth' (W), *rynn-* (N), pt. *dede/n* (SE), *nele* & *nelt* 'will not' (SE); other forms of interest are *peple, moche, sich* & *such/e, fyr, beȝende*. — A somewhat mixed type of Midland language.

G is another ordinary LV MS. An early form is pt. *siȝhid* 'sighed'; late forms are pl. *wommen*, pt. *siþide* 'seethed', and *dead*. Dialect fea-

41

tures are pl. *lapis* 'lap' (N), pt. *heride* 'hired' (SE) and *sterid/e* 'stirred' (SE); other forms of interest are *ony, puple, sich & such, peleris* 'pillars', *vendagis, felleden* 'fell'. — A somewhat mixed SEM MS (the Atlas says Hunts. for the GP in G).

Ha does not differ much from the general type of LV MSS. There are next to no early forms; late forms are adj. *new, streiʒt* 'strait', *away, douʒtful, wom* for 'womb', pl. *fauʒten, doun* 'done'; other forms of interest are *eny & ony, such, þrist/e* 'thirst', pt. *sprad* 'spread'. A dialect feature is *sterid* 'stirred' (SE). — Rather late SEM dialect.

I is perhaps the most interesting MS of LV, combining early (EV) features with late (revised) readings. It has early forms such as *woong* (= *A*) vs. *wang* LV, *adoun* 'down', ptc. *eried*, gen. *modir*, pl. *iʒhen*, pt. *seeþe*; late forms are *away, ooþer*, sg.3 *lijþ*, pt.pl. *aboden, fauʒten*, pt.sg. *ʒildide*. Dialect forms are *bisiloker* (W), *þerstide* (SE), *y-maad* ptc. (S), *them* (N); other forms of interest are *ony, fleische, aʒeinus, nat* 'not', *dewe* 'due', *peple, sich, fijr & fire*, imp.pl. *resteþ!, wirche, silf*, pt. *knewʒ, spradden*. — A late text of mixed Midland character.

K is valuable for its precise date (1408). It has early forms such as *lowʒ* 'low', *adoun* 'down', *liʒgg-*'lie', *hous* pl., pt. *ʒeode/n*; late forms are *batle, wich/e, ʒarde, little*. Dialect features are *fleus* 'fleece' (W), *dijk* (N), *þerstide* (SE), pl. *geytt* (N), pt. *heuld/en* 'held' (W); other forms of interest are *hand, cloiþ* 'cloth' etc., *any & ony, fleiʒssh, aʒenus, sich, mofed* 'moved' etc., *ladde* etc. — Mixed Midland.

L to some extent resembles E. It has late forms such as *perfiʒt, wich, dowter* 'daughter', *brooþer & mooder, douʒtful, purpul*; early forms are rare. Dialect features are *cherche* (SE), *mulne* (stoon, W), *suster* (S), pt.pl. *dedin* (SE); other forms of interest are *hand, moni, ony* or *eny* or *any, peple, muche, such, fyr* and *fire, wirche, hir/e* 'their', pt.pl. *hedden* 'had'. — A mixed, fairly late type of SM dialect.

M has few variations from A. It has the early forms *lowʒ* 'low' and *þreschfold*; late forms are rare. Dialect features are *cherche* 'church' (SE), pt. *þerstide* 'thirsted' (SE), ptc. *y-do* 'done' (S), sg.2 *nelt* 'wilt not' (SE); other forms of interest are *ony, peple, such, fijr*. — A standard MS of the SEM dialect.

Ma is of the general type of LV MSS. Late forms are *perfiʒt* and *þrei-schold* 'threshold'; an early form is *lowʒ* 'low'. A dialect feature is pt. *þerstide* 'thirsted' (SE); other forms of interest are *hand, ony, lenkþe & strenkþe, peple, sich & such, silf*, pl. *hondus* etc. (-*us* abbreviated). — Fairly late SEM dialect.

N does not differ much from the bulk of LV MSS. It has the early forms *lowʒ* 'low', *eiʒtetene & eiʒteti*; late forms are *wich* 'which', *away*, pt.pl. *dranken*, ptc. *ʒoulde*. Dialect features are *þousant* (W), *þerstide* (SE); other forms of interest are *ony*, *deserd* 'desert', *peple*, *moche*, *such*. — Another mixed Midland MS.

O is more individual. Late forms are *away*, *welp* 'whelp', *glaad*, *dymede* 'deemed' & *symede* 'seemed' (vowel-shift), sg.2 *dust* 'doest' & ptc. *doun* 'done' (vowel-shift); Dialectal features are *mulneston* 'millstone' (W), *þerstide* 'thirsted' and *beried* 'buried' (SE). Early forms are *wiʒte* 'weight' and *broʒte* 'brought'. Other forms of interest are *ony*, *aʒenus* 'against' (*-us* abbreviated), *streyngþe*, *sich*, *gisside* 'guessed', pt. *hilde* 'held'. — A rather late SEM copy of LV.

P resembles L (and E). It has late forms such as *naame, purpul, þreshold*, pt.pl. *brakin*; early forms are rare. Dialectal features are *sustir* (S), *dedin* (SE); other forms of interest are *hand*, *ony* & *any*, *hedir* 'hither' & *henis* 'hence' etc., *peple*, *such*, *hir* 'their', pt.pl. *resin* 'rose' etc. — A somewhat late and mixed MS.

Q is like G. It has the early form *siʒhid*, and late forms such as *dead*, *wommen* pl., *fauʒten*. Dialectal features are *steride* 'stirred' and *þerstide* 'thirsted' (SE); other forms of interest are *ony, sich* & *such, streyngþis*. — A SEM text (the Atlas says Beds. for GP) of the normal type.

R differs somewhat from the general type of LV MSS. It has late forms such as *hiþer* & *whiþer, litle*; early forms are rare. Dialectal features are forms of *beelde* 'build' (SE); other forms of interest are *strenkþe, vouʒ* 'vow', *a-boof* 'above', *such, wirche, beire* 'bear', *mowʒ/en* 'may', *beʒende*. — A later, less standardized type of SEM.

S is rather different from the bulk of LV MSS. It has early forms such as *lowʒ* 'low', *eiʒteti*; late forms are *stroong, doore, glaadly, bisiche* 'beseech'. Dialectal features are *þurstide* (W), *soones* 'sons' (N?); other forms of interest are *ony, deserd* 'desert', *biʒounde, nauʒt, sich*, sg.2 *brinkst, ʒhe* 'she'. — A somewhat mixed Midland MS.

U is more individual. It has early forms such as pt. *seeþ* 'seethed', but still more late forms e.g. *myʒddis, hire* 'here' & 'hear', *abouʒte*, *welp* 'whelp', *wroute* 'wrought', *veyners* 'viners' (vowel-shift), *smyʒte* 'smite'. Dialectal features are *kenrede* 'kindred' (SE), *melleston* 'millstone' (SE), *hepe* 'hip' (SE), *kendle* 'kindle' (SE), *fellede* 'filled' (SE), *steride* 'stirred' (SE), *þerstide* 'thirsted' (SE), *berieden* 'buried' (SE), *deden* 'did' (SE), *nelt* & *nele* 'will not' (SE); other forms of interest are *any, melk/e* 'milk', *wil* 'well' adv., *moche, sich, kelliden* 'killed', *hilde/n* 'held', *wete* 'wit' vb., *beʒende*. — Clearly SEM.

W is fairly like A and the majority of LV MSS. Early forms are *lowʒ* & *lowʒere* 'low/er', late forms ptc. *fauʒten* & sg.1 *ouwe*. Dialectal features are *þurstide* (W), ptc. *y-biried* 'buried' (S), *stronde* 'stream' (N) vs.

flodis LV, sg.2 *nelt* 'wilt not' (SE); other forms of interest are *deserd* 'desert', *peple, such, fijr*. — A typically mixed variety of LV.

X is also of the average type of LV. Early forms are *eiȝteti, burgh, adoun, doȝtris*, pt. *droȝ*, pl. *foȝten*; late forms are *haruest, fijr* 'fire'. Dialectal features are *þurstide* 'thirsted' and *hum* 'him' (W); other forms of interest are *ony* & *any, deserd* 'desert', *a-ȝenus* 'against' (*-us* abbreviated), *peple, moche, sich, hirdis* 'hards'. — Again a mixed type of Midland ME, of average age.

EV as a whole is earlier and more mixed than LV. Common to the majority of the EV MSS are early forms like *redels* 'riddles', pl. *wymmen*, comp. *strengerly*, imp. pl. *blesseþ*; late forms common to most of the EV MSS are e.g. *defau/ȝ/ten, spotel* etc. Dialect features are e.g. *nouel* 'navel' (EM), *yuel* 'evil' (EM), *myrye* 'merry' (EM), *þriste* 'thirst' (EM), ptc. *seyande* (NM); other forms of interest are pl. *stappis* 'steps', *mych, sich*, comp. *lasse*, pt.pl. *ladden, eny, fier, puple, meue* & *preue, hider* 'hither', *ford* & *forþ, siþer* 'cider', *twey/ne* 'twain', dem.pl. *þat*. — The EM character of EV is manifest, ranging from NEM via CM to SEM; the age is rather early than late within the time-span.

LV as a whole is later and less mixed than EV. Common to the majority of the LV MSS are late forms like *spotel* etc., *dou/ȝ/teful, wher/e* 'whether', *thre/i/sch-, letcherie, abhomynable*, pt.pl. *abideden*, pt.sg. *felde* 'fell'; early forms are pl. *wymmen, hider* 'hither', *lowȝ* 'low', ptc. *holpen*. Dialect features are *strond/e* = 'stream' (N), *yuel* 'evil' (EM), *e/eld* 'old' (S), *þirst* (EM), *teld-* etc. 'told' (S); other forms of interest are *mych, sich*, comp. *lesse, ony, fier, puple* & *peple, preue, siþer, twey/n/e*, ptc. *ȝouen*. — LV tends more to SEM, ranging from SM via CM to NM; the age is rather late than early within the time-span.

Before we can divide the MSS definitely as to age and dialect, we shall have to consider the *text* contained in the versions and their several MSS. This will be done in the next chapter, The translational evidence. A summing up of the two lots of evidence, finally, will be given in the Summary and Conclusions.

5. The translational evidence

By comparing the Middle English texts and their Latin source, the Vulgate, it is easy to distinguish two modes of translating the Latin text: one fairly literal version and one more idiomatic translation. We have seen that two sets of MSS remain of the Middle English bible: some early MSS from about 1400 called the Early Version (EV) and quite a few later MSS from about 1420 called the Later Version (LV); the denominations correspond to the degree of literalness: the closer a text is to the Latin, the earlier it is. In what follows we shall first compare the two versions, and then briefly study the various MSS of each of them.

1 The first difference between the two versions is typical: Judges 1.1 Vulg. *dicentes* — EV seyynge, LV and seiden; this is one of the points mentioned in the preface to LV called the General Prologue (GP): the *resolution of participles* is characteristic of LV as opposed to EV.

2 In the same verse (1.1) we find *dux belli* — EV duk of bateil, LV duik of *the* batel; the *use of articles* is more frequent in LV.

3 In 1.3 *ait* — EV seith, LV seide; the Latin *present* form has a *past* meaning.

4 1.6 *Fugit autem A.* — EV A. forsothe fleiȝ, LV Forsothe A. fledde; the *word-order* is highly significant: the more like the Latin, the more original the reading.

5 The verse (1.6) goes on: *quem persecuti comprehenderunt* — EV whom pursuynge thei token, LV whom thei pursueden and token; again EV keeps a *participle* whereas LV *resolves* it and *coordinates* it with the finite verb.

6 The continuation of 1.6 is: *caesis summitatibus* — EV kit of the ouermost partis, LV and kittiden the endis; this is a case of the *ablative absolute* treated in the same way as the participles above.

7 The Latin in 6 (above) is followed by the words *manuum eius* — EV of the hoondis *of hym*, LV of *hise* hondis; it is natural to regard EV as literal and hence original.

8 Another *absolute* construction occurs in 1.7: *amputatis ... summitatibus* — EV kut of the ouermore paartis, LV whanne the endis ... weren kit awey; instead of coordination LV here chooses a *temporal* clause.

9 In 1.7 we find *sicut feci* — EV as I haue doo, LV as Y dide; the Latin *perfect* is equalled in EV whereas LV uses the simple past.

10 In 1.8 occurs the expression *in ore gladii* — EV in mouth of swerd, LV bi the scharpnesse of swerd; EV is glaringly *literal*, LV more *idiomatic*.

11 In 1.10 we find *percussit* — EV smoot, LV and Judas killide; both versions use the simple past, but LV *adds* a conjunction and supplies (*repeats*) the subject.

12 1.12 *Qui percusserit* — EV Who smytith, LV hym) that schal smyte; apart from the differing *pronouns* we can notice the *tense* variants.

13 1.14 *Quam pergentem* — EV The which goynge, LV And ... hir goynge; another typical *resolution* mentioned in GP, this time of the *relative* pronoun.

14 1.15 *da et irriguam* — EV ʒif *and* a moyst, LV ʒyue thou *also* a moyst lond; the literal translation of *et* is typical of EV.

15 1.16 *quod est* — EV that is, LV which *desert* is; LV repeats the antecedent, again in keeping with GP.

16 1.19 *falcatis curribus abundabant* — EV thei aboundiden in chaarys *ful of weepnes in maner of sithis*, LV thei weren plenteuouse in yrun charis *scharpe as sithis*; a case of varying translation of a difficult word.

17 1.20 *sicut dixerat Moises* — EV as M. seide, LV as M. *hadde* seid; this is surprising: the simple past in EV used for the Latin pluperfect recalls OE tenses.

18 *usque in praesentem diem* (1.21) — EV vnto the day that is nowe, LV til in to present dai; again somewhat surprising: the roles of the versions seem *reversed*.

19 A typical case of differing translation is seen in 1.26 *Qui dimissus* — EV The which left, LV And he was delyuerede (and; double *resolution* + coordination in LV.

20 1.28 *Postquam autem confortatus est Israel* — EV Forsothe after that Yrael *is* counfortyd, LV Sotheli after that Israel *was* counfortid; Latin versus idiom.

21 1.32 *nec interfecit eum* — EV ne he slewʒ him, LV *and* killide *not* him; LV *resolves* even the negation.

22 A vocabulary item is in 1.34 *arctavit* — EV artide, LV helde streit; the *Latinism* in EV is striking.

23 1.34 also contains the *final* clause *ut ad planiora descenderent* — EV that to the pleyner thei myʒten descende, LV to go doun to pleynere places; instead of a full clause LV uses *to* + *inf*.

24 1.35 *quod interpretatur* — EV that is to seye, LV which is interpretid; another instance of *reversed* roles.

25 In the second chapter verse 2 another *ut*-clause: *ut non feriretis foedus* — EV that ȝe *smyten* no boond of pees, LV that ȝe *schulde* not *smyte* boond of pees; instead of a finite verb form LV uses an aux. + inf.

26 2.4 *Cumque loqueretur angelus Domini* — EV And whanne the aungel of the Lord *hadde spoken*, LV And whanne the aungel of the Lord *spak*; compared to 17 this is somewhat analogous: tense usage seems unsettled.

27 2.7 *servieruntque Domino* — EV And thei serueden *to* the Lord, LV And thei serueden the Lord; Latin construction.

28 The text in 2.7 goes on: *cunctis diebus* — EV alle the days, LV *in* alle the daies; the ablative rendered with or without a *preposition*.

29 2.8 *Mortuus est autem Josue* — EV And J. ... *died*, LV Forsothe J. .... *was deed*; neither version is strictly literal, but as to idiomaticalness the usual roles are *reversed*.

30 2.10 *surrexerunt alii* — EV other risen, LV othere *men* riseden; LV uses a *prop-word*.

31 2.12 *adoraverunt eos* — EV thei honourden *hem*, LV and worschipeden *tho goddis*; LV clarifies the object.

32 2.16 *judices qui liberarent eos* — EV iugis that *shulden* delyuer hem, LV iugis that delyueriden hem; the aux. appears correct in the context (LV possibly from Var. libera/ve/runt?).

33 2.18 *adflictorum gemitus* — EV the weilyngis of the tourmentid, LV the weilyngis of *hem* turmentid; LV underlines the *prop-word* substituted.

34 2.19 *Non dimiserunt adinventiones suas* — EV thei laften not *her* fyndyngis, LV thei leften not *her owne* fyndyngis; LV strengthens the *possessive* pronoun.

35 2.19 goes on: *et viam durissimam* — EV and the *moost hard* weye, LV and the *hardeste* weie; is the superlative absolute or not (cf. MS I: *ful* hard)?

36 2.22 *in ea* — EV in it, LV ther ynne; the use of *pronominal adverbs* is typical of LV.

37 The third chapter, verse 1: *ut erudiret in eis Israelem* — EV *for to lerne* Irael in hem, LV *that* in hem *he schulde teche* Israel; this is almost the reverse of 23.

38 3.3 *quinque satrapas* — EV The fyue princes, LV *He lefte* fyue princes; LV adds (and underlines) a few *explanatory* words.

39 3.4 *ut in ipsis experiretur Israelem* — EV that in hem he *myȝte* haue experiens of I., LV that in hem he *schulde* asaie I; both versions use an aux. for the Latin subj., but not the same.

40 3.4 *utrum audire/n/t* — EV whether thei *wolen* here, LV whethir thei *wolden* here; the aux. is the same but not the tense of it.

41 *quae* (Var. *qui*) *praeceperat* — EV the which (he?) *hath comaundid*, LV whiche he *comaundide*; the tenses do not agree.

42 3.6 *ipsique* etc. — EV And /thei/ etc., LV and *the sones of Israel* etc.; LV expresses more fully the *subject*.

43 3.7 *obliti sunt /domini/ Dei sui* — EV for3eten *of* the Lord her God, LV for3aten her Lord God; Latin constr.

44 3.20 *in aestivo coenaculo* — EV in *the* somer sowpynge place, LV in *a* somer parlour; the articles vary.

45 3.21 *in ventre/?/ eius* — EV into *his* wombe, LV in to the wombe *of the kyng*; LV clarifies the *genitive*.

46 3.25 *donec erubescerent* — EV *to the tyme that* thei weren ashamyd, LV *til* thei weren aschamed; the ME equivalents of *donec* are significantly *distributed*.

47 3.27 *insonuit bucina* — EV he sownede *with tromp*, LV he sownede *with a clarioun*; again variation in the use of articles: EV Ø, LV *a*.

48 3.28 *tradidit enim Dominus* etc. -- EV *(A) forsothe* the Lord (þe L. f. *cet.*) hath taak etc., LV *for* the Lord hath bitake etc.; MS *A* is intermediate between the literal position of the adv. in EV (*cet.*) and the fronted conj. in LV.

49 *habuitque* in chapter 4, verse 2, is translated: EV and hadde, LV and *he* (MS I: *Iabyn*) hadde; LV inserts the *subject* pronoun (and MS I specifies the subject).

50 4.3 *per viginti annos* — EV *bi* twenti 3eer, LV twenti 3eer; EV is *literal*, LV *idiomatic*.

51 4.5 *in omne iudicium* — EV *into* al doom, LV *at* ech dom; EV follows the Latin, LV the sense.

52 4.6 *tollesque* — EV and tak, LV and thou schalt take; EV coordinates the subjunctive with preceding imperatives, whereas LV keeps the *mood*.

53 4.7 *torrentis Cison* — EV of the *streem* of C., LV of the *stronde* of C.; a remarkable use of a N sense.

54 4.8 *si nolueris* etc. — EV if thow *wolt not* etc., LV if thou *nylt* etc.; the contracted form in LV resembles V.

55 4.15 *pedibus (fugeret* — EV on his feet, LV a foote; differing *idiom*.

56 4.17 *erat enim pax* — EV forsothe *there* was pees, LV forsothe pees waas; *cet.*: there was fors. pees — the versions render the Latin by different means.

57 4.18 *ne timeas* — EV *ne* drede thow, drede thou *not*; the versions differ as to the *negations* and their place.

58 4.20 *nullus est*: — EV Noon is, LV No man is *here*; LV adds (and underlines) an explanatory *adverb*.

59 4.21 *defixit* (sc. clavum) — EV piȝt down, LV fastnede *the nail*; LV adds (and underlines) the *object*.

60 4.21 *qui soporem morti /con/socians* — EV the whych felawshipynge sleep to deeth, LV and he slepte and diede to gidere; LV is remarkably free and elegant.

61 Chapter 5, verse 3: *quae* — the whiche EV (þat *C*), LV *the womman* that etc.; LV adds (and underlines) an *antecedent*.

62 5.9 *propria voluntate* — EV bi *propre* wil, LV bi ȝoure owyn wille; again EV is literal, LV idiomatic.

63 5.11 *conlisi* (or *collisi*) — EV hurtlid, LV hurtlid doun to gidere; EV is brief, LV more elaborate.

64 5.11 *in fortes* — EV into the stroonge *men*, LV among the stronge (+ men IW); the versions are at variance in two respects crossing each other.

65 5.14 *o Amalech* — EV *O* Amalech, LV *thou* Amalech; the *interjection* is treated differently.

66 5.14 *qui exercitum ducerent* — EV that oost *shulden lede*, LV that *ledden* oost; cf. 32: Var. duxerunt?

67 5.15 *quasi in praeceps* — EV as into heuedi fallynge, LV as in to a dich (+ hedly I); the meaning is obscure.

68 5.15 *Diviso contra se Ruben* — EV R. aȝens hym diuydide, *While* R. was departid aȝens hym silf; a case like 8.

69 5.19 *nihil tulere praedantes* — EV no thing token *the praytakers*, LV thei token no thing *bi prey*; the present participle caused the variation.

70 5.20 *dimicatum est* — EV it is fouȝten, LV me fauȝt; the neutral *passive* is differently rendered.

71 5.24 *Benedicta inter mulieres Jahel* — EV Blessid among wymmen Jahel, LV Blessyd among wymmen *be* Jahel; LV inserts the *copula*.

72 5.25 *Aquam petenti lac dedit* — EV To the askynge water sche ȝaf mylk, LV *To Sisara* axynge watir sche ȝaf mylk; LV specifies the *indirect* object.

73 5.27 *exanimis* — EV out of lijf, LV with out soule; an example of translational variation (MS I: w.o. lijf).

74 5.28 *pedes quadrigarum illius* — EV the feet of the foure *whelid* cartis of hym, LV the feet of his foure *horsid* cartis; EV shows some ignorance.

75 5.30 *ad ornanda colla* — EV to neckis to be anourned, LV to ourne neckis; a typical case of differing treatment of the *gerund*.

76 5.31 *Domine* — EV *thou* Lord, LV Lord; a case of the *voc.*

77 Chapter 6, verse 2: *Feceruntque sibi* — EV and thei maden to *hem*, LV and thei maden ... to *hem silf*; varying *reflexive* pronouns.

78 6.3 *Cumque s/a/evisset Israel* — EV And whanne Irael *wex feers*, LV And whanne Israel *hadde sowe*; Latin variants.

79 6.4 *apud eos* — anentis *hem* EV, at *the sones of Israel* LV; LV again *specifies* people by adding and underlining.

80 6.4 *in herbis* — EV in grasse, LV in eerbis *ethir grene corn*; the underlining is a *gloss* in LV.

81 6.8 *con/de/scendere* — EV to come *doun*, LV to stie /*up*/; again Latin variants.

82 6.11 *ut fugeret* — EV that he *fleiʒ*, LV that he *schulde fle*; LV alone indicates the *mood* in the final clause.

83 6.14 *hac fortitudine tua* — this thi strength EV, this strengthe of thee; LV deviates from the Latin.

84 6.15 *in quo* — EV in what, LV in what *thing*; LV uses a *prop-word*.

85 6.17 *et ille si inveni inquit gratiam* — EV And *he* If Y haue foundun *he seith* grace, LV And *Gedeon seide* If Y haue foundun grace; LV rearranges the Latin syntax.

86 6.17 *quod tu sis qui loqueris ad me* — EV that thou *be* the which spekist with (to *CELo*) me, LV that thou that spekist to me *art sente of Goddis part*; EV keeps the *mood*, LV adds a *gloss*.

87 6.19 *carnes* — EV fleissh, LV fleischis; LV keeps the *number*.

88 6.19 *ius carnium* — EV the flesh broththe, LV the broth of fleischis; again LV is closer to the Latin.

89 6.22 *heu mihi* — EV Wo me, LV alas to me; different translation of the *interjection*.

90 6.25 *quae est patris tui* — EV that is *of thi fader*, LV which is *thi fadris*; different types of the *genitive*.

91 6.26 *Domino Deo tuo* — EV to the *Lord thi God*, LV to *thi Lord God*; a typical difference in *word-order*.

92 6.26 *lignorum struem* — EV the hepe of *wode*, LV the heep of *trees*; a case like 87.

93 6.28 *surrexissent* — EV *were* rysen, LV *hadde* rise; the two versions form the *pluperfect* differently.

94 6.30 *ut moriatur* — EV that he *be dead*, LV that he *die*; EV seems to be be influenced by the *voice* of the verb.

95 6.37 *si ros in solo vellere fuerit* — EV if dewe in the fleese alone *were*, LV if dew *is* in the flees aloone; the versions differ as to both *tense* and *mood*.

96 6.38 *de nocte* — EV *fro* the (om. *cet.*) niȝt; LV *bi* nyȝt; LV is more *idiomatic*.

97 6.39 *ne irascatur furor tuus* — EV *Ne* wexe *not* wrooth thi woodnes, LV Thi strong veniaunce be *not* wrooth; the *negation* is expressed twice in EV.

98 Chapter 7, verse 2: *Multus tecum est populus* — EV Myche is the puple with thee, LV Myche puple is with thee; both versions differ as to *word-order*.

99 7.3 *Recesseruntque* — EV And *there* wenten aȝen, LV And *thei* ȝeden awei; the *subject* is differently understood.

100 7.3 *reversi sunt* — EV ben turned aȝen, LV turneden aȝen; the *form* is passive (deponential) but the *meaning* active.

101 7.4 *populus multus est* — EV *there* is myche puple, LV the puple is myche; the syntax is differently expressed.

102 7.5 *qui autem curvatis genibus biberint* — EV forsothe thilk that bowid(en) the knees drynkyn(ge), LV sotheli thei that drynken *with* knees bowid; the *ablative* is partly (mis)understood and differently rendered.

103 7.6 *lambuerant* — EV hadden lapid, LV lapiden; cf. 17, 26.

104 7.6 *flexo poplite* — EV the knee bowid, LV knelynge; the *ablative absolute* is kept in EV, freely and idiomatically translated in LV.

105 7.11 *cum audieris* — EV whanne thou *herist*, LV whanne thou *schalt here*; the tense forms are all different.

106 7.12 *cameli quoque innumerabiles erant* — EV forsothe camels vnnoumbrable *there* weren, LV sotheli the camelis weren vnnoumbrable; cf. 101

107 7.13 *in hunc modum* — *in* this maner EV, LV *bi* this maner; varying *prepositions*.

108 7.13 *quasi ... panis ex hordeo volvi* — EV as a loof of barlich ... *to be* trendlid, LV *that* as o loof of barly ... *was* walewid; an example of the *accusative + inf*.

109 7.13 *cumque pervenisset* — and whanne it *were* comyn, LV and whanne it *hadde* come; auxiliaries in different *moods*.

110 7.16 *in tres partes* — EV *in* three parties, LV *in to* thre partis; LV agrees with the Latin.

111 7.17 *quod fecero sectamini* — EV what I *shal doo* folwith, LV sue ȝe that that Y *do*; cf. 105.

112 7.22 *inmisit* — EV sente *yn*, LV sente; EV keeps the *in*.

113 7.22 *mutua se caede truncabant* — EV thei kutten of hem seluen bi sleynge echon other, LV thei killiden hem silf bi deeth ech other;

the idea of *reciprocity* is somewhat awkwardly expressed, particularly in LV.

114 The eighth chapter, verse 1: *cum ad pugnam pergeres* — EV whanne thou *shuldist go* to fi3t, LV whanne thou 3edist to batel; EV imitates the Latin *mood*.

115 8.2 *quale* — EV what, LV what maner thing; LV elaborates the *neutral* pronoun.

116 8.4 *fugientes* — EV fleynge, LV *hem* that fledden; LV *resolves* the participle and *adds* (underlining) an object pronoun.

117 8.6 *responderunt* — EV answerden, LV answeriden *in scorne*; LV *amplifies* the verb by adding two words (underlined).

118 8.7 *cum reversus fuero* — EV whanne Y *were* turned a3en, LV whanne Y *schal* turne a3en; the *tenses* and *moods* do not agree.

119 8.10 *educentium gladium* — EV of drawers out swerd, LV of men drawynge (ledynge *plures*) out swerd; LV retains more of the Latin.

120 8.11 *nihil* — EV no thing, LV not ony thing; LV *resolves* the negation.

121 8.18 *Quales fuerunt viri* — EV What weren the men, LV What maner men weren thei; as usual LV is freer.

122 8.19 *non vos occiderem* — EV Y wold not haue slayn 3ow, LV Y nolde sle 3ou; the context adds to the syntax.

123 8.27 *ephod* — EV a coop, LV ephot *that is a preestis cloth*; LV keeps the Latin word but adds a *gloss*.

124 8.31 *concubina* — EV secoundarye wijf, LV concubyn *that is secoundarie wijf*; again LV keeps the Latin word and adds a gloss which agrees with EV.

125 8.34 *ut esset* — EV that he *were*, LV that he *schulde be*; two ways of rendering the Latin past *subjunctive*.

126 8.34 *recordati sunt Domini Dei sui* — EV thei *recordiden of* the Lord her God, LV thei *hadden mynde of* her Lord God; a typical *vocabulary* item where EV is *latinized*.

127 The ninth chapter, verse 2: *quid vobis est melius* — EV *Whether* is it (om. *H*) betere to 3ou, LV *What* is betere to 3ou; the comparative suggests the alternative.

128 The continuation (of 9.2): *an ut* ... — EV other, LV whether that ...; this rather explains the difficulty.

129 9.3 *cor eorum* — EV the *herte* of hem, LV her *hertis*; the *plural* idea governs LV.

130 9.7 *elevataque voce clamavit* — EV and arerid vp the voice cryede, LV and criede *with* vois reisid; the *ablative* is differently interpreted.

131 9.14 *ramnum* — EV the thorn, LV the ramne *ether theue thorn*;
again LV keeps the Latin word and adds a *gloss*.

132 9.17 *ut erueret vos* — for (om. *C*) *to* delyuer ʒou, LV *that* he *schulde*
(wolde I) delyuere ʒou; with minor variations the same as 37.

133 9.18 *qui nunc surrexistis* — EV *the whiche ʒe* nowe han rysyn, LV
and ʒe han rise now; the usual *resolution* in LV, but EV adds an
explanatory pronoun.

134 9.18 *eo quod frater vester sit* — EV forthi that ʒoure brother he *be*,
LV for he *is* ʒoure brother; EV follows the Latin closely.

135 9.25 *praetereuntibus* — EV goers byside, LV men passynge forth;
two ways of dealing with the *plural participle*.

136 9.27 *factis cantantium choris* — EV the querys maad of syngers, LV
with cumpenyes of syngeris (I y)maad; = 130.

137 9.29 *utinam* — EV Wolde God, LV Y wolde that; idioms.

138 9.29 utinam) *daret aliquis* — EV Wolde God) eny man ʒeue, LV
Y wolde that) sum man ʒaf; differing *moods*.

139 9.31 *et obpugnat adversum te civitatem* — EV and aʒen fiʒtith the
citee aʒens thee, LV and he excitith the citee to fiʒte aʒens thee;
the Latin verb is difficult.

140 9.40 *et in urbem compulit* — EV and in the cytee threste, LV and
constreynede /him IKM/ *to go* (*fle* I) in to the citee; the versions
differ, also from the Latin.

141 9.47 *pariter conglobatos* — EV togidre gedred *in o glob*, LV gaderid
togidere; LV simplifies the expression.

142 9.48 *arrepta securi* — EV takun-to an axe, LV *with* an axe takun;
another instance of an absolute *versus* an instrumental ablative.

143 9.51 *firmissime* — EV moost fastly, LV stronglieste (I ful strongly);
different types of the adverbial *sup*.

144 9.56 *reddidit Deus malum* — EV God ʒeeldide the yuel, LV God
ʒeldide *to Abymelech* the yuel; LV *adds* the indirect object (no
underlining in MSS).

145 9.56 *interfectis septuaginta fratribus suis* — EV slayn his seuenti
bretheren, LV *for* he killide hise seuenti britheren; LV expresses the
cause for the ablative.

146 Chapter ten, verse 3: *Huic successit Iair* — EV To whom cam after
Jayr, LV His successour was Jair; both versions imitate the Latin
but in different ways.

147 10.14 *invocate* — EV inwardli clepith, LV clepe; the Latin *prefix* is
rendered in EV only.

148 Chapter 11, verse 2: *postquam creverant* — EV aftirward that thei
weren waxen, LV aftir that thei *encreesiden*; cf. 103 and 93.

149 11.2 *esse non poteris* — EV thou *shalt not mowe* be, LV Thou *maist not* be; the *tenses* do not agree.

150 11.3 *quos ille fugiens* — EV Whom he fleynge, LV Whiche *britheren* he fledde; LV specifies the *object*.

151 11.5 *quibus acriter instantibus* — EV the whiche sharpli instoondynge, LV and whanne thei contynueden scharpli; double *resolution* in LV (cf. 19).

152 11.7 *nonne vos estis* — EV Ben not ӡe, LV Whethir not ӡe it ben; two ways of expressing the *question*.

153 11.7 (cont.) *qui odistis me* — that *hatiden* me, LV that *haten* me; the Latin tense is ambiguous.

154 11.9 *Si vere venistis ad me* — EV *If* vereyli ӡe ben comen to me, LV *Whether* ӡe camen verili to me; some confusion of *conjunctions*.

155 11.10 *Dominus ... ipse* — EV The Lord ... *he*, LV The Lord *hym silf*; differing translation of the *pronoun*.

156 11.18 *nec voluit intrare* — EV *and* he wold *not* entre, LV *nether* he wolde entre; cf. 21.

157 11.20 *infinita multitudine congregata* — EV a multitude with outen eend gedrid, LV *with* a multitude with out noumbre gaderid to gidere; again LV is *instrumental*.

158 11.25 *nisi forte melior es* — EV but perauenture thow *be* betere, LV /no/ but in hap thou *art* betere; LV (& E^1) use the Latin *ind.*, whereas EV follows ME usage.

159 11.26 *repetitione* — EV askynge, LV axyng *aӡen*; LV is more literal.

160 11.27 *pecco* — EV I synne, LV Y *do* synne; the translation in LV is remarkable.

161 11.30 *si tradideris* — EV If thou *takist* (take *CX*), LV If thou schalt bitake; cf. 105 & 12.

162 11.31 *quicumque primus fuerit egressus* — EV who so euere first *were* gon out, LV who euer *goith* out first; cf. 95.

163 11.33 *usque dum venias* — EV for to that thou *come*, LV til to thou *comest*; the usual difference in *moods*.

164 11.35 *ipsa decepta es* — EV *thi self* art desseyued, LV *thou* art disseyued; the reverse of 155.

165 11.40 *conveniant in unum* — EV comen to gidre *in oon*, LV come togidere; LV *omits* the redundancy.

166 Chapter twelve, verse 1: *transeuntes* — the goers EV, LV thei that passiden; cf. 135.

167 12.1 *ut pergeremus* — that we *wenten* EV, LV that we *schulden go*; cf. 82.

168 12.3 *consurgatis* — EV ʒe rysen, LV ʒe ryse *togidere*; LV follows the Latin more closely.

169 12.5 *Effraim reversurus erat* — EV E. was for (om. *CX*) *to turne* aʒen, LV E. *schulde/n turne* aʒen; a typical instance of the active *periphrastic* conjugation.

170 12.6 *quod interpretatur* — EV that is to mene, LV which is interpretid; cf. 24.

171 Chapter 13, verse 6: *quo nomine vocaretur* — EV what name he *were* clepid, LV bi what name he *was* clepid; EV keeps the Latin *mood*.

172 13.7 *erit enim puer nazareus* — EV forsothe he shal be a Nazare child, LV for the child schal be a Nazarey; different interpretations of the Latin *word-order*.

173 13.8 *qui nasciturus est* — EV that *is to be* born, LV that *schal be* borun; cf. 169.

174 13.11 *Tu es qui locutus es mulieri?* — EV Art thow the which spak to the womman?, LV Art thou he that hast spoke to the womman?; the *antecedent* causes difficulty.

175 13.12 *Quando ... sermo tuus fuerit expletus* — EV Whanne ... thi word *were* fulfillid, LV Whanne thi word *schal be* fillid; cf. 118.

176 13.17 *si sermo tuus fuerit expletus* — EV if thi word *were* fulfillid, if thi word *be* fillid; cf. 175 & 95.

177 13.20 *proni ceciderunt in terram* — EV redi thei fellen *into* the erthe, LV thei felden lowe *to* /þe/ erthe; LV uses the idiomatic *preposition*.

178 13.21 *angelum esse* — EV *to be* the aungel, LV *that he was* an aungel; the typical translations of *acc. + inf.*

179 13.22 *Morte moriemur* — EV Bi deeth *die* we, LV We *schulen die* bi deeth; the *future* with or without an *aux.*

180 13.23 *non suscepisset* — EV he *wold* not haue take, LV he *schulde* (I wolde) not haue take; the *aux.* varies.

181 13.23 *quae sunt ventura* — EV tho thingis that *ben to com*, LV tho thingis that *schulen come*; like 169 & 173, but MS I has *ben to comynge*.

182 13.25 *castris* — EV tentis, LV *castels*; MS I tentus. Both words in the sense of 'camp'.

183 14.4 *quod res a Domino fieret* — EV that the thing *shulde be doo*, LV that the thing *was don*; different interpretation of the clause and its *mood*.

184 14.6 *quasi haedum in frusta concerperet* — EV as he *shulde* to-teer out a kide into gobetis, LV as if he torendide a kide in to gobetis; again EV keeps the *mood*.

185 14.12 *problema* — EV a dowtous word, LV a probleme; LV adds a gloss, which resembles EV.

186 14.15 *ad nuptias* — EV to the brydale, LV to weddyngis; LV imitates the Latin *number*.

187 14.16 *Odisti me* — Thow hatidist me, LV Thou hatist me; cf. 153.

188 14.16 *problema* — EV the redels, LV the probleme; cf 185.

189 14.18 *non invenissetis* — EV ȝe *shulden not haue* foundun, LV ȝe *hadden not* founde; two ways of rendering the Lat.

190 14.19 *quorum ablatas vestes* — EV of whom the takun clothis, LV whose clothis he took awey (and; *resolution*.

191 15.5 *ut ... discurrerent* — EV and (*CELo* þat) thei runnen, LV that thei schulden renne aboute; confusion of *conjunctions*.

192 15.5 *quibus succensis* — EV the whiche sette a-fier, LV *bi* whiche kyndlid; MS I has: wiþ þe whiche *brondis* etc.

193 15.12 *quod non occidatis me* — EV that ȝe *shulen* not *slee* me, LV that ȝe *sle* not me; two variants for the Latin *subjunctive*.

194 15.19 *quibus haustis* — EV the whiche drunkun, LV *bi* whiche (MS I: and whanne he hadde) drunkun; cf. 192.

195 15.19 *invocantis* — EV of the inwardli clepynge, LV of the clepere; MS I has: of þe ynwardly clepere.

196 16.2 *intrasse urbem Samson* — EV S. to haue comen into the citee, LV that S. entride (*had* entrid I) in to the citee; cf. 178.

197 16.2 *ut facto mane exeuntem occiderent* — EV that the morwetide comen him goynge out thei *myȝten* slee, LV that in the morewtid thei *schulden* kille Sampson goynge out; among other things differing *auxiliaries*.

198 16.7 *si ... ligatus fuero* — EV If ... Y *were* bounden, LV If Y *be* boundun; cf. 176.

199 16.8 *ut dixerat* — EV as *she* seide, LV as *he* hadde seide; confusion of the subject pronouns.

200 16.9 *quomodo si rumpat quis* — EV in what maner wise a man *wold breeke*, LV as /if/ a man *brekith*; differing syntax affecting the *verb*.

201 16.9 *tortum* — EV *that is* sponnen, LV writhun; for once EV makes an *addition* to the text.

202 16.11 *aliorum hominum similis* — EV *of* other men lijk, LV lijk othere men; Latin construction in EV.

203 16.16 *animus eius* — EV *hyre* lijf, LV *his* lijf; confusion of the possessive pronouns.

204 16.18 *assumpta pecunia* — EV takun to the money, LV *with* the money takun; MS I: þe m. takun *wiþ þem*.

205 16.25 *sumptis iam epulis* — EV nowe taken meetis, LV *for* thei hadden ete thanne; MS I: and þanne *whanne* etc.

206 16.26 *recliner* — EV Y lene, LV Y be bowid; LV is more like the Latin form.

207 16.29 *alteram ... alteram* — EV the *tother ...* the tother, LV the *oon ...* the tother; EV is literal.

208 17.4 *ut faceret* — EV that he *make,* LV that he *schulde make;* the *subjunctive* is differently rendered.

209 17.9 *ubi potuero* — EV where I *shal mowe,* LV where Y *may;* cf. 149.

210 17.13 *quod benefaciet mihi Deus* — EV that God *wol* doo wel to me, LV that God *schal* do wel to me; different *auxiliaries* for the *future* tense.

211 18.1 *ut habitaret* — EV that he *myȝte* dwelle, LV /MS I for/ to dwelle; cf. 23.

212 18.1 *sortem non acceperat* — EV he hadde takun *no* lot, LV it (Dan I) hadde *not* take eritage; the versions differ slightly.

213 18.2 *ut explorarent terram* — EV that thei *aspien* the loond, LV that thei *schulden aspie* the lond; cf. 208.

214 18.3 *utentesque illius diversorio* — EV and vsynge the restynge place of hym, LV and thei restiden in the yn of hym (in his place I); literal veisus free transl.

215 18.5 *an prospero itinere pergerent* — EV whethir welsum weye thei *shulden goo,* LV whether thei *ȝeden* in weie of prosperite; cf. 183.

216 18.6 *iter quo pergitis* — EV the gaat that ȝe goon, LV the iourney whidur ȝe goon; minor variations.

217 18.7 *nullo eis penitus resistente* — EV no man to hem vtterli withstondynge, LV *for* no man outirli aȝenstood hem; cf. 145.

218 18.8 *sciscitantibus responderunt* — EV to *hem* askynge thei answerden, LV thei answeriden to *britheren* axynge; MS I: ... *hem* enqueringe, adding another variant.

219 18.10 *ad securos* — EV to *the* sikyr, LV to sikir *men;* two ways of expressing the plural.

220 18.10 *in regionem latissimam* — EV in to the regyoun moost brood, LV in to a largeste (ful large I) cuntrey; different equivalents of the *superlative.*

221 18.14 *ad considerandam terram* — to the loond ... to ben biholden, LV to biholde the lond; cf. 75.

222 18.14 *quod in domibus istis sit ephod* — EV that in thes howsis *be* ephot, LV that ephod ... *is* in these housis; cf. 86.

223 18.17 *At illi qui ingressi fuerant domum* — EV And thei the whiche *weren goon* into the hous, LV And thei that *entriden* in to the hows; cf. 148 & 103.

224 18.19 *Quid tibi melius est* — EV *Whether* is it beter to thee, LV *What* is betere to thee; cf. 127 & 128.

225 18.19 *an in una tribu* — EV *other* in o lynage, LV *whether* in o lynage; the continuation of 224 & ref.

226 18.21 *Qui cum pergerent* — EV The whiche whanne *weren goon*, LV And whanne thei ʒeden; cf. 26.

227 18.26 *fortiores se* — EV strenger than *him self*, LV strongere than *he*; differing *reflexive* pronouns.

228 19.1 *Fuit quidam vir levites* — EV A maner man Leuyte was, LV A man was a dekene; differing *word-order*.

229 19.8 *mane facto* — EV erely bigunne, LV whanne the morewtid was maad; different treatment of the *ablative*.

230 19.8 *assumptis viribus* — EV strengthis nomen, LV make thee strong; EV is literal whereas LV takes liberties.

231 19.15 *ut manerent ibi* — EV that thei *myʒten* dwelle there, LV that thei *schulden* (*wolden* I) dwelle there; cf. 197 & 39.

232 19.18 *Profecti sumus* — EV We ben comen, LV We ʒeden forth; an almost *aspectual* difference.

233 19.19 *in meos et ancillae tuae usus* — EV into myn and of thin hand-maydenys vsis, LV in to myn vsis and of thin handmayde; the double *genitive* is awkward in EV.

234 19.24 *ne ... operemini* — EV ne ... ʒe worchen, LV *that* ʒe worche *not*; a rigid *Latinism* in EV.

235 19.30 *quid facto opus sit* — EV what is nede to the deed, LV what is nede to be doon; I adds: *for this dede.*

236 20.6 *piaculum* — EV trespas worthi to be punysshid, LV synne; the five words in EV correspond to one word in LV.

237 20.12 *qui dicerent* — EV the whiche *shulden seye*, LV whiche mes-sangeris *seiden*; cf. 66 & 32.

238 20.14 *ut illis ferrent auxilium* — EV that to hem thei *myʒten* bere helpe, LV to helpe hem; cf. 23.

239 20.16 *ad certum* — EV at certeyn, LV at *a* certeyn *thing*; a typical instance of the difference between EV & LV.

240 20.23 *inite certamen* — EV goth into the strijf, LV bigynne ʒe batel; differing *idioms*.

241 20.25 *tanta in illos caede baccati sunt* — EV [in] so mych slauʒter thei mich wexen wood in hem, LV weren wood aʒens hem *bi* so greet sleyng; the abl. needs a *prep.*

242 20.32 *arte* — EV at the bigynnynge, LV bi craft; here, as elsewhere, we may assume faulty Latin (*ante*?).

243 20.38 *quos ... collocaverant* — EV that weren sett, LV whiche thei hadden set; again EV deviates from the Latin (Var. *qui collocati erant*?)

244 20.39 *Quod cum cernerent filii Israel* — EV The which thing whanne the sones of Yrael ... *shulden biholde*, LV And whanne the sones of Israel ... *sien* this; different interpretation of the Latin *subjunctive*.

245 21.5 *interfici eos qui defuissent* — EV hem to be slayn that thennus weren, LV that thei that failiden /p̄ens I/ *schulden* be slayn; the passive inf. + *aux.* in LV

246 21.7 *non daturos nos* — EV vs not to ȝyue, LV that we *schulen* not ȝyue; the *future* is brought out in LV.

247 21.18 *constricti* — EV bounden, LV *for we ben* boundun; LV links up the *participium conjunctum*.

248 21.18 *Maledictus qui* — EV Cursid that, LV *Be he* cursid that; LV adds the *copula* etc.

249 21.18 (cont.) *qui dederit* — EV that *shal* ȝyue, LV that *ȝyueth*; cf. 12.

250 21.19 *anniversaria* — EV torn/ed/ aboute bi the ȝeer, LV annyuersarie (I: the ȝeris turnyng aboute); difficult to analyze grammatically.

251 21.21 *ad ducendos choros* — EV at the dauncis to be lad, to lede daunsis; the *gerund* typically translated.

252 21.21 *singuli uxores singulas* — EV eche sondry wyues, LV eche man o wijf; again typical translations, *literal* versus *idiomatic*.

253 21.22 *Cum ... venerint* — whanne ... *comen*, whanne ... *schulen come*; cf. 105.

The 253 items above illustrate the types of differences between the two versions. They are not of equal frequency; a rough frequency list, which may also serve as a sort of index to the items above, runs like this:

I *Word-order*. Almost any verse exhibits the basic difference between EV and LV: *literal* versus *free* translation. Examples of various types are 4, 48, 91, 98, 99, 101, 106, 121, 172, 228.

II *Additions*. A characteristic feature in LV is the *adding* of all sorts of *explanatory* words and expressions, including *prop-words* and *glosses* (e. g. 80, 124). Instances are 15, 30, 31, 33, 38, 49, 56, 58, 59, 61, 64, 72, 79, 84, 115, 117, 201, 218, 239, 247; *copula* 71, 248.

III	*Tenses*. This is more complicated; as a rule EV follows the Latin but not always. There is a distinction between the *simple* ME tenses (present & past) and the *compound* ME tenses (perfect & pluperfect). The former are more or less the same in both versions, the latter vary. Examples are 3, 9, 12, 17, 20, 26, 41, 85, 103, 105, 111, 153, 161, 162, 169, 175, 179, 187, 198, 208, 209, 223, 226, 249, 253.
IV	*Articles*. Since Latin has no articles like the ME definite and indefinite articles, the variety *the-a/n/-ø* can be great. EV tends to be less explicit, LV more emphatic. Instances are 2, 44, 47.
V	*Pronouns*. The various types of pronouns together constitute a considerable amount of variations between the versions. Examples are 12, 36, 155, 164, 199, 207; *relative* is 174, *possessive* 34, 62, 83, 203, *refl.* 113.
VI	*Conjunctions*. Owing to differing syntax due to *resolutions* etc. the two versions use conjunctions differently, *co*-ordinating and *sub*-ordinating. Instances are 46, 184, 234; *final* clauses 211, 237, 238.
VII	*Negations*. The main difference here is the *rigid* versus *elastic* positioning in EV & LV respectively. Examples are 54, 57, 97, 120, 156, 212.
VIII	*Moods*. The Latin and ME usage as to modality does not always coincide within the versions. EV is more imitative, almost slavish, whereas LV adapts to idiom. Instances are 82, 86, 95, 109, 114, 118, 134, 158, 163, 167, 171, 176, 183, 213.
IX	*Auxiliaries*. This is intimately bound up with III & VIII. EV uses fewer types than LV, and not always the same as LV. Examples are 32, 39, 40, 66, 93, 180, 193, 197, 210, 231, 245; of the *future* 173, 181, 246, *conditional* 189.
X	*Genitives*. The two types of ME genitives versus one Latin type give rise to variations between the versions. Instances are 7, 45, 90, 233. Cf. also V *possessive*.
XI	*Participles*. Here the main difference is the literalness of EV and the freedom of LV, which frequently *resolves* the forms into *finite* types. Examples are 69, 116, and more under *Absolutes* and *Resolutions*.
XII	*Ablatives*. Apart from its *absolute* use, this peculiar Latin case form must be rendered by *prepositional* expressions in English. The two versions vary in the use (or non-use) of prepositions. instances are 28, 55, 102, 104, 229.
XIII	*Phrases*. Different phrasing is of course inevitable with lan-

guages so unlike as Latin and English. Even so, the versions choose varying equivalents. Examples are 10, 18, 24, 240; of *constructions* 43, 202.

XIV   *Absolutes.* This typical Latin device, particularly the *abl.* abs., is typical also of EV as opposed to LV, which uses various ways of translation. Instances are 6, 8, 68, 157, 192, 194, 204, 205, 217.

XV   *Translations.* This term is of course applicable to all the categories enumerated here. In XV are placed cases which do not readily fit into the other categories. As a rule, and even more noticeably in XV, the basic difference between EV and LV, literalness versus idiomaticalness, prevails. Examples are 16, 60, 67, 73, 74, 122, 170, 190, 214, 216, 230, 236.

XVI   *Omissions.* This is far less common than II *Additions.* In a literal translation no omissions should occur, and this is, apart from inadvertences, the case in EV. In a free translation things may be left out that are considered tautological or unneccessary, e.g. 165; *ellipsis* 52.

XVII   *Agents.* Agent nouns are frequently formed from Latin present participles, either by adding a *prop*-word, or by using the English derivative ending *-er* etc. Instances of differing types are 119, 166, 195.

XVIII   *Prepositions.* Prepositions being an essential part of idiom, differences are bound to appear in a translation. Again EV is closer to the Latin, LV more idiomatic. Examples are 50, 51, 96, 107, 110, 177, 241.

XIX   *Gerunds.* This typical Latin feature has no real counterpart in English, and has to be paraphrased one way or another. EV stiffly imitates Latin, LV is freer. Instances are 75, 221, 251.

XX   *Questions.* This comprises both *direct* speech and, more importantly, *indirect* speech, affecting Latin interrogative particles and conjunctions. Examples of differing translations are 152, 154, 215, 224, 225.

XXI   *Exclamations.* This includes the *vocative* (but not the *imperative*, for which see Verbs). Instances are 65, 76, 89.

XXII   *Voice.* The Latin *active* and *passive* voice is normally kept in the versions. One notable exception is the *deponens*, i.e. a verb formally passive but semantically active; this is mostly treated like Latin in EV, like English in LV. Examples are 29, 100, 206; of *deponentia* also 29, 94, of *passive* 70.

XXIII   *Resolutions.* This is the chief characteristic of LV as opposed to EV: *participles* and *relative pronouns* can, and acc. to GP should, be resolved in to their understood constituents, i.e. a *finite* verb and a *personal* pronoun respectively. Instances are 1, 5, 13, 19, 21, 151.

XXIV   *Superlatives.* As with the genitive, the two types of ME forms versus the one Latin type cause differing translation. Examples are 35, 220.

XXV   *Infinitives.* A special, and very typical case, is the *acc. + inf.* This is preserved in EV, whereas LV uses a full clause. Instances are 108, 178; of *inf.* also 196.

XXVI   *Numbers.* The Latin *singular* and *plural* are mostly kept as such in the versions, but exceptions occur in both though not always parallel. Examples are 87, 88, 92, 186, 252; of *plural* also 219.

XXVII   *Vocabulary.* This is really the most comprehensive area of differences, if *synonyms* are considered items of differing translation. Here only a limited number of words are included because of their importance. Instances are 22, 53, 123, 182, 185, 188.

XXVIII   *Prefixes.* These are treated differently in quite a few cases, again EV being more like the Latin. Examples are 63, 112, 159, 168.

XXIX   *Aspects.* Besides *tense* and *mood* there is the formal distinction called *voice* in verbs; *aspect*, however, may cut through these categories. An instance is 232, where the versions differ.

XXX   *Variants.* Here are meant variants in the Latin text of the *Vulgata* (*Var.* for short). These are often the only clues to explain differing translations of the same word or passage. As a rule EV follows the inferior reading. Examples are 78, 81, 191, 242, 243.

The number of translational variants *within* each of the versions is much smaller than the number of variants *between* the versions. Any one of the surviving nine MSS of EV and of the 24 copies of LV (with one notable exception: MS I) could serve as the text MS of its version, so few are major differences.

In EV, the text MS is *A*. It represents the version in its finished form. The chief difference between *A* and the rest (*cet.* for short) is in *word-order*; where the other MSS follow the Latin pattern in the case of *autem* — 'forsooth', *A* is more modern, e.g. 1.16 *Filii autem Cinei* — *A* Forsothe the sones, *cet.* þe s.f., etc. Other instances are 7.18, 11.35, 12.1, 16.13, 16.17, 19.18. Apart from cases of differing word-order, there are, as in most copied MSS, various errors and dubious readings. Since the text is copied from *A* (with emendations) no further illustration is necessary here.

MS *B*, next, is a uniform copy of EV. It often agrees with *FHWo* in presenting the same dubious or erroneous readings, e.g. 20.34 *instaret interitus* — stood yn deth, *B* etc. stoden in d., 20.41 *versa facie* — turned/e the face, *B* etc. torneden þe f.

MS *C*, unlike *B*, is not a uniform copy of EV. Together with *ELoX*, or with one or two of those MSS, it often deviates from *A* etc., e.g. 4.21 *clavum tabernaculi* — a nail (*A* etc. veyl/e) of the tabernacle. Although on the whole correct, it is erroneous at times: 6.27 *assumptis* — taken-to, *C* takende etc., 18.27 *atque securum* — and (*C* in) siker.

MS *E* is unique among EV MSS in presenting readings of an original character (most of them corrected and thus not representing the actual wording of the authorized MS text). The examples below are taken from my edition of *E*: 3.3 *satrapas* — satrapis, corr. princis, 3.21 *extenditque Ahoth manum sinistram* — & strei ʒte out to Aod þe lift hond, corr. & *Aod* strei ʒte out þe lift hond, 5.6 *per calles devios* — by beest paþis out of þe wey, corr. by streit berid paþis out of þe wey, 5.10 *nitentes* — stronge *E*[1], semynge *E*[2], corr. shynynge, 6.3 *ascendebat Madian* — he sty ʒede opp to Madyan, corr. Madyan sty ʒede opp, 6.28 *lucum* — heriynge place, corr. mawmete wode; 7.23 *persequeba/n/tur Madian* — Madyan was pursuwed, corr. pursueden Madyan, 9.31 *et obpugnat* — begynneþ to ouyrcomyn, corr. & a ʒenfi ʒteþ, 9.44 *obpugnans* — ouyrcomynge, corr. a ʒenfi ʒtynge, 12.6 *in ipso Iordanis transitu* — in þat goynge ouer of (cr. out) Jordan, 16.8 *satrapae* — wise maistres, corr. princis, 16.26 *quibus omnis inminet domus* — on þe whiche leneþ (corr. stant) al þe hous.

On the whole *E* is the most correct MS of EV. It shares one error in common with the other MSS: 9.15 *cedros* — seedis (corr. seed'r'es *Lo*). *E*[1] alone is correct 12.6 *in ipso Iordanis transitu* — in þat goynge ouer *of* (cr. out) Jordan. Together with *CLoX* or with one or two of those MSS it is often correct against the others, e.g. 3.4 *per manum Moysi* — by þe hond (*A* hoondis) of M. *EX*, 3.30 *sub manu Israel* — vnder þe hond (*A* hows) of I. *ELo*, 7.23 *usque ad Bethsecha* — vn to B. *CE* (*A* into B.), 10.9 *in tantum ut* — in (& *A* etc.) so myche þat *CELo*, 10.9 *afflictus* — turmentid (turned *A* etc.) *CELo*, 11.34 *unigenita filia sua* — his onely gotyn dow ʒtyr (dou ʒtris *A* etc.) *CELoX*.

MS *F* is, like *B*, a uniform copy of EV. It often agrees with *BHWo* or with one or two of them in presenting an inferior reading, e.g. 3.11 *Quievitque terra* — And the lond (lord *FWo*) restid, 13.23 *ea quae sunt ventura* — tho thingis that (om. *BFHWo*) ben to com.

MS *H* resembles *B* and *F* in presenting a uniform text of EV. It is less carefully written and has several omissions. It is inferior, alone or together with one or more of *BFWo*, in e.g. 13.17 *si sermo tuus fuerit expletus* — if thi word (lord *H*) were fulfillid, 21.3 *una tribus auferretur* — o lynage be (ben *BFH*) doon awei.

The *Lo* MS, like *CEX*, presents a less standardized text. Its vocabulary is a little different from the other MSS, e.g. 'raise' for 'rear', 'call' for 'clepe'. It often agrees with *CEX* or with one or two of them in its readings, e.g. 11.11 *fecitque eum omnis populus* — and al (om. *A* etc.) þe peple etc. *CELo*.

The *Wo* MS is another uniform MS of EV. As remarked above, it often agrees with one or more of *BFH*, e.g. 4.18 *ingressus tabernaculum* — gooinge (goon *A* etc.) into the tabernacle *Wo* & *F*. Like the other copies it also has errors of its own, e.g. 8.25 *in eo* — out *Wo*.

MS *X*, finally, is one of the 'individual' copies of EV. As mentioned above, it often agrees with *CELo* or one or more of them as against *A* + *BFHWo*, e.g. 19.24 *ut humilietis eas* — that ʒe lowe (louen *A* etc.) hem *CELoX*. It has rather more doubtful readings than *CELo*, however, e.g. 5.20 *ordine* — ordre, cedre(?) *X*, 7.3 *remanserunt* — beden (ben *X*) still, 11.17 *contempsit* — dispisede, dispisende *X*.

In LV, MS A forms the text. It is an ordina y copy of the version with few irregularities. Comparatively few emendations are necessary, and what errors there are in A are the natural consequences of copying, e.g. 14.11 *essent* — schul[d]en be, 19.17 *autem* — forsoþe, þerfor A & N, 20.1 *egressi ... sunt* — ʒeden [out].

MS Ac is very like A and presents few variations. It is erroneous 9.14 *veni* — comaunde (anticipation), 14.3 *mulier* — man, 18.22 *iam* — not; and dubious 10.8 *habitabant* — dwellen, 11.40 *plangant* — biweilide, 17.8 *declinasset* — hadde bowid (lowid Ac).

MS B is also like A with a few more variations than Ac. It is correct 3.28 *transmittunt* — leden (A ledde) ouer, but dubious 5.26 *perforans* — and perside (pereschide B), 11.36 *aperuisti* — openyst, 13.17 *ut* — that (& B). It adds a gloss 20.28, but omits one 8.27.

MS C is very like A, as Ac is, and presents very few variations from it. It is doubtful 9.50 *oppidum* — citee (C citees), 12.5 *quo dicente* — and whanne he seide (hadde seid C). Together with AI it differs from the rest 8.10 *educentium* — drawing (cet. leding) out.

MS Ca presents quite a few linguistic variants but very few translational variations from A. It is doubtful 2.23 *noluit* — nolde (wolde C), 15.14 *vociferantes* — criynge (comynge Ca), erroneous 3.8 *tradidit* — bitook (bitoken Ca).

MS D varies in language about as much from A as Ca, but more in translation. It is corrupt 2.18 *vastantium* — wasteris (watris D), 6.14 *manu* — hond (lond D), 6.21 *evanuit* — vanyschide (rauyschid D), 19.19 *mecum* — with me (þee D); it is dubious 8.2 *quid* — what (whanne D), 10.16 *miseriis* — wretchidnessis (wickidnessis D).

MS E varies considerably from A in both language and translation. It is often corrupt and has many dubious readings, e.g. 1.16 *cognati* — alye (holie E), 5.20 *de* — fro (for E), 5.26 *perforans* — and perside (per-seiued E), 6.5 *greges* — flockis (folks E), 9.9 *venire* — comeþe E, 9.48 *ferens* — and he bar (brak E) it, 10.4 *sedentes* — sittynge (fiȝting E), 13.6 *terribilis* — ferdful (frendful E), 14.18 *arassetis* — hadden ... erid (herd it E).

MS F has, like Ca, more linguistic variants than translational varia-tions from A. It is corrupt 20.37 *caedentibus* — sleeris (fleeres F), dubious 16.24 *videns* — seyinge F, 18.30 *Gersam filii Moysi* — J. sone (sones F) of M.

MS G has about the same number of variations as D. It is corrupt 2.20 *pepigeram* — couenauntide (comaundide GQ), 7.24 *montem* — hil (puple GQ), 8.32 *senectute* — elde (G eende); it is dubious 18.10 *securos* — sikir men (placis G), 20.21 *de* — of (aȝens GQ; repetition?). It omits a gloss 13.6, a past participle 14.9.

MS Ha has rather more language variants than translational varia-tions from A. It is corrupt 11.18 *latere* — side (see Ha), 19.16 *potero* — schal Y mow (now Ha), and dubious 14.14 *cibus* — mete (mede Ha), 15.17 *elevatio* — reisyng (risyng Ha).

MS I really needs an edition of its own. It teems with variations (mostly translational) from A and the rest. It is a curious mixture of EV and (main-ly) LV. Its status will be discussed in the final chapter (Summary and Conclusions). The most frequent deviations from LV (and EV) are changes in *word-order* and *additions* to the text (categories I and II above), e.g. 1.1 *consuluerunt ... Dominum* — counseliden /wiþ I/ þe Lord, 1.8 *percusserunt* — smytiden, þei smoten *it* I, 1.13 *eam* — it, þat *citee* I, 2.18 *afflictorum* — of hem /þat weren I/ turmentid; 3.29 *sed percusserunt Moabitas in tempore illo* — I but in þat tyme þei smeten ... *moabitis*. One might say that MS I continues and strengthens the tendencies displayed by LV versus EV. On the other hand there are relicts of EV retained in I but not in LV, e.g. 16.18 *assumpta pecunia* — EV takun to the monei, LV with the money takun, I the m. taken *wiþ hem*, 19.28 *qua nihil respondente* — EV the which no thing answerynge, LV and whanne sche answeride no thing, I = EV.

MS K, like several of the other LV MSS, has more linguistic than translational variants. It is on the whole correct. Together with A & I it adds an object pronoun 2.1 *introduxi in terram* — Y brouȝte ȝou in to the lond.

MS L is rather like E though it does not vary from A to the same extent. It is corrupt 9.2 *os* — boond L, 9.54 *evagina* — drawe out (not L), 11.23 *terram* — hond L, and dubious 11.34 *unigenita filia sua* — his oon (owne L) gendrid douȝter.

MS M is of the average type, having more linguistic variants than translational ones. It is dubious 18.6 *iter quo pergitis* — the iourney whidur (which LM) ȝe goon.

MS Ma has a fair number of variations. It is dubious 12.4 *vocatis ... ad se* — clepid to hym (cl. togidere Ma), 20.5 *incredibili* — vnbileueful (vnleful GMa). Together with Ac & I it leaves out a gloss 10.16.

MS N does not vary very much from the bulk of LV MSS. It is corrupt 8.27 (gloss) *propir*, purpur N, 11.7 *odistis* — haten (hatiden IU), hadden N, 11.3 *consita* — set aboute (aboue N), and dubious 3.10 *judicavit* — delyuerede N.

MS O varies very little from A. It is dubious 20.18 *surgentes* — riseden (reisiden MaO), 21.22 *ut acciperent* — that thei schulden (O shulen) take.

MS P is very like L, both resembling E but with fewer variations. It is corrupt 11.2 *heres ... esse* — be eir, bere ELP, and dubious 9.57 *quod* — that /þis ELP/ thing.

MS Q is like G but has fewer variations. It is doubtful 8.3 *spiritus eorum* — the spirit of hem (him U, effraym I, þe lord GQ).

MS R is rather more varied than the bulk of LV MSS. It is corrupt 9.19 *laetetur* — be he (ȝe LNR) glad, 18.22 *domo* — hows (hoondis R), and dubious 5.30 *ad ornanda* — to ourne (oure DEMaR). It has a long omission 8.15.

MS S differs somewhat from the average LV MSS. It is inferior 8.26 *praeter* — outakun (vntakun S), 8.35 *bona* — goodis (goddis S), *in domum* — in (vn S) to the hows. It omits glosses 1.28, 2.17, 3.15, 5.18.

MS U has comparatively few variations. It is erroneous 2.18 *caede* — sleyng (fleynge U), and doubtful 18.27 *tulerunt* — token (taken OU).

MS W has about the average number of variations. It is erroneous 16.14 *licio* — strong boond (hond W), and dubious 5.20 *dimicatum est* — me fauȝt (was fauȝten W). Interesting variants are 7.15 *interpretationem* — interpretyng, W interpretacioun, and 7.25 *fluenta* — flodis, W stronde.

MS X, finally, has comparatively few variations. It is doubtful 3.20 *solus* — aloone (aboue X), 11.3 *latrocinantes* — doynge thefte, X gaderinge etc. It omits glosses like S.

6. Summary and Conclusions

In this final chapter the main contents of this third volume of my trilogy will be summarized together with material from the previous two volumes and additions from the present study.

Of the about 200 surviving manuscripts of the Middle English bible, the first full translation of the Latin Vulgate into English, forty MSS have been used for this trilogy of books (I: Prefatory Epistles of St. Jerome, II: Baruch, III: Judges; below referred to as I, II, III respectively). A full list of the MSS including repositories, numbers, and letters can be found at the end of this volume.

The forty MSS fall into two types of texts: a literal version, called the Early Version (EV), and a freer, more idiomatic version, called the Later Version (LV). There are, of the forty MSS, 15 in EV and 28 in LV, the extra three numbers being due to the mixed nature of two MSS (no. 46 & 71) and the binding of two MSS in one codex (no. 87). The letters designating the MSS are for EV in italics (*A* etc.), for LV in ordinary type (A etc.).

Throughout this investigation the Latin source, the Vulgate, has been of paramount importance. It is the fundament of the versions and of their analysis. Almost any reading in any MS of either version can be judged with the help of the Latin behind it. Obviously the Latin text must be reliable; this was important for the translators, and it is so even to-day for investigators. The recent Vatican edition with its full variants is indispensable.

The linguistic evidence from the two versions and the forty various manuscripts is sufficient for a rough dating and localization of them, although the three texts of my MEB do not amount to more than perhaps 5 per cent of the entire bible text. In spite of minor differences as to age and dialect, it is possible to assign to the versions and their MSS dates ranging from the end of the 14th century to the first half of the 15th century, and areas of production in the Midlands with a centre in the middle plus more or less pronounced influxes from adjoining areas. Before we proceed to an attempt at fixing the dates and dialects of the originals more precisely, let us consider the two pieces of evidence together of the various MSS, the language and the translation.

MS *A* (text MS of EV) is rather late among EV MSS. In view of its 'finished' character (partly modernized word-order) and standardized type of language it represents EV in its 'authorized' form. Date: c. 1425. Dialect: mixed CM.

MS *B* is rather early among EV MSS. It is a uniform specimen of the literal version with few textual variants. Date: c. 1400. Dialect: mixed NM.

MS *C* (text MS in II) is one of the earliest MSS of EV. It is less uniform than the bulk of EV MSS but more correct. Date: bef. 1400. Dialect: NM (Atlas).

MS *D* (used in I) is less uniform than the bulk of EV MSS. After the Pentateuch the MS is in LV, called U (below). Date: after 1400. Dialect: SEM.

MS *E* is the earliest MS of EV. It is unique in having corrections of an original character; corrected it agrees with the other EV MSS, particularly *C*. In this volume (III) it shows a 'break' at 7.13 where the second scribe of the MS (a Westerner) is followed by the third scribe of the MS (there are four or five scribes of *E* in all) who is an Easterner. This change of hands does not seem to be reflected in the other MSS of EV or in LV. Date: before 1400. Dialect: WM (bef. 7.13) plus EM (Atlas: Soke).

MS *F* is very like *B*, being also an early copy of EV of the uniform type. Like *B* it has few textual variants. Date: c. 1400. Dialect: mixed NM.

MS *G* (used in II) is rather like *A* but varies a little more. It is an average MS of EV, of medium age and of the standard EM dialect. Date: c. 1425. Dialect: SEM (slightly more northern before Bar. 3.20).

MS *H* is rather like *B* and *F*, being a uniform copy of EV, but less carefully written with ensuing variations. Date: c. 1420. Dialect: EM.

MS *I* (used for EV in I) has prologues in OT in EV, otherwise the MS is in LV and called K (below). It is dated 1408 and written in a mixed CM dialect.

MS *K* (text MS in II) is an ordinary MS of EV of the standard type. It is later than *C*, with which it happens to be bound up, and less correct. Date: c. 1420. Dialect: EM.

MS *Lo* is a fairly early MS of EV and less standardized. It varies from the bulk of EV MSS both in forms and vocabulary. Otherwise it often agrees with *C* & *E*. Date: c. 1400. Dialect: NM.

MS *Wo* is another standard copy of EV, of about the same type as *BFH*, of medium age and mixed M dialect. Date: c. 1420. Dialect: mixed EM.

MS *X* (text MS in I) is rather like *C* and more 'individual' than most EV MSS. It varies from the other EV MSS about as much as *Lo*. Date: 1400—1410. Dialect: NM.

MS *Y* (used in II) is a uniform copy of EV of the standard type. It varies to about the same extent as *K* and *Wo*. Date: c. 1410. Dialect: EM.

MS *Z* (used in II) is a late mutilated copy of EV in a revised type of language in the standard dialect. Date: c. 1430. Dialect: SEM.

Summing up the evidence of the EV manuscripts, we can see a time-span from the earliest MSS *E & C* (both before 1400, perhaps 1390) via the early MSS *BFLo* (all c. 1400) and the fairly early MSS *D* (after 1400, perhaps 1410), *X* (1400—1410, perhaps at the latter end), and *Y* (c. 1410) with MS *I* as an extra sign-post (1408) to the MSS of medium age *HKWo* (c. 1420) and *AG* (c. 1425) with MS *Z* (c. 1430) bringing up the rear.

Geographically, the EV MSS are centred round MSS *A & I* (both mixed CM), from the NM MSS *CLoX & BF* (both mixed) to the WM part of *E* and the EM MSS *HKY & Wo* (mixed) + the EM part of *E* with MSS *DGZ* representing SEM.

MS A (text MS of LV) is an average copy of LV of medium age and standard language. It varies less from the bulk of LV MSS than does *A* from other EV MSS. Date: c. 1420. Dialect: SM (Atlas: Bucks).

MS Ac (formerly Acland) is very like A in most respects, though earlier. Date: c. 1400—1410. Dialect: SM (Atlas: Bucks for GP in Ac).

MS B is also like A with a few more variations from it than Ac, otherwise an ordinary copy of LV in a somewhat mixed dialect. Date: c. 1420. Dialect: CM.

MC C does not vary much from A and Ac. It is also an average MS of LV of medium age and slightly mixed M dialect. Date: c. 1420. Dialect: SM.

MS Ca (not used in I though later found to contain its text) is like the previous MSS of LV an average copy though with more linguistic variants. Date: c. 1420. Dialect: SEM, or mixed SM.

MS D has more later variants than the preceding MSS of LV, otherwise it is an average MS of somewhat mixed dialect. Date: c. 1430. Dialect: mixed SM.

MS E is more varied in language than any of the other LV MSS and has many late and dubious forms and readings. Date: c. 1440. Dialect: very mixed SM.

MS F is rather more varied in language than the other MSS of LV above (except E) of medium age and mixed M dialect. Date: c. 1420. Dialect: mixed CM.

MS G is a little more varied than the average MSS of LV, but otherwise an average copy itself of medium age and standard dialect. Date: c. 1430. Dialect: EM (Atlas: Hunts for GP in G).

MS H (used in II) is a very ordinary copy of LV with very few individual features. It is of medium age and written in standard late ME. Date: c. 1425. Dialect: SEM.

MS Ha varies more in language than in the translation from A, but is otherwise a standard copy of LV as to age and dialect. Date: c. 1430. Dialect: SEM.

MS I is an exceptional MS of LV in that it combines late modernisms of an extreme type with early literalisms of the type of EV. In the main, though, it agrees with LV in a standard type of EM (mixed). Date: c. 1430. Dialect: mixed EM.

MS K (used in II & III) is the same as *I* (above, used in I), thus also dated 1408 and written in a mixed CM dialect.

MS L is rather like E though not varied to the same extent. It is a fairly late copy in a mixed M dialect. Date: c. 1430. Dialect: mixed SM.

MS M is an ordinary MS of LV with about the average number of linguistic and translational variants. Date: c. 1420. Dialect: SEM.

MS Ma is a little later and somewhat more varied than most LV MSS, otherwise fairly standard as to form and language. Date: c. 1430. Dialect: SEM.

MS N is another average MS of LV of the standard type of (mixed) Midland dialect. It does not differ much from A and the bulk. Date: c. 1420. Dialect: SEM.

MS O is a standard MS of LV with fairly few variations from A and the bulk of LV MSS. It is a little later than average copies. Date: c. 1430. Dialect: SEM.

MS P resembles E and L, though E is more extreme than the other two MSS. It is rather late and exhibits a mixed type of M dialect. Date: c. 1430. Dialect: SM (mixed).

MS Q is rather like G though not quite so varied and late as G, but more of medium age and standard dialect. Date: c. 1425. Dialect: SEM (Atlas: Beds for GP in Q).

MS R is a little different from the average MSS of LV being later and less uniform than most copies. Date: c. 1435. Dialect: SEM.

MS Ry (used in II) is an average MS of LV of medium age and standard dialect. It has few variants. Date: c. 1425. Dialect: EM.

MS S is a little different from most of the other LV MSS. It has variants of its own both of language and translation though not material ones. Date: c. 1430. Dialect: mixed EM.

MS U (used in II & III) is the same as *D* (above, used in I). Date: after 1400 (perhaps 1410). Dialect: SEM.

MS V (used in II) is an average MS of LV, of medium age, and of the standard type of the EM dialect. Date: c. 1425. Dialect: SEM.

MS W is a typical MS of LV, of medium age and standard dialect, differing but little from A and the bulk of LV MSS. Date: c. 1420. Dialect: SEM (mixed).

MS X is rather like O, though with more variations. It is yet another typical MS of LV, like W, of medium age and standard dialect. Date: c. 1420. Dialect: SEM.

MS Y, finally, (used in II) is also an average MS of LV, of medium age and comparatively normal dialect. Date: c. 1425. Dialect: SE or SEM.

Summing up the evidence of the LV manuscripts, we get about the same width of the time-span from the earliest to the latest MSS as with EV though beginning and ending about a decade later, i.e. from about the beginning of the 15th century (K 1408) towards the middle of the century (E c. 1440) with the majority of MSS centred round 1425 except the early MSS Ac and U (both c. 1400—1410) and the late MS R (c. 1435).

Geographically, again, the MSS are centred in a fairly coherent area of the country, though with some bias towards the south-east of the Midlands, from a few CM MSS and some more SM MSS to quite a few EM and SEM MSS.

The implications of these dates and dialects for the forty odd MSS listed here will now be considered for the two versions together. We should bear in mind the approximate nature of most of the dates and the often mixed character of the dialects. Still the material is sufficient for drawing some conclusions.

Treating the two versions together the time-span of about half a century (c. 1390— c. 1440) admits of various stages of revisions and copyings. The spectrum assumed by Anne Hudson from a manuscript such as *X* to manuscripts such as A and H does not emerge, though; the two types of texts are clearly distinguishable by their different modes of translation. We must then recognize two translations, one literal and one idiomatic, not just one with subsequent modifications. The interval between the two is difficult to assess: LV did not oust EV as is seen from the contemporary dates of MSS; still there is a difference of about a decade, which we will assume to be the difference of the originals, which are lost.

Before we try to date the lost originals, let us consider the areas within which the MSS of the two versions were written. Two centres have emerged from the preceding survey of the MSS: both in the Midlands, rather more central for EV and more south-eastern for LV. These centres may or may not point to the areas of the originals; the idiom of an original may be preserved by faithful copying or it may disappear more or less completely by 'translating' scribes. We will assume that the dialects of the earliest MSS may represent at least partly the dialects of the originals. Of particular importance, then, are the EV MSS *C* and *E*, and the LV MSS Ac, K, and U.

In the survey of MSS above, *C* is dated bef. 1400 and placed in NM (Atlas), *E* is dated bef. 1400 and placed in WM (bef. 7.13) and EM (Atlas); Ac is dated c. 1400—1410 and placed in SM (Atlas), K is dated 1408 and placed in CM, U is dated after 1400 (1410?) and placed in SEM.

Of these five MSS, *E* alone has the character of an original MS, teeming with corrections, likewise of an original character (for examples see above). I know from my edition of *E* (Bodley 959) that in all these corrected instances, throughout the manuscript, the other EV MSS follow suit and adopt the final reading in *E*. Forshall & Madden were led to believe that this MS is original, and yet a mistake like *seedis* for Lat. cedros (9.15) is enough to prove that *E* was copied from an even earlier text. The state of the MS, on the other hand, cannot be a 'salutary' reminder only of 'the multiple and often textually local effort that went into the modifications' (Anne Hudson), but rather marks it as a proto-type for subsequent copies. That is why it is so important a link in the tradition of the EV text. The dialect shift at 7.13, although not reflected elsewhere, may therefore point to the form of the original behind *E*. Most remarkable is the WM influence before 7.13; no other MS of WB, as far as I know it, can show such a number of W forms. As for the con-tinuation (after 7.13) the Eastern type of language is more natural in a late ME copy, though this also might indicate the linguistic form of *E*'s predecessor.

The other early MS of EV, *C*, is in a consistent NM dialect. Since *C* and the other EV MSS depend for their readings largely on *E*, they cannot throw better light on the original form of EV.

The three early MSS of LV, Ac, K, and U, are all in for WB well attested dialects, and it is hard to point out any one of these dialects, SM, CM, and SEM respectively, as more likely than the others to be the dialect of the original of LV, since none of the three MSS is superior to the rest in the way *E* is superior to all the other MSS of EV. It is noteworthy that there is no MS of LV in a WM or NM dialect, though there may be elements of such in a few MSS, most of the surviving MSS of LV being EM (or SEM) besides a few CM and some more SM MSS.

It is possible that the emerging standard idiom used in many of the LV MSS, and in some EV MSS, tended to obliterate more 'dialectal' forms of the language. Perhaps we should look for the original dialect somewhere in the areas localized for LV MSS in the Atlas, i.e. Bucks, Beds, or Hunts.

As for the date of the originals we must assume at least a decade to have elapsed before the writing of the earliest manuscripts extant to-day, from the composition of the prototypes of E and its counterpart in LV. Assuming again an interval of some ten years between the versions we arrive at approximately 1 380 and 1 390 respectively for the underlying originals of the earliest texts preserved. It does not seem possible to be more precise starting from MS evidence.

So far we have based our conclusions on the materials of chapters 4 and 5, the linguistic and translational evidence. There is one more important source of information: the so-called General Prologue (GP) prefixed to some ten MSS of LV. In it we find descriptions of the books of the Old Testament, some polemics, and, most important, an account of the procedure behind the versions (obviously a conflate document). There are four stages in the process: 1. the establishing of a reliable Latin text to work from; 2. analyzing the text so established with the help of glosses etc.; 3. consideration of knotty points difficult of translation; 4. translation 'to the sentence' followed by correction of the translation. It is clear from 4. and from other references in GP that the last stage (4.) refers to LV. It is equally clear that 1. and 2. cannot refer to EV, which consequently has to be fitted in under 3. where translation is involved. By comparing the Latin Vulgate text and the two versions extant of the Middle English bible we can elicit the meaning of 1. and 2. in the translational context.

The most striking thing, perhaps, about MEB is the literalness of EV, so extreme at times that a modern reader needs the Latin text for enlightenment. This is particularly true of Jerome's prologues (see MEB I for examples) which are difficult enough for an ordinary reader in Latin but far more difficult sometimes in an extremely literal translation into Middle English. This extreme literalness is found chiefly in EV I, less outspoken in EV II and LV (occasionally). It is not consistent even in E, but can be assumed to have been used to a still larger extent in E's predecessor(s). The best explanation of this literalness is to think of 1. and 2. as literally Latin-based pre-stages of EV (3.), 1. perhaps an interlinear gloss, 2. very likely the original 'turning'. What the author of GP describes, then, is his participation in the translational work: 1. preparing word by word the transposition in 2. of a 'nude' literal text in English to serve as the basis for the modified, still largely literal, text of 3. and for the more easily intelligible text in 4. In proof of 1. we have very many extreme literalisms in, above all, EV I; in proof of 2. we have crudities preserved in LV but removed in EV; no proof is needed in the case of 3. and 4., the 15 MSS of EV and the 28 copies of LV in Judges etc. speaking for themselves.

We have mentioned the author of GP as the organizer of the work behind WB. It is time to discuss a little the external circumstances around this undertaking. What we here call the Middle English Bible (MEB) is also known as the Wyclif or Wyclif/f/ite or Lollard Bible (WB). The attribution to Wyclif and his circle is established. There is no reason to doubt that John Wyclif was the prime mover of the project of translating the Bible. Stage 1. is then naturally to be connected with his name. Stage 2., the work of a 'turner', is perhaps to be ascribed to one or more of his associates at Oxford (Trevisa was one of them and David Fowler has shown strong evidence in favour of his participation in the work). Stage 3. is explicitly tied to the name of Nicholas Hereford, one in the Oxford circle. Stage 4., finally, is the work of the author of GP, in co-operation with others, all along, who helped him to correct the work. Since he was active at all the four stages, the prime mover in 1. is also a translator in 4.; the name Wyclif's Bible seems correct. Taken together with the evidence from the MSS the testimony of the General Prologue, in the way it is interpreted here, seems to corroborate the assumptions made above about the dialect of the originals, and to some extent the date. Wyclif's participation in the work sets the limits c. 1370 to 1384; Trevisa's and Hereford's parts in EV can account for the W + E type of language, Wyclif and other Oxford workers for the CM type in LV. The dates, though, will have to be modified: the decade assumed between the originals of EV and LV was probably no more than half, since both were based on the common original version. The four stages of GP would then be: 1. the interlinear version (IV) c. 1370 (Northern?); 2. the original version (OV) c. 1375 (Western?); 3. the early version (EV) c. 1380 (Eastern); 4. the later version (LV) c. 1385 (Central).

It remains to discuss the nature of the remarkable MS I (Bodley 277) in LV but with EV features. Forshall & Madden believed it to be a later amalgamation of the two versions in a revision of its own, Fristedt saw in it the First Revision of EV which later led to LV, i.e. an intermediate version. Both attitudes to it have plus and minus factors: for FM the obvious mixture of EV and LV and the additional modernisms, against FM the apparent inconsistency of keeping ancient features while intro-

74

ducing extremely new ones; for Fristedt the fact that this half EV half LV version is found also partially (not in Judges) in two more MSS, against Fristedt the extreme modernisms found in I which cannot just be explained away as a superstructure.

MS I seems to be based on an original type of translation, see e.g. 2.3 *quam ob rem* — for the whiche thing I (wherefore ELV), 13.23 *sunt ventura* — ben to comynge I (ben to com EV, schulen come LV), 16.11 *infirmus* — lethi I (feble ELV), 16.19 *abicere* — schyue awei I (throwe aw. EV, caste aw. LV). The rare *lethi* is a Trevisa word (cf. MED) and must be a relict, not an innovation. Otherwise EV is often quoted in I, but by and large the form of I is LV, though with very many later changes. On balance, neither FM nor Fristedt can be right, though FM seem to be nearer the truth: MS I is a revision of all the stages of WB, following the principles laid down in GP — to be based on the Latin (IV & OV), to translate not only 'ad verbum' (EV) but first and foremost 'ad sententiam' (LV). MS I is in a way a monument erected in honour of the man who gave England this translation of the Bible — the crown of Middle English scriptural work — John Wyclif.

In strange contrast are the condemning words of Archbishop Arundel (1411) in Deanesly's translation: "to fill up the measure of his malice, he (Wyclif) devised the expedient of *a new translation* (my italics) of the scriptures into the mother tongue." These words are proof of Wyclif's involvement in the work and, in particular, in the Later Version.

II. The Texts

For practical reasons Forshall & Madden's texts of Judges (for EV from *A*, for LV from A) have been used for this edition more or less unchanged, though checked with microfilms of the MSS. The other MSS were also read from copies sent to me. In so doing I noted all the variations from the text MSS except for names and adjectives from names and minor matters such as obvious scribal errors and orthographic variants of no phonetic importance (e.g. *i* for *y* or vice versa). The variants are so numerous that references to them had to be made by line numbers. The Latin text, compiled from Heyse-Tischendorf's edition with variations from the Vatican edition, is numbered, like the EV and LV texts, by the Vulgate verse numbers.

To concentrate on the Latin-based text extra matter such as rubrics and marginal glosses from Lyra in B & C have been left out, as also the short prologue found in M alone.

In the texts a few editorial devices call for comment: square brackets mark additions, round parentheses mark cancellations, and asterisks mark other alterations (information given in the variants).

In the variants accents ('thus') indicate interlinear or marginal insertions. Raised [1] and [2] mark readings pr.v. (prima vice) and sec.v. (secunda vice) respectively, e.g. E^1 and E^2.

A. The Early Version

1. 1 Aftir the deeth of Josue the sones
    of Irael counseilden the Lord, seyynge,
    Who shal stye vp bifore vs aȝens Cha-
  2 nane, and be duk of bateil? And the
    Lord seide, Judas shal stie vp; loo! I   5
  3 haue taak the loond in his hoond. And
    Juda seith to Symeon, his brothir, Sty vp
    with me in my lot, and fiȝt aȝens Cha-
    nane, that I goo with thee in thi lot.

Variants A

1. 1 After *BEFHWo*; deþ *BCFHWoX*; sonus *CX*, sonys *E*
  2 counseyld *BFH*, counseileden *CX*, conseylede *E*, counseylid *LoWo*; lorde
    Wo; seiende *CX*, seying *Lo*
  3 steyȝe *BFLoWo*, steȝe *CX*, styȝe *EH*; opp *E*; befor *C*; aȝeyns *BEFWo*,
    aȝen *CX*, aȝeynes *Lo*
  4 ben *CX*; duyke *BH*, duke *CELoWo*, duyk *F*; bataile *CLoX*, bateyle *EWo*
  5 seyd *B*; steyȝe *BFLoWo*, steȝe *C*, styȝe *EH*, steȝen *X*; opp *E*; lo *CELoX*
  6 ha *C*; taake *B*, take *CEFHWo*, taken *LoX*; lond *CX*, londe *LoWo*; hond
    CX, honde *ELoWo*
  7 seys *Lo*; broþer *cet.*; steyȝ *B*, steeȝ *C*, styȝ *E*, steyȝe *FLoWo*, styȝe *H*,
    steȝe *X*; opp *E*
  8 lott *BFH*, lote *Wo*; fiȝte *Lo*; aȝeyns *BEFWo*, aȝen *CX*, aȝeynes *Lo*
  9 go *CELoWoX*; þe *EWo*; lott *BFH*, loot *Wo*

C. The Latin text

1. 1 Post mortem Iosue consuluerunt filii Israel Dominum,
    dicentes: Quis ascendet ante nos contra Chananeum,
    et erit dux belli?
  2 Dixitque Dominus: Iudas ascendet; ecce tradidi terram
    in manu/s/ eius.

B. The Later Version

1. 1 Aftir the deeth of Josue the sones of
Israel counseliden the Lord, and seiden,
Who schal stie bifor vs aȝens Cananei,
2 and schal be duik of the batel? And the
Lord seide, Judas schal stie; lo! Y haue   5
3 ȝoue the lond in to hise hondis. And Judas seide to Symeon, his brother, Stie
thou with me in my lot, and fiȝte thou
aȝens Cananei, that Y go with thee in thi

Variants B

1. 1 After EFLU; deþ AcCEIOUX; sonys GIQ
2 counceiliden BGHaIMaOQRSX, conseliden C, counceileden CaEFMW,
counceilden D, counseleden LP; the: wiþ þe I; saiden E, þei seiden to him I
3 steie F, stie up I, stiȝe MaNR; bifore BCCaDFGHaIKLMaNRSUWX;
aȝenus AcCNO, aȝeins E; þe men of cananey I
4 duk ELP; bateil DSX, bateyle GR, batele K, batayle U
5 sayde E; steie F, stie up I, stiȝe MaNR; lo: loue S
6 ȝiue E, ȝouen I, ȝofe K; his EFGILPQS; hondes CaF, hoondis R
7 said E; broþir GMaNORS; sti E, steie F, stiȝe MaNR
8 thou: þou up I; into L; lott IKMaR; fiȝth E
9 aȝenus AcCNO, aȝeinus E; that: & þat Ma; þe DE; in: into Ma; þin D

3 Et ait Iudas Simeoni, fratri suo: Ascende mecum in
sorte mea, et pugna contra Chananeum, ut (et) ego
pergam tecum in sorte tua. Et abiit cum eo Simeon.

4 And Symeon wente with hym; and Juda   10
stiede vp. And the Lord took Chanane
and Phereze in to the hoondis of hem,
and thei smyten in Bezech ten thousand
5 of men. And thei foonden Adonybe[ze]ch
in Besech, and thei fouȝten aȝens hym,   15
6 and smyten Chanane, and Phereze. Adonybezech forsothe fleiȝ, whom pursuynge
thei token, kit of the ouermost partis of
7 the hoondis of hym, and [of] feet. And
Adonybezech seide, Seuenti kyngis, kut   20

10 went *BFHWo*
11 steiȝid *BFWo*, steȝede *CX*, styȝede *E*, styȝid *H*, steiȝede *Lo*; opp *E*;
     lorde *Wo*; toke *BFHWo*, toc *CX*
12 hondus *C*, hondys *EHX*, hondes *LoWo*; þem *Lo*
13 smetyn *E*; tenn *BH*; thousend *CX*, þousont *E*, thousande *Lo*
14 founden *BCFHLoWoX*, foundyn *E*
15 foȝten *CX*, fouȝtyn *E*; aȝeyns *BEFHWo*, aȝen *CX*, aȝeynes *Lo*
16 smetyn *E*
17 whome *B*; pursuende *CX*, pursuyng *Lo*
18 tokyn *E*; kutt *BFH*, cut *CEX*, cutte *Lo*, kitt *Wo*; ouermast *Lo*, ouermaste
     Wo, ouermor *X*; paartis *FH*, partyes *LoWo*, partes *X*
19 hondus *C*, hondys *EX*, hondes *LoWo*; feete *Lo*, fete *Wo*; And: om. *B*
20 seuynty *E*; kingus *C*, kynges *LoWoX*; kutt *BFH*, kitte *Wo*

4 Ascenditque Iudas, et tradidit Dominus Chananeum ac
Pherezeum in manus eorum; et percusserunt in Bezech
decem millia virorum.
5 Inveneruntque Adonibezech in Bezech, et pugnaverunt
contra eum, ac percusserunt Chananeum et Pherezeum.
6 Fugit autem Adonibezech; quem persecuti comprehenderunt, caesis summitatibus manuum eius ac pedum.

4 lot. And Symeon ȝede with hym; and
Judas stiede. And the Lord bitook Cananey and Feresei in to the hondis of
hem, and the[i] killiden in Besech ten
5 thousynde of men. And thei founden
Adonybozech in Bezech, and thei fouȝten
aȝens hym, and smytiden Cananei, and
6 Feresey. Forsothe Adonybozech fledde,
whom thei pursueden, and token, and kittiden the endis of hise hondis and feet.
7 And Adonybozech seide, Seuenti kyngis,

10

15

20

10 lott IKMa
11 stiede: stood D, stied E, steiede F, stiede up I, stiȝede NR; bytoke
    ER, bitooke I
12 to: om. ELP; hondus E, hondes F, hoondis R; 12—13 the h. of hem:
    her h. I
13 killeden CaEFLMNPSW
14 þousynd CaMW, þousand DEHaMaQRSX, þousende FO, þousend
    GLNP, þousande K; of: om. I
15 in B.: om. HaMa; fauȝten I
16 aȝenus AcCKNO; smyteden CaKW, smeten EL, smyten FM, þei
    ouercamen I, smetin P
17 Forsothe: & I, forsoþ X; fled DE
18 pursuyden AcQ, pursuweden CaFMW; tooken GKLNOPX; kitteden
    CaEFLMPW, þei kitten off I, kittide R
19 eendis BIKMaQ, endes CaF; his EFHaILOPSX; hondes CaF, hoondis
    LR; of his feet I
20 kynghis E, kynges FHa

7 Dixitque Adonibezech: Septuaginta reges, amputatis
manuum ac pedum summitatibus, colligebant sub mensa
mea ciborum reliquias; sicut feci, ita reddidit mihi
Deus. Adduxeruntque eum in Ierusalem, et ibi mortuus
est.

of the ouermore paartis of hoondis and
of feet, gedreden vndur my bord relyues
of meetis; as I haue doo, so the Lord
hath doo to me. And thei brouȝten
hym into Jerusalem, and there he died.   25
8 Thanne the sones of Juda ouercomynge
Jerusalem token it, and smyten in mouth
of swerd, takynge al the citee to bren-
9 nynge. And afterward descendynge thei
fouȝten aȝens Chanane, that dwellyd in   30
the mounteyns, and at the south, in the
10 wijld feeldis. And Judas goynge aȝens
Chanane, that dwellid in Ebron, whas
name was bi old tyme Caryatharbe,

21   ouermor *C*, ouermost *X*; partis *CE*, partyes *LoWo*, partes *X*; hondus *C*,
hondys *EX*, hondes *LoWo*
22   fete *Lo*, feete *Wo*; geþerden *BF*, gedereden *CWoX*, gederedyn *E*, gadreden
Lo; vnder *BCFHLoWoX*, vndyr *E*; borde *BFHLoWo*; releues *CLo*,
relyfys *E*, releuys *Wo*, releeues *X*
23   metis *BEFHWo*, metus *C*, metes *LoX*; do *CWoX*, doon *ELo*
24   doo: ȝolde *CE²*, do *HWo*, ȝolden *Lo*, don *X*; broȝten *CX*, brouȝtyn *E*
25   dyȝid *BFHWo*, diede *CX*, deyde *E*
26   þann *B*, þenne *E*; sonus *CX*, sonys *E*; ouercomende *CX*, ouercommynge *F*,
ouercomyng *Lo*
27   tokyn *E*; hit *E*; smetyn *E*; mowþe *Lo*
28   swerde *LoWo*; takende *CX*, takyng *Lo*; cyte *BCELoWoX*; brennyng *CLoX*
29   aftirwarde *Lo*; descendende *CX*, descendyng *Lo*
30   foȝten *CX*, fouȝtyn *E*; aȝeyns *BFWo*, aȝen *CX*; dwelte *CX*, dwellede *E*,
dwelled *FWo*
31   mounteines *CLoX*, mounteynys *E*; atte *Lo*; southe *LoWo*
32   wylde *cet.*; feldus *C*, fildys *E*, feldys *Lo*, feeldes *Wo*; gooyng *B*, goende *CX*,
gooynge *F*; aȝeyns *BFWo*, aȝen *CX*
33   dwelt *BFHWo*, dwelte *CX*, twelte *E*; whas *AE*, whos *cet.*
34   olde *LoWo*

8 Oppugnantes ergo filii Iuda Ierusalem ceperunt eam,
et percusserunt in ore gladii, tradentes cunctam
incendio civitatem.
9 Et postea descendentes pugnaverunt contra Chananeum,
qui habitabat in montanis et ad meridiem (et) in
campestribus.
10 Pergensque Iudas contra Chananeum, qui habitabat in
Ebron, cuius nomen fuit antiquitus Cariatharbe,

whanne the endis of hondis and feet
weren kit awey, gaderiden relifs of metis
vndur my bord; as Y dide, so God hath
ȝolde to me. And thei brouȝten hym in
8 to Jerusalem, and there he diede. Ther-   25
for the sones of Juda fouȝten aȝens Jerusalem, and token it, and smytiden bi the
scharpnesse of swerd, and bitoken al the
9 cytee to brennyng. And aftirward thei
ȝeden doun, and fouȝten aȝens Cananey,   30
that dwellide in the hilli places, and at
10 the south, in feeldi places. And Judas
ȝede aȝens Cananei, that dwellide in Ebron,
whos name was bi eld tyme Cariatharbe;

21 when E, whan HaLP; eendis BGHaIKMaR, endes CaF; hendis E, hondes
    F, her hondis I, hondus Ma, hoondis RS; fete E, of her feet I
22 kut ELP, kitte HaK, kitt IMaNS; away Ha; gaderide C, gadereden
    CaELMPW, gadreden F, gadriden GINOR, gederiden K; þe relifs BMa,
    relefs CaLMP, releues EF, relifes K, releues W, relijf X; metes F, meetis
    GQR, mete I
23 vndir BDGHaIKMaNPRSX, vnder FLQ; boord AcBCCaDGIKMMaOQ-
    RSWX; 20−23 I: 70 k. g. rel. of m. vnd. my b. wh. þe e. of her h. & of
    her f. w. k. aw.; haue do I; hath: aþe E; God hath: h. g. Ma
24 ȝolden IKLMa
25 þer L; deide CaW, died E, deiede FM, diȝede R; þerfore
    BCaEFGKLMMaNQRSWX, þanne I
26 sonys GLQ; fauȝten GHaIQ, fouȝtin L, foȝten X; aȝenus AcCNO,
    aȝeins E
27 tooken GKLNOSX, þei token I, tookin P; smyteden CaW, smiten EFM,
    þei smoten it I, smetin LP
28 scharpnes DI; swerde E, sweerd R; bitooken GKLNOSX, þei bitooken I,
    bitookin P
29 cite CaFHaLMPQUW; brennynge DFGMaQU; afterwarde E, afterward
    LU; þai E
30 doune E; aȝenus CNO
31 dwellid D, duelled E, dwelliden I, dwellede LP, dwelleden U; hulli E,
    hillie K; placis EGHaILMaNPQSX
32 at the: atte E; feldi EHaU, þe feldy G, wijlde I, feldie K; placis
    DGHaLMaNPQSX, feeldis I
33 aȝenus AcCNO, aȝeins *E*; dwellid D, dwelled E, dwellede LP, dwelide O
34 elde AcCCaM, oolde DP, called E, oold GKLSX, eelde Ha, olde I, eeld
    MaRW, old NQ

smoot Sisay, and Achyman, and Tholo-

11 may. And thens goon, wenten to the
dwellers of Dabir, whos name was old
Cariathsepher, that is, the citee of lettris.

12 And Caleph seide, Who smytith Caryth-
sepher, and wastith it, I shal ȝyue to

13 hym a wijf, Axam, my douȝter. And
whanne Othonyel, the sone of Senech,
the lasse brother of Caleph, hadde taak
it, he ȝaf to hym a wijf, Axam, hys douȝ-

14 ter. The which goynge in the weie, hir
man monestide, that she shulde axe hir
fader a feeld; the which whanne she
hadde siȝid, sittynge in an asse, Caleph

35 smote *BFHLoWo*, smot *CEX*
36 þenns *BH*, þennus *CX*, þennys *E*, þennes *Lo*; gon *CWoX*; wentyn *E*
37 dwelleris *CLoX*; whose *B*; olde *BEFHLoWo*
38 cyte *BCEHLoWoX*
39 smiteþ *CEWoX*, smytes *Lo*
40 waastiþ *BFH*, wasteþ *CEWoX*, wastes *Lo*; hit *EH*; ȝeue *BEFHLo*
41 wyf *BCFHLoWoX*, wife *E*; doȝter *CX*
42 whenn *B*, whan *CWoX*, whenne *E*, when *H*
43 lesse *Lo*; had *BFLoWo*; take *BEFHWoX*, taken *CLo*
44 hit *E*; ȝaue *BFHWo*, ȝafe *Lo*; wyf *BCFHLoWoX*, wyfe *E*; doȝter *CX*
45 whiche *BCEHLoX*; gooynge *BF*, goende *CX*, goyinge *Wo*; wey *E*, way *Lo*;
   hyre *BFLo*, here *E*
46 monyschid *BFWo*, monestede *CLo*, moneschede *E*, moneschid *H*, mouede
   X; sholde *ELo*, schuld *FWo*; aske *Lo*; hyre *BFLo*, here *E*
47 fadir *BH*, fadre *Lo*; feelde *B*, feld *C*, fild *E*, felde *LoWo*; whiche
   BCEHLoX; whenn *BH*, whan *CEFWoX*
48 had *BFWo*; siȝȝid *BFHWo*, siȝhid *CX*, syȝȝed *E*, syȝed *Lo*; sittende *CX*,
   sittyng *Lo*

percussit Sisay et Achiman et Tholmai;

11 atque inde profectus abiit ad habitatores Dabir,
cuius nomen vetus erat Cariathsepher, id est civitas
litterarum.

12 Dixitque Caleph: Qui percusserit Cariathsepher, et
vastaverit eam, dabo ei Axam, filiam meam, uxorem.

and Judas killide Sisay, and Achyman,   35
11 and Tholmai. And fro thennus he ȝede
forth, and ȝede to the dwelleris of Dabir,
whos eld name was Cariathsepher, that is,
12 the citee of lettris. And Caleph seide, Y
schal ȝyue Axa, my douȝter, wijf to hym   40
that schal smyte Cariathsepher, and schal
13 waste it. And whanne Othonyel, sone of
Seneth, the lesse brother of Caleph, hadde
take it, Caleph ȝaf Axa, his douȝter, wijf
14 to hym. And hir hosebonde stiride hir,   45
goynge in the weie, that sche schulde axe
of hir fadir a feeld; and whanne sche
hadde siȝid, sittynge on the asse, Caleph

35 killid D, killed E, killede FLP
36 from K; þennes Ca FHaIMUW, þens DKMaR, þennis EGNQSX, þenis LP
37 foorþ D, forþe E; ȝede: he came I; the: om. S; dwellers
DEHaIKLMPRSUX, dwelleres F
38 whose C; eeld CaMRWX, elde DGMa, holde E, eelde Ha, oolde I, oold
KL, old NP
39 cite CaFHaLMPQUWX; letters E, lettres S
40 ȝeue BDHaMaQRSU, ȝife K; douȝtir AcBFGHaMaNOPQRSWX,
dowter E; wife E, wif FGHaLPQU
42 waaste DMaNOSX, wast E; whan EFHaLP; þe sone IMa, of s. O
43 lasse CaEK, ȝonger I; broþur E, broþir IPRS; had E
44 tak E, taken I; it: þat citee I; ȝaaf I, ȝafe R; douȝtir
DGHaMaOPQRWX, doutir E; wif EFGHaLPQU
45 hir (1°): her CaMW, here F, hire KS; husbonde BQR, hosebond CHa,
husbond D, hosbonde ELP, housbonde GIMa; stirid D, stired E, steride
GQU; hir (2°): her CaMW, here F, hire GK
46 going E; wey DIU; scholde CaMW, shul E
47 her CaLMW, here F, hire K; fader EFLMMaU; feld U; of hir f. a feeld:
a feeld of hir f. I; whan EFHaLP; ȝhe S
48 had BE; siȝȝid AcBCaELMNOPUW, siȝȝide C, siȝȝed D, siȝȝede F,
siȝhid GQ, siȝide Ha, siȝed IKMaRSX; sitting ELP; upon IMa; hir asse I

13 Cumque cepisset eam Othoniel, filius Cenech, frater
Caleph minor, dedit ei Axam, filiam suam, coniugem.
14 Quam pergentem in itinere monuit vir suus, ut peteret
a patre suo agrum. Quae cum suspirasset sedens /in/
asino, dixit ei Caleph: Quid habes?

15 seide to hir, What hast thou? And she
answerde, 3if to me a blessynge, for a dry
erthe thou hast 3yue to me; 3if and a
moyst with watris. And Caleph 3af to
hir moyst aboue, and moyst bynethe.

16 Forsothe the sones of Cyney, cosyn* to
Moises, stieden vp fro the citee of palmes
with the sones of Juda, into the deseert
of his lot, that is at the south of Arach;

17 and thei dwelliden with him. And Judas wente with Symeon, his brother; and
thei smyten to gidre Chananee, that

49 hyre *BFLo*, here *E*
50 answerede *E*, answerid *Lo*, answered *Wo*; 3eue *BFHLo*, 3yue *Wo*;
blyssynge *BF*, blessing *CLo*, blissing *X*; drye *BCFHLoWoX*, dry3e *E*
51 erþ *B*; 3yue: 3eue *BFH*, 3euen *Lo*, 3oue *X*; 3if: 3eue *BFHLo*, 3yue *Wo*
52 moiste *CLoWoX*; waters *BEH*; And: om. *B*; 3aue *BFHWo*, 3afe *Lo*
53 hyre *BFLo*, here *E*; moyst (2x): most *B* (2°), moiste *CLoWoX*, amoyst *F*
(2°); beneþe *CX*, byneþyn *E*
54 forsoþ *B*; sonus *CX*, sonys *E*; Forsothe the sones: þe s. f. *cet.*; cosyns *A²*
55 stey3id *BFWo*, ste3eden *CX*, styedyn *E*, sty3ede *H*, stei3ede *Lo*; op *E*;
cyte *BCEHLoWoX*; palmys *BEFHWoX*
56 sonys *BEH*, sonus *X*; the: om. *X*; deserte *B*, desert *cet.*
57 lott *BFH*, loot *Wo*; atte þe southe *Lo*
58 dwelten *CX*, dwelledyn *E*
59 went *BFHWo*; and: and þere *Lo*
60 smite *CLo*, smetyn *E*; to gyders *BFH*, togidere *CX*, to geders *E*, to gidres
Lo, to gederes *Wo*

15 At illa respondit: Da mihi benedictionem, quia terram
arentem dedisti mihi; da et irriguam aquis. Deditque
ei Caleph irriguum superius et irriguum inferius.

16 Filii autem Cinei, cognati Moysi, ascenderunt de
civitate palmarum cum filiis Iuda in desertum sortis
eius, quod est ad meridiem Arath, et habitaverunt
cum eo.

17 Abiit autem Iudas cum Simeone, fratre suo; et per-

15 seide to hir, What hast thou? And sche
answeride, ʒiue thou blessyng to me, for   50
thou hast ʒoue a drye lond to me; ʒyue
thou also a moyst lond with watris. And
Caleph ʒaf to hir the moist lond aboue,
16 and the moist lond bynethe. Forsothe
the sones of Cyney, alye of Moyses,   55
stieden fro the citee of palmes with the
sones of Juda, in to the desert of his lot,
which desert is at the south of Arath;
17 and dwelliden with hym. Sotheli Judas
ʒede with Symeon, his brother; and thei   60
smytiden togidere Cananei, that dwellide

49 seid E; her CaMW, here F, hire KLU; haast R; hast thou: haxstow E
50 answerde CaFGMPQUW, answerd D, answed E, answerede L; ʒeue
    BDGHaMaQR, fadir ʒiue I, ʒife K; blissing E, blessynge FGQU, a blessyng
    I
51 haast R; ʒouen GI, ʒofen K; dry E; a drye 1. to me: to me drie lond I;
    ʒeue BDGHaMaQRU, ʒife K
52 also: to me a. I; a: om. I; moiste E; londe E; watirs E, watres F
53 Caleph: hir fadir I; ʒaaf I, ʒaue R; her CaMW, here F, hire KU; the:
    a I; moiste EG
54 the: a I; moisti S; bineeþe R; Forsothe: And whanne I, Forsoþ X
55 sonis ILQ; alye: holie E, þe a. Ma; alye of Moyses: Moyses alije I
56 steieden F, stieden up I, stiʒeden MaNR; from K; cite CaFLMPQW;
    palmys G; the (2°): om. Ma
57 sonys GHaLQ; the: om. BGU; deseert BR; lott IKMaOR
58 whiche G, þe whiche I, wiche K; deseert B, deserd N, deserte R; souþ
    coost I
59 dwellide CO, dwelleden CaFLMPW, dwelledyn E, þei dwelliden I; hym:
    iudas I; sotheli: om. D, Soþli FGLMMaPQUWX, And I
60 ʒede: ʒede foorþ D; with: whit E; broþir BIOPR
61 smyteden CaKW, smiten EFM, smoten I, smetin LP; to gidre DIR, to
    ghedre E; sm. tog.: tog. sm. I; dwelte Ca, dwellid D, dwelled EP, dwellede
    F, dwelliden Ma

dwellid in Sephat, and thei slewen hym;
and the name of the cytee was clepid
18 Horma, that is, cursynge. And Judas
took Gazam with his eendis, and Ascalonem, and Accharon with his teermys.   65
19 And the Lord was with Judas, and the
mounteyns he weeldide; and he my3te
not doo awey the dwellers of the valei,
for thei aboundiden in chaarys ful of
20 weepnes in maner of sithis. And thei   70
3euen* to Caleph Ebron, as Moises seide,

61 dwelte *C*, dwellede *E*, dwelled *Wo*, dwellide *X*; slowen *CLoWoX*, slowyn *E*
62 cyte *cet.*; cleped *E*, kallid *Lo*
63 corsynge *BEFWo*, cursing *CLoX*
64 toke *BFHWo*, toc *CX*; endus *C*, endys *EX*, endes *LoWo*
65 termys *BEFHLoWo*, termes *CX*
67 mounteines *CLoX*, monteyns *E*; weeldyd *BFH*, weldede *C*, weeldede *E*,
    weldid *LoWo*, weldide *X*; my3t *BFHWo*
68 nou3t *Lo*; don *BCX*, doon *EFHLo*, done *Wo*; aweye *BH*; dwelleris *CLoX*
69 aboundeden *BCFHWo*, haboundedyn *E*, abounden *Lo*; chares *CX*, charys
    EFLoWo; full *BF*, fol *E*
70 weppnes *BFHWo*, wepnes *CX*, wepenys *E*, wepenes *Lo*; siþes *CX*
71 3yuen *A*, 3euen *BCFHWo*, 3euyn *E*, 3auen *Lo*, 3eeuen *X*

cusserunt simul Chananeum, qui habitabat in Sephat,
et interfecerunt eum. Vocatumque est nomen urbis
Horma, id est anathema.
18 Cepitque Iudas Gazam cum finibus suis, et Ascalonem,
atque Accaron cum terminis suis.
19 Fuitque Dominus cum Iuda, et montana possedit; nec
potuit delere habitatores vallis, quia falcatis
curribus abundabant.
20 Dederuntque Caleph Ebron, sicut dixerat Moyses, qui

in Sephar, and killiden hym; and the
name of that citee was clepid Horma, that
is cursyng, *ether perfit distriyng, for*
18 *thilke citee was distried outerly.* And
Judas took Gaza with hise coostis, and
Ascolon, and Accaron with hise termes.
19 And the Lord was with Judas, and he
hadde in possessioun the hilli places;
and he my3te not do awey the dwelleris
of the valei, for thei weren plenteuouse in
20 yrun charis, scharpe as sithis. And the
sones of Israel 3auen Ebron to Caleph,

65

70

62 killeden CaEFLP, þei killiden I, killede M
63 cite CaEHaLMPQUW; clepide Ha; that ... outerly (65): om. INSX
64 cursynge DGMaQU, corsing L; eiþer CaFGHaMQRW, or ELP, of Ma,
      eþir O, oþer U; perfi3t BDLMa, perfite ER, parfit F, om. GKMQW;
      distriynge AcDFGQU, destriyng KL, distroiyng R; for ... outerly (65):
      om. CaGHaMQU
65 þilk ER; cite FLPW; distroied ER, destried FKL; outurli Ac, outirly BCW,
      vttirli DKLMaPR, witterli E, vtterly O
66 toke EHaR; his EFGILPQSX; costes EF, costis U
67 whit E; his EFGILPQX; teermes DEMaNPRSX, termys GHaQ
69 had R; in: om. AcCCaDEFGHaKLMMaNOPQRSUX; hadde in p.:
      weeldide I; the: in þe DMaR; hulli E, hillie K, hillis Ma; placis
      DGHaILMaNPQSX, place E
70 he: iudas I; my3t D; awai EHa; dwellers DEHaIKLMPRSX, dwelleres F
71 plenteous BK, plentyuouse CaF, plentyuous DE, plenteuous
      HaILMaPRSX
72 irone BGMaQ, yrene CaFMW, iren EKLPR, ireni L; chares EF, chaaris
      G; yrun charis: ch. ful of wepnes I; scharp BDMa; siþes FKR
73 sonys GLPQ; the s. of: om. I; 3afen K

the which dide awey fro it thre sones of
21 Enach. Jebuse forsothe, the dweller of
Jerusalem, the sones of Beniamyn diden
not awey; and Jebuse dwelt with the   75
sones of Beniamyn in Jerusalem vnto the
22 day that is nowe. Forsothe the hows of
Joseph stiede in to Bethel, and the Lord
23 was with hem. For whanne thei segiden*
the cite, that before was clepid Luza,   80
24 thei seȝyn* a man goynge out of the
cytee, and thei seiden to hym, Shewe to
vs the entre of the cytee, and we shulen

72 whiche *BCEHLoX*; dode *E*; aweye *BH*; from *E*; hit *E*; þree *B*; sonus *CX*,
sonis *E*
73 dwellere *CEX*; *C* deficient from here to 4.4 (line 14)
74 sonys *BEH*, sonus *X*; dode *E*
75 aweye *BH*; dwelte *EX*
76 sonys *BEH*, sonus *X*
77 now *BEHLoWo*; house *BLo*, houȝs *H*; Forsothe the hous: þe h. f. *cet.*
78 steyȝid *BFWo*(+up), styȝede *E*, styȝid *H*, steiȝede *Lo*, steȝede *X*
79 þem *Lo*; whenn *B*, whenne *E*, whann *F*, when *H*, whan *WoX*; segiden:
sugettiden *ABFHWo*, segedyn *E*, byseegiden *Lo*, sogeteden *X*
80 cytee *F*; byfore *BEFHLoWo*, biforn *X*; cleped *E*, kallid *LoWo*
81 seynge *A*, seeyȝin *BF*, syȝyn *E*, seeyȝen *H*, seein(g) *Lo*, seiȝen *Wo*, seȝen *X*;
gooynge *BF*, goyng *HLo*, goende *X*; oute *BF*, ouȝte *H*; off *E*
82 cyte *BEHLoWoX*; seidyn *E*; shew *X*
83 entree *BFH*; cite *ELoWoX*; wee *X*; schuln *BFHWo*, sholyn *E*, schullen *Lo*,
shul *X*

delevit ex ea tres filios Enach.
21 Iebuseum autem habitatorem Ierusalem non deleverunt
filii Beniamin; habitavitque Iebuseus cum filiis
Beniamin in Ierusalem usque in praesentem diem.
22 Domus quoque Ioseph ascendit in Bethel, fuitque
Dominus cum eis.
23 Nam cum obsiderent urbem, quae prius Luza vocabatur,
24 viderunt hominem egredientem de civitate, dixeruntque
ad eum: Ostende nobis introitum civitatis, et faciemus
tecum misericordiam.

as Moises hadde seid, which Caleph dide
21 awei fro it thre sones of Enach. For-   75
sothe the sones of Beniamyn diden not
awei Jebusei, the dwellere of Jerusalem;
and Jebusei dwellide with the sones of
Beniamyn in Jerusalem til in to present
22 dai. Also the hows of Joseph stiede in   80
to Bethel, and the Lord was with hem.
23 For whanne thei bisegiden the citee, that
24 was clepid Lusa bifore, thei sien a man
goynge out of the citee, and thei seiden to
hym, Schewe thou to vs the entrynge of   85
the cytee, and we schulen do mercy with

74 had EI; seide DHaRU, sayde E, boden I; whiche GP, & I, wich K; did E
75 awai E; from K; sonys GQ; Forsothe: but I, Forsop X
76 the: om. C; sonys GQ; dedun E, dide O, dedin P
77 dweller BCaDHaIX, dwellers M, dwelleris N
78 dwellid D, dwelled E, dwellede LP; sonis GLQ
79 til in to: into E, vnto I; present: þe pr. E, þis pr. IK[1]
80 hows: meynee I; stied DE, steiede F, stiȝede HaMaNR, stiede up I, stieden X
82 whan DEHaLP; þai E; bisegeden CaFLMPRSUW, bisegheden E, biseegiden I; cite CaFHaLMPQUW; that: it L
83 seien CaFW, seþ E, siȝen HaKLMaNOX, sawȝen I, sieȝen M
84 goyng EKP; out R; cite CaHaLMQUW
85 sheu E; entryng AcBCCaEFHaIKLMMaNOPRSWX
86 the: þo E; cite CaFHaMPQUW; schullen CaFMUW, schuln D, shul EILP; mercie R; wiþ: to E

25 do with thee merci. The which whanne
   he hadde shewid to hem, thei smyten the   85
   citee in mouth of the swerd; forsothe
   thilk man and al his kynrede thei leften.
26 The which left wente into the lond of
   Sechym, and bilde there a citee, and clepide
   it Luzam; the which is clepid so vnto   90
27 the day that is nowe. Forsothe Manasses
   dide not awey Bethsan, and Thanael with
   his lytyl touns, and the dwellers of Endor, and Geblaam, and Magedo with his
   litil touns; and Chanane bigan to dwel   95
28 with hem. Forsothe after that Yrael is
   counfortyd, he made hem tributaryes,

84 doo *BFHLo*; þe *EWo*; whiche *BEHLoWoX*; whenn *BH*, whan *FWoX*
85 had *BFLoWo*; shewed *EFWo*; þem *LoX*; smetyn *E*
86 cite *ELoWoX*; mouth: þe mowþe *Lo*; the: om. *X*; swerde *BLoWo*; forsoþ *B*;
    forsothe thilke man: th. f. m. *cet.*
87 þulke *E*, þilke *HLo*, þat *X*; alle *BLo*, all *F*; kynreden *Lo*; leftyn *E*
88 whiche *BEHLoWoX*; lefte *LoWo*; went *BFHWo*; lond *EX*, londe *LoWo*
89 bulde *E*, bild *H*; þer *BWo*; cite *EHLoWoX*; clepid *BFHWo*, clepede *E*,
    callid *Lo*
90 hit *E*; whiche *BEHLoX*; cleped *EWo*, callid *Lo*
91 now *EFHWoX*; Forsothe Manasses: M. f. *cet.*
92 dede *E*; aweye *BH*
93 litul *E*, lytel *Wo*, litle *X*; tounys *E*, tounes *LoX*; dwelleris *LoX*
95 lytyll *B*, litul *E*, lytel *Wo*; tounys *E*, tounes *LoX*; bygann *BFH*; dwelle *cet.*
96 þem *LoX*; Forsothe after: a. f. *cet.*; forsoþ *B*; Aftir *LoX*
97 confortyd *BFLoWo*, conforted *E*, counforted *X*; maad *B*; þem *LoX*;
    trybutariys *E*

25 Qui cum ostendisset eis, percusserunt urbem in ore
   gladii; hominem autem illum et omnem cognationem eius
   dimiserunt.
26 Qui dimissus abiit in terram Cethim, et aedificavit
   ibi civitatem, vocavitque eam Luzam; quae ita appella-
   tur usque in praesentem diem.

25 thee. And whanne he hadde schewid to
  hem, thei smytiden the citee bi scharpnes
  of swerd; sotheli thei delyueriden that
26 man and al his kynrede. And he was   90
  delyuerede, and ȝede in to the lond of
  Sethym, and bildide there a citee, and
  clepide it Luzam; which is clepid so til in
27 to present dai. Also Manasses dide not
  awei Bethsan and Thanael with her   95
  townes, and the dwelleris of Endor, and
  Geblaam and Magedo with her townes;
  and Cananei bigan to dwelle with hem.
28 Sotheli after that Israel was counfortid,
  he made hem tributaries, *ethir to paye*   100

87 þe EFR; whan EHaLP; had EI; shewed E
88 smyteden CaW, smetyn EP, smyten FM, smoten I, smeten L; cite
   CaFHaLMPQUW; bi: wiþ þe Ma; sharpnesse AcBCCaFGHa-
   IKLMMaNOPQRUWX, sharpenes E
89 swerde E; soþli FGLMMaPQSUWX, & I; delyuereden CaFGHa-
   ILMMaNPRSUW, delyuerden D, deliuered E
90 alle E; kinred E; he: whanne he CaDGIKNQSX, whan he HaM
91 delyuerid AcBCCaDFKMMaOQSW, deliuered EGHaILNPRUX; and:
   he CaDGHaIKMQSX, om. N, & he O
92 bildid D, bilded E, he bildide I, bildede LP, beeldide R; þer E; cite
   CaFHaLMPQW
93 clepide: clepid D, clepede F; whiche GI, wich K; clepid: cleped E; til:
   om. E; in: om. Ma
94 present: þis pr. EIK[1]; dud E, dede F
95 away HaN; here FIQR, hise Ma
96 townis GIQ, townus I; dwellers DEHaIKLMMaPRX, dwelleres F
97 here FIQR; townis GLQ, townus I
98 bigane R
99 soþli FGILMMaPQSUWX; aftir AcCCaDFGHaIKLMNPQRSWX;
   confortid CKLPSUX, conforted E, comfortid F, cumfortid Q
100 tributaris E; eiþer CaFGHaMMaQW, or ELP, eipir R, oþer U; pay BE

27 Manasses quoque non delevit Bethsan et Thanael cum
  viculis suis, et habitatores Endor et Geblaam et
  Magedo cum viculis suis, coepitque Chananeus habitare
  cum eis.
28 Postquam autem confortatus est Israel, fecit eos
  tributarios, et delere noluit.

29 and doon awey wold he not. Forsothe
   Effraym slewe not Cananee that dwellid
30 in Gazer, but dwellid with hym. Zabu-   100
   lon dide not awey the dwellers of Cethron
   and of Naalon; but Chananee dwelt in
   the mydil of hym, and is maad to hym
31 tributarie. Forsothe Aser dide not aweye
   the dwellers of Cho, and of Sidon, Alab,   105
   and Azenbus, and Alba, and Aphecha-
32 aloa, and Pha, and Roab; and he dwellid
   in the mydil of Chanaan[ei], the dweller of
33 that lond, ne he slew3 him. Neptalim dide
   not awei the dwellers of Bethsames, and   110

 98 don *WoX*; aweye *BH*; wolde *cet.*; no3t *Lo*; forsoþ *B*; Forsothe Effraym:
    E. f. *cet.*
 99 slow *E*, slew *FH*, slow3e *Lo*, slowe *Wo*, slo3 *X*; dwellede *E*, dwelled *Wo*,
    dwelte *X*
100 bot *B*, bote *E*, bute *F*; dwellede *E*, dwelled *Wo*, dwelte *X*
101 dede *E*; aweye *BH*; dwelleris *LoX*, dwelleres *Wo*
102 bot *B*, bote *E*, bute *F*; dwellede *E*, dwellid *Lo*, dwelte *X*
103 mydyll *B*, myddul *E*, myddil *H*, mydel *Lo*, myddel *WoX*; made *BEHLoWo*,
    mad *X*
104 Forsothe Aser: A. f. *cet.*; dede *E*; awey *EFLoWoX*
105 dwelleris *Lo*, dwelleres *X*
107 dwellede *E*, dwelled *Wo*, dwelte *X*
108 mydyll *B*, myddul *E*, myddil *H*, mydel *Lo*, myddel *WoX*; the: om. *X*;
    dwellere *ELoX*
109 loond *BFH*, londe *LoWo*; he: om. *H*; slow3 *EWo*, slow3e *Lo*, slo3 *X*;
    dede *E*
110 a-weye *H*; dwelleris *Lo*, dwelleres *X*

29 Effraim autem non interfecit Chananeum, qui habitabat
   in Gazer, sed habitavit cum eo.
30 Zabulon non delevit habitatores Cethron et Naalon;
   sed habitavit Chananeus in medio eius, factusque est
   ei tributarius.
31 Aser quoque non delevit habitatores Acho, et Sidonis,
   Alab, et Azazib/us/, et Alba, et Aphech, et Roob;

94

29 *tribute*, and nolde do awey *hem*. Sotheli
Effraym killide not Cananei that dwellyde

30 in Gaser, but dwellide with hym. Zabulon dide not awey the dwelleris of Cethron,
and of Naalon; but Cananei dwellide in the   105
myddis of hym, and was maad tributarie

31 to him. Also Aser dide not awey the
dwelleris of Acho, and of Sidon, of Alab,
and of Azazib, and of Alba, and Aphech,
and of Aloa, and of Pha, and of Roob;   110

32 and he dwellide in the myddis of Cananey, dwellere of that lond, and killide

33 not hym. Neptalym dide not awei the
dwelleris of Bethsames, and of Bethanach;

101 tribuyt D, trybut N; 100−1 gloss om. ISX; nolde: wolde not I, noolde
     MaSX; away HaO; *hem*: AI, om. cet.; soþli FGILMMaPQRUWX
102 killid D, killed E, killede FLPSU; dwellid D, dwelled E, dwellede FLPU
103 dwellid D, dwelled E, dwellede LPU
104 dud E; away EHa; dwellers DEHaIKLMPRSUX
105 of: om. X; bot E; dwellid D, dwelled E, dwellede LPU, dwillide O
106 myddes F, middil Ma; made DE; tributari E, trubutarie N
107 to: of R; dud E; away Ha; the: om. U
108 dwellers DEHaIKLMPRUX, dwelleres F; of Alab: & of A. BELP
109 and Aphech: & of A. AcB¹CaDIMaX
111 he: Azer I; dwellid D, dwelled E, dwellede FLPU; myddes F; of: om. E
112 dweller BDEHaLPX, þe dweller I; that: þe D²; killed E, killede FKLSU,
     azer k. I, killid P
113 not hym: him not I; dud E
114 dwellers EHaIKLMPRSUX, dwelleres F, dwellaris N
115 he: Neptalim I; dwelled F, dwellede FGLPU; amonge R; dweller EHaLX,
     þe dw. I

32 habitavitque in medio Chananei, habitatoris illius
    terrae, nec interfecit eum.

33 Neptalim non delevit habitatores Bethsames et Beth-
    anach; et habitavit inter Chananeum habitatorem
    terrae; fueruntque ei Bethsamitae et Bethanitae
    tributarii.

of Bethanach; and he dwellide among
Chanane, the dweller of the lond; and
Bethsamytes and Bethanites weren to
34 him tributaries. And Amorre artide the
sones of Dan in the hil, ne he ȝaf to hem 115
place that to the pleyner thei myȝten
35 descende; and he dwelte in the hil of
Hares, that is to seye, Witnessinge, in
Hailon, and Salabym. And the hond*
of the hous of Joseph is agreggid aȝens 120
Amorre, and he is maad to hym tribu-
36 tarie. Forsothe the terme of Amorre was
fro the stiynge vp of Scorpioun, and Petra, and the heiȝer places.

111 he: om X; dwellid BFHLo, dwellede E, dwelled Wo, dwelte X; amonge
BFHWo
112 dwellere X; loond BFH, londe LoWo
113 weryn E
114 And: om. Lo; artede EX
115 sonys E, sonus X; hyll BFH, hul E, hylle LoWo; ȝaue BFHWo, ȝafe Lo;
þem LoX
116 playner E, pleynere LoX; thei: om. X; myȝt BFHWo, myȝte ELoX
117 descenden BFHLoWo, descendyn E; dwelt BFHLoWo, dwellede E; hyll
BFHWo, hul E, hylle Lo
118 sey BEFLoWoX; wyttnessynge BFH, witnessyng LoX
119 lond A, hoond BFH, honde Lo
120 house BHLo; agredgyd BF, aggregid Lo; aȝeyns BFWo, aȝeynes Lo, aȝen X
121 made EFHLoWo, mad X
122 Forsothe the terme: þe t. f. cet.
123 from X; steyinge BF, styȝynge EH, steiȝinge LoWo, steȝing X; vp: opp E,
om. LoX; scorpyon BEF
124 heeȝer B, hiȝere E, heiȝere X; placis E

34 Artavitque Amorreus filios Dan in monte, nec dedit
eis locum ut ad planiora descenderent;
35 habitavitque in monte Hares, quod interpretatur
testatio, in Hailon et Salabim. Et aggravata est

and he dwellide among Cananey, dwellere
of the lond; and Bethsamytis and Beth-
34 anytis weren tributarie to hym. And
Ammorrey helde streit the sones of Dan
in the hil, and ʒaf not place to hem to go
35 doun to pleynere places; and he dwellide
in the hil of Hares, which is interpretid,
Witnessyng, in Hailon, and in Salabym.
And the hond of the hows of Joseph was
maad heuy, and he was maad tributarie
36 to hym. And the terme of Ammorrei was
fro the stiyng of Scorpioun, and the
stoon, and hiʒere places.

116 the: þat IKMaU; (112) and ... lond (116): om. D
117 tributaryes BCIW, tributaris E; hym: neptalym I
118 held DF, heeld CaELMMaNPSWX, heuld K, heelde Q; streiʒt Ac, strayt
B, streyte DGIQRU; sonys GQ
119 hul E, hill Ma; he ʒaue I
120 playner BI, pleyner DX, plener(re) E, þe pl. M; placis DGLMaNPQSX;
he: dan I; dwellid DF, dwelled E, dwellede LPU
121 hille D, hul E; wich K; wh. is interpretid: þat is to say I
122 witnessynge DGQU, withnessing E, wittessing K
123 honde I; hows: meynee I
124 maad (1°): made DES, maad Ma; heuy aʒe/i/ns amorrei ELP, heuy *or
dul* I; he: ioseph I; maad (2°): made DE; tributari E
125 hym: amorey I; teerme DMaNSX
126 from K; stiynge DGQW, steiynge F, stiyng up I, stiʒinge Ma, stiʒyng NR,
steynge U; þe scorpioun IMa, scorpion EK; the: & fro the I
127 stone E, ston HaIU; and: of MaR; heiʒere CaFMW, hiʒer DKMaRSX,
/þe/ hiere ELP; placis AcDGIKLMaNPQSX

manus domus Ioseph /in Amorreum/ factusque est ei
tributarius.
36 Fuit autem terminus Amorrei ab ascensu scorpionis
et petra et superiora loca.

2. 1 And the angel of the Lord stiede vp
fro Galgala to the place of wepers, and
seith, I haue ladde ʒou out of Egipt, and
brouʒt into the loond, for* the which Y
swore to ʒoure faders, and haue bihoot, 5
that I shulde not maak in veyn my couenaunt with ʒow into with outen eend;
2 so oonly that ʒe smyten no boond of pees
with the dwellers of this loond, and that
ʒe turnen vpsedoun the auters of hem; 10
and ʒe wolden not here my vois. Why
3 thes thingis han ʒe doon? Wher* for
Y wolde not do awey hem fro ʒoure face,
that ʒe han enemyes, and the goddis of

2. 1 aungel *BFHLoWo*, aungil *X*; steyʒid *BFWo*, stiʒede *E*, stiʒid *H*, steiʒede
Lo, steʒede *X*; op *E*, opp *Lo*
  2 weperys *E*, weepers *H*, weperes *X*
  3 seys *Lo*; lad *BEFHWoX*, lede *Lo*; oute *B*, ouʒt *H*
  4 brouʒte *ELo*, broʒt *X*; lond *EX*, londe *LoWo*; for: fro *ABFHWo*; the: om.
X; whiche *BEHLoX*
  5 swor *EFWo*, swoor *X*; ʒour *BFH*; fadres *FLo*, fadris *Wo*; byhoote *BE*,
byhote *FHWoX*, bihette *Lo*
  6 sholde *E*, schold *Lo*, schuld *Wo*; make *cet*; veyne *Lo*; couenaunte *Lo*
  7 wiþ oute *BEX*, wiþ ouʒte *H*; eende *BF*, ende *EHLoWoX*
  8 onely *Lo*, onli *X*; ʒee *LoX*; smytyn *E*, smyte *X;* bonde *BLoWo*, bond *X*;
pese *B*, pes *X*
  9 dwelleris *LoX*; lond *EWoX*, londe *Lo*
  10 ʒee *LoX*; torne *BEFHWo*, turne *LoX*; vpsadoun *BF*, opsodoun *E*,
vpsodoun *LoWoX*; auteres *X*; þem *Lo*
  11 ʒee *LoX*; wold *BF*, wolde *EHLoWo*; heere *FH*, heren *X*; voyce *BFHLoWo*
  12 þese *EX*; þinges *BLoWo*, thingus *X*; ʒee *LoX*; han ʒe: ʒ. h. *cet.*; doone *H*,
don *Wo*, do *X*; wher fore *E*, where fore *Lo*, wheþer for *cet.*
  13 wold *BFWo*; doo *BFH*, doon *E*, don *Lo*; aweye *BH*; þem *LoX*; awey hem:
þem a-wey *Lo*; ʒour *BFH*
  14 ʒee *LoX*; haue *X*; enmyes *BFWo*, enemys *X*; the: om. *X*; goddes *LoWo*,
godis *X*

2. 1 Ascenditque angelus Domini de Galgala ad locum
flentium, et ait: Eduxi vos de Aegypto, et introduxi
/vos/ in terram, pro quo iuravi patribus vestris;
et pollicitus sum, ut non facerem irritum pactum
meum vobiscum in sempiternum;

2. 1 And the aungel of the Lord stiede fro
      Galgala to the place of weperis, and seide,
      Y ledde ȝou out of Egipt, and Y brouȝte
      ȝou in to the lond, for which Y swoor
      to ȝoure fadris, and bihiȝte, that Y schulde   5
      not make void my couenaunt with ȝou in
    2 to with outen ende; so oneli that ȝe schulde
      not smyte boond of pees with the dwelleris
      of this lond, and schulden distrie the
      auteris of hem; and ȝe nolden here my   10
    3 vois. Whi diden ȝe these thingis? Wher-
      fore Y nolde do hem awei fro ȝoure face,
      that ȝe haue enemyes, and that the goddis

2. 1 angel CIL, aungil MaQ; stied DE, steiede F, stiȝede HaMaNR, stiede up
      I; from K
    2 wepers DHaIKLMMaRUX, weperes F; saide E, he seide I
    3 led DE, ladde K; oute R; brouȝt DE
    4 ȝou: AIK, om. cet.; whiche DGQ, wiche K; swore EHaIR, swor LSU;
      for wh. Y sw.: þat I swore fore I
    5 ȝour FK; faderis E, fadres F; bihiȝt E; scholde CaMW, shuld E
    6 void AFI, voide cet.
    7 wiþoute O; eende BHaKMaS, eend R; oonli BCaDGHaIKLMMaNPRSWX,.
      only FIQU; ȝee U; shulen AcCGHaNOQRSUX, schulden BKMa, schullen
      CaM, schuln DF, shul EILP, scholden W
    8 bond EFGQ; pes L; dwellers DEHaIKLMRSUX, dwelleres F
    9 londe I; scholden CaMW, shulen GHaQX, þat ȝe I; distroie AcEMaR,
      destrie HaIKLNU, distruye SX
   10 auters DHaIKLMMaRSUX, autres E, auteres F; the a. of hem: her a. I;
      ȝee U; nolden: wolden not I, noolden SX; heere GKMaNSX
   11 voice EI; dedin EP, deden F; ȝee GU; þes DKNX, þise EU; þinghes E,
      þinges FHa; wherfor AcCDHa, whare fore E, for þe whiche þing I
   12 nolde: wolde not I, noolde SX; away EHa; from K; ȝour FK
   13 ȝee U; hem enmyes I, enemis L, enemyees O; that (2°): om. CS; 13–14.
      the goddis of hem: her goddis I

    2 ita dumtaxat ut non feriretis foedus cum habitator-
      ibus terrae huius, et aras eorum subverteretis; et
      noluistis audire vocem meam; cur haec fecistis?
    3 Quam ob rem nolui delere eos a facie vestra, ut
      habeatis hostes, et dii eorum sint vobis in ruinam.

4 hem ben to ȝou into fallynge. And
whanne the aungel of the Lord hadde
spoken thes wordis to alle the sones of
Yrael, thei rereden vp her vois, and

5 wepten; and the name of that place is
clepid, of wepers, or of terys; and thei

6 offerden [t]her oostis to the Lord. Josue
thanne lefte the puple; and the sones of
Irael wenten awey, echoon into his pos-

7 sessioun, that thei holden it. And thei

serueden to the Lord alle the days of
Josue, and of the eldren that loong tyme
after hym lyueden, and knewe alle the
greet werkis of the Lord, the whiche he

15 þem *LoX*; been *E*, be *X*; fallyng *LoX*
16 whenn *BH*, whenne *E*, whan *FWoX*; angel *E*, aungil *X*; lorde *Wo*; had *BFHLoWo*
17 spoke *BEFHWoX*; þese *ELoX*; wordes *BLoWo*, wrdis *X*; all *F*, al *H*; sonys *BE*
18 reredyn *E*; op *E*; þeir *BFWo*, here *E*, þer *X*; voice *BFHLoWo*
19 weptyn *E*
20 cleped *BEWo*, callid *Lo*; weperis *Lo*, weperes *X*; off *E*; teres *WoX*
21 offredyn *E*, offreden *FLoWoX*; þer *B*, þere *EFHWoX*, þeire *Lo*; hoostys *EWo*, oostes *Lo*, ostes *X*; lorde *Wo*
22 þann *B*, þenne *E*, þan *Wo*; left *BFHWo*; peple *BELoWo*; sonys *E*, sonus *X*
23 went *BFHWo*, wentyn *E*; aweye *BH*; echon *BH*, echone *EFLoWo*, eche *X*; possession *E*
24 holdyn *E*, holde *X*; hit *E*; thei: þe *H*
25 seruedyn *E*; lorde *Wo*; all *F*; dayes *FLoWo*, daȝes *X*
26 eldryn *E*, elderes *X*; longe *BFHLoWo*, long *EX*
27 aftir *Lo*; lyuedyn *E*; knewyn *E*, knew *F*, knewen *LoX*; all *FH*
28 grete *cet.*; werkes *BWoX*, workys *E*

4 Cumque loqueretur angelus Domini haec verba ad omnes
filios Israel, elevaverunt vocem suam, et fleverunt.

5 Et vocatum est nomen loci illius: flentium, sive
lacrimarum; immolaveruntque ibi hostias Domino.

6 Dimisit ergo Iosue populum, et abierunt filii Israel
unusquisque in possessionem suam, ut obtinerent eam;

4 of hem be to ȝou in to fallyng. And
  whanne the aungel of the Lord spak   15
  these wordis to alle the sones of Israel,
  thei reisiden her vois, and wepten; and
5 the name of that place was clepid, of
  weperis, ether of teeris; and thei of-
6 friden there sacrifices to the Lord. Ther-   20
  for Josue lefte the puple; and the sones
  of Israel wenten forth, ech man in to his
  possessioun, that thei schulden gete it.
7 And thei serueden the Lord in alle the
  daies of Josue, and of eldere men that   25
  lyueden aftir hym in long tyme, and
  knewen alle the grete werkis of the Lord,

14 fallynge DGMaQU
15 whan EFGHaLP; angel CEO, aungil MaQ; the a. of the L.: þe lordis a. I;
   spake HaR, had spoke I
16 þes DKNX; wordes CaF; al AcCIOU; sonis GHaLQ, peple I
17 reiseden AcCaDEFKLMPUW; þer E, here FQR; voice DEI; weptin EP,
   wepteden L
18 that: þe I; of (2°): 'þe place' of I
19 wepers DHaIKMMaRUX, weperes F; eiþer CaFGHaMQRW, or EILP,
   eiþir Ma, eþir S, oþer U; teris CaEUW, teres FM, teeres R; offreden
   CaFMPUW, offereden E
20 there: her D, þer E, þe Ha; sacrifisis CaDGKLMNPQRSWX; þerfore
   BCaEFGKLMaNQRSWX, þanne I
21 lafte K; peple CaFILMMaNPSWX; sonis GLQ
22 wentin P, wente R; forþe E; vch E, eche K
23 possessione E, possessioni K; scholden CaMW, schulen O; ghete E, geete
   G, geten U
24 seruyden AcCCGHaIOQ; the (2°): om. B
25 of (2°): om. U; elder BCaDEMPWX, þe eldere GOQ, eeldere Ha, þe eldre
   I, eldre MaR
26 lyuyden GQ, lifeden K; after CaEFILMU; in: om. CaDGHaIKMNOQSX;
   longe BHaIRU
27 knew N; greet D, greete MaOQ; werkes FR

7 servieruntque Domino cunctis diebus Iosue, et
  seniorum qui longo post eum vixerunt tempore, et
  noverunt omnia opera Domini magna, quae fecerat cum
  Israel.

8 dide with* Yrael. And Josue, the ser-
uaunt of the Lord, the sone of Nun, of   30
9 an hundrid and ten ʒeer died; and thei
birieden hym in the eendis of his possessioun, in Thanathsare, in the hil of
Effraym, fro the north coost of the hil of
10 Gaas. And al that generacioun is ge-   35
drid to her fadris; and other risen, that*
knewen not the Lord, and the werkis that
11 he dide with Yrael. And the sones of
Yrael diden yuel in the siʒt of the Lord,
and serueden to Baalym, and Astaroth;   40
12 and laften the Lord God of her fadris,
that ladde hem out of the loond of Egipt,

29 dede *E*; with: to *A*; seruant *E*
31 a *BLo*; hundreþ *B*, hundred *EFLo*; tenn *BH*; ʒere *LoWo*, ʒer *X*; dyʒid
    BFHWo, deʒede *E*, diede *X*
32 byryed *BFHLoWo*, buryedyn *E*; endys *ELoX*, endes *Wo*; possession *E*
33 hyll *BFH*, hul *E*, hille *Wo*
34 northe *Lo*; cost *Wo*, coest *X*; hyll *BFH*, hul *E*, hylle *Wo*
35 alle *Lo*; that: þe *FLoWoX*; generacion *E*, gneracioun *Lo*; geþerde *B*,
    gedered *EWoX*, geþered *F*, gederd *H*, gadride *Lo*
36 her: þeir *BFWo*, here *E*, þer *LoX*; faders *BEHX*, fadres *FLo*; oþere *Lo*;
    rysun *E*; that: & *ABFHLoWoX*
37 knewe *BEHLoWo*, knew *F*; lorde *Wo*; werkes *BWoX*, workys *E*
38 dede *E*; sonys *E*, sonus *X*
39 dedyn *E*; yuyl *E*, euel *WoX*; siʒte *LoX*
40 seruedyn *E*
41 leftyn *E*, leften *X*; lorde *Wo*; her: þeir *BF*, here *E*, þer *LoX*; fadirs *B*,
    faders *EFHX*, fadres *Lo*
42 lede *Lo*; þem *LoX*; oute *B*, ouʒte *H*; lond *E*, londe *LoWo*; the loond of:
    om. *X*

8 Mortuus est autem Iosue filius Nun, famulus Domini,
centum et decem annorum;
9 et sepelierunt eum in finibus possessionis suae,
in Thamnath-sare, in monte Effraim, a/d/ septen-
trionali plaga montis Gaas.
10 Omnisque illa generatio congregata est ad patres
suos; et surrexerunt alii, qui non noverunt Dominum,
et opera quae fecerat cum Israel.

8 whiche he hadde do with Israel. Forsothe Josue, sone of Nun, seruaunt of
the Lord, was deed of an hundrid ʒeer   30
9 and ten; and thei birieden hym in the
endis of his possessioun, in Thannath of
Sare, in the hil of Effraym, at the north
10 coost of the hil Gaas. And al that gene-
racioun was gaderid to her fadris; and   35
othere men riseden, that knewen not the
Lord, and the werkis whiche he hadde
11 do with Israel. And the sones of Israel
diden yuel in the siʒt of the Lord, and
12 thei serueden Baalym and Astaroth; and   40
forsoken the Lord God of her fadris, that
ledde(n) hem out of the lond of Egipt; and

28 which DEF, wiche K, wich L; had EI; y-do E; Forsothe: & I, forsoþ X
29 sone: þe sone EI; 29–30 seruaunt of the Lord: þe lordis seruaunt I
30 lord god W; was deed: diede I, was dead Q; hundred EHa, hunderd LP;
    ʒere E, ʒer ILP; 30–1 was d. of an h. ʒ. and ten: of an h. ʒ. & ten diede I
31 berieden U
32 eendis BGKMaRS, endes FU; possession EIK
33 hille D, hul E; atte north E
34 coste E, cost U; hul E, hill S; generacion *of israel* I, generacion K
35 gadered ELU, gadrid GR, gederid KNX; here EQR, hir L; faders E
36 oþer CELPUX, oþre R; men *of israel* I; risiden BGHaMaOQSX, risen
    EFM, resen up I, resen L, resin P; knew E
37 lorde E; werkes FR; which E, wiche K; had DE; 37–38 h. do: dide I
38 sonys GLQ
39 dedin EP, deden U; yuele AcKN, euel ELPQ, euyle G; siʒte CaDMaU
40 seruyden CGILNOQ, serued E
41 *þei* forsoken I, forsooken P; here QR; faders E, fadres F
42 ledde AcBCaGHaILMaNPQR, led E, ladde K, ledde(n) OX; oute R

11 Feceruntque filii Israel malum in conspectu Domini,
   et servierunt Baalim et Astaroth.
12 Ac dimiserunt Dominum Deum patrum suorum, qui edux-
   erat eos de terra Aegypti, et secuti sunt deos
   alienos, deos populorum, qui habitabant in circuitu
   eorum, et adoraverunt eos; et ad iracundiam con-
   citaverunt Dominum,

103

and folweden alien goddis, goddis of the
puple[s] that dwelten in the viroun of
hem; and thei honourden hem, and to   45
13 wrath stireden the Lord, leuynge hym,
    and seruynge to Baal and to Astaroth.
14 And the Lord, wrooth aȝens Irael, took
    hem into the hoondis of destruyers, the
    whyche token hem, and solden to ene-   50
    myes, that dwelten bi enuyroun; ne thei
15 myȝten aȝenstoond her aduersaries; but
    whidir euere thei wolden goo, the hoond
    of the Lord was vpon hem, as he spak
    and swore to hem; and hugely thei ben   55

43 foloweden *BFH*, folwedyn *E*, folowid *Wo*, foleweden *X*; goddes (2x)
   LoWo(1°), godis *X* (2x)
44 peplis *BEHWo*, puplis *F*, peples *Lo*, puples *X*; dweltyn *E*; in the viroun:
   in enuyron *E*, in þe enuyroun *Wo*, in enuyroun *X*
45 þem *Lo* (2x); honoured *BFHWo*, honourede *ELo*, honoureden *X*
46 wreþ *BHWo*, wraþþe *E*, wrathe *LoX*; styred *BFHWo*, stirede *Lo*; leeuyng
   Lo, lefende *X*
47 seruyng *Lo*, seruende *X*; to (2°): om. *E*
48 wroþ *BFHWoX*, wrothe *Lo*; aȝeyns *BFHWo*, aȝen *X*; tooke *B*, toke *FHWo*,
   toc *X*
49 þem *LoX*; hondys *EX*, hondes *LoWo*; destruers *E*, destreris *Lo*, destroȝeres
   X
50 tooken *E*; þem *Lo*; soldyn *E*; enmyes *BFWo*, enemys *X*
51 dweltyn *E*; enuyron *E*
52 myȝte *B*, myȝt *Wo*; aȝeynstond *B*, aȝeynstonde *EFWo*, aȝenstonde *HX*,
   aȝeynstande *Lo*; þeir *BFWo*, þer *ELoX*; aduersaryys *E*; bot *B*, bote *E*, bute *F*
53 whyþer *B*, whedyr *E*, whidre *Lo*, whider *Wo*; euer *BFWo*, er *E*; wold *B*,
   wolde *EFHLoWo*; goon *BEFHLo*, gon *WoX*; hond *EWoX*, honde *Lo*
54 opon *E*, uppon *Wo*; þem *Lo*; spake *BFWo*
55 swoor *EX*; þem *LoX*; hugeliche *X*; been *E*

13 dimittentes eum, et servientes Baal et Astaroth.
14 Iratusque Dominus contra Israel tradidit eos in
    manus diripientium; qui ceperunt eos, et vendiderunt
    hostibus, qui habitabant per gyrum; nec potuerunt
    resistere adversariis suis;

thei sueden alien goddis, the goddis of
puplis, that dwelliden in the cumpasse
of hem, and worshipeden tho goddis,
and excitiden the Lord to greet wraththe,
13 and forsoken hym, and serueden Baal
14 and Astoroth. And the Lord was wrooth
aȝens Israel, and bitook hem in to the
hondis of rauyscheris, whiche rauyscheris
token hem, and seelden to enemyes, that
dwelliden bi cumpas; and thei myȝten
15 not aȝenstonde her aduersaries; but whidir euer thei wolden go, the hond of the
Lord was on hem, as he spak and swoor
to hem; and thei weren turmentid greetli.

43 suweden CaFM; aliene HaKMR; goddes F (2x); the goddis: om. Ca
44 peplis CaLMMaNPSWX, peples F, þo peplis I, puples R; dwelleden
CaEFLMPUW, dweliden N; the: om. W; cumpas BCCaDFGIKLMMa-
NPSWX, compas E, cumpaas HaQ; 44—5 the c. of hem: her. c. I
45 worschipiden AcBCDGHaLMaNOQRSX, wurschipeden CaFMW, þei
wirschipiden I, worshepeden U; tho: þilke I, þoo R; goddes F
46 exciten Ac, exciteden CaEFKMPUW, þei stiriden I, exitiden O; grete ER,
gret ILPS; wrath E
47 þei forsoken I; seruyden CGNQ; to B. I
48 and A.: & to A. I; wroþe E, wroþ FGILNPQSUX, wroþþe Ha
49 aȝenus AcCNO; bitok EP, bitoke HaR, he bitoke I; him C
50 hondes CaEF, hoondis R; rauyscheris (2x): rauescheris BHaL(1°)P(1°)QS,
rauyschers DMWX, raueschers ELP(2°), raueschers F(1°), om. I(2°),
rauiȝsshers K, rauischeres F(2°)R(2°); which ES, þe whiche I, wiche K
51 tooken CGLNOPSX; selden AcLNPW, solden hem EI, soolden K; enmies
EI
52 dwelleden CaEFLMOP, dwelten W; bi cumpas: bi compas E, aboute I,
bi cumpaas Q; þe[i]Ca, israel I; myȝte I
53 aȝenstonden Ac, withstond E; here FGQR; bot E; whidur
AcBCCaHaMNW, whider EFLMaUW, whidire K, whedir P, whiþer R
54 euere AcCCaGKMMaNQRSWX; thei: israel I; honde E, wraþ I
55 on: aȝaines E, upon I, aȝens LP; spake HaIR; swor BLSU, swore EHaIR
56 were E; turmented E; gretli AcEILPQ

15 sed quocumque pergere voluissent, manus Domini erat
super eos, sicut locutus est et iuravit eis; et
vehementer afflicti sunt.

16 tourmentid. And the Lord areride iugis,
   that shulden delyuer hem fro the hoondis
   of wasters, but and hem thei wolden not
17 here, doynge fornycacioun with alien goddis, and honourynge hem. Soone thei   60
   forsoken the wey, bi the which the faders
   of hem wenten; and herynge the heestis
   of the Lord, alle thingis thei diden con-
18 trarie. And whanne the Lord hadde
   reryd iugys in the dais of hem, he was   65
   bowid bi (more) mercy, and he herde the weilyngis of the tourmentid, and he delyueride hem fro the deeth of wasters.

56   tormentid *EX*, tourmentide *Lo*; arered *BFH*, arerede *E*, arerid *LoWo*,
     rerede *X*; juges *LoX*
57   sholdyn *E*, scholden *Lo*; delyuere *EFLoX*; þem *LoX*; from *E*; hondys *EX*,
     hondes *LoWo*
58   waasters *E*; wasteres *X*; bot *B*, bote *E*, bute *F*; þem *Lo*; wolde
     BEFHLoWo
59   heere *BFH*, heren *X*; doende *X*; fornicacion *E*; aliene *X*; goddes *LoWo*,
     godis *X*
60   honouryng *Lo*, honourende *X*; þem *LoX*; sone *EWo*
61   forsoke *BFHLoWo*, forsokyn *E*, forsooken *X*; weye *BFHX*; whiche
     BEHLoWoX; fadres *FLo*, fadris *Wo*
62   þem *Lo*; wentyn *E*; heerynge *BF*, heryng *Lo*, herende *X*; hestis *BFHWo*,
     hestes *X*
63   lorde *Wo*; all *BF*, al *H*; þinges *BLoWo*, thingus *X*
64   whenn *B*, whenne *E*, when *H*, whan *WoX*; had *BFLoWo*
65   rered *EFHX*, reride *Lo*; juges *LoX*; dayʒis *B*, dayes *FLo*, dawes *Wo*,
     daʒes *X*; þem *Lo*
66   bowed *B*; herd *B*; weylynges *Lo*, weilingus *X*
67   tormentyd *EX*, tourmentyng *Lo*; delyuerd *BH*, delyuerede *ELoX*, delyuerde
     F, delyuered *Wo*
68   þem *LoX*; deþ *BFHWoX*

16 Suscitavitque Dominus iudices, qui liberarent eos de
   vastantium manibus; sed nec illos audire voluerunt,
17 fornicantes cum diis alienis et adorantes eos. Cito
   deseruerunt viam, per quam ingressi fuerant patres
   eorum; et audientes mandata Domini, omnia fecerunt
   contraria.

16 And the Lord reiside iugis, that delyueriden hem fro the hondis of destrieris,
17 but thei nolden here hem, and thei diden
   fornycacioun, *that is, idolatrie,* with alien   60
   goddis, and worschipiden hem. Soone
   thei forsoken the weie, bi which the fadris of hem entriden; and thei herden
   the comaundementis of the Lord, and
18 diden alle thingis contrarie. And whanne   65
   the Lord reiside iugis in the daies of
   hem, he was bowid bi mercy, and he
   herde the weilyngis of *hem* turmentid,
   and he delyuerede hem fro the sleyng of

57 reisid D, reisede EFKLPU, reiside up I; iuges FR; that: & I; delyuereden
   CaEFGHaLMNOPUW, delyuerden D, delyueryde IKMaS
58 from K; hondes CaEF, hoondis R; distrieris AcBCCaGNOQUW,
   distriers DHaMP, destroiers EK, destrieres F, þe destriers I, destriers L,
   distroieris Ma, distroiers RS, distruyers X
59 Bot E; thei: *israel* I; nolden: wolde not I, noolden MaSX; heere
   GHaKMaSX; hem: her iugis I; deden F, dedin P
60 fornication E, fornycacion K; gloss om. SX; whith E; alyene
   BCaEHaKMRW, straunge I
61 goddes F; and: om. N; wurschipeden CaFMW, worshipeden ELP, þei
   wirschipiden I; sone DEFL
62 forsooken NX; wey EI; whiche DGIQ, wiche K; faders E, fadres F;
   62–3 the fadris of hem: her fadris I
63 entreden CaEFMPUW
64 comaundementes E; the c. of the Lord: þe lordis hestis I
65 þei diden I, dedin P; þinges FHa; when E, whan HaLP
66 reisid D, reisede EFKLPU, reiside up I; iughes E, iuges FR; 66–7 d. of
   hem: her d. I
67 bouwid B, bowed EFPLU, bowȝide R; mercie R; he: om. BC
68 herd D; weilinges BCaFHaU, waylingis E, wellingis S; of *hem* t.: of hem
   þat weren t. I
69 delyueride AcBCFKMMaQWX, delyuerid DHa, deliuered E; sleynge
   AcCaDFGLMMaPW, sleeinge Q, fleynge U

18 Cumque Dominus iudices suscitaret in diebus eorum,
   flectebatur misericordia, et audiebat afflictorum
   gemitus, et liberabat eos de caede vastantium.

19 Forsothe after that the iuge was deed,
  thei turneden aȝen, and manye thingis   70
  diden more than diden the faders of hem,
  folwynge alien goddis, and seruynge to
  hem, and honourynge hem; thei laften
  not her fyndyngis, and the moost hard
  weye bi the which thei weren wonyd to   75
20 goo. And the woodnes of the Lord is
  wrooth aȝens Irael, and seith, For this
  folk hath maad at nouȝt my couenaunt
  that I couenauntide with the faders of
  hem, and my vois he dispyside to here;   80
21 and I shal not doo awey the Gentilis,

69 Aftir *LoX*; Forsothe after: a. f. *cet.*; dead *BX*, ded *E*, dede *Wo*
70 torned *BFHWo*, tornede *E*, turnede *Lo*; aȝeyn *BEFHWo*, aȝeyne *Lo*,
    aȝeen *X*; many *BEFHLoWo*; þinges *Lo*, thingus *X*
71 dydden (2x) *BF*, dedyn *E* (2x); þann *B*; fadres *FLo*, fadris *Wo*; þem *Lo*
72 folowynge *BFWo*, folwyng *Lo*, folewende *X*; aliene *X*; goddes *LoWo*,
    godis *X*; seruyng *Lo*, seruende *X*
73 þem (2x) *LoX*; hnouringe *H*, honouryng *Lo*, honourende *X*; laft *BFHWo*,
    lafte *ELo*, leften *X*
74 her: þer *BLoX*, þere *E*, þeir *FWo*; fyndynges *Lo*, findingus *X*; most
    BEFHWoX, moste *Lo*; harde *BFHLoWo*
75 wey *EWo*; whiche *BHLoWoX*; weryn *E*; woned *EFH*, wont *LoWoX*
76 go *EWoX*; wodenes *BH*, wodenesse *FLoWo*, wodnesse *X*
77 wroþ *BFHX*, wrothe *LoWo*; aȝeyns *BFHLoWo*, aȝen *X*; seys *Lo*
78 folke *H*; has *Lo*; made *BEFHLoWo*, mad *X*; noȝt *FX*; couenant *E*,
    couenaunte *Lo*
79 coue[n]auntid *B*, couenauntid *FHWo*, couenauntede *EX*; fadres *FLo*,
    fadris *Wo*
80 þem *Lo*; voyce *BFHLoWo*; he: þey *Lo*; dispysed *BFHLoWo*, despysede *E*;
    heere *BF*, heren *X*
81 doon *E*, do *HWo*, don *X*; aweye *H*; gentyls *F*, gentiles *LoWoX*

19 Postquam autem mortuus esset iudex, revertebantur,
  et multa faciebant maiora quam fecerant patres eorum,
  sequentes deos alienos, et servientes eis, et adorantes illos. Non dimiserunt adinventiones suas,
  et viam durissimam, per quam ambulare consueverant.

108

19 wasteris. Sotheli aftir that the iuge 70
   was deed, thei turneden aȝen, and diden
   many thingis grettere *in yuel* than her
   fadris diden; and thei sueden alien goddis,
   and serueden hem, and worschipiden hem;
   thei leften not her owne fyndyngis, and 75
   the hardeste weie bi which thei weren
20 wont to go. And the strong veniaunce
   of the Lord was wrooth aȝens Israel, and
   he seide, For this puple hath maad voide
   my couenaunt which Y couenauntide with 80
   her fadris, and dispiside to here my vois;
21 also Y schal not do awey folkis, whiche

70 watris D, þe wasters E, wasteres F, *her* destrieris I, wasters MPRX,
   waasters Ma; soþli FGLMMaPQSUWX, but I; after EFLMU; that: om.
   N; the: here I
71 dede E, dead Q; turned E, turnyden GQ; aȝein E; dedin EP
72 manye BGKMaQRUW; þinges FHa; gretter EHaILMPSX; th. gr.: gr.
   th. I; *in yuel*: in euyl GLQ, om. I; þanne CaD; here FGQR
73 faders E, fadres F; dedin EP, deden F; suweden CaFMW; aliene
   BCaHaKMRW; goddes F
74 seruyden AcCGHaQ; wurschipeden CaFMW, wirschipiden I, worshipeden
   PU
75 laften EK, leftin LP; here FQ; owen E; fyndinges BCaFHaR
76 hardist AcDMa, hardiste BGO, hardest EHaLPR, ful hard I; wey DIRU;
   whiche G, wiche K; werin EP; 76–7 bi which thei w. wont to go: þat
   þei w. woned to go *bi* I
77 woned I, wonte R; stronge CCaGHaR; venghaunce E, vengeaunce CK
78 wroþ EFGHaILNPQSUX, wroiþ K; aȝenus AcCNO
79 peple CaFILMMaNPSWX; haþe E; made DE, maade Ha; void FHaI
80 couenaunte E; wich K, þat I; couenauntid D, couenaunted E, comaundide
   GQ, couenauntede P; wh. I c.: om. Ca
81 here FQR; faders EP, fadres F; dispisid D, despisede EKL, dispisede
   FPU, han dispisid I; heere GIKMaNX; voice EI
82 also: & CaDGHaIKMMaNOQSX; away Ha; folkes EFR, þe folkis I;
   þe whiche I, wiche K, which O

20 Iratusque est furor Domini in Israel, et ait: Quia
   irritum fecit gens ista pactum meum, quod pepigeram
   cum patribus eorum, et vocem meam audire contempsit,
21 et ego non delebo gentes, quas dimisit Iosue, et
   mortuus est;

22 the whiche Josue lafte, and is deed; that
   in hem Y haue knoulechynge of Yrael,
   whether thei kepen the weie of the Lord,
   and goon in it, as kepten the faders of

23 hem, or noon. Thanne the Lord lafte alle
   thes naciouns, and wold not anoon ouer-
   turne, ne took into the hoondis of Josue.

3. 1 Thes ben the Gentilis, that the Lord
     lafte, for to lerne Irael in hem, and alle
     that knewen not the bateils of Cha-
   2 nenees; and afterward the sones of hem
     shulden lerne to stryue with enemies, and

5

82 which *F*; laft *BFHWo*; dead *BX*, ded *E*
83 þem *LoX*; knowlechyng *BLoX*
84 wheþere *Lo*; keepen *BF*, kepyn *ELo*, kepe *X*; wey *ELoWo*
85 gon *WoX*; hit *E*; keptyn *E*; fadres *FLo*, fadris *Wo*
86 þem *Lo*; noone *Lo*, nay *X*; þenn *B*, þenne *EHLo*, þann *F*, þan *Wo*; lorde
   Wo; left *BFHWo*, lefte *ELoX*; all *F*
87 þese *E*, þe *X*; nacionys *E*; wolde *BEFHLoX*; anoone *B*, anon *Wo*, anoen *X*;
   ouertorne *BEHWo*
88 toke *BFHWo*, toc *X*; hondys *EHX*, hondes *LoWo*

3. 1 þese *BEHX*; been *E*; gentyles *Lo*; lorde *Lo*
   2 laft *BFHWo*, lefte *E*; lern *BH*, leerne *FWo*; þem *Lo*; all *F*, al *H*
   3 knewe *BEFH*, knew *Wo*; bateylys *EF*, batayles *Lo*, bateyles *Wo*, batailis *X*
   4 aftirwarde *Lo*; sonys *BEH*, sonus *X*; þem *Lo*
   5 sholdyn *E*, schold *Lo*; lern *B*, leerne *F*; enmyes *BFWo*, ennemyes *H*,
     enemys *X*

22 ut in ipsis experiar Israel, utrum custodiant viam
   Domini, et ambulent in ea, sicut custodierunt patres
   eorum, an non.
23 Dimisit ergo Dominus omnes has nationes, et cito
   subvertere noluit, nec tradidit in manus Iosue.

22 Josue lefte, and was deed; that in hem
Y asaie Israel, whether thei kepen the
weie of the Lord, and goen ther ynne, as
23 her fadris kepten, ether nay. Therfor
the Lord lefte alle these naciouns, and
nolde destrie soone, nethir bitook in to
the hondis of Josue.

3. 1 These ben the folkis whiche the Lord
lefte, that in hem he schulde teche Israel,
and alle men that knewen not the batels
2 of Cananeis; and that aftirward the sones
of hem schulden lerne to fi3te with ene-   5

83 lafte K; dede E, dead Q; l. and was d.: þat is d. l. I
84 assaye BCaEHaIKLMPQW, asay D; wher AcBCaFGHaKLMMaNOPQRS-
UWX; where DEI; kepten O, kepin P
85 wey DEIMaU; goon CaKLMMaPW, gone E, gon GHaIQU; þere BR
86 here QR; faders ELU, fadres F; kepten *it* I; eþir BO, eiþer
CaFGHaMMaQW, or EILP, eiþir R, oþer U; no I; þerfore
BCaEGIKLMMaNPQRWX, for O, fore S²
87 left D, lafte EK, lefte *alijue* I; þes DKNRX; nationes E, nacions KQ
88 wolde Ca, he wolde not I, noolde MaQSX; distrie AcBCCaDFGHaMNO-
PQUW, destroie EK, destrie hem I, distroie MaR, distruye SX; sone EF;
neþer AcBCDKLNPX, neiþer CaFGHaIMQW, noþer EU, neiþir MaR;
bitok E, bitoke HaR, he bitoke *hem* I
89 the: om. MW; hondes EF, hond I

3. 1 Thes DN; bene E; folkes EFR, foolis N; wiche K, which S; lorde E
2 lafte EK, lefte alyue I; scholde CaMW, shuld E; teeche G
3 al E; bateyls GX, batailis I, batelis K, batails L, bateilis S, bataides U
4 afterward ELNU; sonys GQ; 4—5 the s. of hem: her s. I
5 scholden CaMW, schulde D; lern E; enmyes I

3. 1 Hae sunt gentes, quas Dominus dereliquit, ut erudiret
in eis Israelem, et omnes, qui non noverant bella
Chananeorum;
2 et postea discerent filii eorum certare cum hostibus,
et habere consuetudinem proeliandi:

3 to haue vsage of fiȝtynge in batayl. The
fyue princes of Philistynys, and al Chanane, and Sydon, and Euee the whiche
dwelten in Liban hil, fro the hil of Baal
of Hermon vnto the entre of Emath.   10
4 And he lafte hem, that in hem he myȝte
haue experiens of Yrael, whether thei
wolen here the heestis of the Lord, the
which hath comaundid to the faders of
hem by the hoond(is) of Moyses, or noon.   15
5 And so the sones of Yrael dwelten in the
mydil of Chananeei, Ethei, and Amorrei, and Pherezei, and Euei, and Jebusei.

6 han *X*; fiȝtyng *Lo*, fiȝte *X*; bateyl *BFWo*, bateile *EH*, batayle *LoX*
7 princis *BEFHWo*; all *B*, alle *X*
8 which *FWo*
9 dweltyn *E*, dwelte *X*; hil (2x): hyll *BFH*, hul *E*, hylle *Wo*
10 of (1°): om. *X*; entree *BH*
11 left *BFHWo*, lefte *ELoX*; hem (2x): þem *LoX*(1°); myȝt *BFHWo*
12 han *X*; experience *EX*
13 wyln *BFWoX*, wolyn *E*, wolden *H*, wille *Lo*; heere *BF*, heren *X*; hestis *FH*,
   hestes *WoX*; lorde *Wo*
14 whiche *BEHLoX*; hath: has *Lo*, 'he' haþ *X*; comaunded *E*, comaundide *Lo*;
   fadres *FLo*, fadris *Wo*
15 þem *LoX*; hond *EX*, hondes *LoWo*; noone *Lo*, none *Wo*, nai *X*
16 sonys *E*, sone *Lo*, sonus *X*; dweltyn *E*
17 mydyll *B*, myddul *E*, myddil *H*, mydel *Lo*, myddel *WoX*; off *X*

3 quinque satrapas Philistinorum, omnemque Chananeum,
et Sidonium, atque Eveum, qui habitabant in monte
Libano, de monte Baal-hermon usque ad introitum
Emath.
4 Dimisitque eos, ut in ipsis experiretur Israelem,
utrum audirent mandata Domini quae praeceperat
patribus eorum per manum Moysi, an non.
5 Itaque filii Israel habitaverunt in medio Chananei,
Ethei, et Amorrei, et Pherezei, et Evei, et Iebusei;

3 myes, and to haue custom of batel. *He
lefte* fyue princes of Filistees, and al Cananei, and the puple of Sidon, and Euey
that dwelliden in the hil Liban, fro the
hil Baal Hermon til to the entryng of   10
4 Emath. And he lefte hem, that in hem
he schulde asaie Israel, whethir thei wolden
here the heestis of the Lord, whiche he
comaundide to her fadris bi the hond of
5 Moises, ethir nai. And so the sones of   15
Israel dwelliden in the myddis of Cananei,
of Ethei, and of Ammorrei, and of Feresei,

6 custum BCaDHaMMaQSWX, þe vse I; of: to R; bateil DSX, fiȝting I,
   batele K, bateile R, bataile U
7 lafte EK; pryncis DGIKLMaNPQSWX; Filistees: þe f. I
8 peple CaFILMMaNPSWX
9 dwelleden CaLP, dwellid D, dwelledyn E, dwellide FGHaIK²MMaQW;
   hul E; þat *hiȝte* liban I, of liban AcKS; from K
10 hille D, hul E; of baal AcIMa; of hermon I; til to: vnto I, in to E;
   entrynge DGMaQRU
11 he: þe *lord* I; laft E, laft E, lafte K; that in hem: om. G; hem: om. W
12 scholde CaMW; assaie CaEFGHaILMPQWX, assay D; al israel I; wher
   AcBCaFGHaKLMMaNOPQRSUW, where CDEI, wheþer X
13 heere GMaNPX; hestis CaEIPQUW, hestes F, heestes R; the heestis of
   the Lord: þe lordis hestis I; which F, wiche K
14 comaundid D, comaunded E, comaundede LP; here QR; faders E, fadres
   F; honde E, witnesse *'or hond'* I, hoond R
15 eþer AcBCDKNOSX, eiþer CaFGHaIMMaQRW, oþer U; sonis EGLPQ,
   sonus Ma
16 dwelleden CaFMUW, dwelledyn E; myddes F, myȝddis U
17 and of Ammorrei: & A. Ha; and of Feresei: & f. C
18 weddeden CaFLMPW, weddedyn E, þei weddiden I, weeldiden N

113

6 And wyues thei token douȝtres of hem,
  and [thei] token her douȝtris to the sones   20
  of hem, and serueden to [the] goddis of
7 hem. And thei diden yuel in the siȝt of
  the Lord, and forȝeten of the Lord her
  God, seruynge to Baalym, and to Asta-
8 roth. And the Lord, wrooth aȝens Yrael,   25
  took hem into the hoondis of Chusanra-
  sathaym, kyng of Mesopothanye, and thei
9 serueden to him eiȝt ȝeer. And thei crieden to the Lord, the which areryde to
  hem a saueour, and delyuerde hem, that   30
  is, Othonyel, the sone of Cenez, the lasse

19 wyuys *BEFWo*, wyfys *H*; tooken *B*, tookyn *E*; douȝters *BF*, douȝtris
    EWo, doȝtris *X*; þem *LoX*
20 tooken *B*, tookyn *E*; þeir *BFWo*, here *E*, þer *LoX*; douȝtren *BFHLoWo*,
    doȝtris *X*; sonis *EH*, sonus *X*
21 þem *Lo*; seruedyn *E*; goddes *LoWo*, godus *X*
22 þem *LoX*; dedyn *E*, dydden *F*; yuyl *E*, yuele *Lo*, euel *WoX*; siȝte *LoX*
23 forȝetyn *E*; þeir *BFWo*, here *E*, þer *LoX*
24 seruyng *Lo*, seruende *X*
25 wroþ *BFHWoX*, wrothe *Lo*; aȝeyns *BEFLoWo*, aȝen *X*
26 tooke *BFHLoWo*, toc *X*; þem *LoX*; hondys *EX*, hondes *LoWo*
27 kynge *FLoWo*
28 seruedyn *E*; eiȝte *ELoX*; ȝere *LoWo*, ȝer *X*; crydyn *E*, cried *Wo*
29 lorde *Wo*; whiche *BEHLoWoX*; arerid *BHWo*, arerede *EX*, arered *F*,
    reysede *Lo*
30 þem *LoX*; sauyour *E*, saueoure *Lo*; delyuered *LoWo*, deliuerede *X*; þem
    LoX
31 off *E*; lesse *LoX*

6 et duxerunt uxores filias eorum, ipsique filias suas
  filiis eorum tradiderunt, et servierunt diis eorum.
7 Feceruntque malum in conspectu Domini, et obliti
  sunt Domini Dei sui, servientes Baalim et Astaroth.
8 Iratusque Dominus contra Israel tradidit eos in
  manus Chusanrasathaim regis Mesopotamiae, servieruntque ei octo annis.

6 and of Euey, and of Jebusey, and weddiden wyues, the douȝtris of hem; and
the sones of Israel ȝauen her douȝtris to
the sones of hem, and serueden the

7 goddis of hem. And the sones of Israel
diden yuel in the siȝt of the Lord, and
forȝaten her Lord God, and serueden

8 Baalym, and Astaroth. And the Lord
was wrooth aȝens Israel, and bitook hem
in to the hondis of Cusanrasathaym, kyng
of Mesopotanye, and thei serueden hym

9 eiȝte ȝeer. And thei crieden to the Lord,
and he reiside to hem a sauyour, and delyuerede hem, that is, Othonyel, sone of

20

25

30

19   wiuis EQ, wifes K; douȝtres EF, douȝters U
20   sonis GPQ; ȝaf E, ȝafen K; here FGQR, þer K; douȝtres EF
21   sonis GLPQ; the sones of hem: her sones I; seruyden CG, þei
     seruyden I
22   goddes EF; 21−22 the goddis of hem: to her goddis I; sonis GLPQ
23   dedin EP, deden U; euel E, euyle G, euil LPQ; siȝte CaU, shiȝt E; lorde
     E; the siȝt of the Lord: þe lordis siȝt I
24   þei forȝaten I, forȝatin LP; her: þe G, þer K, here Q; seruyden CGIQ,
     seruedin E
25   lorde E
26   wroþe E, wroþ GHaILPQRSUX; aȝenus AcCNO; bitoken Ca, bitooke D,
     bitoke EHaIR, bitok U
27   the: om. E; hondes CaF, hoondis R; þe king E
28   seruyden CGIOQ; him: om. R
29   ȝere E, ȝer ILP; cried E
30   reisede EFKP, reiseden L; saueour BCaFHaLMPW, sauyoure D; to hem
     a s. and: om. D; delyueride AcBCCaFIKOQWX, delyuerid D, deliuered
     E, deliuyriden S
31   þe sone I

9 Et clamaverunt ad Dominum, qui suscitavit eis
salvatorem, et liberavit eos, Othoniel videlicet,
filium Cenez, fratrem Caleph minorem.

10 brother of Caleph. And the spiryt of
the Lord was in hym, and he demyde
Irael. And he wente out to fiȝt, and the
Lord took into the hoondys of hym Chu-   35
sanrasathaym, the kyng of Syrie, and
11 oppresside hym. And the loond restid
fourti ȝeer; and Othonyel, the sone of
12 Cenez, died. Forsothe the sones of Yrael
addiden to doon yuel in the siȝt of the   40
Lord; the which counfortide aȝens hem
Eglo, the kyng of Moab, for thei diden
13 yuel in the siȝt of the Lord. And he
cowplid to hem the sones of Amon and
of Amalech; and he wente, and smoot   45
Yrael, and he weeldide the citee of

32 spirite *BFLo*, spiriȝte *H*
33 demyd *BFHWo*, demede *EX*
34 went *BFHWo*; oute *B*, ouȝte *H*; fiȝte *Lo*, fiȝten *X*
35 lorde *Lo*; tooke *B*, toke *FHLoWo*, toc *X*; hondys *EX*, hondes *LoWo*
36 kynge *BFWo*
37 oppressed *BFH*, oppressede *E*, oppressid *Wo*, opressede *X*; lond *EX*, lord
FWo, londe *Lo*; restede *EX*, restyd *FWo*
38 ȝere *LoWo*, ȝer *X*
39 dyȝid *BHWo*, deide *E*, dyȝed *F*, dyede *LoX*; Forsothe the sones : þe s. f.
cet.; sonys *BEH*, sonus *X*
40 addeden *BFWo*, addedyn *E*; do *EWo*, don *X*; yuyl *E*, euel *WoX*; siȝte *LoX*
41 whiche *BHLoX*, wheche *E*; confortyd *BF*, conforted *E*, counfortid *HWo*,
confortide *Lo*, counfortede *X*; aȝeyns *BEFLoWo*, aȝen *X*; þem *Lo*
42 kynge *FLo*; dydden *BF*, dedyn *E*
43 yuyl *E*, euel *WoX*; siȝte *LoX*
44 couplede *EX*, couplide *Lo*; þem *LoX*; sonys *BEH*, sonus *X*
45 went *BFHWo*; smote *BFHLoWo*, smot *EX*
46 weeldyd *BFH*, weeldede *E*, weldide *LoX*, weldid *Wo*; cite *EHLoWoX*

10 Fuitque in eo spiritus Domini, et iudicavit Israel.
Egressusque est ad pugnam, et tradidit Dominus in
manus eius Chusanrasathaim, regem Syriae, et op-
pressit eum.
11 Quievitque terra quadraginta annis, et mortuus est
Othoniel, filius Cenez.

10 Ceneth, the lesse brother of Caleph. And
the spirit of the Lord was in hym, and he
demyde Israel. And he ȝede out to batel,
and the Lord bitook in to hise hondis   35
Cusanra[sa]thaym, kyng of Sirie; and *Otho-*
11 *nyel* oppresside hym. And the lond restide
fourti ȝeer; and Othonyel, sone of Ceneth,
12 diede. Forsothe the sones of Israel ad-
diden to do yuel in the siȝt of the Lord;   40
and he counfortide aȝens hem Eglon, the
kyng of Moab, for thei diden yuel in the
13 siȝt of the Lord. And the Lord couplide
to hym the sones of Amon and Ama-
lech; and he ȝede, and smoot Israel, and   45
hadde in possessioun the citee of Palmes.

32 the lesse: þe lasse EK, & þe ȝōnger I
33 spirite E, spiritt K, spiriȝt L; lorde E; in: wiþ G, maad in Ma¹
34 demede BCaFKMPRUW, demyd D, demed E, deemede LMaX, delyuerede
    N; ȝeod E; oute R; bateil DRSX, batail I, bataile KU
35 bitoke EHaIR, bitok U; his EFILPSX; hondes F, hoondis R
37 oppressid DF, oppressed E, oppressede P; restid D, restede ELP, r. *in pes* I
38 ȝere E, ȝer LP; þe sone EI
39 deide CaW, died E, deiede FM, diȝede R; Forsothe: & I, fforsoþ R;
    sonis ILQ; addeden CaEFLMPSW
40 don G; euel ELP, euyl GQ; siȝte CaU; the s. of the L.: þe lordis siȝt I
41 counfortiden Ac, confortid C, counfortid D, conforted E, counfortede F,
    confortide IKLMSWX, confortede P, cumfortide Q; aȝenus AcCaNO
42 thei diden: israel dide I, þei dedin P; yuele BMaN, euel ELP, euyl GQ
43 siȝte MaUW; s. of the L.: lordis siȝt I; couplid D, coupled E, couplede FP
44 hym: eglon I; sonys GQ; and of Amalech BIMaX
45 he: eglon I; smote EHaIR, smot G
46 had E, he hadde I, haddē O; possession EIK; cite CaEFHaLMPQW;
    palmys GQ, psalmis Ha

12 Addiderunt autem filii Israel facere malum in conspectu Domini; qui confortavit adversum eos Eglon,
regem Moab, quia fecerunt malum in conspectu
Domini.
13 Et copulavit ei/s/ filios Amon et Amalech; abiitque
et percussit Israel, atque possedit urbem palmarum.

14 Palmys. And the sones of Yrael serueden to Eglon, the kyng of Moab,
15 eiȝteen ȝeer. And aftirward thei cryeden
   to the Lord; the which reryde to hem a   50
   saueour, Aod bi name, the sone of Gera,
   sone of Gemyny, the which either hoond
   vside for the riȝt. And the sones of
   Yrael senden bi hym ȝiftis to Eglon, the
16 kyng of Moab; the which maade to hym   55
   a swerd bitynge in eche side, hauynge in
   the mydil a pomel of lengthe of the palm
   of an hoond; and he is gird with it
   vndur the coot armure, in the riȝt hipe.
17 And he offerde ȝiftis to Eglon, the kyng   60
   of Moab; forsothe Eglon was myche fat.

47 palmys *LoX*; sonys *BEH*, sonus *X*; seruedyn *E*
48 kynge *FLoWo*
49 eyȝtene *BFHLoWo*, eiȝtetene *EX*; ȝeere *B*, ȝere *LoWo*, ȝer *X*; afterward
   BEFHWoX, aftirwarde *Lo*; crydyn *E*, criden *Wo*
50 whiche *BEHLoWoX*; rerid *BFHWo*, rerede *EX*, reysede *Lo*; þem *LoX*
51 sauyour *E*, sauyoure *Lo*
52 whiche *BEHLoX*; hond *EWoX*, honde *Lo*
53 vsyd *BFH*, vsede *ELoX*, vsed *Wo*; riȝte *Lo*; sonys *E*
54 senten *X*; ȝiftes *LoWoX*
55 kynge *BFLo*; whiche *BEFHLoX*; maad *B*, made *EHLoWo*, maden *X*
56 swerde *LoWo*; bitende *X*; ech *Wo*; hauende *X*
57 mydyll *B*, myddul *E*, myddil *H*, mydel *Lo*, myddel *WoX*; pomell *BF*;
   leyngþ *BF*; palme *BFHLoWo*
58 hond *EX*, honde *LoWo*; gerd *E*, gyrde *Lo*; hit *E*
59 vnder *BEFHWoX*, vndre *Lo*; the: om. *Lo*; coote *BFLo*, coot- *E*, cote *Wo*,
   coete *X*; -harmure *E*, armour *HX*; riȝte *Lo*; hypp *BFWo*, hupe *E*, hippe
   HLo
60 offerd *B*, offrede *ELoX*, offred *FH*, offrid *Wo*; ȝiftes *LoX*; kynge *BFLoWo*
61 off *E*; forsothe Eglon: E. f. *cet.*; moche *E*; fatt *BFHWo*, fatte *Lo*

14 Servieruntque filii Israel Eglon, regi Moab, decem
   et octo annis.
15 Et postea clamaverunt ad Dominum; qui suscitavit
   eis salvatorem, vocabulo Aod, filium Gera, filii
   Gemini, qui utraque manu utebatur pro dextera.
   Miseruntque filii Israel per illum munera Eglon
   regi Moab.

118

14 And the sones of Israel serueden Eglon,
15 kyng of Moab, eiȝtene ȝeer. And aftirward thei crieden to the Lord; and he
reiside to hem a sauyour, Aioth bi name,   50
the sone of Gera, sone of Gemyny, which
Aioth vside euer either hond for the riȝt
hond. And the sones of Israel senten bi
him ȝiftis, *that is, tribute,* to Eglon, kyng
16 of Moab; which Aioth made to hym a   55
swerd keruynge on euer either side, hau-
ynge in the myddis a pomel of the lengthe
of the pawm of an hond; and he was
gird therwith vndir the sai, *that is, a*
17 *knyȝtis mentil,* in the riȝt hipe. And   60
he brouȝte ȝiftis to Eglon, the kyng of

47 sonis GQ; serued E, seruiden GIQ
48 kyng: þe k. K; eiȝtē I; ȝere E, ȝer P; afterward EU
49 cried E, criden W
50 reisid D, reisede EFKLPU; saueour BCaEFHaLMPW
51 whiche G, þe whiche I, wiche K
52 vsid D, usede EFKLP; eþer C, eiþ[er] E, eiþir MaQSX; honde E; riȝth E
53 honde E; sonys GLQ; senden I
54 ȝiftes EFR; gloss om. ISX
55 whiche G, þe which I, wiche K
56 swerde E; keruyng EL; euer either: eueri E, euer eiþir NOS, euir eiþer Q; hauyng DE
57 myddes F; lenkþe Ma
58 the: a IR; pawme AcBCaDEGHaIKMMaNQRSUWX; honde E, hand Ma
59 girt EP; þere wiþ B; vndur AcCCaMW, vnder FLU; the: a I; sei E, sayȝ I
60 knyȝtes FHa; mentel CaDFMW, mantel EHaKLRW, mantil P; *kn. m.*: *coote armure* I; gloss om. S; in: on I; hepe U; 59–60 gird þerwiþ on þe riȝt hipe vndir a sayȝ *þat is a coote armure* I
61 brouȝt D; ȝiftes F, ȝeftis L; the: om. BCEGIMPQRX

16 Qui fecit sibi gladium ancipitem, habentem in medio
capulum longitudinis palmae manus, et accinctus est
eo subter sagum in dextro femore.
17 Obtulitque munera Eglon regi Moab. Erat autem Eglon
crassus nimis.

18 And whanne he hadde offerd to hym
ʒiftis, he folwide felawis that with hym
19 camen; and turned aʒen fro Galgalis,
where weren the mawmettis, seide to the   65
kyng, A preue word Y haue to thee,
O kyng. And he comaundide silence.
And alle men goon out, that weren about
20 hym, Aod wente in to hym; forsothe he
sat in the somer sowpynge place alone.   70
And he seide, The word of God Y haue
to thee. The which anoon roos fro the
21 troon. And Aod strauʒte out the left
hoond, and he took the swerd fro his
riʒt hipe; and he putte into his wombe   75

62 whenn *BH*, whenne *E*, whan *FWoX*; had *BFLoWo*; offred *BFH*, offrede
    ELo, offrid *WoX*
63 ʒiftes *Lo*, ʒeftes *Wo*; folowid *BWo*, folwede *E*, folowyd *FH*, folowide *Lo*,
    folewede *X*; felowis *BEFH*, felawes *LoX*, felowes *Wo*
64 coomen *BF*, comyn *E*, comen *HLoWo*; tornyd *BH*, torned *E*, turnede *Lo*;
    aʒeyn *BEFHWo*, aʒeyne *Lo*, aʒeen *X*; from *Lo*
65 wern *B*, were *E*; maumetys *ELoWo*, maumetes *X*
66 kynge *BFLoWo*; pryue *ELoX*, preuee *Wo*; worde *LoWo*, wrd *X*; þe *EWo*
67 kynge *FLo*; comaundyd *BFHWo*, comaundede *E*, cōmaundide *Lo*
68 all *FH*; gon *WoX*; oute *B*, ouʒt *H*; weryn *E*; aboute *BEFLo*, abouʒte *H*,
    abouten *X*
69 went *BWo*; 69–70 forsothe he sat: he sat f. *cet.*
70 satt *BEFH*, satte *Lo*, sate *Wo*; souppyng *Lo*, souping *X*; doon *BFHWo*
71 worde *LoWo*, wrd *X*
72 þe *EWo*; whiche *BEHLoX*; anoone *Lo*, anon *Wo*, anoen *X*; rose *Wo*,
    roes *X*
73 trone *BEFHLoX*, throne *Wo*; strauʒt *BFHWo*, streiʒte *E*, straʒte *X*; ouʒt
    H; lift *EHX*, lyfte *Lo*
74 hond *EWoX*, hande *Lo*; tooke *B*, toke *FHWo*, toc *X*; swerde *LoWo*; from
    E
75 riʒte *Lo*; hipp *BFHWo*, hupe *E*, hippe *Lo*; putt *BFH*, piʒt *Lo*[2], put *Wo*,
    putte *X*; woombe *E*

18 Cumque obtulisset ei munera, persecutus est socios,
   qui cum eo venerant.
19 Et reversus de Galgalis, ubi erant idola, dixit ad
   regem: Verbum secretum habeo ad te, o rex. Et ille
   imperavit silentium. Egressisque omnibus qui circa
   eum erant,

18 Moab; forsothe Eglon was ful fat. And
whanne he hadde ʒoue ʒiftis to the kyng,
he pursuede felowis that camen with hym;

19 and he turnede aʒen fro Galgalis, where   65
idolis weren, and he seide to the kyng,
A kyng, Y haue a priuei word to thee.
And he comaundide silence. And whanne
alle men weren goon out, that weren aboute

20 hym, Aioth entride to hym; forsothe he   70
sat aloone in a somer parlour. And Aioth
seide, Y haue the word of God to thee.

21 Which roos anoon fro the trone. And
Aioth helde forth the left hond, and took
the swerd fro his riʒt hype; and he   75

62 forsothe: & I, forsoþ X; fatt IKMaR
63 whan EGHaLP; had E; ʒofe K; ʒiftes EHa, ʒeftis L
64 pursuyde AcQ, pursuwide CaMW, pursued DE, pursuwede F, suyde forþ
    aftir I; felawis CaDMW, felows E, felowes FLP, his f. I; camyn S
65 turned DE, turnyde GHaIQW; aʒein BE; from K
66 idols CCaHaKMMaRSX, ydoles F; idolis weren: weren ydolis I; seid E
67 O kyng I, aa k. NX; priuy AcBCHaMaNORSUX, priue CaFMW, pryuye
    D, preuy GPQ, preuey I; worde E; to þe EF
68 he: þe king I; comaundid D, comaunded E, comaundede LP; scilens D;
    when E, whan GLP
69 al E; were GMOQ; gon AcFGHaILNQU, goen BDOR, a gone E, gone K;
    oute R; wheren E; abouʒte L
70 hym: þe kyng I, hem R; entrid D, entred E, entrede PU; forsothe: & I,
    forsooþe S, forsoþ X; he: þe kyng I
71 sate DIR, satt KMa; allone C, alone CaFKMPW, al on E, aloon IR,
    aboue X; somir GQ
72 saide E; worde E; to þe EMaR
73 whiche EG, þe whiche I, wich K; roos up E, roose I; anone E, anon PQ;
    from K; the: his I; troone AcGMaX
74 heeld CaFMMaNPSWX, held GL, heuld K, hilde O, heelde R; forþe E;
    the: his I; lefte CRU, lift EFHaKLMaOP; honde U; toke ER, tooke Ha
75 the: his I; swerde E; from K; his: þe BN

20 ingressus est Aod ad eum; sedebat autem in aestivo
cenaculo solus. Dixitque: Verbum Dei habeo ad te.
Qui statim surrexit de throno.

21 Extenditque Aod sinistram manum, et tulit sicam de
dextro femore suo, infixitque /eam/ in ventrem eius,

22 so strongly, that the pomel folwide the
    yren in the wound, and that with moost
    fat grees it was streyned; ne he drewe
    out the swerd, but so as he smoot, he
    lafte in the bodi; and anoon bi the pry-   80
    uetees of kynde the tordis of the wombe
23 bursten out. Forsothe Aod, closyde moost
    bisilich the doris of the sowpynge place,
24 and fastnyd with lok, wente out bi the
    postern. And the seruauntis of the kyng   85
    goon yn, seȝyn* the ȝatis of the sowp-
    inge place closid, and seiden, Perauenture
    he purgith the wombe in the somer sowp-

---

76 strongely *Lo*; pomell *B*; folowid *BFH*, folwede *E*, folowed *Wo*, folewede *X*
77 yrun *E*; wounde *cet.*; most *BEFHWoX*, moste *Lo*
78 fatt *BFHWo*, fatte *Lo*; grece *cet.*; hit *E*; streynyd *BH*, streynede *Lo*; drowȝ
    BEHWo, drewȝ *F*, drowe *Lo*, droȝ *X*
79 oute *B*, ouȝt *H*; swerde *EHLoWo*; bot *B*, bote *E*, bute *F*; smote
    BFHLoWo, smot *X*
80 laft *BFHWo*, lefte *ELo*; anone *Wo*, anoen *X*; pryuytees *E*, preuetees *F*,
    priuytes *X*
81 tordes *Wo*, turdus *X*
82 burstyn *E*, brusten *Lo*, brosten *X*; oute *BF*, ouȝte *H*; Forsothe Aod: A. f.
    cet.; closed *BEFH*, closede *Lo*, closid *WoX*; most *BE²FHWoX*, moste *Lo*
83 bysylyche *B*, bysileche *E*, bisily *LoX*; dores *LoX*; souppyng *Lo*, souping *X*
84 fastned *BEFHWoX*, festenede *Lo*; locke *Wo*; went *BFHWo*; ouȝt *H*, oute *X*
85 posterne *EFLoWoX*; seruauntes *BLo*, seruauns *X*; kynge *B*
86 gon *X*; seynge *A*, seeynge *BFH*, seyȝen *E*, seein(g) *Lo*, seȝynge *Wo*,
    seende *X*; ȝates *Lo*; souppynge *Lo*, souping *X*
87 closed *BEFH*, closide *Lo*; par auenture *X*
88 purgeþ *EWoX*, purges *Lo*; woombe *B*; souppynge *Lo*, souping *X*

---

22 tam valide, ut capulus sequeretur ferrum in vulnere,
    ac pinguissimo adipe stringeretur; nec eduxit
    gladium, sed ita ut percusserat, reliquit in corpore;
    statimque per secreta naturae alvi stercora pro-
    ruperunt.
23 Aod autem, clausis diligentissime ostiis cenaculi
    et offirmatis sera,
24 per posticum egressus est; servique regis ingressi
    viderunt clausas fores cenaculi, atque dixerunt:
    Forsitan purgat alvum in aestivo cenaculo.

22 fastnede in to the wombe of the kyng
so strongli, that the pomel, *ether hilte,*
suede the yrun in the wounde, and was
holdun streite in the thickeste fatnesse
with ynne; and he drow not out the   80
swerd, but so as he hadde smyte, he lefte
in the bodi; and anoon bi the priuetees
of kynde the tordis of the wombe braste

23 out. Forsothe whanne the doris of the
parlour weren closid moost diligentli, and   85

24 fastned with lok, Aioth ȝede out bi a
posterne. And the seruauntis of the
king entriden, *not in the parlour, but in
the porche,* and thei sien the doris of the
parlour closid, and seiden, In hap he   90
purgith the wombe in the somer parlour.

76 fastenyde Ac, fastnyde CGHaMaQ, fastned DE, putte it I, fastynede O;
to: om. Ma; wombe of the kyng: kyngis wombe I; kings E, kynge U;
76—77 putte it so strongly in to þe kyngis wombe I

77 ether: or ELP, eiþer FRW, oþer U; þe hilt E, hilt R; gloss om.
AcCCaDGHaIKMMaNOQSX

78 suwide CaMW, sued DE, suwede F, suyde GQ; yrone B, yren
CaEFIKLMMaPRW; it was I

79 holden CaDEFGHaIKLMMaPRSUW, hooldun O; streiȝte Ac, streyt
BCaFIMUW, streiȝt HaK; in the: wiþ I; þickiste AcMaOU, þickist
BDELPR, þickest FHa, moost I; fatnes E, fattnesse K

80 withynne þe wombe I; he: aioth I; drouȝ AcCaGHaKMMaNQWX,
drowe DR, drewe I, drew LP; not: om. M; oute R, om. S

81 swerde ER, sweerd P; bot E; had E; smitte E, smyte *eglon* I; left AcD,
lafte EK, lefte it I

82 the (1°): his I; anon EFHaPQ; priuytees AcILMaORSUX, pryuytes CN,
preuytees GQ, priuetes Ha

83 kynd Ha; toordis AcBCCaDKLMMaNOPQUW, tordes F, orduris I;
woombe E; barsten AcBCCaDFHaIKLMMaNOQRSUWX, barstin EP,
bursten G

84 oute R; Forsothe: & I, forsoþ X; whan EGLP; dores CaEFHaI

85 parloure E; were M; closed ELP, closide K; most CCaEFHaPQU; bisily I

86 fastid D, fastined E, fastnyd GHaNPQSW, fastnede KR; lock RU;
oute ER

87 the (1°): om. E; seruauntes EFHa; 87—88 s. of the king: kyngis seruauntis I

88 entreden CaEFMPW; in (2x): in to AcBCCaDEFGHaI(2°)KLMMa-
NOPQRSUWX; bot E; not ... but: om. I

89 seien CaEFW, siȝen GHaKMaNRSX, sawen I, seiȝen M; dores CEFHaR;
89—90 d. of the p.: p. d. I

90 parloure DE; cloosid K, closed ELP; þei seiden I, seide O; happe EK;
he: þe kyng I

91 purgeþ EFHaK, pourgiþ Ma, puyrgeþ R; the (1°): his I

25 ynge place. And abidynge long, to the
tyme that thei weren ashamyd, and se- 90
ynge that no man opnyde, thei token the
keye, and opnynge thei foonden her lord
26 liggynge deed in the erthe. Forsothe
Aod, while thei weren disturbid, flowȝ
awey, and he passide the place of maw- 95
mettis, whens he turnede aȝen; and he
27 cam into Seyrath. And anoon he sownede with tromp in the hil of Effraym;
and the sones of Yrael dessendiden with

89   abidyng *Lo*, abidende *X*; longe *cet.*
90   were *E*; aschamed *BEHX*, aschamede *Lo*; seeyng *BLo*, seeynge *FH*, seȝinge *Wo*, seende *X*
91   opnyd *BF*, openede *ELoX*, openyd *HWo*; tokyn *E*
92   key *Wo*, keȝe *X*; openynge *EHWo*, openyng *Lo*, openende *X*; founden *BHLoWoX*, foundyn *E*, fonden *F*; þeir *BFWo*, þer *ELoX*
93   lyȝynge *E*, liende *X*; dead *BX*, ded *E*, dede *Wo*; erþ *B*; 93 – 94 Forsothe Aod: A, f. *cet.*; forsoþ *B*
94   þe while *Lo*, whyl *WoX*; were *Wo*; distourbyd *BH*, distourblyd *FWo*, distourblede *Lo*; flowe *B*, flow *EFWo*, flewȝ *H*, flewe *Lo*, fleiȝ *X*
95   aweye *BH*; passed *BFHWo*, passede *ELoX*; maumetys *EFLoWo*, maumetes *X*
96   whenns *B*, whennys *E*, whennes *Lo*, whan *X*; torned *BH*, tornede *E*, turned *FWo*; aȝeyn *BEFLoWo*, aȝeen *X*
97   come *BLoWo*, coom *E*, coome *FH*; anone *LoWo*, anon *X*; sowned *BFHWo*
98   trompe *BEFHLo*, trumpe *WoX*; hyll *BFH*, hul *E*, hylle *LoWo*
99   sonys *EH*, sonus *X*; descendedyn *E*

25 Exspectantesque diu, donec erubescerent, et videntes
quod nullus aperiret, tulerunt clavem; et aperientes
invenerunt dominum suum iacentem in terra mortuum.
26 Aod autem, dum illi turbarentur, effugit, et per-
transiit locum idolorum, unde reversus fuerat;
venitque in Seirath.

124

25 And thei abididen longe, til thei weren
aschamed; and thei sien that no man
openede, and thei token the keie, and
thei openyden, and founden her lord lig- 95
26 gynge deed in the erthe. Sotheli while
thei weren disturblid, Aioth fledde out,
and passide the place of idols, fro
whennus he turnede aȝen; and he cam in
27 [to] Seirath. And anoon he sownede with a 100
clarioun in the hil of Effraym; and the
sones of Israel camen doun with hym, and

92 abiden C²HaLMMaNX, abideden CaFKW, abidden E, aboden I, abedin
P; long DEHa, 'so' long Ha, so longe I; til: to E; were D, where E, werin
P
93 ashamyd GLPQ; seiȝen CaM, seien FW, siȝen GHaKMaNRSX, sawȝen I
94 openyde AcCNOQR, opened DE, openyden G, openid Ha, opnede þe
dore I; tooken CGNSX, tookin P; key E
95 openeden BCaDFKLMMaPRSWX, opened E, opneden I; fonde E, þei
founden I; here Q; liggind E, liȝgginge K, liginge U
96 dead Q; in: on I; eerþe RS; soþli FGLMMaPQUWX, & I; whiles E, whil
GKLPR
97 where E, werin P; distourblid CaMW, disturbled E, distorblid L, distroublid
Ma; fled DE; oute R
98 passid D, passed E, he p. I, passede KLP; idolis DEGILOPQW, ydoles F;
from K
99 whennes CaFHaKM, whens DIMaR, whennis EGLNQS, whenis P,
whenns U; turned D, turnid E, turnyde GHaQ; aȝein B; came R, caam S

27 Et statim insonuit bucina in monte Effraim; descenderuntque cum eo filii Israel, ipso in fronte
gradiente.

28 hym, hym goynge in the frount. The 100
which seide to hem, Folwe ʒe me, forsothe the Lord hath taak oure enemyes,
Moabitis, into oure hoondis. And thei
wenten doun after hym, and thei occupyeden the foordis of Jordan, that ouer- 105
29 senden in to Moab. And thei sufferden
not eny man to passe ouere, but thei
smyten Moabites that tyme about ten
thowsand, alle myʒti and stronge men;
30 noon of hem myʒte ascaape. And Moab 110
is mekid that day vndur the hows of
Yrael, and the loond restide foure scoor

100 gooyng *BF*, goende *X*; frounte *Lo*
101 whiche *BEHLoWoX*; seyd *B*; þem *LoX*; folowe *BFHWo*, folewe *X*; ʒee
LoX; 101—102 forsothe the Lord: þe L. f. *cet.*
102 has *Lo*; take *BEFHWo*, taken *LoX*; our *BF*; enmyes *BFWo*, enemys *X*
103 our *F*; hondys *EHX*, hondes *LoWo*
104 wentyn *E;* aftir *Lo*; occupyʒeden *E*, occupyden *LoWo*, ocupieden *X*
105 fordis *BEFHWo*, forthes *Lo*, forþis *X*; ouersendyn *E*
106 sufferd *BH*, soffrede *E*, suffred *F*, suffreden *LoX*, suffrid *Wo*
107 noʒt *Lo*; any *X*; passen *X*; ouer *cet.*; bot *B*, bote *E*, bute *F*
108 smetyn *E*; aboute *BEFLoX*, abouʒte *H*, abouten *Wo*; tenn *BH*
109 þousont *E*, þousande *FLo*, thousend *X*; all *F*, al *H*
110 & noen *X*; þem *Lo*; myʒt *BFHWo*; aschape *BF*, ascape *EHLoWo*, scape *X*
111 meekid *B*, meked *E*, meeked *H*, mekyde *Lo*; vndir *B*, vnder *EFHWoX*,
vndre *Lo*; hows: house *BH*, hond *E*, honde *Lo*
112 lond *EWoX*, londe *Lo*; restyd *BFHWo*, restete *E*, restede *LoX*; four *B*;
score *cet.*

28 Qui dixit ad eos: Sequimini me; tradidit enim
Dominus inimicos nostros Moabitas in manus nostras.
Descenderuntque post eum, et occupaverunt vada
Iordanis, quae transmittunt in Moab; et non di-
miserunt transire quemquam,

28 he ȝede in the frount. Which seide to hem,
   Sue ȝe me, for the Lord hath bitake oure
   enemyes, Moabitis, in to oure hondis. And   105
   thei camen doun after hym, and ocupi-
   eden the forthis of Jordan, that ledde ouer
29 in to Moab. And thei suffriden not ony
   man to passe, but thei smytiden Moabitis in that tyme aboute ten thousande,   110
   alle myȝti men and stronge; no man of
30 hem myȝte ascape. And Moab was maad
   low in that dai vndur the hond of Israel,
   and the lond restide fourescoor ȝeer.

100 to: om. A; anon EFPQ; souned D, sownyde GHaQR
101 clarion E; hul E
102 sonis GLQ, sonus Ma, soones S; come E; a doune E; with: to W
103 in: to E; front DO, frounte R; whiche DGHa, þe whiche I, wiche K; seid E
104 suwe CaFMW; ȝee U; haþe E; bitak C, be take E, take GHaQ; out E
105 enmyes I; hondes CaF, hoondis R
106 comen E; a doune E; aftir AcBCCaDGHaKMaNOPQRWX; occupiede C,
     þei ocupieden I, occupieden EGHaMaO
107 foorþis DMa, forþes EF, foordis IK, fordis R; leden BW, led D, lad E,
     ledden HaI, ladde K
108 suffreden CaEFHaKMPW; eny Ha
109 bot E; smyteden CaW, smityn E, smyten FLU, smeten I, smetin P
110 abouȝte L; þousynde AcBCOU, þousand CaDEHaMaQRSX, þousend
     FGLP, þousynd IMW; 109 − 10 but in þat tyme þei smeten aboute ten
     þousynd of (exp. & cr. out) *moabitis* I
111 al Ca²D; miȝtie K; strong DE
112 myȝt D; made DHa; 112 − 13 & in þat day was moab maad lowe vndir
     þe hond of I. I
113 lowe CDGILR, lowȝ KMMaW; vndir BDIKMaNPRSX, vnder EFGLQU;
     hond: boond N
114 restid CaD, restede EFP, r. *in pes* I; foure scoore Ac, foure score
     CaGIMaQ, eiȝti KM, xviii L, eiȝteti NSX, seuenti W; ȝere E, ȝer LP

29 sed percusserunt Moabitas /in/ tempore illo circiter
   decem millia, omnes robustos et fortes viros;
   nullus eorum evadere potuit.
30 Humiliatusque est Moab /in/ die illo sub manu Israel,
   et quievit terra octoginta annis.

31 ʒeer. After this was Sangar, the sone of
Anath, that smoot of Philistiym six hundrid men with a shaar; and he forsothe
defendide Irael.

4. 1 And the sones of Yrael addeden to doo
yuel in the siʒt of the Lord, after the
2 deeth of Aod. And the Lord took hem
in to the hoondis of Jabyn, kyng of Chanaan, that regned in Asor, and hadde a
duk of his oost, Siseram bi name; and

(margin: 115)

(margin: 5)

113 ʒere *LoWo*, ʒer *X*; aftyr *BX*
114 smote *BLoWo*, smot *X*; sixe *cet.*; hundriþ *B*, hundred *EFLo*
115 an *BFHLoWo*; shar *EX*, schaare *Lo*
116 defendyd *BFWo*, defendede *E*

4. 1 sonys *E*, sonus *X*; addedyn *E*, addiden *HLoWo*; do *EWo*, don *X*
2 yuyl *E*, yuele *Lo*, euel *WoX*; siʒte *LoX*
3 deþ *BFHWoX*; lorde *Wo*; toke *BFHLoWo*, toc *X*; þem *Lo*
4 hondys *EWoX*, hondes *Lo*
5 ryngned *B*, regnede *EHX*, he reygnede *Lo*, regnyd *Wo*; had *LoWo*
6 duyk *BF*, duke *ELoWo*, duyke *H*; hoost *BEFH*, ooste *Lo*, ost *X*

31 Post hunc fuit Samgar, filius Anath, qui percussit
de Philistiim sexcentos viros vomere; et ipse quoque
defendit Israel.

4. 1 Addideruntque filii Israel facere malum in conspectu
Domini post mortem Aod,
2 et tradidit illos Dominus in manus Iabin, regis
Chanaan, qui regnavit in Asor; habuitque ducem
exercitus sui nomine Sisaram, ipse autem habitabat
in Aroseth gentium.

31 Aftir hym was Samgar, the sone of
Anath, that smoot of Filisteis sixe hundrid men with a schar; and he also defend[id]e Israel.

4. 1 And the sones of Israel addiden to do
yuel in the siȝt of the Lord, aftir the
   2 deeth of Aioth. And the Lord bitook hem
in to the hondis of Jabyn, kyng of Canaan,
that regnede in Asor; and he hadde a
duyk of his oost, Sisara bi name; and he

115 After EFLU; hym: om. I
116 Anath: anath *iuge* I; that: þe whiche I; smote EHaIR; six I; hundred E, hunderd LP
117 schare BN, schaar Ca, char D; he also: also he GI; defendid D, defended E, defendede LP, defende AS

4. 1 sonis GILNQ; addeden CaFLMW
   2 euel E, euyle G, euil LPQ, yuele N; siȝte CaGQU; s. of the Lord: lordis s. I; after BEFLNU
   3 deþ AcEFPSUX, lijf I; bitok EU, bitoke HaIR
   4 hondes F, hoondis R
   5 regnyde AcGHaIQR, regned DE; he: Iabyn I; had E
   6 duk EHa, duke LP; his: om L; ost U; he: iabyn I

3 he dwellyd in Aroseth of Gentilis. And
the sones of Yrael crieden to the Lord;
forsothe he hadde nyne hundred chaaris,
ful of wepenes, the maner of sithis, and   10
bi twenti ȝeer greetli he oppresside hem.
4 Forsothe Delbora was a prophetesse, wijf
of Laphidoth, that demyde the puple in
5 that tyme; and she sat vndur the palm
tree, the which bi name of hir was   15
clepid, bitwix Rame and Bethel, in the
mount of Effraym; and the sones of
Yrael stieden vp to hir into al doom.

7 dwellede *E*, dwelled *Wo*, dwelte *X*; gentyles *Lo*
8 sonys *EH*; cryden *BEWo*
9 forsothe he hadde nyne hundred: 900 f. he h. *cet.*; had *Wo*; hundreþ *B*,
   hundrid *EHWoX*; charys *EWo*, chares *X*
10 full *BF*, fol *E*, fulle *LoWo*; wepenys *BEFHWo*, wepnes *X*; manere *E*;
   siþes *EX*
11 ȝere *LoWo*, ȝer *X*; gretely *BF*, gretly *EHLoWoX*; oppressede *E*, oppressed
   FH, oppressid *LoWo*, opressede *X*; þem *Lo*
12 Forsothe Delbora: D. f. *cet.*; prophetisse *BHWo*, prophetis *Lo*; wyf
   BFHWoX, wyfe *ELo*
13 demyd *BFHWo*, demede *ELoX*; peple *BEFHLoWo*; in: om. *X*
14 satt *BEFHWo*, satte *Lo*; vnder *cet*; pallme *B*, palme *CEFHLoWo*
15 tre *Wo*; the which: þe whiche *BEHLoWoX*, þat *C*; hyre *BFLo*, here *E*
16 cleped *E*, callid *Lo*; bytwixe *BEFHLoWo*, betwe *C*, bitwen *X*
17 mounte *Lo*; sonys *BEH*, sonus *X*
18 steyȝid *BFWo*, steȝeden *CX*, styȝede *E*, stiȝid *H*, steiȝede *Lo*; opp *E*;
   hyre *BF*, here *ELo*; alle *BLoX*; dome *B*, dom *CX*

3 Clamaveruntque filii Israel ad Dominum; nongentos
enim habebat falcatos currus, et per viginti annos
vehementer oppresserat eos.
4 Erat autem Delbora prophetis, uxor Lapidoth, quae
iudicabat populum in illo tempore.
5 Et sedebat sub palma, quae nomine illius vocabatur,
inter Rama et Bethel in monte Effraim; ascendebant-
que ad eam filii Israel in omne iudicium.

130

3 dwellide in Aroseth of hethene men. And
the sones of Israel crieden to the Lord;
for he hadde nyn hundrid yrone charis,
keruynge as sithis, and twenti ȝeer he   10
4 oppresside hem greetli. Forsothe Del-
bora was a prophetesse, the wijf of Lapidoth, which Delbora demyde the puple
5 in that tyme; and sche sat vndur a palm
tree, that was clepid bi her name, bitwixe   15
Rama and Bethel, in the hil of Effraym;
and the sones of Israel stieden to hir at

7 dwelte Ca, dwellid D, dwelled E, dwellede LPU; Aroseth: A. *a citee* I;
   heþen BCDEILN
8 sonis GILQX; cried E, criden W
9 he: iabyn I; had E; nyne AcCaGIKMMaNQRSWX; hundred EHa,
   hunderd LP; yrene CaMMa, irun DX, iren EILPR, yron G; chares
   CaER, chaaris K, chares *ful of wepnessis* I
10 keruyng ELP, scharpe I; siþes KR; ȝere E, ȝer ILP
11 oppressid DF, oppressed E, oppressede LP; hem: israel I; gretli
   AcEIOPRU, grettli L, greteli R; Forsothe: And I, forsoþ X
12 profettesse D; wif EGHaLPQU
13 whiche G, þe whiche I; deemede BLMaX, demede CaFKMPRSU, demyd
   D, demed E; peple CaFLMMaNPSWX, puple *of israel* I
14 sate DIR, satt KMa; vndir BDHaIKMaNPQRSX, vnder FGLU; palme
   BCEGHaKQR
15 tre BCDEHaIMNQRSX; clepide R; hir BEIMaNSX, here FGHaQ,
   hire K; bitwix DEHaQ
16 hul E
17 sonis GLQ; stiden CE, steieden F, stieden up I, stiȝeden MaNR; her
   CaMUW, here F, hire KS

6 The which sente, and clepide Barach,
the sone of Abynoen, of Cedes of Nepta-   20
lym, and she seide to hym, The Lord
God of Irael hath comaundide to thee,
Go, leed the oost into the hil of Thabor,
and tak with thee ten thowsand of fiȝtynge men of the sones of Neptalym and   25
7 of the sones of Zabulon. Forsothe I shal
brynge to thee, in the place of the streem
of Cyson, Sisaram, prince of the oost of
Jabyn, and the chaaris of hym, and al
the multitude; and Y shal taak hem in   30

19 whiche *BCEFLoX*; sent *BFHWo*, sende *ELo*; clepyd *BFH*, clepede *C*,
    cleped *EWo*, callid *Lo*
21 seid *B*
22 has *Lo*; comaundid *BCFHWoX*, comaunded *E*, commaundide *Lo*; þe *E*
23 goo *BFHLoWo*; led *C*, lede *FLoWo*; hoost *BFH*, ost *CX*, (h)oost *E*;
    hyll *BFH*, hul *E*, hylle *LoWo*
24 take *BFHLoWo*, taak *E*; þe *EWo*; tenn *BH*; thousend *CX*, þousount *E*,
    þousande *FLo*; fiȝting *CHLoX*
25 sonys *BE*, sonus *CX*
26 sonys *EH*; Forsothe I: I f. *cet.*
27 thee: þe *EWo*; streme *BFHWo*, strem *CX*
28 prince: þe pr. *X*; ost *CWoX*, (h)oost *E*, hoost *H*
29 charis *CE*, chares *X*; alle *BLo*, all *F*
30 take *cet.*; þem *CX*

6 Quae misit, et vocavit Barach, filium Abinoen, de
Cedes Neptalim; dixitque ad eum: Praecepit tibi
Dominus Deus Israel, vade, /et/ duc exercitum in
montem Thabor, tolle/s/que tecum decem millia pugnatorum, de filiis Neptalim et de filiis Zabulon.
7 Ego autem ducam ad te, in loco torrentis Cison,
Sisaram principem exercitus Iabin, et currus eius,
atque omnem multitudinem, et tradam eos in manu tua.

132

6 ech dom. And sche sente, and clepide
  Barach, the sone of Abynoen, of Cedes of
  Neptalym, and sche seide to hym, The   20
  Lord God of Israel comaundide to thee,
  Go thou, and lede an oost in to the hil of
  Thabor, and thou schalt take with thee
  ten thousande of fiȝteris of the sones of
  Neptalym and of the sones of Zabulon.   25
7 Sotheli Y schal brynge to thee, in the
  place of the stronde of Cison, Sisara,
  prince of the oost of Jabyn, and his
  charis, and al the multitude; and Y schal

18 eche IK; doom AcBCCaDFGHaIKMMaNOQSWX, dome ER; sent E; clepid DE, clepede F; of (3°): om. U
20 sayde E
21 comaundeþ E, comaundede LP; þe EFMa
22 leede BKS, leede þou G; host E; hul E
23 þe ER
24 þousynde AcBCOU, þousynd CaFIMW, þousand DHaMaNQRSX, þousend GLP; of (1°): om. I; fiȝters DEHaKLMMaPRX, fiȝtinge men I, fiȝteres U; sonys GLQ
25 sonys GLQ
26 sothli EFGLMMaPQSUWX, and I; bring E; thee: þe ELS; 26–7 And in þe place of þe stronde of cison I schal bringe to þee S. I
28 þe prince I; ost RU; the oost of J.: Jabyns oost I; hise AcBCCaDHaKMMaNORSUW, hijs E
29 chares FR; alle EMa

8 thin hoond. And Barach seide to hyr,
  If thow comest with me, Y shal goo; if
  thow wolt not come with me, Y shal not
9 goo. The which seide to hym, Forsothe
  Y shal goo with thee; but in this while   35
  victory shal not be witid to thee; for in
  the hoond of a womman Sisara shal be
  taak. And so Delbora roos, and wente
10 with Barach in to Cedes. The which,
  clepid Zabulon and Nepthalym, stiede vp   40
  with ten thousand of fiȝtynge men, hau-

31 þine *Lo*; hond *CEWoX*, honde *Lo*; hyre *BFLo*, here *E*
32 ȝif *BEFHWo*, ȝife *Lo*; commist *BF*, comyst *EH*, commest *LoWo*; go
    CLoWoX; ȝyf *BEFHWo*, ȝife *Lo*
33 wylt *BCFX*; comme *BF*
34 go *CELoWoX*; whiche *BCELoWoX*; 34−35 Forsothe Y shal goo: Y sh.
    g. f. *cet.*; go *CEWoX*
35 þe *EWo*; bot *B*, bote *E*
36 victorie *CELoWo*; wited *LoX*; þe *E*
37 hoonde *B*, hond *CEWoX*, honde *Lo*; ben *X*
38 take *BCEFHWo*, taken *LoX*; ros *CX*; went *BFHWo*
39 in: -ym *FWo*; whiche *BCEHLoX*
40 cleped *E*, callid *Lo*; steyȝid *BFWo*, steȝede *CX*, styȝede *E*, styȝid *H*,
    steiȝed *Lo*; opp *E*
41 tenn *BF*; thousend *CX*, þousont *E*, þousande *FLo*; fiȝting *CLoX*; hauende
    CX, hauyng *Lo*

8 Dixitque ad eam Barach: Si venis mecum, vadam; si
  nolueris venire mecum, non pergam.
9 Quae dixit ad eum: Ibo quidem tecum, sed in hac vice
  victoria non reputabitur tibi, quia in manu mulieris
  tradetur Sisara. Surrexit itaque Delbora, et perrexit cum Barach in Cedes.
10 Qui, accitis Zabulon et Neptalim, ascendit cum decem
  millibus pugnatorum, habens Delboram in comitatu suo.

8 bitake hem in thin hond. And Barach   30
   seide to hir, If thou comest with me, Y
   schal go; if thou nylt come with me,
9 Y schal not go. And sche seyde to hym,
   Sotheli Y schal go with thee; but in this
   tyme the victorie schal not be arettide to   35
   thee; for Sisara schal be bitakun in the
   hond of a womman. Therfor Delbora
   roos, and ȝede with Barach in to Cedes.
10 And whanne Zabulon and Neptalym weren
   clepid, he stiede with ten thousynde of   40
   fiȝteris, and hadde Delbora in his felou-

30   bitak E; þine E, þijn K, þe O; honde EU
31   saide E; to: om. W; her CaMU, here F, hire KQ, om. W; ȝif E; comist
     DGLPQ, cummist E
32   nelt CaMUW, wilt not I; cum E
33   shalt Ac; goo GS; said E
34   shoþeli E, soþli FGLMMaPQUWX, And I; þe DE; bot E
35   victori E; not be: be not M; arrettid S, arettid cet.
36   to thee: to þe EO, þe to S¹; for: & for S; be: om. DG, ben Ma; bitakun:
     takun Ac, bitaken CaFIKLMMaQRUW, taken E, bitakin P; in: in to DI,
     om. S
37   honde E; wumman CaFMW, woman E; þerfore BCaEFGKMaNQRSWX,
     And so I
38   ros E, roose I; to: om. I
39   whan EGHaLP
40   cleped E, clepide K; he: barach I; stied DE, steiede F, stiȝede
     GHaMaNR, stiede up I; þousynd CaMW, þousand DEHaMaNQRSX,
     þousend GILP, þousande K
41   fiȝters DEHaIKLMMaPRX, fiȝteres U; had E, haddē L; hise K;
     felowschip DEHaIRX, felauschipe MW, feloschipe Ma, folowschipe O,
     felauschip S

11 ynge Delbora in his felawship. Forsothe
   Aber Cynee wente awey sumtyme fro
   other Cynees his britheren, the sones of
   Obbab, cosyn of Moyses; and he strei3te   45
   tabernaclys vnto the valey, that is clepid
12 Sennym, and was biside Cedes. And it
   is told to Cysare, that Barach, the sone
   of Abynoem, hadde stied vp into the hil
13 of Thabor. And he gedryd nyn hundryd   50
   chaaris, ful of wepenys, maner of sithis,
   and al the oost fro Aroseth of gentilis to

42 felawschipe B, felashipe CX, felouscheep E, felowschip F, felawschippe Lo;
   42−43 Forsothe Aber: A. f. cet.
43 went BFH; aweye BH; somtyme E, somme t. LoWo; from E
44 oþere C; breþeren BFHLoWo, breþern CX, bryþryn E; sonys E
45 cosyne Lo; stra3te CX, strei3t Wo
46 thabernaclis Lo, tabernacles X; valeie E; cleped E, called Lo
47 bysydis BEFH, beside C, bisydes LoWo; hit E
48 tolde HLoWo
49 had BFWo; stey3id BFWo, ste3id CX, sty3ed E, sty3id H, stei3ed Lo;
   op E; hyll BFH, hul E, hille Wo
50 geþerd B, gederede CEX, geþered F, gederid H, gaderid Lo, gidered Wo;
   nyne CEFHLoWoX; hundreþ B, hundret E, hundred F
51 charis CEHWo, chares X; full BF, fol E; wepnes CX, wepenes Lo;
   manere F, in maner LoX; siþes CEX
52 alle B, all F; ost CX, (h)oost E; from E; gentyles LoX

11 Aber autem Cineus recesserat quondam a ceteris Cineis
   fratribus suis, filiis Obab, cognati Moysi; et te-
   tenderat tabernacula usque ad vallem, quae vocatur
   Sennim, et erat iuxta Cedes.
12 Nuntiatumque est Sisarae, quod ascendisset Barach,
   filius Abinoen, in montem Thabor.
13 Et congregavit nongentos falcatos currus omnemque
   exercitum de Aroseth gentium ad torrentem Cison.

11 schipe. Forsothe Aber of Cyneth hadde
   departid sum tyme fro othere Cyneys hise
   britheren, sones of Obab, alie of Moises;
   and he hadde set forth tabernaclis til to   45
   the valei, which is clepid Sennym, and
12 was bisidis Cedes. And it was teld to
   Sisara, that Barach, sone of Abynoen,
13 hadde stiede in to the hil of Thabor. And
   he gaderide nyn hundrid yronne charis,   50
   keruynge as sithis, and al the oost fro
   Aroseth of hethene men to the stronde

42 Forsothe: And I, soþeli KLO, forsoþ X; had E
43 departed E, departide Ha; from K; oþer EHaX; Cyneys: men of cyney I;
    his EFGHaILPQX; 42–43 A. of C. hadde dep. sum tyme: sumtyme a.
    of. c. hadde dep. I
44 breþren CaFMW, breþeren EHaLPUX, briþren G, breþern K; sonys
    GLQ, þe sonus I; alie of Moises: moyses alije I
45 he: om. Ma; had EI; sette DHaR, sett IKMaNX; tabernacles CaFR; til
    to: to E, vnto I
46 whiche G, þat I, wiche K
47 was: he was I; bisides FGHaKU, besidis P; teeld BDGMaNQS²WX,
    told CEILP, telde Ha, toold K, tolde R
48 þe sone I
49 had E; stied AcBCCaDEGKLMOPQSUWX, steied F, stied up I, stiȝed
    MaN, stiȝede R; hul E
50 he: sisara I; gaderid D, gadred E, gadrede F, gadride GR, gedride I,
    gederide K, gadirede L, gaderede P; nyne AcCaGIKMMaNQSWX;
    hundred EHa, hunderd LP; irone AcBCDFHaKMaNOQ, yrene CaM,
    iren EGILPRW, irun SX, irunne U; chares FHaR, charis *fulle of wepnes* I,
    chaaris N
51 keruing E; siþes KR; all X; ost E; fro: of KS
52 heþen BDEILNPX; strond D, stroonde Ma

14 the streem of Cyson. And Delbora seide
   to Barach, Rise, this is forsothe the day,
   in the which the Lord hath taak Sysa-   55
   ram into thin hoondys; loo! he is thi
   leder. And so Barach descendide fro the
   hil of Thabor, and ten thowsand of fiȝt-
15 ynge men with hym. And the Lord
   feeryde Sisaram, and alle the chaaris of   60
   hym, and al the multytude, in the mouth
   of swerd, at the siȝt of Barach, in so
   myche that Sisara of the chaar lepynge
16 doun on his feet fliȝ. And Barach pursuede the fleynge chaaris and the oost   65
   vnto the see vnto Aroseth of Gentilis;
   and al the multitude of enemyes fell(en)

53 streme *BFHLoWo*, strem *CX*
54 ris *CX*; forsoþ *B*; the day: om. *H*
55 the which: þe whiche *BEFLoWoX*, whiche *C*; has *Lo*; take *BCEFHWoX*,
    taken *Lo*
56 þine *Lo*; hondis *BEX*, hondus *C*, hondes *LoWo*; lo *CELoX*
57 leeder *BF*, ledere *CEX*; descendyd *BFHLoWo*, descendede *CE*
58 hyll *BFH*, hul *E*, hille *Wo*; tenn *BH*; thousend *CX*, þousont *E*, thousande
    Lo; fiȝting *CLo*, fiȝtende *X*
60 fered *BFHWo*, ferede *CEX*, feride *Lo*; all *F*; charis *CEWo*, chares *X*
61 alle *BLo*, all *FH*; the (2°): om. *X*; mouþe *BLo*
62 swerde *FHLoWo*; siȝte *CLo*
63 moche *E*, mych *FWo*; off *BF*; char *CX*, chaare *LoWo*; lepyng *BLo*, lepende
    CX, leepynge *F*
64 fete *LoWo*; fleiȝ *CHLoX*; pursued *BHLo*
65 fleeȝinge *BH*, fleende *CX*, fleeyȝinge *F*, fleing *Lo*, fleyȝinge *Wo*; charis
    CE, chares *X*; ost *CX*, (h)oost *E*
66 se *CX*; Gentyles *Lo*
67 alle *BHLoWo*, all *F*; enmyes *BFWo*, enmeys *CX*; fell *BEH*, fel *CWoX*,
    ful *E¹*, fyl *E²*, felle *Lo*

14 Dixitque Delbora ad Barach: Surge, haec est enim
   dies, in qua tradidit Dominus Sisaram in manus tuas;
   en ipse ductor est tuus. Descendit itaque Barach de
   monte Thabor, et decem millia pugnatorum cum eo.
15 Perterruitque Dominus Sisaram, et omnes currus eius,
   universamque multitudinem, in ore gladii ad con-

14 of Cison. And Delbora seide to Barach,
  Rise thou, for this is the day, in which
  the Lord bitook Sisara in to thin hondis;   55
  lo! the Lord is thi ledere. And so Barach
  cam doun fro the hil of Thabor, and ten
15 thousynde of fyȝteris with hym. And the
  Lord made aferd Sisara, and alle the charis
  of hym, and al the multitude, bi the   60
  scharpnesse of swerd, at the siȝt of Ba-
  rach, in so myche that Sisara lippide doun
16 of the chare, and fledde a foote. And
  Barach pursuede the charis fleynge and
  the oost til to Aroseth of hethene men;   65
  and al the multitude of enemyes felde doun

53 said E
54 Rise thou: arise þou C, rise þou up I; wich EK, whiche GI
55 bitoke EHaR, haþ bitake I; þine CaEMRW, þi K; hondes CaF, hoondis R
56 lede DHaK, ledar E, leedere G
57 com E, came R; doune E; from K; hul E
58 þousynd CaMW, þousand DEHaKMaNQRSX, þousend FGLP; fiȝters
   DEFHaIKMMaRX, fiȝteres U
59 mad D; afeerd BIKMaNX, aferde R; made af. Sisara: m. c. af. I; chares
   CaF; 59—60 the ch. of hym: his charis I
60 and: om. ELP; the (2°): om. ELP
61 scharpnes DEIMa, scharpenesse R; swerde ER; siȝte CaUW
62 moche CaFNX, muche L, mych R; lippid D, leppid E, lippede F, leppide
   G, lepide I; doune E
63 chare: charyte B, chaar CaMW; fled E; on foote AcDLMaNP, afoot C,
   on fote CaKM, on foot EI, a fote FHaQRSW
64 pursuyde Ac, pursuwide CaMW, pursued DE, pursuwede F, pursuide Q;
   chares EFR, chaaris G; fleyng EL
65 ost E; til to: to E, vnto I; heþen BDELMNPX
66 alle C; enmies EI, enemis L; felden BMa, fel CaELMPW, fild D, fellen
   FI; a doun E

  spectum Barach, in tantum ut Sisara de curru de-
  siliens pedibus fugeret,
16 et Barach persequeretur fugientes currus et
  exercitum usque ad Aroseth gentium, et omnis hostium
  multitudo usque ad internecionem caderet.

17 doun vnto [the] deeth. Sisara forsothe
   fleynge cam to the tent of Jahel, wijf of
   Aber Cynei; forsothe there was pees bi-   70
   twix Jabyn, the kyng of Asor, and the
18 hows of Aber Cynei. Jahel thanne goon
   out in to aȝen comynge of Sisare, seide
   to hym, Com in to me, my lord; ne drede
   thow. The which goon into the taber-   75
   nacle of hyr, and couerd of hir with a
19 mantel, he seide to hir, ȝif to me, Y biseche, a litil of water, for Y thriste
   myche. The which openyde a botel of
   mylk, and ȝaf to hym to drynk, and   80

68   doun: om. *cet*; deþ *BCFHWoX*; forsoþ *B*
69   fleeȝynge *BF*, fleende *CX*, fleeynge *H*, fleing *Lo*, fleȝinge *Wo*; coome *BFH*,
     coom *E*, come *LoWo*; tente *CELo*; off *E*; wyfe *BELo*, wif *CFHWoX*
70   forsothe there was: th. w. f. *cet.*; þer *cet.*; pes *CX*; betwen *C*, bytwixe
     EFLoWo, bitwe *X*
71   kynge *BLo*
72   house *BLo*; þann *BF*, þenne *E*, þan *Wo*; gon *CWoX*
73   oute *B*, ouȝte *H*; aȝeyn *BEFHWo*, aȝeyne *Lo*, aȝen- *X*; commyng *BLo*,
     comyng *CX*, commynge *F*
74   comme *BF*, cum *CX*, coom *E*, come *HLoWo*; dreede *BF*
75   þu *B*; whiche *BCEHLoX*; gon *CX*, gooinge *F*, goynge *Wo*
76   hyr (2x): hyre *BFLo*, here *E*; couered *CWoX*, keuered *E*, couerde *Lo*
77   mantyll *BF*, mantil *CHWoX*; hyre *BFLo*, here *E*; ȝeue *BFHLo*, ȝiue *Wo*;
     beseche *CX*
78   lytyll *BF*, litul *E*, lytel *Wo*; watre *Lo*; þrest *BFH*, þerste *E*, þruste *Lo*,
     þirst *Wo*, þreste *X*
79   moche *E*, mych *FWo*; whiche *BCEHLoX*; opnyde *B*, openede *CELoX*,
     opnyd *FH*, openyd *Wo*; botell *BF*; off *E*
80   mylke *EH*; ȝaue *BFHWo*, ȝafe *Lo*; drynke *cet.*

17 Sisara autem fugiens pervenit ad tentorium Iahel,
   uxoris Aber Cinei; erat enim pax inter Iabin, regem
   Asor, et domum Aber Cinei.
18 Egressa igitur Iahel in occursum Sisarae, dixit ad
   eum: Intra ad me, domine mi, /intra ad me/, ne

17 til to deeth. Sotheli Sisara fledde, and
   cam to the tente of Jahel, the wijf of Aber
   Cyney; forsothe pees waas bitwixe Jabyn,
   kyng of Asor, and bitwixe the hows of   70
18 Aber Cyney. Therfor Jahel ȝede out in
   to the comyng of Sisara, and seide to hym,
   My lord, entre thou to me, entre thou to
   me; drede thou not. And he entride in
   to the tabernacle of hir, and was hilid of   75
19 hir with a mentil. And he seide to hir,
   Y biseche, ȝyue thou to me a litil of
   watir, for Y thirste greetli. And sche
   openyde a botel of mylk, and ȝaf to hym

67 til to: to E, vnto I; deþ AcCFILOPQUX, deþe E; soþli FGLMMaPQSUX,
    & I; fled DE
68 com E, came R; tent EHa; wif EFGHaLPQU
69 forsothe: for I, forsoþ X; pes IP; was cet.; bitwix DEHaQ
70 bitwene D, om. E, bitwix Q
71 þerfore EFGIKMaNQRSWX; ȝede: wente CaDGHaIKMNOQSX; oute R
72 to: om. S; comynge CaDFGMMaQUW; saide E, sche seide I
73 entre þou to me my lord entre to me I; entre thou to me: 1x MaN
74 entrid D, entred E, entrede PU
75 her CaMUW, here F, hire K; the tabernacle of hir: hir t. I; he was I;
    hilide B, hiled EK
76 hir (1°): her CaMW, here F, hire K; mentel CaDFMW, mantil ELNP,
    mantel IKR; hir (2°): her CaMUW, here F, hire K
77 biseche þe E, biseche þee I; ȝeue BDGHaLMaQRU, ȝif ES, ȝife K;
    thou: om. GHaIQ; to: om. EFGHaIQS; a drink a etc. E; litul E,
    litel FKL; of: om. EGHaIKNQS
78 water EFKMMaUX; þurste CaDF, þriste HaKU; gretli AcDILOU,
    grete E
79 openede BCaFKLMMaPSUWX, opened DE, opnede I; botele K; milke EI,
    melke U; botel of m.: mylke botel I; ȝaaf I, ȝaue R; to: om. EI

timeas. Qui ingressus tabernaculum eius, et opertus
   ab ea pallio,
19 dixit ad eam: Da mihi, obsercro, paululum aquae, quia
   sitio valde. Quae aperuit utrem lactis, et dedit ei
   bibere, et operuit illum.

20 couerde hym. And Sisara seide to hir,
Stoond before the dore of the tabernacle,
and whanne there cometh eny man, ask-
inge thee, and seiynge, Whether here is
eny man? thou shalt answere, Noon is. 85
21 And so Jahel, the wijf of Aber, took a
neyl* of the tabernacle, takynge there
with an hamer; and she goon out priue-
lich, and with silence putte vpon the
templis of his heed a neyl*, and smyten 90
with an hamer piȝt down into the brayn
vnto the erthe; the whych, felawshipynge

81 couerd *BFH*, couerede *C*, keuerede *E*, couered *Wo*, coouerede *X*; hyre
BFLo, here *E*
82 stonde *BFHWo*, stond *CX*, stont *E*, stande *Lo*; byfore *BEFLoWo*, befor *CX*
83 whenn *B*, whan *CFWoX*, whenne *E*, om. *H*; þer *BCEFHWoX*; commiþ *B*,
commeþ *F*, comiþ *H*, comes *Lo*; any *CX*; askende *CX*, askyng *Wo*
84 þe *E*; seying *BLo*, seiende *CX*, sayinge *E*; her *C*, heer *EX*, heere *FLo*
85 any *CX*; þu *B*; noen *X*
86 the: om. *F*; wyf *BCFHWoX*, wyfe *ELo*; toke *BEFHLoWo*, toc *CX*
87 veyl *ABFH*, nail *CELoX*, veyle *Wo*; thabernacle *Lo*; takende *CX*, takyng
Lo; þer *cet.*
88 a *Lo*; hamor *Lo*; gon *CX*; oute *B*, ouȝte *H*; preueliche *B*, priueli *CLoX*,
pryueileche *E*
89 putt *BFH*, put *CELoWo*; opon *E*, uppon *Wo*
90 temples *LoX*; heued *BCFHWo*, hed *E*, hede *Lo*, heid *X*; veyl *ABFHWo*,
nail *CEX*, nayle *Lo*; smetyn *E*, smytyng *Lo*
91 hamor *Lo*; piȝte *CELoX*; breyn *BFHWo*, brayne *Lo*
92 erþ *B*; whiche *BCEHLoX*; felawschepynge *B*, felashipende *C*,
felouschepynge *E*, felawschipyng *Lo*, felashipinge *X*

20 Dixitque Sisara ad eam: Sta ante ostium tabernaculi,
et cum venerit aliquis interrogans te et dicens:
Numquid hic est aliquis? respondebis: Nullus est.
21 Tulit itaque Iahel, uxor Aber, clavum tabernaculi,
assumens pariter malleum; et ingressa abscondite et

20 to drynke, and hilide hym. And Sisara   80
   seide to hir, Stonde thou bifor the dore
   of the tabernacle, and whanne ony man
   cometh, and axith thee, and seith, Whether ony man is here? thou schalt an-
21 swere, No man is *here*. And so Jahel,   85
   the wijf of Aber, took a nayl of the tabernacle, and sche took also an hamer; and
   sche entride pryueli, and puttide with
   silence the nail on the temple of his
   heed, and sche fastnede *the nail* smytun   90
   with the hamer in to the brayn, til to
   the erthe; and he slepte, and diede to

80 drink E; hilid D, hiled E, hilede FKU, *sche* hilide I
81 said E; her CaMW, here F, hire GK; thou: om. R; bifore
   AcBCCaDEGHaIKLMMaNPQRSUWX; dor E
82 whan EHaLP; any KU
83 comyþ DEPS; axet E, axeþ HaLR; þe ERS; seit E; where BCDE, wher
   cet.
84 eni EHa; heere GKMaN; shal S; onswer E
85 *heere* GK
86 wif EFGHaLPQU; tok FU, toke HaIR; nayle R
87 toke EIR, tooke Ha, tok U; also: om. P; hamir Q
88 entrid D, entred E, entrede PU; pryuyli CHaMaNOSX, preuily GPQ;
   puttid D, putted E, putte FIM, piȝcchide K, puttede LP, picchide MaOSX,
   puthide S; 88−89 p. with silence: wiþ s. sche p. I
89 silens D; nayle DER; on: of B, in E, vpon I; of: on B
90 heued EHa, hed I; fastenyde Ac, fastned CD, fastened E, fastnyde GHaQ;
   naile E; smyten CaFGIKMMaQRW, smytyn D, smetyn EP, smeten L;
   90−1 sche f. the n. sm. w. the h.: þe n. sm. wiþ þe h. sche f. it I
91 the (1°): om. CGQ; hamir EPQ; the (2°): his I, þee X; brayne ER; til to:
   in to E, vnto I
92 eerþe R; slepped E; deide CaFW, died DE, deiede M, diȝede R; to gidre
   DIR, to gider E

cum silentio posuit supra tempus capitis eius clavum,
percussumque malleo defixit in cerebrum usque ad
terram; qui soporem morti socians defecit, et mortuus
est.

22 sleep to deeth, faylide, and died. And lo!
   Barach* folwynge Sisaram cam; and Jahel,
   goon into aȝen comynge of hym, seide to   95
   hym, Com, and Y shal shewe to thee a
   man, whom thow sechist. The whych,
   whanne he hadde goo in to hir, he sawȝ
   Sisaram liggynge deed, and a neyl* piȝt
23 into his templis. God therfor lowide in   100
   that day Jabyn, the kyng of Chanaan,
   bifore the sones of Yrael; the whiche
   woxen eche day, and with strong hoond
   beren doun Jabyn, the kyng of Chanaan,
   to the tyme that thei hadden doo hym   105
   awey.

---

93   slep *CX*, slepe *LoWo*; deþ *BCFHWoX*; feylid *BFHWo*, failede *CE*, fayled
     Lo; dyȝid *BFH*, diede *CX*, deyȝede *E*, deyȝid *Wo*; loo *FH*
94   Balach *A*; folowynge *BH*, folewende *CX*, folowyng *FLoWo*; coome *BWo*,
     coom *E*, come *FHLo*
95   gon *CLoWoX*; aȝeyn *BEFHWo*, a-ȝeyne *Lo*; commynge *BF*, -comyng *CX*,
     commyng *Lo*; saide *E*
96   comme *BF*, cum *CX*, coom *E*, come *HLoWo*; schalle *Lo*; þe *EHWo*
97   whome *BFWo*; sechest *Lo*; whiche *CEHLoX*
98   whenn *BH*, whan *CFWoX*, whenne *E*; had *BFHLoWo*; go *CWo*, goon *Lo*,
     gon *X*; hyre *BFLo*, here *E*; he: om. *X*; sawe *BLoWo*, saȝ *CX*, saw *EF*
99   lyȝinge *BEFHWo*, liende *CX*, lyinge *Lo*; dead *BCX*, ded *E*, dede *Wo*;
     veyl *ABFHWo*, nail *CE*, nayle *Lo*; piȝte *ELo*
100 temples *X*; þerfore *BCEFHWoX*, þere-fore *Lo*; lowyd *BFH*, lowede *E*,
     lowed *Wo*; in: om. *X*
101 kynge *Lo*
102 beforn *C*, bifor *X*; sonus *CX*, sonis *E*; which *FWo*
103 wexen *CLoX*, woxyn *E*; stronge *BFLoWo*; hond *CX*, hoonde *F*, honde
     LoWo
104 beeren *C*, beryn *E*, baren *Lo*; kynge *B*
105 hadde *CX*, haddyn *E*; don *C*, doon *ELo*, do *Wo*, done *X*
106 aweye *BH*

22 Et ecce Barach sequens Sisaram veniebat; egressaque
   Iahel in occursum eius dixit ei: Veni, et ostendam
   tibi virum, quem quaeris. Qui cum intrasset ad eam,
   vidit Sisaram iacentem mortuum, et clavum infixum
   in tempora eius.

22 gidere, and failide, and was deed. And
lo! Barach suede Sisara, and cam; and
Jehel ȝede out in to his comyng, and seide   95
to hym, Come, and Y schal schewe to thee
the man, whom thou sekist. And whanne
he hadde entrid to hir, he siȝ Sisara liggynge deed, and a nail fastnede in to hise
23 templis. Therfor in that day God made   100
low Jabyn, the kyng of Canaan, bifor the
sones of Israel; whiche encresiden ech dai,
and with strong hond oppressiden Jabyn,
the kyng of Canaan, til thei diden hym
awey.   105

93 failede CFKLP, failid D, failed E, he failide *liif* I; dede E, ded L, dead Q
94 lo: so L; suwide CaMW, sued E, suwede F, suide Q; came GR, caam HaQ;
   B. suede S. and cam: B. cam & suede S. I
95 oute R; in to: int N; comynge DFGMaPQU; saide E
96 cum E; sheu E; þe EF
97 wam E, þat I; sekest EFHaR; whan EGHaLP
98 had EI; entred E, entride HaL; her CaM, here F, hire KU; seiȝ CaFMW,
   sie E, sawȝe I, siȝe R; ligging EL, ligynge G, liȝgginge K
99 dede E, dead Q; fastnyde Ac, fastned BCCaDFIKMMaNORSUWX,
   festid E, fastnyd GPQ, fastenid Ha, fastened L; his EFGHaILPUX
100 temples FR; Therfore CaFGIKMMaNQRSWX; maade R; 100−01 made
   low: lowide I
101 lowȝ CaKMMaSW, lowe DEGR; bifore AcBCCaDEGHaIKMaNQRSWX
102 sonis ILQ; þe whiche I, wiche K, which L; encreessiden AcBMaQ,
   encressiden CGIO, encreseden CaEFP, encresseden M, encrededen S,
   encreesseden W; vche E, eche FKN
103 stronge CHaR; honde E, hoond I; oppresside C, oppresseden
   CaEFKLMPW, *þei* oppressiden I
104 til: to E; þai E; dide Ma, dedin P, deden U; hem N

23 Humiliavit ergo Deus in die illo Iabin, regem
Chanaan, coram filiis Israel;
24 qui crescebant quotidie, et forti manu opprimebant
Iabin, regem Chanaan, donec delerent eum.

5. 1 And Delbora and Barach, the sone of
2 Benoem, songen in that day, seiynge, ȝe
that wilfully offerden of Yrael ȝoure lyues
3 to peryl, blissith to the Lord. Here, ȝe
kyngis; perseyue, ȝe princes, with eeris;   5
Y am, Y am, the whiche to the Lord
shal synge, and seye salm to the God of
4 Yrael. Lord, whanne thow wentist out
fro Seyr, and passidist bi the regiouns of
Edom, the erthe is meued, and heuens   10
5 and clowdis droppeden with watris; hillis
floweden fro the face of the Lord, and
Synai fro the face of the Lord God of

5. 2 sungen *CX*; sayinge *BH*, seiende *CX*, seying *Lo*, seyȝinge *Wo*; ȝee *CLoX*
3 wilfolly *E*; offreden *CX*, offredyn *E*; ȝour *BCFHWo*; lyuys *BF*, lyfys *E*
4 peryle *BCFLoWoX*, perel *E*; blesseþ *CEWo*, blisseþ *FX*, blessiþ *H*, blessis
Lo; heere *CEFWoX*; ȝee *CLoX*
5 kingus *CX*, kynges *Lo*; ȝee *CLoX*; princis *BCEFHWo*; erys *BCFHWo*,
eeres *Lo*, eres *X*
6 the whiche: þat *C*, þe which *F*; lorde *LoWo*
7 and: & schal *H*; say *BFHWo*, sei *CE*, seyn *X*; psalm *BCFH*, psalme
ELoWo; the: om. *H²*
8 whenn *B*, whan *CFWoX*, whenne *E*, when *H*; wentest *Lo*; oute *B*, ouȝte *H*
9 passedist *BCEFHX*, passedest *Lo*, passidest *Wo*; regyons *E*, regyoun
FWoX, regiounes *Lo*
10 erþ *E*; moued *CX*, meuyde *Lo*; heuenus *C*, heuenys *E*, heuenes *LoX*
11 clowdes *Lo*; droppyden *Lo*; waters *BEH*, watres *Lo*; hullys *E*, hylles
LoWoX
12 flowede *X*; the Lord: oure 1. *Lo¹*

5. 1 Cecineruntque Delbora et Barach, filius Abinoen,
in illo die, dicentes:
2 Qui sponte obtulistis de Israel animas vestras ad
periculum, benedicite Domino.
3 Audite, reges; percipite auribus, principes: Ego
sum, ego sum quae Domino canam, psallam /Domino/
Deo Israel.

5. 1 And Delbora and Barach, sone of Aby-

2 noen, sungen in that dai, and seiden, ȝe

men of Israel, that offriden wilfuli ȝoure

3 lyues to perel, blesse the Lord. ȝe kingis,

here, ȝe princes, perceyueth with eeris;   5

Y am, Y am *the womman*, that schal synge

to the Lord; Y schal synge to the Lord

4 God of Israel. Lord, whanne thou ȝedist

out fro Seir, and passidist bi the cuntrees

of Edom, the erthe was moued, and he-   10

uenes and cloudis droppiden with watris;

5 hillis flowiden fro the face of the Lord,

and Synai fro the face of the Lord God

5. 1 þe sone IMa
    2 songen FR; saiden E
    3 offreden CaEFMPUW; wilfully BCaDEFGHaIKMMaNOQRWX, welfulli
       U; o. w.: han wilfully offrid I; ȝour K
    4 lifes K, lymes N, lyuis Q; peril E, pereyl GQ, perele K; blesse ȝe
       CaEHaIQ, blesse ȝee G; the: om. E; ȝe: þe E, ȝee U; kynges FHaOR;
       4—5 ȝe k. h.: h. ȝe kyngis I, k. h. ȝe K²
    5 heere DGKNSX, heere ȝe Ma; ȝe: om. I, & ȝe Ma, ȝee U; pryncis
       DGIKMaPQSX; perceyue AcBCDEGHaKLMaNOPQRSUX, parceyue
       CaFMW, perceyue ȝe I; ȝe pr. p.: pr. p. ȝe K²; eris CaMW, eres EF,
       eeres R
    6 Y am: 1x EGR²; wumman CaFMW, woman E; 6—7 Y ... Lord: om. R
    7 syng Ha
    8 whan EGHaLP; ȝedest EFHaL, ȝedeste R
    9 oute R; fro: of GW, from K; passedist CaMNW, passedest EFLP,
       passidest HaU, passideste R; cuntreis AcBCCaDFGHaKLMMaOQRSUWX,
       cuntres E
   10 mouyd AcCGOQRUW, meued ELP, mofed K, mooued SX; heuenys
       AcCGLPQU, heuens E
   11 cloudes CaFL; droppeden CaEFLMPW; watres F, watirs I
   12 hullis E, hilles FKLR; floweden BCaDEFILMPW, flowȝiden R; from K;
       face of the Lord: lordis f. I
   13 Synal: fro S. I; from K; God: om. D

4 Domine, cum exires de Seir, et transires per

regiones Edom, terra mota est, caelique ac nubes

stillaverunt aquis;

5 montes fluxerunt a facie Domini, et Sinai a facie

Domini Dei Israel.

6 Israel. In the dais of Sangar, sone of
 Anath, in the dais of Jahel, restiden the   15
 paththis, and tho that wenten in bi hem
 ȝeden awey bi streyt beryd paththis out
7 of the weye. Stronge men seseden in
 Yrael, and restiden, to the tyme that
8 Delbora roos, moder in Yrael. Newe   20
 bataylis hath chosun the Lord, and the
 ȝatis of enemyes he ouerturnede; swerd
 and speer aperyde not in fourti thowsand
9 of Yrael. Myn herte shal loue the princis
 of Yrael; ȝe that bi propre wil han offrid   25

14 In: & *X*; daȝes *CX*, dayes *FLoWo*
15 daȝes *CX*, dayes *FLoWo*; resteden *CLoX*, restedyn *E*
16 paþis *BCEFHWoX*, paþes *Lo*; þoo *C*; wentyn *E*; þem *CLoX*
17 ȝiden *CX*, ȝedyn *E*; aweye *B*; streiȝte *Lo*; berede *Lo*, bered *X*; paþis
 BCEFHWoX, paþes *Lo*; oute *B*, ouȝt *H*
18 wey *ELoWo*; sesedyn *BE*, cessiden *H*, cesseden *Lo*
19 resteden *CLoX*, restedyn *E*
20 ros *CX*, rose *Lo*; modyr *ELo*
21 bateylis *FWo*, batailes *CLoX*, bateyls *BE*, bateyles *H*; has *Lo*; chosen
 BCFHLoWoX, chosyn *E*
22 ȝatus *C*, ȝates *LoX*; enmyes *BFHWo*, enemys *CX*; ouertorned *BFHWo*,
 ouertornede *E*; swerde *LoWo*
23 spere *BCFHLoWoX*, sper *E*; apeerid *BF*, aperede *CX*, apereden *E*,
 aperid *HWo*, apperid *Lo*; thousend *CX*, þousondys *E*, þousande *FLo*
24 my *BEFHLoWo*; hert *Wo*; looue *C*; princes *LoX*
25 ȝee *CLoX*; propyr *E*, proper *X*; wyll *BFH*, wille *ELoWo*; offerd *BFH*,
 offrede *E*, offered *Lo*, offred *Wo*

6 In diebus Sangar, filii Anath, in diebus Iahel,
 quieverunt semitae; et qui ingrediebantur per eas,
 ambulaverunt per calles devios.
7 Cessaverunt fortes in Israel, et quieverunt, donec
 surgeret Delbora, mater in Israel.
8 Nova bella elegit Dominus, et portas hostium ipse
 subvertit; clypeus et hasta non apparuerunt in
 quadraginta millibus Israel.

6 of Israel. In the daies of Sangar, sone
   of Anach, in the daies of Jahel, paththis   15
   restiden, and thei that entriden bi tho
7 ʒeden bi paththis out of the weie. Stronge
   men in Israel ceessiden, and restiden, til
8 Delbora roos, a modir in Israel. The
   Lord chees newe batels, and he destriede   20
   the ʒatis of enemyes; scheeld and spere ap-
   periden not in fourti thousynde of Israel.
9 Myn herte loueth the princes of Israel;
   ʒe that offriden ʒou to perel bi ʒoure owyn

14   þe sone I
15   of (1°): om. C²; paþis AcGIKMaU, paþes EF
16   resteden CaEFMPW; entreden CaEFMPW; tho: hem N, þoo R
17   þei ʒeden I; paþis AcGIKMMaSUWX, paþes EF; oute R; wey DKR,
     waie E; strong DE
18   ceesseden CaMW, ceceden EFL, cessiden Ha, ceeceden P, ceesiden KR,
     ceciden SU; resteden CaELMPW; til: to E, & til W
19   rose I; moder EFMMaU; & þe I
20   chese E; new E; bateles E, batelys HaS, bateils KQX, batailes U; distriede
     AcBCaFGMMaNOPQW, distried CD, destroied E, destroiede HaK,
     distroiede R, distruyde S, distroyde U, distruyede X
21   ʒates CaEFHa; enmies EIL; scheelde C, scheld HaI, sheel L; speere G,
     sper NX; appereden CaEFMPU, appeerid D, apperede L, aperiden R,
     apperide W
22   þousynd CaIMW, þousand DHaMaNQRSX, þousend EFGLP, þousande
     K; of (exp. & cr. out) men of I
23   mijn K, my I, myne R; loueʒ E; pryncis GIKMaNPQSWX; 23: om. D
24   ʒee U; offreden CaEFILMPUW; peril EHaU, perele K; be S; ʒour KLM;
     owen E, owne cet.

9 Cor meum diligit principes Israel; qui propria
   voluntate obtulistis vos discrimini, benedicite
   Domino.

10 ӡou to peryl, blissith to the Lord; ӡe
that stien vp vpon shynynge assis, and
sittith aboue in doom, and goon in the
11 weye, spekith. Where the chaaris ben
hurtlid, and the oost of the enemyes is 30
queynt, there the riӡtwisnessis of the
Lord ben told, and mercy into the
stroonge men of Yrael; thanne the puple
of the Lord cam doun to the ӡatis, and
12 hadde the prynshod. Ryse, ryse, Del- 35
bora, ryse, and spek the dyte of songe;
ryse, Barach, and thou, sone of Abynoem,
13 tak thi chaytyues. The relyues of the
puple ben saued; the Lord in stronge men

26 perile *CFLoWoX*, perel *E*; blesseþ *CEWo*, blessiþ *H*, blessis *Lo*, blisseþ *X*;
ӡee *C*
27 steyӡen *BFLoWo*, steӡen *CX*, styӡen *EH*; opp *E*; apon *B*, opon *E*, vppon
Wo; schynyng *B*, shinende *CX*, schynyng *Lo*
28 sitten *CX*, sittes *Lo*, sitteþ *Wo*; aboun *BF*, abouen *ELoWo*; dome *BFHLoWo*,
dom *CX*; gon *CWoX*
29 wey *ELo*; spekeþ *CEX*, spekes *Lo*; wher *C*, wheer *E*; charis *BCEFH*,
chares *X*; been *E*
30 hurtlud *E*, hurtlide *Lo*; hoost *BEH*, ost *CWoX*; the: om. *X*; enmyes
BFWo, enemys *CX*
31 queynte *Lo*; riӡtwisnesses *CX*, riӡtwisnes as *Lo*
32 lorde *LoWo*; been *E*; tolde *BFHLoWo*
33 stronge *cet.*; of Y.: om. *H*; þann *B*, þenne *E*, þan *HLoWo*; peple
BEFHLoWo
34 coome *BF*, coom *E*, come *HLoWo*; ӡates *LoX*
35 had *BFHWo*; princehode *BFHLoWo*, princehod *C*, prinshood *E*,
princehed *X*; ris (2x) *CX*
36 ris *CX*; speke *BFHLoWo*; detee *E*, deete *Lo*; song *CEHX*
37 ris *CX*; þu *B*, þ^u *E*
38 take *BFHLoWo*; caitiues *CWoX*, chaytyfs *E*, caytifes *Lo*; relyfys *E*, reeliues
Lo, relyfes *X*
39 peple *BEFHLoWo*; been *E*; sauede *Lo*; lorde *Lo*

10 Qui ascendi/s/tis super nitentes asinos, et sedetis
supra in iudicio, et ambulatis in via, loquimini.
11 Ubi collisi sunt currus, et hostium suffocatus est
exercitus, ibi narrentur iustitiae Domini, et
clementia in fortes Israel; tunc descendit populus
Domini ad portas, et obtinuit principatum.

10 wille, blesse ȝe the Lord; speke ȝe, that   25
    stien on schynynge assis, and sitten aboue

11 in doom, and goen in the wey. Where
    the charis weren hurtlid doun to gidere,
    and the oost of enemyes was straunglid,
    there the riȝtfulnessis of the Lord be   30
    teld, and mercy among the stronge of
    Israel; thanne the puple of the Lord
    cam doun to the ȝatis, and gat prinsehod.

12 Rise, rise thou, Delbora, rise thou, and
    speke a song; rise thou, Barach, and thou,   35

13 sone of Abynoen, take thi prisoneris. The
    relikis of the puple ben sauyd; the Lord

25 wil IMaU; bles E; ȝe (1°): om. BC², ȝee U; ȝe (2°): om. L, ȝee U;
    25−27 ȝe þat ... gon in þe wey speke ȝe I
26 steien F, stiȝen KMaNR, stien up I; on: vpon I; schynyng BCEF, þe s.
    N; asses FR; sittin P; aloone Ha (cr. out), abouen K, a boof R, aboute SX
27 dome EHaR, dom U; goon CaFKLMMaW, gon EGHaILPQSUX; weie
    AcBCCaDFGHaKLMMaNOPQRSUWX; wher CaF, of werre E
28 scharis CQU, charris D, chares F, sharris N; hurteled E, hurlid I, hirtlid L;
    to gidre DIR, to ghider E
29 ost EU; enemis E, enmyes I; strangled E, stranglid cet.
30 þer U; riȝtfulnesses FORU; riȝtf. of the L.: lordis riȝtwisnesse I; ben DHa
31 teeld BCaDGMMaNOQSWX, tolde ER, told out I, toold K, told LP;
    his mercy I, mercie R; amonge R; strong CDE, stronge men IW
32 þan EFHa; peple CaFILMMaNPSWX; p. of the Lord: lordis p. I
33 com E, came R; ȝates F; gate IR, gaatt K; prynshod AcN, princehood
    BCaFKMMaORSWX, prinshode D, princehode E, þe princehood I
34 Rise (1°): om. B
35 spek L; songe R; rise: 2x RX
36 prisoners DIKLMPRUX, prisones E, prisoneres FHa, presoneris G,
    presoners S
37 relikes CaFKR, reliks HaSX, relifs I; peple CaFILMMaNPSWX; been E,
    be W; saued BCaDEFHaIKLMMaNOPSUX

12 Surge, surge Delbora, surge et loquere canticum;
    surge Barach, et apprehende captivos tuos, fili
    Abinoen.

13 Salvatae sunt reliquiae populi, Dominus in fortibus
    dimicavit.

14 hath fouȝten. Fro Effraym he hath doon   40
   hem awey into Amelech, and after hym
   fro Beniamyn in to thi puplis, O Amalech. Fro Machir princis descendiden,
   and fro Zabulon, that oost shulden lede
15 to fiȝt. Dukis of Ysachar weren with   45
   Delbora, and the steppis of Barach thei
   folweden, the whiche, as into heuedi fallynge and helle, he ȝaf hym silf to peryl.
   Ruben aȝens hym diuydide, of greet willi
16 men is foundun stryuynge. Whi dwellist   50
   thow bitwix two teermys, that thow
   here the noysis of flockis? Ruben aȝens
   hym dyuydide, of greet willi men is

40 has *Lo* (2x); fouȝte *BEFH*, foȝte *CX*, fouȝt *Wo*; do *CX*, don *Wo*
41 þem *CLoX*; aweye *BH*; aftir *X*
42 thi: þe *X*; peplis *BEFHWo*, peples *Lo*, puples *X*; O: of *X*
43 from *E*; princes *LoX*; descendeden *BCF*, descendedyn *E*, descenden *Lo*
44 ost *CX*, (h)oost *E*; sholdyn *E*; leede *BFHWo*, leden *X*
45 fiȝten *CX*, fiȝte *ELo*; duykis *BFH*, dukes *LoX*; weryn *E*
46 stappis *BEFHWo*
47 foloweden *BFHWo*, folewiden *C*, folwedyn *E*, foleweden *X*; which *FWo*;
    hedi *CELoX*; fallyng *BCLoX*
48 hell *BF*, hil *X*; ȝaue *BFHWo*, ȝafe *Lo*; self *BCEFHLoX*; perile *CLoX*,
    perel *E*
49 aȝeyns *BEFLoWo*, aȝen *CX*; dyuydid *BEFHLoWoX*, deuyded *C*; grete
    BFHLoWoX, gret *C*
50 founden *BFHLoWo*, founde *CX*, foundyn *E*; striuende *CX*, stryuyng *Lo*;
    dwellest *Wo*
51 betwe *C*, bytwixe *BEFHLoWo*, bitwe *X*; termys *BEFHLoWo*, termes *CX*
52 heere *EFWo*; noises *CX*, voycis *Wo*; flockes *X*; aȝeyns *BEFLoWo*, aȝen *CX*
53 dyuydid *BFHLoWoX*, deuyded *C*, deuydid *E*; grete *BFHLoWoX*, gret *C*;
    willily *Lo*

14 Ex Effraim delevit eos in Amalech, et post eum ex
   Beniamin in populos tuos, o Amalech. De Machir
   principes descenderunt et de Zabulon, qui exercitum
   ducerent ad bellandum.
15 Duces Isachar fuerunt cum Delbora, et Barach
   vestigia sunt secuti, qui quasi in praeceps ac

14 fauʒt aʒens stronge men of Effraym. He
dide awei hem in Amalech, and aftir hym
of Beniamyn in to thi puplis, thou Ama-   40
lech. Princes of Machir and of Zabulon
15 ʒeden doun, that ledden oost to fiʒte. The
duykis of Isachar weren with Delbora, and
sueden the steppis of Barach, which ʒaf
hym silf to perel, as in to a dich, and in   45
to helle. While Ruben was departid aʒens
hym silf, the strijf of greet hertyd men
16 was foundun. Whi dwellist thou bitwixe
tweyne endis, that thou here the hiss-
yngis of flockis? While Ruben was de-   50
partid aʒens hym silf, the strijf of greet

38 fauʒte BDHaILMaNR; aʒenus AcCNO; strong DES; of: fro I
39 dud E; away Ha; þem E, hym R; in: in to CaDGHaIKMMaNOQSX;
after BDFLU
40 of: fro I; peples CaF, puple D, peplis ILMMaOPSWX, peple N, puples R
41 pryncis DEGIKMaNPQSX; of: fro I (2x)
42 doune E; ladden K; oste E, þe oost IK
43 dukis BCCaGPQW, dukes EFL, duykes R
44 suede AcMa, suweden CaFMW; steppes FR; whiche G, þat I, wich K;
ʒaaf I, ʒaue R
45 self CaEFKLMPRUW; peril E, perele K; diche CDELNPR, dich
'[h]edely' Ha, diche hedly I, dijk K, dijch X
46 wille E, whil KLPR; departed EF, dipartid O; aʒenus AcCNO, aʒenes I
47 self CaEFIKLMPRUW; strif EFGHaLNPU; grete EHaILRUW, greete
GQ, gret P; hirtid C, hertide KL
48 founden CaDEFGHaKLMMaPRW, founden or perceyued I; dwellest
CFHaL, dwellis E; bytwix EGQ
49 tweye BQ, tweyn ELPU, twey G, two I, twene N; eendis BKMaR, endes
F, termes I; heere GKMaNS, heer X; hissinges BCaFHaLR, priuey noyse I
50 flockes FR, flokis O; wil E, whiles Q, whil KLPR; departed E
51 aʒenus AcCNO; hem Ac, it B; self CaEFIKMPRUW; strif EFHaILPU;
grete AcBCaEHaIKNORSUWX, greete GQ, gret LP

baratrum se discrimini dedit. Diviso contra se Ruben,
magnanimorum reperta contentio est.
16 Quare habitas inter duos terminos, ut audias sibilos
gregum? Diviso contra se Ruben, magnanimorum reperta
est contentio.

17 foundun a strijf. Gad biȝonde Jordan
   restide, and Dan tentide to shippis. Aser   55
   dwellid in the brenk of the see, and in
18 hauens abood. Forsothe Zabulon and
   Neptalym offerden her lyues to deeth,
19 in the regioun of Moreme. Kyngis
   camen, and fouȝten; fouȝten the kyngis   60
   of Chanaan in Thanath, biside the watris
   of Magedan; and neuerthelater no thing
20 token the praytakers. Fro heuene it is
   fouȝten aȝens hem; sterrys dwellynge in
   ordre and in her course aȝens Sysaram   65

54   founde(n) *B*, founde *CEFHWoX*, founden *Lo*; a: þe *cet.*; stryfe *BFLo*,
      stryf *HWoX*; byȝond *BFWo*, beȝunde *CX*
55   restyd *BFHLoWo*, restede *CE*; tented *BFHWo*, tentede *CEX*; shipis *C*,
      schippes *LoX*
56   dwelte *CX*, dwellyde *E*; brynke *cet.*; se *CX*
57   haauens *BFH*, hauenees *C*, hauenys *E*, haauenes *Lo*, hauenes *X*; aboode
      BF, abod *CX*, abode *LoWo*; Forsothe Zabulon: Z. f. *cet.*
58   offriden *C*, offredyn *E*, offreden *LoX*; her: þeir *BFWo*, þer *CE²LoX*;
      lyuys *E*; deþ *BCFHWoX*, þe deeþ *Lo*
59   region *E*; kingus *CX*, kynges *Lo*
60   coomen *BF*, comyn *E*, comen *HLoWo*; fouȝten (2x): foȝten *CX*(1°; 2° om.),
      fouȝtyn *E*; kingus *C*
61   bysydis *BEFH*, beside *C*, bisides *LoWoX*; waters *BEH*, watres *Lo*
62   ner þe latere *CX*, ner þe later *E*, neuere þe later *Lo*, neuer þe latter *Wo*;
      þinge *BFLoWo*
63   tokyn *E*; pray-: prayȝe *BFWo*, prei *CX*, preyȝe *E*, praye *H*, preye *Lo*;
      -takers: takeres *CX*, takeris *Lo*; from *E*; heuen *BFWo*, heuenes *Lo*; hit *E*
64   foȝten *CX*, fauȝtyn *E*; aȝeyns *BEFWo*, aȝen *CX*, a-ȝeynes *Lo*; þem *Lo*;
      sterres *X*; dwellende *CX*, dwellyng *Lo*
65   ordre: cedre(?) *X*; þeir *BFWo*, þer *CLoX*, here *E*; cours *CELoX*; aȝeyns
      BEFH, aȝen *CX*, a-ȝeynes *Lo*

17 Gad trans Iordanem quiescebat, et Dan vacabat nav-
   ibus; Aser habitabat in litore maris, et in portibus
   morabatur.
18 Zabulon vero et Neptalim obtulerunt animas suas
   morti, in regione Moreme.

17 hertid men was foundun. Gad restide bi-
ȝendis Jordan, and Dan ȝaf tent to schippis.
Aser dwellide in the brenke of the see,

18 and dwellide in hauenes. Forsothe Za-   55
bulon and Neptalym offriden her lyues to
deeth, in the cuntre of Morema, *that*

19 *is interpretid, hiȝ.* Kyngis camen, and
fouȝten; kyngis of Canaan fouȝten in
Thanath, bisidis the watris of Magedon;   60
and netheles thei token no thing bi prey.

20 Fro heuene me fauȝt aȝens hem; sterris
dwelliden in her ordre and cours, and

---

52 hirtid C; founden CaDEFGHaIKLMMaPRW; restid D, restede EFP;
biȝondis BDEGQ, biȝendes FU, biȝonde IKX, biȝende R, biȝounde S
53 ȝaaf I, ȝaue R; tente BLRU, schippes FR
54 dwellid D, dwelled E, dwellede LP, dwelde U; brynke cet.; br. of the see:
see br. I
55 dwellid D, dwelled E, dwellede FLP, he dwellide I, dwelde U; hauens EI,
hauenis Q; Forsothe: & I, forsoþ X
56 offreden CaEFMPUW; here GQRU; lifes K, lyuis Q
57 deþ AcCEHaLPQRSUX, þe deþ I; cuntrei AcBCCaDFGHaMMaOQRUW,
cuntree IK
58 heiȝ CaFMW; gloss om. ISX[1]; kynges FHaR; camyn S
59 fauȝten I (2x); kynges FHa; k. of C. f.: om. D
60 besidis EP, bisides FHaLU; watres F, waters U
61 naþeles BI; tooken GKLNPSX; pry D, prai EK
62 fro: for E, from K; heuen R, heþen E; men E; fauȝte BDHaLNORUX;
me fauȝt: it was fouȝten I, me was fauȝten W; aȝenus AcCNO; sterres
FLR
63 dwelleden CaEFLMPW, dwelden U; hire L, here Q; ordir BN, ordris G;
course ER, in her c. I

---

19 Venerunt reges et pugnaverunt, pugnaverunt reges
Chanaan in Thanach, iuxta aquas Magedon; et tamen
nihil tulere praedantes.

20 De caelo dimicatum est contra eos; stellae manentes
in ordine et cursu suo, adversus Sisaram pugnaverunt.

21 fouȝten. The streem of Syson drowȝ the
careyns of hem, the streem of Cadunym,
streem of Cyson. Treed thou, my soule,
22 stronge men. Cleas of hors fullen hem
fleynge with feerse, and bi heedlynge   70
fallinge the moost stroonge men of ene-
23 myes. Curse ȝe to the loond of Meroth,
seide the aungel of the Lord, curse ȝe to
the dwellers of it, for thei camen not to
the help of the Lord, in to the help of   75
24 the moost stronge men of hym. Blessid
among wymmen Jahel, the wijf of Aber
Cynei; be she blessid in hir tabernacle.

66   foȝten *CX*, fouȝtyn *E*; streme *BFHLoWo*, strem *CX*; droȝ *CX*, drowe *Lo*
67   careines *CLoX*, careynys *E*; þem *CLo*; streme *BFHLoWo*, strem *CX*
68   streme *BFHLoWo*, strem *CX*; trede *cet.*
69   cles *CX*, clees *ELo*; horse *E*; fellen *C*, fullyn *E*, follen *Lo*; þem *CLo*
70   fleeȝinge *BFH*, fleende *CX*, fleȝinge *Wo*; ferse *B*, feers *WoX*; heuedlynge
BFHWo, hedling *CLo*, hed long *E*, hedli *X*
71   fallyng *BLoX*, fallende *C*; moste *BLo*, most *CEFHX*; stronge *cet.*; enmyes
BFWo, enemys *CX*
72   corse *BEFWo*, cursse *Lo*; ȝee *CLoX*; lond *CEX*, londe *LoWo*
73   aungell *B*, aungil *CX*, angel *E*; corse *BEFHWo*, cursse *Lo*; ȝee *CLoX*
74   dwelleris *CLoX*; hit *E*; coome *BF*, come *EHLoWo*
75   help (2x): helpe *CF*(2°)*Lo*(2°)*Wo*(1°)*X*; lorde *Wo*; off *E*
76   most *BCEFHWoX*, moste *Lo*; blyssed *BF*, blessed *E*, blissid *X*
77   amonge *BFHLoWo*; wyf *BCFHLoWoX*, wife *E*
78   blyssed *BF*, blessed *E*, blissid *X*; hyre *BFLo*, here *E*, her *H*; thabernacle *Lo*

21 Torrens Cison traxit cadavera eorum, torrens Cadumim,
torrens Cison; conculca, anima mea, robustos.
22 Ungulae equorum ceciderunt, fugientibus impetu et
per praeceps ruentibus fortissimis hostium.
23 Maledicite terrae Meroth, dixit angelus Domini,
maledicite habitatoribus eius, quia non venerunt ad
auxilium Domini, in adiutorium fortissimorum eius.
24 Benedicta inter mulieres Iahel, uxor Aber Cinei,
benedicatur in tabernaculo suo.

21 fouȝten aȝens Sisara. The stronde of
Cyson drow the deed bodies of hem, the   65
stronde of Cadymyn, the stronde of Cy-
son. My soule, to-trede thou stronge
22 men. The hors howis felden, while
the strongeste of enemyes fledden with
23 bire, and felden heedli. Curse ȝe the lond   70
of Meroth, seide the aungel of the Lord,
curse ȝe the dwelleris of hym, for thei
camen not to the help of the Lord, in
to the help of the strongeste of hym.
24 Blessyd among wymmen be Jahel, the   75
wijf of Aber Cyney; blessid be sche in

64 fowten E, þei fouȝten I; aȝenus AcCNOX; strond D, stroonde Ma
65 drowȝ CaGHaKMMaNQSW, drowe DR, drewe I, droȝ X; deede
    BGKNPQ, dede CaFLMW; the d. b. of hem: her d. b. I
66 strond D (2x), stroonde Ma (2x); & þe CaGHaIKMMaN²OQSX
67 (to)-trede Ac, to treede GQ, totride W; thou: þe G; strong DE
68 The: om. I; horse HaNO, horsis W; howues AcBCaDEFHaLMMaNPSW,
    hows C, howuis GKRQX, hooues I, houes O; fellen CaEFLMPW, filden
    D, fellen awey I; wil E, whil KPR
69 strongiste B, strongist D, stronghest E, strongest Ha, strengest I, strengist
    Ma; enmyes ILO; fledde O; 69—70 wiþ bire fledden Ma
70 bir EHaLPW; fellen CaFLMW, fellin EP, fellen doun I, feelden QR;
    hedli EILP, heedlyng G; ȝee U
71 angel CE, aungil MaQ; aungel of the Lord: lordis aungel I
72 ȝee GU; dwellers DEHaKLMRSUX, dwelleres F; hem E; the dw. of
    hym: his dwellers I
73 the: om. DI; to: in to MW; helpe CEGHaQR; ne in I; 73—74 in ... hym:
    om. Ma
74 helpe EGPQR; strongiste B, strongist D, strongest E, moost stronge I,
    strengeste W
75 blessed KL; amonge R; wommen BGQ, alle wymmen D
76 wif EFGHaLPQU; blissed E, blessed L

25 To the askynge water sche ȝaf mylk, and
   in the viole of pryncis she brouȝte forth   80
26 butter. The left hoond she putte to the
   nayl, and the riȝt to the hamers of
   smythis; and she smoot Cisaram, sechynge in the heed the place of the wound,
27 and the temple myȝtilich thrillynge. Bi-   85
   twix the feet of hir he felle, failid, and
   dyede; and he was wrappid bifore the
   feet of hir, and he lay out of lijf, and

79   askende *CX*, askyng *Lo*; watir *CEX*, watre *Lo*; ȝaue *BFWo*, ȝafe *Lo*;
     mylke *HLo*
80   viol *X*; princes *LoX*; brouȝt *BFHWo*, broȝte *CX*; forþe *HLo*
81   botter *BEFHWo*, bootere *C*, butre *Lo*, botere *X*; lift *CEX*, lyfte *Lo*; hond
     CEWoX, hande *Lo*; put *Lo*, putt *Wo*
82   nayle *LoWo*; hameres *CX*, hamoris *Lo*
83   smyþes *CLoX*, smeþys *E*; smott *B*, smot *CX*, smote *FLoWo*; sechende *C*,
     seching *Lo*, sekende *X*
84   heuede *BFH*, heued *CWo*, hed *EX*, hede *Lo*; wounde *cet.*
85   myȝtily *cet.*; thirlende *CX*, þurlynge *E*, thirllyng *Lo*; bytwixe *BEFHLoWo*,
     betwe *C*, bitwe *X*
86   fete *LoWo*; hyre *BFLo*, here *E*; fell *BFHX*, fil *C*, ful *E*, fylle *Wo*; failede *C*,
     faylede *E*, failed *Lo*, failide *X*
87   dyȝid *BFHWo*, deyde *E*, dyed *Lo*; and: om. *E²*; wrapped *EWo*; befor *C*,
     bifor *X*
88   feete *B*, fete *LoWo*; hyre *BFLo*, here *E*; oute *B*, ouȝt *H*; lyf *BFHLoWoX*,
     life *E*

25 Aquam petenti lac dedit, et in phiala principum
   obtulit butyrum.
26 Sinistram manum misit ad clavum, et dexteram ad
   fabrorum malleos; percussitque Sisaram, quaerens
   in capite vulneris locum, et tempus valide perforans.
27 Inter pedes eius ruit; defecit, et mortuus est;
   volvebatur ante pedes eius, et iacebat exanimis et
   miserabilis.

25 hir tabernacle. *To Sisara* axynge watir
   sche ȝaf mylk, and in a viol of princes
26 sche ȝaf botere. Sche puttide the left
   hond to a nail, and the riȝt hond to *the*   80
   hameris of smyȝthis; and sche smoot Si-
   sara, and souȝte in the heed a place of
   wounde, and perside strongli the temple.
27 He felde bitwixe the feet of hir, he
   failide, and diede; he was waltryd bifor   85
   hir feet, and he lay with out soule, and

77 her CaFLMW, hire K; tabernaclis AcMa, tabernacle O; axing EKP;
    watre Ca, water EFKMU; *To S.* axynge watir: to þe axynge '*þat is Sisera*'
    w. I
78 ȝaf him E, ȝaaf I, ȝaue R; mylke DI, melk U; viole CaFIRW, vessel M;
    pryncis DEGHaIKMaNPSX
79 ȝaaf him I, ȝaue R; boter B, buttir D, botre I, buttere N; puttid DF,
    putted E, putte IM, puttede LP; lift BKLMaOP, lefte EHaR
80 hond (1°): hoond S; to: in to Ha; a: þe I; naile DE; the: hir I; rith E;
    hond (2°): hand K, hoond R; *the*: om. BW
81 hamers DHaLX, hamere E, hameres F, hamer IN; smyþis
    AcBCCaDGHaKLMMaPQRWX, smþis E, smiþes F, smyteris O, smiþþis
    S; h. of sm.: smyþes hamer I; smot EPU, smote HaIR
82 the: his I; hed EL, heued Ha; plaace S
83 wound R; pereschide B, peerside CaMaNRX, peersid D, perseiued E,
    persede FKP, sche perschide I; strongheli E; his temple I
84 fel CaEFLMPW, filde D, felle I; bitwix EFQ; fete R; her CaMW, here F,
    hire K; the feet of hir: hir feet I; & he B
85 failid D, failed E, failede FKLPU; deide CaFW, died E, diȝede K, deiede
    M, diȝed R; waltred E; bifore BCaDEGHaIKMaNQRSWX
86 her CCaEFMW, hire QR; fete R; laiȝ K; wiþ oute CaFGHaLMMaNPR-
    SWX, whit out E, wiþouten IK; soule: lijf I

28 wretchidful. Bi the wyndow biholdynge
ʒollide the moder of hym; and fro the 90
sowpynge place she spak, Whi tarieth to
turn aʒen the chaar of hym? Whi tary-
eden the feet of the foure whelid cartis
29 of hym? Oon wiser than that other
wijfis of hym to the moder in lawe thes 95
30 wordis answerde, Perauenture now he
dyuydith spuylis, and the moost feyr of
wymmen is chosun to hym; clothis of
dyuers colours to Sysare ben taak into
praye, and dyuerse portenaunce to neckis 100

89 wrytchidfull *BF*, wrecchedfol *E*, wreccheful *Lo*; wyndowe *BCFLoWoX*;
beholdende *C*, biholdyng *Lo*, biholdende *X*
90 ʒollid *BFHWo*, ʒellede *C*, ʒollede *E*, ʒellide *X*; modir *BEH*, modre *Lo*
91 souping *CX*, souppynge *Lo*; spake *BWo*; taries *Lo*
92 torne *BEFHWo*, turnen *C*, turne *LoX*; aʒeyn *BEFLoWo*, aʒeen *CX*; char
CX, chare *EWo*, chaare *FLo*; tariedyn *E*
93 fete *LoWo*; the: om. *X*; four *BFH*; wheled *BEFH*, wheelid *C*, whelide *Lo*
94 oone *H*, oen *CX*; wisere *CX*; þann *BF*; that: þe *CX*; oþere *CX*, oþur *Lo*
95 wyfis *BEFHWo*, wiues *CLo*, wifes *X*; modir *BEH*, modre *Lo*; þese *CEX*
96 wordes *BLoWo*, woordus *C*, wrdis *X*; answerede *E*, answeride *Lo*, answered
Wo; par auenture *X*; nowe *BFLo*
97 deuydeþ *BCE*, diuydes *Lo*, deuydiþ *X*; spoiles *C*, spulys *E*, spoylis *Lo*,
spoilis *X*; most *BCEFHWoX*, moste *Lo*; fair *CEWoX*, faire *Lo*
98 chosen *BFHLoWoX*, chose *C*, chosyn *E*; cloþes *Lo*; off *E*
99 diuerse *CELoWoX*; colouris *C*, coloures *LoWoX*; been *E*; take *BFHWo*,
taken *CLoX*, takyn *E*
100 prayʒe *BFHWo*, prei *CX*, preyʒe *E*, preye *Lo*; purtenaunce *CEHLoX*,
purtynaunce *Wo*; nekkes *EX*

28 Per fenestram respiciens, ululabat mater eius; et
de cenaculo loquebatur: Cur moratur regredi currus
eius? Quare tardaverunt pedes quadrigarum illius?
29 Una sapientior ceteris uxoribus eius haec socrui
verba respondit:
30 Forsitan nunc dividit spolia, et pulcherrima femin-
arum eligitur ei; vestes diversorum colorum Sisarae
traduntur in praedam, et supellex varia ad ornanda
colla congeritur.

28 wretchidful. His modir bihelde bi a wyndow, and ȝellide; and sche spak fro the
soler, Whi tarieth his chaar to come aȝen?
Whi tarieden the feet of his foure horsid   90
29 cartis? Oon wisere than othere wyues of
hym answeride these wordis to the modir
30 of hir hosebonde, In hap now he departith
spuylis, and the faireste of wymmen is
chosun to hym; clothis of dyuerse colouris   95
ben ȝouun to Sisara in to prey, and dy-
uerse aray of houshold is gaderid to ourne

87 wrecchedful E; moder EFLU; biheeld CaFGLMMaNPQWX, biheld
    DS, biheuld K, biheelde R, bihilde U; wyndowe BDGHaIMaQ
88 ȝellid D, ȝelled E, ȝellede FLPU; spake DHaIR; from K
89 soleer GQ; chare AcBCDEHaIKLMaNPRSX, char GQ; forto I; cum E,
    comen O
90 tariden E, tarien I; fete E; hise AcBCCaGKMMaNOQUW, þe E;
    horseden E, horsed FL, horsede K, horside W
91 cartes F; one E, on U; wyser DEILR; þanne CaD; oþer E; wyuis EGHaQ,
    wifes K; 91 – 92 othere wyues of hym: an oþer of his wyues I; of hym:
    om. D
92 answerde CaEFMPQW, answerd D, om. G, answerede L; þes DKNX,
    om. G; wordes CaF, woordis P; moder EFLMU
93 her CaLMW, here F, hire K; husbonde BDMaPQ, husbond ER, housbonde
    GI, hosbonde L; happe K; departeȝ E, departeþ FHaKL
94 spoiles CaFL, spoilis EGMMaNOPQ, spuyles HaK; fairiste B, fairist DI,
    fairest HaLP, fairste X; wommen BGQ
95 chosen CaFGHaIKMMaQRUW, chose ELP; cloþes FKL; dyuers DMa;
    colours EFHaIKLMOPRSX, coloures W
96 be DMa, bene E; ȝouen CaEFILMMaOPRUW, ȝofene K; pray BEKLP,
    preie CIR, pry D; dyuers DEFILMaNPQRSX
97 housholde CE, houshoold MaWX; gadrid FR, gadered HaL, gederid
    KSX; oure DEMaR, ourne wiþ I

31 to be anourned is born to gidre. So
perischen alle thin enemyes, thou Lord;
forsothe thoo that louen thee, as the
sunne in his rysynge shyneth, so glit-
32 teren thei. And the loond restide bi
fourti ӡeer.

6. 1 The sones forsothe of Yrael diden yuel
in the siӡt of the Lord, the which took
hem in the hoond of Madian seuen ӡeer.
2 And thei ben oppressid greetli of hem;
and thei maden to hem caaues, and spe-
lunkis in hillis, and moost defensable

101 ben CX, been E; anournede B, enourned CX, onorned E, anoured H,
anourenede Lo; bore BEFHWo, borne Lo; to geþers B, togidere C, to
geders EH, to gyþers F, to gidres Lo, to gideres Wo, togiþere X
102 pershen C, peryschyn E, pershe X; all F; þine Lo; enmyes BFWo, enemys
CX; þu B, om. X; lorde Wo
103 forsoþ H; þo BEFHLoWoX; forsothe thoo: þ. f. cet.; loouen C, louyn E;
þe EWo
104 sonne ELo; risyng CX; schyniþ BFH, schynes Lo; gleteren BFLoWo,
glitere C, gleteryn E, glemeren H
105 lond CEWoX, loonde F, londe Lo; restyd BFHWo, restede ELoX
106 ӡeer: wynter B, ӡere LoWo, ӡer X

6. 1 sonus C, sonys E; deden C, dedyn E; euel CWoX, yuil E, yuele Lo
2 siӡte CLoX; whiche BCEHLoWoX; tooke B, toc CX, toke FHLoWo
3 þem CLo; in: in to Lo; hond CEWoX, honde Lo; seuene ELoWoX; ӡere
BLoWo, ӡer CX
4 been E; opressid CX, oppressed BEFH, oppresside Lo; gretely BF, gretli
CEHLoWoX; þem CLoX
5 made E; þem CLoX; cauys BEFHLoWo, caues CX; spelonkis BFHWo,
spelumpkys E, spelonkes Lo, spelunkes X
6 hullys E, hilles Lo; most BCEFHWoX, moste Lo

31 Sic pereant omnes inimici tui, Domine; qui autem
diligunt te, sicut sol in ortu suo splendet, ita
rutilent.
32 Quievitque terra per quadraginta annos.

31 neckis. Lord, alle thin enemyes perische
so; sotheli, thei that louen thee, schyne
so, as the sunne schyneth in his risyng.   100
And the lond restide fourti ӡeer.

6. 1 Forsothe the sones of Israel diden yuel
in the siӡt of the Lord, and he bitook
hem in the hond of Madian seuene ӡeer.
   2 And thei weren oppressid of hem greetly;
and thei maden dichis, and dennes to hem   5
silf in hillis, and strongeste places to fiӡte

98 neckes FR; lorde E; þine CaEIKLMNPQRSWX; enemis E, enmyes I;
    peresche B, pershe EL, periӡsshe K, perisch R
99 soþli FGLMPQSUWX, & I; þai E; loue GHaQ; þe EMR; schyne þei I
100 sonne E; shineӡ E, schӯneþ O, shiniþ P; his: her L; risynge DGMaQRU
101 londe E; restid D, rested E, r. *fro batel* I, restede P; ӡere E, ӡer ILP

6. 1 Forsothe: And I, Forsoþ X; sonys GQ; dedin EP; euel E, euyl FLPQ,
       euyle G
    2 siӡte CaGUW; siӡt of the Lord: lordis siӡt I; bitok EFHa, bitoke IR
    3 in to AcF¹IK²MaO; honde E, hoond X; seuen CaGIMW; ӡere E, ӡer P
    4 thei: israel I; weren: was I; oppressed EL, oppresside K, opressid U;
       gretli AcILPU, greteli ER
    5 thei: israel I; made I; diches EFM, dich S; dennys BGLMaPQSX; 5—6 d.
       & d. to hem self: to h. s. d. & d. I
    6 self CaEFIKMPRUW; hilles F; strongiste B, strongist D, stronghes E,
       moost stronge I, strongest L; placis AcDGHaIKLMaNPQSX; fiӡt E

6. 1 Fecerunt autem filii Israel malum in conspectu
Domini; qui tradidit eos in manu Madian septem annis;
   2 et oppressi sunt valde ab eis. Feceruntque sibi
antra et speluncas in montibus, et munitissima ad
repugnandum loca.

163

3 placis to withstonden. And whanne Irael
  wex feers, Madian stiede vp, and Ama-
4 lech, and other of the est naciouns; and
  anentis hem pitchinge tentis, as thei weren   10
  in grasse, alle thingis thei wastiden vnto
  the entre of Gaze, and no thing perteynynge to the lijf vtterli thei laften in
5 Yrael, ne sheep, ne oxe[n], ne asses. Forsothe thei and alle the flockis of hem   15
  camen with her tabernaclis, and at the
  licknes of locustis alle placis fulfillide
  the vnnoumbrable multitude of men and
  of camels, and wastynge what euere thing

7 places LoX; wiþstoonden BF, wiþstonde C, wiþstondyn E; whenn B, whan
   CWoX, whenne E, whann F
8 wexe BFHLoWo, wax E; fers E; stey3id BFWo, ste3ede CX, sty3ede E,
   sty3id H, stei3ede Lo; opp E
9 oþere CX; eest BEFLo; nacionys E
10 anentus C, anuntys E, anent X; þem CLo; picchende CX, picching Lo;
   tentus C, tentes X; weryn E
11 gras CE, gres X; all F, al H; thingus CX, þinges Lo; wasteden CLoX,
   wastedyn E
12 entree B; þinge BLoWo; perteynyng B, pertenende CX
13 lyf BCFHWoX, life ELo; laftyn BE, leften CX, laft H, lafte Lo; in: om.
   BFWo
14 scheepe B, shep CX, schepe HLoWo; oxen C, oxyn E; assis BCEFHLoWo;
   14—15 Forsothe thei: þei f. cet.
15 all F; flockes X; þem CLo
16 coomen BFH, coomyn E, comen LoWo; þeir BFWo, þer CLoX, here E;
   thabernaclis Lo, tabernacles X
17 licnesse CX, liknes EWo, lickenes Lo; locustes LoWoX; all F; places LoX;
   fulfilliden BFHWo, fulfilden CX, folfulleden E, fulfilde Lo
18 vnnoumbreable BFH, innoumbreable Lo
19 chamels BFH, chamailes C, chameylys E, kamelis Lo, camailes X; waastynge
   BF, wastende CX, wastyng Lo; euer BCFWo, er E; þinge BWo

3 Cumque s(a)evisset Israel, ascendebat Madian et
  Amalech et ceteri orientalium nationum;
4 et apud eos figentes tentoria, sicut erant in herbis,
  cuncta vastabant usque ad introitum Gazae; nihilque
  omnino ad vitam pertinens relinquebant in Israel,
  non oves, non boves, non asinos.

164

3 aȝen. And whanne Israel hadde sowe,
   Madian stiede, and Amalech, and othere
4 of the naciouns of the eest; and thei settiden tentis at *the sones of Israel*, and
   wastiden alle thingis as tho weren in
   eerbis, *ethir grene corn*, til to the entryng of Gaza, and outirli thei leften not
   in Israel ony thing perteynynge to lijf,
5 not scheep, not oxun, not assis. For thei
   and alle her flockis camen with her tabernaclis, and at the licnesse of locustus thei
   filliden alle thingis, and a multitude of
   men and of camels was with out noumbre,
   and wastiden what euer thing thei touch-

10

15

20

7 aȝein B, aȝen *madian* I; whan EGHaLP; had EI; souwe F, sowen I
8 stied E, steiede F, stiȝede GHaNR, stiede up I; oþer EL
9 nacions CEKQ; est E; n. of the e.: eest naciouns I; setteden CaEFLPW,
   setten M, settidin S
10 tentes F, her tentis I; at: bisidis I; *sonis* GQ
11 wasteden CaEFMPW, þei wastiden I, waastiden MaX; þinges F; tho: þo
   þat KMa, þoo R, þei X; wherin E, werin P
12 erbis DEGIK, herbes F; eþer AcBCDKSX, eiþer CaGHaMMaQRW, or
   EILP, oþer FU; greene AcCGNX; corne ER; til to: vn to EI; entrynge
   DGMaQU
13 vttirli DGMaPQX, utturli E, outerly FU, outurli Ha, vtterli LN; laftin E,
   laften K, leftin P
14 pertynynge D, pertening E, perteynyng F, perteninge LP; to: vn to E;
   life E, lyf FGHaLPQU
15 not (1°): ne I; shepe E; not (2°): ne I; oxen CaEFGHaKLMMaPRW;
   not (3°): ne EI; asses F
16 here HaQRU; folks E, flockes FR; her: alle E, here QR; tabernacles FR
17 and: om. U; at the: atte E; liknes DX, lickenesse G, licknesse KR, lijknesse
   Ma; locustis AcCCaDEGHaIKLMMaNPQRWX, locustes F
18 filleden CaFLMQW, felledin E, fulfilliden I; þinghes E, þinges FHa
19 camelis EGILPQ, cameles F; was: om. Ac; wiþoute CaFGLMMaNPR-
   SUWX, wiþouten IK
20 wasteden CaEFMPW, þei w. I, waastiden MaX; euere FGKQWX;
   toucheden CaFLMPUW, towchedyn E

5 Ipsi enim et et universi greges eorum veniebant cum
   tabernaculis suis, et instar locustarum universa
   complebant, innumera multitudo hominum et camelorum,
   quidquid tetigerant devastantes.

6 thei touchiden. And Yrael is mekid greetli

7 in the siȝt of Madian. And he cryede to
the Lord, askynge help aȝens Madianytis;

8 the which sente to hem a man prophete,
and spak, Thes thingis seith the Lord
God of Yrael, I haue maad ȝou to come
doun fro Egipt, and haue brouȝt ȝou out

9 fro the hous of seruage, and delyuerd fro
the hoond of Egipciens, and of alle the .
enemyes that tourmentiden ȝow; and
haue throwun hem out at* ȝoure entree,
and haue taak to ȝow the loond of hem;

20 toucheden *BCFLoX*, touchedyn *E*; meekid *C*, meked *EWo*, mekede *Lo*;
gretely *BFWo*, gretli *CEHLoX*
21 siȝte *CLoX*; cryed *BFHWo*, cride *E*
22 askende *CX*, askyng *HWo*; helpe *CHLoX*; aȝeyns *BEFLoWo*, aȝen *CX*
23 whiche *BCELoX*; sende *ELo*, sent *FHWo*; þem *CLoX*; propheet *E*
24 spake *Wo*; þese *CEX*; þinges *BELo*, thingus *CX*; seys *Lo*
25 made *BEHLoWo*, maade *F*, mad *X*; comme *F*
26 from *E*; broȝt *CX*, brouȝte *Lo*; oute *B*, ouȝte *H*, ouȝt *Lo*
27 house *B*, houȝs *H*; deliuered *CEHWo*, deliuerede *Lo*, deliuerid *X*
28 hond *CEWoX*, honde *Lo*; all *F*, al *H*
29 enmyes *BFHWo*, enemys *CX*; tormenteden *CX*, tormentedyn *E*
30 ha *C*; þrou *BF*, þrowe *CEWo*, þrouȝ *H*, throwen *LoX*; þem *CLo*; oute *B*,
ouȝt *H*; at: of *A*; ȝour *BCFH*; entre *CELoWoX*
31 ha *C*; take *BCEFHWoX*, taken *Lo*; lond *CEWoX*, londe *Lo*; þem *LoX*

6 Humiliatusque est Israel valde in conspectu Madian.

7 Et clamavit ad Dominum, postulans auxilium contra
Madianitas.

8 Qui misit ad eos virum prophetam, et locutus est:
Haec dicit Dominus Deus Israel: ego feci vos con-
/de/scendere de Aegypto, et eduxi vos de domo
servitutis,

9 et liberavi de manu Aegyptiorum, et omnium inimic-
orum, qui affligebant vos; eiecique eos ad introitum
vestrum, et tradidi vobis terram eorum;

6 iden. And Israel was maad low greetli
7 in the siȝt of Madian. And Israel criede
  to the Lord, and axyde help aȝens Ma-
8 dianytis; and he sente to hem a man, a
  profete, and he spak, The Lord God of   25
  Israel seith these thingis, Y made ȝou to
  stie fro Egipt, and Y ledde ȝou out of the
9 hows of seruage, and Y delyueride *ȝou* fro
  the hond of Egipcians, and of alle ene-
  myes that turmentiden ȝou; and Y cast-   30
  ide out hem at ȝoure entryng, and Y ȝaf

21 made DER; lowe CDMaR, lowȝ CaKMNW; maad low: lowed I; gretli
   AcEGIOPU, grettli L, greteli R
22 siȝte CaMaU; Israel: he I; cride CaUW, cried E
23 axed E, axede PU; and axyde: axynge I; helpe EGQRU; aȝenus AcCNO,
   a-ȝeinus E
24 sent E
25 profeete G, prophet I; spake ER, spake *to hem* I
26 seit E; þes DKNX; þinges FHa; maade G; to: om. R
27 steie F, stiȝe HaMaNR, stie up I; from K; lad E, ladde K; oute R
28 delyuerid D, deliuered E, delyuerede GHaLMNPUX, deliride S; ȝou: om.
   AcBCCaDEFGHaLMMaNOPQRSUWX; from K
29 honde EI; þe enmyes I
30 turmenteden CaFMPUW, turmented E, tourmentiden I; castid D,
   castede EFP, þrewe I
31 oute R; out hem: hem out I; ȝour CFKL; entrynge DGLMaQU, entree
   I; ȝaaf I, ȝaue R

10 and seide, I the Lord ȝoure God; ne
drede ȝe the goddis of Amorreis, in whos
loond ȝe dwellen; and ȝe wolden not here
11 my vois. Forsothe the aungel of the   35
Lord cam, and sat vndur the ook, that
was in Effra, and perteynede to Joas, the
fader of the meyne of Ezry. And whanne
Gedeon, the sone of hym, shockide out,
and purgide whetis in the pressynge   40
12 place, that he fleiȝ Madian, the aungel of
the Lord apperide to hym, and seith, The
Lord with thee, moost stroong of men.

32 ȝour *CFHLo*
33 dreed *B*, dreede *F*; ȝee *CLoX*; godis *CX*, goddus *F*, goddes *Wo*
34 lond *CEWoX*, londe *Lo*; ȝee (2x) *CLoX*; dwellyn *E*; wolde *BEFHLoWo*;
 heren *CX*, heere *F*
35 voyce *BFHLoWo*; forsoþ *B*; aungell *B*, aungil *CX*, angel *E*; Forsothe the
 aungel: þe a. f. *cet.*
36 lorde *Wo*; coom *BEF*, coome *H*, come *LoWo*; satt *BFH*, satte *Lo*, sate *Wo*;
 vndir *BEFHWo*, vnder *CX*, vndre *Lo*; ooke *BFHLoWo*, oc *CX*
37 perteyned *BEHWo*, pertenede *CX*
38 fadir *BE*, fadre *Lo*; whenn *B*, whan *CFWoX*, whenne *E*
39 shocked *BFHWo*, shakede *C*, shekede *E*, shokede *X*; oute *B*, ouȝt *H*
40 purgyd *BFHWo*, purgede *ELoX*; whetes *LoX*; pressing *CLoX*
41 fliȝ *BEFHLo*[2]; aungil *CX*, angel *E*
42 apeerid *BF*, aperede *CX*, apperede *E*, aperid *HWo*; seys *Lo*
43 lorde *Lo*; þe *LoWo*; most *BCEFHWoX*, moste *Lo*; stronge *BE*[1]*FHLoWo*,
 strong *CE*[2]*X*

10 et dixi: Ego Dominus Deus vester; ne timeatis deos
Amorreorum, in quorum terra habitatis. Et noluistis
audire vocem meam.
11 Venit autem angelus Domini, et sedit sub quercu,
quae erat in Effra, et pertinebat ad Ioas, patrem

10 to ȝou the lond of hem; and Y seide,
   Y am ȝoure Lord God; drede ȝe not
   the goddis of Ammorreis, in whose lond
   ȝe dwellen; and ȝe nolden here my vois.   35
11 Forsothe an aungel of the Lord cam, and
   sat vndur an ook, that was in Effra, and
   perteynede to Joas, fadir of the meinee
   of Ezri. And whanne Gedeon, his sone,
   threischide out, and purgide wheetis in   40
12 a pressour, that he schulde fle Madian, an
   aungel of the Lord apperide to hym, and
   seide, The Lord be with thee, thou strong-

32   the lond of hem: her londe I; saide E
33   ȝour FKL; ȝoure Lord God: þe lord ȝoure god I; dreede G; ȝee U
34   goddes F; in: & N; whos AcBCCaDEFGHaIKLMaNPQRWX; londe EI
35   ȝe (1°): ȝee U; dwelin E, dwellin P; ȝe (2°): ȝee U; nolde CER, wolden
     not I, noolden MaX; heere GHaMaNX; voice EI
36   Forsothe: And I, Forsoþ X; angel CE, aungil MaQ; the: om. L; came
     IR, cam doun Ma
37   sate DIR, satt KMa; vndir BDEGHaIKNPQRX, vnder FLMaU; oke
     DR, ok U
38   perteyned DE, perteynide HaQR, it perteynede I, perteynde CaSW; þe
     fadir EI, fader LMaU; meyne CaEFHaLMPQW, m[e]yne G
39   whan EHaLP; hise O; his sone: þe sone of ioas I
40   þreschide BCaFIMRW, þrischide C, þreisschid D, þreshed E, þreiȝsshide
     K, þreshede LP; out: om. I, oute R; purgid D, purgede EFKLPU, puyrgide
     R; wheetes BMaO, whetis CaEFLMPRW, whetes Ha, whete I
41   pressoure D, pressur U; scholde CaMW, shul E; flee CaEFGLP
42   angel CEI, aungil MaQ; apperid D, a-pered E, apperede FP, appeeride I,
     aperide R
43   saide E; þee: þe F; strongiste B, strongist DMa, strongest EHaLPQU,
     strengist I, stronge O

familiae Ezri. Cumque Gedeon, filius eius, excuteret
atque purgaret frumenta in torculari, ut fugeret
Madian,
12 apparuit ei angelus Domini, et ait: Dominus tecum,
   virorum fortissime.

13 And Gedion seide to hym, Y biseche, my
   lord, if the Lord is with vs, whi thanne   45
   han taak vs alle thes yuels? Where ben
   the merueyls of hym, the whiche oure
   faders tolden, and seiden, The Lord hath
   lad vs out of Egipt? Now forsothe he
   hath forsakun vs, and takun in the hoond   50
14 of Madian. And the Lord bihelde to
   hym, and seith, Go in this thi strength,
   and thou shalt delyuer Yrael fro the
   hoond of Madian; wite thow, that Y

44 seyd *B*; beseche *CX*
45 ȝif *BEFHWo*, ȝife *Lo*; þan *B*, þenne *E*, þann *FHWo*
46 take *BEFHWo*, taken *CLoX*; all *F*, om. *H*; þese *CEWoX*; euelis *C*, yuyls
    E, yueles *Lo*, eueles *WoX*; wher *CF*; been *E*
47 merueiles *CX*, merueylys *EWo*, meruailes *Lo*; which *CF*; our *F*
48 fadris *LoWo*, fadres *X*; toldyn *E*; seidyn *E*; has *Lo*
49 ladde *Lo*; oute *B*, ouȝte *H*; nowe *FLo*
50 hath: om. *H*, has *Lo*; forsaken *BCFHWoX*, forsake *E*, forsakyn *Lo*; taken
    BCFHLoWoX, takyn *E*; hoonde *B*, hond *CEX*, honde *LoWo*
51 beheeld *C*, byheld *EF*, biheeld *X*
52 seys *Lo*; goo *BF*; streyngþ *BF*, strengþe *CEHLoWoX*
53 þu *B*; deliuere *CELoX*; from *Lo*
54 honde *BLo*, hond *CEWoX*; witte *Lo*, wete *Wo*; that: in þat *X*

13 Dixitque ei Gedeon: Obsecro, domine mi, si Dominus
   nobiscum est, cur ergo apprehenderunt nos haec omnia
   mala? ubi sunt mirabilia eius, quae narraverunt
   patres nostri, atque dixerunt: de Aegypto eduxit
   nos Dominus? Nunc autem dereliquit nos, et tradidit
   in manu Madian.
14 Respexitque Dominus ad eum, et ait: Vade in hac
   fortitudine tua, et liberabis Israel de manu Madian;
   scito, quod miserim te.

13 este of men. And Gedeon seide to hym,
   My lord, Y biseche, if the Lord is with   45
   vs, whi therfor han alle these yuels take
   vs? Where ben the merueils of hym,
   whiche oure fadris telden, and seiden, The
   Lord ledde vs out of Egipt? Now forsothe he hath forsake vs, and hath bitake   50
14 vs in the hond of Madian. And the
   Lord bihelde to hym, and seide, Go thou
   in this strengthe of thee, and thou schalt
   delyuere Israel fro the hond of Madian;

44 of men: man R; said E
45 biseeche I
46 þerfore BCaFGKMaQRSUW, þarfor E, þanne I; þes DKNX; haue R;
    yuelis AcBCaDIMaOSUW, euelis ELPQ, yueles F, euylis G; tak E, taken
    FGIQ, takun N
47 wher CL, where P; meruels AcL, merueylis BDEGIMaNOPQWX, meruelis
    CU, merueiles CaFR, meruailis S; hym: þe lord I
48 which EF, wiche K; our E; faders E, fadres F; tolde E, teelden GMaQX,
    tolden IKLPR; saiden E
49 lad E, haþ led I, ladde K; 49–50 Now forsothe: for now I
50 hat E; forsak E, forsaken K
51 vs: om. AcBCFGHaLMMaNOPQRSUWX; in: in to AcK²Ma; honde EI
52 lorde E; biheeld CaGHaLMMaPQWX, biheld DS, biheuld K, biheelde R,
    bihilde U; hem R; saide E
53 this: þe E; strenkþe MaR; þe EF; schal Ha
54 delyuer R; from K; hond: lond D, honde EI

15 haue sent thee. The which answerynge 55
seith, My lord, Y biseche, in what shal
Y delyuer Yrael? Loo! my meyne is
lowest in Manasse, and Y leest in the
16 hows of my fader. And the Lord seide
to hym, I shal be with thee, and thow 60
17 shalt smyte Madian as o man. And he,
If Y haue foundun, he seith, grace before thee, ȝif to me a tokne, that thou
18 be, the which spekist with me; ne goo
thou hens, to the tyme that I turne aȝen 65
to thee, bryngynge sacrifice, and offrynge
to thee. The which answerde, Y shal

55 sende *ELo*; þe *EWo*; whiche *BCEHLoWoX*; answerende *CX*, answeringe
H, answeryng *Lo*
56 seys *Lo*; beseche *CX*
57 deliuere *CELo*, deliueren *X*; lo *CELoX*; meynee *BF*
58 lowist *BEFHWo*; Y: om. *X*; lest *BCEFHWoX*, leste *Lo*
59 house *B*, houȝs *H*; fadir *BEH*, fadre *Lo*
60 þe *EWo*
61 oo *BEFH*
62 ȝif *BEFHWo*, ȝife *Lo*; founde *BCEFHWo*, founden *LoX*; seys *Lo*; byfore
BEFHLoWo, befor *C*, bifor *X*
63 þe *EWo*; ȝeue *BFHLo*, ȝiue *Wo*; tooken *BF*, tookne *E*, token *HWo*
64 the which: whiche *BHLoX*, þat *C*[1]; spekest *CLo*; with: to *CELo*[2]; go
CELoWoX
65 henns *BF*, hennes *CLo*, hennys *E*, hennus *Wo*, henes *X*; torne *BEFHWo*;
aȝeyn *BEFWo*, aȝeen *CX*, aȝeyne *Lo*
66 þe *EWo*; bringende *CX*; offryng *BX*
67 þe *EWo*; whiche *BCEHLoX*; answerede *E*, answeride *Lo*, answered *Wo*

15 Qui respondens ait: Obsecro, Domine mi, in quo
liberabo Israel? ecce familia mea infima est in
Manasse, et ego minimus in domo patris mei.
16 Dixitque ei Dominus: Ego ero tecum, et percuties
Madian quasi unum virum.

15 wite thou, that Y sente thee. Which   **55**
Gedeon answeride, and seide, My lord,
Y biseche, in what thing schal Y delyuere
Israel? Lo! my meynee is the loweste
in Manasses, and Y am the leeste in the
16 hows of my fadir. And the Lord seide   **60**
to hym, Y schal be with thee, and thou
17 schalt smyte Madian as o man. And
Gedeon seide, If Y haue foundun grace
bifor thee, ȝyue to me a signe, that thou,
that spekist to me, art *sente of Goddis*   **65**
18 *part*; go thou not awei fro hennus, til
Y turne aȝen to thee, and brynge sacrifice,
and offre to thee. Which answeride, Y

55   wete U; sent E, haue sent I; þe EF; Which: And I, whiche K, whiche LP
56   answerde CaEFGMPQUW, answerid D, answerede L
57   biseeche GI, beseche U; diliuer E
58   loo S; meyne CaDEFGHaLMPQUW, lowist DIR, lowest EFHaU, lowiste LMaO
59   Manasses: þe lynage of M. I; leest AcDRU, leste EFMPW
60   house E; fader EFGLU; saide E
61   thee: þe ER
62   shal E; smyte *or skunfite* I, smyȝte U; o: a E, oo GHaKLPQR
63   founde AcBCCaEHaIKLMMaNOPRSWX, founden DGU
64   bifore BCCaDEGHaIKMaNQRWX; þe E; ȝeue BDGHaLMaQ, ȝif EU, ȝife K, ȝyue þou M; signe: tokene I
65   spekest EHaLR; to: wiþ K; sent AcBCaDEFGHaIKLMMaNOPQSUWX
66   parte R; & go CaIKX; awai E, aweie R; from K; awei fro: om. AcDGHaIK¹Ma²NOQSX; hennes CCaFHaMUW, hens DEGMaQR, henis LP, hennys NSX; til: to E
67   þe EFR; bryng DE; sacrifice: s. to þee X; 67−68 & br. s. & o. to thee: om. D, & br. s. to þee & o. X
68   offer E, offrere O, offere S; to thee: om. X; þe EF; whiche G, þe lord I, wich K; answerde CaEFGMPQUW, answerd D, answerede L

17 Et ille, Si inveni, inquit, gratiam coram te, da
mihi signum, quod tu sis, qui loqueris ad me;
18 ne/c/ recedas hinc, donec revertar ad te, portans
sacrificium, et offerens tibi. Qui respondit: Ego
praestolabor adventum tuum.

19 abide thi comynge. And so Gedeon
  wente in, and sethide a kydde, and of a
  busshel of flour therf looues, and fleish 70
  puttynge in the leep; and the flesh
  broththe puttynge in to the pot, he took
  alle thingis vndur the ook, and offerde
20 to hym. To whom seide the aungel of
  the Lord, Tak the flesh, and the therf 75
  looues, and putte vpon the stoon, and the
  broththe heelde there vpon. And whanne

68 commynge *BF*, comyng *CX*, commyng *Lo*
69 went *BFWo*; in: om. *H*, inne *Lo*; seeþid *BFH*, seeþede *C*, seþede *ELo*,
  seþid *Wo*, seth *X*; kide *CLoX*, kede *E*
70 buschell *B*; floure *LoWo*; þerue *CX*, þerfe *Lo*; loouys *BFWo*, loues *CX*,
  louys *E*; flesche *BLo*, flesh *CEFHWoX*
71 puttende *CX*; lep *CX*, lepe *Lo*, leepe *Wo*; flesche *BHLo*
72 broþ *CX*, brooþ *E*, brothe *Lo*; puttyng *BLo*, puttende *CX*; pott *BFHWo*,
  potte *Lo*; tooke *B*, toc *C*, toke *FHLoWo*
73 all *F*, al *H*; thingus *C*, þinges *Lo*; vndir *B*, vnder *CEFHWoX*, vndre *Lo*;
  ooke *BFHLoWo*, oc *CX*; offerd *B*, offride *C*, offrede *EX*, offred *FHWo*,
  offeride *Lo*
74 whome *BFLo*; aungil *CX*, angel *EWo*
75 take *BFHLoWo*; flesche *HLo*; þerfe *BLo*, þerue *CX*
76 loouys *BFHWo*, loues *C*, louys *E*, loeues *X*; putt *BFLo*, put *CELoX*; apon
  BH, opon *E*, uppon *Wo*; the (1°): þat *BCEFHLoWo*; ston *CWoX*
77 broth *CX*, brooþ *E*, brothe *Lo*; heeld *BCFX*, helde *EHWo*; þer *BCEFHWoX*;
  opon *E*, uppon *Wo*, on *X*; whenn *BH*, whan *CFWoX*, whenne *E*

19 Ingressus est itaque Gedeon, et coxit haedum, et de
  farinae modio azymos panes; carnesque ponens in
  canistro, et ius carnium mittens in ollam, tulit
  omnia sub quercu/m/, et obtulit ei.
20 Cui dixit angelus Domini: Tolle carnes et azymos
  panes, et pone super petram illam, et ius desuper
  funde. Cumque fecisset ita,

19 schal abide thi comyng. And so Gedeon
   entride, and sethide a kide, and took   70
   therf looues of a buyschel of mele, and
   fleischis in a panyere; and he sente the
   broth of fleischis in a pot, and bar alle
   thingis vndur an ook, and offride to
20 hym. To whom the aungel of the Lord   75
   seide, Take thou the fleischis, and therf
   looues, and putte on that stoon, and
   schede the broth aboue. And whanne

69 comynge DFGLMMaPQRU
70 entrid D, entred E, ȝede in I, entrede PU; seid E, seþede FKLP, siþide G,
   seeþe I, seeþ U; kid Ha, kede U; tok EFU, tooke Ha, he took I, toke R
71 þeerf C, therue Ha, þerff I, þerfe KR, þerof L¹; loues DEFR, loouys GQ;
   busschel CaDEFGHaILMOPQRW, buyȝscheel K, boishel N; meele GQ
72 flesschis CaELMPQRW, flesches F, fleish I, fleiȝsshis K; in: in to C;
   panyer BCCaEFHaIKMMaNRWX; sent AcEO, putte IM
73 brooþ AcMaR; flesshis CaELMPQRW, flesches F, þe fleshe I, fleiȝsshis
   K; in: AC, in to cet.; pott IKMaX; bare CDHaR, baar EKNPX, he bare I
74 þinges FHa, þese þingis I; vndir BDGHaIKMaNPQRS, vnder FLUX;
   an: þe I; ooke E, oke R; offrid D, offred E, offride þo I, offrede PU,
   offeride S
75 wam E; angel CI, anghel E, aungil Ma
76 saide E; flesschis CaLMPQRW, flesshes EF, fleshe I, fleiȝsshis K; and: of
   Ac; þerue Ha, þe þerff I, þerfe KR
77 loues DEF, loouys GQ; put CEFS, putte hem I, putt R; stone E, ston HaU
78 sheede G, helde I, shedde LO, scheed U; the: om. S; brooþ AcMaR,
   broþe E; a boof R; whan EHaLP

175

21 he hadde doo so, the aungel of the Lord
strei ʒte out the vttermost paart of the
ʒeerde that he heelde in hoond, and he   80
touchid the flesh, and the therf looues;
and fier stiede up fro the stoon, and con-
sumede the flesh, and the therf looues.
Forsothe the aungel of the Lord va-
nysshide awey fro the eyen of hym.   85
22 And Gedeon seynge that it was the aun-
gel of the Lord seith, Wo me, Lord God,
for Y haue seen the aungel of the Lord
23 face to face. And the Lord seide to hym,
Pees with thee; ne drede thow, thou   90

78 had *BFLoWo*; do *CEHWoX*, doon *Lo*; soo *BWo*; aungil *CX*, angel *EWo*
79 straʒte *CX*, streiʒt *Wo*; oute *BF*, ouʒte *H*; vttermast *BH*, vtmost *CX*,
   otemost *E*, vttermaste *Lo*; parte *BFHLo*, part *CEWoX*
80 ʒerde *BCFHLoWoX*, ʒerd *E*; helde *BEFHLoWo*, heeld *CX*; hond *CX*,
   hoonde *H*, honde *LoWo*
81 touchide *C*, touchede *ELoX*, touʒchid *H*; flesche *Lo*; the: om. *X*; þerfe
   BFLoX, therue *C*; loues *CWoX*, louys *E*
82 fijr *C*, fuyr *E*, fuyre *LoWo*; steyʒid *BFWo*, steʒede *CX*, styʒede *E*, styʒid *H*,
   steiʒed *Lo*; opp *E*; stoone *BF*, ston *CX*, stone *HWo*; consumed *BFHWo*
83 flesche *HLo*; þerue *CX*, therfe *Lo*; loues *CWo*, louys *E*, loeues *X*
84 Forsothe the aungel: þe a. f. *cet.*; aungil *CX*, angel *E*; vanyschid *BFHWo*,
   vanshide *C*, vanysched *E*, vanyschede *Lo*, vanshede *X*
85 aweye *BH*; eyʒen *BFHLoWoX*, eʒen *C*, yʒyn *E*
86 And: om. *C*; seeynge *BFH*, seande *C*, seeing *Lo*, seʒinge *Wo*, seende *X*;
   hit *E*; aungil *CX*, angel *EWo*
87 saiþ *E*, seys *Lo*
88 seeyʒen *BFH*, seyn *E*, seiʒen *Wo*; aungil *CX*, angel *EWo*; lorde *Wo*
89 seid *B*
90 pese *B*, pes *CX*; þe *EWo*; dreed *B*

21 extendit angelus Domini summitatem virgae, quam
tenebat in manu, et tetigit carnes et azymos panes;
ascenditque ignis de petra, et carnes azymosque
panes consumpsit; angelus autem Domini evanuit ex
oculis eius.

21 he hadde do so, the aungel of the Lord
   helde forth the ende of the ȝerde which   80
   he helde in the hond, and he touchide
   the fleischis, and the therf looues; and
   fier stiede fro the stoon, and wastide the
   fleischis, and therf looues. Forsothe the
   aungel of the Lord vanyschide fro hise   85
22 iȝen. And Gedeon siȝ that he was an
   aungel of the Lord, and seide, Lord God,
   alas to me, for I siȝ the aungel of the
23 Lord face to face. And the Lord seide to
   hym, Pees be with thee; drede thou not,   90

79 he: Gedeon l; had EI; angel CEI, aungil MaQ
80 heeld CaGLMMaPQWX, held FN, heuld K; forþe E, foorþ P; eende
   BHaIKMa, end E; ȝerd HaN, ȝarde K, ȝeerd R; e. of the ȝ.: ȝerdus
   eende I; which: þat I, wich K
81 heeld CaDGLMMaNPQWX, held F, heuld K; the: his I; honde E;
   touchid D, touched E, touchede PU
82 flesschis CaLMPQRW, fleshes EF, fleshe I, fleiȝsshis K; þerue Ha, þerff I,
   þerfe R; loues DEFR, loouys GQ; 82 and … looues (84): om. GHaQ
83 fiȝr CaIMW, fire DE, fyr FLP; stied DE, steiede F, stiede up I, stiȝede
   MaNR; from K; stone E, ston U; waastide CCaMaX, wastid D, wasted E,
   wastede FKP, deuowride I
84 flesschis CaLMPRUW, fleisch D, fleshes EF, fleshe I, fleiȝsshis K; þe þerf
   I, þerfe K, þe þerfe R; loues DEFM, loouis L; for[so]þe Ac, & I
85 angel CEI, aungil MaQ; vaneschide B, rauyschid D, uanised E, vanyschede
   FILU, vaniȝshide K, vanishde P; from K; his EFGILPQX
86 eiȝen CaFMUW, iȝhen I; seiȝ CaFMW, sawȝe I, siȝe R; that: whase (?) E
87 angel CE, aungil Ma; an a. of the L.: þe lordis angel I; said E, he s. I
88 allas K; seiȝ CaFMW, sawȝe I, seȝ L¹, siȝe R; angel CEI
89 saide E
90 pes I; with: to GQ; þe E; dreede G; nouȝt L

22 Vidensque Gedeon, quod esset angelus Domini, ait:
   Heu mihi, Domine Deus, quia vidi angelum Domini
   facie ad faciem.
23 Dixitque ei Dominus: Pax tecum; ne timeas, non
   morieris.

24 shalt not dye. Thanne Gedeon bilde there
an auter to the Lord, and he clepide it
the Pees of the Lord, vnto the day that is
now. And whanne ȝit he hadde be in
25 Effra, that is the meyne of Ezry, that 95
nyȝt the Lord seide to hym, Tak the bole
of thi fader, and another bole of seuen
ȝeer, and thou shalt distruye the auter of
Baal, that is of thi fader, and the wode,

91 schal *X*; dyȝe *BFHWo*, deyȝe *E*, dien *X*; þann *B*, þenne *E*; bulde *E*; þer
BEFH
92 autere *Lo*; lorde *Wo*; cleepe *B*, clepede *C*, cleep *EF*, clepid *H*, callid *Lo*,
clepe *Wo*; hit *E*
93 pese *B*, pes *CX*; lorde *Wo*
94 nowe *BLo*; whenn *BH*, whan *CLoWoX*, whenne *E*, whann *F*; ȝitt *BFH*;
had *LoWo*; ben *Lo*
95 meynee *BFH*
96 nyȝte *Lo*; take *BFHLoWo*, taak *E*; boole *C*
97 fadir *B*, fadre *Lo*; boole *C*; seuene *CEHLoWoX*
98 ȝere *BLoWo*, ȝer *CX*; destruye *BFWo*, destroȝe *C*, destrue *E*, destrye *H*,
destroye *Lo*, distroȝe *X*
99 fadir *BEH*, fadre *Lo*

24 Aedificavit ergo ibi Gedeon altare Domino, vocavitque illud Domini pax, usque in praesentem diem.
Cumque adhuc esset in Effra, quae est familia/e/
Ezri,
25 nocte illa dixit Dominus ad eum: Tolle taurum patris
tui, et alterum taurum annorum septem, destruesque
aram Baal, quae est patris tui; et nemus, quod circa
aram est, succide;

24 thou schalt not die. Therfor Gedeon
bildide there an auter to the Lord, and
he clepide it the Pees of the Lord, til in
to present dai. And whanne he was ʒit
in Effra, which is of the meynee of Ezri,   95
25 the Lord seide to hym in that nyʒt, Take
thou the bole of thy fadir, and anothir
bole of seuene ʒeer, and thou schalt distrie
the auter of Baal, which is thi fadris,
and kitte thou doun the wode, which is   100

91 schal E; deie CaFMW, diʒe R; þerfore BCaFGKLMMaNQRSWX,
   þanne I
92 bildid D, bilde E, bildede LP, beeldide R; þer ES; auteer G, aunter Ha
93 he: om. U; clepid DEP, clepede F; pes I; til: om. EI; in: vn I
94 present: þe pr. E, þis pr. IK¹; wan E, whan GHaLP; he: Gedeon I; ʒut E,
   ʒitt Ma
95 þe whiche I, wich K; meyne CCaDEFGHaLMPQUW; of (2°): om. N
96 seid E; s. to hym in that n.: in þat n. s. to him I; tak E
97 the: om. S; boul E, boole Ma; fader CaFNU; the b. of thy f.: þi fadris
   bole I; an oþere Ac, an oþer BCCaDFGHaIKLMNPQRSUW, an oþur E
98 bool D, boul E, boole Ma; seuen CaM; ʒere E, ʒer LP; destroie E, destrie
   IK, distroie MaRU, distruye X
99 auteer G; which: þat I, wich K

26 that is about the auter, hew doun; and 100
thou shalt bilde an auter to the Lord thi
God in the ouermost of this stoon, vpon
the which thou puttist before sacrifice;
and thou shalt take the secounde bole,
and offer brent sacrifice vpon the hepe of 105
wode, that thou hast kut of the wode.
27 Thann Gedeon taken-to ten men of his
seruauntis, dide as the Lord comaundide
to hym. Forsothe dredynge the hows of
his fader, and the men of that cytee, by 110
day he wold not doon, but alle thingis

100 aboute BCEFLoX, abouȝte H; hewe BFHLoWoX
101 bulde E; autere Lo
102 ouemost E, ouermaste Lo; stone Wo, ston CX; opon E, vppon Wo
103 the: om. C; whiche BCEHLoWoX; puttest LoWoX; byfore BEFHLoWo,
beforn C, biforn X; sacrefice Wo
104 secunde X; boole C
105 offre CEFHLoWoX; sacrefice Wo; opon E, vppon Wo; hep CX, heep EF
106 woode (2x) E; þu B; cutt BFHWo, cutte Lo
107 þanne CLoX, þenne E, þan HWo; takende C, takyn E; tenn BH
108 seruauntus C, seruauntes Lo, seruauns X; dede CE; lorde Wo; comaundid
BFHWo, comaundede CE
109 Forsothe dredynge: dr. f. cet.; dredende CX, dreedynge F, dredyng Lo;
houȝs H
110 fadir BEH, fadre Lo; cyte BCEHLoWo
111 wolde CEFHLoWoX; do C, don WoX; bot B, bote E, bute F; al BHLo,
all F; þinges Lo, thingus X

26 et aedificabis altare Domino Deo tuo in summitate
petrae huius, super quam posuisti ante sacrificium;
tollesque taurum secundum, et offeres holocaustum
super struem lignorum, quae de nemore succideris.
27 Assumptis igitur Gedeon decem viris de servis suis,
fectit sicut praeceperat ei Dominus. Timens autem
domum patris sui, et homines illius civitatis, per
diem noluit facere, sed omnia nocte complevit.

180

26 aboute the auter; and thou schalt bilde
an auter to thi Lord God in the hiȝnesse
of this stoon, on which thou puttidist
sacrifice bifore; and thou schalt take the
secounde bole, and thou schal offre brent   105
sacrifice on the heep of trees, whiche
27 thou kittidist doun of the wode. Therfor
Gedeon took ten men of hise seruauntis,
and dide as the Lord comaundide to hym.
Sotheli Gedeon dredde the hows of his   110
fadir, and the men of that citee, and nolde
do bi dai, but fillide alle thingis bi nyȝt.

100 kitte thou: kitto E; doune E; wood Ha, wote S; whiche DG, wich EK,
     þat I
101 a bout E, abouȝte L; auteer G; beelde R
102 auteer GQ; heiȝnesse CaFMW, hiȝnes E, hiȝenesse RSX
103 ston HaU; on: vpon I, in N; whiche AcDGLQ, þe whiche I, wiche K;
     puttedist CaMNW, puttedest EFLPU, puttidest HaK, puttideste R, p.
     þis X
104 bifor LU; shal E; the: þis KX
105 secunde BCEMaNQR, secound DP, seconde K; boole D, boul E; shalt
     AcBCCaDEGHaKLMNPQRSUWX; offren B; brente R, brende U
106 on: upon I; hepe E; the h. of: om. S; which EFRSX, þe whiche I, wiche K
107 kittidest BHa, kittedist CaNUW, kittedest EKLP, kittest F, kittist M,
     kittideste R; doune E; woode G, wood Ha; þerfore BCaEGKLMMaN-
     QRUWX, þanne I
108 toke HaIR; men: om. GHaQ; his EFGIPQX, om. L; seruaunteȝ EFGHa
109 did E, he dide I; as the: aste E; comaundid D, comandid E, comaundede
     LP
110 Sotheli: soþli FGLMMaPQUWX, & I; dred E; [h]ys E
111 fader EFLM; cite FHaMQWX; nolde: he wolde not I, noolde MaX
112 daie CaM; bot E; fillid D, fu[l]filled E, fillede FLP, he fulfillide I; al E;
     þinges FHa; nyȝte CaDLMNPW, night E, niȝtis Ma

28 the nyȝt he fulfilde. And whanne the
men of his burgh toun(s) erly weren rysen,
thei seen the auter of Baal destruyed,
and the mawmet woode hewun doun, 115
and another bole set vpon the auter, that
29 thanne was bild vp. And thei seiden
to gidre, Who hath doon this? And
whanne thei souȝten the doer of the dede,
it is seide, Gedeon, the sone of Joas, dide 120
30 alle thes thingis. And thei seiden to
Joas, Bryng forth thi sone hider, that he
be deed, for he hath destruyed the auter

112 nyȝte *Lo*; fulfillide *B*, folfullede *E*, fulfyllid *FWo*; whenn *BH*, whan
CFLoWo, whenne *E*
113 borgh *BFH*, burȝ *CX*, borw *E*, borghe *Lo*; were *E*; risun *E*
114 seeyȝen *BF*, seȝe *C*, syȝyn *E*, seeȝen *H*, sawen *Lo*, seyȝen *Wo*, seȝen *X*;
autere *Lo*; destruyȝid *BFH*, destroȝid *C*, destrued *E*, distroyede *Lo*,
distroȝed *X*
115 maumett *BFHWo*, maumete *CELo*; wode *cet.*; hewe *BCEFHWoX*, hewen
Lo
116 boole *C*; sett *BEFHWo*, sette *Lo*; apon *B*, opon *E*, uppon *Wo*, on *X*;
autere *Lo*
117 þann *BF*, þenne *E*, þan *LoWo*; bylde *BFHLoWo*, buld *E*; opp *E*; seidyn *E*
118 to giþers *BF*, togidere *CX*, to geders *E*, to gyders *H*, to gidres
Lo, to gideres *Wo*; has *Lo*; don *CWo*, done *H*, do *X*
119 whenn *BH*, whan *CFLoWoX*, whenne *E*; soȝten *CX*, souȝtyn *E*; doere
CLoX; deede *CX*
120 hit *E*; seid *CX*; dede *E*
121 all *BF*; þese *CEX*; þinges *BLo*, thingus *CX*; seide *BFHWo*, seidyn *E*
122 brynge *BHLoWo*; forþe *Lo*; hyþer *BF*, hedur *E*, hidre *Lo*
123 dead *BCX*, ded *EH*, dede *LoWo*; has *Lo*; destroȝed *CX*, destrued *E*,
destroyede *Lo*

28 Cumque surrexissent viri oppidi eius mane, viderunt
destructam aram Baal, lucumque succisum, et taurum
alterum impositum super altare, quod tunc aedifica-
tum erat.
29 Dixeruntque ad invicem: Quis hoc fecit? Cumque per-

28 And whanne men of that citee hadde rise
eerly, thei sien the auter of Baal distried,
and the wode kit doun, and the tothir bole   115
put on the auter, that was bildid thanne.
29 And thei seiden to gidere, Who hath do this?
And whanne thei enqueriden the doer(is) of
the dede, it was seid, Gedeon, the sone of
30 Joas, dide alle these thingis. And thei   120
seiden to Joas, Brynge forth thi sone
hidur, that he die, for he distriede the
auter of Baal, and kittide doun the wode.

113   whan EHaLP; þe men I; cite FHaMPQW; hadden AcBCCaDEFGHa-
IKLMMaNOQRSWX, haddin P; risen L, rese U
114   erly EGLQU; & þei Ac; seiȝen CaM, siȝen EGKMaNQR, seien FW, seen
Ha, sawȝen I; auteer G; distriede AcO, destroied E, destried I, distroied
KR, distruyed X
115   wood Ha; kitte D, kutt K, kitt MaX; doune E; toþer
AcBCCaDFGHaIKLMMaNOPQRUWX, oþer E; bool DE, boole R
116   putte DHa, putt KMa; upon I; auteer G; bilded EKL, beldid R; þan E
117   to gidre DIR, to ghider E, togider P; Wo E; haþe E
118   when E, whan GLMP; enquereden CaEFMPUW, enquerden D; doere
AcCaFGLMMaNOPQSUW
119   deede GLMaP, deed R; seide DRU, saide E
120   did E; þes DKNX, þise EU; þinges FHa; þai E
121   saiden E; Bring EGU; forþe E; 121–22 thi sone hidur: hidir þi sone I
122   hider EF, om. GQ, hidir IKMaNUX, hedir LP, hiþer R; deie CaFMW,
diȝe R; distried D, destroied E, destroiede Ha, haþ destried I, distroiede
KR, destriede L, distruyede X
123   auteer G; kittid D, kitt E, haþ kit I, kittede KLP, kitte U; a-doune E;
wood DHa, woode G, wode *aboute it* I

quirerent auctorem facti, dictum est: Gedeon,
filius Ioas, fecit haec omnia.
30 Et dixerunt ad Ioas: Produc filium tuum huc, ut
moriatur, quia destruxit aram Baal, et succidit
nemus.

31 of Baal, and hewen doun the wode. To
  whom he answerde, Whether ȝe ben   125
  wrechers of Baal, that ȝe fiȝten for hym?
  who is the aduersarye of hym, dye he,
  before the morwetide liȝt come; if he is
  God, venge he hymsilf of hym that hath
32 deluen vp the auter of hym. Fro that   130
  day Gedeon is clepid Jeroboal, forthi that
  Joas seide, Baal taak veniaunce of hym
  that hath doluen down the auter of hym.
33 Therfor al Madian, and Amelech, and the
  este puplis ben gedrid to gidre, and pass-   135
  ynge ouer Jordan settiden tentis in the

124 hewe *BCEFHWoX*
125 whome *BFLoWo*; answerd *B*, answerede *E*, answeride *Lo*, answered *Wo*;
    wher *H*, where *Lo*; ȝee *CLoX*; been *E*; 125−6 ȝe ben wrechers: wr. ȝ. b.
    *CELo*²
126 wreechers *B*, wrekeris *C*, wrekers *E*, wrekers *Lo*, wrekeres *X*; ȝee *CLoX*;
    fiȝt *BFHWo*, fiȝte *CELoX*
127 aduersary *FHWo*; dyȝe *BFHWo*, deyȝe *E*
128 byfore *BEFHLoWo*, befor *C*, biforn *X*; morwtyde *BFHWo*, morntid *CX*,
    morwe tide *Lo*; liȝte *Lo*; comme *BF*; ȝif *BEFHWo*, ȝife *Lo*
129 hymself *cet.*
130 doluen *CHLoX*, deluyn *E*; opp *E*
131 cleped *E*, callid *Lo*
132 take *cet.*; vengeaunce *Lo*
133 has *Lo*; dolue *BCE*
134 þerfore *BCEFHWoX*, þerefore *Lo*
135 est *CX*, eest *ELoWo*; peplis *BEFHWo*, peples *Lo*, puples *X*; been *E*;
    geþerd *BF*, gedered *CEWoX*, gederd *H*, gaderide *Lo*; to giþers *BF*, togidere
    CX, to geders *E*, to gyders *H*, to gidres *Lo*, to gideris *Wo*; passende *CX*,
    passyng *HLo*
136 setten *CX*, settedyn *E*, setteden *Lo*; tentus *C*, tentes *X*

31 Quibus ille respondit: Numquid ultores estis Baal,
  ut pugnetis pro eo? qui adversarius est eius, moriatur, antequam lux crastina veniat; si Deus est,
  vindicet se de eo, qui suffodit aram eius.
32 Ex illo die vocatus est Gedeon Ierobaal, eo quod

31 To whiche he answeride, Whether ȝe ben
the venieris of Baal, that ȝe fiȝte for hym? 125
he that is aduersarie of hym, die, bifor
that the liȝt of the morew dai come;
if he is God, venge he hym silf of hym
32 that castide doun his auter. Fro that dai
Gedeon was clepid Gerobaal, for Joas 130
hadde seid, Baal take veniaunce of hym
33 that castide doun his auter. Therfor al
Madian, and Amalech, and the puplis of
the eest weren gadirid to gidere, and passiden Jordan, and settiden tentis in the 135

124 which F, whom I, wiche K; he: ioas I; answerde CaFGMPQUW, answerid
D, answerd E, answerede L; where DEI, wher cet.; ȝee GU; been E
125 vengeris AcBCaGMaPQW, veniers DIMX, vengers EHaLR, vengeers K;
ȝee HaU
126 deie CaMW, dye he I, diȝe R; bifore BCaDEGHaIKMaNQRW
127 that: om. I; morewe AcCCaFGMOUW, morn B, morwe DLNPQ, morowe
EHaIKMaRX; liȝt of the morew dai: morowe liȝt I
128 if: And L; venie O; self CaEFIKMPRUW, sif Ma
129 castid D, cast E, castede FP, haþ cast I, caste U; a-doune E; auteer G;
from K
130 for: for þat CaDMaOS², for þi þat GHaIKNQS¹X
131 had EI; seide DRU, said E; tak L; Baal take: Take B. I; vengeaunce GK
132 castid D, castede EFP, haþ cast I, castiden S, caste U; doune E; his: þin
E; auteer G; þerfore BCaEGIKLMaNQRWX
133 peplis CaLMMaNPWX, puples E, peples FI
134 est EQ; werin P; gaderid AcBCaDFHaMMaNOPQSW, gederid CKX,
gadered ELU, gadrid GR, gedrid I; to gidre DIR, to ghiders E, to gider P;
passeden CaFLMPW, passed E, þei passide ouer I
135 setteden CaEFLMPUW, þei settiden I; tentes F

dixisset Ioas: Ulciscatur se de eo Baal, qui suffodit altare eius.
33 Igitur omnis Madian, et Amalech, et orientales
populi congregati sunt simul, et transeuntes
Iordanem castrametati sunt in valle Iezrael.

34 valey of Jezrael. Forsothe the spyryt of
the Lord clothide Gedeon; the which
criynge with tromp clepide to gidre the
hows of Abiezer, for he shulde folwe   140
35 hym. And he sente messangers into al
Manassen, the which and he folwide
hym; and other messangers into Aser,
and Zabulon, and Neptalym, the whiche
36 aȝen camen to hym. And Gedeon seide   145
to the Lord, If thow makist saaf bi myn
hoond the puple of Irael, as thow hast

137 Forsothe the spyryt: þe sp. f. *cet.*; spyryte *BFLo*, spiriȝte *H*, sperit *X*
138 cloþid *BFH*, cloþede *CELo*, cloþed *Wo*; whiche *BCEHLoWoX*
139 criende *CX*, crying *Lo*; trompe *BEFHLo*, trumpe *CWoX*; clepid *BFHWo*,
    clepede *CEX*, callid *Lo*; to giþers *BF*, togidere *CX*, to geders *E*, to gyders
    H, to gidres *Lo*, to gideres *Wo*
140 houȝs *H*; sholde *ELo*, schuld *Wo*; folowe *BFHLoWo*, folewen *C*, folewe *X*
141 sent *BFHWo*, sende *ELo*, messageres *CX*, messungers *E*, messageris *Lo*,
    messangeres *Wo*; alle *BLo*, all *F*
142 whiche *BCEHLoX*; folowid *BFHWo*, folewide *C*, folwede *E*, folwed *Lo*,
    folewede *X*
143 oþere *C*; messageres *CWoX*, messungers *E*, messagers *Lo*
144 which *FWo*
145 aȝeyn *BEFWo*, aȝeen *C*, aȝeyne *Lo*, aȝen *X*; commen *B*, comyn *E*,
    commenn *F*, comen *HLoWoX*
146 lorde *Wo*; ȝif *BEFHWo*, ȝife *Lo*; makest *LoX*; saue *BFWo*, sue *H*, saufe *Lo*
147 hond *CWoX*, honde *Lo*; peple *BFHLoWo*

34 Spiritus autem Domini induit Gedeon, qui clangens
bucina convocavit domum Abiezer, ut sequeretur se.
35 Misitque nuntios in universum Manassen, qui et ipse
secutus est eum; et alios nuntios in Aser, et
Zabulon, et Neptalim, qui occurrerunt ei.
36 Dixitque Gedeon ad Dominum: Si salvum facis per
manum meam /populum/ Israel, sicut locutus es,

34 valey of Jezrael. Forsothe the spirit of the
Lord clothide Gedeon; and he sownede
with a clarioun, and clepide to gidere the
hows of Abiezer, that it schulde sue hym.

35 And he sente messangeris in to al Ma-   140
nasses, and he suede Gedeon; and *he sente*
othere messangeris in to Aser, and Zabulon, and Neptalym, whiche camen to

36 hym. And Gedeon seide to the Lord, If
thou makist saaf Israel bi myn hond, as   145

136 forsoþ X; spiritt K, spiriȝt L; of: om. S
137 cloþid D, cloþed E, cloþide '*or fulfillide*' I, cloþede KLPR; and he: þe
   whiche I; sownyde AcGHaQR, sowned DE, sownynge I
138 clarioune E, trumpe I, clarion K; and: om. I; clepid DE, clepede F; to
   gidre DI, to ghider E, togider P
139 hows: meynee I, sones X; scholde CaMW, shuld E; suwe CaFMW
140 sent E; messangers DIMX, messageres EHa, messangeres FR, messagers K,
   messengers LP, massangeris O; alle C¹E
141 he: om. L; suwide CaMW, suwede F, sue L, suide Q; sent E
142 oþer ELP, om. G; messangers CDFIMRX, messangeris E, messangeres Ha,
   messagers K, messengers L, massangeris O, messengeris P; and Z.: & to
   Z. CaDGHaIKMMaNOQSX
143 and N.: & to N. O; which EL, & þei I, wiche K; come E
144 saide E
145 makest EFHaLR; saue E; myne ER; honde E

37 spokun, Y shal put this fleese of wul in
   the floore; if dewe in the fleese alone
   were, and in al the erthe drouȝth, Y shal   150
   wyte, that bi myn hoond, as thou hast
38 spokun, thow shalt delyuer Yrael. And
   it is doo so. And fro the niȝt risynge,
   thrust out of the fleese, he fulfillide an
39 holwȝ vessel with dew; and eft he seide   155
   to the Lord, Ne wexe not wrooth thi
   woodnes aȝens me, if ȝit ones Y tempte
   a tokne sechynge in the fleese; Y preye,
   that oonli the fleese be drye, and al the

148 spoken *BFHLoWoX*, spoke *C*, spokyn *E*; putt *BWo*, putte *CEFHX*; flees
    CLoX, fluys *E*, flese *HWo*; wull *BF*, wlle *CX*, wolle *EWo*, wulle *H*, woole *Lo*
149 flore *BFHWo*, floor *CEX*, flor(þ)e *Lo*; ȝif *BEFHWo*, ȝife *Lo*; dew *CEX*;
    flees *CX*, fluys *E*, flese *HWo*; aloon *BFH*, allone *ELo*, aloone *Wo*
150 alle *B*, all *F*; erþ *BF*; drouȝþe *CEHLoWo*, droȝte *X*
151 wete *Wo*; hond *BCEWoX*, honde *Lo*; has *Lo*
152 spoke *BCEFHWoX*, spoken *Lo*; deliuere *CELo*, delyueren *X*
153 hit *E*; do *CHWoX*, doon *Lo*; the: om. *cet.*; nyȝte *Lo*; risende *CX*
154 þrest *CX*, þruste *E*, thriste *Lo*; oute *B*, ouȝt *H*; of: om. *X*; flees *C*, fluys *E*,
    flese *Wo*; fulfilled *BWo*, fulfilde *CLoX*, folfullede *E*, fulfillyd *FH*; a *Lo*
155 holu *C*, holwe *E*, holowȝ *HWo*, holowȝe *Lo*, holȝ *X*; vessell *B*; dewe
    BFHLoWo; efte *Lo*
156 lorde *Lo*; waxe *CELoX*; wroþe *BFHLoWo*, wroþ *CX*; thi: in *B*
157 wodenesse *BLoWo*, wodnesse *CX*, woodenesse *FH*; aȝeyns *BEFWo*, aȝen
    CX; ȝif *BEFHWo*, ȝife *Lo*; ȝitt *BFHWo*, ȝet *E*; oons *BH*, onys *EWo*,
    oonys *F*
158 tooken *BFH*, tookne *E*, token *LoWo*; sechende *CX*, seching *H*; flees *CX*,
    fluys *E*, flese *Wo*; prey *BEFH*, preȝe *CX*, preyȝe *Lo*, pray *Wo*

37 ponam hoc vellus lanae in area; si ros in solo
   vellere fuerit, et in omni terra siccitas, sciam,
   quod per manum meam, sicut locutus es, liberabis
   Israel.
38 Factumque est ita. Et de nocte consurgens, expresso
   vellere concham rore implevit.

37 thou hast spoke, Y schal putte this flees
of wolle in the corn floor; if dew is in
the flees aloone, and drynesse is in al the
erthe, Y schal wite, that thou schalt dely-
uere Israel bi myn hond, as thou hast   150
38 spoke. And it was don so. And he roos
bi nyȝt, and whanne the flees was wrongun
39 out, he fillide a pot with deew; and he
seide eft to the Lord, Thi strong veniaunce
be not wrooth aȝens me, if Y asaie, *that*   155
is, axe a signe, ȝit onys, and seke a signe
in the flees; Y preye, that the flees aloone
be drie, and al the erthe be moist with

146 tou E; haast R; spoken I; put ER; fles D, flese E, fleus K
147 wulle CaMW, wol E, wole R; corn: drie I, corne R; flore DEHaR, flor U;
   deew AcBKLMaSU, dewe DR, þe dewe I
148 flese E, fleus K; alone CaEFKLMPUW, aloon R; drienesse
   AcBCCaHaMMaNOSUWX, drines E, driȝnesse HaKQR; alle E; the: om.
   B
149 eerþe Ca; þat: 2x Ha; schal Ha; diliuer E
150 myne E, my K; honde E; haast R
151 spoken K; doon BCaFKMMaW, done ER; he: Gedeon I; rose EFK
152 nyȝte CaEKLMMaPUW; whan EHaLP; flese E, fleus K; wrungen CaMW,
   wrongon E, wrongen FGHaIKLMaPRS, wrungun X
153 oute L; fillid D, filled E, fillede FKLP, fellede U; pott IKMa; dew
   CCaEFGHaMNOPQSX, dewe DIR
154 said E; efte ELR; stronge AcCCHaLRU; vengeaunce GIKR
155 wroþ CEFHaLNPQUX, wroiþ K; aȝenus AcCNO, a ȝeins E; ȝif E;
   assaie CaKLMPW, seie G, say Ha
156 is: om. G; aske ELP; sing E; gloss om. IX; ȝitt IMa; oonys BDGHaMaN
   PQX, ones Ca, oons I, oones KL; seche I; signe: tokene I
157 flees (2x): flese E, fleus K; praie W; alone CaEFKLMW
158 dri E, driȝe K; and: & þat I; eerþe R; moiste Ma

39 Dixitque rursus ad Dominum: Ne irascatur furor tuus
contra me, si adhuc semel temptavero, signum quaerens in vellere. Oro ut solum vellus siccum sit, et
omnis terra rore madens.

40 erthe with dew moyst. And the Lord   160
    dide that ny3t, as he axide; and there
    was drou3th in the fleese alone, and
    dewe in al the erthe.

7. 1 Thanne Jeroboal,
    the which and Gedeon, fro ny3t rysynge,
    and al the puple with hym, cam to the
    wel that is clepid Arad. Forsothe the
    tentis of Madian weren in the valey, at   5
    the north coost of the hi3e hil.
  2 And the Lord seide to Gedeon, Myche
    is the puple with thee, and lest Yrael
    glorie a3ens me, Madian shal not be taak
    into the hoondis of hym, and lest he seye,   10

159 onli *CWoX*; flees *CX*, fluys *E*, flese *Wo*; dry3e *BEFHWo*; alle *B*, all *F*
160 erþ *B*; dew: þe dewe *BFHLoWo*, þe dew *EX*; moiste *CLo*, be moiste *X*
161 dede *E*; ny3te *Lo*; axed *BFHWo*, axede *CEX*, askide *Lo*; þer *BCEFWoX*
162 dro3te *CX*, drou3þe *EHLo*; flees *CX*, fluys *E*, flese *Wo*; aloon *BFWo*,
    aloone *H*, allone *Lo*
163 deu *CEX*; alle *BLoWo*, all *F*; erþ *B*

7. 1 þann *BF*, þenne *E*, þan *HWo*
  2 whiche *BCEHLoX*; ny3te *Lo*; rysyng *B*, risende *CX*
  3 alle *B*, all *F*; peple *BEFLoWo*; come *BLoWo*, coom *E*, coome *F*; the: om. *H*
  4 well *BF*, welle *CEHLoWoX*; cleped *E*, callid *Lo*; forsoþ *B*
4—5 Forsothe the tentis: þe t. f. *cet.*; tentus *C*, tentes *X*; weryn *E*; atte *Lo*
  6 northe *Lo*; cost *CEWoX*, cooste *Lo*; of: at *Wo*; hee3e *C*, hy(e) *Lo*, he3e *X*;
    hyll *BFH*, hul *E*, hylle *LoWo*
  7 mych *B*, moche *ELo*
  8 peple *BEFLoWo*; þe *EWo*; leste *Lo*
  9 a3eyns *BEFWo*, a3en *CX*, a-3eynes *Lo*; take *BEFHWoX*, taken *CLo*
  10 hondis *BEX*, hondus *C*, hondes *LoWo*; leste *Lo*; say *E*, sey *FWo*

40 Fecitque Dominus /in/ nocte illa, ut postulaverat; et
    fuit siccitas in solo vellere, et ros in omni terra.

7. 1 Igitur Ierobaal, qui /est/ et Gedeon, de nocte con-
    surgens, et omnis populus cum eo, venit ad fontem
    qui vocatur Arad. Erant autem castra Madian in valle
    ad septentrionalem plagam collis excelsi.

40 deew. And the Lord dide in that ny3t,
as Gedeon axide; and drynesse was in 160
the flees aloone, and dew was in al the
erthe.

7. 1 Therfor Jerobaal, which also Gedeon,
roos bi ny3t, and al the puple with hym,
and cam to the welle which is clepid
Arad. Sotheli the tentis of Madian weren
in the valey, at the north coost of the hi3 5
2 hil. And the Lord seide to Gedeon, Mych
puple is with thee, and Madian schal not
be bitakun in to the hondis ther of, lest
Israel haue glorie a3ens me, and seie, Y

159 dew CCaEFGHaLMNOPQWX, dewe DIR; ni3th E
160 axed E, axede P; drienesse AcBCCaDHaMMaNUWX, drines E, dri3nesse
     GKQ, dri3enesse R
161 flese E, fleus K; aloone: om. Ac, alone CaFKMNW, aloon DI, al on E;
     deew BMaUX, dewe DHaIKLR
162 erthe: drie flore I

7. 1 þerfore BCaEFGKMaNQR, Thanne I, Therefore W; þe whiche I, wich K;
      also: also is C², also was I, was also Ma
   2 rose E, roose I; ny3te CaEFKLMMaPUW; al: of W; peple
      CaFILMMaNPWX; hem R
   3 he came I, came R; wel D; whiche EGHa, þat I, wiche K
   4 soþli EFGLMMaPQSUWX, & I; tentes F; werin E
   5 nort E; cost QU; hei3 CaFMW, hi3e D, hie E
   6 hille D, hul E; sayde E; myche AcBCCaDGHaIKLMOPQSUW, Much
      E, moche FN
   7 peple CaFILMMaNPWX; þe EF
   8 be: om. D; bitakun: takun Ac, bitaken BCaDFHaIKLMMaQRW, taken
      E, bitakin P; hondes EF, hoondis R; ther of: of it I; leste BE
   9 haue: om. I; a3enus AcCNO, a3enes I; sey I

2 Dixitque Dominus ad Gedeon: Multus tecum est
populus, nec tradetur Madian in manus eius, ne
glorietur contra me Israel, et dicat: Meis viribus
liberatus sum.

3 Bi my strengthis I am delyuerd. Spek
to the puple, and alle herynge, preche,
Who is feerful and dredy, turne he aȝen.
And there wenten aȝen fro the hil of
Galaad, and ben turned aȝen of the pu- 15
ple two and twenti thowsand of men;
4 and onely ten thowsand beden stil. And
the Lord seide to Gedeon, ȝit there is
myche puple; lede hem to the watris,
and there I shal preue hem, and of whom 20
Y shal seye to thee, that goo with thee,
he goo; whom I shal defende to goo,

11 streyngþis *BF*, strengþes *Lo*; deleuered *C*, delyuered *EWoX*, deliuerede *Lo*;
   speke *BFHLoWo*
12 peple *BEFLoWo*, om. *H*; all *F*; heryng *BLo*, herende *CX*
13 ferfull *B*, ferful *CFH*, ferfol *E*, ferdful *LoWo*; torne *BEFHWo*; aȝeyn *BEF*,
   aȝeen *CX*, a-ȝeyn(e) *Lo*
14 þer *BCEHLoWoX*; went *BFHWo*, wente *ELo*; aȝeyn *BEFWo*, aȝeen *CX*,
   a-ȝeyn(e) *Lo*; hyll *BFH*, hul *E*, hylle *LoWo*
15 been *E*; torned *BEFHWo*, turnede *Lo*; aȝeyn *BEFWo*, aȝeen *CX*; peple
   BEFHLoWo
16 thousend *C*, þousont *E*, þousande *FLo*
17 oonly *BEFHLo*, onli *CWoX*; tenn *BH*; thousend *CX*, þousont *E*, thousande
   FLo; biden *CH*, bedyn *E*, a-biden *Lo*, abyden *Wo*, ben *X*; styll *B*, stille
   CEFHLoWoX
18 ȝitt *BFHWo*, ȝet *E*; þer *BCEFHWoX*
19 moche *ELo*, mych *Wo*; peple *BEFHLoWo*; leed *BEX*, led *C*, leede *FWo*;
   þem *CLo*; waters *BEH*, watres *Lo*
20 þer *B*; proue *C*; þem *CLoX*; whome *BF*
21 say *E*, sei *CLoWoX*; too *X*; þe (2x) *EWo*; go *CELoWoX*
22 go *BCELoX*; he g.: g. he *Lo*; whome *BFWo*; defend *Lo*, defenden *X*; go
   CEWoX

3 Loquere ad populum, et cunctis audientibus praedica:
Qui formidolosus et timidus est, revertatur. Recesseruntque de monte Galaad et reversa sunt ex
populo viginti duo millia virorum, et tantum decem
millia remanserunt.

3 am delyuerid bi my strengthis. Speke   10
   thou to the puple, and preche thou, while
   alle men heren, He that is ferdful in
   herte, and dredeful with outforth, turne
   aȝen. And thei ȝeden awei fro the hil of
   Galaad, and two and twenti thousynde of   15
   men turneden aȝen fro the puple; and oneli
4 ten thousynde dwelliden. And the Lord
   seide to Gedeon, ȝit the puple is myche;
   lede thou hem to the watris, and there
   Y schal preue hem, and he go, of whom   20
   Y schal seye, that he go; turne he aȝen,

10 delyuered CEHaILMaRUX; strengþes FK, strenkþis MaR; spek EU
11 peple CaFILMMaNPWX; whil EGKLPR
12 heeren DGKMaNR; ferful U, feerdful MaX; 12–13 in herte: om. I
13 dredful CEILPU; wiþ oute forþ CaFGKLMNPUWX, wiþoutforþe E, om. I
14 thei: þe sones of Israel I; aweie G; from K; hul E
15 þousynd CaHaIMW, þousand DMaNQX, þousend FG, þousande KRS,
    þousende LP
16 turned E, turnyden GQ; aȝein E; from K; the: þat CaGHaIKMNO²QSX;
    peple CaFILMaNPWX; oonli BCaDGHaIKLMMaNPRWX, only FQU
17 þousynd CaIMW, þousand DEHaMaNQX, þousend FGL, þousande KR,
    þousende P; dwelleden CaEFLMPW, abiden I, dwelden U
18 said E; ȝut E, ȝitt I; peple CaFILMMaNPWX:, much E, moche
    FNUX, mych R
19 leede BG, leed U; watres EF; 19–20 and there Y schal preue hem: & I
    I schal preue hem 'þere' I
20 he go: go he ELP, go he wiþ þee I; of: om. R; wam E
21 sai E, sey I; And turne I; aȝein B

4 Dixitque Dominus ad Gedeon: Adhuc populus multus est;
   duc eos ad aquas, et ibi probabo illos; et de quo
   dixero tibi ut vadat tecum, ipse pergat; quem ire
   prohibuero, ipse revertatur.

5 he turne aȝen. And whanne the puple
was goon doon to the watris, the Lord
seide to Gedeon, Thilk that with hoond   25
and with tonge lapen the watris, as
houndis ben woned to lape, thou shalt
seuere hem aside; forsothe thilk, that
bowid(en) the knees drynkyn(ge), in that
6 other paart shulen be. And so was the   30
noumbre of hem, that with hoond throwynge to the mouth watris hadden lapid,
thre hundrid men; forsothe al that other

23 torne *BEFHWo*; he t.: t. he *Lo*; aȝeyn *BEFWo*, aȝeen *CX*, aȝeyne *Lo*;
whenn *B*, whan *CEFLoWoX*, whenne *H*; peple *BEFHLo*
24 go *CE*, gon *WoX*; doun *cet.*; waters *BEH*, watres *Lo*
25 thilk: þoo *C*, þulke *E*, þilke *FH*, þo *LoX*; hond *CWoX*, honde *ELo*
26 tunge *CX*, tounge *E*; lapyn *E*, laapen *Lo*; waters *BEH*, watres *Lo*
27 houndus *CX*, houndes *LoWo*; been *E*; wont *BCEFHWoX*, wonte *Lo*;
lapen *CX*
28 seueren *BFHWo*, seueryn *E*; hem: om. *CE*[1], þem *LoX*; aaside *Lo*; forsothe
thilk: th. f. *cet.*; thilk: þoo *C*, þulke *E*, þilke *FH*, þo *LoX*
29 bowid *BCFHLoWo*, bowed *E*; kneeȝis *BF*, knes *CE*; drinken *C*, drynkyn
E, drinkin(ge) *Lo*, drinkende *X*; that: þe *CX*
30 other: toþer *C*; part *cet.*; shul *CX*, sholyn *E*, schuln *BFWo*, schullen *H*,
schulle *Lo*; ben *BFHLoWoX*, been *E*
31 þem *Lo*; hoond: þe hond *CE*, hoonde *F*, honde *LoWo*, hond *X*; þrowende
CX, throwing *Lo*
32 mouthe *Lo*; waters *BEFH*, watres *Lo*; haddyn *E*, hadde *X*; laped *E*
33 hundreþ *BF*, hundred *E*, hundrede *Lo*; forsothe al: a. f. *cet.*; alle *BHLoX*,
all *F*; that: þe *CX*; other: toþer *C*

5 Cumque descendisset populus ad aquas, dixit Dominus
ad Gedeon: Qui manu et lingua lambuerint aquas,
sicut solent canes lambere, separabis eos seorsum;
qui autem curvatis genibus biberint, in altera
parte erunt.
6 Fuit itaque numerus eorum, qui manu ad os proiciente
aquas lambuerant, trecenti viri; omnis autem reliqua
multitudo flexo poplite biberat.

194

5 whom Y schal forbede to go. And whanne
the puple hadde go doun to watris, the
Lord seide to Gedeon, Thou schalt departe
hem bi hem silf, that lapen watris with   25
hond and tunge, as doggis ben wont to
lape; sotheli thei, that drynken with
knees bowid, schulen be in the tothir
6 part. And so the noumbre of hem, that
lapiden watris bi hond castynge to the   30
mouth, was thre hundrid men; forsothe
al the tothir multitude drank knelynge.

22   wham E; forbed C, forbeede LP; whan EGHaLP
23   peple CaFILMMaPWX, peplis N; had E; doune E; watres E, þe watris I
24   seid E; depart D
25   self CaEFILMPRUW; lapin ELMaPSU, lapis GQ; watres F, waters U;
     25 – 26 that lapen watris with hond and tunge: þat wiþ h. & t. lapen
     watris I
26   tonge B, tong E; dogghis E, dogges FHaR, houndis I; be E; wond L,
     wonte R
27   lapen O; soþli EFGLMMaPQUWX, & I; þai E, þo I; drinkin P, drinkun
     S
28   knes GR, þe knees I; bowyde EK, bowed FGHaL, foolden I, bowȝid R;
     schullen CaFMW, schuln D, shul EILP; toþer AcBCCaDFHaIKLMMa
     NQUW, oþer E
29   parte R; noumber E
30   lapeden CaEFMPW, lapide L; watres EF; þe hond CD[1]IK[2]Ma, honde R;
     casting E
31   hundred EHa, hunderd LP; forsoþ EX, & I
32   toþer AcBCCaEFGHaIKLMMaOQUWX; drank watir Ac[1], dranke
     BHaIR; kneling DE, kneelynge Ha
33   said E; to: om. S
34   hundred Ha, hunderd LP; lapeden CaEFMPW

7 multitude the knee bowid dronke. And
the Lord seith to Gedeon. In three hun-   35
drid men, that lapiden watris, I shal
delyuer ʒou, and taak Madian in thin
hoond; forsothe al that other multitude
8 be turned aʒen into his place. And so
metis taken for the noumbre, and trom-   40
pis, al that othir multitude he comaundide to goon to her tabernaclis; and
he, with thre hundrid men, ʒaf hym silf
to the bateil. Forsothe the tentis of Ma-
9 dian weren vndur in the valey. The   45
same nyʒt the Lord seide to hym, Rise,
and go doun into the tentis, for Y haue

34 kne *CEWoX*; bowed *BEFH*, bowide *Lo*; dranc *CX*, dronken *Lo*
35 lorde *Lo*; seys *Lo*; þre *cet.*; hundred *ELo*, hundreþ *BF*
36 lapeden *CWoX*, lapedyn *E*, laapiden *Lo*; waters *BEF*, watres *Lo*
37 deliuere *CX*, delyuere *EF*, diliuer *Lo*; take *cet.*
38 hond *CEX*, honde *LoWo*; forsothe al: a. f. *cet.*; all *F*, alle *LoX*; that: þe
    CX; other: toþer *C*
39 tornede *B*, torned *EFWo*, turnede *Lo*; aʒeyn *BEFHWo*, aʒeen *CX*, a-ʒeyne
    Lo
40 metus *C*, metes *X*; takyn *E*; trumpis *C*, trompes *Wo*, trumpes *X*
41 alle *BLo*, all *F*; that: þe *CX*; oþer *BEFHLoWoX*, toþer *C*; comaundyd
    BFHWo, comaundede *CE*, commaundede *Lo*, coomaundide *X*
42 go *CLoX*, gon *HWo*; to: into *H*; þeir *BFWo*, þer *CLoX*, here *E*;
    thabernaclis *Lo*
43 hundreþ *BF*, hundride *Lo*, hundred *X*; ʒaue *BFHWo*, ʒafe *Lo*; self *cet.*
44 bataile *CELoX*, bateyle *H*; Forsothe the tentis: þe t. f. *cet.*; tentus *C*,
    tentes *X*
45 weryn *E*; vnder *BCFHWo*, vndir *E*, vndre *Lo*; in: om. *H*; valeye *EH*
46 nyʒte *Lo*; lorde *Lo*; ris *CX*
47 goo *BFH*; tentus *C*, tentes *X*

7 Et ait Dominus ad Gedeon: In trecentis viris, qui
lambuerunt aquas, liberabo vos, et tradam Madian in
manu tua; omnis autem reliqua multitudo revertatur
in locum suum.
8 Sumptis itaque pro numero cibariis et tubis, omnem

196

7 And the Lord seide to Gedeon, In thre
hundrid men, that lapiden watris, Y schal
delyuere ʒou, and Y schal bitake Madian   35
in thin hond; but al the tothir multi-
8 tude turne aʒen in to her place. And
so whanne thei hadden take meetis and
trumpis for the noumbre, he comaundide
al the tothir multitude to go to her taber-   40
naclis; and he, with thre hundrid men,
ʒaf hym silf to batel. Sothely the tentis
of Madian weren bynethe in the valey.
9 In the same nyʒt the Lord seyde to hym,
Ryse thou, and go doun in to the castels   45
of Madian, for Y haue bitake hem in

35   deliuer E; bitak E, bitaken L, betake P
36   in to F; þine ER; honde EI; Bot E, And I; alle ELMaP; toþer
     AcBCCaDFGHaIKLMNPQRUW, oþer EX, toþere Ma
37   aʒein B; in: om. Ma; hir L, here QRS
38   so: om. I; whan EHaLP; þai E; had E, haddin P; taken EMa; metis
     AcBCCaDEIKLMMaNOPSUWX, metes F
39   trumpes FP, trompis L; for: fro Ha; noumbre of hem I; comaundid D,
     comaunde E, comaundede LP, comandide S; 39—40 he com. al the t. m.:
     al þe t. m. he c. I
40   the tothir: þe toþer AcCCaFGHaIKLMMaPQUW, þe oþer E, þat oþir N;
     here FQRU; tabernacles ER
41   he: Gedeon I; whith his E; hundred EHa, hunderd LP
42   ʒaaf I, ʒafe R; self CaEFKLMPRUW; bateil DGX, bateile KR, bataile
     U; soþli FGLMMaPQUWX, & I; tentes F
43   bineþþen S; valeie CR
44   said E; hym: Gedeon I
45   doune E; in: om. Ha; castelis EG, castelles U; 45—46 the c. of M.: her
     tentis I
46   bitaken K; in: into AcMa

reliquam multitudinem abire praecepit ad tabernacula
sua; et ipse cum trecentis viris se certamini dedit.
Castra autem Madian erant subter in valle.
9 Eadem nocte dixit Dominus ad eum: Surge, et descende
in castra, quia tradidi eos in manu tua.

10 taak hem in thin hoond; forsothe if alone
   thou dredist to goo, go doun with thee
11 Phara, thi child. And whanne thou herist   50
   what thei speken, thanne thin hoondis
   shulen be counfortid, and sikerer thou
   shalt goo doun to the tentis of the* enemyes. Thanne descendide he, and Phara,
   his child, into a paart of the tentis, where   55
12 weren the watchis of armed men. For-
   sothe Madian, and Amalech, and alle the
   este puplis shed layen in the valey, as
   multitude of locustis; forsothe camels vnnoumbrable there weren, as grauel that   60

48 take *BCEFHWoX*, taken *Lo*; þem *CX*; þine *Lo*; hond *CEX*, honde *LoWo*;
   forsothe if: if f. *cet.*; forsoth *B*; ȝif *BEFHWo*, ȝife *Lo*; aloon *B*, aloone
   FHWo, allone *Lo*; 48−49 forsothe if alone thou dredist to goo: If f. þou
   dr. to g. alone *X*
49 dredest *CLo*; goo: goon *BEFHLo*, go *C*, gon *WoX*; go: goo *BFHWo*; þe
   Wo
50 childe *ELoWo*; whenn *BH*, whan *CLoWoX*, whenne *E*, whann *F*; heerist
   BF, herest *CLoX*
51 spekyn *E*; þann *BF*, þenne *E*, þan *LoWo*; þine *Lo*; hondus *C*, hondys *EX*,
   hondes *LoWo*
52 schuln *BFHWo*, shul *CX*, sholyn *E*, schullen *Lo*; ben *BFHLoWo*; confortyd
   BWo, counfortid *C*, conforted *E*, comfortyd *F*, counfortide *H*, confortede
   Lo, counfortid *X*; sykirer *BF*, sikerere *CEX*
53 goon *BEFHLo*, go *CX*, gon *Wo*; tentus *C*, tentes *X*; the: þin *A*; enmyes *BFWo*,
   enemys *CX*
54 þann *B*, þenne *E*; descendyd *BFHLoWo*, descendede *CE*
55 childe *LoWo*; parte *BEFH*, part *CWoX*, paarte *Lo*; off *E*; tentus *C*, tentes
   X; wher *CE*
56 weryn *E*; wacches *LoWo*; armyd *BEFHWo*, armede *Lo*; forsoþ *B*
57 Forsothe Madian: M. f. *cet.*; all *BF*, al *Wo*
58 est *CEWoX*, eest *Lo*; peplis *BEFHLoWo*, puples *X*; schedde *Lo*; layȝen
   BEFHLoWo, leȝen *CX*
59 locustes *LoX*; forsothe camels: c. f. *cet.*; chamels *BFH*, camailis *C*,
   kameylys *E*, chamelis *Lo*, camailes *X*; vnnoumbreable *BFHLo*
60 þer *BCEFWo*; grauell *BF*, graueil *E*

10 Sin autem solus ire formidas, descendat tecum Phara
   puer tuus.
11 Et cum audieris quid loquantur, tunc confortabuntur
   manus tuae, et securior ad hostium castra descendes.

10 thin hond; sotheli if thou dredist to go
aloone, Phara, thi child, go doun with thee.

11 And whanne thou schalt here what thei
speken, thanne thin hondis schulen be   50
counfortid, and thou schalt go down si-
kerere to the tentis of enemyes. Therfor
he ȝede doun, and Phara, his child, in to
the part of tentis, where the wacchis of

12 armed men weren. Forsothe Madian, and   55
Amalech, and alle the puplis of the eest
layen spred in the valey, as the multitude
of locustis; sotheli the camelis weren vnnoumbrable, as grauel that liggith in the

47 þine ER, þijn K; honde E, hoondis R; soþli FGLMMaPQUWX, & I;
    ȝif E; dredest EFHaL, dreedist G
48 alone CaEFKMW, aloon R; thi: þe L; childe E, chijld K; adoune E; þe
    ER
49 whan EGHaLP; heere DGHaMaNOX; thei: þe madianytis I
50 spekin EP, schul speke I; þan E; þi C, þine CaEKMRW; hondes F, hoondis
    R; schullen CaMW, schuln DF, shul EILPU; ben S
51 confortid CCaEIKLMPX, cūfortid Q; doune E; siker BW, sikerer
    DEILMaNPRX, sikur Ha
52 to: in to D; tentes F; þe enmyes I; þerfore AcCaEFGKLMMaPQRWX,
    þanne I, & þerfore N
53 he: Gedeon I; doune E; chijld K
54 the: a I; parte E; tentes F, þe t. EI; wher L; wecchis C, wacches EF,
    waiȝcches K
55 armyd GPQS, aarmed HaX, armede KU; weeren S; forsoþ X, And I
56 the (1°): om. B; peplis CaILMMaNPWX, puples ER, peples F; est EQ
57 layn I, laiȝen K; spredde C, sprad HaO, spred abrod I, spradde K
58 locustes EPR, locustus O; soþli FGLMMaPQUWX, & I; camels
    AcBCaDHaILMMaNOPRUX, cameles F; werin E; innommerable E,
    vnnoumbreable I, vnnumerable LP, vnnoumberable R
59 grauele K, graueil X; liggeȝ E, liggeþ FHaLR, lijþ I, liȝggeþ K
60 brink EQ, brynke cet.; br. of the see: see br. I; whan EGHaLMP

Descendit ergo ipse et Phara, puer eius, in partem
castrorum, ubi erant armatorum vigiliae.

12 Madian autem et Amalech, et omnes orientales populi
fusi iacebant in valle, ut locustarum multitudo;
cameli quoque innumerabiles erant, sicut harena
quae iacet in litore maris.

13 lieth in the brenk of the see. And whanne
Gedeon was comen, a man tolde a sweuen
to his neiȝbore, and in this maner he
toolde that he sawȝ, Y sawȝ a sweuen,
and it semed to me, as a loof of barlich   65
maad vndir asshen to be trendlid, and
into the tentis of Madyan to goo doun;
and whanne it were comyn (in) to the tabernacle, it smoot it, and turnede vpsedoun,

61 lyȝiþ *BFH*, liþ *CWoX*, liþe *E*, liggeþ *Lo*; brynke *cet.*; se *CX*; whenn *BH*,
    whan *CFWoX*
62 commen *BF*, comyn *E*; told *BF*; sweuene *CELoWoX*
63 neȝhebore *CEX*, neyȝebore *HLo*; manere *F*
64 tolde *BCEHLoWoX*, told *F*; saȝ (2x) *CX*, sawgh (2x) *ELo*(1°), sawe *Lo*
    (2°); sweuene *CELoWoX*
65 hit *H*; semyd *BFHWo*, semede *CELoX*; lof *C*, loif *E*, loofe *FHLoWo*,
    loef *X*; barli *CLoX*, barliche *HWo*
66 made *BFHLoWo*, mad *X*; vnder *BCFHWoX*, vndre *Lo*; asken *BCFHWoX*,
    askyn *E*; ben *BEFHLoWoX*; trendelid *LoWo*
67 tentes *BX*, tentus *C*; goon *BFHLo*, go *CX*, gon *EWo*
68 whenn *BH*, whan *CFLoWoX*, when *E*; commen *BF*, come *C*, comen
    HLoWoX; thabernacle *Lo*
69 smote *BFHLo*, smot *CEWoX*; tornede *B*, turnyde *E*, torned *FH*, turned
    WoX; vpsadoun *BFH*, vp so doun *CELoWoX*

13 Cumque venisset Gedeon, narrabat aliquis somnium
proximo suo; et in hunc modum referebat quod vid-
erat: Vidi somnium, et videbatur mihi, quasi sub-
cinericius panis ex hordeo volvi, et in castra
Madian descendere; cumque pervenisset ad tabernaculum, percussit illud, atque subvertit, et terrae
funditus coaequavit.

13 brenke of the see. And whanne Gedeon   60
hadde come, a man tolde a dreem to his
neiȝbore, and telde bi this maner that,
that he hadde seyn, I siȝ a dreem, and it
semyde to me, that as o loof of barly
bakun vndur the aischis was walewid,   65
and cam doun in to the tentis of Madian;
and whanne it hadde come to a tabernacle,
it smoot and distriede that tabernacle,
and made euene outirly to the erthe.

61 had EI; come *doun* I; telde AcCDFHaIMOSUX, teelde BCaGMaNQW,
    toolde K; dreme E, drem LU
62 neiȝebore GILMaNRSX; teld AcDS, teelde BGMaNQX, told E, he telde
    I, tolde KLPR; this: his N; manere CaGIMQW
63 that: at E; had EIR; seyen BGHaQ, seen IMa, seyne R; seiȝ CaEFMW,
    sawȝe I, siȝe R; dreme DER
64 seemede BX, semede CaFKLMMaNPRU, semyd D, semed E, symede O;
    o: a BIW, oo CGHaKLPQR; loue E, lof Q; barlei K; loof of barly: barly
    loof I
65 baken BCaFGIKLMMaQRW, bakin EP; vndir DEGIKMaNPQRX,
    vnder FLU; the: om. CaGHaIKNOSX; asschis CaEFHaLMPSW, asches
    R; walowid DHaKMa, walwid EP, walwed L, walewed U
66 com E, came HaR, it cam I; doune E; the: om. L; tentes FHa
67 whan EGHaLP; hadde: om. D, had EI; cum E; a: þe R
68 smot EU, smote HaR, smote it I; distried D, distroide E, destriede FIK,
    destroide Ha, distroiede Ma, distroied R, distruyede X; that tabernacle:
    þe t. CE, it I
69 maade G, made it I; euen DEIR; vttirli DGHaKMaPQX, witterly E,
    outerly IUW, vtterli LN; eerþe IR

14 and al doun to the erthe euenede. He,   70
    to whom he spak, answerde, This is noon
    othere thing, but the swerd of Gedeon,
    sone of Joas, a man of Irael; forsothe
    the Lord hath takun into the hoondis of
    hym Madian and alle the tentis of it.   75
15 And whanne Gedeon hadde herd the
    sweuen, and the remenynge of it, he
    heryede, and, turned aȝen to the tentis of
    Yrael, seith, Ryse ȝe; forsothe the Lord
    hath takun into oure hoondis the tentis   80
16 of Madian. And he dyuydide the thre
    hundred men in thre parties, and he ȝaf
    trompis in the hoondis of hem, and voyd
    wyn pottys, and laumpis in the myddis

70 alle *Lo*; erþ *B*; euened *X*
71 whome *BF*; spake *BWo*; answerd *B*, answeride *Lo*, answered *Wo*; non *Wo*,
    noen *X*
72 oþer *BCFHLoWoX*, ooþer *E*; þinge *LoWo*; bot *B*, bute *F*; sweerd *E*, swerde
    LoWo
73 forsothe the Lord: þe l. f. *cet.*
74 has *Lo*; taken *BFHLoWo*, take *CX*, takyn *E*; hondus *C*, handis *E*;
    hondes *LoWoX*
75 all *F*, al *Lo*; tentus *C*, tentes *X*; hit *H*
76 whenn *B*, whan *CEFLoWoX*, whenne *H*; had *BFLoWo*; herde *HLoWo*
77 sweuene *CELoWoX*; remenyng *CELoX*
78 heryed *BFHWo*; tornyd *BF*, torned *HWo*, turnede *Lo*; aȝeyn *BFWo*,
    aȝeen *CX*; tentus *CX*
79 seys *Lo*; ȝee *CELoX*; forsothe the Lord: þe l. f. *cet.*
80 has *Lo*; taken *BFHLoWo*, take *CX*, takyn *E*; our *F*; hondus *C*, handis *E*,
    hondes *LoWo*, hondis *X*; tentus *C*, tentes *X*
81 deuidede *CEX*, dyuydid *Wo*
82 hundreþ *BF*, hundrid *CEHWo*; partis *CX*; ȝaue *BFHWo*, ȝafe *Lo*
83 trumpis *CEX*; hondes *BLoX*, hondus *C*, handis *E*; þem *CLo*; voyde *cet.*
84 wyne *BFHLoWo*; pottes *LoX*; lampes *Lo*, laumpes *X*; myddus *C*, myddes *X*

14 Respondit is, cui loquebatur: Non est hoc aliud,
    nisi gladius Gedeonis, filii Ioas, viri Israelitae;
    tradidit enim Dominus in manus eius Madian, et
    omnia castra eius.
15 Cumque audisset Gedeon somnium, et intepretationem
    eius, adoravit; et reversus ad castra Israel ait:

202

14 That man answeride, to whom he spak,   70
This is noon other thing, no but the
swerd of Gedeon, sone of Joas, a man of
Israel; for the Lord hath bitake Madian
and alle tentis therof in to the hondis of
15 Gedeon. And whanne Gedeon had herd   75
the dreem, and the interpretyng therof,
he worschypide *the Lord*, and turnede
aȝen to the tentis of Israel, and seide,
Ryse ȝe; for the Lord hath bitake in to
16 oure hondis the tentis of Madian. And   80
he departide thre hundrid men in to thre
partis, and he ȝaf trumpis in her hondis,
and voyde pottis, and laumpis in the

70 That: And þat IKX; answerde CaFGMPQUW, answerid D, answered E,
answerede L; spake EIR
71 none E; oþere AcR, oþir GNO, ooþer L; no: om. I
72 swerde ER; sone of Joas: ioas sone I
73 for: forsoþe I; lord god K; haþe E
74 þe tentis EKUX, tentes FHa; tentis therof: her tentis I; of in to the
hondis: om. L; hondes CaF, hoondis R
75 whan DHaILP, when E, om. G; had AEI, hadde cet.; herde EHa
76 dreme ER; interpretinge CaDEGLMaQU, remeenyng I, interpretacioun
W; therof: of it I
77 wurschipide CaMW, worschipid D, worshepid E, wurshipede F, wirschipide
I, worshepide PU; turned DE, turnyde GHaQ
78 aȝein B; in to I; tentes F
79 arise E; ȝee U; haþe E
80 oure: ȝoure D; hondes CaF, hoondis R; tentes F
81 departid D, departede EFLP; þe þre I; hundred EHa, hunderd LP
82 partise E, partes FI; he: om. HaS; ȝaaf hem I, ȝaue R; trumpes F,
trumpus P; into N; here FQRU; hondes CaF, hundis L, hoondis R
83 voyde: empty I; pottes FHa; laumpes F, l. *brennynge* I, lampis O; the:
om. Ca

Surgite, tradidit enim Dominus in manus nostras
castra Madian.
16 Divisitque trecentos viros in tres partes, et dedit
tubas in manibus eorum, lagenasque vacuas, ac
lampades in medio lagenarum.

17 of the pottis. And he seide to hem,   85
   What ȝe seen me doon, that doo ȝe; Y
   shal goo into a paart of the tentis, and
18 what I shal doo, folwith. Whanne the
   trompe fulsowneth in myn hoond, forsothe ȝe bi the enuyroun of the tentis   90
   trompith, and crieth to gidre, To the Lord
19 and to Gedeon. And Gedeon wente in,
   and thre hundred men that weren with
   hym, into a part of the tentis, bigynnynge the watchis of the mydnyȝt; and   95
   the kepers reryd, thei bigunnen with
   trompis to cryen, and clappen togidre

85 pottes *X*; þem *CLoX*
86 ȝee *CELoX*; seeyȝen *BF*, seeȝen *H*, seyȝen *Wo*; doon: to do *C*, to don
    E, to doon *Lo*, don *WoX*; doo: do *CEWoX*; ȝee *CEHLoX*
87 go *CHLoWoX*, gon *E*; part *BCEFHWoX*, paarte *Lo*; tentus *C*, tentes *X*
88 do *CWoX*, don *E*; folowiþ *BFHWo*, folewith *CX*, foleweth *E*, folweþ *Lo*;
    whenn *BH*, whan *CFLoWoX*; 88−89 Whanne the trompe fulsowneth:
    Wh. f. þe tr. *cet.*
89 trumpe *CEWoX*; fulsounneþ *H*; hoonde *BFH*, hond *CX*, hand *E*, honde
    LoWo; forsoþ *B*; 89−90 forsothe ȝe: ȝ. f. *cet.*
90 ȝee *CELoX*; the (1°): om. *C*; tentus *CX*
91 trumpiþ *BCFHWo*, trumpeþ *EX*, trompes *Lo*; cryes *Lo*; to giþer *BF*,
    togidere *CE*, to gyder *H*, to giders *Wo*, togiþere *X*
92 went *FWo*
93 hundreþ *BF*, hundrid *CEHWoX*; weryn *E*
94 parte *Lo*; tentes *BX*, tentus *C*; begynnende *C*, begynny[n]ge *E*,
    bigynnende *X*
95 wacches *LoX*; mydnyȝte *Lo*
96 keperis *CELo*, keperes *X*; reryde *Lo*, rered *X*; begunne *C*, begunnyn *E*,
    by-gonne *Lo*, bigunne *X*
97 trumpis *CE*, trumpes *Wo*, tru[m]pis *X*; clappe *C*, clappyn *E*; to giþer *BF*,
    togidere *CEX*, togyder *HWo*

17 Et dixit ad eos: Quod me facere videritis, hoc facite; ingrediar partem castrorum, et quod fecero
   sectamini.
18 Quando personuerit tuba in manu mea, vos quoque per
   castrorum circuitum clangite, et conclamate, Domino
   et Gedeoni.

17 myddis of the pottis. And he seide to
hem, Do ȝe this thing which ȝe seen me   85
do; Y schal entre in to a part of the tentis,

18 and sue ȝe that, that Y do. Whanne the
trumpe in myn hond schal sowne, sowne
ȝe also bi the cumpas of tentis, and crye
ȝe togidere, To the Lord and to Gedeon.   90

19 And Gedeon entride, and thre hundrid
men that weren with hym, in to a part
of the tentis, whanne the watchis of mydnyȝt bigunnen; and whanne the keperis
weren reysid, thei bigunnen to sowne   95
with trumpis, and to bete togidere the

84 myddes F; pottes F; 83−84 and (2°) ... pottis: om. GQ; said E
85 ȝe (1°): ȝee BU; whiche DP, wiche E, þat GHaIQ, wich K; ȝe (2°):
    ȝee OU; se DHaQ, sen G, siȝen L, seyn U
86 don U; shall L, shalt Q; a: the X; parte ER; the: om. X; tentes F
87 suwe CaFMW, swe K; ȝee KU; that (2°): at E; whan EHaLMP, And
    whanne Ma
88 myne E, my KO; honde E
89 ȝee GU; the: om. CaGHaKMO²QX; bi the cumpas of: al aboute I;
    tentes F, þe t. I
90 ȝee GU; to gidre DIR, to ghider E, togider P
91 entrid D, entred E, entrede PU; þe þre I; hundride B, hundred EHa,
    hunderd LP
92 a: þe E; parte R
93 the: her I; tentes F; whan EGHaLP; wacches FR, waȝcchis K; of: at B;
    þe mydnyȝt Ha; 91−94 & whanne þe mydnyȝt wacchis bigunnen G.
    entride in to a part of her tentis & þe þre hundrid men þat weren wiþ him
    I
94 when E, whan GHaLP; kepers DEKLMMaPRX, keperes FHaU, kepers
    of her wacchis I
95 reysed ELU, reisede K; thei: Gideon & hise I
96 trumpes FKPR; beete GQ; to gidre DIR

19 Ingressusque est Gedeon, et trecenti viri, qui
erant cum eo, in partem castrorum, incipientibus
vigiliis noctis mediae; et custodibus suscitatis,
coeperunt bucinis clangere, et complodere inter se
lagenas.

20 bitwix hem seluen the wyn pottis. And
whanne bi enuyroun of the tentis in thre
placis thei fulsowneden, and the stenys   100
hadden broken, thei heelden with the
left hoondis the laumpis, and with the
riȝt the sownynge trompis; and thei crieden, The swerd of the Lord and of

21 Gedeon; stondynge eche in his place, by   105
enuyroun of the enemyes tentis. And
so alle the tentis ben disturblid; and

22 criynge out and ȝellynge, flowen; and
neuerthelater the thre hundryd men
stoden to stedfastly, sownynge with trom-   110
pis. And the Lord sente yn swerd in alle
the tentis, and thei kutten of hem seluen

98 bytwen *B*, betwe *C*, betwen *E*, bytwene *FHLoWo*, bitwe *X*; þem *CLoX*;
    self *CX*, seluyn *E*; wyne *BFHLoWo*; -pottus *C*, pottes *X*

99 whenn *B*, whan *CLoWoX*, whann *F*, whenne *H*; tentus *C*, tentes *X*

100 places *LoX*; fulsownedyn *E*, fulsounneden *H*, full souneden *X*; stenes *LoX*

101 hadde *C*, haddyn *E*; broke *BCFHWo*, brokyn *E*; heelde *C*, heeldyn *E*,
    helden *HLoWo*

102 lifte *Lo*, lift *Wo*, lift *X*; hondis *CH*, -handis *E*, hondes *LoWo*, hendes *Wo*,
    hond *X*; laumpes *WoX*; the (2°): om. *Lo*

103 riȝte *X*; sounende *CX*, sounnynge *FHWo*, sownnyng *Lo*; trumpis *CE*,
    trumpes *X*; kriedyn *E*, cried *Wo*

104 swerde *BLoWo*; lorde *Lo*

105 stondende *CX*, stondyng *Lo*

106 enmys *B*, enemys *CEX*, enmyes *FHWo*; tentus *C*, tentes *X*

107 all *F*, al *H*; tentes *BX*, tentus *C*; distourblid *BFHWo*, disturbid *CX*,
    distroublede *Lo*

108 criende *CX*, crying *FWo*; oute *B*, ouȝte *H*; ȝellende *CX*; floun *CX*, flowyn *E*

109 neuer þe latter *BWo*, ner þe latere *CX*, neuerþelatere *E*, neuere þe later
    HWo; hundreþ *BF*, hundrede *Lo*

110 stoodyn *E*; to: so *Wo*, om. *X*; stedefastli *CEX*, stidfastly *Wo*; sounende *CX*,
    sounnynge *H*, sowndynge *Lo*; with: þe *Wo*; trumpis *CE*, trumpes *WoX*

111 sent *BFHWo*, sende *ELo*; inne *Lo*; swerde *BHWo*; all *BF*, al *H*

112 tentus *C*, tentes *X*; kuttyn *E*, kitten *Wo*; þem *CLoX*; selue *BEFHWo*;
    self *CLoX*

20 Cumque per gyrum castrorum in tribus personarent
locis, et hydrias confregissent, tenuerunt sinistris
manibus lampades, et dextris sonantes tubas; clamaveruntque: Gladius Domini et Gedeonis;

21 stantes singuli in loco suo, per circuitum castrorum

20 pottis among hem silf. And whanne thei
sowneden in thre places bi cumpas, and
hadden broke the pottis, thei helden
laumpis in the left hondis, and sownynge   100
trumpis in the riȝt hondis; and thei crieden, The swerd of the Lord and of Ge-
21 deon; and stoden alle in her place, bi
the cumpas of the tentis of enemyes.
And so alle the tentis weren troblid;   105
and thei crieden, and ȝelliden, and fled-
22 den; and neuertheles the thre hundrid
men contynueden, sownynge with trumpis.
And the Lord sente swerd in alle the
castels, and thei killiden hem silf bi deeth   110

97 pottes FHa; amonge RU; self CaEFKLMPRUW; when E, whan FHaLP
98 sownyden GQR; placis AcDEGHaIKLMaNPQSX
99 hadde HaU, haddin P; broken EU, broke *togidre* I; pottes FHa; heulden
    K, heelden LMaNPQRX, hilden U
100 lampis EI, laumpes FL; the: her I; lift BEGHaKMaPQ, lefte IR, lifte L,
    lef- O; hondes CaF; sounyng E; 99–100 in her lefte hondis þei helden
    lampis I
101 trumpes FPR; in: with R; the: her I, þer E; hondes CaF; 100–1 &
    trumpis sowny[n]ge in her riȝt hondis I; criden EUW
102 swerde ER, sweerd L
103 stooden GKLNX, þei stoden I; here FQ; 103–4 bi the cumpas of: aboute I
104 the: om. MMa; tentes FHa; her enmyes I, enmyes O
105 tentes FHa; troublid CaDFGHaLMMaNOPRWX, storbled E, troublide
    K; alle þei weren troblid in her tentis I
106 crieden 'out' I, criden UW; ȝelleden CaFLMPUW, ȝelledden E; fledden
    awey I
107 nerþeles ELP, neþeles GIMaQX, neuereþeles K; the: om. D; hundred
    EHa, hunderd LP
108 sounyng EF; trompis E, trumpes FPR
109 lorde E; sent E; swerde HaR, sweerd L
110 castels: tentis I, castelis LS; killeden EFLMPW, kelliden U; self
    CaEFKLMNPRUW; deþ AcCEFIOPQRSUX

hostilium. Omnia itaque castra turbata sunt, et
vociferantes ululantesque fugerunt;
22 et nihilominus insistebant trecenti viri, bucinis
personantes. Immisitque Dominus gladium in omnibus
castris, et mutua se caede truncabant,

23 bi sleynge echon other, fleynge into Beth-
saka, and bi the cop of the brenke, fro
Elmonla into Thebbath. The men of 115
Irael forsothe criynge togidre, of Neptalym, and Aser, and al Manasse, pursueden Madian; and the Lord ȝaf to
the puple of Yrael victory in that day.

24 And Gedeon sente messangers into al the 120
hil of Effraym, seiynge, Comith doun
into a ȝen metynge of Madian, and occu-
pieth the watres vnto Bethhem and Jordan. And al Effraym criede, and forn
occupiede the watres and Jordan vnto 125

113 sleyng *CX*; echon: eche *CX*, echeon *E*, echone *Lo*; ooþer *E*; fleeȝing *B*,
fleande *C*, fleeȝinge *FH*, fleing *Lo*; fleȝinge *Wo*, fleende *X*; into: vn to *CE*
114 copp *BFH*, coppe *LoWo*; brynke *cet.*; from *X*
116 criende *CX*, cryenge *E*; to giþer *BF*, togidere *CEX*, togyder *HWo*
117 all *BF*, alle *Lo*; pursuede *BLo*, pursued *H*
118 ȝaue *BFHWo*, ȝafe *Lo*
119 peple *BFHLoWo*; victorie *CELo*
120 sent *BFHWo*, sende *Lo*; messagers *B*, messageres *CWoX*, messageris *ELo*;
alle *BLo*, all *F*
121 hyll *BFH*, hille *LoWo*; seyand *BFWo*, seiende *CX*, seyande *ELo*, seying *H*;
commiþ *BF*, comeþ *CEX*, comes *Lo*
122 a ȝeyn *BFWo*, a-ȝeyne *Lo*; meeting *C*, metyng *EX*, mettyng *Lo*; ocupieþ
CX, occupyes *Lo*
123 waters *BH*, watris *CFWoX*, wateris *E*
124 all *F*, alle *Lo*; cryed *Wo*; forn: bifore *Lo*
125 occupied *BFHWo*, ocupiede *CX*; waters *BH*, watris *CEFWoX*

23 fugientes usque Bethsecha, et per crepidinem ab El-
meula in Thebbath. Conclamantes autem viri Israel,
de Neptalim, et Aser, et omni Manasse, persequebantur
Madian. Et dedit Dominus victoriam populo Israel in
die illa.

24 Misitque Gedeon nuntios in omnem montem Effraim,
dicens: Descendite in occursum Madian, et occupate
aquas usque Bethbera atque Iordanem. Clamavitque
omnis Effraim, et praeoccupavit aquas atque Iordanem
usque Bethbera.

23 ech other; and thei fledden til to Bethsecha, and bi the side, fro Elmonla in to
Thebbath. Sotheli men of Israel crieden
togidere, of Neptalym, and of Aser, and
of alle Manasses, and pursueden Madian;   115
and the Lord ʒaf victorie to the puple of
24 Israel in that day. And Gedeon sente
messangeris in to al the hil of Effraym,
and seide, Come ʒe doun aʒens the com-
yng of Madian, and ocupie ʒe the watris   120
til to Bethbera and Jordan. And al
Effraym criede, and bifore ocupide the

111 vche E, eche K; oþere AcDG, oþir NOS; til to: to E, vn to I
112 and: om. Ma; the side: a *priuei* side I; fro: *þei wenten* fro I, from K
113 soþli FGLMMaPQSUWX, & I; criden UW
114 to gidre DIR, to gyder E
115 al cet.; pursuweden CaFMW, þei pursueden I, pursuiden Q
116 ʒaaf I, ʒaue R; peple CaFILMMaNPWX
117 sent E
118 messangers DIMX, messagers EK, messangeres HaRU, messengers L,
     massangeris O, messengeris P; hille D, hul E, puple GQ
119 said E, he seide I; cum E; ʒee U; doune E; aʒenus AcCO, aʒen N;
     the: om. D; comynge CaDFGLMaPQUW
120 occupie CGHaILMaSU; ʒee U; the: om. I; watres EF
121 til to: to E, vn to I
122 cride CaUW, cried E; and: om. B, & þei I; bifor Ac; ocupiede
     AcBCaFIKMNOPQRSUWX, ocupiede CGHaLMa, ocupied DE,
     ocupieden I

25 Bethhara. And two men of Madian
   takun, Oreb and Zeb, he slowȝ; Oreb in
   the stoon of Oreb, forsothe Zeb in the
   pressynge place of Zeb; and thei pur-
   suden Madian, the heedys of Oreb and   130
   of Zeb berynge to Gedeon, ouer the
   floodis of Jordan.

8. 1 And the men of Effraym seiden to
   hym, What is this that thou woldest doo,
   that thou clepedist not vs, whanne thou
   shuldist go to [the] fiȝt aȝens Madian?
   chidynge stronglich and almest violence   5

127 taken *BCFHLoWoX*, takyn *E*; slewȝ *BFH*, sloȝ *CX*, slowȝe *Lo*
128 ston *CEHX*, stone *Wo*; forsothe Zeb: Z. f. *cet.*
129 pressing *CEX*; pursueden *BCFHLoWoX*, pursuwedyn *E*
130 heuedis *BFH*, hedis *CEX*, hedes *Lo*, heuedes *Wo*
131 berende *CX*; ouyr *E*
132 flodis *BCEFH*, flodes *LoWo*, flodus *X*

8. 1 seidyn *E*
   2 this: om. *X*; woldist *BEFHX*; doon *BFLo*, do *C*, don *EWo*, doone *H*
   3 cleepe *B*, clepedest *CLo²X*, clepe *EWo*, cleep *FH*, kalle *Lo¹*; noȝt *Lo*;
     whenn *BH*, whan *CFLoWoX*
   4 shuldest *CEWo*, scholdest *Lo*; goon *BFLo*, gon *EWo*, goo *H*; fiȝt: þe fiȝt
     BCEFHWo, þe fiȝte *Lo*, fiȝte *X*; aȝeyn *BFWo*, aȝen *CEHX*, aȝeyne *Lo*

25 Apprehensosque duos viros Madian, Oreb et Zeb, interfecit; Oreb in petra Oreb, Zeb vero in torculari Zeb.
   Et persecuti sunt Madian, capita Oreb et Zeb portant-
   es ad Gedeon, trans fluenta Iordanis.

8. 1 Dixeruntque ad eum viri Effraim: Quid est hoc, quod
   facere voluisti, ut non nos vocares, cum ad pugnam
   pergeres contra Madian? iurgantes fortiter, et prope
   vim inferentes.

25 watris and Jordan til to Bethbera. And
Effraym killide twei men of Madian, Oreb
and Zeb; *he killide* Oreb in the stoon of
Oreb, forsothe *he killide* Zeb in the pressour of Zeb; and thei pursueden Madian,
and baren the heedis of Oreb and of Zeb
to Gedeon, ouer the flodis of Jordan.

125

8. 1 And the men of Effraym seiden to
hym, What is this thing, which thou
woldist do, that thou clepidist not vs,
whanne thou ȝedist to batel aȝens Madian? And thei chidden strongli, and

5

---

123 watres EF; and: of KMa; til to: to E, vn to I
124 killid DE, killede FLP, kilde U; tweye BCaQW, two I; '*cheef*' men I
125 killid D, killed E, killede FLP, kilde U; *he killide* Oreb: O. he k. I; stone
E, ston I
126 forsothe: & I, forsoþ X; killid D, kylled E, killede FL, kille[de] P, kilde U;
he k.: om. I; pressure I
127 thei: Effraym I; pursuyden AcQ, pursuweden CaFMW, pursuede I
128 barin ELPU, baaren KX, þei baren I; hedis CaMRW, hedes EF, heedes U
129 ouir Q; floodis AcCDGHaKLMaOPX, flodes EFR, stronde W

8. 1 sayden E
2 hym: Gedeon I; whiche G, þat I, wiche K
3 woldest CEFHaLP; clepidist CaIMNW, clepedest EFP, clepidest HaKL,
clepidiste R
4 whan EFGHaLP; ȝedest EFHaL, ȝediste R; bateil DKX, batail I, bateile
R, bataile U; aȝenus AcCNO
5 chidden *wiþ him* I

2 brynggynge yn. To whom he answerde,
What siche thing forsothe myȝte Y doo,
what ȝe han doon? Whether is not betere the graape of Effraym than the
3 vendage of Abiether? Into ȝoure hoondis   10
the Lord hath takun the princis of Ma-
dian, Oreb and Zeb. What siche thing
miȝte Y doo, what thing ȝe han doo?
The which thing whanne he hadde
spoken, the spyryt of hem took rest, bi   15
the which thei bolneden aȝens hym.

5 chidende CX; strongli CX, strongliche EWo, strongely Lo; almost CX, almoste Lo
6 bringende CX, bryngen[de] E, bringynge LoWo; inne Lo; whome BFLo; answerd B, answeride Lo, answered Wo
7 such CEX, suche Lo; þinge BFLoWo; miȝt BFHWo; do CWoX, don E
8 ȝee CELoX; do CX, don EWo; wheþere Lo; no Lo; better BFHWo, bettere E, betre Lo
9 grape cet.
10 vindage CEX; ȝour BCFHLoWo; hondus C, handis E, hondes LoWo, hondis X
11 lorde Wo; has Lo; take BFHWoX, taken CLo, takyn E; prynces ELoX
12 such CEX, sich FWo, suche Lo; þinge BFWo
13 myȝt BFHWo; do CEWoX; þinge BHWo; ȝee CEHLoX; do CWoX, don E, doon Lo
14 whiche BCEHX; þinge BFLoWo; whenn BH, whan CELoWoX, whann F; had BFLoWo
15 spokyn E; spirite BFLo, spiriȝte H; þem CLoX; toke BFHLoWo, toc CX; reste CEFLoWoX
16 whiche BCEHLoX; bolnyden BFHWo, bolnedyn E; aȝeyn BFH, aȝen CEWoX, a-ȝeynes Lo

2 Quibus ille respondit: Quid enim tale facere potui,
quale vos fecistis? nonne melior est racemus Effraim
vindemiis Abiezer?
3 In manus vestras Dominus tradidit principes Madian,
Oreb et Zeb. Quid tale facere potui, quale vos fec-

2 almest diden violence. To whiche he
answeride, What sotheli siche thing myȝte
Y do, what maner thing ȝe diden? Whethir a reisyn of Effraym is not betere
3 than the vindagis of Abiezer? (And) the   10
Lord bitook in to ȝoure hondis the princes
of Madian, Oreb and Zeb. What sich
thing myȝte Y do, what maner thing ȝe
diden? And whanne he hadde spoke
this thing, the spirit of hem restide, bi   15

6 almeest BK, almoste E, almost HaPR, welnyȝ I, almoost LMa; þei diden
   to him I, dedin P, deden U; which DE, whom I, wiche K
7 answerde CaFGMPQUW, answerid D, answede E, answerede L; what
   sotheli: whanne s. D, and what I; soþli FGLMMaPQRUWX; sich
   AcBCGIKMaOQSUX, such CaEHaLMNPRW, suche DF; miȝt DE,
   myȝti S
8 do: haue do I, doo S; manere FGW; ȝee GU; deden F, han do I, dedin P;
   where DI, wher cet.
9 reisen BDGHaLOQS, resen E; bettir DR, better E, bettere KMaN
10 þanne D; the: om. L; vyndages CaFR, vendagis G, windagis S; And: om.
   A²B²
11 bi-toke ER, bitok F, haþ bitake I; ȝour F, oure B; hondes F, hoondis R;
   pryncis DGHaKLMaNPQX; 11—12 the princes of Madian Oreb and Zeb:
   O. & Z. þe princis of m. I
12 such CaEFGHaLMMaNPRW, suche D
13 myȝt DE, myȝti S; do: haue do I, doo S; manere GW; ȝee U
14 deden FU, han do I, dedin P; wan E, whan HaLP; he: Gedeon I; had EI
15 spiritt K, spiriȝt L; hem: þe Lord GQ, effraym I, him U; restid D, restede
   EFP

istis? Quod cum locutus esset, requievit spiritus
eorum, quo tumebant contra eum.

4 And whanne Gedeon was comyn to Jordan, he passide it with thre hundrid
men, that weren with hym; and for
werynes, fleynge thei my3ten not pursue.   20
5 And he seide to the men of Socchoth,
Y biseche, 3yueth looues to the puple,
that is with me; for greetlich thei de-
fauten, that we mowen pursue Zebee
6 and Salmana, kyngis of Madian. The   25
princis of Soccoth answerden, Perauen-
ture the palmes of the hoondis of Zebee
and of Salmana ben in thin hoond, and
therfor thow askist, that we 3euen to

17 whenn *B*, whan *CLoWoX*, when *EH*, whann *F*; commen *BF*, come *C*,
comen *HLoWoX*
18 passed *BFWo*, passede *CX*, passid *HLo*; hundreþ *BF*, hundrede *Lo*
19 weryn *E*
20 werynesse *cet.*; flee3inge *BFH*, þe fleande *C*, fle3inge *Wo*, þe fleende *X*;
my3tyn *E*, my3te *Lo*; pursuen *BFHLoWo*, pursuwyn *E*
22 Y biseche 3yueth: 3. Y b. *cet.*; beseche *BCEX*; 3euiþ *BFH*, 3efeþ *E*,
3yues *Lo*, 3eueþ *Wo*; loues *C*, louys *E*, loeues *X*; peple *BFHLoWo*
23 gretliche *BEH*, gretli *CLoX*, gretlich *F*, gretelich *Wo*; defawtyn *E*, defau3ten
H
24 wee *EX*; moun *C*(+not)*E*; pursuen *BFHLoWo*, pursuwyn *E*
25 kingus *CX*, kynges *Lo*
26 prynces *ELoX*; answerdyn *E*, answeriden *Wo*; parauenture *BCEFHX*
27 palmys *EFLoWo*; handus *C*, handis *E*, hondis *HWoX*, hondes *Lo*
28 þine *Lo*; hond *CWoX*, hand *ELo*²
29 þerfore *BCEFHWoX*, þerefore *Lo*; askest *CLoX*; wee *CEX*; 3iue *CX*,
3ifyn *E*, gyuen *Lo*, 3iuen *Wo*

4 Cumque venisset Gedeon ad Iordanem, transivit eum
cum trecentis viris, qui secum erant; et prae lassi-
tudine, fugientes persequi non poterant.
5 Dixitque ad viros Soccoth: Date, obsecro, panes
populo, qui mecum est, quia valde defecerunt, ut
possimus persequi Zebee et Salmana, reges Madian.
6 Responderunt principes Soccoth: Forsitan palmae
manuum Zebee et Salmana in manu tua sunt, et idcirco
postulas, ut demus exercitui tuo panes.

4 which thei bolneden aȝens hym. And
whanne Gedeon hadde come to Jordan,
he passide it with thre hundrid men, that
weren with hym; and for weerynesse thei
5 myȝten not pursue hem that fledden. And   20
he seide to the men of Socoth, Y biseche,
ȝyue ȝe looues to the puple, which is
with me; for thei failiden greetli, that we
moun pursue Zebee and Salmana, kyngis
6 of Madian. The princes of Socoth an-   25
sweriden *in scorne*, In hap the pawmes of
the hondis of Zebee and of Salmana ben
in thin hond, and therfor thou axist, that

16   whiche GI, wich K; bolnyden GHaQR, bolnden M; aȝenus AcCNO
17   whan EGLP; had EI; cum E
18   passid DF, passed E, passede PU; it: om. E; hundreþe E, hunderd LP
19   werynesse AcBCCaFGHaIKLMMaNQRUWX, wirinesse E; þai E
20   miȝt E, miȝte L; pursuwe FMW; fled E
21   he: Gedeon I; seid E; the: om. L; bisech E
22   ȝeue BDGHaLMaQR, ȝif E, ȝife K; ȝee SU; loues DFGLR, bred I,
     þe looues Ma, loouis Q; peple CaFILMMaNPWX; whiche G, þat I,
     wich K
23   faileden CaDEFLMNPW, failede U; gretli AcEILOPQSU
24   mowen *þanne* I, mowe K, mowen U; pursuwe CaFMW; kings E, kynges
     FHa, þe kyngis I
25   The princes: þe princis DGMaNPQSWX, And þe princis I; answerden
     CaDEFGMPQUW, answereden LN
26   scorne AR, scoorn GMa, scorn cet.; happe K; pawmys GQ
27   the: om. X; hondes CaF, hoondis R; and of Salmana: & S. DI
28   þi K; honde E, hondis I; and: om. GOQ; þerfore BCaEGIKMaNQRWX;
     axest EFHa

7 thin oost looues. To whom he seith, 30
Whanne therfor the Lord shal taak into
myn hoondis Zebee and Salmana, and
whanne Y were turned aȝen ouercomer
in pees, Y shal to-teren ȝoure flesh with
8 thornes and breris of deseert. And thens 35
goynge he cam into Phanuel; and he
spak to the men of that place lijk thingis,
and to whom thei answerden, as an-
9 swerden the men of Soccoth. And to
hem he seide also, Whanne Y were turn- 40
ed aȝen ouercomer in pees, Y shal de-

30 þine *Lo*; ost *CX*, host *E*; loouys *BFWo*, loues *C*, louys *E*, loeues *X*; whome
BFLo; seys *Lo*
31 whenn *BH*, whan *CLoWoX*, whann *F*; þerfore *BCEFHWoX*, þere fore *Lo*;
take *BCFHLoWo*, takyn *E*, taken *X*
32 hondis *CX*, handis *E*, handes *Lo*, hondes *Wo*
33 whenn *BH*, whan *CLoWoX*, whenne *E*, whann *F*; wer *B*; tornyde *B*,
turnyd *E*, turnyde *FH*, turnede *Lo*, torned *Wo*; aȝeyn *BFHLoWo*, aȝeen
CEX; ouercommer *BFLo*, ouercomere *CE*
34 pese *BE*, pes *CX*; to-tern *CE²X*; ȝour *BCEFHLoX*; flesche *HLo*
35 þornys *BEFHWo*; breres *X*; desert *BCEFHWoX*, deserte *Lo*; þenns *B*,
þennus *C*, þennys *E*, þennes *LoX*
36 gooynge *BF*, goende *CX*, going *Lo*; coom *BFH*, come *LoWo*
37 spake *BWo*; the: om. *X*; lyke *cet.*; thingus *CX*, þinges *Lo*
38 Whome *BFLo*; answerdyn *E* (2x); as answerden: om. *B*
40 þem *CLoX*; he: om. *H*; whenn *BH*, whan *CLoWoX*, whenne *B*; tornyd
BFH, turnyd *E*, turnede *Lo*, torned *Wo*
41 aȝeyn *BFWo*, aȝeen *CEX*; ouer-commer *BFLo*, ouercomere *CX*, ouyrcomere
E; pese *BE*, pes *CX*; destroȝe *C*, destroien *E*, destruye *FHWo*, destroye
Lo, distroȝe *X*

7 Quibus ille ait: Cum ergo tradiderit Dominus Zebee
et Salmana in manus meas, et cum reversus fuero
victor in pace, conteram carnes vestras cum spinis
tribulisque deserti.
8 Et inde conscendens venit in Phanuel; locutusque

216

7 we ȝyue looues to thin oost. To whiche
  he seide, Therfor, whanne the Lord schal   30
  bitake Zebee and Salmana in to myn
  hondis, and whanne Y schal turne aȝen
  ouercomere in pees, Y schal to-reende ȝoure
  fleischis with the thornes and breris of
8 deseert. And he stiede fro thennus,   35
  and cam in to Phanuel; and he spak lijk
  thingis to men of that place, to whom also
  thei answeriden, as the men of Socoth
9 hadden answerid. And so he seide to
  hem, Whanne Y schal turne aȝen ouer-   40
  comere in pees, Y schal distrie this tour.

29 ȝeue DGHaMaQRU, ȝif E, ȝife K; loues CaEF, loouys GHaNQ; þine E;
    ost E; which DE, whom I, wiche K
30 he: and he Ac, Gedeon I; said E; þerfore BCaEGIKMaNQRWX; whan
    EFHaLP, whane S
31 myne CaEKMRW
32 hondes CaFL, hoondis RS; whan EGHaLP; aȝein B
33 ouercomer BDEHaRX; pes E; 32−33 in pes I schal turne aȝen ouercomere
    I; torende AcBCCaDEGMMaRUW, torente Ha; ȝour FK
34 flesshis CaEFLMPRUW, fleshe I, fleiȝsshis K; the: om. EI; þornys GMaQ;
    breres EKRU, breeris GI, brerers Ha; of: in D
35 desert AcCCaEFGHaKLMNOPQSUWX, þe desert I, deserte R; he:
    Gedeon I; stied DE, steiede F, stiede up I, stiȝede MaNR, ȝede S; from
    K; þennes CaFHaKMUW, þens DEMaR, þennys GNQSX, þenns I,
    þenis LP
36 came DIR; spake IR, spaac K; lik CFGU, like DEHaLP
37 þinges CaFHa, þings E; wom E; also: alle R
38 þai E; answerden CCaDEFGMPQUW, answereden L
39 had E, haddin P; answerd DEF, answeride Ha, answerde LU; so: om.
    AcCCaDEFGHaKLMMaNOPQRSUX; he: Gedeon I
40 when E, whan FGHaLP; aȝein E; ouercomer DEHaIRX
41 pese E; destroi E, destrie IL, distroie KMaR, distruye X; toure DE

est ad viros loci illius similia. Cui et illi responderunt, sicut responderant viri Soccoth.
9 Dixit itaque /et/ eis: Cum reversus fuero victor in
  pace, destruam turrim hanc.

10 struy this tour. Zebee forsothe and Salmana restiden with al her oost; forsothe
   fifteen thowsand men abiden stil of alle
   the cumpanyes of the [est] puplis, sleyn   45
   an hundryd and twenty thousandis of
11 fiȝters and of drawers out swerd. And
   Gedeon stiynge vp bi the weye of hem
   that dwelliden in tabernaclis at the eest
   coost of Nobee and Lecaa, he smoot the   50
   tentis of the enemyes, that weren siker,
   and no thing of aduersyte ortroweden.
12 And Zebee and Salmana flowen, whom
   pursuynge Gedeon took, disturblid al the

---

42   toure *LoWo*; forsoþ *B*
43   resteden *CLoX*, restidyn *E*; alle *BLo*, all *F*; þer *BCLoX*, þeir *EFWo*; ost *CX*,
     host *E*, ooste *Wo*; 43–44 forsothe fifteen: fift. fors *BCEFHWoX*; fyftene
     cet.
44   þousande *BFLo*, thousend *CEX*; abidyn *E*; styll *BF*, stille *CEHLoWoX*;
     all *F*, al *HX*
45   companyes *BEFLoWo*; est: om. *ABFHWoX*, eest *Lo*; peplis *BFHLoWo*;
     slawen *BFHWo*, slain *CX*, slawyn *E*, slayne *Lo*
46   a *Lo*; hundreþ *BF*, hundred *LoX*; thousend *CX*
47   fiȝteres *CX*, fiȝteris *ELo*; draweres *CX*, draweris *ELo*; oute *B*, ouȝte *H*,
     out of *X*; swerde *BFLoWo*; An[d] *E*
48   steyȝinge *BFWo*, steȝende *CX*, steynge *E*, styȝinge *H*, steiȝing *Lo*; wey
     LoWo; þem *CLoX*
49   dwellen *C*, dwelledyn *E*, dwelleden *H*, dwelten *X*; thabernaclis *Lo*; este
     BF, est *CEHLoX*
50   cost *CE*, coest *X*; smote *BLoWo*, smot *CEX*
51   tentus *C*, tentes *X*; enmyse *B*, enemys *CEX*, enmyes *FHWo*; weryn *E*;
     sikyr *E*
52   þinge *BFWo*; ortrowidyn *E*, ouertroweden *WoX*
53   floun *CX*, flowyn *E*; whome *BFLo*
54   pursuyng *B*, pursuende *CX*, pursuwynge *E*; toke *BFLoWo*, toc *CX*;
     distourblyd *BFHWo*, disturbid *CX*, destourblede *Lo*

---

10 Zebee autem et Salmana requiescebant cum omni
   exercitui suo; quindecim enim millia viri remanserant ex omnibus turmis orientalium populorum,
   caesis centum viginti millibus bellatorum et educentium gladium.
11 Ascendensque Gedeon per viam eorum, qui in taberna-

10 Forsothe Zebee and Salmana restiden
with al her oost; for fiftene thousynde
men leften of alle the cumpenyes of the
puplis of the eest, whanne an hundrid 45
and twenti thousynde of fiȝteris and of
men drawynge out swerd weren slayn.

11 And Gedeon stiede bi the weye of hem
that dwelliden in tabernaclis at the eest
coost of Nobe and of Lethoa, and smoot 50
the tentis of enemyes, that weren sikur,
and supposiden not ony thing of aduersite.

12 And Zebee and Salmana fledden, whiche
Gedeon pursuede and took, whanne al the

42 Forsothe: And I, forsoþ X; resteden CaFLMPW, restendē E
43 here FGQR; oste E; for: om. E, and I; þousynd CaIMW, þousand
   DEHaMaNQRX, þousend FGL, þousande KS, þousende P
44 laften EK, leftin P; al Ma; the: om. L; cumpanyes
   BCaGILMMaNPQRUWX, companies E; the (2°): om. GHaQ; 44−45
   the puplis of: om. E
45 peplis CaIMMaNPWX, peples FL, puples R; est EGQ; whan EFGHaLP;
   hundred Ha, hunderd LP; 43−45 and of alle þe companyes of þe eest
   peplis fiftene þousynd men leften I
46 þousynd CaIMW, þousand DHaMaNQRX, þousend FGL, þousande KS,
   þousende P; fiȝters DEHaKLMMaRX, fiȝteres U; 46−47 of fiȝteris and
   of men: of fiȝtynge men I
47 drawynge: ledynge AcBCaDFGHaMMaNOQRSUWX, drawing C, leding
   EKLP; sweerd FL; were GMQ; slayne KR
48 stied DE, steiede F, stiede up I, stiȝede MaNR; wey DEHaIMaU
49 dwelleden CaFLMPW, dwelledden E, dwelden U; tabernacles EFPR; at
   the: atte E; est EQ
50 coost: ost E, cost Q; smote EHaIR, smot U
51 tentis of enemyes: enmyes tentis I; sikir AcCaDGIMMaNPQSUWX,
   siker BEFKLR
52 supposeden CaEFLMPUW, subposiden O; eny Ha, any X;
   aduersytee BGKMa
53 which EFHaQ, whom I, wiche K
54 pursuyde AcQ, pursuwide CaMW, pursued DE, pursuwede F; tok E,
   toke R; whan EGHaLP; alle CS

culis morabantur, ad orientalem plagam Nobee et
Lechaa, percussit castra hostium, qui securi erant,
et nihil adversi suspicabantur.

12 Fugeruntque Zebee et Salmana, quos persequens Gedeon
comprehendit, turbato omni exercitu eorum.

13 oost of hem. And he turnynge aȝen fro 55
14 the bateyl before the sunne rysynge, he
took a child of the men of Soccoth; and
he askyde hym the names of the pryncis,
and of the eldren of Soccoth; and he dis-
criuyde seuenty and seuen men bi noum- 60
15 bre. And he cam to Socoth, and seide to
hem, Loo Zebee and Salmana! vpon the
whiche ȝee mysseyden to me, seiynge,
Perauenture the hoondys of Zebee and
Salmana in thin hoondis ben, and therfor 65
thou askist, that we ȝeuen to the men,
that ben wery and han defautid, looues.

55 ooste B, ost CX, host C; þem CELo; tornynge BFHWo, turnende CX;
aȝeyn BFHWo, aȝeen CEX
56 bataile CELoX, bateyle H, batayl Wo; beforn BEH, befor C, byforn F,
bifore LoX, biforne Wo; sonne Lo; rising CX; he: om. CE²
57 toke BFHLoWo, toc CX; chylde BLoWo
58 askede CEX, askyd FHWo; namys BEFHWo; prynces ELoX
59 elder B, eldere CEX, eldre FHLoWo; he: om. H; discryuyd BFH,
discriuede CELoX, discreuyd Wo
60 seuene LoWoX; and s. men: men & s. X
61 coom BFH, come LoWo; to: in to H
62 þem CLoX; lo CE; apon BFWo
63 which F; ȝe BWo; mysseidyn E; seiende CX
64 par auenture EX; hondus C, handis E, handes Lo, hondes Wo, hondis X;
64–65 and Salmana: & of S. CELo
65 þine Lo; hondus C, handis E, hondis HX, handes Lo, hondes Wo; þerfore
BCEFHWoX, þerefore Lo
66 askest LoWoX; wee CEX; ȝiue CX, ȝifen E, ȝyuen LoWo; the: þee F,
þi Wo
67 werye Lo; defawted E, defauȝtid H, defautede Lo; loouys BFH, loues C,
louys EWo, loeues X

13 Revertensque de bello ante solis ortum,
14 apprehendit puerum de viris Soccoth; interrogavitque
eum nomina principum et seniorum Soccoth, et de-
scripsit septuaginta septem viros numero.
15 Venitque ad Soccoth, et dixit eis: En Zebee et Sal-

13 oost of hem was disturblid. And he   55
   turnede aȝen fro batel bifor the risyng of
14 the sunne, and took a child of the men
   of Socoth; and he axide hym the names
   of the princes and eldere men of Socoth;
   and he descryuede seuene and seuenti men   60
15 in noumbre. And he cam to Socoth, and
   seide to hem, Lo Zebee and Salmana! of
   whiche ȝe vpbreideden* me, and seiden, In
   hap the hondis of Zebee and of Salmana
   ben in thin hondis, and therfor thou axist,   65
   that we ȝyue looues to men, that ben weeri

55 ost E; 54—55 the oost of hem: her oost I; distourblid CaFMW, desturblid
    E, distroublid Ma; he: Gedeon I
56 turned DE, turnyde GHaQR; a-ȝein E; from K; bateil DQX, bataile KU,
    bateile MaR; bifore BCaDEGHaIKMaNQRWX; risinge CaDGMaQUW
57 sonne EK; 56—57 risyng of the sunne: sunne rysyng I; toke ER, he took
    I; childe E, chijld K
58 axid D, axed E, axede FPU; namys GQ
59 princis DEGHaIKLMaNPQSWX; elder CaDELMPW, of þe eldre I,
    eldre MaRX
60 he: om. GHaQ, Gedeon I; discryuede AcBCHaLMMaNPRUW, discryuede
    DE, discriuyde GIQ; seuene and seuenti men: seuenti & seuen/e/ men
    CaMW, seuenti men & seuen/e/ GIQ
61 came R
62 seid E; loo K; Zebee and Salmana: Z. & S. ben taken I
63 which EO, wiche K; ȝe: om. E, ȝee U; vpbroididen AAc, upbreydiden
    BGHaMaQSUX, vpbraididen CO, vpbreideden CaDIKMNW, vmbreideden
    E, vpbraideden F, vnbreideden LP; saiden E; 62 of ... S. (64): om. R
64 happe K; hondes CaF; and of Salmana: & S. DEGHaQU¹X
65 bene E; þi C, þine CaKMMaRW; hondes CaF, hoondis R; þerfore
    BCaGIKMaNQRWX; axest EF
66 ȝeue BDGMaQRU, ȝeuen Ha, ȝife K; loues DEF, loouis HaQ; þe men Ma;
    bene E; wery BCCaDEFGHaILMMaNPQSUWX, werie KR

mana, super quibus exprobrastis mihi, dicentes:
Forsitan manus Zebee et Salmana in manibus tuis sunt,
et idcirco postulas, ut demus viris, qui lassi sunt
et defecerunt, panes.

16 He took thanne the eldre of the cyte,
and thornes of deseert and breris, and to-
rente with hem, and distruyede the men 70
17 of Socoth; forsothe the tour of Phanuel
he turnede vpsedoun, slayn the dwellers
18 of the cyte. And he seide to Zebee and
to Salmana, What weren the men, whom
ȝe slowen in Thabor? The whiche an- 75
swerden, Lijk thee, and oon of hem as
19 the sone of a kyng. To whom he, My
britheren thei weren, the sones of my
moder; God lyueth, if ȝe hadden kepte

68 toke *BFHLoWo*, toc *CX*; þann *BF*, þan *Wo*; eldere *CE*, eldere men *X*;
the: þat *X*; cytee *F*
69 þornys *BEFHWo*; desert *BCEFHWoX*, deserte *Lo*; breres *X*; to rent *Wo*
70 þem *CELoX*; destruyed *BFHWo*, destroȝede *C*, destroiede *E*, destroye *Lo*,
distroȝede *X*
71 forsoþ *B*; forsothe the tour: þe t. f. *cet.*; toure *LoWo*
72 torned *BFHWo*; vpsadoun *BFH*, vp so doun *CELoWoX*; slawen *BFHWo*,
slawyn *E*; dwelleris *CELoX*
74 to: om. *Wo*; weryn *E*; whome *BFHLo*, þat *X*
75 ȝee *CELoX*; slowyn *E*; which *FWo*; answerdyn *E*
76 lyke *BCFHLoWo*, lik *EX*; þe *Wo*; oone *HLoWo*, oen *X*; þem *Lo*
77 kynge *BLo*; whome *BFLoWo*
78 breþeren *BEFHLoWoX*, breþern *CX*; weryn *E*; sonys *BEFH*, sonus *CX*
79 modir *BEH*, modre *Lo*; lyfiþ *BH*, lyuiþ *F*, lyues *Lo*; ȝif *BFHWo*, ȝife *Lo*;
ȝee *CELoX*; hadde *CH*, haddyn *E*; kept *BCEFHWoX*

16 Tulit ergo seniores civitatis, et spinas deserti ac
tribulos, et contrivit cum eis atque comminuit viros
Soccoth.
17 Turrim quoque Phanuel subvertit, occisis habitatoribus civitatis.
18 Dixitque ad Zebee et Salmana: Quales fuerunt viri,
quos occidistis in Thabor? Qui responderunt: Similes
tui, et unus ex eis quasi filius regis.
19 Quibus ille ait: Fratres mei fuerunt, filii matris
meae. Vivit Dominus, si servassetis eos, non vos
occiderem.

16 and failiden. Therfor Gedeon took the
eldere men of the citee, and thornes and
breris of deseert, and he to-rente with
tho, and al to-brak the men of Socoth;   70
17 also he destriede the tour of Phanuel,
whanne the dwelleris of the citee weren
18 slayn. And he seide to Zebee and Salmana, What maner men weren thei, whiche
ȝe killiden in Thabor? Whiche answer-   75
iden, *Thei weren* lijk thee, and oon of
19 hem was as the sone of a kyng. To
whiche he seide, Thei weren my britheren, the sones of my modir; the Lord
lyueth, if ȝe hadden saued hem, Y nolde   80

67 faileden CaDEFIKLMNPUW, failen R; þerfore BCaEFGIKMaNQRWX;
   toke DER
68 elder CaDFLMPX, eldur E, eeldere Ha, eldre IMaR; cite FHaMPQW;
   and (1°): om. N, & *also* I; þornis EGMaQ
69 breres EFHaKSU, breeris L; desert AcCCaDEFGHaKLMNOPQSUWX,
   þe desert I, þe deseerte R; he: om. S; torent hem E, torende L, to-reente
   S; with: om. E
70 al to-brake DHaIR; 69−70 & wiþ þo he torente & alto brake I
71 he: Gedeon I; distride Ac, distriede BCCaFGHaIMNOPQSW, distried D,
   distroied E, distroiede MaR, distroide U, distruyede X; toure DE, hous G
72 when E, whan GLP; dwellers DEHaIKLMPRX, dwelleres F; cite
   CaFHaLMPQW; were MQ
73 slawne K, slayne R; saide E; and Salmana: & to S. IMa
74 manere FGIQRW; wer E, were HaQ; þai E; which E, þat I, wiche K
75 killeden CaFLMNW, kilden EU, killden P; which ELP, þe whiche I, wiche
   K; answerden CaDEGMPQUW, answereden FL
76 like DELP, lyk FGHaQSU; lijk þᵉ *þei weren* I; one E
78 which EF, whom I, wiche K; he: Gedeon I; saide E; breþren CaFM,
   breþern EK, briþren G, breþeren HaILNPUWX
79 sonys GQ; moder EFU, mooder L
80 liueþe E, lifeþ K; ȝif E; ȝee U; haddin P; sauyd AcCNQRSW, sauede Ha;
   nolde: wolde not I, noolde MaX

20 hem, Y wold not haue slayn ʒow. And   80
he seide to Jepter, his fyrst gotun, Ryse,
and sle hem. The which drewe not out
the swerd; forsothe he dredde, for a
21 child he was ʒit. And Zebee and Salmana seyden, Thow ryse, and fal into vs;   85
for after age and strength thow art of a
man. Gedeon roos, and slewe Zebee and
Salmana, and took the ournementis, and
billis, with the whiche the neckis of kyngis
22 chamels ben wonyd to be anourned. And   90
alle the men of Yrael seiden to Gedeon,
Haue lordship of vs, thow, and thi sone,
and the sone of thi sone; for thow hast

80 þem *CELo*, wolde *CEFHLoX*; han *CEX*; slawe *BFHWo*, slawyn *E*, sclayne
Lo
81 firste *CEH*; goten *BCFHX*, gotyn *E*, geten *LoWo*; ris *CEX*
82 slea *B*, slee *FHLo*, þem *CLoX*; whiche *BCEHLoX*; droʒ *CX*, drowʒ *EWo*,
drowe *Lo*; oute *B*, ouʒt *H*
83 swerde *FHLoWo*; forsothe he dredde: he dr. f. *cet.*; dredd *F*; 83−84 for
a child he was ʒit: for ʒit he was a child *X*
84 childe *LoWo*; ʒitt *BFHWo*
85 seidyn *E*; þu *B*; Thow ryse: rise þou *Lo*; ris *CEX*; fall *BFH*, falle *LoWo*
86 aftyr *E*; streyngþ *BF*, strengþe *CEHLoWoX*; ert *BFH*
87 rose *BWo*, ros *CEFHX*; slooʒ *C*, slow *E*, slowʒe *Lo*, slowe *Wo*, sloʒ *X*
88 toke *BFHLoWo*, toc *CX*; ornamentys *Lo*, ournamentis *Wo*, ournemens *X*
89 billes *Lo*; which *BFWo*; nekkes *WoX*; kynges *Lo*, kyngus *WoX*
90 camailes *CX*, chamailys *E*, chamelis *Lo*, camels *Wo*; wont *CWoX*, woned
EH, wonte *Lo*; ben *BCEFLoWo*; enourned *CX*, enournyd *E*, anoured *H*,
enournede *Lo*
91 all *F*; seidyn *E*
92 lordschipe *BCEFLoWoX*; þu *B*

20 Dixitque Iepther, primogenito suo: Surge, et inter-
fice eos. Qui non eduxit gladium; timebat enim,
quia puer adhuc erat.
21 Dixeruntque Zebee et Salmana: Tu surge, et irrue in
nos, quia iuxta aetatem et robur es hominis. Surrexit Gedeon, et interfecit Zebee et Salmana; et

20 sle ȝou. And he seide to Jepther, his
firste gendrid sone, Rise thou, and sle hem.
Which drow not swerd; for he dredde,
21 for he was ȝit a child. And Zebee and
Salmana seiden, Ryse thou, and falle on   85
vs; for thou art bi the age and strengthe
of man. Gedeon roos, and killide Zebee
and Salmana, and took the ournementis,
and bellis, with whiche the neckis of
kyngis camels ben wont to be maad fair.   90
22 And alle the men of Israel seiden to Ge-
deon, Be thou lord of vs, thou, and thi
sone, and the sone of thi sone; for thou
delyueridist vs fro the hond of Madian.

81 slee CaFGHaKQRW, haue slawe I; he: Gedeon I; said E
82 first DGHaQR; gendred Ha, goten I, gendride R; slee CaGHaKQW
83 which: And iepther I, wiche K; drowȝ CaFHaKMMaNWX, drowe DG,
    drewe out I, drowȝe R; swerde E, sweerd L, his sw. I; dred E
84 ȝitt Ma; childe EU, chijld K
85 saiden E, s. *to gedeon* I; on: in to I
86 and: of G; stre[n]gþe DEX, strenkþe MaR
87 rose EI; killid D, killed E, killede FLP, kilde U
88 toke ER, tooke Ha, he toke I; ornamentis E, ournementes FHa,
    ournamentis I, ornementis U
89 and: of Ca; belles FL, þe bellis I; with: bi I; which E, wiche K; neckes
    FR; n. of: om. Ma; of: om. Ca
90 kyngis: om. Ca, kynges FHa, þe kyngis I; camelis EGILQ; wonte R;
    made DE, mad LMaR; faire DER
91 the: om. AcCCaDEFGHaIKLMMaNOQRSUX; saiden E
94 delyueredist CCaFGMMaNUWX, delyuerdist D, deliueredest ELP,
    deliueridest HaK, hast delyuered I, deliuerediste R; from K; hond: power
    I, hoond R, honde U

tulit ornamenta ac bullas, quibus colla regalium
camelorum decorari solent.
22 Dixeruntque omnes viri Israel ad Gedeon: Dominare
nostri, tu, et filius tuus, et filius filii tui;
quia liberasti nos de manu Madian.

23 delyuerd vs fro the hoond of Madian. To
   whom he seith, I shal not haue lordship   95
   of ȝou, ne my sone shal haue lordship in
24 ȝou, but the Lord shal haue lordship. And
   he seide to hem, Oon askynge I aske of
   ȝow, ȝeueth to me the eere ryngys of
   ȝoure praye; forsothe Ysmaelitis weren   100
25 woned to han golden eereryngis. The
   whiche answerden, Moost glaadly we
   shulen ȝeue. And spredynge abrood vpon
   the erthe a mantil, thei threwen forth in

94 deliuered *CWoX*, delyuerid *E*, deliuerede *Lo*; hond *CWoX*, hand *E*, honde
    Lo
95 whome *BFLoWo*; seys *Lo*; han *CEX*; lordschipe *BCEFLoWoX*
96 han *CEX*; lordschipe *BCEFLoWoX*
97 bot *B*, bute *F*; han *CE*; lordschipe *BCEFWoX* (+ in ȝou *WoX*)
98 þem *CELoX*; oen *X*; asking *CEX*
99 ȝiueþ *CWoX*, ȝefeþ *E*, ȝeue *Lo*; errynges *B*, ereringus *CX*, er-ryngis *E*,
    ere-ryngis *FHWo*, ereyngis *Lo*
100 ȝour *BCFHLo*; prayȝe *BFHWo*, prei *CX*, preye *E*; forsoþ *F*; forsothe
    Ysmaelitis: Y. f. *cet.*; weryn *E*, were *LoWo*
101 wont *CWoX*, wonyd *E*, wonte *Lo*; haue *Lo*; goldene *CEX*; erringis *B*,
    ereringus *CX*, ereryngys *EFHWo*, ereyngis *Lo*
102 which *FWo*; answerdyn *E*; most *BCEFHWoX*, moste *Lo*; gladly *cet.*; wee
    CEX
103 schal *BFHLoWo*, shul *CX*, schuln *E*; ȝeuen *BFH*, ȝiue *CX*, ȝifen *E*, gyfen
    Lo, ȝyuen *Wo*; spredende *CX*, spredyng *Lo*; abrode *BFHWo*, abrod *CEX*,
    a-broode *Lo*; uppon *Wo*
104 erp *B*; mantyll *BF*, mantel *Lo*; þrewe *CX*, threwyn *E*; forþe *HLoX*; 104−5
    in it: out *Wo*

23 Quibus ille ait: Non dominabor vestri, nec dominabitur in vos filius meus, sed dominabitur Dominus.
24 Dixitque ad eos: Unam petitionem postulo a vobis:
   date mihi inaures ex praeda vestra. Inaures enim
   aureas Ismaelitae habere consueverant.
25 Qui responderunt: Libentissime dabimus. Expandentes-
   que super terram pallium, proiecerunt in eo inaures
   de praeda;

23 To whiche he seide, Y schal not be lord 95
of ȝou, nethir my sone schal be lord on
24 ȝou, but the Lord schal be lord. And he
seide to hem, Y axe oon axyng of ȝou,
ȝyue ȝe to me the eere ryngis of ȝoure
prey; for Ismaelitis weren wont to haue 100
25 goldun eere ryngis. Whiche answeriden,
We schulen ȝyue moost gla(l)dli. And thei
spredden for[th] a mentil on the erthe,
and castiden forth therynne eere ryngis

95 which BEL, whom I, wiche K
96 neþer AcBCDEKLNSUX, neiþer CaFGHaIMQRW, neiþir Ma; on: of DE
97 bot E; lord: lord of ȝou D¹, lord on ȝou D²I; he: Gedeon I
98 seid E; on EU; axinge CaDGLMaPQU
99 ȝeue BDGHaMaQRU, ȝife K; ȝee U; to: om. Ha; ere CaEFMW, eer I;
    rynges CaFHa; ȝour FK
100 pry D, pray EKLP; were Ha; wonte R
101 goldene CaFGW, golden DEIKLMMaPRU; ere BEMW; rynges FHa;
    which ES, þe whiche I, wiche K; answerden CaDEFGMPQUW,
    answereden L
102 schullen CaMW, schuln DF, shul EILP; ȝeue BDGHaMaQR, ȝiue þee
    þese I, ȝife K; most CaEFHaOPQ, ful I; gladli: MS A glaldli, gladdly O,
    glaadly S
103 spreden E, spradden IK, spreddin P; foorþ D, forþe E; mantel BEIKR,
    mentel CaFMW, mantil GHaLPQ; on: upon I; eerþe IR
104 casteden CaEFLMPW, casten U; foorþ D, forþe E; therynne: om. CMa,
    þere ynne BFR, þer in E, þer upon I; ere CaEMW, þe eer I; ringes
    CaFHa; & þer upon þei castiden forþ þe eer ryngis I

26 it the eere ryngis of the praye; and the
weiȝt of the askid eereryngis was a thousand and seuenti siclis of gold, with outen
the ournementis and* brochis and purpur
clooth, the which the kyngis of Madian
weren wont to vse, and biside the goldun

27 beeȝis of chamels. And Gedeon maad of
it a coop, and putte it in Effra his citee;
and al Yrael dide fornycacioun in it; and
it was maad to Gedeon and to al the

105 erryngis *B*, ereringus *CX*, ereryngis *EFHWo*, ereyngis *Lo*; prayȝe *BFHWo*, prei *CX*, preye *E*
106 weiȝte *CLoX*, wiȝt *E*; asked *BH*, askede *Lo*; errynges *B*, ereringus *CX*, ereryngis *EFHWo*, ereyngis *Lo*; thousend *CX*, þousande *FLo*
107 sicles *LoX*; golde *Lo*; withoute *CEX*, wiþ ouȝten *H*
108 ournementus *C*, ornamentys *Lo*, ournamentis *Wo*, ournemens *X*; and: of *A*; broches *Lo*, brooches *X*; purpre *CEX*, purpure *Lo*
109 cloþe *BFHLoWo*, cloþ *CEX;* the which: þe whiche *CHX*, wiþ þe whiche *E¹Lo¹*; kingus *CX*, kynges *LoWo*
110 wer *C*, weryn *E*, were *WoX*; wonte *Lo*; vsen *BCFHLoWoX*, vsyn *E*; beside *C*, besiden *E*; golden *BFLoMo*, goldene *CEX*
111 beȝes *CX*, beeyȝes *E*, byeeys *Lo*; camailis *C*, chamelys *ELo*, camels *Wo*, camailes *X*; made *cet.*
112 cope *BCEH*, coope *FLo*, cuppe *Wo*, coepe *X*; putt *BFHWo*, put *Lo*; cyte *BCEHLoWoX*
113 all *BF*, alle *Lo*; hit *H*
114 made *BFHLoWo*, mad *CX*; alle *BLo*, all *F*

26 et fuit pondus postulatarum inaurium mille septingenti auri sicli, absque ornamentis et monilibus et
veste purpurea, quibus reges Madian uti soliti erant,
et praeter torques aureas camelorum.
27 Fecitque ex eo Gedeon ephod, et posuit illud in
civitate sua Ephra; fornicatusque est omnis Israel
in eo, et factum est Gedeoni et omni domui eius in
ruinam.

26 of the prey; and the weiȝte of eere ryngis   105
    axid was a thousynde and seuene hun-
    drid siclis of gold, with out ournementis
    and brochis and cloth of purpur, whiche
    the kyngis of Madian weren wont to vse,
27 and outakun goldun bies of camels. And   110
    Gedeon made therof ephot, *that is, a*
    preestis cloth, and propir cloth of the
    hiȝeste preest, and he puttide it in his
    citee Ephra; and al Israel diden forny-
    cacioun, *that is ydolatrie,* ther ynne;   115
    and it was maad to Gedeon and to al his

105   pray EKLP; wiȝt B, weiȝt EI, wiȝte O; ere EHaMW rynges CaF
106   axide CaLR, þat he axide I; þousynd CaIMW, þousand DEHaMaNQRX,
       þousend FGLP, þousande K; seuen CaIM; hundred EHa,
       hunderd P
107   sicles R; wiþoute CaFGKLMaNPRSWX, wiþouten IMU; ornamentis E,
       ournementes F, ournamentis I, ourenementis L, ornementis U
108   broochis AcGLPX, broches FR; and: of O; clooþ AcCaDMMaRW,
       cloþe E, cloiþ K; purpul ELP, purpre W; which EFO, wiche K
109   kynges FHa; of M.: om. R; werin EP; wonte R
110   and (1°): om. Ma; out taken CaFMW, outakyn DP, out tak E, outaken
       GKLMaQRU, outake I, outtakun NX, vntakun S; golden
       CaDEGIKLMMaPRU, goldene FW; beies FMW, biȝes KR, biyes N;
       camelis E
111   maade G; þeroff I, þere of R; ephot: a prestis coope I
112   prestis AcBCCaDGHaKMOPQRSUW, prestes EP; cloth (2x): clooþ
       AcCaDG(2°)K(1°)LMMaRW, cloþe E, cloiþ K(2°); propre C, proper
       EFMa, propur HaL, purpur N; and propir cloth: om. W
113   hiȝest AcBDEHaKLPR, heiest Ca, heiȝeste FGW, heiȝest M, hijeste S;
       prest AcBCGHaMOPRSUW, preste E, biȝsshop K; gloss om. B¹IX;
       puttid D, putted E, putte IM, puttede LP, putide U; it: om. G
114   cite CaFHaMQW; al: om. S; dide AcBCaDFGHaKLMMaNOPRSUWX,
       did E; fornicatione E, fornycacion K
115   gloss om. BIX; þere ynne BR, þeryn D; dide *þerynne* fornycacioun I
116   made E; alle CS

28 hows of hym into fallynge. Forsothe 115
   Madian is mekid before the sones of
   Yrael, ne thei myȝten more ouer reer vp
   the nollis; but the loond restide bi fourty
   ȝeer, in the which Gedeon was in dignyte.
29 And so Joroboal, the sone of Joas, 120
30 ȝede, and dwelte in his hows; and he
   hadde seuenti sones, that camen out of
   the hype of hym, forthi that he hadde
31 many wyues. Forsothe the secoundarye
   wijf of hym, that he had in Sichem, gat 125

115 houȝs *H*, house *Lo*; falling *CX*; 115—6 Forsothe Madian: M. f. *cet.*
116 mekide *Lo*; befor *C*, beforn *E*, byfore *FHLoWo*, bifor *X*; sonys *BEFH*,
     sonus *CX*
117 nee *X*; myȝtyn *E*, myȝte *F*, myȝt *Wo*; mor *C*; ouyr *E*; reren
     BCFHLoWoX, reryn *E*
118 bot *B*, bute *F*; lond *CWoX*, land *E*, londe *Lo*; restyd *BFHWo*, restede *LoX*
119 ȝeere *B*, ȝer *CX*, ȝere *LoWo*; whiche *BCEHLoWoX*; dignete *CEX*,
     dyngnyte *F*
121 ȝide *CX*; dwelt *BWo*, dwellede *E*; houȝs *H*
122 had *BFLoWo*; sonys *BEFH*, sonus *CX*; coomen *BF*, comyn *E*, comen
     HLoWo; oute *BLo*, ouȝte *H*
123 hypp *BFH*, hepe *E*, hippe *LoWo*; had *BFWo*
124 manye *CELoX*; wifes *E*; Forsothe the secoundarye: þe s. f. *cet.*; secundarye
     Lo
125 wyf *BCEFHX*, wyfe *LoWo*; hadde *CEHLoX*; gatt *BEFHWo*, gate *Lo*

28 Humiliatus est autem Madian coram filiis Israel,
   nec potuerunt ultra cervices elevare; sed quievit
   terra per quadraginta annos, quibos Gedeon praefuit.
29 Abiit itaque Ierobaal, filius Ioas, et habitavit in
   domo sua;
30 habuitque septuaginta filios, qui egressi sunt de
   femore eius, eo quod plures haberet uxores.
31 Concubina autem illius, quam habebat in Sichem,
   genuit ei filium nomine Abimelech.

28 hows in to fallyng. Forsothe Madian
was maad low bifor the sones of Israel,
and thei myȝten no more reise nollis;
but the lond restide fourti ȝeer, in whiche   120
29 Gedeon was souereyn. And so Jerobaal,
sone of Joas, ȝede, and dwellide in his
30 hows; and he hadde seuenti sones, that
ȝeden out of his thiȝ, for he hadde many
31 wyues. Forsothe a concubyn, *that is,*   125
secoundarie wijf, of hym, whom he
hadde in Sichem, gendride to hym a sone,

117 hows: meynee I; fallynge DFGMaQU; Forsothe: But I, Forsoþ X
118 made DER, mad O; lowȝ CaKMW, lowe DGILMaR, law E; bifore
     AcBCCaEGHaIKMaNQRWX; sonys GQ, sonus I
119 reise up I; nolles EF, her n. I
120 but: bᵗ D, bot E, & I; loond R; restid D, rested E, restede LP; ȝere E,
     ȝer LP; & fourti ȝeer þe lond restide I; which BCEFHaLOQR, wiche K
121 souereyn O, souereyne R
122 þe sone I; ȝede: wente I; dwellid D, dwelled E, dwellede LP, dwelde U
123 had E; sonis GQ
124 oute R; þeiȝ CaFMW, þiȝh D, þiȝe I; for: for þi þat I; had E, hade G;
     manye BGKMaQR, moni L
125 wifes K, wyuis Q; Forsothe: & I; concubine EILMaPRW
126 secundarye BDEHaNQRSX, secoundari C, a secundarie IMa, a secoundarie
     K; wif EFGHaLNPQU
127 had E; gendrid CD, gendred E, gendrede P

32 hym a sone, Abymalech bi name. And
    Gedeon, the sone of Joas, is deed in a
    good age, and biryed in the sepulcre of
    Joas his fader, in Efra, of the meyne of
33 Ezry. Forsothe after that Gedeon is deed,   130
    the sones of Irael ben turned awey, and
    han doo fornycacioun with Baalym; and
    thei smyten with Baal couenaunt of pees,
34 that he were to hem into God, ne thei
    recordiden of the Lord her God, the   135
    which delyuerde hem fro the hoond of
35 alle her enemyes bi enuyroun; ne thei
    diden mercy with the hows of Joroboal
    Gedeon, after alle the good thingys that
    he dide to Yrael.   140

126 to hym C
127 dead BCEX, ded(e) Lo, dede Wo
128 gode BF, goode HWo; buryed Wo
129 fadyr EH, fadre Lo
130 Forsothe after: a. f. cet.; Aftyr EX; dead BCEX, ded H, ded(e) Lo, dede Wo
131 sonus CX, sonys BEFH; torned BFH, tornede Lo, tornyd Wo; aweye BH
132 haue Lo; do CWoX, don E, doon Lo
133 smyte C, smytyn E; couenaunte Lo; pese BE, pes CX
134 þem CLoX
135 recordeden CX, recordidyn E, recorden Lo; þeir BFWo, þer CELoX
136 the which: þe whiche BEHLoX, þat C; delyuerd BFH, deliuerede CELoX,
     delyuered Wo; þeym BF, þem CELoX; hond BCWoX, hand E, honde Lo
137 all F; þeir BEFWo, þer CLoX; enmys B, enemys CEX, enmyes FWo
138 didyn E; houȝs H
139 aftyr ELo; all FH; gode BFWo, goode CEHX; thingus CX, þinges Lo

32 Mortuusque est Gedeon, filius Ioas, in senectute
    bona, et sepultus in sepulchro Ioas patris sui, in
    Ephra, de familia Ezri.
33 Postquam autem mortuus est Gedeon, aversi sunt filii
    Israel, et fornicati sunt cum Baalim; percusserunt-
    que cum Baal foedus, ut esset eis in deum;
34 nec recordati sunt Domini Dei sui, qui eruit eos de
    manu omnium inimicorum suorum per circuitum;
35 nec fecerunt misericordiam cum domo Ierobaal Gedeon
    iuxta omnia bona, quae fecerat Israeli.

32 Abymelech bi name. And Gedeon, sone
of Joas, diede in good elde, and was biried
in the sepulcre of Joas, his fadir, in Ephra,   130
33 of the meynee of Ezri. Forsothe aftir
that Gedeon was deed, the sones of Israel
turneden awey *fro Goddis religioun,* and
diden fornycacioun, *that is, idolatrie,*
with Baalym; and thei smytiden boond   135
of pees with Baal, that he schulde be to
34 hem in to God, nether thei hadden mynde
of her Lord God, that delyuerede hem
fro the hond of alle her enemyes bi cum-
35 pas; nether thei diden merci with the   140
hous of Gerobaal Gedeon, bi alle the
goodis whiche he hadde do to Israel.

128 be R; sone: þe sone I
129 deide CaFIW, died E, deiede M, diȝede R; gode E; eelde
AcBCCaIKLMaNOPQSUWX, eende G, eeld HaR; biriede Ha, b[i]ried O,
y-biried W, beried U
130 sepul[c]ra B; fader EFU; in ephra in þe sepulcre of ioas his fadir I
131 meyne CaEFHaLMPQR; Forsothe: & I, forsoþ X; after EFU
132 ded L, dead Q; sonys GQ, sonus Ma
133 turned E, turnyden GQ; away Ha; from K; goddes F; religion K; gloss
om. I
134 deden FU, þei diden I, dedin P; fornycacion K; adolatrie E; gloss om.
B¹IX¹
135 thei: om. S; smyteden CaOW, smitin E, smyten FM, smoten I, smeten LU,
smetin P; bond CaFGHaMQU, bonde E
136 pes I; scholde CaMW, shuld E
137 hem: om. Ca; neiþer CaFGHaIMMaUW, noþer E, neþir NOS, neiþir QR;
thei: israel I; haddyn EP, hadde I
138 her: þer E, here FQ; delyueride AcBCCaFKMaQRWX, delyuerid D,
deliuered E, hadde delyuered I, deliuyride S
139 from K; honde EI, lond G; al O; here FGQR; enmyes I, enemyees O;
bi cumpas: aboute I
140 neþir BNOS, neiþer CaFGHaIMMaRUW, neiþir Q; dedin EP; mercie R;
with: to I
141 hous: meynee I; of: om. Q; 140−1 with the hous of: om. G; ierobaal
þat is G. I; bi: aftir I
142 godes F, gode þingis I, godis QR, goddis S; which ES, wiche K, þat I;
had E; hadde do: dide I; don O, to S

233

9. 1 Abymalech, the sone of Jeroboal, ȝeed
for[so]þ into Sichem to the britheren of
his moder; and he spak to hem, and to
al the kynrede of the hows of his modir,
seiynge, Spek to alle the men of Sychem,   5

2 Whether is it betere to ȝou, that seuenti
men, alle the sones of Jeroboal, han
lordship of ȝow, other o man be lord to
ȝow? and togidre bihold ȝe, for ȝoure

3 boon and ȝoure flesh Y am. And the   10
britheren of his moder speken of hym to
alle the men of Sichem alle thes wordes;
and thei boweden the herte of hem after
Abymalech, seyinge, Oure brother he is.

9. 1 ȝide *CX*, ȝede *EFLoWo*, ȝeede *H*
   2 breþeren *BEFHLoWo*, breþern *CX*
   3 modir *BEH*, modre *Lo*; spake *BWo*; þem *LoX*
   4 kynreden *Lo*; houȝs *H*; moder *CFWoX*, 'fader &' modre *Lo*
   5 seyand *BFWo*, seiende *CX*, seyande *ELo*; speke ȝe *BFWo*, speke ȝee
      CELoX, speke *H*; all *F*, al *H*
   6 is it: is *H*, it is *X*; better *BFHWo*, bettere *E*, betre *Lo*
   7 al *BLo*, all *F*, of alle *X*; sonys *BEFH*, sonus *CX*; haue *LoX*
   8 lordshipe *CEFWoX*, lordschippe *Lo*; other: or *CLoX*, ouþer *E*; oo *BFH*,
      oon *E*
   9 to giþer *BF*, togidere *CEX*, to gyder *HWo*; byholde *BFHLoWoX*, beholde
      CE; ȝee *CELoX*; ȝour *BCFH*
  10 bon *CEX*; ȝour *BCFH*; flesche *Lo*
  11 breþeren *BEFHLoWo*, breþern *CX*; modyr *EH*, modre *Lo*; speeken *CX*,
      spekyn *E*, spoken *Lo*
  12 alle (2x): al *B* (2°) *Lo*, all *F*; þese *CEX*; wordis *BFH*, woordis *CE*, wrdis *X*
  13 bowedyn *E*, bowiden *Wo*; þem *Lo*; aftyr *ELo*
  14 seiende *CX*; our *B*; broþere *Lo*

9. 1 Abiit autem Abimelech, filius Ierobaal, in Sichem
ad fratres matris suae; et locutus est ad eos, et
ad omnem cognationem domus matris suae, dicens:

2 Loquimini ad omnes viros Sichem: quid vobis est
melius, ut dominentur vestri septuaginta viri, omnes
filii Ierobaal, an ut dominetur vobis unus vir?

9. 1 Forsothe Abymelech, the sone of Gero-
       baal, ȝede in to Sichem to the britheren of
       his modir; and he spak to hem, and to al
       the kynrede of the hows of his modir,
    2 and seide, Speke ȝe to alle the men of   5
       Sichem, What is betere to ȝou, that seuenti
       men, alle the sones of Gerobaal, be lordis
       of ȝou, whether that o man be lord to ȝou?
       and also biholde, for Y am ȝoure boon,
    3 and ȝoure fleisch. And the britheren of   10
       his modir spaken of hym alle these wordis
       to alle the men of Sichem; and bowiden
       her hertis aftir Abymelech, and seiden,

9. 1 Forsoþ X; the: om. C; of: om. G
    2 the: om. R; breþren CaFMW, breþeren EHaILPUX, briþren G, breþern K
    3 moder CaEFLM; spake IR; alle C
    4 kenrede U; house E; moder FHaLU; the h. of his m.: his modir hous I
    5 spek E; al Ma; the: om. CaGHaIKMNOQSX
    6 bettir DR, better E, bettere KN, betre U
    7 sonis GQ; lordes F
    8 ȝoue E; wheþir BINORSX; wh. th.: þat wh. Ha; that: om. R; oo
       GHaKLPQR; to: of R
    9 biholde ȝe AcBCCaDEFGHaIKLMMaOQRSWX, bihold ȝe P, biholde
       ȝee U; for: þat KX; ȝour FK; bon EIU, boond L
   10 ȝour K; flesch CaEFLMPRUW, fleishe I, fleiȝssh K; breþren CaFMW,
       breþern EK, briþren G, breþeren HaILPUX
   11 his: abymalechus X; moder EFMaPU, moooder L; spak E, spakin LP,
       speken S; of: to D; þes DEKNPX; wordes CaEFP; sp. alle þese wordis
       of him G
   12 the: om. Ac; boweden CaEFMPUX, þei boweden I, bouȝiden R, bouweden
       W
   13 hire L, here Q; hertes EF; after BCaEFMU; seide U

       simulque considerate, quia os vestrum et caro vestra
       sum.
    3 Locutique sunt fratres matris eius de eo ad omnes
       viros Sichem universos sermones istos; et inclinav-
       erunt cor eorum post Abimelech, dicentes: Frater
       noster est.

4 And thei ʒauen to hym seuenti pownde   15
   of siluer of the hethen temple of Baal
   Berith; the which hiride to hym of it
   nedi men and vagaunt, and thei folweden
5 hym. And he cam into the hows of his
   fader in Ephra, and he slewʒ his bri-   20
   theren the sones of Jeroboal, seuenti men,
   vpon o stoon. And Joatham, the sone
   of Jeroboal, the leest, abood stil, and is
6 hid. And alle the men of Sichem, and
   al the meynee of the cite of Mello, ben   25
   gedred togidre, and wenten, and ordeyn-
   eden hem a kyng, Abymalech, biside the

15 ʒeuen *BFHWo*, ʒeue *C*, ʒeuyn *E*, ʒafen *Lo*, ʒeeuen *X*; pound *CEHX*
16 seluer *C*, seluyr *E*, siluere *Lo*; heþene *CELoX*
17 whiche *BCEHLoX*; hyred *BFH*, hirede *CLoX*, herede *E*, hyrid *Wo*
18 vagaunte *Lo*; foloweden *BFHWo*, folewiden *C*, folewedyn *E*, foleweden *X*
19 coome *B*, coom *FH*, come *LoWo*; house *B*, houʒs *H*
20 fadir *BE*, fadre *Lo*; sloʒ *CX*, slowʒ *EWo*, slewe *H*, slowʒe *Lo*, breþeren
    BEFHLoWo, breþern *CX*
21 sonys *EF*, sonus *X*
22 uppon *Wo*; oo *BFH*, a *C*, oon *EWo*; ston *BCEHWoX*, stoone *Lo*
23 lest *BFHWo*, leste *CEX*; abod *CX*, aboid *E*, aboode *H*, abode *LoWo*;
    styll *BF*, stille *CEHLoWoX*
24 hydde *BFHLoWo*; al *BHLo*, all *F*
25 alle *B*, all *F*; meine *CEHLoWoX*; cytee *F*; bēn *H*
26 geþerd *B*, gadered *C*, gaderid *E*, geþered *FX*, gederid *H*, gaderide *Lo*,
    gedered *Wo*; to giþer *BF*, togidere *CEX*, to gyder *HWo*; went *BFHWo*,
    wentyn *E*; ordeynden *BFH*, ordeynedyn *E*, ordeynede *Lo*, ordeyned *Wo*
27 þem *CLo*; kynge *BLo*; beside *C*, bisydyn *E*

4 Dederuntque illi septuaginta pondo argenti de fano
   Baal-berith. Qui conduxit sibi ex eo viros inopes
   et vagos, secutique sunt eum.
5 Et venit in domum patris sui in Ephra, et occidit
   fratres suos filios Ierobaal, septuaginta viros,
   super lapidem unum; remansitque Ioatham, filius
   Ierobaal minimus, et absconditus est.

4 He is oure brother. And thei ȝauen to
  hym seuenti weiȝtis of siluer of the tem-   15
  ple of Baal Berith; and he hiride to hym
  therof men pore and hauynge no certeyn
5 dwellyng, and thei sueden hym. And
  he cam in to the hows of his fadir in
  Ephra, and killide hise britheren the   20
  sones of Gerobaal, seuenti men, on o
  stoon. And Joathan, the leste sone of
6 Gerobaal, lefte, and was hid. Forsothe
  alle the men of Sichem, and alle the
  meynees of the citee of Mello, weren   25
  gadirid to gydere, and thei ȝeden, and
  maden Abymelech kyng, bysidis the ook

14 is: his O; broþir IMaORS; ȝafen K
15 weiȝtes FL; siluere C, seluer L, siluir MaQ
16 hirede CLOP, hirid D, hired E, heride G
17 þeroff I, þere of R; þ. men: m. þ. Ma; men pore: pore men Ha; hauyng
   ER; noo Ha, noon K; certeyne R
18 dwellynge DMaQR, duelynge G; suweden CaFMW, sued E, suiden Q
19 came DR; in to: to D, in Ha; the: om. Ha; house E; fader EFLMaU;
   the h. of his f.: his fader hous I
20 killid DE, killede FLP, kilde U; his EFGILPQUX; breþren CaFMW,
   breþern EK, briþren G, breþeren HaILPUX
21 sonis LQ; oo GHaKLPQR, a I; 20−22 upon a stoon he killide seuenti men
   his breþren þe sones of ierobaal I
22 stone E; leeste AcBGHaKMaNQX, leest DR, ȝungist I
23 left E, was left 'vnslayn' I, lafte K; was: om. I; hidde E; Forsothe: And I,
   forsoþ X
25 meynes C, meyneis L; cite AcCaFLPQW, citees DM
26 gaderid AcBCCaDFHaMMaOPQW, gadred E, gadrid GR, gedrid IN,
   gederide K, gadered LSU, gederid X; to gidre DIR, to gidris E, togidir P
27 þei maden I; bisides FK; oke E; 26−28 ȝeden bisidis þe ook þat stood in
   sichem & þei maden abymalech kyng I

6 Congregati autem sunt omnes viri Sichem, et uni-
  versae familiae urbis Mello; abieruntque et con-
  stituerunt regem Abimelech iuxta quercum, quae stabat in Sichem.

7 ook that stood in Sichem. The which
  whanne was told to Joatham, he ȝede, and
  stood in the cop of the hil of Garysym,   30
  and, arerid vp the voice, cryede, and
  seyde, Here ȝe me, men of Sichem, so
8 that God here ȝou. Treese wenten for
  to anoynte vpon hem a kyng; and thei
  seiden to the olyue, Comaund thou to vs.   35
9 The which answerde, Whethir may Y
  forsake my fatnes, the which and Goddis
  vsen and men, and come, that bitwix
10 trees Y be auansid? And the trees seiden
  to the fige tree, Com thou, and tak kyng-   40

---

28 ooke *BFHLoWo*, oc *CEX*; stod *CX*, stoode *F*, stode *BHLoWo*; whiche
    BCEHLoX
29 whenn *B*, whan *CLoWoX*, whann *F*, whenne *H*; was: it was *Lo*; tolde
    LoWo; ȝide *CX*
30 stode *BFHLoWo*, stod *CX*; copp *BFH*, coppe *LoWo*; hyll *BFH*, hylle
    LoWo
31 arered *BEFHLo*, rered *CX*; vois *CX*; cryed *FHWo*
32 heere *EF*; ȝee *CELoX*
33 heere *F*; Trees *CEHLoWoX*; wentyn *E*; for: om. *C*
34 anoynten *BFHLoWo*, enointen *CX*, anoyntyn *E*; vppon *Wo*; kynge *BLo*
35 seidyn *E*, seyde *Lo*; comaunde *BCEFHWoX*, commaunde *Lo*
36 whiche *BCEHLoX*; answerd *BF*, answeride *Lo*, answerid *Wo*; wheþer *cet.*
37 forsakyn *E*; fattnesse *BH*, fatnesse *CEFLoWoX*; whiche *BCEHLoX*; and:
    om. *Wo²X*; goddes *Lo*, godis *X*
38 vsyn *E*; comme *BFH*, comen *CX*, comyn *E*; bytwene *BFHLoWo*, betwe *C*,
    betwen *E*, bitwe *X*
39 treese (2x) *BFH*; auaunsede *Lo*; seydyn *E*
40 tre *Lo*; comme *BF*, cum *CX*, come *HLoWo*; þu *B*; take *BFHWoLo*;
    kingdam *CEX*, kyngdome *LoWo*; 40−41 tak kyngdom vpon vs: vp. vs
    k. t. *cet.*

---

7 Quod cum nuntiatum esset Ioatham, ivit, et stetit
  in vertice montis Garizim; elevataque voce clamavit
  et dixit: Audite me, viri Sichem, ita ut audiat vos
  Deus.
8 Ierunt ligna, ut unguerent super se regem; dixeruntque olivae: Impera nobis.

238

7 that stood in Sichem. And whanne this
  thing was teld to Joathan, he ʒede, and
  stood in the cop of the hil Garisym, and   30
  criede with vois reisid, and seide, ʒe men
  of Sichem, here me, so that God here ʒou.
8 Trees ʒeden to anoynte a kyng on hem;
  and tho seiden to the olyue tre, Comaunde
9 thou to vs. Which answeride, Whether   35
  Y may forsake my fatnesse, which bothe
  Goddis and men vsen, and come, that Y
10 be auaunsid among trees? And the trees
  seiden to the fige tree, Come thou, and

28 stode ER, stoode Ha, stod U; whan EFGHaLP
29 teeld BCaDGMaNWX, tolde ER, told IL, toold KP; ʒeode K
30 stode EHaIR, stod U; coppe I; hille D, hul E; hil of G. KO[1]
31 cride CaSUW, cried DE, he criede I; uoice EIU; reised EKL, reiside R;
    with v. r.: wiþ hiʒe voice I; ʒee U
32 here (1°): here ʒe F, here GKMaNX, hereþ I; so: & R; here (2°): heere
    GHaKMaNX
33 on: upon I
34 tho: þei I; olyif K; tree CaDEGKLNOPRUX
35 whiche DGR, þe whiche I, wich K; answerde CaFGMPQUW, answerd D,
    answered E, answerede L; where DI, wher cet.
36 forsak E; fattnesse K; whiche EFG, þe whiche I, wiche K
37 goddes FM; comeþe E
38 auaunced EKLR; amonge R
39 saiden E; fike E, fig O; tre BCDEHaMPQSU; cum E, com Ha; thou: om.
    G

9 Quae respondit: Numquid possum deserere pinguedinem
  meam, qua et dii utuntur et homines, et venire, ut
  inter ligna promovear?
10 Dixeruntque ligna ad arborem ficum: Veni, et super
  nos regnum accipe.

239

11 dom vpon vs. The which answerde to
hem, Whether may Y forsake my swetnes
and moost swete fruytis, and goo that
12 bitwix other trees Y be auansid? And
13 the trees speken to the viyn, Com, and   45
comaund to vs. The which answerde,
Whether may I forsake my wyn, that
gladith God and men, and bitwix other
14 trees be auansid? And alle the trees
seiden to the thorn, Com, and comaund   50

41 uppon *Wo*; whiche *BCEHLoWoX*; answerden *B*, answeride *Lo*
42 þem *CLoX*; wheþir *X*; forsaken *C*, forsakyn *E*; swettnesse *BFH*,
    swetnesse *CELoWoX*
43 most *BCEFX*, moste *LoWo*; frutis *CX*, fruytes *Lo*; go *CWo*, gon *ELoX*
44 bytwene *BFHLoWo*, betwe *C*, between *E*, bitwen *X*; oþere *CEX*; treese *BF*;
    auansed *BH*, auansede *Lo*
45 treese *BF*; speeken *CX*, speekyn *E*, spoken *Lo*; vyne *BCEHLoWoX*;
    comme *BFH*, cum *CEX*, come *LoWo*
46 comaunde *cet*; whiche *BCEHLoX*; answeride *Lo*
47 forsaken *C*, forsakyn *E*; wyne *BFLoWo*, vyne *H*
48 gladeþ *CEWo*, glades *Lo*; bytwene *BFHLoWo*, betwe *C*, betwen *EX*;
    oþere *CX*, ooþere *E*
49 treese *B*; ben *BEFHLoWoX*; auaunsed *BH*, auaunsede *Lo*; all *F*, al *Lo*;
    treese *B*
50 seydyn *E*; thorne *Lo*; comme *BFH*, cum *CEX*, come *LoWo*; comaunde
    BCEFHWoX, commande *Lo*

11 Quae respondit eis: Numquid possum deserere dulce-
dinem meam, fructusque suavissimos, et ire, ut inter
cetera ligna promovear?
12 Locuta /quo/que sunt ligna ad vitem: Veni, et impera
nobis.
13 Quae respondit: Numquid possum deserere vinum meum,
quod laetificat Deum et homines, et inter cetera
ligna promoveri?
14 Dixeruntque omnia ligna ad ramnum: Veni, et impera
super nos.

11 take the rewme on vs. Which answeride 40
to hem, Whether Y may forsake my swetnesse and swetteste fruytis, and go that

12 Y be auaunsid among othere trees? Also
the trees spaken to the vyne, Come thou,

13 and comaunde to vs. Which answeride, 45
Whether Y may forsake my wyn, that
gladith God and men, and be auaunsid

14 among othere trees? And alle trees seiden
to the ramne, *ether theue thorn*, Come

40 take þou G; on: 'up' on I; whiche G, þe whiche I, wiche K; answerde
CaFGMPQUW, answerd D, ansuerede EL
41 to hem: om. X; whether AE, where DI, wher cet.
forsak C; swetnes E, sweetnesse K, fatnesse M
42 swettiste AcBKR, swettist DMa, swetest E, swettest HaL, *my* ful swete I,
swittiste U; froites E, fruytes FHa, fruy3tis KMa, frutis L, frutes P
43 auaunsed EKLP; amonge R; oþer EFLP, oþre R
44 the trees: þei I; spaken: seiden G, spakin P; come: comaunde Ac, cum E
45 commaunde R; whiche G, þe whiche I, wiche K; answerde CaFGMPQUW,
answerd DE, answerede L
46 whether AF, where D, wher cet.; for-sak E; my: om. N; wijn BKMaX,
wyne DEIR
47 gladet E, gladeþ FHaKL; auanced EKLP
48 e-mong E, amonge R; oþer ELP; trees (2°): þe trees CI; saiden E
49 rampne I, ramme O; eiþer CaFGHaMQRW, or EILP, eiþir Ma, eþir
NOSX, oþer U; þe þeeue I, þew Ma, þeef R; þorne HaR; cum E

15 thow vpon vs. The which answerde to
hem, If verreily me kyng ȝe han ordeynde to ȝou, cometh, and vnder my
shadewe restith; forsothe if ȝe wolen not,
go out fier fro the thorn, and deuowre   55
16 the seed[r]is of Liban. Nowe thanne if
riȝtly, and withouten synne ȝe han ordeynde vpon ȝou a kyng, Abymalech,
and wel han doo with Jeroboal, and with
the hows of hym, and han ȝolden while   60
to his benfeetis, the which fauȝt for ȝou,
17 and his lijf ȝaf to peryls, for to delyuer

51 uppon *Wo*; whiche *BCEHLoWoX*; answeride *Lo*
52 þem *CLoX*; ȝif *BFHWo*, ȝife *Lo*; verreli *CEHX*; kynge *B*; me kyng: k.
   me *Lo²X*; ȝee *CELoX*; ordeyned *CX*, ordeynyd *EWo*, ordeynd *F*,
   ordeynede *Lo*
53 commiþ *BF*, comiþ *H*, comes *Lo*; vndir *BEH*, vndre *Lo*
54 schadowe *BFHLoWo*; resteþ *CEX*, restes *Lo*; forsothe if: /ȝ/if f. *cet.*;
   ȝif *BFH*, ȝife *LoWo*; ȝee *CELoX*; wyll *BF*, wiln *CX*, wilyn *E*, wole *HLo*,
   wyl *Wo*
55 goo *BFH*; oute *B*, ouȝte *H*; fijr *CE*, fyre *Lo*, fuyre *Wo*; thorne *Lo*;
   deuowre: d. hem *H*
56 sedis *C*, seed'r'es *Lo*, seedes *Wo*, sedes *X*; Now *CEHLoWoX*; þann *BF*,
   þan *Wo*; ȝif *BFHWo*, ȝife *Lo*
57 riȝtely *Lo*; withoute *CEX*, wiþ ouȝten *H*, wiþ out *Wo*; ȝee *CELoX*;
   ordeined *CEWoX*, ordeynede *Lo*
58 uppon *Wo*; kynge *Lo*
59 wele *BF*, weel *E*; doon *BFHLoWo*, do *CX*, don *E*
60 houȝs *H*; ȝolde *CX*, ȝooldyn *E*; whyl *BFH*, wel *Lo*
61 hise *E*; benfetis *BFLo*, benefetus *C*, benefetys *EHWo*, benefetes *X*; whiche
   BCEHLoX; faȝt *CX*, fauȝte *HLo*
62 lyf *cet.*; ȝaue *BFHWo*, ȝafe *Lo*; perilis *CFH*, perelis *E*, periles *LoWoX*; for:
   om. *C*; deliuere *CLoX*, delyueryn *E*

15 Quae respondit eis: Si vere me regem vobis con-
stitui/s/tis, venite, et sub umbra mea requiescite.
Si autem non vultis, egrediatur ignis de ramno, et
devoret cedros Libani.
16 Nunc igitur, si recte et absque peccato constitu-

15 thou, and be lord on vs. Which an-   50
sweride to hem, If ȝe maken me verili
kyng to ȝou, come ȝe, and reste vndur
my schadewe; sotheli, if ȝe nylen, fier
go out of the ramne, and deuoure the ce-
16 dris of the Liban. Now therfor if riȝt-   55
fuli and without synne ȝe han maad
Abymelech kyng on ȝou, and ȝe han do
wel with Jerobaal, and with his hows, and
ȝe han ȝolde while to the benefices of
17 hym, that fauȝt for ȝou, and ȝaf his lijf to   60
perelis, that he schulde delyuere ȝou fro

50 on: of E, up on I; whiche G, þe whiche I, wich K; answerde
    CaEFGMPQUW, answerd D, answerede L
51 ȝif E; ȝee U; make D, makin EP; verrely CaFIMW, verrili D, uereli E,
    verri N
52 cummeþ E; ȝe: om. ELP, ȝee GU; resteþ I, reste 'ȝe' KMa; vnder BFLU,
    vndir DGHaIKMaNPQRSX
53 schadowe BHaKMaNRX, shadwe ELOP; soþli FGLMMaPQUWX, & I;
    ȝee U; nillen E, wole not I; fijr CaIMW, fire D, fyr EFLP
54 oute R; ramme O; cedres FHa
55 the: om. CaDGHaIKMMaNOQSX; þerfore BCaFGIKMaNQRW;
    riȝtfully BCaDFGHaIKMaNQRW; 55—56 if ȝe han riȝtfully & wiþoute
    synne maad I
56 wiþ oute CaFGIKLMMaNPQSUWX, syn E; ȝee GU; haue R; made
    DEHaR
57 on: vpon I; and: & if CaDGHaIKMMaNQX, & ȝif OS; ȝee U; haue R
58 weel MaS, wil U; with: to R; and: & if CaDGHaIKMMaNOQSX
59 ȝee U; haue R; ȝolden BK, ȝoulde N; whil R; the: om. M; benefetis
    BGX, beneficis CaDMaNQW, manyfold wel doyngis I
60 fauȝte BHaILNR; ȝaaf I, ȝaue R; lyf EFGHaLNPQU; to: for
    AcCCaDE²FHaKLMMaNOPQRSUX
61 perels AcBDFHaIKMMaNOQSUWX, pereylis G, perils R; scholde
    CaMW, shuld E, wolde I; diliuer E; from K

istis super vos regem Abimelech, et bene egistis
cum Ierobaal, et cum domo eius, et reddidistis
vicem beneficiis eius, qui pugnavit pro vobis,
17 et animam suam dedit periculis, ut erueret vos de
manu Madian,

18 ȝou fro the hoond of Madian; the whiche
ȝe nowe han rysyn aȝens the hows of my
fader, and han slayn his sones, seuenti   65
men, upon o stoon, and han ordeynde a
kyng, Abymalech, the sone of the werk
womman of hym, vpon the dwellers of
Sichem, forthi that ȝoure brother he be;
19 if thanne riȝtly and with outen vice ȝe   70
han doo with Jeroboal and the hows of
hym, to day glade ȝe in Abymalech, and

63 hond *BCWoX*, hand *E*, hande *Lo*; which *FWo*
64 ȝee *CEFLoX*; now *BCEFHWoX*; ȝe nowe: n. ȝ. *Lo*; rysen *BCFHLoWoX*;
    aȝenst *BELo*, aȝen *CX*, aȝeynst *FHWo*; houȝs *H*, house *Lo*
65 fadir *BEH*, fadre *Lo*; slawen *BFHWo*, slan *C*, slawyn *E*, sclayne *Lo*;
    hise *E*; sonys *BEFHWo*, sonus *C*
66 uppon *Wo*; oo *BCFHWo*, oon *E*, a *Lo*; ston *CEX*, stoone *Lo*; ordeyned
    CWoX, ordeynyd *E*, ordeynede *Lo*
67 kynge *BLo*; werke *HLo*
68 dwelleris *CELo*, dwelleres *X*
69 ȝour *BFH*; broþere *Lo*
70 ȝif *BFHWo*, ȝife *Lo*; þann *F*, þan *HWo*; riȝtliche *E*, riȝtely *Lo*; withoute
    CX, wiþ ouȝten *H*, wiþ out *Wo*; ȝee *CELoX*
71 doon *BFHLo*, do *CX*, don *E*, done *Wo*; houȝs *H*
72 ȝee *CELoX*

18 qui nunc surrexistis contra domum patris mei, et
interfecistis filios eius, septuaginta viros, super
unum lapidem, et constituistis regem Abimelech,
filium ancillae eius, super habitatores Sichem, eo
quod frater vester sit;
19 si ergo recte et absque vitio egistis cum Ierobaal
et domo eius, hodie laetamini in Abimelech, et ille
laetetur in vobis.

244

18 the hond of Madian; and ȝe han rise
now aȝens the hows of my fadir, and han
slayn hyse sones, seuenti men, on o stoon,
and han maad Abymelech, sone of his   65
handmayde, kyng on the dwelleris of
19 Sichem, for he is ȝoure brother; therfor
if ȝe han do riȝtfuli, and with out synne
with Gerobaal and his hows, to dai be ȝe
glad in Abymelech, and be he glad in ȝou;   70

62 honde I; and: & ȝif Ca, & if DGHaKMMaNOQSX; ȝee U, om. W;
   haue IR; risen E, risun X; 62−63 & now ȝe haue rise I
63 aȝenus AcCKNO; fader EFU; ȝe han I
64 slawe I, slayne R, slayen S, sleyn U; his EFGIPQSX; sonys GLQ; on:
   upon I; a DI, oo GHaKPQR; stone E, ston HaU; 63−64 & ȝe han slawe
   his seuenti sones men upon a stoon I
65 haue R; made DEHaR; þe sone I; hise N
66 hondmayde B, concubyne CaDGHaIKLMMaNOQSX, hondemayden E,
   concubyn X; on: of E, upon I; dwellers DEIKLMMaRUX, dwelleres F;
   of: om. O; 65−66 and abymalech þe sone of his concubyne ȝe han maad
   kyng upon þe dwellers I
67 ȝoure: oure B, ȝour K; broþir INORSX; þerfore BCaGIMaNQW, &
   þerfore K
68 ȝif E; ȝee U; haue R; don D; riȝtfully BCaEFGHaIKMMaNQRW; wiþ
   oute CCaFGIKLMMaNPRSUWX
69 and: & wiþ N; ȝee GU; to dai be ȝe: be ȝe to dai I
70 glad (1°): glade C, glaad O; be he: he be FMa, be ȝe LNR

20 he glade in ȝou; forsothe if shrewidli,
fier goo out of hym, and waast the
dwellers of Sichem, and the burȝ toun of   75
Mello; and go out fier fro the men of
Sichem, and fro the burgh toun of Mello,

21 and deuowre Abymalech. The whiche
thingis whanne he hadde seid, he fleiȝ,
and wente into Bereram, and dwelte there,   80
for drede of Abymalech, his brothir.

22 And Abymalech regnede vpon Yrael thre

23 ȝeer. And God sente the worst spiryte
bitwix Abymalech and the dwellers of
Sichem, the whiche bigunne to wlaat   85

73 forsothe if: ȝif f. *cet.*; ȝif *BFHWo*, ȝife *Lo*; schrewdly *B*, schreudeli *CX*, shrewedely *E*, schrewedly *H*
74 fijr *CE*, fire *Lo*, fuyr *Wo*; go *BCELoWoX*; oute *B*, ouȝte *H*; waste *CELoWoX*
75 dwelleris *CELo*, dwelleres *X*; bourgh *BH*, borwȝ- *E*, borgh *FWo*, bourghe *Lo*
76 goo *FH*; ouȝt *H*; fijr *CE*, fire *Lo*, fuyr *Wo*
77 bourgh *BH*, burȝ *C*, borwȝ *E*, borgh *FWo*, bourghe *Lo*
78 deuour *BFWo*; which *FWo*
79 thingus *CX*, þinges *Lo*; whenn *B*, whan *CEFLoWoX*, when *H*; had *BFLoWo*; seyde *HLoWo*; fleeȝ *Lo*
80 went *BWo*; dwellede *E*, dwelt *HWo*, dwellide *Lo*; þer *Wo*
81 broþer *cet.*
82 ryngned *BF*, reignede *ELo*, regnyd *Wo*; vppon *Wo*
83 ȝer *CX*, ȝere *LoWo*; sent *FWo*, sende *Lo*; werste *BCEHWoX*, werst *F*, worste *Lo*; spirit *CEWoX*, spiriȝte *H*
84 bytwene *BFHLoWo*, betwen *CE*, bitwen *X*; dwelleris *CELo*, dwelleres *X*
85 which *FWo*; bygunnen *BFHWoX*, begunnen *C*, begunnyn *E*, by-gonnen *Lo*; wlaten *BCFHWoX*, wlatyn *E*, wlate *Lo*

20 Sin autem perverse, egrediatur ignis ex eo, et con-
sumat habitatores Sichem, et oppidum Mello; egredi-
aturque ignis de viris Sichem, et de oppido Mello,
et devoret Abimelech.

21 Quae cum dixisset, fugit, et abiit in Berara; habitavitque ibi metu Abimelech, fratris sui.

20 but if ȝe han do weiwardli, fier go out of
   hym, and waste the dwelleris of Sichem,
   and the citee of Mello; and fier go out
   of the men of Sichem, and of the citee
21 of Mello, and deuoure Abymelech. And   75
   whanne he hadde seid these thingis, he
   fledde, and ȝede in to Berara, and dwellide
   there, for drede of Abymelech, his brother.
22 And Abymelech regnede on Israel thre
23 ȝeer. And the Lord sente the worste   80
   spirit bitwixe Abymelech and the dwell-
   eris of Sichem, whiche bigynnen to holde

71 ȝif E; ȝee U; haue R; don CG; waywardli E, weiwarli L; fire DI, fyr
   EFLP, fijr CaMW; oute R; of: fro CaDGHaIMMaNOQSX, from K
72 hym: abymalech I; waaste AcMaNRX, wast E; dwellers DEHaIKLM-
   OPRSUX, dwelleres F
73 cite CaHaLMPQW; fijr CaIMW, fire D, fyr EFP, þe fier Ha; 73 and (2°) ...
   Mello (75): om. L
74 of (1°): fro CaDGHaIMNOQSX, from K; of (2°): fro GI; cite
   CCaFHaMPQW
76 whan EGHaLP; he: ioathan I; had EI; said E, seide DHaR; þes DKNX,
   þise U; þinges FHa
77 fled E; dwellid D, dwelled E, dwellede FLP, he dwelte I, dwelde U
78 þare E, þer N; þe dreede G; broþir BRS
79 regnyde AcGHaIQR, regned DE; on: upon I; þree K
80 ȝere E, ȝer LP; sent E; wurste CaFMW, wherst E, werste P
81 spiritt K, spiriȝt L; bitwix EFQ; dwellers DEFHaIKLMMaPRSUX
82 which E, þe whiche I, wiche K; bigunnen CCaDEGHaIKLMMaNOPQSWX,
   bigonnen F

22 Regnavitque Abimelech super Israel tribus annis.
23 Misitque Deus spiritum pessimum inter Abimelech et
   habitatores Sichem; qui coeperunt eum detestari,

24 hym, and the hidows gilt of the slauȝter
of the seuenti sones of Jeroboal, and the
shedynge of blod of hem, to ȝeelde into
Abymalech, his brothir, and into the
tother princis of Sichemytis, that hym 90
25 helpeden. And thei puttiden aspies
aȝens hym in the cop of hillis; and while
thei biden the comynge of hym, thei
hawntiden theftis, takynge prayes of the
goers byside; and it is told to Abyma- 95
26 lech. Forsothe Gaal, the sone of Obed,
with his bretheren cam, and passide into
Siccymam; at whos comynge reryd the

86 hydouse *BCEFLo*, hydouȝse *H*; gilte *CELoX*; slaȝter *CX*, slawtyr *E*,
sclauȝter *Lo*
87 sonys *BFH*, sonus *CX*
88 sheding *CELoX*; of blod: of þe bl. *cet.*; blode *BFHLoWo*; þem *CLo*;
ȝeelden *BCFHX*, ȝeeldyn *E*, ȝelden *LoWo*
89 his: her *X*; broþer *cet.*
90 toþere *CEX*; pryncis *ELoX*
91 holpen *CX*, helpedyn *E*, helpiden *Lo*; putten *CX*, puttyn *E*, putteden *Lo*
92 aȝeynst *BFHWo*, aȝen *CX*, aȝenst *ELo*; in: in to *Wo*²*X*; copp *FHWo*,
coppe *Lo*; hilles *E*, þe hylles *Lo*; whil *CX*, þe while *Lo*
93 bidyn *E*; commyng *B*, comyng *CEX*, commynge *F*
94 haunteden *CLoX*, hawntidyn *E*; theftus *C*, þeftes *Lo*; takyng *BWo*, takende
CX; prayȝis *BHWo*, preȝes *C*, preyes *EX*, preyȝis *F*
95 gooers *BFH*, goeres *CX*, goaris *E*, goeris *Lo*; beside *C*, besiden *E*; tolde
HLoWo
96 Forsothe Gaal: G. f. *cet.*
97 hise *E*; breþern *CX*; coom *BFH*, come *Lo*, coome *Wo*; passyd *BFHLoWo*,
passede *CX*
98 Att *E*; whose *BFWo*, whois *E*; commynge *BF*, comyng *CHX*, commyng
Lo; reryd: reysid *Lo*, rered *X*

24 et scelus interfectionis septuaginta filiorum Ierobaal, et /ef/fusionem sanguinis eorum conferre in
Abimelech, fratrem suum, et in ceteros Sichimorum
principes, qui eum adiuverant.
25 Posueruntque insidias adversus eum in summitate
montium; et dum illius praestolabantur adventum,

24 hym abomynable, and to arette the felony
of sleyng of seuenti sones of Gerobaal,
and the schedyng out of her blood, in to   85
Abymelech her brother, and to othere
princes of Sichem, that hadden helpid
25 hym. And thei settiden buyschementis
azens hym in the hiznesse of hillis; and
the while thei abideden the comyng of   90
hym, thei hauntiden theftis, and token
preies of men passynge forth; and it was
26 teld to Abymelech. Forsothe Gaal, the
sone of Obed, cam with his britheren,
and passide in to Siccima; at whos en-   95
tryng the dwelleris of Sichem weren reisid,

83 hym: þe king I; abhomynable AcBCCaDEGHaKLMMaNPQRSUWX; rette
U; felonye CaEGHaKLMMaPQRUW
84 sleynge AcCaDGHaLMMaPQRW; þe seuenti I; sonis GHaLQ
85 schedynge DGMaQRUW; here FQ; blode ER, blod U
86 broþir OS, brooþer L; to: in to CaDGHaIKMMaNOQSX; oþer EL,
oþire O, oþre R
87 pryncis DGIKLMaNPQX; haddin P, hadde R; holpen GHaKU, holpe IX,
helpen Q, helpi(d)n S
88 thei: men of sichem I; setteden CaELMPW, setten FIU; busschementis
CaDEILMOW, buschmentes FHa, bushmentis GPQ, boizschementis K,
boyshmentis N, boyschementis U
89 azenus AcCNO, azeins E, azenis P; hym: þe king I; hizenesse CR,
heiznesse CaFMW, hinesse E, hiznes Ma, hizenes X; hullis E, hilles FR
90 the (1°): om. DIMa; abididen AcBCDGHaMaOQSX, abiden FM, aboden
I, abeden U; comynge CaDFGLMaPQUW; 90−1 the c. of hym: his
comyng I
91 haunteden CaELMPW, hauntede F, haundeden U; þeftes F, þeeftis O;
tooken KLNOX, tookin P
92 pries D, prayes EKLP; passyng BEFGS; foorþ D, forþe E, þerforþ I
93 teeld BGMaNWX, telde C, told ELP, toold K, tolde R; to: om. G;
Forsothe: & I, forsoþ OX
94 of: om. EL; 93−94 the s. of O.: obeþ sone I; came IR; hise
CHaKMMaNORSUW; breþeren ILPUX, breþren MW
95 passiden AcCGMaQR, passid D, passed E, he passide I, passede L,
passeden PU; whose C, whoos K; entringe DFGHaQU
96 dwellers DEHaIKLMRUX; reisede K, reised LU

exercebant latrocinia, agentes praedas de praetereuntibus; nuntiatumque est Abimelech.
26 Venit autem Gaal, filius Obed, cum fratribus suis,
et transivit in Siccimam; ad cuius adventum erecti
habitatores Sichem,

27 dwellers of Sichem, wenten out into
    feeldis, wastynge vynes, and grapis tred-   100
    ynge; and the querys maad of syngers
    thei wenten into the temple of her God,
    and bytwix meetis and drynkis thei curs-
28 eden*/ to Abymalech, criynge Gaal, the
    sone of Obed, Who is this Abymalech?   105
    And what is Sichem, that we seruen to
    hym? Whether is not he the sone of Jero-
    boal, and set a prince, Zebul his seruaunt,
    vpon the men of Emor, the fader of Si-
    chem? Whi thanne shulen we serue to   110

99 dwelleris *CLo*, dwellris *E*, dwelleres *X*; wentyn *E*, wente *Lo*; oute *B*, ouȝte *H*
100 feeldis: þe feldis *C*, þe feeldys *ELo*, feldes *Wo*; waastynge *BFH*, wastende *CX*; vynys *BFHWo*; grapes *LoX*; tredende *CX*, tredyng *Lo*
101 qweres *LoX*; made *HLoWo*, mad *X*; singeres *CX*, syngerys *ELo*
102 wentyn *E*; þeir *BEFWo*, þer *CLoX*
103 bitwene *BFHLoWo*, betwe *C*, betwen *E*, bitwe *X*; metis *BEFHWo*, metus *C*, metes *LoX*; drinkus *C*, drinkes *Lo*; burseden *ABFH*, kursedyn *E*, cursseden *Lo*
104 crying *B*, criende *CX*
106 wee *CEX*; serue *BCFHLoWoX*, seruyn *E*
108 sett *BFHWo*, sette *CELoX*; seruaunte *Lo*
109 apon *BFHWo*; the (2°): om. *CE²Lo²*; fadir *BEFHWo*, fadre *Lo*
110 þann *BF*, þan *HWo*; schal *BFHLoWo*, shul *CEX*; wee *CEX*; seruen *BH*, seruyn *E*

27 egressi sunt in agros, vastantes vineas uvasque
    calcantes; et factis cantantium choris, ingressi
    sunt fanum dei sui, et inter epulas et pocula male-
    dicebant Abimelech,
28 clamante Gaal, filio Obed: Quis est iste Abimelech,
    et quae est Sichem, ut serviamus ei? numquid non
    est filius Ierobaal, et constituit principem Zebul,
    servum suum, super viros Emor, patris Sichem? Cur
    igitur serviemus ei?

27 and ʒeden out in to feeldis, and wastiden
vyneris, and to-traden grapis; and with
cumpenyes of syngeris maad thei entriden
in to the temple of her God, and among   100
metis and drynkis thei cursiden Abyma-
28 lech, while Gaal, *the* sone of Obed,
criede, Who is this Abymelech? And
what is Sichem, that we serue hym?
Whether he is not the sone of Jerobaal,   105
and made Zebul his seruaunt prince on
the men of Emor, fadir of Sichem? Whi

97   out: out *togidre wiþ gaal* I; feldes EU, feeldes F, þe feeldis I; wasteden
     CaFLMP, wasted E, waastiden MaX
98   vyners DEHaIKMPR, vyneres F, veyners U; to trediden B, to tradden
     DLOPQSW, al-to traden I; grapes FR
99   cumpeny AcF, cumpanyes BCaGIKLMNPQUWX, cumpenyes DO,
     companyes E, cumpanye Ma; syngers DEHaIKLMPRX, syngeres F;
     made D; c. y-maad of s. I; entreden CaFMPUW, entred E
100 here Q; the temple of her God: her goddis t. I; amonge R
101 metes F, meetis GPQS, her etyngis I; drynkes FMRU, drynkingis I;
     curseden AcCaEFKLMPUW; Abymalech: her kyng I
102 while: whil EGPR, while þat I; *the*: AI, om. cet.
103 cride CaUW, cried DE; wo E; he þis I
104 seruen OS
105 where CDE, wher cet.; nat I
106 he haþ maad I; seruant E, seruaunte DR; on: of EHaS, upon I
107 fader EFGLU, þe fadir I

29 hym? Wolde God eny man ȝeue this
   puple vnder myn hoond, and I shulde
   doo awey fro the mydil Abymalech. And
   it is seid to Abymalech, Gedre a multi-
30 tude of oost, and com. Forsothe Zebul,   115
   the prince of the cytee, herd the wordis
   of Gaal, the sone of Obed, is ful wrooth;
31 and sente preueli to Abymalech messagers, seiynge, Loo! Gaal, the sone of
   Obed, cam into Siccymam with his bri-   120
   theren, and aȝen fiȝtith the citee aȝens
32 thee; aryse also the nyȝt with the puple,
   that is with thee, and lurk in the feeld;

111 wold *BE*; any *CEX*; ȝyue *Wo*
112 peple *BFHLoWo*; vndir *BE*, vndre *Lo*; hond *CEX*, honde *LoWo*; scholde
     Lo, schuld *Wo*
113 do *BCWo*, don *EX*; aweye *BH*; mydyll *BH*, myddel *CEWoX*, mydel *Lo*;
     fro þe m. A.: A. fro þe m. *C*
114 seide *BFHLoWo*; geþer *BF*, gedere *CEX*, geder *HWo*, gadre *Lo*
115 hoost *BFH*, ost *CX*, host *E*; comme *BF*, cum *CEX*, come *HLoWo*;
     Forsothe Zebul: Z. f. *cet.*
116 cyte *BCEFHLoWo*; herde *HLoWo*; woordus *C*, woordis *E*, wordes *LoWo*,
     wrdis *X*
117 the: om. *CX*; full *BFH*; wroþ *CEWoX*, wroþe *Lo*
118 sent *BFHX*, sende *Lo*; priuyly *CX*, pryuely *ELoWo*; messageres *CWoX*,
     messageris *ELo*, messangers *H*
119 seyand *B*, seiende *CX*, seyande *EFLoWo*; lo *CEWoX*
120 coome *BFH*, come *LoWo*; hise *E*; breþeren *BEFLoWo*, breþern *CX*
121 aȝeyn- *BFHWo*; -fiȝtep *CEWoX*, fiȝtes *Lo*; cyte *BCEFHLoWo*; aȝeyns
     BFWo, aȝen *CX*, aȝenst *E*, a-ȝeynes *Lo*
122 ris *CX*, rise *Lo*; nyȝte *Lo*; peple *BFHLoWo*
123 thee: þe *Wo*; lurke *CELoX*; feld *C*, felde *LoWo*

29 Utinam daret aliquis populum istum sub manu mea, et
   auferrem de medio Abimelech. Dictumque est Abimelech: Congrega exercitus multitudinem, et veni.
30 Zebul enim princeps civitatis, auditis sermonibus
   Gaal filii Obed, iratus est valde,

252

29 therfor schulen we serue hym? Y wolde,
that sum man ȝaf this puple vndur myn
hond, that Y schulde take awei Abime-   110
lech fro the myddis. And it was seid to
Abymelech, Gadere thou the multitude of
30 oost, and come thou. For whanne the
wordis of Gaal, sone of Obed, weren herd,
Zebul, the prynce of the citee, was ful   115
31 wrooth; and he sente priueli messangeris
to Abymelech, and seide, Lo! Gaal, sone
of Obed, cam in to Siccymam, with hise
britheren, and he excitith the citee to fiȝte
32 aȝens thee; therfor rise thou bi nyȝt with   120
the puple, which is with thee, and be

108 þerfore BCaFGIKLMaNQRUW; schullen CaMW, schuln DF, shul
    EILP; 108–9 Y wolde that: wolde god I
109 ȝaf: wolde ȝiue I, ȝafe R; this: his E; peple CaFLMMaNPWX; vndir
    BDGHaIKMaNPQRX, vnder FLU; myne ER, mijn K
110 that: & CaDGHaIKMMaNOQSX; shuld E, scholde MW; take: do I;
    away Ha
111 from K; myddes F, myddis of sichem I; seide DRU, said E
112 Gader E, gadre G, Gedre I, gedere KX, gaderere S
113 þe oost AcK²Ma, ost EU, an oost I; cum E; thou: þou aȝens gaal I;
    whan EGHaLP
114 wordes F; þe sone GIU; wheren E, werend S; herde KR
115 cite CaFHaMQW
116 wroþ EFGHaILNPQX; sent E; pryuyli CDMaNPX, preuyly GQ, preueli
    U; messangers DHaIMX, messagers EK, messangeres FU, messengers L,
    massangeris O, messengeris PS
117 he seide I; loo K; þe sone GI
118 came DR, is come I; his EFGILPQSX
119 breþren CaEFMW, briþren G, breþeren HaILPUX, breþern K; exciteþe E,
    exciteþ FHaKR; cite CaEFHaKMPQW; fiȝt E
120 aȝenus AcCNO; þerfore BCaEFGIKLMaNQRWX; nyȝte
    CaDFKMMaUW
121 peple CaFILMMaNPWX; whiche GL, þat I, wich K; thee: þe E

31 et misit clam ad Abimelech nuntios, dicens: Ecce,
   Gaal filius Obed venit in Siccimam cum fratribus
   suis, et oppugnat adversum te civitatem.
32 Surge itaque nocte cum populo, qui tecum est, et
   latita in agro;

253

33 and first eerli rysynge the sunne, fal vpon
   the cite; forsothe hym goynge out aʒens   125
   thee with his puple, do to hym that thow
34 mayst. And so Abymalech with al his
   oost roos the nyʒt, and sette bushementis
35 biside Siccymam, in foure placis. And
   Gaal, the sone of Obed, wente out, and   130
   stood in the entre of the ʒate of the cytee.
   Forsothe Abymalech roos, and al the oost
   with hym, fro the place of the busshe-

124 erly *cet.*; risende *CX*, risyng *E*; sonne *Lo*; fall *BF*, falle *HLoWo*; uppon *Wo*
125 forsothe hym: h. f. *cet.*; gooynge *BF*, goende *CX*, goyng *E*; oute *BWo*,
    ouʒte *H*; aʒeynst *B*, aʒen *CX*, aʒenst *ELo*, aʒeyns *FWo*
126 þe *Wo*; peple *BFHLoWo*; doo *BFH*
127 soo *X*; alle *B*, all *F*
128 hoost *BFH*, ost *CX*, host *E*; rose *BFWo*, ros *CEX*, roose *Lo*; nyʒte *Lo*;
    sett *BFHWo*; buschementus *C*, buschmentis *FWo*, buschemens *X*
129 beside *C*, besiden *E*; four *BFHWo*; places *ELoX*
130 went *BFHWo*; oute *B*, ouʒte *H*
131 stode *BFHLoWo*, stod *CX*; cyte *cet.*
132 Forsothe Abymalech: A. f. *cet.*; rose *BFWo*, ros *CEX*, roose *Lo*; alle *BLo*;
    hoost *BFH*, host *E*, ost *C*
133 buschmentes *B*, busshementus *C*, buschmentis *ELoWo*, buschemens *X*

33 et primo mane oriente sole, irrue super civitatem;
   illo autem egrediente adversum te cum populo suo,
   fac ei quod potueris.
34 Surrexit itaque Abimelech cum omni exercitu suo
   nocte, et tetendit insidias iuxta Siccimam in
   quattuor locis.
35 Egressusque est Gaal, filius Obed, et stetit in
   introitu portae civitatis. Surrexit autem Abimelech
   et omnis exercitus cum eo de insidiarum loco.

33 thou hid in the feeld; and first in the
morewtid, whanne the sunne rysith, falle
on the citee; forsothe whanne he goth
out with his puple aȝens thee, do thou to   125
34 hym that that thou maist. Therfor Abyme-
lech roos with al his oost bi nyȝt, and settide buyschementis bisidis Siccimam, in
35 foure places. And Gaal, the sone of Obed,   130
ȝede out, and stood in the entryng of the
ȝate of the citee. Forsothe Abymelech
and al the oost with hym roos fro the

122 hid: om. X; felde E, feld Ha, fild U; þe firste C, firste L; in to O
123 morntid BMa, morewetide CaMW, morwetide DLP, morowtide E,
     morewetid FGOS, morowtid HaU, morewtijd I, morowtijd K, morwetyd N,
     morwetijd Q, morewtide RX; whan EFHaLP; son E, om. G; riseþe E,
     ryseþ FHaKLRS; fall U, falle þou I; 122–23 & whanne þe sunne risiþ
     first in þe morewtijd I
124 on: upon I; cite CaFHaMQW; forsoþ EX, & I; whan EGHaLP; he:
     gaal I; goiþ AcBCDKMaNORX, gooþ CaMW, goþe E
125 oute R; peple CaFILMMaNPWX; aȝenus AcCNO; þe ER
126 that (1°): om. Ma; that (2°): at E; thou: tou E; may E, maiȝt LP;
     þerfore BEGKMaNQRW, & so I
127 rose E, roose I; his: þe R; ost E; nyȝte CaDEFKMMaPUW; settid D,
     setted E, sette FIMU, settiden G, settede LPW
128 busschementis CaDEFLMW, bushmentis GHaIPQ, boiȝsshementis K,
     boyshmentis N, buyschmentis O; bisides EFHa
129 placis EGHaIKLMaPQ
130 ȝeed R; stode ER, stoode HaI; entrynge DGMaQRU
131 cite FHaLMPQW; ȝate of the citee: citee ȝate I; Forsothe: And I, forsooþ
     R, forsoþ X
132 alle E; ost ES; ros E, roose I; from K

36 mentis. And whanne Gaal hadde seen
the puple, he seide to Zebul, Loo! fro 135
the hillis a multitude descendith. To
whom he answerde, The shadewis of hillis
thow seest as mennus heedis, and by this
37 errour thou art desseyued. And eft Gaal
seith, Loo! the puple fro the nouel of the 140
erthe cometh doun, and o cumpanye commeth bi the weye that biho[l]dith the ook.

134 whenn *B*, whan *CFLoWoX*, when *E*, whenne *H*; had *LoWo*; sen *Wo*
135 peple *BFHLoWo*; lo *CEWoX*
136 hilles *LoWoX*; descendeþ *CWo*, om. *H*, descendis *Lo*; a multitude descendith:
descendiþ a m. *X*
137 whome *BFLo*; answerd *B*, answeride *LoWo*; schadowis *Lo*, shadewes *X*;
hillis *LoWoX*
138 mens *BH*, mennys *ELo*, mennes *F*; heuedis *BFHWo*, hedus *C*, hedis *EX*,
hedes *Lo*
139 erroure *Lo*; ert *BH*; disceyued *BFHWoX*, deceyuede *Lo*; efte *Lo*
140 seys *Lo*; lo *CEX*; peple *BFHLoWo*; nouell *BH*, nouyle *C*, nauell *Lo*[2],
nouele *X*
141 erþ *B*; cometh: commiþ *BF*, comiþ *H*, commes *Lo*; oo *BFHWo*, oon *E*;
company *BEHWo*, companye *F*; commeth: commiþ *BF*, comeþ *CEWoX*,
om. *H*, comes *Lo*
142 wey *LoWo*; beholdeþ *CEWo*, bi-holdes *Lo*, biholdeþ *X*; oc *CX*, ooke *LoWo*

36 Cumque vidisset populum Gaal, dixit ad Zebul: Ecce
de montibus multitudo descendit. Cui ille respondit:
Umbras montium vides quasi hominum capita, et hoc
errore deciperis.
37 Rursumque Gaal ait: Ecce populus de umbilico terrae
descendit, et unus cuneus venit per viam, quae respicit quercum.

256

36 place of buyschementis. And whanne Gaal
hadde seyn the puple, he seide to Zebul,
Lo! a multitude cometh doun fro the   135
hillis. To whom he answeride, Thou
seest the schadewis of hillis as the heedis
of men, and thou art disseyued bi this
37 errour. And eft Gaal seide, Lo! a puple
cometh doun fro the myddis of erthe, *that*   140
is, fro the hiȝnesse of hillis, and o cumpeny
cometh bi the weie that biholdith the ook.

133 busschementis CaDEGILMPW, buschementes F, bushmentis HaQ,
boiȝsshementis K, boishmentis N, biyschementis U; whan EFGLP, om. Ha
134 had EI; seyen BGHaQS, seen IMa, seie L, seyne R; peple
CaFILMMaNPWX; seid E; Zebul: Z. 'his priuee e[nmy]' I
135 cumeȝ E, comiþ GIQ; doune E; from K
136 hullis E, hilles F; he: ȝebul I; answerde CaFGMPQUW, answerd D,
answered E, answerede L
137 seist G, seeste R; schadowis BHaMaNX, shadues ELP, schadewes FU,
shadows K, schadewe R; hullis E, hilles F; hedis CaEMW, hedes F;
136–7 the heedis of men: mennus hedis I
138 arte E; deceieued EHaLP, disceyuid GQ, desseued U
139 efte ELR; saide E; peple CaFILMMaNPWX, multitude G
140 cumeȝ E, comyþ IQ; from GK; the: om. I; middes EF; þe erþe CIU,
eerþe R
141 from G; hiȝenesse AcRS, heiȝnesse CaFMW, hiȝnes D; hullis E, hilles FR;
gloss om. IX[1]; oo GHaKLPQR; cumpanye BCaIKMMaRUW, cumpany
EGLNPQX, cumpenye Ha
142 cumeȝ E, comyþ IQ, commeþ R; wey DHaIMa; biholdeþ DFHaKLR,
bi-holdeȝ E, bihooldiþ X; oke E

38 To whom seide Zebul, Where is nowe
thi mowth, bi the which thou speek, Who
is Abymalech, that we seruen to hym? 145
Whether is not this the puple, whom
thow despisedist? Go out, and fiȝt aȝens
39 hym. Gaal thanne wente, abidynge the
puple of Sichemys, and fauȝte aȝens Aby-
40 malech. The which pursuede hym fle- 150
ynge, and in the cytee threste; and there
fellen of the parti of hym many vnto the
41 ȝate of the cyte. And Abymalech sat in
Rana*; Zebul forsoth Gaal and his fe-
laws he putte out of the cyte, ne in it 155

143 whome *BFLo*; seid *B*; now *CEHWoX*
144 mouþe *BLo*; whiche *BCEHLoX*; speke *ELoWo*, speeke *X*
145 wee *CEX*; serue *BCFHLoWoX*, seruyn *E*
146 the: om. *Lo*; peple *BFHLoWo*; whome *BFL*
147 þu *B*; despisedist *BFHWo*, despisedest *C*, dispisedest *LoX*; goo *BFH*;
oute *B*, ouȝt *H*; feiȝt *BF*, fiȝte *Lo*; aȝenus *B*, aȝen *CX*, aȝenst *E*, aȝeyns *F*,
aȝeynes *Lo*, aȝeynst *Wo*
148 þann *BF*, þan *Wo*; went *BFWo*; abidende *CX*
149 peple *BFHLoWo*; fauȝt *BEFWo*, faȝt *CX*; aȝeyns *BFWo*, aȝen *CX*,
aȝenst *E*
150 whiche *BCEHLoX*; pursued *BFWo*; fleeȝinge *BF*, fleende *CX*, fleyng *Lo*,
fleȝinge *Wo*
151 cyte *cet.*; þrest *Wo*; þer *CEFWoX*
152 fellyn *E*; partye *Lo*, part *X*; manye *CEX*; the (2°): om. *Lo*
153 satt *BEFHWo*, satte *Lo*
154 Bana *A*; forsoþe *cet.*; hise *E*; felawis *BCEFHLo*, felawes *WoX*
155 he: om. *CX*; putt *BFH*, put *LoWo*; oute *B*, ouȝte *H*

38 Cui dixit Zebul: Ubi est nunc os tuum, quo loque-
baris: Quis est Abimelech ut serviamus ei? Nonne
iste est populus, quem despiciebas? Egredere, et
pugna contra eum.
39 Abiit ergo Gaal, expectante Sichimorum populo, et
pugnavit contra Abimelech;

38 To whom Zebul seide, Where is now thi
mouth, bi which thou spekist, Who is
Abymelech, that we serue hym? Whether   145
this is not the puple, whom thou dispisidist? Go thou out, and fiȝte aȝens hym.
39 Therfor Gaal ȝede, while the puple of
Sichen abood; and he fauȝt aȝens Aby-
40 melech. Which pursuede Gaal fleynge,   150
and constreynede *to go* in to the citee;
and ful many of his part felde doun til
41 to the ȝate of the citee. And Abymelech
sat in Ramna; sotheli Zebul puttide Gaal
and hise felowis out of the citee, and suf-   155

143   wam E; wher ILU; thi: þe X
144   mouþ *of boost* I; whiche GIO, wiche K; spakest FLR, spakist cet.
145   *he þis* abymalech I; where CDE, wher cet.
146   peple CaFILMMaNPWX; dispisidist CaKMNUW, despisedest EL,
      dispisedest FP, dispisedeste R
147   fiȝt EU; aȝenus AcCN, aȝenns O
148   þerfore CaEGKLMaNQRW, þanne I; ȝede out I; while: w^t E, whil
      LPR; peple CaFILMMaNPWX
149   abode E, abood *in þe citee* I; fauȝte BDEILNPR; aȝenus AcCNO;
      Abymelech: abymalech þat *ouercame* gaal I
150   whiche DG, and I, wich K; pursuwide CaMW, pursued DE,
      pursuwede F, pursuyde GQ; Gaal: him I; fleyng EL
151   constreynde CaW, constreyned DEU, constreinyde GHaQR,
      constreynede *him* IKM, constrainede L; go: fle I; cite CaFHaMQUW
152   manye BCaFGKMMaNQRWX; his part: þe partie of gaal I; felden BKX,
      filde D, fel EFLP, fellen CaIM; adoun E; til to: vn to EI
153   ȝates E, ȝatee Ma; cyte BCaFHaLMPQW
154   sate BDIR, satt KMa; soþli EGKLMMaQUWX, And I; puttid D, puttede
      EFL, putte IM
155   his CEGILPQX; felawis CaMW, felous EX, felawes F, felowes I; oute R;
      cite CaFHaMQW, c. *of sichem* I; suffride: s. *hem* B, suffrid D, suffred E,
      suffrede FLPUW, he s. hem I

40 qui persecutus est eum fugientem, et in urbem compulit; cecideruntque ex parte eius plurimi usque ad
portam civitatis.
41 Et Abimelech sedit in Rama; Zebul autem Gaal et
socios eius expulit de urbe, nec in ea passus est
commorari.

42 he suffrede to dwelle. Thanne the day
   folowynge the puple ȝede out into the
   feeld; the which whanne it was toold to
43 Abymalech, he took his oost, and dyuydide in thre companyes, settynge   160
   busshementis in the feeldis; and seynge
   that the puple wente out of the cytee, he
44 roos, and felle into hem with his oost,
   aȝenfiȝtynge and biseegynge the cytee.
   Forsothe two companyes, opynly ren-   165
   nynge hidir and thidir bi the feeld, the

156 sufferd *BH*, suffride *CE*, suffred *FWo*; dwellen *BFHLoWo*, dwellyn *E*;
    þann *F*, þan *HWo*
157 folewende *CX*, folewynge *E*, folwynge *Lo*; peple *BFHLoWo*; ȝide *CX*,
    went *Wo*[1]; oute *B*, ouȝte *H*
158 feld *C*, felde *LoWo*; whiche *BCEHLoX*; whenn *B*, whan *CEFWoX*, whenne
    H; tolde *BHLoWo*, told *CEFX*
159 toc *CX*, toke *FHWo*, tooke *Lo*; hoost *BFH*, ost *CX*, host *E*; dyuydyd
    BFHLoWo, deuidede *CEX*
160 cumpanyes *CEX*; settyng *B*, settende *CX*
161 buschmentis *Wo*, busshemens *X*; feldis *C*, feldes *Wo*; seeynge *BEFH*,
    seande *C*, seende *X*
162 peple *BFHLoWo*; went *BFWo*; oute *B*, ouȝte *H*; cyte *BCEFLoWoX*
163 rose *BFHWo*, ros *CEX*, roose *Lo*; fell *BF*, fel *CEHX*; þem *CLoX*; hoost
    BFH, ost *CX*, host *E*
164 aȝen-: aȝeyns *B*, aȝeyn- *FHWo*, a-ȝeynes *Lo*; -fiȝtynge: feyȝtinge *B*,
    fiȝtende *CX*; besegende *CX*, besegynge *E*, bysegynge *HWo*; cite *CEFLoWoX*
165 Forsothe two: tw. f. *cet.*; twei *E*; cumpanyes *CEX*; opeli *C*, openly
    HLoWoX; rynnynge *BF*, rennende *CX*, rennyng *Lo*
166 hiþer *BFX*, hider *CEHWo*, hidre *Lo*; and: om. *H*; þider *BCEFWoX*, om.
    H, þidre *Lo*; feelde *BFH*, feld *C*, felde *LoWo*

42 Sequenti ergo die egressus est populus in campum.
   Quod cum nuntiatum esset Abimelech,
43 tulit exercitum suum, et divisit in tres turmas,
   tendens insidias in agris; vidensque quod egredere-
   tur populus de civitate, surrexit, et irruit in eos,

42 fride not to dwelle ther ynne. Therfor
in the dai suynge the puple ȝede out in to
the feeld; and whanne this thing was teld
43 to Abymelech, he took his oost, and departide in to thre cumpenyes, and settide   160
buyschementis in the feeldis; and he siȝ
that the puple ȝede out of the citee, and
44 he roos, and felde on hem with his cumpeny, and enpugnyde and bisegide the
citee. Sothely twei cumpenyes ȝeden   165
aboute opynli bi the feeld, and pursueden

156 þer in E, þere ynne BR; Therfor: for Ac, þerfore BCaGIKMaNQRUWX
157 suwinge CaFMW, sygned E; peple CaFILMMaNPWX; ȝeden Ma
158 felde EHa; whan EFGHaLP; thing: om. Ca; teeld BDFGMaOWX,
told EI, toold KLP, tolde R
159 tok E, toke I, tooke R; ost E; departid D, departed E, departide it I,
departede P
160 to: om. I; þree K, þe L; cumpanyes BCaEGHaIKLMMaNPQUWX;
settid D, setted E, sette FU, he sette I, settede LP
161 busschmentis CaGHaPQW, busschementis DEFILM, boiȝsshementis K,
boyshmentis N; in: to D; feldes E, feeldes F, feldis HaU; seiȝ CaFMW,
sawȝe I, siȝe R
162 peple CaFLMMaNPWX, peple of gaal I; the (2°): om. E; cite
CaFHaMPQW
163 ros E, roose I, om. W; and: om. W; fel CaEFLMPW, filde D, felle I;
on: upon I; cumpanye BDEINW, cumpany CaGLMPQUX, cumpenye
DHaR, companye K
164 enpugnede BCFKLPRX, enpungnede CaMMaSU, enpugned DE, fauȝte
aȝens hem I, enpungnyde W; bisegid D, byseged E, ensegide I, bisegede
LPX
165 cite EFHaLMPQW; soþli FGLMMaPQUWX, & I; tweie CaMMaQRW,
two I; cumpanyes BCaEGIKLMMaNPQUWX; ȝede R
166 openli AcCaEFGLMMaNPQW; felde ER, feld Ha; pursuweden CaFMW,
pursuyden GQ

44 cum cuneo suo oppugnans et obsidens civitatem; duae
autem turmae palantes per campum adversarios persequebantur.

45 aduersaryes pursueden. Forsothe Abymalech al that day ouercam the cytee,
the which he took, slayn the dwellers of
it, and it destruyede, so that salt in it 170
46 he sprengide. The which thing whanne
hadden herd thei that dwelten in the
tour of Sychemys, wenten into the temple
of her god Beryth, where a boond of pees
with hym thei couenauntiden; and of it 175
the place took name, the which was
47 greetli strengthid. And Abymalech herynge the men of the tour of Sichemys
togidre gedre[d] in o glob, *or company*,

167 pursuedyn *E*
168 all *BF*; ouercoome *BF*, ouyrcam *E*, ouercome *HLoWo*; cyte *cet.*
169 whiche *BCEHLoX*; toke *BFHWo*, toc *CX*, tooke *Lo*; slawen *BFHWo*,
     slawyn *E*, slaw3en *Lo*; dwelleris *CELoX*
170 distruyde *BFH*, destro3ed *C*, destried *E*, destroyed *Lo*, destruyed *Wo*,
     distro3ede *X*
171 he: om. *H*; sprenged *BFH*, sprengde *CEX*, sprengid *Wo*; whiche
     BCEHLoX; þinge *FLoWo*; whenn *BH*, whan *CELoWoX*, whann *F*
172 had *BFHLoWo*, haddyn *E*; herde *BHLoWo*; dwelledyn *E*
173 toure *Lo*; wentyn *E*
174 þeir *BFWo*, þer *CELoX*; bonde *BLo*, bond *CEX*, boonde *Wo*; pese *BE*,
     pes *CX*
175 couenaunteden *CX*, couenauntidyn *E*
176 toke *BFHLoWo*, toc *CX*; whiche *BCEHLoX*
177 gretely *BFH*, gretli *CELoWoX*; streyngþid *BF*, strengþede *Lo*; heerynge
     BEF, herende *CX*
178 toure *LoWo*
179 to giþer *BF*, togidere *CEX*, to gyder *HWo*; tog. gedred: g. tog. *Lo*; geþerd
     BF, gadered *CE*, gaderd *H*, gaderide *Lo*, gidered *Wo*, gedered *X*; oon
     BEFHWo; globb *BFHWo*, glubbe *CX*, globbe *ELo*; *or company*: om. *cet.*

45 Porro Abimelech omni illo die oppugnabat urbem;
quam cepit, interfectis habitatoribus eius, ipsaque
destructa, ita ut sal in ea dispergeret.
46 Quod cum audissent, qui habitabant in turre Sichimorum, ingressi sunt fanum dei sui Berith, ubi foed-

45 aduersaries. Certis Abymelech fauȝt
a ȝens the citee in al that dai, which
he took, whanne the dwelleris weren
slayn, and that citee was destried, so that   170
46 he spreynte abrood salt ther ynne. And
whanne thei, that dwelliden in the tour of
Sichem, hadde herd this, thei entriden in
to the temple of her god Berith, where
thei hadden maad boond of pees with   175
hym; and of that the place took name,
47 which place was ful strong. And Abymelech herde the men of the tour of Si-

167 her aduersaries I; certes F, & I; fauȝte BEHaILNR; 167–68 & al þat day
    abymalech fauȝte aȝens þat citee I
168 aȝenus AcCNO; the: þat I; cite CaFHaLMQW; in: om. I; whiche G,
    þe whiche I, wiche K
169 tok E, toke HaIR; when E, whan LP; dwellers DEHaKLMPRUX, dwelleres
    F, dw. þerof I; were F, werin P
170 slayne EKR; that: þe Ca; cite CaFHaMPQW; distried AcBCaDFGMN-
    OPQSUW, distroied EMaR, distruyed X
171 he: abymalech I; spreynt AcBCDF, sprent E, sprengid K, spreynde U,
    sprenge W, sprengide X; abrode DER, abroode Ha, abrod I; salte E;
    þere ynne BR, þer in E
172 whan EFGLP; þai E; that: om. E; dwelten Ca, dwelledin E, dwelleden
    FLMPW, dwellid R, dwelden U
173 hadde AO, hadden cet.; herde EHaU; entreden CaEFMPW
174 here Q; where: wh. *bi a-vowis makyng* I
175 haddin P; made DEHaR; bond CCaLPQU, bonde E; þe pees E[1]
176 that: þat *ydole* I; the: om. C; toke EIR, tooke Ha; þe name IK
177 whiche GL, þe whiche I, wich K; stronge GHaR
178 herd D; the: om. FGHaQ, þat I; toure E

us cum eo pepigerant, et ex eo locus nomen accepit,
qui erat munitus valde.
47 Abimelech quoque audiens viros turris Sichimorum
pariter conglobatos,

48 stiede vp into the hil of Selmon with al   180
   his puple; and takun-to an axe he kytte
   of a braunche of a tree, and putte on the
   shuldir berynge, he seide to felawis, That
   ȝe seen me doo, that anoon doo ȝe.
49 Thanne stryuyngly of the trees kut-   185
   tynge of braunchis thei foleweden the
   duyk; the whiche enuyrounynge the
   place of socour, brenten vp; and so is
   doon, that thurȝ smook and fier a thowsand men weren slayn, men togidre and   190
   wymmen, of the dwellers of the tour of

180 steyȝid *BFWo*, steȝede *CEX*, styȝid *H*, steiȝede *Lo*; hyll *BFH*, hylle *LoWo*;
     alle *BLo*, all *FH*
181 peple *BFHLoWo*; taken *BFHLoWo*, take *CX*, takyn *E*; ax *CEX*; kytt
     BFHWo, cutte *CELo*
182 off *B*; braunch *CEWoX*; tre *EWo*; put *CEWo*, putt *X*
183 schulder *BCFHWoX*, scholdre *Lo*; berende *CX*; felawes *LoX*
184 ȝe (1°): ȝee *BCELoX*; doo (1°): do *CWoX*, don *E*; anoone *Lo*, anoen *X*;
     doo (2°): do *CEWoX*; ȝe (2°): ȝee *BCEFHLoX*
185 þann *BF*, þan *Wo*; striuendeli *CX*, striuyngeli *ELo*, stryuynglye *Wo*;
     treese *B*; cuttende *C*, kittinge *Wo*, kittende *X*
186 brawnches *ELoX*; þe *HX*; foloweden *BFHLoWo*, folewedyn *E*
187 duyke *BH*, duke *CELoWoX*; which *FWo*; enuyrounyng *B*, enuyrounende
     CX, enuyrounnynge *HLo*
188 socoure *Wo*; brenden *C*, brendyn *E*, brente *X*
189 don *CEWo*, done *H*, do *X*; þorȝ *B*, þurgh *EWo*, þoruȝ *FHLo*; smoke
     BCEFHWoX, smeke *Lo*; fijr *CE*, fire *Lo*, fuyre *Wo*; thousend *CX*, þousande
     FLoWo
190 slawe *BFWo*, slawyn *E*, slawen *H*, sclayne *Lo*; to giþer *BF*, togidere *CE*,
     to gyder *HWo*, togiþere *X*
191 dwelleris *CELoX*; toure *Lo*

48 ascendit in montem Selmon cum omni populo suo; et
   arrepta securi praecidit arboris ramum, impositumque
   ferens humero, dixit ad socios: Quod me videtis facere, hoc cito facite.
49 Igitur certatim ramos de arboribus praecidentes,
   sequebantur ducem. Qui circumdantes praesidium suc-
   cenderunt; atque ita factum est, ut fumo et igne
   mille hominum necarentur, viri pariter et mulieres,
   habitatorum turris Sichem.

264

48 chem gaderid togidere, and he stiede in
   to the hil Selmon with al his puple; and   180
   with an axe takun he kittide doun a
   boow of a tre, and he bar it, put on the
   schuldur, and seide to felowis, Do ȝe
49 this thing, which ȝe seen me do. Ther-
   for with strijf thei kittiden doun bowis   185
   of the trees, and sueden the duyk; whiche
   cumpassiden and brenten the tour; and
   so it was doon, that with smooke and fier
   a thousynde of men weren slayn, men
   togidere and wymmen, of the dwelleris   190

179 gaderide B, gadered E, gadrid GR, weren gederid round I, gedrid K,
    gederid NX; to gidre DIR, to gyder E, to gedere U; stied DE, steiede F,
    stiede up I, stiȝede KMaNR
180 hulle E; of Selmon BC¹CaDGHaIKMMa²NQX; alle E; peple
    CaFLMMaNPWX
181 an: 'a' E; ax AcCEFKLMMaNOPQSUX; taken BCaEFHaIKMMaRW,
    takin LP; kittid D, kitted E, kittede GLP, kitte I; adoun KX
182 bow BCEFHaOPQUX, bowȝ CaGIMMaR, bowe D, boowȝ KS, bouwȝ
    W; a: þe B, om. C; tree AcCaDEGHaIKLMaOWX; bare CDHaIR, brak
    E, baar KNX; put: om. Ca, putte D, putt IKMa; vp on CaI; the: his IN
183 shuldir AcBKX, schuldre CaDGHaIMaNQRW, shulder EFLPU; saide E,
    he seide I; felawis CaMW, felawes F, his felowis I, felows X; ȝe: ȝe anoon
    I, ȝee U
184 this: þis þis I (sic); whiche G, þat I, wich K; ȝee U; sene DE, sen G,
    sawȝen I, seene R; don U; þerfore BCaEGKMaNQRWX, þanne I
185 with: a I; strif EFGHaLPSU; þai E; kittide C, kitteden CaLMPUW, kitted E,
    kitten F, kittidin S; adoun I; bouwis BWX, bowes EFI, bo'o'wȝes K
186 the: om. BI; suweden CaFMW, sweden E, suiden Q; duk E, duke LP;
    wiche EK, which F, þe whiche I
187 cumpaceden CaEFLMPW, cumpasiden þe tour I, cumpasseden U;
    brenten: br. it up I, brenden U; toure DE
188 don AcDGHaILNPQUX, done ER; smook P, smoke cet.; fijr CaIMW,
    fire DE, fyr FLP
189 þousynd CaMW, þousand DEHaMaNQX, þousend FGLP, þousande KR;
    of: om. IR; were FHaMW; slaine EKR
190 to gidre DI, to gyder E; wommen BDGQ; 189—90 men & wymmen
    togidere I; the: om. E; dwellers DEHaIKLMMaRUX, dwelleres F

50 Sichem. Forsothe Abymalech thens go-
    ynge cam to the burgh toun Thebes, the
    which enuyrounnynge bisegide with oost.

51 Forsothe the tour was hiȝe in the mydil   195
    cytee, to the which flowen togidre men
    and wymmen, and alle the princis of the
    cytee, closid moost fastly the ȝate; and
    vpon the roof of the tour stondynge by

52 the pynnaclis. And Abymalech comynge   200
    nyȝ biside the tour fauȝt strongli, and
    neiȝynge to the dore, he was about to

192 forsoþ B; Forsothe Abymalech: A. f. *cet.*; þenns BF, þennus CWoX,
     þennes ELo; gooynge BF, goende CX
193 come BLoWo, coome FH; bourgh BH, burȝ C, borgh F, bourghe Lo
194 whiche BCEHLoX; enuyrounynge BEFWo, enuyrounende CX, envirounnyng
     Lo; byseegyd BFH, besegede CE, biseegede Lo, bysegid Wo, bisegede X;
     hoost BFH, ost CX, host E
195 forsoþ BH; Forsothe the tour: þe t. f. *cet.*; toure Lo; heeȝe BF, heeȝ C,
     heeyȝ E, hye Lo, heiȝe Wo, hiȝ X; mydyll B, middel CEWoX, myddyl FH,
     mydel Lo
196 cyte BCHLoWo, of þe cyte X; whiche BCEHLoX; floun CX, flowyn E,
     flewen Lo; to giþer BF, togidere CEX, to gyder HWo
197 all FH, al Lo; prynces ELoX
198 cyte BCEHLoWoX; closed BEFH, closide Lo; most BCEHWoX, moste Lo
199 uppon Wo; roofe BFHLo; toure Lo; stoondynge BF, stondende CX
200 the: om. X; pynaclis BCWo, pynacles ELoX; commyng B, comende CX,
     commynge FLo
201 neeȝ C, neegh E, neiȝ Wo; besyde BC, besiden E; toure Lo; faȝt CX,
     fowȝt(ȳ) E, fauȝte Lo; strongely Lo
202 neȝhende CX, neȝynge E; aboute BCFLoX, aboutyn E, abouȝte H

50 Abimelech autem inde proficiscens venit ad oppidum
    Thebes, quod circumdans obsidebat exercitu.

51 Erat autem turris excelsa in media civitate, ad quam
    confugerant viri simul ac mulieres, et omnes prin-
    cipes civitatis, clausa firmissime ianua, et super
    tectum turris stantes per propugnacula.

50 of the tour of Sichem. Forsothe Abymelech wente forth fro thennus, and cam
to the citee of Thebes, which he cum-
51 passide, and bisegide with an oost. For-
sothe the tour was hiʒ in the myddis of   195
the citee, to which men togidere and
wymmen fledden, and alle the princes of
the citee, while the ʒate was closid stronglieste; and thei stoden on the roof of the
52 tour bi toretis. And Abymelech cam bi-   200
sidis the tour, and fauʒt strongli. and he
neiʒede to the dore, and enforside to putte

191 toure CDE; forsoþ EX, And I
192 went E; foorþ D, forþe E; from K; þennys BGNQSX, þennes
     CCaFHaIKMW, þens DEMa, þenis LPR, þenns U; came DIMaR
193 citees CDFMOX, cite CaHaPQW; whiche CFG, þe whiche I, wiche K;
     cumpacide CaMW, cunpassid D, cumpacede EFLP
194 bisegid D, biseged E, bisegede FLOP, besegide S; ost E; Forsothe: & I,
     forsoþ X
195 þe (1°): om. G; toure DE; heiʒ CaFM, hiʒe D, hye E; the (2°): om. I;
     myddes F
196 cite CaEFHaMPQRW; whiche BGHaLMaPQX, whiche EK, whom I;
     to gidre DIR
197 wommen BGQ; 196−97 men & wymmen fledden togidre I; al AcE, all N;
     pryncis DGHaIKLMaNPQSWX
198 cite FGHaMQW; whille E, whil PR; ʒates E, ʒat N; wher E; closeed E,
     closed KL; strongliest AcDEFGHaKMaNQX, ful strongly I, strongest U
199 thei: men I; stooden GKLNOQX; upon I; rof U; r. of the: om. S
200 toure D; torrettis AcIRS, torettis CaDGMMaOQUW, torettes F, touretis K,
     tourettis N, turetis X; came DIR; bisides EHaKU
201 the: þis G; toure D; fauʒte BDHaILNR; strongly aʒens it I
202 neiʒide AcBS, neʒide C, neiʒʒide CaMW, nyʒed D, neiʒʒede F,
     neiʒede I; to: nyʒ I; enforsid D, enforced E, enforcede FLPU, enforside
     him I, enfoorside K, enforsiden O; put AcEOSU, putt R

52 Accedensque Abimelech iuxta turrim, pugnabat fortiter, et appropinquans ostio ignem supponere nite-
batur;

53 put vndir fyre; and, loo! a womman the
brekynge of a mylnstoon from aboue
throwynge hurtlide to the heed of Aby- 205
54 malech, and brak his brayn. The which
clepide anoon his squyer, and seith to
hym, Drawe out thi swerd, and smyte
me, lest perauenture it be seid, that of
a womman I am slayn. The which, ful- 210
55 fillynge the heest, slewȝ him; and him
slayn, alle that with hym weren of Yrael
56 ben turned aȝen to her seetis. And God
ȝeeldide the yuel that Abymalech dide
aȝens his fader, slayn his seuenti bre- 215

203 putt *BFWo*, putte *CHLo*, puttyn *E*, putten *X*; vnder *CFHWoX*, vndre *Lo*;
fijr *CE*, fyer *FX*, fuyre *Wo*; lo *CELoX*
204 breking *C*; mylne ston *CEX*, mylstoon *H*, mylne stoon *Lo*, mylnston *Wo*;
fro *CEX*; abouen *E*
205 þrowende *CX*; hurtlede *CLoX*, hurtlyd *Wo*; heued *BFHWo*, hed *CX*,
heuyd *E*, hede *Lo*
206 brake *BLoWo*; brayne *Lo*; whiche *BCEHLoX*
207 clepid *BFHWo*, clepede *CE*, callid *Lo*; a-noone *Lo*, anoen *X*; squyere
LoWo; seys *Lo*, seide *X*
208 drawȝ *CE*, draȝ *X*; oute *BLo*, ouȝte *H*; swerde *LoWo*; smyt *CEX*
209 leste *Lo*; par auenture *EX*; seyde *BHLoWo*
210 woman *Lo*; be *Wo*; slawen *BFHWo*, slawyn *E*, sclayne *Lo*; whiche
BCEHLoX; fulfillende *CX*, fyllynge *Lo*
211 hestis *BEFH*, hestus *C*, heestis *Lo*, hestes *WoX*; slewe *BFH*, slooȝ *C*,
slowȝ *E*, slowȝe *Lo*, slowe *Wo*, sloȝ *X*
212 slayne *BFWo*, sclayne *Lo*; all *FH*; weryn *E*
213 tornede *B*, turnyd *E*, torned *FHWo*, turnede *Lo*; aȝeyn *BFWo*, aȝeen *CX*,
aȝeyne *Lo*; þeir *BFWo*, þer *CELoX*; setys *BFHWo*, setes *X*
214 ȝeeldid *B*, ȝeeldede *C*, ȝeldede *E*, ȝeldide *Lo*, ȝeldyd *Wo*, ȝeld *X*; euel
CWoX, yuele *Lo*
215 aȝeyns *BFWo*, aȝen *CX*, aȝenst *E*, a-ȝeynes *Lo*; fadir *BEH*, fadre *Lo*;
slayne *Lo*; breþern *C*

53 et ecce una mulier fragmen molae desuper iaciens,
illisit capiti Abimelech, et confregit cerebrum eius.
54 Qui vocavit cito armigerum suum, et ait ad eum:
Evagina gladium tuum, et percute me, ne forte dica-
tur quod a femina interfectus sim. Qui iussa per-
ficiens, interfecit eum.

268

53 fier vndur; and lo! o womman castide
fro aboue a gobet of a mylnestoon, and
hurtlide to the heed of Abymelech, and   205
54 brak his brayn. And he clepide soone
his squyer, and seide to hym, Drawe out
thi swerd, and sle me, lest perauenture it
be seid, that Y am slan of a womman.
Which performede the comaundementis,   210
55 and killide Abymelech; and whanne he
was deed, alle men of Israel that weren
with hym turneden a3en to her seetis.
56 And God 3eldide to Abymelech the yuel
that he dide a3ens his fadir, for he killide   215

203 fijr CaIMW, fire D, fyr EFLP; vndir BDGHaKMaNPQX, vnder FLRU,
      vndir it I; o: a AcDEGIMaNX; wumman CaFMW, woman E; castid DF,
      casted E, þrewe doun I, castede P
204 from K; a boof R; gobett IK; mylnstoon D, mylne-stone EHa, mylle
      stoon I, mulne stoon L, mulneston O, melleston U
205 hurtele E, hurtelid F, sche hurlide it I, hurtlede LP, hurlide U; hede E,
      hed U; the heed of Abymelech: abymalech heed I
206 brake DHaR, it brake I, braak K; brayne R; clepid DE, cleepide S;
      sone EFQR, anoon I
207 squiere F; said E; Draw EU; out: not L, oute R
208 swerd anoon I, sweerd L, swerde R; slee CaFGKLPQR; leste BK, leest R
209 seide DRU; that: om. GQ; slayne R, slayn cet.; a: oo L; wumman CaFM,
      woman E
210 whiche G, þe whiche I, wiche K; perfourmede AcX, parfourmede Ca,
      perfourmed D, performed E, parformede FMSU, performyde GHaOQ,
      fulfillide I, parfoormede Ma, perfourmyde NR, parfourmyde W; the: his I;
      comaundement E, hestis I
211 killid D, killed E, killede FLP, slew3 I, kilde U; Abymelech: him I; whan
      EFHaLP; he: abymelech I
212 dede E, dead Q; alle þe men EIR
213 turnyden GHaQ; a3ein B; here GQ, hir O; citees E, placis I, setis MQRW
214 3eeldide CaR, 3ildid D, 3elded E, 3ildide I, 3eldede LPU; euel E, euyl
      FGLPQ
215 dud E; a3enus AcCNO; to U; fader FU; killid D, killed E, killede FLP,
      kilde U

55 Illoque mortuo, omnes qui cum eo erant de Israel,
reversi sunt ad sedes suas.
56 Et reddidit Deus malum, quod fecerat Abimelech
contra patrem suum, interfectis septuaginta fratribus suis.

57 theren. And to the Sichemys is ʒoldun
that thei wrouʒten, and is comen vpon
hem the cursynge of Joatham, sone of
Jeroboal.

10. 1 Aftir Abymalech roos a duyk in Yrael,
Thola, the sone of Phua, the faders brothir of Abymalech, a man of Ysachar,
that dwellide in Sanyr, of the hil of Ef-
2 fraym; and he demyde Irael thre and   5
twenti ʒeer, and he is deed, and biried in
3 Sanyr. To whom cam after Jayr Galadites, that demede Irael bi two and twenti

216 ʒolden BCEFHLoWo, ʒolde X
217 wroʒten CX, wrowʒtyn E; commen BF, comyn E, come LoX; uppon Wo
218 þem Lo; cursing CEHX, cursynge Lo

10. 1 After BFHWo; rose BF, ros CE, roose Lo, roes X; duyke BH, duc C,
duke ELoWoX
2 fadyres E, fadris Lo; broþer cet.
4 dwellyd BFHLoWo, dwelte CX, dwellede E; hyll BFH, hille LoWo
5 demed BFH, demede CX, demyd Wo
6 ʒer C, ʒere LoWo; dead BCEX, dede LoWo; buried Wo
7 whome BFLo; coom BH, coome F, come LoWo; aftyr ELoWoX
8 demyd BFHWo, demyde C

57 Sichimis quoque, quod operati erant, retributum est,
et venit super eos maledictio Ioatham, filii Ierobaal.

10. 1 Post Abimelech surrexit dux in Israel Thola, filius
Phua, patrui Abimelech, vir de Isachar, qui habitavit in Sanir, montis Effraim;
2 et iudicavit Israel viginti et tribus annis, mortuusque est, ac sepultus in Sanir.
3 Huic successit Iair Galaadites, qui iudicavit Israel
per viginti et duos annos,

57 hise seuenti britheren. Also that thing
was ʒoldun to men of Sichem, which thei
wrouʒten, and the curs of Joathan, sone
of Jerobaal, cam on hem.

10. 1 Aftir Abymelech roos a duyk in Israel,
Thola, the sone of Phua, brother of the
fadir of Abymelech; *Thola was* a man of
Ysachar, that dwellide in Sanyr, of the
2 hil of Effraym; and he demyde Israel thre
and twenti ʒeer, and he was deed, and
3 biriede in Sanyr. His successour was
Jair, a man of Galaad, that demyde Israel

5

216 his CEFGHaILPQX; breþren CaEFMW, briþren G, breþeren
HaILPUX, breþern K; & þat Ac; þat þis ELP; thing: yuel I
217 ʒolden CaDEFGHaIKLMMaPRUW; whiche G, þat I, wich K
218 curse E; þe sone I
219 came IR; on: upon I, to O; him DE

10. 1 After ELU; ros EU, roos up I; duke EP, duk L; roos a duyk: a d. r.
INR
2 of (1°): om. C; brother: þe broþer I, broþir ORS
3 fader CaEFLU; 2−3 the fadir of A.: abymalechus fadir I
4 dwellid D, dwelled E, dwellede LP, dwelde U
5 hille D, hul E; demede BCaFLMMaPRU, demed DE, deemede KX
6 ʒere E, ʒer LP; was deed: diede I, was dead Q
7 was biried I, beried U, biried cet.; successoure DE
8 deemede BMaX, demede CaFKLMPR, demed DE, dymyde O

4 ȝeer; hauynge thretti sones, sittynge vpon
thretti coltis of assis, and princis of thretti   10
cytees, the whiche of the name of hym
ben clepid Anochiayr, that is, the burghis
of Jayr, vnto the day that is nowe, in the
5 loond of Galaad. And Jayr is deed, and
biryed in the place to the which is the   15
6 name Camon. Forsothe the sones of Yrael
to oold synnes ioynynge newe, diden yuels
in the siȝt of the Lord, and serueden to
mawmettis, Baalym and Astaroth, and to
goddis of Syrye, and of Sidon, and of   20
Moab, and of the sones of Amon, and of
Philistiym; and thei laften the Lord,

9   ȝer C, ȝere LoWo; hauende CX, hafynge E; þrytty BFHLoWo; sonus CX,
    sonys EF; sytynge B, sittende CX, sittyng E; uppon Wo
10 þrytty (2x) BFHLoWo; coltes X; asses X; princes CELoX
11 cites CEX; which HWo
12 cleped C, callid Lo; the: om. X; bourghis BF, burȝis C, bourowis H,
    bourghes Lo, burȝs X
13 now CEHWoX
14 lond CWoX, land E, londe Lo; off X; dead BCEX, dede LoWo
15 biriede Lo; whiche BCEHLoX
16 Forsothe the sones: þe s. f. cet.; sonus CX
17 olde cet.; synns B, synnys H; ioynende CX; dydden B, didyn E; euelis C,
    euylis E, yuelis Lo, eueles WoX
18 siȝte CELoX; seruedyn E
19 maumetys C, mawmetis ELo, mawmetes X
20 godis CX, goddes Lo; of (2°): om. X
21 sonus CX, sonys EF
22 laftyn E, leften X

4 habens triginta filios, sedentes super triginta
pullos asinarum, et principes triginta civitatum,
quae ex nomine eius sunt appellatae Anothiair, id
est oppida Iair, usque in praesentem diem, in terra
Galaad.
5 Mortuusque est Iair, ac sepultus in loco, cui est
vocabulum Camon.
6 Filii autem Israel peccatis veteribus iungentes
nova, fecerunt mala in conspectu Domini, et servi-

4 bi two and twenti ʒeer; and he hadde
  thretti sones, sittynge aboue thretti coltis   10
  of femal assis, and thretti princes of
  citees, whiche ben clepid bi his name,
  Anoth Jair, that is, the citees of Jair, til
  in to present day, in the lond of Galaad.
5 And Jair was deed, and biriede in a   15
6 place to which the name is Camon. For-
  sothe the sones of Israel ioyneden newe
  synnes to elde synnes, and diden yuels in
  the siʒt of the Lord, and serueden to the
  idols of Baalym, and of Astoroth, and to   20
  the goddis of Sirie, and of Sidon, and of
  Moab, and of the sones of Amon, and of
  Filistiym; and thei leften the Lord, and

9   bi: om. CIKNRX; two: þre AcEKMNX, iii BCFGLOPQRSU; ʒere E,
    ʒer LP; & (2°): om. D; had E
10 þritti AcCaIMNWX, thirty E; sonys GLPQ, sonus I; sittynge: fiʒting E,
    sitting KLP; aboue: upon I; þritti AcCaIMNWX, thirty E; coltes F
11 female EMaR, sche I; asses FR; þritti AcCaIMNRWX, þirti E; pryncis
    DEGLMaNPQSWX
12 cites L; 11–12 & þei weren princis of þritti citees I; þe whiche I, wiche K;
    bene E; clepide K; his name: her fadir name I, his naame P
13 cites L; til: om. EI; 13–14 til … day in … Galaad: in … Galaad /til/ …
    day GIKNO²QSX, til … day in … G. til … day Ha
14 in to: vn to EI; þis present EIK¹
15 ded P, dead Q; was deed: diede I; was biried I, biriid P, birieed S, biried
    cet.
16 whiche FGLMaS, wiche K; is: om. O; to wh. the name is C.: þat hiʒte C.
    I; forsoþ EX, certis I
17 sonys GLQ; ioined E, ioynede O, ioyniden Q; new E
18 synnes (1°): synnis LQ; eelde CaHaMaWX, eeld D, holde E, oolde GKQ,
    olde ILPR; synnes (2°): synnis LPQ, synnus Ma; dedin P; yuels
    AcBCaDIKMaNOSW, yuel C, euel E, yueles FU, euylis G, euels L,
    euelis PQ
19 siʒte CaGU; siʒt of the Lord: lordis siʒt I; seruyden AcCGQ, þei seruyden
    I; the (2°): om. I
20 idolis DLW, ydoles FI; of (2°): to I; and (2°): om. GQ
21 goddes F
22 sonis GMaQ
23 laftyn E, laften K, leftin P

erunt idolis Baalim et Astaroth, et diis Syriae ac
Sidonis et Moab et filiorum Ammon et Philistiim; di-
miseruntque Dominum, et non colebant eum.

7 and heryeden not hym. Aȝens whom the
Lord wexe wrooth, and took hem into
the hoondis of Philistiym, and of the   25
8 sones of Amon. And thei ben tourmentid, and hidously oppressid bi eiȝteen
ȝeer, alle that dwelliden biȝonde Jordan
in the loond of Ammorre, that is in Ga-
9 laad, in* so mych, that the sones of Amon,   30
Jordan ouerpassid, wastiden Judam and
Beniamyn and Effraym; and Yrael is
10 turmentid* wel myche. And criynge to
the Lord thei seiden, We han synned to
thee, for we han forsakun oure God, and   35

23 heriedyn *E*, worschipede *Lo*; nott *X*; aȝeyns *BFHWo*, aȝen *EX*, a-ȝeynes
Lo; whome *BLo*
24 lorde *Lo*; wex *CEX*; wroþþe *B*, wroþ *CEX*, wrooþe *F*, wroþe *HLoWo*;
tooke *B*, toc *CX*, toke *FHLoWo*; þem *Lo*
25 hondus *C*, handis *F*, hondes *LoWo*, hondis *X*
26 sonus *CX*, sonys *EFHWo*; tourmentyde *BLo*, tormentid *CX*, turmentid *E*
27 hydouȝsly *H*, hidousely *Lo*; oppressed *BFH*; eyȝtene *BEHLoWo*,
eiȝtetene *CX*, eiȝteene *F*
28 ȝere *BLoWo*, ȝer *CX*; all *FH*, al *Lo*; dwelten *CX*, dwelledyn *E*, dwelleden
Wo; beȝunde *C*, beȝonde *E*, biȝunde *X*
29 lond *CWoX*, land *E*, londe *Lo*
30 in: & *ABFHWoX*; myche *BCEHLoWoX*; sonus *CX*, sonys *E*
31 ouer-passed *BFHWo*, ouyrpassed *E*, ouer passide *Lo*; waastyden *BFH*,
wasteden *CLoX*, wastidyn *E*
33 turmentid: turned *A*, torned *BFHWo*, tormentid *C*, tourmentide *Lo*,
turned *X*; wel: ful *C*, wol *E*; mych *FWo*; criende *CX*, cryyng *E*
34 lorde *Lo*; thei: om. *X*; seidyn *E*; wee *CEX*; synnede *Lo*
35 þe *Wo*; wee *CEX*; forsake *BFHWoX*, forsaken *CLo*, forsakyn *E*; our *CF*

7 Contra quos iratus est Dominus, et tradidit eos in
manus Philistiim et filiorum Amon.
8 Afflictique sunt, et vehementer oppressi per annos
decem et octo, omnes qui habitabant trans Iordanem
in terra Amorrei, quae est in Galaad;

7 worschipiden not hym. And the Lord was
wrooth aȝens hem, and he bitook hem in 25
to the hondis of Filistiym, and of the sones
8 of Amon. And alle that dwelliden ouer
Jordan in the lond of Ammorrey, which
is in Galaad, weren turmentid and op-
9 pressid greetli bi eiȝtene ȝeer, in so myche 30
that the sones of Amon, whanne thei hadden passid Jordan, wastiden Juda and
Benjamyn and Effraym; and Israel was
10 turmentid greetli. And thei crieden to
the Lord, and seiden, We han synned to 35
thee, for we forsoken oure God, and ser-

24 wurschipeden CaFMW, worschepeden E, wirschipiden I, worschipide L,
worschipeden NPU
25 wroþ EFHaLNPQU, wroiþ K; aȝenus AcCNO, et aȝens E; he: AIR, om.
cet.; bitok ESU, bitoke HaR
26 hondes CaF, hoondis R; sonis GHaLQ, sonus I
27 alle þe sones of israel I; dwellen AcO, dwelleden CaFLMPW, dwelledin
E, dwelden U; ouer: oure E, biȝonde I
28 the: om. E; whiche G, þat I, wich K
29 wheren E; tormentid F, turmentide K; oppresside KR, oppressed L
30 gretli AcIOPQSU, greteli DHa, gretteli E, grettli L; eyten E; ȝer ELP;
moche CaFNX, much E, mych R
31 sonys GLQ; whan EGLP; haddin P
32 passed EK; Jordan: A²IW, om. cet.; wasteden CaEFLMPW, waastiden
MaX
34 tourmentid I; gretli AcCEILOPQSU, greteli Ha; criden U
35 haue R; synnyd GPQ, synnede Ha, synneden L
36 þe ER; forsooken KX, forsookin P; seruyden ACGQ, serueden cet.

9 in tantum, ut filii Amon, Iordane transmisso, vasta-
rent Iudam et Beniamin et Effraim; afflictusque est
Israel nimis.
10 Et clamantes ad Dominum dixerunt: Peccavimus tibi,
quia dereliquimus Deum nostrum, et servivimus Baalim.

11 serueden to Baalym. To whom the Lord
spak, Whether not the Egipciens, and
Amorreis, and the sones of Amon, and of

12 Philistiym, Sidoneus forsothe, and Amalech, and Chanaan oppressiden ȝou, and
ȝe han cried to me, and Y haue dely-

13 ueryd ȝou fro the hoondis of hem? And
neuerthelater ȝe han forsake me, and
heried alien goddis; therfor I shal not
adde, that eny more I delyuer ȝou.

14 Gooth, and inwardli clepith the goddis
the whiche ȝe han chosen; delyuer thei

40

45

36 serued *BCX*, seruyd *E*, seruede *FHLoWo*; whome *BF*
37 spake *BWo*; the: om. *X*
38 sonys *BEFH*, sonus *CX*; of (2°): om. *B*
39 Ph.: om. *H*; forsoþ *B*
40 oppresseden *BFWo*, opresseden *C*, oppressedyn *E*, oppressid *LoX*
41 ȝee *CEX*; cryede *Lo*; hafe *E*; delyuerd *B*, deliuered *CFWoX*, delyuerde *H*,
deliuerede *Lo*
42 hondus *C*, handis *E*, hondes *LoWo*, hondis *X*; þem *CLo*
43 ner þe latere *CX*, neuerlatere *E*, neuere þe later *HLo*, neuer þe latter *Wo*;
ȝee *CELoX*; forsakyn *E*
44 heryede *Lo*; aliene *CE*; godis *CX*, goddes *LoWo*; þerfore *CEFHWoX*,
þere fore *Lo*
45 addyn *E*; any *CEX*; deliuere *CEFX*, deliuerede *Lo*
46 goþ *CEWoX*, goos *Lo*; inwardely *Lo*; clepeth *EWoX*, kallis *Lo*; godus *C*,
goddes *LoWo*, godis *X*
47 the whiche: þat *CX*, þe which *FWo*; ȝee *CELoX*; chose *C*, chosyn *E*;
deliuere *CELoX*

11 Quibus locutus est Dominus: Numquid non Aegyptii et
Amorrei, filiique Amon et Philistiim,

12 Sidonii quoque et Amalech et Chanaan oppresserunt
vos, et clamastis ad me, et erui vos de manibus
eorum?

13 Et tamen reliquistis me, et coluistis deos alienos;
idcirco non addam, ut ultra vos liberem.

14 Ite, et invocate deos, quos elegistis; ipsi vos lib-
erent in tempore angustiae.

11 uyden Baalym. To whiche the Lord spak,
Whether not Egipcians, and Ammorreis,
and the sones of Amon, and of Filistiym,

12 and Sidonyes, and Amalech, and Canaan, 40
oppressiden ȝou, and ȝe crieden to me,
and Y delyuerede ȝou fro the hondis of

13 hem? And netheles ȝe forsoken me, and
worschipiden alien goddis; therfor Y schal

14 not adde, that Y delyuere ȝou more. Go 45
ȝe, and clepe goddis whiche ȝe han
chose; delyuere thei ȝou in the tyme of

15 angwisch. And the sones of Israel seiden
to the Lord, We han synned; ȝelde thou

37 which EFL, whom I, wiche K; spake DEHaR, seide I
38 where D, were E, wher cet.; þe egipcians I
39 sonis GLQ; of (2°): om CaDGHaIMMa²NOQS
41 oppresseden CaEFLMPW, han oppressid I; ȝee U; criden U; 41 and …
   ȝou (42): om. L
42 delyueride AcCCaFHaKMMaQRSW, delyuerid D, diliuered E, delyuerde
   I; from K; hondes CaEF, hoondis R; 42–43 the hondis of hem: her
   hondis I
43 And: om. R; naþeles B; ȝee U; forsokin E, han forsake I, forsooken K,
   forsookin P
44 wurschipeden CaFMW, worshipeden EKOP, han wirschipid I; aliene
   HaKMRW; goddes EF; þerfore BCaGIKMNPQRWX
45 adde to I; deliuer E, delyueride O; moore B, nomore K¹
46 clepeþ N; goddes F, þo goddis I; which CE, þat I, wiche K; ȝee U; haue R
47 chosen EGU, chose to ȝou I; the: om. I
48 aungwisch CG, angwische DHaI, anguissis E, angwijss K; sonis GLQ
49 haue R; synnyd GLPQ, synnede Ha; ȝeelde CaMW, ȝilde D, ȝeld U

15 ȝou in the tyme of angwish. And the
sones of Yrael seiden to the Lord, We
han synned; ȝeeld thou to vs what euere 50
thing plesith to thee; oneli nowe delyuer
16 vs. The whiche ledynge alle thingis fro
her coostis, threwen out the mawmettis
of alien goddis, and serueden to the
Lord; the which sorewide vpon the 55
17 wrecchidnes of hem. And [so] the sones
of Amon criynge togidre in Galaad
piȝten tentis, aȝens whom the sones of
Yrael gedryd in Masphat setten tentis.

48 the (1°): om. *CX*; angwysche *HLo*
49 sonis *BEFH*, sonus *CX*; seidyn *E*; wee *CEX*
50 synnede *BLo*; ȝeld *C*, ȝeelde *FX*, ȝelde *LoWo*; euer *BCFWo*
51 þinge *BFLoWo*; pleseþ *CEX*, plesis *Lo*; þe *HWo*; oonly *BFHLoWo*, onli
   CEX; now *CEHLoWoX*; deliuere *CELoX*
52 which *FWo*; ledende *CX*; all *F*; thingus *CX*, þinges *Lo*
53 þeir *BFWo*; þer *CELoX*; costus *C*, coistis *E*, coostes *LoWo*, coestus *X*;
   threwyn *E*; oute *B*, ouȝte *H*; maumetus *CX*, mawmetis *ELo*
54 aliene *E*; godus *C*, goddes *LoWo*, godis *X*; seruedyn *E*
55 whiche *BCEHLoX*; sorowed *BFHWo*, sorewede *EX*, sorowide *Lo*; vppon
   Wo
56 wrecchedenesse *CE*, wrecchednes *Lo*, wrecchidnesse *Wo*, wrecchednesses *X*;
   þem *CLo*; sonus *CX*, sonys *EFHWo*
57 criende *CX²*; to giþer *BF*, togidere *CEX*, to gyder *HWo*
58 piȝtyn *E*; tentus *C*, tentes *X*; aȝeyns *BFHWo*, aȝen *CX*, aȝenst *E*, a-ȝeynes
   Lo; whome *BLo*; sonys *BEFH*, sonus *CX*
59 geþerd *BF*, gadered *C*, gaderid *E*, gederd *H*, gaderide *Lo*, gedered *Wo*,
   geþered *X*; settyn *E*, setteden *X*; tentus *C*, tentes *X*

15 Dixeruntque filii Israel ad Dominum: Peccavimus;
redde tu nobis, quidquid placet tibi; tantum nunc
libera nos.
16 Quae dicentes, omnia de finibus suis alienorum de-
orum idola proiecerunt, et servierunt Domino; qui
doluit super miseriis eorum.
17 Itaque filii Amon conclamantes in Galaad fixere
tentoria; contra quos congregati filii Israel in
Masphat castrametati sunt.

16 to vs what euer thing plesith thee; oneli 50
delyuere vs now. And thei seiden these
thingis, and castiden forth fro her coostis
alle the idols of alien goddis, and serueden
the Lord; which hadde rewthe, *ether*
compassioun, on the wretchidnessis of 55
17 hem. And so the sones of Amon crieden
togidere, *that is, clepyden hem silf togidere*
to batel, and excitiden aȝens Israel, and
settiden tentis in Galaad, aȝens whiche
the sones of Israel weren gaderid, and 60

---

50 wat E; euere AcGKMaQX; pleseȝ E, pleseþ FHaLR, pleesiþ GQ, pleeseþ
K; thee: to þee D¹GIQ; þe EF; oonli BCaDGHaIKLMMaNPRWX,
only FQU
51 deliuer E; now delyuere us I; seiden: seiynge GIQ, seynge Ha; þes
CDKNX
52 þings E, þinges Ha; and: om. GHaIQU; casteden CaEFLMPW; foorþ D;
from K; hir EP, here FGQ; costis U
53 idolis CaDGLQW, idoles EFIP; alyene BCaHaKMRW; goddes F;
seruyden CGIOQ
54 whiche G, wiche K, þe whiche I; had E; ruþe DHaLMaNQRX;
eiþer CaFGHaMQR, & E, or LP, eþir O, oþer U, eiþir W
55 compassion EKP; c. 'eþer r.' B; gloss om. AcMaI; on: of E, upon I;
wrecchidnesse AcGHaIMaQ, wickidnessis D, wrechednesse EL,
wrecchidnesses RU; 55—56 the wr. of hem: her wrecchidnesse I
56 sonis GLQ; so: om. M¹X
57 togidere (1°): to gidre DIR, to gyder E; clepeden CaEFMW; self
CaEFKLMPRUW; togidere (2°): to gidre DRX, togider ELP, om. C
58 bateil DKQ, bateile MaR, bataile U; exciteden CaEFKMNPW; aȝenus
AcCNO; gloss om. *text* I, 'ech mouynge "oþer" to batel aȝens israel'
marg. I
59 setteden CaEFLMPW, þei settiden I, setten U; aȝenus AcCNO; which CE,
whiche KN
60 sonys GLQ; were ELP; gadered EL, gadrid GR, gederide K, gedered P,
gederid X; 59—60 in G. And þe sones of I. weren gaderid aȝens hem I

279

18 And the princis of Galaad seiden eche to
his neiȝbors, He, that first of ȝou aȝen the
sones of Amon bigynneth to fiȝt, shal be
the duyk of the puple of Galaad.

11. 1 There was also in that tyme Jeptee
Galadites, a man moost strong and fyȝter,
the sone of a womman strompet, that is
2 born of Galaad. Forsothe Galaad hadde
a wijf, of whom he took sones, the
whiche aftirward that thei weren waxen,
kesten out Jeptee, seiynge, Eyre in the
hows of oure fader thou shalt not mowe
be, for of avowtresse modir thou art

60 prynces *ELoX*; seydyn *E*; ech *BWo*
61 hise *E*; neiȝbours *BF*, neȝhebores *CX*, neȝebores *E*, neyȝebores *H*,
neiȝebore *Lo*, neiȝboures *Wo*; firste *H*; aȝeynst *BFWo*, aȝenst *EHLo*
62 sonis *BFH*, sonus *CX*; begynneþ *CE*, bygynniþ *H*, bygynnes
Lo; fiȝte *BCFHLoX*, fiȝtyn *E*; shal: he shal *X*; ben *CEX*
63 the: om. *F²LoWoX*; duyke *BH*, duke *CELoWo*, duk *X*; peple *BHLoWo*

11. 1 þer *BCEFHWoX*
2 most *BCEFHWoX*, moste *Lo*; stronge *BHLoWo*; fiȝtere *CEFX*
3 a: om. *X*; woman *Lo*; strompett *BWo*, strumpet *CEX*
4 borne *BHLo*; Forsothe Galaad: G. f. *cet.*; had *BFLoWo*
5 wyf *cet.*; whome *BF*; tooke *BF*, toc *CX*, toke *LoWo*; sonys *BEFH*, sonus
CX
6 which *FLoWo*; afterward *BCFHWo*, afterwarde *Lo*, aft[er]-ward *X*; wexyn *E*
7 casten *CLo*, kastyn *E*; oute *B*, ouȝte *H*; seiende *CX*; eir *CEX*, heyre *H*
8 houȝs *H*; our *BF*; fadir *BEHWo*, fadre *Lo*; moun *CEX*, nowe *Lo*
9 ben *CELo*; of: om. *H*; moder *BCFWoX*, modre *Lo*; ert *BFH*

18 Dixeruntque principes Galaad singuli ad proximos
suos: Qui primus ex nobis contra filios Amon coep-
erit dimicare, erit dux populi Galaad.

11. 1 Fuit itaque in illo tempore Iepte Galaadites, vir
fortissimus atque pugnator, filius mulieris mere-
tricis, qui natus est de Galaad.

18 settiden tentis in Masphat. And the
princes of Galaad seiden ech to hise neiȝ-
boris, He, that bigynneth first of vs to
fiȝte aȝens the sones of Amon, schal be
duyk of the puple of Galaad. 65

11. 1 And so in that tyme Jepte, a man of
Galaad, was a ful strong man, and fiȝtere,
the sone of a womman hoore, which
2 Jepte was borun of Galaad. Forsothe
Galaad hadde a wijf, of which he hadde 5
sones, whiche aftir that thei encreesiden,
castiden out Jepte, and seiden, Thou maist
not be eir in the hows of oure fadir, for
thou art born of a modir auoutresse.

61 setteden CaEFLMPW, setten U; tentes F
62 princis DGIKLMaNPQSWX; eche KL; his AcCaEFGHaILMaPQX;
neȝboris C, neiȝbore EK, neiȝbores FHaPR, neiȝebore GMa, neiȝeboris
LNSX
63 bigynneȝ E, bigynnif G, biginniþ PQS; firste BU
64 fiȝt R; aȝenus AcCNO, aȝen E; sonis GLQ, sonus Ma
65 duke ELP, dwyk G, duk Ha; peple CaFLMMaNPWX

11. 2 stronge CHaR; a fiȝter I, fiȝter MX
3 wumman CaFMW, woman E; hore D¹EFMU, strompet I; þe whiche I,
wiche K
4 born CaDEFGHaIKLMMaOPWX, borne R, boren U; Forsothe: And I,
forsoþ X
5 had E; wife E, wif FGHaLNPQU; whiche GR, whom I, wiche K; had E
6 sonis GLQ; which DEHaLQ, þe whiche I, wiche K; after EFLUX; that:
om. I; þai E; encreessiden AcBCMaNOQS, encresseden Ca, encresiden
DHaKRUX, entreden E, encreseden FLP, encressiden G, weren woxe I,
encreesseden MW
7 casteden CaFLMPW, casten E; seid E; myȝt E, maiȝt LP, maiste R
8 not: om. S; eire D, heir R; be eir: bere ELP; in: to Ha; our DL; fader
CaDFLRU
9 borun AcBCNOQSU, borne R; moder FLU

2 Habuit autem Galaad uxorem, de qua suscepit filios;
qui postquam creverant, eiecerunt Iepte, dicentes:
Heres in domo patris nostri esse non poteris, quia
de adultera matre natus es.

3 born. Whom he fleynge and shonnynge 10
dwellide in the loond of Tob; and there
ben gedrid to hym nedi men and ste-
4 lynge, and as prince thei sueden. In
thoo days fou3ten the sones of Amon
5 a3ens Yrael; the whiche sharpli instoond- 15
ynge, the more thur3 birth wenten fro
Galaad for to take into her help Jeptee
6 of the loond of Tob; and thei seiden to
hym, Com, and be oure prince, and fi3t

10 borne *Lo*; whome *BF*; flee3ynge *BFH*, fleande *C*, fle3inge *Wo*, fleende *X*; shonende *CX*, schonynge *ELo*
11 dwellid *BFHLoWo*, dwelte *CX*; lond *CWoX*, land *E*, londe *Lo*; þer *cet.*
12 geþerd *BF*, gadered *C*, gaderid *E*, gedered *HWoX*, gaderide *Lo*; stelende *CX*
13 prince: a prince *X*; sueden: s. hym *C*, suedyn *E*
14 thoo: þat *BEFHLo²Wo*, þo *X*; da3es *CX*, daies *EFHLoWo*; fo3ten *CX*, fou3tyn *E*; sonys *BFH*, sonus *CX*
15 a3eyns *BFWo*, a3en *CX*, a3enst *E*, a-3eynes *Lo*; which *FWo*; instondende *CX*, in-stondynge *EFHWo*, inne stondynge *Lo*
16 þor3 *BF*, þurgh *E*, þoru3 *HLo*; birþe *CEHLoWoX*; wentyn *E*
17 takyn *E*; þeir *BFWo*, þer *CELoX*; helpe *BCEHLoX*
18 lond *CWoX*, land *E*, londe *Lo*; seidyn *E*
19 comme *BF*, cum *CEX*, come *HLoWo*; fi3te *Lo*

3 Quos ille fugiens atque devitans, habitavit in terra
Tob; congregatique sunt ad eum viri inopes et latrocinantes, et quasi principem sequebantur.
4 In illis diebus pugnabant filii Amon contra Israel.
5 Quibus acriter instantibus, perrexerunt maiores natu
de Galaad, ut tollerent in auxilium sui Iepte de
terra Tob;
6 dixeruntque ad eum: Veni, et esto princeps noster,
et pugna contra filios Amon.

3 Whiche britheren he fledde, and eschew-   10
ide, and dwellide in the lond of Tob;
and pore men and doynge thefte weren
gaderid to hym, and sueden as a prince.
4 In tho daies the sones of Amon fouȝten
5 aȝens Israel; and whanne thei contynu-   15
eden scharpli, the grettere men in birthe
of Galaad, ȝeden to take in to the help of
6 hem silf Jepte fro the lond of Tob; and
thei seiden to hym, Come thou, and be
oure prince, and fiȝte aȝens the sones of   20

10 which E, wiche K; breþren CaEFMW, briþren G, breþeren HaLPUX,
    breþern K; fled D; & he fledde his briþeren I; escheuede ELP, eþchewide
    hem I
11 dwellid D, dwelled E, he dwellide I, dwellede LP, dwelde U; londe E
12 doing ELP, gaderinge X; ȝeft E, þeefte O, þeft R; doynge thefte: þeues I
13 gadered ELU, gadrid GR, gederide K, gederid X; suweden CaFMW,
    suiden GQ, sueden him I
14 þoo R; sonys GQ; fouten E
15 aȝenus AcCNO; whan EGL
16 scharply 'here enmytees' I; grettir Ac, gretere C, gretter CaDFHaNX,
    greter E; burþe F
17 the: om. MaR; helpe EGQR; 17–18 take iepte fro þe lond of tob in her
    owne help I
18 self CaEFKLMPRUW; from K
19 cum E
20 our L; fiȝte þou I, fiȝt U; aȝenus AcCNO, aȝen D; sonis GLQ

7 aȝens the sones of Amon. To whom he   20
answerde, Ben not ȝe, that hatiden me,
and kesten out fro the hows of my fader,
and nowe ȝe ben comen to me thurȝ nede

8 constreyned? And the princis of Galaad
seiden to Jepte, For this cause thanne   25
nowe to thee we ben comen, that thou
goo with vs, and fiȝt aȝens the sones of
Amon, and be duyk of alle that dwellen

9 in Galaad. Forsothe Jeptee seide to hem,
If verreyli ȝe ben comen to me, that I fiȝte   30
for ȝow aȝen the sones of Amon, and the
Lord take hem into myn hoondis, shal

20 aȝeyns *BFWo*, aȝen *C*, aȝenst *E*, a-ȝeynes *Lo*; sonys *BFH*, sonus *CX*;
whome *BF*
21 answeride *Lo*, answered *Wo*; be *X*; ȝee *CEFLoX*; hatydden *B*, hateden *CX*,
hatedyn *E*
22 casten *C*, kastyn *E*; oute *BLo*, ouȝte *H*; from *E*; houȝs *H*; fadir *BE*, fadre
Lo
23 now *BCEFHWoX*; ȝee *CELoX*; commen *BF*, come *C*, comyn *E*; þorȝ *BF*,
þurgh *E*, þoruȝ *HLo*
24 constreynyd *E*, constreynede *Lo*; princes *ELoX*
25 seidyn *E*; þann *BFH*, þan *LoWo*
26 now *CEFWoX*; to thee: to þe *Wo*, om. *X*; wee *CEX*; commen *BF*, come
CX, comyn *E*
27 go *CELoWoX*; fiȝte *CELoX*; aȝeyns *BFWo*, aȝen *CX*, aȝenst *E*, a-ȝeynes
Lo; sonys *BEFH*, sonus *CX*
28 duc *CX*, duke *ELoWo*, duyke *H*; all *F*, al *H*; dwellyn *E*
29 forsoþ *B*; Forsothe Jeptee: J. f. *cet.*; þem *CEFLoX*
30 ȝif *HWo*, ȝife *Lo*; verreli *CEWoX*, verili *H*; ȝee *CELoX*; be *C*; commen
BF, come *CX*, comyn *E*; fiȝt *BFHWo*
31 aȝeyn *BFWo*, a-ȝeyne *Lo*; sonys *BEFH*, sonus *CX*
32 þem *CELoX*; myn *E*; hondus *C*, handis *E*, handes *Lo*, hondes *Wo*, hondis *X*

7 Quibus ille respondit: Nonne vos estis, qui odistis
me, et eiecistis de domo patris mei, et nunc venistis ad me necessitate compulsi?

8 Dixeruntque principes Galaad ad Iepte: Ob hanc igitur causam nunc ad te venimus, ut proficiscaris

284

7 Amon. To whiche he answeride, Whethir not ȝe it ben, that haten me, and
castiden me out of the hows of my fadir,
and now ȝe camen to me, and weren com-

8 pellid bi nede? And the princes of Galaad   25
seiden to Jepte, Therfor for this cause
we camen now to thee, that thou go with
vs, and fiȝte aȝens the sones of Amon; and
that thou be the duyk of alle men that

9 dwellen in Galaad. And Jepte seide to   30
hem, Whether ȝe camen verili to me, that
Y fiȝte for ȝou aȝens the sones of Amon,
and if the Lord schal bitake hem in to
myn hondis, schal Y be ȝoure prince?

21   which E, þe whiche I, wiche K; answerde CaFGMPQUW, answerd D,
     answered E, answerede L; where D, wheþer E, wher cet.
22   ȝee U; it be not ȝe E; hatiden IU, hadden N, hatin P
23   casteden CaFLMPW, caste E, þrewen I; fader CaFLMU, fadris E
24   ȝee U; sum E, han come I, comen Ma; compelled E, compellide Q;
     24–25 and weren compellid bi nede: & bi neede weren compellid I, om. S;
25   princis DGIKLMaNPQWX
26   saiden E; þerfore BCaGKLMaNQRW, þanne I; cause: case Ha; For þis
     cause þanne I
27   camen AB, com E, comen cet.; þe EF; now to thee: to þee now GI
28   fiȝt EU; aȝenus AcCNO; sonys GLQ
29   the: om. DM; duke ELP; al R
30   dwellin EP
31   whether AE, where DI, wher cet.; ȝee U; com E, comen I; werrely Ca,
     verrili DMa, uereli E, verrely FMW; verrily 'wiþoute fraude' I; v. to me:
     to me v. I
32   aȝenus AcCNO; sonys GLQ
33   ȝif E; betake EP; hem: amon I
34   myne CaEKMMaRW; hondes CaF; ȝour F

nobiscum, et pugnes contra filios Amon, sisque dux
omnium qui habitant in Galaad.

9 Iepte quoque dixit eis: Si vere venistis ad me, ut
pugnem pro vobis contra filios Amon, tradideritque
eos Dominus in manus meas, ego ero princeps vester?

10 Y be ȝoure prynce? The whiche answerden to hym, The Lord, that thes
thingis herith, he meene and witnes is,   35
11 that oure biheestis we shulen doo. And
so Jeptee ȝede with the princis of Galaad, and the puple made hym ther(e)
prince; and Jeptee spak alle his wordis
12 before the Lord in Maspha. And he   40
sente messagers to the kyng of the sones
of Amon, the which of his persone shulde
seye, What to me and to thee is, for thou
art comun aȝens me, that thou waste(st)

33 ben *EX*; ȝour *BFHLoWo*; which *F*; answerdyn *E*, answereden *Wo*
34 þese *CEX*
35 þinges *BLo*, thingus *CX*; hereþ *CEX*, heeriþ *FWo*, heres *Lo*; mene *cet.*;
    wyttnes *BF*, witnesse *CELoWo*, wittnesse *H*
36 our *B*; byhestis *BFH*, behestis *CE*, byhestes *WoX*; wee *CE*; schuln *BEFHWo*,
    shul *CX*, scholden *Lo*; do *CWoX*, don *E*, doon *Lo*
37 ȝide *CX*; princes *ELoX*
38 the puple: þe peple *BFHWo*, al þe puple *CE*, al þe peple *Lo*; þeir *B*, þer
    CLoX, her *H*
39 spake *BWo*; all *FH*; hise *E*; woordis *CE*, wordes *LoWo*, wrdus *X*
40 beforn *BEH*, befor *C*, byforn *FWo*, bifore *Lo*, bifor *X*
41 sent *BFHWo*, sende *Lo*; messageres *CX*, messageris *ELo*; kynge *BLo*;
    sonus *CX*, sonys *EFHWo*
42 the which: þat *C*, þe whiche *EHLoX*; shulden *CX*, schuldyn *E*,
    scholde *Lo*, schuld *Wo*
43 seyn *cet.*; þe *Wo*; is: om. *X*
44 ert *BFHWo*; commen *BFWo*, come *CX*, comyn *E*, comen *HLo*; aȝeynst *BF*,
    aȝen *CX*, aȝenst *EHWo*, a-ȝeynes *Lo*; waast *BH*, waaste *F*, wast *Wo*

10 Qui responderunt ei: Dominus, qui haec audit, ipse
mediator ac testis est, quod nostra promissa faciemus.
11 Abiit itaque Iepte cum principibus Galaad, fecitque
eum /omnis/ populus principem sui; locutusque est
Iepte omnes sermones suos coram Domino in Maspha.
12 Et misit nuntios ad regem filiorum Amon, qui ex
persona sua dicerent: Quid mihi et tibi est, quia
venisti contra me, ut vastares terram meam?

10 Whiche answeriden to hym, The Lord   35
hym silf, that herith these thingis, is me-
diatour and witnesse, that we schulen do
11 oure biheestis. And so Jepte wente
with the princes of Galaad, and al the
puple made hym her prince; and Jepte   40
spak alle hise wordis bifor the Lord in
12 Maspha. And he sente messangeris to
the kyng of the sones of Amon, whiche
messangeris schulden seie of his persoone,
What is to me and to thee, for thou hast   45

35   which EFL, þe whiche I, wiche K; answerden CaFGMPQUW, answerd
D, answed E, answereden L
36   self CaEFKLMPRUW; heryt E, hereþ FHaLR, heeriþ GMaNOU, heereþ
K; þis E, þes DKNU; þinges FHaP; mediatoure D, a m. Ha
37   wittenes E; schullen CaFMW, schuln D, shul EILP; do: fulfille I
38   oure: ȝour E; bihestis CaEFMPUW, bihestis *to þee* I, biheestes R; so:
þanne I; went E, wente forþ IL
39   pryncis DGIKLMaNPQSX; alle E
40   peple CaFILMMaPWX; maden F; hem N; here FGQR
41   spake CDHaIR; his ELPQX, her I; wordes CaF, wordus I; bifore
BCaDEGHaIKLMaNPQRWX
42   sent E; messagers EK, messangers DFMX, messengers LP, massangeris O,
messangeres Ha
43   sonys GHaLQ; which ES, þe whiche I, wiche K
44   messangers DFIMX, messageris E, messangeres HaU, messagers K,
messengers LP, massengeris O; scholden CaMW, shuld E, schul I, shulen
O; saye E, sey I; of: to I; his: þe kyngis owne I; persone CaDEFLMPSUW
45   þe EF; for: þat KX; haast R

13 my loond? To whom he answerde, For   45
    Yrael took my loond, whanne he stiede
    vp fro Egipt, fro the coostis of Arnon
    vnto Jaboth and Jordan, nowe thanne
14 with pees ȝeeld to me it. Bi whom eft
    Jeptee sente, and comaundide to hem, that   50
    thei shulden seye to the kyng of Amon,
15 Thes thingis seith Jeptee, Yrael took not
    the loond of Moab, ne the loond of the
16 sones of Amon; but whanne fro Egipt
    thei styeden, he ȝede bi wildernes vnto   55

45   lond *CX*, land *E*, londe *LoWo*; too *X*; whome *BF*; answerd *B*, answeride
    Lo, answerid *Wo*
46   toke *BFHLoWo*, toc *CX*; lond *CWoX*, land *E*, londe *Lo*; whann *BH*,
    whan *CEFLoWoX*; steyȝed *BF*, steȝede *CEX*, styȝed *H*, steiȝede *Lo*,
    steiȝid *Wo*
47   costus *C*, costis *E*, coestes *X*
48   now *CELoWoX*; þann *BF*, þan *Wo*
49   pese *BE*, pes *CX*; ȝeelde *BF*, ȝelde *HLoWo*, ȝeld *X*; me: om. *H*; be *E*;
    whome *BF*; efte *Lo*
50   sent *BFHWo*, sende *Lo*; comaundede *C*, comaundid *Wo*; þem *CLoX*
51   schuldyn *E*, scholde *Lo*; say *BH*, sei *CLoWoX*, seyn *E*; kynge *BLoWo*
52   þese *CEWoX*; þinges *BELo*, thingus *CX*; seys *Lo*; toke *BFHLoWo*, toc *CX*
53   lond (2x) *CH*(1°)*WoX*, land *E*, londe *Lo*
54   sonus *CX*, sonys *EF*; bot *B*, bute *F*, butt *X*:, whenn *BH*, whan *CLoWoX*,
    whenne *E*, whann *F*
55   steyȝeden *BFLoWo*, steȝeden *CX*, steȝedyn *E*, styȝeden *H*; ȝide *CX*,
    ȝeede *H*, ȝode *Lo*; wyldernesse *BCEFHLoWo*; vnto: in to *Lo*

13 Quibus ille respondit: Quia tulit Israel terram
    meam, quando ascendit de Aegypto, a finibus Arnon
    usque ad Iaboch atque Iordanem; nunc igitur cum
    pace redde mihi eam.
14 Per quos rursum mandavit Iepte, et imperavit eis,
    ut dicerent regi Amon:
15 Haec dicit Iepte: Non tulit Israel terram Moab, nec
    terram filiorum Amon;
16 sed quando de Aegypto conscenderunt, ambulavit per
    solitudinem usque ad mare rubrum, et venit in Cades.

13 come aȝens me to waaste my lond? To
whiche the kyng answeride, For Israel
whanne he stiede fro Egipt took awei my
lond, fro the coostis of Arnon til to Jaboch and to Jordan, now therfor ȝeelde it 50
14 to me with pees. Bi whiche massangeris
Jepte sente eft, and comaundide to hem,
that thei schu[l]den seie to the kyng of
15 Amon, Jepte seith these thingis, Israel
took not the lond of Moab, nether the 55
16 lond of the sones of Amon; but whanne
thei stieden fro Egipt, he ȝede bi the
wildirnesse til to the Reed See, and cam

46 cum E, comen K; aȝenus AcCNO; aȝ. me: om. I; waste
BCCaFGHaKLMOQRUW, waast D, wast E
47 which BDEFHaPQR, 'þe' whiche messangers I, wiche K; answerde
CaEGMPQUW, answerd D, answerede FL
48 whan EGHaLP; stied DE, steiede F, stiȝede HaKMaNR, stiede up I; from
K; toke EHaIR, tok U; away EHa
49 from K; costes EF, coostus I, costis U; til to: vnto EI
50 now: om. L; þerfore CaEFGIKNQRUWX; ȝelde AcBCEFHaIKLM-
MaNOPQRSUX, ȝilde D
51 to me: to me aȝen I; with: in W; which ER, þe whiche I, wiche K;
messangeris AcBCCaMaNQRUW, messangers DIMX, messagers EFK,
mensangeris G, messangeres Ha, messengers PL, messongerus O, messageris
S
52 sent AcE; efte EHaLR, eft aȝen I; comaund E, comaundede LP
53 þai E; scholden CaMW, shuld E; say E, sey I
54 sayt E; þes DKNX, þise E; þings E, þinges FHa
55 tok EF, toke HaR; neiþer CaFGHaIMQRW, neiþir Ma, neþir OPS
56 sonys GLQ, sonus I; Bot E; whan EGLP
57 þai E; stied E, steieden F, stiȝeden HaKMaR, ȝeden up I, stiȝede N;
from K; he ȝede: israel wente I
58 wildernes E, wildurnesse Ha, wildernesse LMaRU, wildirnes X; til to: vnto
EI; rede EFLMMaUWX, reede GKQ; came CDIR, com E

17 the Reed See, and cam into Cades; and
   he sente messagers to the kyng of Edom,
   seiynge, Let me (not), that I passe bi thi loond;
   the which wold not assente to his preiers.
   And he sente to the kyng of Moab, the   60
   which and he dispiside to ȝyue passynge;
18 and so he abood in Cades, and enuyrounde aside the loond of Edom, and the
   loond of Moab; and he cam to the eest
   coost of the loond of Moab, and he sette   65
   tentis biȝonde Arnon, and he wold not
   entre the teermys of Moab; forsothe Arnon is niȝ coost to the loond of Moab.

56 rede *BCEFHWoX*; se *CX*; coome *BF*, come *HLoWo*
57 sent *BFHWo*, sende *Lo*; messageres *CX*, messagerys *ELo*; kynge *B*
58 seiende *CX*; lete *BFHLoWo*; thi: þe *Lo*; lond *CEWoX*, londe *Lo*
59 whiche *BCEHLoX*; wolde *cet.*; assenten *BCFHLoWo*, assentyn *E*; hise *E*;
   prayers *B*, preyȝeeris *C*, preyeres *E*, preyeris *Lo*, prayeres *Wo*, preieeres *X*
60 sent *BFHWo*, sende *Lo*; kynge *BLo*
61 whiche *BCEHLoX*; dispised *B*, despisede *CE*, dispisyd *FHLoWo*, dispisende
   X; ȝeue *BFH*, ȝifen *E*, gyue *Lo*; passing *CX*
62 abode *BLoWo*, abod *CX*, aboid *E*, aboode *FH*; enuyrouned *BFWo*,
   enuyrownyde *E*, environned *H*, environede *LoX*
63 lond *CHWoX*, land *E*, londe *Lo*
64 lond *BCWoX*, land *E*, londe *Lo*; coome *BFH*, come *LoWo*; este *BF*, est
   CEHX
65 cost *C*, coist *E*, coest *X*; lond *CWoX*, land *E*, londe *Lo*; sett *BHWo*
66 tentus *C*; byȝond *BFHWo*, beȝunde *C*, beȝondyn *E*, biȝunde *X*; wolde
   CEHLoX
67 entryn *E*; termys *BEFHWo*, termes *CLoX*; forsoþ *B*; forsothe Arnon:
   A. f. *cet.*
68 neeȝ *CE*, neiȝ *Wo*; cost *CWo*, coist *E*, coest *X*; lond *BCWoX*, land *E*,
   londe *Lo*

17 Misitque nuntios ad regem Edom, dicens: Dimitte me,
   ut transeam per terram tuam; qui noluit acquiescere
   precibus eius. Misit quoque ad regem Moab, qui et
   ipse transitum praebere contempsit. Mansit itaque
   in Cades,

17 in to Cades; and he sente messangeris to
 the kyng of Edom, and seide, Suffre thou   60
 me, that Y go thoruȝ thi lond; which
 kyng nolde assente to his preyeres.
 Also Israel sente to the kyng of Moab,
18 and he dispiside to ȝyue passage; and so
 Israel dwellyde in Cades, and cumpasside   65
 bi the side the lond of Edom, and the lond
 of Moab; and he cam to the eest coost
 of the lond of Moab, and settide tentis
 biȝende Arnon, nether he wolde entre in
 to the termes of Moab; for Arnon is the   70

59 send E; messageris C, messangers DFIMX, messagers EK, messangeres
  Ha, messengers LP, massangeris O
60 said E
61 þorouȝ AcGIKLOPU, þoru B, þorou CR, þorow E, þurȝ NX, þorouþ S;
  whiche G, þe whiche I, wiche K
62 nolde: wolde not I, noolde X; assent E; hise AcBCCaDGHaKMMaNQ-
  RSUW; preieris AcBCCaGMaNOQSUW, preiers DHaKLMRX, praiers E,
  praieris I; his pr.: þe praieris of israel I
63 sent E
64 dispisid D, despised E, dispisede FKLPU; ȝeue BDHaLMaQR, ȝiue israel
  I, ȝife K; so: om. X
65 dwellid D, dwelled E, dwellede FLP, dwelde U; cumpacide CaMW,
  cumpassid D, cumpacede EFLP; 65−66 & bi þe side he cumpasside I
66 side: see Ha; the (1°): of þe C¹Ca
67 of: om. E; he: israel I; came DIR, com E; est EGQ; cost EQU
68 of þe lond: om. R; settid DU, sette EF, he settide IMa, settede LP; tentes
  FHa
69 biȝonde BDHaIKQX, bi-ȝend E, biȝondis G; neiþer CaFGHaIMQRW,
  neiþir Ma, neþir OPX; wolde: noolde Ma; entren F
70 teermes DMaRX, termys GQ; is: is in N

18 et circuivit ex latere terram Edom et terram Moab;
 venitque ad orientalem plagam terrae Moab, et
 castrametatus est trans Arnon, nec voluit intrare
 terminos Moab; Arnon quippe confinium est terrae
 Moab.

19 And so Yrael sente messagers to Seon,
   the kyng of Ammorreis, that dwellide in   70
   Esebon; and seide to hym, Leete me, that
20 Y passe bi thi loond vnto the flood. The
   which and he, dispisynge the wordis of
   Yrael, leete hym not passe bi his teermys,
   but a multitude with outen eend gedrid   75
   wente out aȝens hym into Gessa, and
21 strongli withstood. And the Lord took
   hym into the hoondis of Yrael with al
   his oost; the which smoot hym, and
   weeldide al the loond of Ammorree, the   80

69 sent *BFWo*; messangers *BH*, messageres *CWoX*, messageris *ELo*
70 kynge *BLo*; dwelte *CX*, dwellid *FHLo*, dwelled *Wo*
71 seyden *BCFHLoWoX*, seidyn *E*; lete *BFHWo*, let *CEX*, late *Lo*
72 thi: þe *Lo*; lond *CWoX*, land *E*, londe *Lo*; flode *BFHLoWo*, flod *CX*
73 whiche *BCEHLoX*; despisende *C*, despisinge *Wo*, dispisende *X*; woordus *C*,
    woordis *E*, wordes *LoWo*, wrdis *X*
74 leet *CEX*, lete *HLoWo*; passyn *E*; hise *E*; termys *BEFH*, termes *CLoWoX*
75 bot *B*, bute *F*; withoute *CX*, wiþ outyn *E*, -ouȝten *H*; ende *CEHLoWoX*,
    eende *F*; geþerd *BF*, gedered *CX*, gederid *E*, gederd *H*, gaderide *Lo*
76 went *BFHWo*; oute *B*, ouȝte *H*; aȝeyns *BFWo*, aȝen *CX*, aȝenst *E*,
    a-ȝeynes *Lo*
77 wiþstode *BFHLoWo*, wiþstod *C*; toke *BFHLoWo*, toc *CX*
78 hondus *C*, handis *E*, hondes *LoWo*, hondis *X*; alle *BLo*, all *F*
79 hoost *BFH*, ost *CWoX*, host *E*; whiche *BCEHLoWoX*; smote *BFHLoWo*,
    smot *CX*, smoit *E*
80 weldede *CX*, weldide *ELo*, weeldid *FH*, weldid *Wo*; alle *BLo*; lond *CWoX*,
    land *E*, londe *Lo*

19 Misit itaque Israel nuntios ad Seon regem Amorreorum, qui habitabat in Esebon, et dixerunt ei: Dimitte /me/, ut transeam per terram tuam usque ad
   fluvium.
20 Qui et ipse, Israel verba despiciens, non dimisit
   eum transire per terminos suos, sed infinita multi-

19 ende of the lond of Moab. And so Israel
sente messangeris to Seon, kyng of Ammorreis, that dwellide in Esebon; and
thei seiden to hym, Suffre thou, that Y
passe thorouȝ thi lond til to the ryuer.   75
20 And he dispiside the wordis of Israel, and
suffride not hym passe bi hise termes, but
with a multitude with out noumbre gaderid to gidere he ȝede out aȝens Israel,
21 and aȝenstood strongli. And the Lord   80
bitook hym with al his oost in to the
hondis of Israel; and Israel smoot hym,
and hadde in possessioun al the lond of

71 eende BHaIKMa, eend R
72 sent E; messangers DFIMX, messagers EK, messangeres Ha, messengers L,
massangerus O, messangeris P; þe kyng I
73 dwellid D, dwellede ELP, dwelde U
74 thei: þe messangers I; suffree U
75 þoru B, þorou CLR, þoruȝ CaDFHaMMaQW, þorow EP, þurȝ NX,
þorouþ S; til to: vnto EI
76 dispisid D, despised E, despisede FL, dispisede KP; wordes FHaX
77 suffrid D, suffred E, suffrede PU, sufferide S; not hym: him not I, hem
not Ma; to passe IMa; his EFGILPQSX; teermes DMaNRX, termys GLQ
78 wiþoute CaFGHaIKLMMaNPRSUWX, wit out E; noumble R; gadered
EL, gadrid GI, gadride R, gederid KO
79 to gidre DIR, to gyders E; aȝenus AcCNO; 78–79 esebon ȝede out aȝens
israel wiþ a multitude wiþoute noumbre gadrid togidre I
80 aȝeinstood B, aȝeinstod E, aȝenstode HaR, aȝenstode him I, aȝenstod U
81 bitok EF, bitooke HaI, bitoke R; hym: esebon I; ost EU
82 hondes CaF, hoondis R; 81–82 him in to þe hondis of I. wiþ al his oost
W; Israel (2°): he I; smote EHaIR, smot U
83 had E; possessione E, possession IK

tudine congregata egressus est contra eum in Iessa,
et fortiter resistebat.
21 Tradiditque eum Dominus in manus Israel cum omni
exercitu suo; qui percussit eum, et possedit omnem
terram Amorrei, habitatoris regionis illius,

22 dweller of that regioun, and al the coost[is]
of it fro Arnon vnto Jaboch, and fro the
23 wildernes vnto Jordan. The Lord than
God of Israel turnede* vpsedoun Amorre,
fiʒtynge aʒens hym to his puple Yrael.   85
And thou nowe wolt weelde the loond
24 of hym? Whether not thoo thingis, the
whiche weeldith Camos, thi god, to thee
thurʒ riʒt ben owid? Forsothe thingis
that the Lord oure God ouercomer heelde,   90
25 in oure possessioun shulen falle; but perauenture thow be betere than Baalach,
the sone of Sephor, kyng of Moab, othere
thou mayst teche, that he stroue aʒens

81 dwellere CELoX; alle BCELo, all F; costis E, coost BFHWoX, coostis Lo,
cost X
82 fro (1°): from Lo; vn too E
83 wyldernesse cet.; þann BF, þanne CELoX
84 turnynge A, torned BFHWo, tornede Lo; vpsadoun BFH, vp so doun
CELoWoX
85 fiʒtende CX; aʒeynst BFWo, aʒen CX, aʒenst EH, aʒeynes Lo; peple
BFLoWo
86 now cet.; wylt BCEFHX; nowe wolt: wilt now X; welde CWoX, weldyn
E; lond CWoX, land E, londe Lo
87 þo BFHLoWoX; þinges BLo, thingus CX; 87—88 the whiche: that C¹,
þe which FWo
88 weeldis BFWo, weldeþ CEX; to thee: to þe Wo
89 þorʒ BF, þurgh E, þoru H, þoruʒ Lo; riʒte Lo; owid: aʒt C, owede Lo;
Forsothe thingis: th. f. cet.; thingus CX, þinges Lo
90 our F; ouer commer BFWo, ouercomere CX, ouyrcomere E; heeld BCEFHX
helde Lo
91 our BF; schuln BEFWo, shul CX, schullen HLo; fallen BFHLoWoX,
fallyn E; bot B, bute F; par auenture EX
92 þu B; be: art E¹; better BFHWo, bettere E, betre Lo; þann B
93 kynge Lo; ouþer BEFHWo, or CX, oþer Lo
94 techen BFHLoWo, techyn E; stroof BFH, strof CWoX, stroif E, stroffe Lo;
aʒeynst BFWo, aʒen CX, aʒenst EH, a-ʒeynes Lo

22 et universos fines eius de Arnon usque /ad/ Iaboch,
et de solitudine usque ad Iordanem.
23 Dominus ergo Deus Israel subvertit Amorreum, pugn-
ante contra illum populo suo Israel; et tu nunc vis
possidere terram eius?
24 Nonne ea, quae possedit Chamos, deus tuus, tibi iure

22 Ammorrey, dwellere of that cuntrey, and
al the coostis therof fro Arnon til to Ja-   85
boch, and fro the wildirnesse til to Jordan.
23 Therfor the Lord God of Israel distriede
Ammorrey, fiȝtynge aȝens hym for his
puple Israel. And wolt thou now haue
24 in possessioun his lond? Whether not   90
tho thingis whiche Chamos, thi god,
hadde in possessioun, ben due to thee bi
riȝt? Forsothe tho thingis whiche oure
Lord God ouercomere gat, schulen falle
25 in to oure possessioun; no but in hap   95
thou art betere than Balach, the sone of
Sephor, kyng of Moab, ether thou maist
preue, that he stryuede aȝens Israel,

84 dweller BDLPX, þe dweller I; contre E, cuntre LPQR, cuntray S
85 alle AcBCCaDEFGHaIKLMMaNQRWX; costis FU; þere of R; from K;
   til to: vnto I
86 wildernes E, wildernesse FLNU, wildurnesse Ha; til to: to E, vnto I
87 þerfore BCaEGKMMaNQRWX, And þanne I; distried D, distroied E,
   distroiede HaKR, destriede IL, distrieden O, distroide U
88 fiȝttyng E; aȝenus CNO
89 peple FILMMaPWX; wolt thou: woltow B, wltou E, wolte þou I, wilt
   þou LP; 89—90 haue his lond in possessioun I
90 possessione E, possession K; lond: hond L; whether AI, where D, wher cet.
91 þoo IR; þinges FHa; which EL, þe whiche I, wiche K
92 had E; possession K; duwe CaFKMWX, deu E, dewe I; þe EF
93 Forsothe: soþely I, forsoþ X; tho: om. E, þoo R; þinges FHa; wyche E,
   wich K; our E; 93—94 oure Lord God: þe lord oure god IU[1]
94 ouercomer DEILPRX; gat: haþ goten I, gatt K, gate R; schullen CaGMW,
   schuln DF, shul EILP
95 possession K; no: om. CaDGHaIKMMa[2]NOQSX; happe KR
96 bettir DR, better E, bettere MaN; þanne D; the: om. Ca
97 eiþer CaEFGHaIMMaQRW, oþer U; myȝt E, maiȝt LP, maiste R;
   thou maist: maist þou I
98 preue: sey I; he: balach I; stryued DE, stryuyde GIQ,
   str'i'euede U; aȝenus AcCKN

debentur? Quae autem Dominus Deus noster victor obtinuit, in nostram cedent possessionem;
25 nisi forte melior es Balach, filio Sephor, rege Moab;
aut docere potes, quod iurgatus sit contra Israel,
et pugnaverit contra eum,

295

26 Yrael, and fauȝt aȝens hym, whanne he   95
    dwelte in Esebon, and in the litil touns
    of it, and in Aroer and hys litil touns,
    and in alle the cytees beȝonde Jordan,
    by thre hundred ȝeer. Whi so mych
    tyme no thing vpon this askynge thou   100
27 asaydist? Therfor I synne not in thee,
    but thou aȝens me dost yuel, bryngynge
    in to me bataylys not ryȝtwise; deme the
    Lord, domysman of this day, bitwexe
28 Yrael and the sones of Amon. And the   105
    kyng of the sones of Amon wold not
    assente to the wordis of Jeptee, the

95 faȝt *CX*, fauȝte *Lo*; aȝeyns *BFWo*, aȝen *CX*, aȝenst *EH*, a-ȝeynes *Lo*; whenn *BH*, whan *CFLoWoX*, whenne *E*
96 dwelt *BFHWo*, dwellede *E*; lytyll *BF*, litle *CE*, lytel *Wo*; tounus *C*, townys *E*, tounes *LoX*
97 hys: hise *E*, in his *Wo*; lytyll *BF*, litle *C*, litile *E*, lytel *Wo*; tounes *CLoX*, townys *E*
98 all *F*; the: om. *C*; cites *CX*; beȝunde *C*, beȝende *E*, byȝond *F*, by-ȝonde *LoWo*, biȝunde *X*
99 þree *F*; hundreþ *BF*, hundrid *CEH*, hundride *Lo*; ȝere *Lo*, ȝer *X*; myche *BCEFHLoX*
100 þinge *LoWo*; asking *CX*
101 asaȝedest *CX*, asaiedest *E*, assaydest *LoWo*; þerfore *BCEFHWoX*, þere fore *Lo*; þe *X*
102 bot *B*, bute *F*; aȝeynst *BFWo*, aȝen *CX*, aȝenst *EH*, a-ȝeynes *Lo*; doost *BFH*, doist *E*, doest *Lo*; euele *C*, euyle *E*, yuele *Fo*, euel *WoX*; bringende *CX*, bringyng *H*
103 batayls *B*, batailes *ELoX*, bateyls *FH*, bateyles *Wo*; riȝtwisse *Wo*
104 domesman *CELoWo*, domes aman *X*; bytwene *BFHLoWo*, betwe *C*, betwen *E*, bitwen *X*
105 sonus *CX*, sonys *EFH*
106 kynge *BLoWo*; sonus *CX*, sonys *EFH*; wolde *CEFHLoWoX*
107 assenten *BFHLoWo*, assentyn *E*; woordis *CE*, wordes *LoWo*, wrdes *X*; 107−08 the whiche: þat *C*[1]

26 quando habitavit in Esebon, et viculis eius, et in
    Aroer et villis illius, et in cunctis civitatibus
    trans Iordanem, per trecentos annos. Quare tanto
    tempore nihil super hac repetitione temptasti/s/?
27 Igitur non ego pecco in te, sed tu contra me male

26 and fauȝt aȝens hym, whanne he dwellide
in Esebon, and in townes therof, and in   100
Aroer, and in townes therof, and in alle
citees biȝende Jordan, bi thre hundrid
ȝeer. Whi in so myche time assaieden ȝe
27 no thing on this axyng aȝen? Therfor not
Y do synne aȝens thee, but thou doist yuel   105
aȝens me, and bryngist in batels not iust
to me; the Lord, iuge of this dai, deme
bitwixe the sones of Israel and bitwixe
28 the sones of Amon. And the kyng of the
sones of Amon nolde assente to the   110
wordis of Jepte, whiche he sente bi mes-

99 fauȝte BDHaILNOR; aȝenus AcCNO; whan EHaLPS; he: israel I;
dwellid D, dwelled E, dwellede LPU, dwelliden O
100 in (2°): om. M; townis EGHaLQ; þere of R; and (2°) ... therof (101):
om. S
101 townys GHaLQ; þeroff I
102 þe citees B, cites L; biȝonde BDEGHaIKLOQX; þree O; hundret E,
hundred Ha, hunderd LP
103 ȝere E, ȝer ILP; whiy E; moche CaFNUX, ınuch E, mich R; asaieden
AcDMaORSUX; ȝee U
104 not no S; on: of E; axynge DFGMaQU; þerfore BCaEGIKLMMa-
NQRWX; 104−05 not Y do: I do not EI
105 doo K; aȝenus AcCNO; þe FR; bot E; dost EFILPQ, doost MW, dust O;
yuele AcHaKN, euel EL, euyl GPQ
106 aȝenus AcCNO, aȝenis P; bringiste B, bringest EFHaL, bryngeste R,
brinkst S; bateils DX, batelis I, bateilis MaQ, batailis U; iuste KX;
106−07 yn to me not iust batelis I
107 *iust* iuge I; deeme BMaNX, deme he G
108 bi-twix EQ; sonys GLQ; bi-twix EQ
109 sonys GQ, sonus I; And: om. U
110 sonys GLPQ; nolde: wolde not I, noolde MaX; assent E, asente R; the:
þo C
111 wordes EF; which ELQ, wiche K; sent E; messangers DFM, messegers E,
messangeres Ha, þe messangers IX, messagers K, messengers L, massangerus
O, messengeris PS

agis, inducens mihi bella non iusta; iudicet Dominus
arbiter huius diei inter Israel et inter filios Amon.
28 Noluitque acquiescere rex filiorum Amon verbis Iepte,
quae per nuntios mandaverat.

29 whiche bi messagers he sente. Thanne
is doon vpon Jeptee the spyrit of the
Lord, and he enuyrounnynge Galaad and   110
Manasse, Maspha and Galaad, and thens
30 passynge (in) to the sones of Amon, he
vowide a vowe to the Lord, seiynge, If
thou takist the sones of Amon into myn
31 hoondis, who so euere first were gon out   115
fro the ȝatis of myn hous, and aȝen
cometh to me turnynge aȝen with pees
fro the sones of Amon, I shal offre hym
32 brent sacrifice to the Lord. And Jeptee
passide forth to the sones of Amon, for   120
to fiȝte aȝens hem, whom the Lord took

108   which *FWo*; messageres *CWoX*, messageris *ELo*, messangers *FH*; sent
     BFHWo, sende *Lo*; þann *BF*, þan *LoWo*
109   don *CEWoX*, done *H*; uppon *Wo*; spiryte *BFLo*
110   he: om. *HWo*; enuyrounynge *BEFWo*, enuyrounende *CX*
111   þennus *CX*, þennys *E*, þennes *Lo*
112   passende *CX*; sonys *BEFH*, sonus *C*
113   uowid *BFHWo*, vouwede *CEX*, vowede *Lo*; vow *CEFHWoX*; seiende *CX*,
     seying *Lo*; ȝif *BFHWo*, ȝife *Lo*
114   take *CX*, takest *ELo*; sonys *BFH*, sonus *CX*; my *BEH*
115   hondis *C*, handis *E*, handes *Lo*, hondes *Wo*, hondus *X*; euer *BFWo*;
     firste *H*; goon *BFHLo*; oute *B*, ouȝte *H*
116   ȝates *LoX*; my *BEFHLoWo*; houȝs *H*, house *Lo*; aȝeyn *BFHWo*, a-ȝeyne
     Lo
117   commiþ *BF*, comiþ *H*, comes *Lo*, commeþ *Wo*; turnende *CX*, tornynge
     FWo; aȝeyn *BFH*, aȝeen *CEX*, a-ȝeyne *Lo*; pese *BF*, pes *CX*
118   sonys *BFH*, sonus *CX*; schalle *Lo*; offer *B*, offryn *E*
119   brente *Lo*; sacrefice *Wo*
120   passed *BFHWo*, passede *CE*, passid *Lo*; foorþ *F*, forþe *Lo*; sonys *BEFH*,
     sonus *X*; for: om. *C*
121   fiȝt *BHWo*, fiȝten *CX*, fiȝtyn *E*; aȝeyns *BFWo*, aȝen *CX*, aȝenst *E*,
     a-ȝeynes *Lo*; þem *ELo*; whome *BF*; tooke *B*, toc *CX*, toke *FHLoWo*

29 Factus est ergo super Iepte spiritus Domini, et
circumiens Galaad et Manasse, Maspha quoque Galaad,
et inde transiens ad filios Amon,
30 votum vovit Domino, dicens: Si tradideris filios
Amon in manus meas,

29 sangeris. Therfor the spirit of the Lord
was maad on Jepte, and he cumpasside
Galaad and Manasses, Maspha and Ga-
laad; and he passide fro thennus to the   115
30 sones of Amon, and made a vow to the
Lord, and seide, If thou schalt bitake the
31 sones of Amon in to myn hondis, who
euer goith out first of the dores of myn
hows, and cometh aȝens me turnynge aȝen   120
with pees fro the sones of Amon, Y schal
offre hym brent sacrifice(s) to the Lord.
32 And Jepte ȝede to the sones of Amon, to
fiȝte aȝens hem, whiche the Lord bitook

112 þerfore BCaEGIKLMaNQRWX; spiritt K, spiriȝt L
113 made DHa, mad Ma; upon I; and: om. Ma; cumpacide CaLMW,
cumpassid D, cumpaced E, cumpacede FP
114 & Maspha Ma
115 passid D, passed E, passede FLP; from K; þennes CCaFHaIKMW, þens
DMaQRU, þennis EGLNSX, þenis P
116 sonys GLQ; he made I; vowe I, vouȝ R
117 seid E; ȝif E; bi-tak E
118 sonys GLQ, sone U; myne CaMRW, my K; hondes CaF, hoondis R
119 euere AcCaGIKMMaQRUWX; gooþ CaMW, goþe E, goþ FGHaILPQ;
doris AcBDEGHaIKMMaNQRUWX; myne ER
120 comyt E, comiþ GIPQ; aȝenus AcCNO; turning E
121 pes L; from K; sonys GLQ
122 offer E; brente RU; sacrifisis CaDMPQX, sacrifice BGIRW, sacrifices cet.
123 sonys GHaLPQ, sonus I
124 aȝenus AcCNO; him X; which E, wiche K; bitoke EIR, bitok HaU

31 quicumque primus fuerit egressus de foribus domus
meae, mihique occurrerit revertenti cum pace a
filiis Amon, eum holocaustum offeram Domino.
32 Transivitque Iepte ad filios Amon, ut pugnaret
contra eos; quos tradidit Dominus in manus eius.

33 into the hoondis of hym; and he smoot
   fro Aroer for to that thou come into
   Mennyth, twenti citees, and vnto Abel,
   that is with vynes set, with a wel greet   125
   veniaunce; and the sones of Amon ben
34 mekid of the sones of Yrael. Forsothe
   to Jeptee turnynge aȝen(s) into Maspha,
   his hous, aȝen cam(en) to hym his oonli
   goten douȝter* with tymbrys and chorys;   130
   forsothe he had* noon other free chil-

122 hondis *CX*, handis *E*, hondes *LoWo*; smote *BFHLoWo*, smot *CEX*
123 comme *BF*
124 cites *CX*
125 vynys *BFHWo*; sett *BEFHWo*, sette *Lo*; woll *BF*, wol *E*, ful *HX*, well *Wo*;
    grete *BWo*, gret *CX*, grett *EFH*, grette *Lo*
126 vengeaunce *ELo*; sonys *BFHWo*, sonus *CX*
127 meked *E*, mekede *Lo*; sonus *C*, sonys *EFHWo*; 127−8 Forsothe to Jeptee:
    to J. f. *cet.*
128 tornynge *BFHWo*, turnende *CX*; aȝeyn *BFWo*, aȝeen *CEX*, aȝen *H*,
    a-ȝeyne *Lo*
129 houȝs *H*; aȝeynst *BFWo*, aȝenst *EH*, a-ȝeyne *Lo*; coome *BFH*, come *LoWo*;
    onli *CX*, onely *E*
130 gotyn *E*, geten *Lo*, gote *X*; douȝters *BFH*, doȝter *CX*, dowȝtyr *E*, douȝtris
    AWo; tymbres *LoX*; cheris *FWo*, chores *LoX*
131 haþ *ABFHWoX*, hadde *CE*, had *Lo*; none *E*, noen *X*; ooþere *E*, oþere
    X; fre *BEFLoWo*; childer *BCX*, childre *EH*
132 which *FWo*; seene *Lo*; kutt *BFHLo*, cutte *CEX*, kitt *Wo*; hise *E*

33 Percussitque ab Aroer usque dum venias in Mennith,
   viginti civitates, et usque ad Abel, quae est vineis
   consita, plaga magna nimis; humiliatique sunt filii
   Amon a filiis Israel.
34 Revertenti autem Iepte in Maspha, domum suam, occurrit ei unigenita filia sua cum tympanis et choris;
   non enim habebat alios liberos.

33 in to hise hondis; and he smoot fro   125
Aroer til to thou comest in to Mennyth,
twenti citees, and til to Abel, which is
set aboute with vyneris, with ful greet
veniaunce; and the sones of Amon weren
34 maad low of the sones of Israel. For-   130
sothe whanne Jepte turnede aȝen in to
Maspha, his hows, his oon gendrid douȝter cam to hym with tympanys and
croudis; for he hadde not othere fre chil-

125 his EFGHaILPQSX; hondes F, hoondis R; smote ER, smote *or ouercame*
I, smot U; from K
126 til to: til to þat AcCaDFHaKLMMaNOPRSX, vn to þat E, til þat GIQ;
thou comest: he cam AcCaDFGHaKLMMaNOPQSX, he com E, he came
IR
127 cites LS; til to: to E, vnto I; which: þat I, wich K
128 sette DE, sett IKMaNU; abouȝte L, aboue N; vyners DEHaIKMQRUX,
vyneres F; wit E; grete ER, gret L
129 vengeaunce KR; sonys GLQ
130 made DEK, mad Ma; lowȝ CaMNW, lowe DGHaILMaQR, lowȝe K;
sonys GLQ, sonus I; of: om. C; Forsothe: And I, forsoþ X
131 whan EFGHaLP, turned DE, turnyde GHaQ; aȝen: aȝein B, om. L
132 oon: owne L, on SU; gendrid: bigotun I, gendride W; douȝtir
AcGHaIKMaNOPQRWX, douȝtre D, dowter E
133 com E, came IR; to: aȝens B, to meete I; tympans AcBCCaDFGHaIK-
MMaNOQRUWX
134 croudes F, croudis daunsynge I; had DE; oþer EL, oþre R; free CaKMa;
childrin EP

35 dren. The whiche seen, he kytte his
 clothis, and seith, Allas! douȝter myn,
 thou hast disseyued me, and thi self art
 desseyued; forsothe Y haue openyd my   135
 mouth to the Lord, and I shal not mowe
36 doo other thing. To whom she answerde, Fader myn, if thou hast openyd
 thi mouth to the Lord, do to me what
 euere thing thou hast bihoot, grauntid to   140
 thee veniaunce and victorye of thin ene-
37 myes. And she seide to the fader, This
 oonli ȝif to me, that I praye; leete me,
 that two monthis Y enuyroun the hillis,
 and weyle my maydenhod with my fe-   145

133 cloþes *BEHLo*; seys *Lo*; doȝter *CX*, dowȝtyr *E*
134 disceyuede *B*, deceiued *CE*, deceyuede *Lo*, disceyuyd *Wo*; silf *Wo*
135 disceyued *BFHWoX*, deceyuede *Lo*; forsoþ *B*; hafe *E*; opnyd *BF*, opened *CX*, openede *Lo*
136 mowþe *Lo*; 136−37 I shal not mowe doo other thing: o. th. d. I sh. n. m. *cet.*; mown *BCEFX*, mowen *HLoWo*
137 don *BCEX*, doon *FLo*, done *HWo*; ooþer *E*; þinge *LoWo*; whome *BFLo*, whon *H*; answerd *B*, answeride *Lo*, answered *Wo*
138 fadir *BCH*, fadre *Lo*; ȝif *BFHWo*, ȝife *Lo*; opnyd *BF*, opened *CEX*, openede *Lo*
139 mowþe *LoWo*; doo *BF*
140 euer *BCEFWo*; þinge *LoWo*; byhoten *BFHWoX*, behoten *C*, behotyn *E*, by-hette *Lo*; grauntede *Lo*
141 vengeaunce *E*; victory *BFH*; þi *E*, þine *Lo*; enmys *BF*, enemys *CEX*, enmyes *Wo*
142 seid *Wo*; fadir *BH*, fadre *Lo*
143 onli *CWoX*, oneli *E*, oonely *H*; ȝeue *BFHLo*, ȝyue *Wo*; pray *BWo*, preȝe *C*, preye *ELoX*, prey *FH*; lete *BFHWo*, let *CX*, lett *E*
144 twei *E*; moneþs *BF*, moneþis *CHX*, moneþes *E*, monþes *Lo*; enuyrounne *C*, enuyrowne *EX*; hilles *LoWoX*
145 meydenhode *BH*, maidenhed *CX*, maydenhode *FLoWo*; felawes *ELoWoX*

35 Qua visa, scidit vestimenta sua, et ait: Heu, filia
 mea, decepisti me, et ipsa decepta es; aperui enim
 os meum ad Dominum, et aliud facere non potero.
36 Cui illa respondit: Pater mi, si aperuisti os tuum
 ad Dominum, fac mihi, quodcumque pollicitus es, con-
 cessa tibi ultione atque victoria de hostibus tuis.

302

35 dren. And whanne sche was seyn, he ⁣ 135
to-rente his clothis, and seide, Allas! my
douȝtir, thou hast disseyued me, and thou
art disseyued; for Y openyde my mouth
to the Lord, and Y may do noon other
36 thing. To whom sche answeride, My fa- ⁣ 140
dir, if thou openydist thi mouth to the
Lord, do to me what euer thing thou bi-
hiȝtist, while veniaunce and victorie of
37 thin enemyes is grauntid to thee. And
sche seide to the fadir, ȝyue thou to me ⁣ 145
oneli this thing, which Y biseche; suffre
thou me that in two monethis Y cumpasse
hillis, and biweile my maidynhed with my

135 whan EFGHaLP, wh. while Ma; sche: he L; seyen BGQS, seen Ma,
seyne R; wh. he sawȝe hir I
136 to-rent E; hise AcBCCaDGHaKMMaNRW; clooþis G; saide E; Allas
ABEU, alas cet.
137 douȝter CCaFIKLMSU, dowter E; haste R; desceyued E, deceyuede Ha,
deceiued LPX, disceiuid Q
138 deceyued EHaLP, disceiuyd GQ; for: certis I; openede
BCaFKLMMaPUX, opened DE, opnede I; mouþe E, mouȝ S
139 to the Lord: to þe lord vowynge a vowȝ I; doon K; none E, non FL;
oþere Ac, oþir PR; 139−40 noon oþer þing do I
140 sche: he L; answerde CaEFGMQUW, answerid D, answerede L; My: om.
B; fader CaEFLRU
141 ȝif E; openedist AcCCaDFKMMaNWX, openyst B, openedest ELP,
opnedist I, openediste R; mouþe E; to: so to I
142 wat E; euere GKMaQRWX; bihiȝtest CFHa, bihiȝtiste R
143 whil KR; vengeaunce K; victori E
144 þine CaKMMaRWX; enmyes EI; grantid E; þe EFR
145 saide E; the: hir I; fader FILU, fadre X; ȝeue BDHaMaQR, ȝif E, ȝife K
146 oonli BCaDFGHaIKLMMaNPRWX, onli EQSU; which: þat I, wich K,
whiche P; biseche þe E, biseeche G, bisech N
147 twei AcKMNOX, tweie CaMaW; moneþes CEPRU, monþis GHaQ;
cumpace CaEFMPW, cumpacid L; 147−8 þat I cumpasse hillis in two
moneþis I
148 hullis E, hilles FR; biwaylen E, biweilen LP; myn Ac; maidenhed
AcCLNOPSU, maydenheed BKMaX, maidenhede CaEFMW, maydenhode
D, maydenhod GHaQ, maidenhood I, maydenhoode R; my (2°): om. D

37 Dixitque ad patrem: Hoc solum mihi praesta, quod de-
precor; dimitte me, ut duobus mensibus circumeam
montes, et plangam virginitatem meam cum sodalibus
meis.

38 lawis. To whom he answerde, Go. And
he lafte hir two monthis. And whanne
she was goon with felawis and hir com-
peers, she wepte hyr maydenhod in the

39 hillis. And fulfillid two monthis, she is   150
turned aȝen to hir fader, and he dyde to
hire, as he auowide; the which knewe
not man. Therfor maner spronge in

146 whome *BFH*; answeride *Lo*; goo *BFH*
147 left *BFHWo*, lefte *CELoX*; hyre *BEFLo*; twey *E*; moneþis *BCHX*, moneþes
E, monþes *Lo*; whenn *BH*, whan *CEFLoWoX*
148 go *CX*, gon *EWo*; felawes *ELoWoX*; hire *BEFLo*; compers *BFHWo*,
cumperes *C*, comperis *ELo*, cumperis *X*
149 wept *BFHLo*; hyre *BEFLo*; meydenhode *BH*, maidenhed *CEX*, maydenhode
FLoWo
150 hilles *ELoWoX*; fulfild *CEX*, fulfilde *Lo*; twei *EWo*; moneþs *B*, moneþis
CEHX, monþes *Lo*
151 turnede *BLo*, torned *FWo*; aȝeyn *BFWo*, aȝeen *CX*, a-ȝeyne *Lo*; hyre
BEFLo; fadir *BE*, fadere *Lo*; dydde *B*
152 hir *CWoX*; auowid *BFH*; vouwide *C*, a-vowed *LoWo*, vouwede *X*; whiche
BCEHLoWoX; knew *C*, knewȝ *E*, kneȝ *X*
153 þerfore *BCEFHWoX*, þere fore *Lo*; manere *Lo*:, sprong *CEX*

38 Cui ille respondit: Vade. Et dimisit eam duobus
mensibus. Cumque abiisset cum sociis ac sodalibus
suis, flebat virginitatem suam in montibus.

39 Expletisque duobus mensibus, reversa est ad patrem
suum, et fecit ei sicut voverat; quae ignorabat virum. Exinde mos increbruit in Israel, et consuetudo
servata est,

38 felowis. To whom he answeride, Go thou.
And he suffride hir in two monethis. And   150
whanne sche hadde go with hir felowis
and pleiferis, sche biwepte hir maydyn-
39 hed in the hillis. And whanne twey
monethis weren fillid, sche turnede aȝen
to hir fadir, and he dide to hir as he   155
avowide; and sche knew not fleischli a
man. Fro thennus a custom cam in (to)

149 felawis CaMMaW, felowes EP, felawes F, felows X; wham E; he: hir
     fadir I; answerde CaFGMQUW, answerd D, answered E, seide I, answerede
     LP
150 suffrid D, suffred E, suffrede LPU; her CaMUW, here F, hire K; in: bi I;
     twei AcKNX, tweie CaMMaOW, to L; moneþes E, monþis GHaQ
151 whan EGHaLP; had EI; goon F, gon forþ I; her BCaELMPUW, here F,
     hire K; felawis CaMW, felows EX, felawes F, felowes P
152 pleieferis Ac, plaiferis E, pleiferes FKR, playeferis Ha, hir pleiferis I,
     pleyueris U, pleyfeeris X; her CaEFMPW, hire K; maidenhed
     AcCEFLNOSU, maydenheed BKMa, maidenhede CaMPW, maidenhode
     DG, maydenhod HaQ, maidenhood IRX
153 the: om. CaDGHaIMNOQSX²; hullis E, hilles F; when E, whan P; two
     BDGHaILQ, tweie CaMa
154 moneþs E, monþis GHaLQ, moneþes P; wheren E, were Q; filled EKL,
     fulfillid I; sche: he L; turned DE, turnyde GHaQ; aȝein B, a-ȝene E
155 her BCaLMW, here F; fader EFLU; did E; her BCaMW, here F, hire KL
156 avowed CE, auowid D, avouwede F, auouwede LPU, auouwide CX,
     avouȝide R; knewe CDGHaR, knewȝ IKM, kneew Ma; fleisli C, fleschly
     CaEFLMPRUW, fleihli Ha, fleiȝssli K, fleisly S; a: om. BGHaKNQX;
     knewȝ no man fleishly I
157 from K; thennus: þennes CaFHaKMW, þens DEMaQR, om. G, þat tyme
     I, þenis LP, þenns U, þennis X; a: þe AcCaDEFGHaKLMMaNOPQRSUX;
     custum BCaDGHaMMaQSWX; came DR, com E, caam N

40 Yrael, and vsage is kept, that after the
sercle of o ʒeer the douʒtris of Yrael
comen to gidre in oon, and weylen the
douʒter of Jeptee Galadyte foure dayes.

12. 1 Loo! forsothe in Effraym is sprongun
a debate; forsothe the goers aʒen the
north seiden to Jeptee, Whi goynge to
the fiʒt aʒens the sones of Amon thou
woldist not clepe vs, that we wenten
with thee? Therfor we shulen brenne

5

154 kepte *Lo*; aftyr *EX*
155 circle *Lo*; oo *BFHWo*, a *CE*; ʒere *BLoWo*, ʒer *CX*, ʒeere *H*; douʒters
BH, doʒtris *CX*, douʒtres *Lo*
156 coomen *F*; to gyder *BFHWo*, togidere *CEX*; one *H*, oone *Lo*, oen *X*;
weilyn *E*, waylen *Lo*
157 doʒter *CX*, dowʒtyr *E*; days *BH*, daʒes *CX*

12. 1 Lo *cet.*; sprongen *BFHLoWo*, sprunge *C*, sprongyn *E*, sprungen *X*
2 debat *C*; gooers *BF*, goeris *CELo*, goeres *X:*, aʒeyns *BFWo*, aʒenst *E*,
aʒens *H*, a-ʒeyne *Lo*
3 northe *HLo*; seydyn *E*; gooynge *BF*, goende *CX*
4 fiʒte *Lo*; aʒeynst *BFWo*, aʒen *CX*, aʒenst *EH*, a-ʒeynes *Lo*; sonys
BEFH, sonus *CX*; 4—5 thou woldist not clepe vs: cl. us þ. w. n.
BCEFHLo
5 woldest *LoWo*; clepen *BCEFHWoX*, kalle *Lo*; wee *CEX*; wente *CX*,
wentyn *E*
6 þe *Wo*; þerfore *BCEFHWoX*, þere fore *Lo*; wee *CEX*; schuln *BEFWo*,
shul *CX*, schullen *Wo*, schulle *Lo*; brennen *BFHLoWo*, brennyn *E*

40 ut post anni circulum conveniant in unum filiae Israel, et plangant filiam Iepte Galaaditae diebus
quattuor.

12. 1 Ecce autem in Effraim orta est seditio, nam transeuntes contra aquilonem dixerunt ad Iepte: Quare

40 Israel, and the custom is kept, that aftir
the ende of the ȝeer the douȝtris of Israel come togidere, and biweile the douȝtir of Jepte of Galaad foure daies.

12. 1 Lo! forsothe discencioun roos in Effraym; for whi thei, that passiden aȝens
the north, (and) seiden to Jepte, Whi ȝedist thou
to batel aȝens the sones of Amon, and
noldist clepe vs, that we schulden go
with thee? Therfor we schulen brenne

158 the: þat I; custum BCaDGHaMMaQWX; kepte ER; after CEFLMaU
159 eende BHaKMaS; ȝere E; ȝeris ende I; the (3°): om. I, of þe DO; dowtris
E, douȝtres F, douȝters U
160 comyn E, comen ILMaPRS; to gidre DIR, to gyders E; biweilide Ac,
biwaile E; douȝter BCCaEFKMNQRSU, douter L; 160–61 & bi foure
daies þei biweilen iepteus douȝter of galaad I

12. 1 Lo: om. AcMaR; forsothe: And I, forsoþ X; Lo! forsothe: Forsoþe 'lo'
Ac, And lo I; discencion EK; a-roos E
2 whi: A²I, om. cet.; that: om. AcBCEFLPRUW; passeden
CaEFKLMPRUW; aȝenus AcCNO, toward I
3 norþe ER; & seiden A¹AcBCFLPRUW, & seide E; ȝedist thou: ȝedestow
E, ȝedest þou FHaL, ȝedeste þou R
4 batels CaFHaMOR, bateil DX, bateles E, bateilis GQ, batele K, batails
L, batelis P, batailis U; aȝenus AcCNO; sonys GLQ
5 noldest EFL, nolde Ha, woldist not I, noldiste R, nooldist X; scholden
CaMW
6 wit E; þe EF; þerfore BCaEFGIKLMMaNQRWX; schullen CaEMW,
schuln DF, schul ILP; bren E

vadens ad pugnam contra filios Amon vocare nos
noluisti, ut pergeremus tecum? Igitur incendemus
domum tuam.

2 thin hows. To whom he answerde, An
hydows debate was to me and my puple
aȝen the sones of Amon, and ȝow Y
clepyde, for ȝe shulden ȝyue help to me,   10
3 and ȝe wolden not doon. The which
biholdynge Y putte in myn hondis my
lijf; and Y passide to the sones of Amon,
and the Lord took hem into myn hoondis;
what haue Y disserued, that aȝens me ȝe   15

7 þi *BEFHLoWo*; houȝs *H*, house *Lo*; whome *BF*; answeride *Lo*, answerid *Wo*
8 hidouse *E*, hydouȝs *H*; peple *BFHLoX*
9 aȝeyn *BFWo*; sonys *BEFH*, sonus *CX*
10 clepid *BFH*, clepede *CEX*, callid *Lo*, cleped *Wo*; ȝee *CELoX*; schuldyn *E*,
   schulde *Wo*; ȝeue *BFHLo*, ȝefyn *E*; helpe *BCEHLo*
11 ȝee *CELoX*; wold *BF*, woldyn *E*, wolde *HLoWo*; do *C*, don *EFWoX*,
   doone *H*; whiche *BCEHLoX*
12 beholdende *C*, beholdynge *E*, biholdende *X*; putt *BFHWo*; hoondis *BFH*,
   handis *E*, hondes *LoWo*
13 lyf *BCE²FHWoX*, sowle *E¹*, life *Lo*; passed *BFWo*, passede *CEHLoX*;
   sonys *BEFH*, sonus *CX*
14 toke *BFHLoWo*, toc *CX*; þem *CELoX*; my *E*, myne *Lo*; hondus *C*, handes
   E, hondes *LoWo*, hondis *X*
15 hafe *E*; deserued *BCFHX*, deseruyd *EWo*, deseruede *Lo*; aȝeynst *BF*,
   aȝen *CX*, aȝenst *EHWo*, a-ȝeyns *Lo*; ȝee *CELoX*

2 Quibus ille respondit: Disceptatio erat mihi et
populo meo contra filios Amon vehemens; vosque voca-
vi, ut praeberetis mihi auxilium, et facere noluistis.
3 Quod cernens posui in manibus meis animam meam,
transivique ad filios Amon, et tradidit eos Dominus
in manus meas. Quid commerui, ut adversum me consurgatis in proelium?

2 thin hows. To whiche he answeride,
  Greet strijf was to me and to my puple
  aȝens the sones of Amon, and Y clepide
  ȝou, that ȝe schulden ȝyue help to me,   10
3 and ȝe nolden do. Which thing Y siȝ,
  and puttide my lijf in myn hondis; and
  Y passide to the sones of Amon, and the
  Lord bitook hem in to myn hondis; what
  haue Y disseruyd, that ȝe ryse togidere   15

7   þine CaE; which EF, whom I, wiche K; answerde CaFGMQUW, answerd
    D, answered E, answerede L
8   grete ER, gret FI; strif EFHaLNPU, strijf I; peple CaFILMMaNPWX
9   aȝenus AcCNO; sonys GLQ; clepid DE; 8−9 to me & to my peple was
    gret strijf I
10 ȝee U; scholden CaFMW, shuld E, shulde L; ȝeue BDGHaMaQRU,
    ȝif E, ȝife K; helpe GHaLPQR; schulden haue holpen me I
11 nolden: wolden not I, noolden MaX; do so I; whiche G, wich K; seiȝ
    CaFMW, siȝe R; And I seynge þat I
12 and: om. I; puttid DEF, puttede U; lif EFGHaLPQU; myne CaMMaRW,
    my K; hondes Ca, hoondis R
13 passid D, passed E, passide forþ I, passede LP; sonys GLQ; 13−14 the
    Lord: god I
14 bitooke C, bitoke ER; myne CaMRW, my K; hondes Ca, hoondis R
15 disseruyde Ac, disserued BCCaDFIKMMaNOSUWX, deserued ELPR,
    deseruyd GQ, deseruede Ha; ȝee U; rijse I; to gedere C, to gidre DI

4 rysen into batayl? And so clepid to him
alle the men of Galaad, he fauȝt aȝens
Effraym; and the men of Galaad smyten
Effraym; for he seide, Fugitiue is Galaad
fro Effraym, and dwellith in mydil of   20
5 Effraym and Manasse. And Galadites
men occupiden the forthis of Jordan, bi
whiche Effraym was for to turne aȝen.
And whanne a man of the noumbre of
Effraym fleynge was comyn to tho*   25
fordis, and hadde seyde, Y preye, that
ȝe leten me passe, Galaaditis seiden to
hym, Whether art thou an Effrate? The

16 rijsen *CE*; in: om. *C*; bateyl *BFH*, bataile *CELoWoX*; clepid: callid *Lo*
17 all *FH*; the: om. *H*; faȝt *CX*, fauȝte *Lo*; aȝeyn *BFHWo*, aȝen *CX*, aȝenst
    E, a-ȝeyne *Lo*
18 smytyn *E*
19 fugitif *CEX*; 19—20 for … Effraym: om. *Wo*
20 and … Effraym (21): om. *F*; dwelleþ *EX*, dwellis *Lo¹*; mydyll *B*, þe myddel
    CE, myddil *H*, þe mydel *Lo*, þe medyl *Wo*, myddel *X*
22 occupyeden *BFHLoWo*, ocupieden *CX*, occupiedyn *E*; forþes *BEFX*,
    fordis *H*, fordes *Wo*
23 þe whiche *ELo²*, which *FWo*; for: om. *CX*; tornen *BFHWo*, turnen *E²Lo*;
    aȝeyn *BFWo*, aȝeen *CEX*, a-ȝeyne *Lo*
24 whenn *BH*, whan *CLoWoX*, whenne *E*, whann *F*; of (2°): off *E*
25 fleeȝinge *BFH*, fleende *CX*, fleȝinge *Wo*; commen *BF*, comen *CHLoWoX*;
    þoo *CE*, þe *AFLoWoX*
26 forþis *BCFLoX*, forþes *E*, fordes *Wo*; had *BFHLoWo*; seid *CE²X*; pray
    BWo, preȝe *CX*, prey *FH*, praye *Lo*
27 ȝee *CELoX*; lete *CX*, letyn *E*, late *Lo*, letten *Wo*; passyn *E*; seidyn *E*
28 ert *BFHWo*

4 Vocatis itaque ad se cunctis viris Galaad, pugnabat
  contra Effraim; percusseruntque viri Galaad Effraim,
  quia dixerat: Fugitivus est Galaad de Effraim, et
  habitat in medio Effraim et Manasse.
5 Occupaveruntque viri Galaaditae vada Iordanis, per

4 aȝens me in to batel? Therfor whanne
alle the men of Galaad weren clepid to
hym, he fauȝt aȝens Effraym; and the
men of Galaad smytiden Effraym; for he
seide, Galaad is fugitif *ether exilid* fro   20
Effraym, and dwellith in the myddis of
5 Effraym and of Manasses. And the men
of Galaad ocupieden the forthis of Jordan, bi whiche Effraym schulden turne
aȝen. And whanne a man fleynge of the   25
noumbre of Effraym hadde come to tho
forthis, and hadde seid, Y biseche, that
thou suffre me passe, men of Galaad
seiden to hym, Whether thou art a man
of Effraym? And whanne he seide, Y   30

16 aȝenus AcCNO; bateyl GKX, bataile U; þerfore BCaEGIKLMaPQRWX;
   whan EGLP
17 cleped E; 17—18 to hym: togidere Ma
18 hym: iepte I; fauȝte BCDGHaILNOR; aȝenus AcCNO; the: om. I
19 smyteden CaOUW, smetyn ELP, smyten FM, smoten I
20 said E; fugitif: om. I, fugitijf KMaRX; *ether*: eiþer CaFGHaMQRW, or
   ELP, om. I, eiþir Ma, eþir NO, oþer U; exiled EKL, excilid Ma; gloss om.
   X; from K
21 dwellid D, dwelliȝ E, dwelleþ FHaLR, ȝit he dwelleþ I; myddes F, myddil I
23 ocupiede C, occupieden EHaLMaS; foorþis DP, forþes EF, foordis IMa,
   fordis K
24 which DEL, þe whiche I, wiche K; schulden AS, scholde CaMW, shulde
   cet.; turnen G
25 aȝeyn B; whan EGHaLP; fleyng E
26 cummen E, comen I; to: in to Ac; tho: þe AcDEFGHaIKMMaNQRWX,
   om. L
27 foorþis DLMaP, forþes EF, fordis IK; hadde: om. DGHaIQ, had ES;
   seide DHaIR, saide E; biseeche G, biseche ȝou I
28 thou: ȝe DGHaIKMNOQSX; suffur E; þe men I
29 saiden E; where D, wher cet.
30 whanne: whan EFGHaLP, om. W; hadde seid C, said E

quae Effraim reversurus erat. Cumque venisset ad ea
de Effraim numero fugiens atque dixisset: Obsecro,
ut me transire permitta/ti/s; dicebant ei Galaaditae: Numquid Effrateus es? quo dicente: Non sum,

6 which seiynge, Y am not, thei askiden
hym, Seye thanne Sebolech*, that is to   30
mene, an eere. The which answerde,
Thebolech*, bi the same lettre an eere not
my3ti to bryngen out. And anoon takyn
thei kyttiden his throot in that goynge
ouer Jordan; and there fellen in that   35
tyme of Effraym two and fourti thow-
7 sandis. And so Jeptee demyde Galaadites of Yrael sexe 3eer; and he is deed,
8 and biryed in his citee of Galaad. After
this demyde Yrael Abethsan of Beth-   40

29   whiche *BCEHLoX*; seiende *CX*; askeden *CLoX*, askedyn *E*
30   sey *BCEFHWoX*; þann *BF*, þan *Wo*; Sobolech *A*
31   meenen *BFHWo*, meenyn *E*, menen *LoX*; ere *BFHWo*, er *CEX*; whiche
     BCEHLoX; answerede *Lo*, answerid *Wo*
32   thebolech *CELo*, shebolech *cet.*; letter *Wo*; ere *BFHLoWo*, er *CEX*
33   bryngyn *E*; oute *BLo*, ou3te *H*; anoen *X*; taken *BCFHLoWo*, take *X*
34   þe[i] *X*; kuttiden *BFH*, cutten *C*, kuttyn *E*, cutteden *LoX*; þrote *cet.*;
     gooynge *BF*, going *CX*
35   Jordan: of J. *E*¹; þer *BCEFHWoX*; fillen *BFWo*, fellyn *E*
36   þousandes *BELo*, thousend *CX*
37   demyd *BFHWo*, demede *CELoX*
38   sex *BLo*, sixe *CEHWoX*; 3eere *B*, 3er *CX*, 3ere *Lo*; dead *BCEX*, dede
     LoWo
39   biriede *Lo*; cyte *BCLoWoX*; aftir *Lo*
40   demyd *BFHWo*, demede *CELoX*

6 interrogabant eum: Dic ergo sebolech, quod interpretatur spica. Qui respondebat: thebolech, eadem
littera spicam exprimere non valens. Statimque ap-
prehensum iugulabant in ipso Iordanis transitu. Et
ceciderunt in illo tempore de Effraim quadraginta
duo millia.
7 Iudicavit itaque Iepte Galaadites Israel sex annis;
et mortuus est, ac sepultus in civitate sua Galaad.
8 Post hunc iudicavit Israel Abethsan de Bethleem;

6 am not, thei axiden hym, Seie thou therfor Sebolech, which is interpretid, an
eer of corn. Which answeride, Thebolech, and my3te not brynge forth an eer
of corn bi the same lettre. And anoon 35
thei strangeliden hym takun in thilke
passyng of Jordan; and two and fourti
thousynde of Effraym felden doun in that
7 tyme. And so Jepte, a man of Galaad,
demyde Israel sixe 3eer; and he was 40
deed, and biried in his citee Galaad.
8 Abethsan of Bethleem, that hadde thretti

31 þai E; axeden CaEFLMPW; sei EIU; þerfore BCaEFGIKMaNQRWX
32 which AAcBFG, wich CaK, þat I, whiche cet.; interpretid: to sey I;
32—33 a corn eer I
33 ere EW, eere HaKMaOQX; corne ER; þe whiche I, wiche K, whiche O;
answerde CaFGMPQUW, answerd DE, answeride & seide I, answerede L
34 mi3t E, he my3te I; bring E; foorþ D, forþe E; ere E, eere HaKQX
35 corne R; lettir D, letter EHa; anon EPQ
36 þei token & strangliden him I; strangliden AcBCDGHaLMaRUX,
strangleden CaMPW, strangled E, strangeleden F; taken BCaEFHaKM-
MaOQRUW, takin LP; þilk BHa
37 passinge CaDMaQRU; twei E; fourti & two W
38 þousynd CaMW, þousand DEHaMaNQRX, þousend FG, þousynde men
I, þousande K, þousende LP; fellen CaFILMW, filden D, fellin EP
39 a man: om. GHaIMQ
40 deemede BMaX, demede CaFKLMP, demyd D, demed E; sex E, six I;
3ere E, 3er LP
41 dede E, dead Q; 40—41 was deed: diede I; deed and: om. D; biried:
was b. I, beried U; his owen E; cite CaFHaLMPQW
42 had E; þritti AcCaEIMMaNWX

313

9 leem, that hadde thretti sones, and so
feele douȝtris, the whiche sendynge out
to housbondis he ȝaf, and of the same
noumbre to his sones he took wyues,
bryngynge yn to his hows; the which 45
10 seuen ȝeer demyde Yrael, deed, and by-
11 ryed in Bethlem. To whom cam aftir
Degelon Zabulonyt, and demyde Yrael
12 ten ȝeer, and is deed, and byried in Zabu-
13 lon. After hym demyde Yrael Abdom, 50
14 the sone of Elel, Pharatonyt*; the which
hadde fourty sones, and thretti of hem
sones sones, stiynge vp vpon seuenti
coltis of assis, and he demyde Yrael eiȝt

41 had BWo; þritty BFHLoWo; sonys BEFH, sonus CX
42 fele cet.; douȝters BH, doȝtris CX, doȝtres E, douȝtres Lo; which FWo; sendende CX; ouȝte H, oute Lo
43 husbondis BEX, husbondus C, housebondis H, housebondes Lo, husbondes Wo; ȝaue BFHWo, ȝafe Lo
44 sonus CX, sonys EFH; toke BFHLoWo, toc CX; wyfis BH, wifes E
45 bringende CX; house BLo, houȝse H; whiche BCEHLoX
46 seuene CLo; ȝer CX, ȝere LoWo; demyd BFHWo, demede CELoX; dead BCEX, ded H, dede LoWo; buried Wo
47 whome BF; coome BF, come LoWo; after BCFHWo
48 demyd BFHWo, demede CLoX, demed E
49 tenn B; ȝer CX, ȝere LoWo; is: he is X; dead BCEX, ded H, dede LoWo; byriede Lo
50 Aftyr E; demyd BFHWo, demede CELoX
51 Pharatonyk A; whiche BCEHLoWo
52 had BFLoWo; sonys BEFH, sonus CX; þritty BFHLoWo; þem CLo
53 sones sones: sonus sonys C, sonys sonys EFWo, sonys sones H, sonus sonus X; steyinge BF, steȝende CX, steȝynge E, styȝinge H, steiȝinge LoWo; apon BFH, on CEX, uppon Wo
54 cooltis Lo, coltes X; asses ELoX; demyd BFHWo, demede CELoX; eiȝte CLoX, eghte E

9 qui habuit triginta filios, et totidem filias, quas
emittens foras maritis dedit, et eiusdem numeri
filiis suis accepit uxores, introducens in domum
suam; qui septem annis iudicavit Israel;
10 mortuusque est, ac sepultus in Bethleem.
11 Cui successit Ahialon Zabulonites, et iudicavit Israel decem annis;

314

9 sones, and so many dou3tris, demyde Israel
aftir Jepte; whiche dou3tris he sente out,
and 3af to hosebondis, and he took wyues   45
to hise sones of the same noumbre, and
brou3te in to hys hows; which demyde
10 Israel seuene 3eer; and he was deed, and
11 biried in Bethleem. Whos successour was
Hailon of Zabulon; and he demyde Israel   50
12 ten 3eer; and he was deed, and biried in
13 Zabulon. Aftir hym Abdon, the sone of
14 Ellel, of Pharaton, demyde Israel; which
Abdon hadde fourti sones, and of hem
thretti sones, stiynge on seuenti coltis of   55
femal assis, *that is, mulis*, and he

43 sonis GLQ; manye BGHaKMaQR; dowters E, dou3tres F, dou3ters U;
   demede BCaKLMPR, demyd D, demed E, deemyde G, deemede MaX
44 after BEFU; which EX, þe whiche I, wiche K; dowtris E, dou3tres F,
   dou3ters U; sent EF; oute R
45 3aue hem I, 3aue R; hosebondes CaF, housbondis EGI, hosbondis LP,
   husbondis MaQR; toke ER; wifes K, wyuis Q
46 his EFGILPQX; sonys GHaLQ, sonus IMa
47 brou3t D, brouth E, he brou3te *hem* I; whiche Ac, And abechsan I,
   wiche K; deemede BMaX, demede CaFKLMPRU, demed DE, dymede O
48 seuen CaEIMW; 3ere E, 3er P;.dead Q; was deed: diede I
49 was biried I, biriid P, biriede R; whois K; successor E, successur U
50 deemede BMaX, demede CaFKLMPR, demyd D, demed E, demymede O
51 3er EPS, 3ere G; dede E, ded L, dead Q; beried OU
52 after EIU; the: om. N
53 deemede BMaX, demede CaFKLMPR, demyd D, demed E; whiche GLP,
   þe whiche I, wiche K
54 had E; sonis GLQ
55 þritti AcCaGMNQWX, þirti E, weren þritti I; sonys GL; stying E, steyinge
   F, sti3inge MaN, sti3yng R; upon I; coltes F
56 femel D, sche I, female RX; asses F; mules EFLP; gloss om.
   AcCaGHaIKMMaNOQSX; he: abdon I

12 mortuusque est, ac sepultus in Zabulon.
13 Post eum iudicavit Israel Abdon, filius Ellel
Pharatonites;
14 qui habuit quadraginta filios, et triginta ex eis
nepotes, ascendentes super septuaginta pullos asinarum, et iudicavit Israel octo annis;

15 ʒeer; and he is deed, and biried in Pharaton, the loond of Effraym, in the hil of
Amalech.

13. 1 And eft the sones of Yrael diden yuel
in the siʒt of the Lord, the which took
hem in to the hoondis of the Philisteyns
2 fourti ʒeer. And there was a maner man
of Saraa, and of the lynage of Dan,
Manue bi name, hauynge a wijf bareyn.
3 To whom aperyde the aungel of the
Lord, and seide to hyre, Bareyn thou art,
and with out free children; but thou shalt

5

55 ʒer *CX*, ʒere *Lo*, ʒeere *Wo*; dead *BCEX*, ded *H*, dede *LoWo*; beried *E*,
buryed *Wo*
56 lond *CWoX*, land *E*, londe *Lo*; hill *BFH*, hylle *LoWo*

13. 1 efte *Lo*; sonys *BEFH*, sonus *CX*; euel *CX*, euyl *E*, yuele *Lo*
2 siʒte *CELoX*; whiche *BCEHLoX*; toke *BFHLoWo*, toc *CX*
3 þem *Lo*; hondus *CX*, handys *E*, hondes *LoWo*; the (2°): om. *LoX*
4 ʒer *CX*, ʒere *LoWo*; þer *BCEFHWoX*
5 and: om. *X*
6 hauende *CX*, hafynge *E*; wyfe *BLo*, wif *CEFHWoX*; bareyne *ELo*
7 whome *BF*; apeerd *B*, aperede *CEHX*, apeerid *F*, apperid *Lo*, aperid *Wo*;
aungil *CX*, angel *Wo*
8 lorde *Lo*; seyd *B*; hir *CHWoX*, here *E*; bareyne *H*, barayne *Lo*; ert *BF*
9 wiþ oute *BCEFX*, wiþ ouʒte *H*; fre *CELoWoX*; childer *CX*, childre *E*;
bot *B*, bute *F*

15 mortuusque est, ac sepultus in Pharaton, terra
Effraim, in monte Amalech.

13. 1 Rursumque filii Israel fecerunt malum in conspectu
Domini, qui tradidit eos in manus Philistinorum
quadraginta annis.

15 demyde Israel eiȝte ȝeer; and he was
deed, and biried in Pharaton, in the
loond of Effraym, in the hil of Amalech.

13. 1 And eft the sones of Israel diden yuel
in the siȝt of the Lord, which bitook
hem in to the hondis of Filisteis fourti
2 ȝeer. Forsothe a man was of Saraa, and   5
of the kynrede of Dan, Manue bi name,
3 and he hadde a bareyn wijf. To which
wijf an aungel of the Lord apperide,
and seide to hir, Thou art bareyn, and
with out fre children; but thou schalt   10

---

57 deemede BMaX, demede CaFKLMPR, demyd D, demed E; ȝer EP
58 dead Q; was deed: diede I; was biried I, beried U
59 lond cet.; hille D, hul E

13. 2 eft: efte BLR, om. F; sonys GLQ; dedin ELP; euel EL, euyle G, yuele N,
    euil PQ
3 siȝte CaDGMaU; s. of the L.: lordis siȝt I; whiche G, & he I, wiche K;
    bitoke EHaIR, bitok F
4 in to: in GIQ; hondes CaE, hond FN, hoondis R
5 ȝere E, ȝer P; Forsothe: And I, forsoþ NX; and: om. CDW
6 kynred E, kinreede S; M. bi name: þat hiȝte manue I
7 had E, hade O; barayn E, baren Ha, bareyne KLPRW, barayne U; wif
    EFGHaLPQU; whiche GX, wiche K; 7—8 wh. w.: hir I
8 wyf EFGHaLPQU; an: om. E, þe I; angel CL, aungil MaQU; apperid D,
    appered E, apperede FLPU, appeeride I
9 to hir: om. B; her CaMW, here E, hire K; bareine LRU
10 wiþoute CaFGHaIKLMMaNPRWX, wiþouten U; free CaKMa; childrin P;
    bot E

---

2 Erat autem quidam vir de Saraa, et de stirpe Dan,
nomine Manue, habens uxorem sterilem.
3 Cui apparuit angelus Domini, et dixit ad eam:
Sterilis es, et absque liberis; sed concipies et
paries filium.

4 conseyue, and bere a sone. Be war thanne,   10
  lest thou drynke wyn and sither, ne eny
5 thing vnclene thou eete; for thou shalt
  conseyue, and bere a sone, whos heed
  shal no rasure towche; forsothe he shal
  be a Nazare of God from his childhod, and   15
  fro the wombe of the moder; and he shal
  bygynne to delyuer Yrael fro the hoond

10 conceyuyn *E*, conceyuen *X*; bern *CEX*; þann *BF*, þan *LoWo*
11 drynk *B*; wyne *BFHLoWo*; sider *Wo*; any *CE*
12 þinge *BFLoWo*; þu *B*; ete *cet.*
13 conceyuyn *E*; bern *CEX*; whose *BFWo*; heued *BFHWo*, hed *CEX*, hede *Lo*
14 rasoure *B*, rasour *CEX*, rasur *H*; touchyn *E*; forsothe he shal be: he sh.
    be f. *cet.*
15 ben *CE*; fro *cet.*; childehode *BFLoWo*, childhed *CX*, childhode *H*
16 modir *BEH*, modre *Lo*
17 begynne *C*, begynnen *E*; deliuere *CLo*, delyueryn *E*, diliuere *X*; hand *CE*,
    honde *Lo*, hond *WoX*

4 Cave ergo, ne bibas vinum ac siceram, nec immundum
  quidquam comedas;
5 quia concipies, et paries filium, cuius non tanget
  caput novacula; erit enim nazareus Dei ab infantia
  sua, et ex matris utero, et ipse incipiet liberare
  Israel de manu Philistinorum.

4 conseyue, and schalt bere a sone. Therfor be thou war, lest thou drynke wyn,
and sydur, nethir ete thou ony vnclene
5 thing; for thou schalt conceyue and schalt
bere a sone, whos heed a rasour schal not 15
towche; for he schal be a Nazarei of
God fro his ȝong age, and fro the modris
wombe; and he schal bigynne to dely-

11 schalt: om. CaGHaIK¹M¹MaNOQSX; beire R; þerfore CaEGIKLMa-
NQRWX
12 ware D; lest thou: leste þou BK, lestou E, leest þou R; drink E; wijn
BDKMaX, wyne ER
13 and: eiþer G; sidir CaDEGKLMPQRX, siþer FU, syþir IMa; neþer
AcCDEKLNPX, neiþer BCaFGHaIMQUW, neiþir MaR; eete GR; eni
EL, ani P; vncleene AcBG
14 schalt (2°): om. EIMaX
15 beere GQ, beire R; rasur E
16 a Nazarei: anaȝarei 'þat is holi' K²P
17 God: þe lord P; from K; ȝonge BGHaMaRU, ȝunge D, ȝoung I, ȝong
wexinge M; from K; the: his C; moderis D, modres F, moderes L
18 An[d] E; deliuer E

6 of the Philistiens. The which, whanne
she was comen (in) to hire housbond, seide
to hym, A man of God cam to me, hau-   20
ynge an aungelis chere, feerful wel myche;
whom whanne I hadde askid, who he
was, and whennus he was comen, and
what name he were clepid, he wold not
7 to me seye; but thus he answerde, Loo!   25
thou shalt conseyue, and bere a sone;
be war that thou drynke no wyn ne
sither, ne eete eny thing vnclene; forsothe he shal be a Nazare child of the
Lord, fro his ʒongth and fro the wombe   30
of the moder into the day of his deeth.

18 the: om. *LoWo*; whiche *BCEHLoX*; whenn *BH*, whan *CEFLoWoX*
19 commen *BF*, come *C*, comyn *E*; hir *CEHWoX*; husboond *B*, husbonde
    CEX, housbonde *F*, houʒsebonde *H*, housebonde *Lo*, husbond *Wo*
20 coome *BFH*, come *LoWo*; hauende *CX*, hafynge *E*
21 an: om. *X*; aungels *BFHWo*, aungel *Lo*; cheere *BCEFWo*; ferfull *BFWo*,
    ferful *CEHX*, ferdful *Lo*; well *BF*, ful *CLoX*, wol *E*
22 whome *BF*; whenn *BH*, whan *CFLoWoX*; had *BLoWo*; asked *CEX*,
    askide *Lo*
23 whenns *BFWo*, whennys *E*, whens *H*, whennes *LoX*; commen *BFLoWo*,
    come *CX*, comyn *E*
24 callid *Lo*; wolde *cet.*
25 to me s.: s. to me *Lo*; sey *B*, sein *CEX*, seyen *Lo*; bot *B*, bute *F*; answerd
    B, answeride *Lo*, answered *Wo*; lo *CWoX*
26 conceyuyn *E*; bern *CEX*
27 drynk *B*; wyne *BFHLo*
28 sider *Wo*; ete *cet*; any *CE*; þinge *BLoWo*; 28 – 29 forsothe he shal be:
    he sh. be f. *cet.*
29 ben *E*; childe *Lo*
30 lorde *Wo*; ʒouþ *CF*, ʒouþe *CEHLoWoX*
31 the: his *X*; modyr *EH*, modre *Lo*; deþ *BCEHWoX*

6 Quae cum venisset ad maritum suum, dixit ei: Vir
Dei venit ad me, habens vultum angelicum, terribilis nimis. Quem cum interrogassem, quis esset, et
unde venisset, et quo nomine vocaretur, noluit
mihi dicere;
7 sed hoc respondit: Ecce concipies, et paries filium; cave ne vinum bibas nec siceram, ne aliquo

320

6 uere Israel fro the hond of Filisteis. And
whanne sche hadde come to hir hosebonde,   20
sche seide to hym, The man of God cam
to me, and hadde an aungel[s] cheer, and
he was ful ferdful, *that is, worschipful*
and reuerent; and whanne Y hadde axyde
hym, who he was, and fro whannus he   25
cam, and bi what name he was clepid, he
7 nolde seie to me; but he answeride this,
Lo! thou schalt conseyue, and schalt bere
a sone; be thou war, that thou drynke
not wyn ne sidur, nether ete ony vn-   30
cleene thing; for the child schal be a Na-
zarey, *that is, hooli* of the Lord, fro his
ʒonge age and fro the modris wombe

19 from K; honde EI
20 whan EGHaLP, whane U; had EI; com E; her CaLMW, here F, hire K;
    husbonde BEMaQR, husbond D, housbonde GI, hosbonde LPU,
    hosebounde S
21 The: A I; came DIMaR, com E
22 had E, he hadde I; an: om. EHaMaS; aungels AcBDFGHaIKMMaNRSX,
    angelis C, aungelis CaELPQW, angels O, aungles U; chere EHaIR, cheere
    GLP, cher U
23 feerdful BKMaR, frendful E; wurschipful CaMW, worshipeful Q; gloss om.
    B¹GI¹NX
24 *and reuerent*: om. BCaGHaIKMNOQSX; whan EGHaLP, whane S;
    Y: he Ha; had E; axyde AHaR, axed EL, axid cet.
25 wo E; from K; whennus AcBKO, whennes CCaFHaMW, whens DEIMaQR,
    whennys GLNSX, whenis P, whenns U
26 com E, came R; cleped E
27 nolde: wolde not I, noolde MaX, nol S; sai E, sey IS; answerde
    CaFGMPQUW, answerd DE, answerede L; þus CaDEGHaIKLMNOQSX
28 schalt (1°): schal M; schalt (2°): om. I; beire R
29 ware D; drink E
30 not: no E; wijn BKMaX, wyne DER; ne: neþer AcBCDLNOSU, neiþer
    CaFHaIMMaRW, noþer E, neþir PX, neiþir S; siþir CaIMa, sidir
    DEGKLMNPQRX, siþer FU; neiþer CaFGHaIMMaQRSW, neþir OP;
    eete GQS, ete þou I; eni E; vnclene CCaDEHaIKLMMaNPQRSUWX
31 chijld K, childe U
32 holy BCaDEFKMMaQW; gloss om. I; from K
33 ʒong BCCaEHaKLMMaPQRWX, ʒunge D, ʒoung I; age: om. S; the:
    his EM; moderis D, modres F, modir I; womb E

vescaris immundo; erit enim puer nazareus Domini
ab infantia sua, et ex utero matris usque ad diem
mortis suae.

8 And so Manue preyede the Lord, and
seith, Y biseche, Lord, that the man of
God, the which thou sentist, com eft,
and teche vs, what we owen to doo of 35
9 the child, that is to be born. And the
Lord herde Manue preiynge; and eft
aperide the aungel of the Lord to his
wijf sittynge in the feeld; forsothe
Manue hir housboond was not with hir. 40
The which, whanne she hadde seen the
10 aungel, hiede, and ranne to hir man, and
tolde to hym, seiynge, Loo! the man

32 prey3id *BFH*, pre3ede *CX*, prayed *Wo*
33 seys *Lo*; beseche *CEX*, bisech *Wo*
34 the which: þat *CX*, þe whiche *BEHLo*; sendest *Lo*, sentest *X*; comm *BF*,
   come *CEHLoWoX*; efte *Lo*
35 wee *CEX*; owyn *E*; do *CEWoX*
36 childe *LoWo*; ben *ELo*; borne *Lo*
37 pre3ende *CX*, preynge *E*, prey3inge *F*, prayinge *Wo*; efte *Lo*
38 apeerid *BF*, aperede *CEHX*, apperide *Lo*, aperid *Wo*; aungil *CEX*
39 wyf *BCEFHWoX*, wyfe *Lo*; sittende *CX*, sittyng *E*; feelde *BFHLo*, feld
   CX, felde *Wo*; 39—40 forsothe Manue: M. f. *cet.*
40 hyre *BF*; husboond *B*, husbonde *CEWoX*, housbonde *F*, housebonde *HLo*;
   hyre *BEFLo*
41 whiche *BCEHLoX*; whenn *B*, whan *CLoWoX*, whann *F*, whenne *H*; had
   BF; sene *Lo*
42 aungil *CEX*; hy3id *BFHWo*, hee3ede *CE*, hi3ede *LoX*; rann *BH*, ran
   CEFWoX; hyre *BFLo*; to hir man: om. X^2
43 told *F*; to hym: to hir man *X*; seyand *BWo*, seiande *CEFLo*, seiende *X*;
   lo *C*

8 Oravit itaque Manue Dominum, et ait: Obsecro, Domine, ut vir Dei, quem misisti, veniat iterum, et
doceat nos, quid debemus facere de puero, qui
nasciturus est.
9 Exaudivitque Dominus precantem Manue, et apparuit
rursum angelus Domini uxori eius sedenti in agro.

8 til to the dai of his deeth. Therfor

Manue preiede the Lord, and seide, Lord,   35

Y biseche, that the man of God, whom

thou sentist, come eft, and teche vs, what

we owen to do of the child, that schal

9 be borun. And the Lord herde Manue

pre[i]ynge; and the aungel of the Lord ap-   40

peride eft to his wijf sittynge in the feeld;

forsothe Manue, hir hosebonde, was not

with hir. And whanne sche hadde seyn

10 the aungel, sche hastide, and ran to hir

hosebonde, and telde to hym, and seide,   45

Lo! the man whom Y siȝ bifore, apperide

---

34 til to: vn to EI; deþ AcFIOPQUX, deþe E; þerfore BCaGIKLMaNPQRWX,
þerfo S

35 preide CaIMUW, preied D, praied E, preede S; Lord: lond S; said E;
Lord: om. I, Lo S

36 biseeche G, bisiche S; wham E, which X

37 sentest EFL, sentiste R; cum E; efte ER; teeche G

38 owy S; chil[d] S; schal: om. S

39 born CaDEFGHaIKLMMaNPWX, borne R; herd AcCD

40 preiynge AcBCCaDGHaIKMMaNOPQRSWX, praying E; angel CIN,
aungil MaU; apperid D, appered E, appeeride I, apperede LP, aperide O

41 efte ER; his: þe his G, hijs S; wif EFHaMPQU; sitting E; felde EHa, feld
S, fild U

42 forsothe: & I, forsoþ X; her CaELMPW, here F; husbonde
BILMaPQR, husbond DE, housbonde G, hosebond Ha, hosebounde S,
hosbonde U

43 her CaEMW, here F, hire K; whan EGHaLP, om. S; ȝ'h'e S; had DEIR;
seen DIMa, seien GHaQ, seyne R

44 angel CI, aungil MaQ; hastid D, hasted E, hastede FLP, haastide NRX;
ron E, rane R; her CaLMW, here F, hire K

45 husbonde DIMaQR, hosbonde ELPU, housbonde G, hosebounde S;
teelde BGMaNX, teld D, tolde EILPR, toolde K, saide E; to: om. N

46 loo K; wham E; seiȝ CaFMW, seie E, sawȝe I, siȝe R, saiȝ X; apperid D,
appered E, appeeride I, apperede FPU

Manue autem maritus eius non erat cum ea. Quae cum
vidisset angelum,

10 festinavit, et cucurrit ad virum suum, nuntiavitque
ei, dicens: Ecce apparuit mihi vir, quem ante vid-
eram.

11 aperide to me, whom before I saw₃. The
    which roos, and folewide his wijf; and   45
    comynge to the man he seide to hym,
    Art thow the which spak to the wom-
12 man? And he answerde, Y am. To
    whom Manue, Whanne, he seith, thi
    word were fulfillid, what wolt thou, that   50
    the child doo, or fro what thing shal he
13 kepe hym silf? And the aungel of the
    Lord seide to Manue, Fro alle thingis
    that Y spak to thi wijf, absteyne he hym.

44 apeerid *BF*, aperede *CEX*, aperid *HWo*, apperide *Lo*; the man aperide to
    me: ap. to me þe m. *cet.*; whome *BF*; byfore *BFHLoWoX*; sa₃ *CX*,
    sawe₃ *F*, sawe *LoWo*
45 whiche *BCEHLoX*; rose *BF*, ros *CEX*, roose *Lo*; folowid *BFHWo*, folwede
    Lo, folewede *X*; wyf *BCEFHWoX*, wyfe *Lo*
46 commynge *BF*, comende *CX*
47 the which: þe whiche *BEHLo*, þat *CX*; spake *BWo*, speke *X*
48 answerd *BWo*, answeride *Lo*
49 whome *BF*; whenn *BH*, whan *CLoWoX*, whann *F*; seys *Lo*
50 woord *CE*, worde *LoWo*, wrd *X*; fulfild *CEX*, fulfilled *LoWo*; wylt
    BCEFHWoX
51 chylde *BLoWo*; do *CEWoX*; þinge *BLoWo*
52 kepen *C*, kepyn *E*; self *BCFHLoWoX*, selue *E*; aungil *CX*
53 all *F*, al *Lo*; thingus *CX*, þinges *Lo*
54 spake *BWo*; wyf *BCEFHWoX*, wyfe *Lo*; abstene *BCFWoX*, absteene *E*

11 Qui surrexit, et secutus est uxorem suam; veniens-
    que ad virum, dixit ei: Tu es qui locutus es muli-
    eri? Et ille respondit: Ego sum.
12 Cui Manue: Quando, inquit, sermo tuus fuerit ex-
    pletus, quid vis, ut faciat puer, aut a quo se ob-
    servare debebit?
13 Dixitque angelus Domini ad Manue: Ab omnibus, quae
    locutus sum uxori tuae, abstineat se;

11 to me. Which roos, and suede his wijf;
and he cam to the man, and seide to
hym, Art thou he, that hast spoke to
the womman? And he answeride, Y am.   50
12 To whom Manue seide, Whanne thi word
schal be fillid, what wolt thou, that the
child do, ethir fro what thing schal he
13 kepe hym silf? And the aungel of the
Lord seide to Manue, Absteyne he hym   55
silf fro alle thingis whiche Y spak to thi

47   whiche G, þe whiche I, wiche K; suwide CaMW, sued D, swed E, suwede
      F, suyde GQ, swede P; wif EFGHaLPQU
48   came DR, com E; said E
49   thou: tow E; haast R; spok E
50   the: þis I; wumman CaFMW, woman P; answerde CaFGMPQUW,
      answerid D, answerd E, answerede L; am *he* I
51   wham E; sayde E; wanne E, whan GHaLP; worde E
52   fulfillid I, filled EFKL; wolt thou: woltow BE, wilt þou LP
53   childe EU, chijld K; eþer AcBCDKNOSX, eiþer CaFGHaIMQW, or
      ELP, eiþir MaR, oþer U; from K
54   self EFKLMPRUW, selue Ca; angel CO, aungil MaQ; 54—55 þe lordis
      aungel I
55   said E; abstene E, abstyne DU
56   self CaFKLMPRUW, selue E; from BK; þinges FHa; which EF, wiche K;
      spake HaIR

14 And what euer thing growith of the vyn 55
eete he not, wyn and sithir drynk he
not, noon vnclene thing eete he; and that
I haue comaundid to hym, fulfille he and

15 kepe. And so Manue seide to the aungel
of the Lord, I biseche thee, that thou 60
assente to my preiers, and we maken to

16 thee a kidde of the she geet. To whom
answerde the aungel, If thou me constreynest, Y shal not eete thi looues;
forsothe if thou wolt doo brent sacrifice, 65
offre thou that to the Lord. And Manue
wiste not, that it was the aungel of the

55 euere *ELoX*, eeuere *H*; þinge *BLoWo*; growis *Lo*, groweþ *Wo*; vyne *cet.*
56 ete *cet.*; wyne *BFHLoWo*; siþer *BCEFHLoX*, sider *Wo*; drynke *cet.*
57 noen *X*; þinge *BLo*; ete *cet.*
58 hafe *E*; comaunded *C*, commaundide *Lo*; fulfill *B*
59 keep *B*; aungil *CEX*
60 beseche *CEX*; þe *Wo*
61 assent *BHWo*; prayers *B*, prei3eeris *C*, preyeres *ELo*, prey3ers *F*, prayeres *Wo*, pre3eeres *X*; wee *CEX*; make *CX*, makyn *E*
62 þe *Wo*; kide *CELoX*; schee *E*; geyte *BFHLoWo*, got *CX*, gett *E*; whome *BF*
63 answeride *Lo*, answered *Wo*; aungell *B*, aungil *CEX*, angel *Wo*; 3if *BFHWo*, 3ife *Lo*; constreynyst *BFH*, constrenest *C*, constreyne *X*
64 ete *BCFHLoWoX*, etyn *E*; loouys *BF*, loues *C*, louys *EWo*, loeues *X*
65 forsothe if: /3/if f. *cet.*; 3if *BFHWo*, 3ife *Lo*; þu *B*; wylt *BCEFHX*; do *CX*, don *E*; brente *Lo*
67 wist *BFHWo*; aungil *CEX*

14 et quidquid ex vinea nascitur, non comedat; vinum
et siceram non bibat, nullo vescatur immundo; et
quod ei praecepi, impleat atque custodiat.

15 Dixit itaque Manue ad angelum Domini: Obsecro /te/,
ut acquiescas precibus meis, et faciamus tibi haedum de capris.

16 Cui respondit angelus /Domini/: Si me cogis, non
comedam panes tuos; si autem vis holocaustum facere, offer illud Domino. Et nesciebat Manue, quod
angelus Domini esset.

14 wijf. And ete he not what euer thing
cometh forth of the vyner, drynke he not
wyn and sidur, ete he not ony vncleene
thing and fille he and kepe that, that   60
15 Y comaundide to hym. Therfor Manue
seide to the aungel of the Lord, Y biseche, that thou assente to my preieris,
and we aray to thee a kide of the geet.
16 To whom the aunge[l] of the Lord an-   65
sweride, Thouȝ thou constreynest me, Y
schal not ete thi looues; forsothe if thou
wolt make brent sacrifice, offre thou it to
the Lord. And Manue wiste not, that it

57 wif EGHaLPQU; eete GQ; wat E; euere CGKMaX
58 comyþ DIQ, comeþe E; forþe E, om. Ma; drink E
59 wijn BKMaNOX, wyne DEIR; siþir CaMaP, sidir DGKNQX, siþer
     EFILU; eete GQ; eni EHa; vnclene CaDFHaIKLMMaNPQRSUWX,
     vncle[ne] E
60 fulfille I; that (2°): at E
61 comaunde AcDFMaW, comau[n]ded E, haue comaundid I, comaundede
     KLP, comaundid O; to: om. KX; þerfore CaGIKLMaNQRWX
62 saide E; angel EI, aungil MaQ; a. of the L.: lordis angel I; biseeche þee I
63 that thou: þattou E; assent E, asente Ma; preiers DHaIKLMRX, praieres
     E
64 and: þat E; aray AE, araie cet.; we aray: araie we I; thee: þe EF; kyd
     EHa, kede U; gete D, get HaQ, geytt K; k. of the g.: geet kide I
65 wom E; angel CEI, aungil MaQ; answerde CaEFGNPQUW, answerd D,
     answerede L
66 constreyneste AcR, constreyne I, constrainedest L, constreinist Q
67 eete GQ; loues DEF, loouys GQ, breed I; forsoþ X, But I; ȝif EK
68 wilt EILPU; brente DR, brint E; it: þat I
69 wist E

17 Lord. And he seide to hym, What is
name to thee, that if thi word were ful-
fillid, we doon worship to thee? To   70
18 whom he answerde, Whi askist thou my
19 name, that is merueylows? And so Manue took a kidde of the geet, and sacrifices of licours, and putte vpon the stoon,
offrynge to the Lord that doth mer-   75
ueylows thingis. Forsothe he and the
20 wijf of hym biheelden. And whanne the
flawme of the auter stiede into heuene,
the aungel of the Lord togidre in the
flawme stiede vp. The which thing   80
whanne Manue hadde seen and his wijf,

68 lorde *Wo*
69 þe *H*; ʒif *BFHWo*, ʒife *Lo*; woord *CE*, lord *H*, worde *LoWo*, wrd *X*;
   fulfild *CEX*, fulfilde *Lo*, fulfilled *Wo*
70 wee *CEX*; do *CX*, don *EWo*; wirschip *BF*, worshipe *C*, woorschipe *E*,
   worschippe *Lo*, wrshipe *X*; þe *Wo*
71 whome *BFLo*; answerd *B*, answeride *Lo*; askis *BFWo*, askest *LoX*
72 merueylouse *BFHWo*
73 toke *BFHWo*, toc *CX*, tooke *Lo*; kyd *BFH*, kide *CELoX*; geyt *BFHWo*,
   get *CX*, gett *E*, geyte *Lo*; sacrificis *CFWo*, sacrifice *X*
74 licouris *CE*, licoures *LoX*; putt *F*, put *LoWo*; ston *CEX*, stone *Wo*
75 offeringe *Lo*, offrende *X*; dooþ *F*; merueylouse *BCEFHWo*
76 thingus *C*, þinges *LoX*; Forsothe he: he f. *cet.*
77 wyf *BCEFHWoX*, wife *Lo*; beheelden *CX*, beheeldyn *E*, byhelden *HLo*;
   whenn *B*, whan *CFLoWoX*, whan *H*
78 autere *Lo*; steyʒid *BFWo*, steʒede *CE*, styʒid *H*, steiʒede *Lo*, steʒede vp *X*;
   heuen *BHWo*
79 aungil *CE*; to giþer *BF*, togidere *CE*, to gyder *HWo*, togiþere *X*; 79–80
   in the flawme stiede vp: st. vp in þe fl. *X*
80 steyʒid *BFWo*, steiʒ *C*, steʒede *E*, styʒid *H*, steiʒede *Lo*, steʒede *X*;
   whiche *BCHLoWoX*; þinge *BLoWo*
81 whenn *BH*, whan *CELoWoX*, whann *F*; had *BFHLoWo*; sene *Lo*; hadde
   seen and his wijf: & his w. had s. *Lo*; wyf *cet.*

17 Dixitque ad eum: Quod est tibi nomen? ut, si sermo
   tuus fuerit expletus, honor/ific/emus te.
18 Cui ille respondit: Cur quaeris nomen meum, quod
   est mirabile?
19 Tulit itaque Manue haedum de capris, et libamenta,
   et posuit super petram, offerens Domino, qui facit

17 was an aungel of the Lord. And Manue   70
   seide to hym, What name is to thee, that
   if thi word be fillid, we onoure thee?
18 To whom he answeride, Whi axist thou
19 my name, which is wondurful? Therfor
   Manue took a kide of the geet, and   75
   fletynge sacrifices, and puttide on the
   stoon, and offryde to the Lord that doith
   wondirful thingis. Forsothe he and his
20 wijf bihelden. And whanne the flawme
   of the auter stiede in to heuene, the aun-   80
   gel of the Lord stiede togidere in the
   flawme. And whanne Manue and his wijf
   hadden seyn this, thei felden lowe to erthe.

70 angel CEI, aungil MaQU; an a. of the L.: þe lordis angel I
71 seid E; thee: þe EF; that: & B
72 filled EKL, fulfillid I; honoure IMaNR; þe EF
73 answerde AcCaFGMPQUW, answerd D, answed E, answerede L; axest EF
74 myn B; which: þat I, þe wiche K; wondirful BDEGHaKMaNPQRSX,
   wundurful CaMW, wundirful F, merueilous I, wonderful LU; þerfore
   BCaGIKMaNQRWX
75 toke EHaR, tooke I; kyd EHa, kede U; the: a E; gete D, geytt K, get Q;
   k. of the g.: geet kide I
76 fletyng EK, fleetynge G; sacrifisis CaDGMaQWX; puttid D, putted E,
   putte FMU, he putte hem I, puttede LP; on: upon I; the: a EI
77 ston U; offrid D, offred E, he offride hem I, offrede PU; dooþ CaMW,
   doþe E, doþ FGHaILPQR
78 wondurful AcCO, wundurful CaMW, wonderful FLN; þinges FHa;
   forsoþ X, & I
79 wif EFGHaLPQU; byheelden CaGILMaNQRWX, bi-heeldin EP, biheulden
   K, bihilden U; whan EGHaLP
80 auteer GQ; stied DE, steiede F, stiȝede HaMaNR, stiede up I; heuen L;
   angel CE, aungil GMaQ
81 stied DE, steiede F, stiȝede HaNR, stiede up I; to gidre DIR, to gyder E
82 whan EFGHaLP, whane N; wif EFGHaILPQU
83 haddin EP; seen DIMa, seie GQS, seien Ha, seyne R; fellen CaFLMW,
   filden D, fellin EP, fellen doun I; low BCE; þe erþe DEIKU[1]

mirabilia. Ipse autem et uxor eius intuebantur.
20 Cumque ascenderet flamma altaris in caelum, angelus
   Domini pariter in flamma ascendit. Quod cum vid-
   isse/n/t Manue et uxor eius, proni ceciderunt in
   terram.

21 redi thei fellen into the erthe. And na-
more to hym aperide the aungel of the
Lord. And anoon Manue vndurstood to
22 be the aungel of the Lord. And he seide   85
to hys wijf, Bi deeth die we, for we han
23 seen the Lord. To whom answerde the
womman, If the Lord wold slee vs, of
oure hoondis brent sacrifice and offryngis
of licours he wold not haue take; but   90
alle thes thingis he wold not haue shewid
to vs, ne tho thingis that ben to com

82 fell *BF*, fellyn *E*, fel *H*, felle *Wo*; erþ *B*; no *CELoX*
83 hem *E*, þem *C*; apeered *BF*, aperede *CEHX*, apperide *Lo*, apperid *Wo*;
to h. aperide: ap. to /t/h. *CX*; aungil *CEWoX*
84 anoone *Lo*, anon *Wo*, anoen *X*; vnderstode *BHWo*, vnderstod *CX*,
vndirstood *E*, vndirstode *F*, vndrestode *Lo*
85 ben *CEX*; aungil *CEX*; lorde *Lo*
86 wyf *BCEFHWoX*, wyfe *Lo*; deþ *cet.*; dyȝe *BFH*, deyȝe *Wo*; wee (2x) *CEX*
87 sene *Lo*; whome *BF*; answerd *B*, answeride *Lo*, answered *Wo*
88 ȝif *BFHWo*, ȝife *Lo*; lorde *Lo*; wolde *cet.*; slen *BCEFX*, sleen *HLoWo*
89 our *F*; hondis *CX*, handis *E*, hondes *LoWo*; brente *Lo*; sacrifises *X*;
offringus *C*, offerynges *Lo*
90 licourus *C*, licowris *E*, licoures *LoX*; wolde *CEFHLoWoX*; han *BCEFHWoX*;
takyn *E*, taken *LoX*; bot *BF*
91 al *BH*, all *F*; þese *CEWoX*; þinges *BLo*, thingus *C*; wolde *CEFHLoWoX*;
han *CEX*
92 þoo *CE*; thingus *CX*, þinges *Lo*; that: om. *BFHWo*; to: om. *H*; commen
BF, come *CX*, comyn *E*, comen *HLoWo*

21 Et ultra non eis apparuit angelus Domini. Statimque
intellexit Manue, angelum esse Domini,
22 et dixit ad uxorem suam: Morte moriemur, quia vidimus Dominum.
23 Cui respondit mulier: Si Dominus nos vellet occidere, de manibus nostris holocaustum et libamenta
non suscepisset, sed nec ostendisset nobis haec
omnia, neque ea, quae sunt ventura, dixisset.

21 And the aungel of the Lord apperide no
more to hem. And anoon Manue vndur- 85
stood, that he was an aungel of the
22 Lord. And he seide to his wijf, We
schulen die bi deeth, for we sien the
23 Lord. To whom the womman answeride,
If the Lord wolde sle vs, he schulde not 90
haue take of oure hondis brent sacrifices,
and moiste sacrifices, but nether he schulde
haue schewid alle thingis to vs, nether he
schulde haue seid tho thingis, that schu-

84 angel CE, aungil GMaQ; appered DE, appeeride I, apperede LPU
85 onon E, anon HaP; vndirstood BDFGKNPSX, vndurstode E,
vndirstode HaIR, vnderstood LMaQ, vndirstod U
86 an: þe I; angel C, aungil MaQ
87 wif EFGHaILPQU
88 schullen CaMW, schuln DF, shul EILP; deie CaFMW, diʒ R; deþ
AcCEFILOPQSUX; seiʒen CaM, seyen EFUW, siʒen GKLMaNR, han
seen I
89 lorde E; wumman CaFMW, woman E; answerde CaFGMQUW, answerd
D, answerid E, answerede L
90 slee CaGKLQ; scholde CaFMW, shuld E, wolde I; nauʒt S
91 of: om. L; hondes CaF, hoondis R; brente KR; sacrifisis
CaDEGKMMaPQWX
92 moist AcBCaDFHaIMMaQ, sacrifisis CaDEGKLMMaPQRX; neiþer
CaFGHaIMMaQRW, neþir S, noþer U; scholde CaMW, schuld F, wolde I
93 shewed EL, sheewid G, schewide HaR; þis þingis E, þinges FHa, þese
þingis I; neiþer CaFGHaIMQW, neþir EOP, neiþir MaR, noþer U; he:
om. I
94 scholde CaMW, shuld E, schold F, om. I; haue: a G; saied E, seide DRS,
seid to us I; þoo R; þinges FHa; shul ELP, schullen CaFMW, schuln D

24 haue seid. And so she beere a chi[l]d,
and clepide the name of him Sampson;
and the child wexe, and the Lord bless-   95
25 ide to hym. And the spyrit of the Lord
began to be with hym in the tentis of
Dan, bitwix Saraa and Eskahol.

14. 1 Sampson thanne dessendide in to Thannatha, and seynge there a womman of
2 the douȝtris of Philistien, stiede vp, and
tolde to his fader and his moder, seiynge,
I sawȝ a womman in Thannatha of the   5
douȝtris of Philistiens, whom, Y biseche,

93 han *CELoX*; seide *BFHLoWo*; beer *BFH*, bar *CEX*, bare *Lo*, bere *Wo*;
childe *LoWo*
94 clepid *BFHWo*, clepede *CX*, callid *Lo*
95 childe *LoWo*; wex *CEX*; blissed *B*, blissede *CX*, blessed *F*, blessid *HLoWo*
96 spirite *BFLo*, spiriȝte *H*, sperit *X*
97 bygann *BF*, bygan *HLoWoX*; ben *EX*; tentus *C*, tentes *X*
98 bytwen *B*, betwe *C*, betwen *E*, bytwene *FHLoWo*, bitwe *X*

14. 1 þann *BFH*, þan *LoWo*; descendid *BFHWo*, descendede *C*; to: om. *cet.*
2 seeynge *BEFLo*, seande *C*, seeyng *H*, seende *X*; þer *E*; womm[an] *H*
3 douȝters *BH*, doȝtris *CX*, douȝtres *Lo*; steyȝid *BFWo*, steȝede *CEX*,
styȝid *H*, steiȝede *Lo*
4 told *F*; fadir *BEFH*, fadre *Lo*; modir *BEH*, modre *Lo*; seynge *E*, seiende *CX*
5 sawe *BFLoWo*, saȝ *CX*, sawȝe *H*; woman *Lo*
6 douȝters *BH*, doȝtris *CX*, douȝtres *Lo*; whome *BFLoWo*; beseche *CEX*

24 Peperit itaque filium, et vocavit nomen eius Samson.
Crevitque puer, et benedixit ei Dominus.
25 Coepitque spiritus Domini esse cum eo in castris
Dan inter Saraa et Estahol.

14. 1 Descendit igitur Samson in Thannatha. Vidensque ibi
mulierem de filiabus Philistiim,
2 ascendit, et nuntiavit patri suo et matri suae,
dicens: Vidi mulierem in Thannatha de filiabus
Philistinorum, quam quaeso, ut mihi accipia/ti/s
uxorem.

24 len come. Therfor sche childide a sone,   95
and clepide his name Sampson; and the
child encreesside, and the Lord blesside
25 hym. And the spirit of the Lord bigan
to be with hym in the castels of Dan,
bitwixe Saraa and Escahol.   100

14. 1 Therfor Sampson ȝede doun in to Thannatha, and he siȝ there a womman of the
2 douȝtris of Filisteis; and he stiede, and
telde to his fadir and to his modir, and
seide, Y siȝ a womman in Thannatha of   5
the douȝtris of Filistees, and Y biseche,

95 cum E, ben to comynge I; þerfore BCaEFGKMMaNQRWX, and so I;
     childid D, childed E, childede KLP
96 clepid DEU, clepede F
97 childe EU; encresside CaMS, encresid D, encrescede E, encresede FLPU,
     encreside HaNX, wexide I, encreeside KR; blessid AcD, blessed E, blessede
     LPU
98 spiritt K, spiriȝt L; bigane R
99 castels: tentus I, castelis S
100 bitwix EQR

14. 1 þerfore BCaFGKMaNQRWX, Thanne I, Thefor O
    2 seiȝ CaFMW, seȝ E, sawȝe I, siȝe R; þer E; wumman CaFMW
    3 douȝtres F, doutris L, douȝters U; 2—3 of the d. of F.: of philistees
       douȝtris I; stied D, steiede F, stiede up I, stiȝede MaNR
    4 teelde BCaGMaNX, tolde EKLPR, tolde þis I; fader EFHaLMMaU; to
       his (2°): om. I; moder EFLU
    5 seiȝ CaFMW, sie E, sawȝe I, siȝe R, saiȝ X; wumman CaFMW
    6 douȝtres F, doutris L, douȝters U; d. of F.: philistees douȝtris I; biseeche
       L

3 that thou take to me wijf. To whom
  seiden the fader and his moder, Whether
  is there no womman in the douȝtres of
  thi britheren and in al thi puple, for   10
  thou wolt take a wijf of Philistien, that
  ben vncircumcidid? And Sampson seide
  to his fader, This tak to me, for she
4 pleside to myn eyen. His fader and   15
  moder wisten not, that the thing shulde
  be doo of the Lord, and he shulde seche
  occasioun aȝens the Philistien; forsothe
  that tyme Philistien lordshipide to Yrael.

7 wyf *BCEFHWoX*, wyfe *Lo*; whome *BF*
8 seidyn *E*, seyde *FLoWo*; fadir *BE*, fadre *Lo*; his: þe *Wo*; modir *BE*,
   modre *Lo*
9 þer *BCEFHWo*, om. *X*; douȝtren *BFHLoWo*, doȝtris *CX*, dowȝtryn *E*
10 breþeren *BEFHLoWo*, breþern *CX*; alle *BLo*, all *F*; þe *Lo*; peple *BFHLoWo*
11 wilt *BCEFHWoX*; taken *BFHWoX*, takyn *E*; wyf *BCEFHWoX*, wyfe *Lo*
12 ben: om. *H*; vncircumcidide *Lo*
13 fadyr *EH*, fadre *Lo*; take *BFHLoWo*
14 plesid *BFHWo*, plesede *CLoX*; my *E*; eyȝen *BFHLoWo*, eȝen *CX*, eȝyn *E*;
   fadir *BEH*, fadre *Lo*
15 modir *BEH*, modre *Lo*; wist *BFHWo*, wyste *Lo*; þinge *BLoWo*; schuld *B*
16 ben *E*; don *CEX*, doon *Lo*, do *Wo*; schuld *B*, scholde *Lo*; sechen
   BCEFHWoX, seke *Lo*
17 occasyon *BH*, ocasioun *CX*; aȝeynst *BFHWo*, aȝen *CX*, aȝenst *E*, aȝeynes
   Lo; 17–18 forsothe that tyme: þ. t. f. *cet.*
18 lordschipiden *BFHWo*, lordshipeden *CX*, lordschipedyn *E*, lordschippeden
   Lo

3 Cui dixerunt pater et mater sua: Numquid non est
  mulier in filiabus fratrum tuorum, et in omni populo
  tuo, quia vis accipere uxorem de Philistiim, qui
  incircumcisi sunt? Dixitque Samson ad patrem suum:
  Hanc mihi accipe, quia placuit oculis meis.
4 Parentes autem eius nesciebant, quod res a Domino
  fieret, et quaereret occasionem contra Philistiim.
  Eo enim tempore Philistiim dominabantur Israeli.

3 that ȝe take hir a wijf to me. To whom
his fadir and modir seiden, Whether no
womman is among the douȝtris of thi
britheren and in al my puple, for thou
wolt take a wijf of Filisteis, that ben
vncircumcidid? And Sampson seide to his
fadir, Take thou this wijf to me, for sche
4 pleside myn iȝen. Forsothe his fadir
and modir wisten not, that the thing was
don of the Lord; and that he souȝte occa-
siouns aȝens Filisteis; for in that tyme

10

15

7 ȝee U; her CaMW, hur E, here F, hire K; a: om. I; wif EFGHaLPQU
8 fader CaFGLU; moder FLU; saiden E, seide O; Whether AE, where D,
   wher cet.; 8—9 no womman is: þer is no womman I
9 womman: man AcFRU, wumman CaMW, woman EHa; amonge R;
   douȝtres F, douȝters U
10 breþren CaFMW, breþern E, briþren G, breþeren HaLPUX, briþern K;
   peple CaFILMMaNPWX
11 wolte B, wol E, wil LP; tak E; wif EFGHaLPQU; þe philistees I
12 vncircumcized E, vncircumcided KL; said E
13 fader EFHaLOU; thou: om. R; wif EFGHaLPQU
14 plesid D, pleseȝ E, haþ plesid I, plesede KLP, pleeside Q; myne
   CaEHaKMRW; eiȝen CaFMUW; forsoþ X, But I; fader ILU
15 and modir: om. D; moder LU; wiste O; the: þis I
16 doon BCaFKMMaQW, om. D, done ER; he: sampson I; southe E;
   occasions EKQ
17 aȝenus CN; þe philistees IN

5 And so Sampson dessendide with his fader and moder in to Thannatha; and   20
   whanne thei weren comen to the vynes
   of the bourʒ toun, and there aperide a
   feers whelp of a lyoun and rorynge, and
6 aʒen cam to hym. The spyrit of the
   Lord forsothe felle into Sampson, and he   25
   taar the lioun, as he shulde to-teer out
   a kide, into gobetis, no thing vtterli hauynge in hoond; and that to fader and
7 moder he wold not shewe. And he
   dessendide, and spak to the womman,   30

19 descendede *C*, descendid *Wo*; fadir *BCEH*, fadre *Lo*
20 modir *BEH*, modre *Lo*; to: om. *X*
21 whenn *BH*, whan *CLoWoX*, whenne *E*, whann *F*; were *Wo*; commen *BF*,
    come *CX*, comyn *E*; vynys *BFHWo*
22 bourgh *BFH*, burʒ *CX*, burgh *EWo*, bourghe *Lo*; þer *CEX*; apeerid *BF*,
    aperede *CEX*, aperid *HWo*, apperide *Lo*
23 feerse *BH*, ferse *F*, fers *Wo*; whelpe *Lo*; leoun *CX*; rorende *CX*; and: om.
    H
24 aʒeyn *BEFHWo*, aʒeyne *Lo*; coom *BFH*, come *LoWo*; spirite *BFLo*,
    spiriʒte *H*, sperit *X*; 24−25 The spyrit of the Lord forsothe: þe sp. f. of
    þe l. *Lo*
25 fell *BF*, fel *CEHX*
26 tar *CEX*, taare *LoWo*; leoun *CX*; scholde *Lo*, schuld *Wo*; to: om. *X*;
    tere *BFHLoWo*, tern *CX*, teryn *E*; oute *BLo*, ouʒt *H*; 26−27 out a kide:
    a k. out *X*
27 kyd *BFHWo*; goobitis *B*, gobytis *F*, gobbettis *H*, gobyttes *Lo*, gobetes *X*;
    þinge *BLoWo*; owtyrli *E*, outerli *X*; hauende *CX*, hafynge *E*
28 hond *CWoX*, hand *E*, hoonde *F*, hande *Lo*; fadir *BEH*, fadre *Lo*
29 modir *BEH*, modre *Lo*; wolde *CEFHLoWoX*; schewyn *E*
30 descendede *C*, descendid *FHWo*; spake *BWo*

5 Descendit itaque Samson cum patre suo et matre in
   Thannatha. Cumque venissent ad vineas oppidi, apparuit catulus leonis saevus et rugiens, et occurrit ei.
6 Irruit autem spiritus Domini in Samson, et dilacer-

5 Filisteis weren lordis of Israel. Therfor
Sampson ȝede doun with his fadir and
modir in to Thannatha; and whanne thei   20
hadden come to the vyneris of the citee,
a fers and rorynge whelp of a lioun ap-
6 peride, and ran to Sampson. Forsothe
the spirit of the Lord felde in to Sampson, and he to-rente the lioun, as if he   25
to-rendide a kide in to gobetis, and
outerli he hadde no thing in the hond;
and he nolde schewe this to the fadir
7 and modir. And he ȝede doun, and spak
to the womman, that pleside hise iȝen.   30

18 þe philistees I; lordes F, lorddis U; þerfore BCaGIKMaQR
19 hise N; fader CaFLMU
20 moder FLRU, modur O; whan EFGLP; thei: he N
21 hadde EGNS; cum E; vyneeris B, vyners DHaIKMRX, vyneres F, vineers
    Q; cite CaFHaILMPQW
22 feers BGKLMaNPQ; a roryng CEHa, a rorynge DGIN, roring LP;
    whelpe ER, welp OU; lyon EK; wh. of a l.: liouns whelp I; apperid D,
    appered E, appeeride L, apperede LP
23 ranne D, rane R; forsoþ X, and I
24 spiritt K, spiriȝt L; lorde E; fel CaEFLMPW, filde D, felle I
25 torentid D, to-rent E; lione E, lion K; if: om. L; he (2°): om. Ca; 25–26
    as if he to-r. a k. in to g.: in to g. as if he hadde tor. a k. I
26 torentide AcHaMaNSU, toreendide B, torentid D, to-rented E, torente
    FGM, hadde torente I, torentede LP; kyd Ha; gobettis DGU, gobites E,
    gobetes F
27 outirli AcBCCaIKMW, vttirli DGMaPQ, utterly EHaLN, outurly O,
    outtirli RX; had E; the: his EI; hondis C, honde IR, hand LP
28 noolde MaX, wolde not I; shew E; the: his I, om. S; fader FLMU
29 moder FLU; spake HaIR
30 wumman CaFMW; plesid D, plesed E, plesede FLP, pleeside Q; his
    EFGHaILNPQX; eiȝen CaFMW

avit leonem, quasi haedum in frusta decerperet,
nihil omnino habens in manu; et hoc patri et matri
noluit indicare.
7 Descenditque, et locutus est mulieri, quae placu-
erat oculis eius.

8 that pleside to his eyen. And after a
fewe days turnynge aʒen for to take hir,
he wente aside for to se the careyn of the
lioun; and loo! a swarm of beese was in
the mouth of the lioun, and an hony   35
9 coombe. The which whanne he hadde
takun in hoondis, he ete in the weye;
and comynge to his fader and moder, he
ʒaf to hem part, the which and thei
eeten; and neuerthelater he wold not   40
shewe to hem, that the hony he took of
10 the mouth of the lioun. And so his fader
dessendide to the womman, and made to
his sone Sampson a feest; forsothe so

31 plesed *BF*, plesede *EX*, plesid *HWo*; hise *E*; eyʒen *BFHLoWo*, eʒen *CX*,
eʒeen *F*; aftyr *BLo*
32 daʒes *CX*, daies *EFLoWo*; tornynge *BFHWo*, turnende *CX*; aʒeyn
BFHWo, aʒeen *CEX*, a-ʒeyne *Lo*; taken *BCFHWoX*, takyn *E*; hyre *BFLo*
33 went *BFHWo*; for: om. *C*[1]; see *BHLoWo*, seen *CE*; careyne *Lo*
34 leoun *CX*; lo *CX*; swarm *BFHLoWo*; bees *CEHLoWoX*
35 mouþe *HLo*; leoun *CX*; a *Lo*
36 comb *CEX*, combe *LoWo*; whiche *BCEHLoX*; whenn *B*, whan *CEFLoWoX*;
had *BFHLoWo*
37 taken *BFHLoWoX*, take *C*, takyn *E*; hondus *C*, handis *E*, handes *Lo*,
hondes *Wo*, hondis *X*; eet *CX*, eett *E*, ett *Lo*; wey *Wo*
38 commynge *BF*, comende *CX*; fadir *BEH*, fadre *Lo*; modir *BEH*, modre *Lo*
39 ʒaue *BFH*, ʒafe *Lo*; þem *CLoX*; paart *BFHWo*, parte *Lo*; whiche
BCEHLoX
40 eetyn *E*, eten *LoWo*; nerþelatere *CX*, neuerþelatere *E*, neuere þe later *Lo*;
wolde *CEHLoWoX*
41 schew *B*, schewyn *E*; þem *CLoX*; tooke *B*, toc *CX*, toke *FHLoWo*
42 mowþe *Lo*; leoun *CX*; fadir *BEH*, fadre *Lo*
43 descendede *C*, descendid *Wo*
44 feste *BCEHWoX*, feeste *F*; forsoþ *B*; forsothe so: so f. *cet.*

8 Et post aliquot dies revertens, ut acciperet eam,
declinavit, ut videret cadaver leonis, et ecce ex-
amen apium in ore leonis erat ac favus mellis.
9 Quem cum sumpsisset in manibus, comedebat in via;
veniensque ad patrem suum et matrem, dedit eis
partem, qui et ipsi comederunt; nec tamen eis voluit indicare, quod mel de ore leonis assumpserat.

8 And aftir summe daies he turnede aȝen
to take hir *in to matrimonye*; and he
bowide awey to se the careyn of the
lioun; and lo! a gaderyng of bees was
in the mouth of the lioun, and a coomb   35
9 of hony. And whanne he hadde take it
in hondis, he eet in the weie; and he
cam to his fadir and modir, and ȝaf part
to hem, and thei eeten; netheles he nolde
schewe to hem, that he hadde take hony   40
10 of the mouth of the lioun. And so his
fadir ȝede doun to the wommon, and made
a feeste to his sone Sampson; for ȝonge

---

31 after EFU; sum DF; daes S; turned DE, turnyde GHaQR; a-ȝein E, om.
   S²
32 her CaMW, hur E, here F, hire KL; *in to m.*: om. I; matrimoyne E
33 bowed E, bowede FLPU, wente I, bowȝide R; awey: aside I, aweie R;
   see CaFGLMRW; careyne EGKLMaPRU; 33—34 c. of the l.: liouns
   careyn I
34 lione E, lion K; loo CO; gaderynge CaDGMaQU, swarm I, gedering KN,
   gadryng R
35 mouþe U; lion K; m. of the l.: lioun mouþ I; comb
   BCaEFGHaKLMaOPQUW, combe DIR
36 hoony O; 35—36 a c. of h.: an hony combe I; whan EGHaLP; he:
   Sampson I; had EI; it: þe combe I
37 hondes F, his hondis I, hoondis R; eet it B, ete E, eete HaR, eete it I;
   wey I
38 com E, came GR; fader FLMU; moder FLMaU; ȝafe R; 38—39 ȝaf p.
   to hem: ȝaue hem part þerof I
39 eten CaDEFHaMUW, eetin LP; naþeles B, & neþeles CaM; noolde MaX,
   wolde not I, nolde R, nolde not W
40 shew E, chewe S; had EI; tak E, om. G; þat hony I
41 mouþe E; lion EK; m. of the l.: lioups mouþ I
42 fader CaFLU; wumman CaFMW
43 feste CaEFLMUW, feest DHaIKQR; his sone S.: Sampson his sone I;
   ȝunge CaD, ȝonge EP, ȝounge I; 43—44 for ȝ. men weren w. to do so:
   for so ȝ. m. w. wont to do I

10 Descendit itaque pater eius ad mulierem, et fecit
filio suo Samson convivium. Sic enim iuvenes facere consueverant.

11 ʒong men weren wont to doo. Whanne   45
   thanne the cyteseyns of that place hadden
   seen him, thei ʒouen to him bord felawis
   thretti, the whiche shulden be with hym.

12 To whom spak Sampson, Y shal purpose
   to ʒow a dowtous word, the which if ʒe   50
   soylen to me with ynne seuen dais of the
   feest, I shal ʒyue to ʒou thretti lynnen

13 clothis, and so fele cootis; forsothe if ʒe
   mowen not assoyle, ʒe shulen ʒyue to me
   thretty lynnen clothis, and of the same   55
   noumbre cootis. The whiche answerden
   to hym, Purpos the probleme, that we

45 ʒonge *BEFHLoWo*, ʒunge *CX*; weryn *E*; were *Wo*; wonte *Lo*; do *CEFWo*,
    don *X*; whenn *BH*, whan *CLoWoX*, whann *F*; 45—6 Whanne thanne:
    þ. wh. *Lo*
46 þann *BF*, þan *HWo*; cyteeseyns *BF*, citeseines *CEX*, citeʒeynes *Lo*; haddyn
    E
47 seeyn *BH*, sene *Lo*; ʒeuen *BCFHX*, ʒefyn *E*, ʒauen *Lo*, ʒyuen *Wo*; to:
    om. *FWo*; borde *BFHLoWo*, boord *CE*; felowes *Lo*, felawes *WoX*
48 þrytty *BFHLoWo*; the whiche: þat *C*, þe which *FWo*; schuldyn *E*; ben *EX*
49 whome *BF*; spake *BFWo*; schalle *Lo*; purposyn *E*, purposen *X*
50 dotous *BCEFWoX*, dotouʒs *H*; woord *CE*, worde *LoWo*, wrd *X*; whiche
    BCEHLoX; ʒif *BFHWo*, ʒife *Lo*; ʒee *CELoX*
51 soilyn *E*; sefne *E*, seuene *LoWoX*; daʒis *C*, daies *EFHLoWo*, daʒes *X*
52 feste *BCEHX*, feeste *FLoWo*; ʒeue *BFH*, ʒifen *E*; þritty *BFHLoWo*;
    linene *CEX*
53 cloþes *ELo*; feele *Lo*; cotis *CEH*, cootes *Lo*, cotes *Wo*, coetes *X*; forsoþ *B*;
    forsothe if: if f. *cet.*; ʒif *BFHWo*, ʒife *Lo*; ʒee *CELoX*
54 mown *BCEFWoX*; assoylen *BFHLoWo*, asoile *C*, assoilyn *E*, asoilen *Lo*;
    ʒee *CELoX*; schuln *BFWo*, shul *CEX*, schullen *H*, schulle *Lo*; ʒeue
    BFHLo, ʒifen *E*
55 þritty *BCFHLoWoX*; line *C*, lynene *EX*; cloþes *ELo*
56 cotis *CE*, cootes *Lo*, coetes *X*; which *FWo*; answerdyn *E*
57 purpose *cet.*; the: þi *X*; wee *CEX*

11 Cum igitur cives loci illius vidissent eum, dederunt ei sodales triginta, qui essent cum eo.

12 Quibus locutus est Samson: Proponam vobis problema;
   quod si solveritis mihi intra septem dies convivii,
   dabo vobis triginta sindones, et totidem tunicas;

13 sin autem non potueritis solvere, vos dabitis mihi
   triginta sindones, et eiusdem numeri tunicas. Qui
   responderunt ei: Propone problema, ut audiamus.

11 men weren wont to do so. Therfor
   whanne the citeseyns of that place had-   45
   den seyn hym, thei ȝauen to hym thretti
   felowis, whiche schul[d]en be with hym.
12 To whiche Sampson spak, Y schal putte
   forth to ȝou a probleme, *that is, a douȝte-*
   ful word and priuy, and if ȝe asoilen   50
   it to me with ynne seuen daies of the
   feeste, Y schal ȝyue to ȝou thretti lynnun
   clothis, and cootis of the same noumbre;
13 sotheli if ȝe moun not soyle, ȝe schulen
   ȝyue to me thretti lynnun clothis, and   55
   cootis of the same noumbre. Whiche
   answeriden to hym, Sette forth the pro-

44 wond L; þerfore BCaGIKMaNQRWX; 44−45 Therfor whanne: wh.
    þerfore I
45 when E, whan LP; citesens D, citeseynis GQ, citeseynes R; had E, haddin P
46 seyen BGHaQS, seen DIMa, i-sein E, seyne R; hym: sampson I; þai E;
    ȝafen K; þritti AcCaIMNWX, thirti E
47 felawis CaMW, felous DX, felawes EF, felowes LP; which E, þe whiche I,
    wiche K; schulden BCDGHaIKMaNOQSX, schullen CaM, shul ELP,
    schuln F, scholden W; wit E
48 whiche: whom I, wiche K; spake IR; put ER
49 forþe E; probleeme G, problem Ma; doutful DE, douȝtful HaL, douteful
    cet.
50 pryue CaFMW, preui EGLPQ, pryuey KR; ȝif O; ȝee U; assoylen BCaD-
    HaKMW, asoile E, assoile LP; gloss 49−50: or 'a' priuy douteful word I;
    50−51 & if ȝe tellen to me þe vndirstonding þerof I
51 seuene AcGHaKNQWX, seue O; dais E; the: þis I
52 feest DEGHaKQR, feste FMUW; ȝeue BDHaMaQR, ȝife K; þritti
    AcCaMMaNWX, þirti E; lynnen CaDEFIKMMaNRW, lynnyn LP,
    lynen G, lynene Q
53 clooþis D, cloþes EFK; cotis CaHaMRW, cotes EF; numbre E; and etc.:
    & as many cootis I
54 soþli FGLMMaPQUWX, & I; ȝif EG; ȝee (1°) GU; moun: mou E,
    cunnen I, mowen Ma; not: om. D; soyle: soule D, asoyle GR, assoile it I;
    ȝee (2°) BU; schullen CaMW, schuln DF, shul EILP
55 ȝeue BDHaMaQRU, ȝif E, ȝife K; to: om. I; þritti AcMNWX, þirti E;
    lynnen CaDEFIKMMaNPRW, lynen G, linnyn L, lynun Q; clooþis Ac,
    cloþes F
56 cotis CaMRW, cotes EF; noumber E; 55−56 & as many cootis I; which
    DE, þe whiche I, wiche K
57 answeridin B, answerden CaDEFGMQUW, answereden L, answerdin P;
    set D, put I, sett U; forþe E; the probleme: þi sotil axyng I

14 heren. And he seide to hem, Of the
eter ȝede out meete, and of the strong
wente out swetnes. And thei miȝten not   60
15 bi thre days soylen the proposicioun. And
whanne the seuenthe day was nyȝ, thei
seiden to the wijf of Sampson, Faage to
thi man, and meue hym, that he shewe
to thee what bitokeneth the probleme.   65
The which thing if thou wold not doo,
we shulen brenne thee and the hows of
thi fader. Whether therfor ȝe han clepid

58   heeren *BF*, here *C*, heeryn *E*; þem *CLoX*
59   etere *CEX*; ȝide *CX*; oute *BLo*, ouȝte *H*; mete *cet.*; stronge *cet.*
60   went *FHWo*; oute *BLo*, ouȝte *H*; swettnes *BF*, swetnesse *CELoWoX*,
   swettnessis *H*; myȝtyn *E*, myȝte *Lo*
61   daȝes *CX*, daies *EFLoWo*; soile *C*, soilyn *E*
62   whenn *BH*, whan *CEFWoX*; seuenþ *BH*, seuen *FWo*; dayes *FWo*; neeiȝ *C*,
   neegh *E*, neiȝ *Wo*
63   seidyn *E*, seyde *Lo*; wyf *BCEFHWoX*, wife *Lo*; fage *CEHLoX*; to: om. *X*
64   moue *CX*, moeue *E*
65   bytokeniþ *BFH*, betocneþ *CE*, by-tokenes *Lo*, bitocneþ *X*
66   whiche *BCEHX*; þinge *BLoWo*; ȝif *BFHWo*, ȝife *Lo*; wylt *BCEFHWoX*,
   wolt *Lo*; do *CEHWo*
67   wee *CEX*; schal *BFHLoWo*, shul *CX*, schuln *E*; brenn *BHX*, brennyn *E*;
   þe *Wo*; houȝs *H*
68   fadir *BH*, fadre *Lo*; where *Lo*; þerfore *BCEFHWoX*, þerefore *Lo*; ȝee
   CELoX; ha *X*; callid *Lo*, cleped *Wo*

14 Dixitque eis: De comedente exivit cibus, et de forti
egressa est dulcedo. Nec potuerunt per tres dies
solvere propositionem.
15 Cumque adesset dies septimus, dixerunt ad uxorem
Samson: Blandire viro tuo, et suade ei, ut indicet
tibi, quid significet problema. Quod si facere nolueris, incendemus te, et domum patris tui. An idcirco vocastis nos ad nuptias, ut spoliaretis?

14 bleme, that we here *it*. And he seide to
hem, Mete ȝede out of the etere, and swetnesse ȝede out of the stronge. And bi thre   60
daies thei myȝten not assoile the proposicioun, *that is, the resoun set forth.*

15 And whanne the seuenthe dai cam, thei
seiden to the wijf of Sampson, Glose thin
hosebonde, and counseile hym, that he   65
schewe to thee what the probleme signy-
fieth. That if thou nylt do, we schulen
brenne thee and the hous of thi fadir.
Whether herfor ȝe clepiden vs to wed-

58   heere GHaKMaNO²RX; *it*: AINS, om. cet.; seid E
59   meete GQ, mede Ha; ȝeode K; oute R; eetere GLQ, eeter Ha, eter IR;
     swettenesse E, sweetnesse K
60   ȝeode K, om. R, ȝe S; oute R; strong E
61   miȝt E; asoile AcCCaDMaNORSUX; proposicion EK, om. I
62   *that is* the: om. I; resoune E, reson K, reesoun Q; sette D, put I, sett
     KNRX; forþe E, forþ *of sampson* I
63   when E, whan HaLP; seueþe B, seuent E, seuenþ R; com E, came GIR;
     thei: þese men I
64   said E; wif EFGHaLPQU; the w. of S.: sampsons wijf I; gloose K, fage I;
     þine EW, þi K
65   husbonde BDIMaQ, hosbond E, housbonde G, hosbonde LPU, husbond
     R; councele AcBCKN, moue I, counseil L; hum X
66   shew E; thee: þe EFR; the: om. E; problem E, probleeme G, sutel axyng
     I, proble N; signefieþ AcBCCaFOSW, signifieȝ E, meneþ I
67   nelt CaMW, wilt not I; do it I; schullen CaMW, schuln DF, shul EILP
68   bren E; thee: þe E; fader EFLU; the h. of thi f.: þi fadris hous I
69   Whether AE, where D, wher cet.; herfore BCaEGKLMaNPQRWX,
     þerfore I; ȝee U; clepeden CaEFLMPW; weddinges BCaFha, wedyngis O

16 vs to the brydale for to robben? The
   which shedde anentis Sampson teeris, and   70
   pleynede, seiynge, Thow hatidist me, and
   not louest, and therfor the redels, that
   thow hast purposid to the sones of my
   puple, thou wolt not to me expowne. He
   answerde, To my fadir and moder I wold   75
   not seye, and to the shal I mowe shewe?
17 Therfore seuen days of the feest she wepte
   anentis hym; at the last the seuenthe dai
   whanne she was heuy to hym, he ex-
   pownede. The which anoon tolde to hir   80

69 robbyn *E*
70 whiche *BCEHLoX*; shadde *C*; anentus *C*, anent *X*; teris *BCEFH*, teres *X*
71 pleyned *Wo*; seiende *CX*; hatedest *CLo*, hatedist *X*
72 loouest *CE*; þerfore *BCEFHWoX*, þere-fore *Lo*; redelis *CELo*, ridels *Wo*,
    redeles *X*
73 purposede *BF*, purposide *HLo*; sonys *BEFH*, sonus *CX*
74 peple *BFHLoWo*; wilt *BCEFWoX*; expownen *BFHWo*, expownyn *E*; He:
    & he *CEFHLoWo*
75 answeride *Lo*, answered *Wo*; fader *BCFWoX*, fadre *Lo*; modyr *EFH*, modre
    Lo; wolde *CEFHLoWoX*
76 seyn *BEFHWoX*, sei *C*, seyne *Lo*; þee *BCEFHLoX*; moun *CEX*, mow
    FWo, mowen *Lo*; schewen *BFHLoWo*, schewyn *E*
77 Therfore seuen: s. þ. *cet.*; seuene *CLoWoX*, sefne *E*; daȝes *CX*, daies
    EFHLoWo; feste *BCEFHX*; wept *BFWo*
78 anentus *C*, anent *X*; the (1°): om. *X*; laste *CELo*, om. *X*; seuenþ *BF*
79 whann *B*, whan *CEFHLoWoX*; expowned *BFHWo*
80 whiche *BCEHLoX*; anon *BX*, anoone *Lo*; told *BF*; hyre *BFLo*

16 Quae fundebat apud Samson lacrimas, et querebatur,
   dicens: Odisti me, et non diligis; idcirco problema,
   quod proposuisti filiis populi mei, non vis mihi ex-
   ponere. At ille respondit: Patri meo et matri nolui
   dicere; et tibi indicare potero?
17 Septem igitur diebus convivii flebat apud eum; tan-
   dem/que/ septimo die, cum ei esset molesta, exposuit.
   Quae statim indicavit civibus suis.

16 dyngis, that ʒe schulden robbe vs? And 70
   sche schedde teerys at Sampson, and
   pleynede, and seide, Thou hatist me, and
   louest not, therfor thou nylt expowne
   to me the probleme, which thou settidist
   forth to the sones of my puple. And he 75
   answeride, Y nolde seie to my fadir and
   modir, and schal Y mow schewe to thee?
17 Therfor bi seuene dayes of the feeste, sche
   wepte at hym; at the laste he ex-
   pownede in the seuenthe dai, whanne 80
   sche was diseseful to hym. And anoon

70 ʒee GU; scholden CaFW, scholde M; robben E
71 sched D, schedde out I; teris CaMW, teres EF
72 playnede AcBCCaFKLNOPSUWX, pleyned D, playned E, playnide
    GHaQ, complaynede I, pleynide R; hateste E, hatest F, hatiste R; 72—73
    and l. not: & no't' louest I
73 louist GQ, louest *me* K; þerfore BCaGIKLMMaNQRW; nelt CaFMW,
    wolt not I, om. S; expowne: vndo I
74 the probleme: þis sutel axyng I; whiche BGOP, þat I, wiche K; settedist
    CaMNW, settist DU, settedest EFLP, settidest Ha, hast put I, settidiste R
75 foorþ D; the: om. G; sonys GHaQ, sone R; my: al my N; peple
    CaFILMMaNPWX; he: sampson I
76 answerde CaFMPQUW, answerid D, ansuerd E, answerde G, answerede L;
    nold E, wolde not I, noolde Ma; sey E, sey þis þing I; fader FLU
77 moder HaLU, my modir X; mowe AcIKMaX, now DEGHaNQSW,
    mouwe F, mowʒ R; schewe it I; þe ER
78 þerfore BCaEGIKMaNQRWX; seuen CaELMP; dais E; feste CaEFILM-
    OUW, feest DHaKQR
79 at (1°): upon I; at the laste: at þe last D, atte last E, and at þe laste I;
    expowne B, expowned D, expounde E, expownyde GHaQRS, tolde it to
    hir clerly I; 79—80 he expownede in the seuenthe dai: in þe seuenþe day he
    tolde etc. I
80 seueþe B, seuent E; when E, whan LP
81 sche: he Ha¹; disseseful D, dissest-ful E, diseeseful GKQX, disseful Ha,
    diseesful I, deseseful L, diseful Ma; anon EHaP

345

18 citeseyns. And thei seiden to him the
   seuenthe day before the sunne goynge
   doun, What is swetter than hony, and
   what is stronger than a lyoun? The
   which seide to hem, If ȝe hadden not   85
   er(r)yd in my she calf, ȝe shulden not
19 haue foundun my proposicioun. And so
   the spyryt of the Lord felle into hym;
   and he wente doun to Aschalonem, and
   he smoot there thretti men, of whom the   90
   takun clothis he ȝaf to hem that the
   redilis soileden; and wroot[h] wel myche
   he stiede vp into the hows of his fader.

81 cyteeseyns *BF*, citeseynus *C*, citeseynes *EX*, citeȝeynes *Lo*; seydyn *E*
82 seuenþ *BFH*; day: om. *FWo*; byfore *BFHLoWo*, befor *C*, beforn *E*, bifor
    X; sonne *Lo*; gooyng *BF*, going *CEX*
83 swettere *CEX*; þann *B*, þanne *Lo*
84 strenger *B*, strengere *CEX*; a: þe *CE*; leoun *CX*
85 whiche *BCEHLoX*; þem *CLoX*; ȝif *BFHWo*, ȝife *Lo*; ȝee *CELoX*; had
    BFLoWo, haddyn *E*, hadde *H*
86 eride *Lo*, ered *X*; calfe *Lo*; ȝee *CELoX*; schuld *BWo*, shulde *CFH*, schuldyn
    E
87 ha *C*, han *EX*; founden *BFHLo*, founde *CX*, fowndyn *E*
88 spirite *BLo*, spiriȝt *H*, sperit *X*; fell *BFH*, fel *CEWoX*
89 he: om. *Lo*; went *BFWo*; to: into *Wo*
90 smot *CEHX*, smote *LoWo*; þer *Wo*; þritty *BFHLoWoX*; whome *BF*; the:
    om. *Lo²*
91 taken *BCFHLoWoX*, takyn *E*; cloþes *CELo*; ȝaue *BFHWo*, ȝafe *Lo*;
    þem *CELoX*
92 redils *BF*, redelis *CELo*, redels *H*, ridels *Wo*, redeles *X*; soiledyn *E*; wroth
    BCEHWoX, wroþe *Lo*; ful *CX*, wol *E*; mych *F*
93 steyȝid *BFWo*, steȝede *CEX*, styȝid *H*, steiȝede *Lo*; houȝs *H*, house *Lo*;
    fadir *BEH*, fadre *Lo*

18 Et illi dixerunt ei die septimo ante solis occubit-
   um: Quid dulcius melle, et quid fortius leone? Qui
   ait ad eos: Si non arassetis in vitula mea, non invenissetis propositionem meam.
19 Irruit itaque in eum spiritus Domini, descenditque
   Ascalonem, et percussit ibi triginta viros, quorum
   ablatas vestes dedit his, qui problema solverant.

18 sche telde to hir citeseyns. And thei
seiden to hym in the seuenthe dai bifor
the goyng doun of the sunne, What is
swettere than hony, and what is strengere 85
than a lioun? And he seide to hem, If
ȝe hadden not erid in my cow calf, that is
my wijf, ȝe hadden not founde my pro-
19 posicioun. Therfor the spirit of the Lord
felde in to hym; and he ȝede doun to 90
Ascalon, and killyde there thretti men,
whose clothis he took awey, and he ȝaf
to hem that soiliden the probleme; and
he was ful wrooth, and stiede in to the

82 teelde BGNX, teeld D, told E, tolde it I, tolde KLPR; her BCaELMRW,
hire DK, here F; citesens D, citeȝains E, cyteseynis GQ, citeȝeynes R
83 saiden E; hym: Sampson I; seueþe BE; bifore BCaDEGHaIKMaNOQRWX
84 goinge CaDGLMPQRUW; doune E; sonne EK
85 swetere C, swetter DEFHaMNORX; strongere AcCGKMMaNQU,
stronger BCaDFHaOX, stronghar E, strenger IR
86 lion E; he: sampson I; seid E
87 ȝee U; haden E, had I; erid: herd it E, errid GR, erride Ha, eried 'or
bisied ȝou' I; 87—88 cowe calff or wijf I
88 wif EFGHaLPQU; ȝee U; had EI, haddin P, hadde U; founden DIL,
found E; proposicion K
89 þerfore BCaGIKMaQRWX; spiritt K
90 fel CaEFLMPW, filde D, felle I; hym: sampson I; to: into GK²MaN
91 killid D, killed E, killede FKLP, kilde U; þer E; þritti AcCaGIMNWX,
thirty E; men: men 'of goddis enmyes' I
92 whos AcDFGHaIKLMaPQRX, wos E; cloþes EFK; tok E, toke IR;
away Ha; he: om. CaDGHaIKMNO²QSX; ȝaue IR
93 soileden CCaDFKLMNPUW, soylede E, assoiliden I; the probleme: his
resoun I
94 he: sampson E; wroþ EHaILNPQUX, wroiþ K; stied DE, steiede F,
stiede up I, stiȝede MaNR; in to: vn to S; 94—95 the hows of his fadir:
his fadris hous I

20 Forsothe the wijf of hym took an hous-
 boond, oon of hir freendis and wowers.   95

15. 1 Aftir a litil forsothe of tyme, whanne
 the dais of whete ripynge stooden yn,
 cam Sampson wilnynge to se his wijf,
 and he brouȝte to hir a kide of the she
 geet; and whanne he wold goo into the   5
 bedde of hir, as he was wont, the fadir

94 Forsothe the wijf: þe w. f. *cet.*; wyfe *BLo*, wif *CEFHWoX*; toke *BFHLoWo*,
    toc *CX*; an: a *Lo*; husboond *B*, husbonde *CEWoX*, housbonde *F*,
    houȝsbonde *H*, housebonde *Lo*
95 one *H*, oone *Lo*, oen *X*; hyre *BFLo*, his *CE²*; frendis *BEH*, frendus *CX*,
    frendes *LoWo*; wowerus *C*, woweris *ELo*, woweres *X*

15. 1 After *BCFHWo*; lytyll *BF*, lytel *Wo*; Aftir a litil forsothe: A. f. a l. *CX*;
       whenn *BH*, when *E*, whann *F*, whan *CLoWoX*
    2 daȝes *C*, dayes *FHLoWo*, daȝis *X*; repynge *BFHLoWo*, reping *CEX*;
       stoden *CLoWoX*, stoodyn *E*; inne *Lo*
    3 coom *BF*, come *LoWo*; willende *CX*, willynge *EH*; see *BHLo*, seen *CEX*;
       wyf *BCEFH*, wife *LoWoX*
    4 brouȝt *BFHWo*, broȝte *CEX*; hyre *BEFLo*; kyd *BFHWo*
    5 geyt *BFWo*, get *C*, gett *E*, geyte *Lo*, got *X*; whenn *BH*, whan *CLoWoX*,
       whann *F*; wolde *CEFHLoWoX*; goon *BFHLo*, go *C*, gon *EWoX*
    6 bed *CEWoX*; hyre *BFLo*; fader *CFWoX*, fadre *Lo*

20 Iratusque nimis ascendit in domum patris sui.
 Uxor autem eius accepit maritum unum de amicis eius
 et pronubis.

15. 1 Post aliquant/ul/um autem temporis, cum dies tritic-
 eae messis instarent, venit Samson, invisere volens
 uxorem suam, et attulit ei haedum de capris. Cumque
 cubiculum eius solito vellet intrare, prohibuit eum
 pater illius, dicens:

348

20 hows of his fadir. Forsothe his wijf   95
took an hosebonde, oon of the frendis
and keperis of hir.

15. 1 Forsothe aftir sum del of tyme, whanne
the daies of wheete heruest nei ȝiden, Sampson cam, and wolde visite his wijf, and
he brou ȝte to hir a kide of geet; and
when he wolde entre in to hir bed bi cus-   5
tom, the fadir of hir forbeed hym, and

95 fader CaFLMU; forsoþ X, and I; wif EFGHaLPU
96 tok E, tooke Ha, toke IR; husbonde BIMaQ, husbond DR, hosbonde ELP,
housbonde G; one E, on U; the: his DGHaI; freendis AcMaR, frendes EF,
frendes of hir O
97 and: om. Ma; kepers CEKLR, pryue keperis Ca, pryuy kepers DHa,
keperes F, preuye keperis G, priuey kepers I, pryueie kepers K, priue
kepers M, priui kepers Ma, pryuy keperis NS, priuei keperis O, preuy
keperis Q, pryuy kepers X; k. of hir: of hir p. k. DGHaINQSX, of hire
p. k. K; of hir: of here F, of her MW, om. O

15. 1 Forsothe: But I, forsoþ X; after EFU; deel BCaKMMaOSWX; aftir sum
del of tyme: a litil tyme aftir I; whan EGLP
2 dais E; whete CaDEFHaILMPRUW; herueste ER, haruest X; nei ȝeden
BEGHaIKLMaNOPQRUX, nei ȝȝeden CaFMW, ny ȝeden D
3 com E, came IR; wif EFGHaLPQU
4 brou ȝt D, bro ȝte O; her CaM, here F, hire KL; kid Ha; gete DR, geytt K;
k. of g.: geet kide I
5 whanne AcBCCaDFIKMMaNOQRSUWX, whan EGHaLP; wold E; her
CaMW, here F, hire K; custum BCaDGHaMMaOQWX; entre etc.: bi c.
entre in to hir bed I
6 fader EFLU; her CaMW, here F, hire KL; the f. of hir: hir fadir I; forbede
CDHaR, forbed EGQ, forbeede I

2 of hir defendide hym, seiynge, I wende
that thou haddist hatid hyr, and therfor
I took hir to thi freend; but she hath
a sister, that is ȝonger and feyrer than   10
3 she, be she to thee for hir a wijf. To
whom Sampson answerde, Fro this day
blame shal not be in me aȝens the Philistiens, Y shal doo to ȝou [forsothe] yuels.
4 And he ȝede, and took thre hundryd   15
foxys, and the taylis of hem he ioynede
to the taylis, and broondis he boond in

7 hyre *BFLo*; defendede *C*; seiende *CX*; wenede *Lo*
8 haddest *CLoX*; hatide *HLo*; hyre *BFLo*; þerfore *BCEFHWoX*, þere-fore *Lo*
9 toke *BFHLoWo*, toc *CX*; hyre *BFLo*; freende *BF*, frend *CHX*, frende *LoWo*;
    bot *B*, bute *F*
10 sistyr *E*, sustre *Lo*; ȝungere *CX*, ȝongere *E*; fairere *CEX*, fayrer *FLoWo*;
    þann *B*, þanne *Lo*
11 þe *Wo*; hyre *BFLo*; wyfe *BLo*, wif *CEFHWoX*
12 whome *BF*; answeride *Lo*, answered *Wo*
13 ben *E*; aȝeynst *BFWo*, aȝen *CLoX*, aȝenst *EH*
14 do *CHWoX*, don *ELo*; to ȝou forsothe: f. to ȝ. *CELo*[2]; euelis *C*, euylis *E*,
    yuelis *Lo*, euels *Wo*, eueles *X*
15 ȝide *CX*; toke *BFHLoWo*, toc *X*; hundreþ *BF*, hundrede *Lo*
16 foxes *BEFLoWoX*; tailes *CELoWoX*; þem *CLo*; ioyned *BFHWo*
17 tailes *CELoWoX*; brondis *CEHX*, brondes *LoWo*; bond *CEX*, bonde *LoWo*

2 Putavi, quod odisses eam, et ideo tradidi illam
amico tuo; sed habet sororem, quae iunior et pulch-
rior illa est, sit tibi pro ea uxor.
3 Cui Samson respondit: Ab hac die non erit culpa in
me contra Philisteos; faciam enim vobis mala.
4 Perrexitque et cepit trecentas vulpes, caudasque
earum iunxit ad caudas, et faces ligavit in medio;

2 seide, Y gesside that thou haddist hatid
hir, and therfor Y ȝaf hir to thi freend;
but sche hath a sistir, which is ȝongere
and fairere than sche, be sche wijf to   10
3 thee for hir. To whom Sampson an-
sweride, Fro this day no blame schal be
in me aȝens Filistees, for Y schal do yuels
4 to ȝou. And he ȝede, and took thre hun-
drid foxis, and ioynede the tailis of hem   15
to tailis, and boond brondis in the

7 seid E; gessid DW, ghessid E, gisside O, gessede PU; haddest FHaL;
   hated E, hatide Ha
8 hir (1°): her CaEMW, here F, hire KL; þerfore BCaFGIKLMaNQRW;
   ȝaue IR; hir (2°): her CaMW, here F, hir wijf I, hire K; frend AcBCCa-
   FGHaIKLNOPSUX, frende E
9 haþe E; sister CFKNU, sustir CaP, suster EL; wiche K, þat I; ȝonger
   DEHaLMRX, ȝunger I
10 fairer CaDEFHaIMNRWX; schee S; wif EFGHaLPQU; 10−11 wijf to
   thee: þi wijf I
11 þe EF; her CaMW, here F, hire K; answerde CaEFGMPQUW, answerid
   D, answerede L
12 from K; day: day forþ I; blam E; ben S
13 in: to HaNQ; aȝenus AcCNO, aȝenes EP; yuelis AcBCaDIMMaUW,
   euelis EPQS, yueles F, euylis G, euels L
14 toke EHaIR; vndred E, hundred Ha, hunderd P
15 foxes FI; ioyned DE, ioynide HaQR, he ioynede togidre I; tailes
   CEFHaIKR; the t. of hem: her tailis I
16 tayles BFIK, tails C; bond CaEGLPQU, bonde HaR, he bonde I; brondes
   CaFHa, firy br. I, broondis MaX; the: om. I

5 the myddil, the whiche teendynge with
fier he lafte, that* hidir and thidir thei
runnen; the whiche anoon wenten into   20
the cornys of the Philistiens, the whiche
sette a-fier, and the fruytis now brouȝt
to gidre, and the ȝit stoondynge in the
stobil, ben brent, in so mych that vynes
6 and olyues the flawm wastide. And the   25
Philistiens seiden, Who hath doon this
thing? To whom it is seide, Sampson,
the sone in lawe of Thannath, for he
took his wijf, and ȝaf to another, thes
thingis he hath wrouȝt. And the Phi-   30
listiens stiden vp and brenten as wel the

18 the: om. *C*; mydyl *BF*, myddes *C*, myddel *EWoX*, mydel *Lo*; which *FWo*;
   teendende *CX*, tendynge *HLoWo*
19 fijr *CE*, fyre *Lo*, fuyre *Wo*, fyr *X*; laft *BFH*, lefte *X*; þat *CELo*, and *cet*;
   heþer *BF*, hider *CEHWoX*, hidre *Lo*; þider *BCHWoX*, þeder *E*, þidre *FLo*
20 runnyn *E*, ronnen *LoWo*; which *FWo*; anon *BWo*, anoen *X*; wentyn *E*
21 cornes *CLoX*; which *BFWo*
22 sett *BCEFHWo*, set *X*; a-fijre *C*, afire *ELoX*, afuyre *Wo*; frutus *C*, fruytes
   Lo, frutes *X*; nowe *Lo*; broȝt *CEX*, brouȝte *Lo*
23 togidere *CEX*, to gyder *HWo*; ȝitt *BFH*; the ȝit: ȝ. þe *Lo*; stondynge
   BHLoWo, stondende *CX*, standynge *E*
24 stobul *Lo*; myche *BCEHLoX*; vynys *BFHWo*
25 olyuys *BFHWo*; flawme *cet.*; wastede *CLoX*, wastid *Wo*
26 seidyn *E*; has *Lo*; do *CX*, don *EWo*, done *H*
27 þinge *BLoWo*; whome *BF*; seid *CEFX*
29 toke *BFHLoWo*, toc *CX*; wyf *BCEFHWoX*, wyfe *Lo*; ȝafe *Lo*, ȝaue *Wo*;
   an ooþer *E*; þese *CEX*
30 þinges *BLoWo*, thingus *CX*; wroȝt *CEX*, wrouȝte *Lo*
31 steyȝeden *BFLo*, steȝeden *CX*, styȝeden *H*, steyȝiden *Wo*; brendyn *E*;
   wele *BF*

5 quas igne succendens, dimisit, ut huc illucque discurrerent. Quae statim perrexerunt in segetes Philistinorum. Quibus succensis, et comportatae iam
fruges et adhuc stantes in stipula, concrematae
sunt, in tantum ut vineas quoque et oliveta flamma
consumeret.
6 Dixeruntque Philistiim: Quis fecit hanc rem? Quibus
dictum est: Samson gener Thannathei, quia tulit
uxorem eius, et alteri tradidit, haec operatus est.
Ascenderuntque Philistiim, et combusserunt tam
mulierem quam patrem eius.

5 myddis, whiche he kyndlide with fier,
and leet *hem*, that thei schulden renne
aboute hidur and thidur; whiche ȝeden
anoon in to the cornes of Filisteis, bi   20
whiche kyndlid, bothe cornes borun now
to gidere and ȝit stondynge in the stobil,
weren brent in so myche that the flawme
wastide vyneris, and places of olyue

6 trees. And Filisteis seiden, Who dide   25
this thing? To whiche it was seid, Samp-
son, hosebonde of the douȝtir of Thannathei, for he took awey Sampsones
wijf, and ȝaf to another man, wrouȝte
this thing. And Filisteis stieden, and   30
brenten bothe the womman and hir fadir.

17 myddes F, myddil *of þe tailes* I; which E, þe whiche *brondis* I, wiche K;
   kyndli[de] Ac, kyndelide BHaIKMa, kyndelid D, kyndeled E, kyndlede
   GP, kindelede L, kyndlid R; fijr CaIMW, fire D, fyr EFLP
18 lete EHa, made I; *hem*: þe foxes I, om. cet.; scholden CaFMW, shuld E;
   that thei schulden: to I; ren E
19 about E, abouȝte L, aboue N; hidir DGMaPQX, hider FLU, hidere IK,
   hiþir R; þidir DGMaQRX, þider EFL, þidre I, þidere K, þedir PU;
   whiche AAcBCFGLMMaNOUX, þe whiche I, wiche K, which cet.;
   ȝeden: runnen I, ȝeoden K
20 onon E, anon HaP; cornis GMaQ, corne Ha, corn I; þe philistees I; bi:
   wiþ I
21 which E, þe whiche *brondis* I, wiche K; kyndelid BDFIK, kindeling E,
   kindelide Ma, kyndlide N; bothe: boþe þe cet.; cornis EGMaQ, corne Ha;
   born CCaDFKLMMaNPWX, brent E, borne R; now: om. E; b. now: þat
   weren now b. I; 21−22 now to gidere: togidere now M
22 to gidre DIR, to gyders E; ȝut E, þat weren ȝitt I, riȝt L, ȝitt Ma;
   stubbil CaDFMW, stobul ELP, stuble I, stobbile K, stoble R, stubil X
23 brente KR; moche CaEFNUX, mich R
24 waastid D, wasted E, waastide MaX, wastede P; vyners DHaKLMPRUX,
   vineres E, vyneners G, her vyners I; placis DGKMaNPQSX, þe placis I;
   of her olyue I
25 þe philistees I; saiden E; dud E
26 which AcDELR, whom I, wiche K; seide DHaRU, saide E
27 husbonde BLMaPQR, þe hosebonde C¹, husbond D, hosbond E, housbonde
   G, þe husbonde I; douȝter BCEFKMSU; the d. of Th.: þe thannathei/s/
   douȝtir HaI
28 tok E, toke IR; away Ha, aweie R; sampsones: his I
29 wif EFGHaLPQU, om. S; ȝaue hir I, ȝaue R; an oþere Ac, anoþir
   GMaOSX; wrouȝt DE, om. I, wrouȝte U
30 this thing: om. I; þe philistees I; steieden FM, stieden up I, stiȝeden MaNR
31 brend E; booþ R; wumman CaMW, woman E; her CaMW, here F, hire
   K; fader EFL

7 womman as hir fader. To whom seith
Sampson, Al be it that thes thingis ȝe
han doon, neuerthelater ȝit of ȝou I shal
aske a veniaunce, and thanne I shal   35
8 reste. And he smoot hem with a greet
veniaunce, so that astonyinge thei putten
on the calf of the leg to the hipe; and
he dessendynge dwellide in the spelunk
9 of the stoon of Ethan. Than Philistiens   40
stiynge vp into the loond of Juda setten
tentis in the place, the which afterward
is clepid Lethi, that is, a cheek boon,

---

32 hyre *BEFLo*; fadir *BEH*, fadre *Wo*; whome *BF*
33 þese *CEHX*; þinges *BLo*, thingus *CX*; ȝee *CELoX*
34 do *CX*, don *EWo*, done *H*, doone *Lo*; nerþelatere *CX*, neuer þe latere *E*, neuere þe later *HLo*; ȝitt *BF*
35 asken *CEHX*; a: om. *C*; vengeaunce *E*; þann *B*, þan *Wo*
36 resten *BFHLoWoX*, restyn *E*; smote *BFLoWo*, smot *CEX*; þem *CLoX*; grete *BFHLoWo*, gret *CX*, grett *E*
37 vengeance *E*, vengeaunce *Lo*; astoneyinge *BFHWo*, astoneande *C*, astoneynge *E*, a-stonnynge *Lo*, astoneiende *X*; puttyn *E*
38 calfe *Lo*; of: on *Lo*; legg *BFHLo*, legge *Wo*; hypp *BFWo*, hepe *E*, hyppe *HLo*
39 descendende *CX*; dwellid *BFHWo*, dwelte *CX*; spelonke *BFHLo*, spelunke *CEWoX*
40 ston *CEWoX*; þann *BF*, þanne *CEHLo*, þane *X*
41 steyinge *BFWo*, steȝende *CX*, steȝynge *E*, styȝinge *H*, steiȝinge *Lo*; lond *CWoX*, land *E*, londe *Lo*; settyn *E*, setteden *Lo*
42 tentus *C*, tentes *X*; the which: þe whiche *BEHLo*, þat *CX*; aftyrward *E*, aftirwarde *Lo*
43 clepid: callid *Lo*; cheeke *BFHLo*, cheke *CEWoX*; bon *CEX*, bone *Lo*

7 Quibus ait Samson: Licet haec feceritis, tamen adhuc ex vobis expetam ultionem, et tunc quiescam.
8 Percussitque eos ingenti plaga, ita ut stupentes
suram femori imponerent. Et descendens habitavit in
spelunca petrae Ethan.
9 Igitur ascendentes Philistiim in terram Iuda castrametati sunt in loco, qui postea vocatus est Lethi,
id est maxilla, ubi eorum /ef/fusus est exercitus.

7 To whiche Sampson seide, Thouȝ ȝe han
  do this, netheles ȝit Y schal axe veniaunce of ȝou, and than Y schal reste.

8 And he smoot hem with greet wounde,   35
  so that thei wondriden, and puttiden the
  hyndrere part of the hipe on the thiȝ;
  and he ȝede doun, and dwellide in the

9 denne of the stoon of Ethan. Therfor
  Filisteis stieden in to the lond of Juda,   40
  and settiden tentis in the place, that was
  clepid aftirward Lethi, that is, a cheke,
  where the oost of hem was spred abrood.

32 which DEL, þe whiche *philistees* I, wiche K; saide E; þauȝ E; ȝee U;
     haue R
33 don DS; ȝis E, þis þing HaIK¹; naþeles B; ȝitt Ma; axe & *take* I;
     vengeaunce K
34 of: on X; than AEHa, þanne cet.; rest R, reeste S
35 he: Sampson I; smote EHaIR, smot U; hem: þe philistees I; grete DEHaR,
     a greet I, gret P; wounde: veniaunce I
36 þai E; wundreden CaFMW, wondreden ELP; putteden CaLMP, putted
     EF, puttide U
37 hynderer D, hynder EX, hindere KMa, hinderere LP, hyndrer M, hyndre
     R; parte R; hip E; þeiȝ CaFMW, þie E, þiȝe I; 36—37 & þei smoten þe
     þiȝe wiþ þe calf of þe leg *so faste þei fledden* I
38 he: Sampson I; dwellid D, dwelled E, dwellede LP, dwelde U; in the:
     om. G
39 den CaEFKLMPW, om. G; ston EISU; þerfore BCaGKMaNQRWX,
     þanne I
40 þe philistees I; stied E, steieden F, stieden up I, stiȝeden MaNR; to: om.
     W; londe I
41 setteden CaELMPW, setten F, þei settiden I; tentes FHa
42 clepide R; afterwarde E, afterward LU
43 ost E; the o. of hem: her oost I; spred: set EL, sprad K, spreed O, sett P,
     spredde R; abrode DHa, aboute E

10 where the oost of hem is hellid. And
   thei of the lynage of Juda seiden to hem,   45
   Whi han ȝe stied vp aȝens vs? The
   whiche answerden, That we bynden
   Sampson we ben comen, and we ȝeelden
   to hym that in vs he hath wrouȝt.
11 Thanne thre thousand of men of Juda   50
   dessendiden to the den of the flynt of
   Ethan; and thei seiden to Sampson, Wost
   thou not, that [the] Philistiens comaunden
   to vs? Whi this thing woldist thou doo?
   To whom he seith, As thei diden to me,   55

44 wher *C*; hoost *BFH*, ost *C*, host *EX*; þem *CLo*; held *CELoX*
45 seydyn *E*; þem *CLoX*
46 ȝee *CELoX*; steyȝid *BFWo*, steȝid *CEX*, stiȝid *H*, steiȝede *Lo*; aȝeynst
   BFWo, aȝen *CX*, aȝenst *E*, a-ȝeynes *Lo*
47 which *Wo*; answerdyn *E*, answereden *Lo*; wee *CEX*; binde *CX*, byndyn *E*
48 wee (1°) *CEX*; been *Lo*; commen *BF*, come *CX*, comyn *E*; wee (2°) *CX*;
   ȝelden *BFHLoWo*, ȝeelde *CX*
49 wroȝt *CEX*, wrouȝte *Lo*
50 þann *BF*, þan *Wo*; þree *B*; þousande *BFLo*, thousend *CX*
51 descendeden *CLo*, descendidyn *E*; denn *BFHWo*, denne *Lo*; flynte *Lo*
52 seidyn *E*; woste *Lo*
53 comawndyn *E*, comaundiden *H*, commaunden *Lo*, comaundeþ *Wo*
54 þinge *BWo*; woldest *CEWo*, woste *Lo*; do *CWoX*, don *E*
55 whome *BF*; seys *Lo*; didyn *E*

10 Dixeruntque ad eos /viri/ de tribu Iuda: Cur ascend-
   istis adversum nos? Qui responderunt: Ut ligemus
   Samson venimus, et reddamus ei quae in nos operatus
   est.
11 Descenderunt ergo tria millia virorum de Iuda ad
   specum silicis Ethan; dixeruntque ad Samson: Nescis,
   quod Philistiim imperent nobis? quare hoc facere
   voluisti? Quibus ille ait: Sicut fecerunt mihi,
   feci eis.

10 And men of the lynage of Juda seiden to
hem, Whi stieden ȝe aȝens vs? Whiche 45
answeriden, We comen that we bynde
Sampson, and ȝelde to hym tho thingis

11 whiche he w[r]ouȝte in vs. Therfor thre
thousynde of men of Juda ȝeden doun to
the denne of the flynt of Ethan; and thei 50
seiden to Sampson, Woost thou not, that
Filisteis comaunden to vs? Why woldist
thou do this thing? To whiche he seide,

44 said E
45 stieden ȝe: stied ȝe E, steieden ȝe F, stiȝeden ȝe HaMaNR, han ȝe stied
   up I, stieden ȝee U; aȝenus AcCNO; which ES, þe whiche I, wiche K
46 answerden CaDEFGMPQUW, answereden L, answeden O; com E, camen
   I; abidden E, bynden GLPU
47 ȝeelde CaRW, ȝilde D; þoo R; þinges FHa
48 which DE, þe whiche I, wiche K; wroȝte C, wrouȝt DE, haþ wrouȝt I,
   brouȝte L, wroute U; in: aȝens I; þerfore BCaGIKMaNQRWX
49 þousynd CaFIMW, þousand DEHaMaNQRX, þousend GLP, þousande K;
   of (1°): om. B
50 den CaEFIKLMPW; the (2°): om. Ha; flinte K; of (2°): om. Ac
51 sayd E; wost þou CFGHaKLPQU, wostou E, wotiste þou R
52 comaunden to us 'þat is þei han lordschip on u[s]' I; wi E; woldest þou
   CFHaLN, woldestou E
53 doo K; þing to hem I; wiche EK, whom I; saide E

12 Y dide to hem. To bynden thee, thei
seyn, we ben comen, and to take into the
hoondis of Philistiens. To whom answerde Sampson, Swerith, and bihotith

13 to me, that ȝe shulen not slee me. And
thei seiden, We shulen not slee thee,
but bounden we shulen ȝyue. And thei
bounden hym with two newe coordis,
and token hym fro the stoon of Ethan.

56 þem *CELoX*; binde *C*, byndyn *E*; þe *Wo*
57 seyen *Lo*; wee *CEX*; commen *BFWo*, come *CX*, comyn *E*; taken *BEFHLoWo*
58 hondus *CX*, handis *C*, hondes *LoWo*; whome *BF*; answerd *BWo*, answeride *Lo*
59 swereþ *CE*, sweris *Lo*, swerþ *X*; behoteþ *CE*, by-hetis *Lo*, bihoteþ *X*
60 ȝee *CELoX*; sshuln *BEFWo*, shul *CX*, schullen *H*, schulle *Lo*; slen *BEFHWo*, sle *CX*, sclee *Lo*
61 seidyn *E*; wee *CEX*; schuln *BEFWo*, shul *CLoX*; slen *BEFHWoX*, sle *C*, scle *Lo*
62 bot *B*, bute *F*; bounde *CX*, bowndyn *E*; wee *CEX*; schuln *BEFWo*, shul *CX*, schullen *H*, sshulle *Lo*; ȝeuen *BFHWo*, ȝifyn *E*, ȝyuen *Lo*
63 bowndyn *E*, bounde *X*; twey *Wo*; cordus *C*, cordis *EH*, coordes *Lo*, cordes *X*
64 tookyn *E*; stone *BH*, ston *CEWoX*

12 Ligare, inquiunt, te venimus, et tradere in manus
Philistinorum. Quibus respondit Samson: Iurate et
spondete mihi, quod non occidatis me.

13 Dixeruntque: Non te occidemus, sed vinctum trademus.
Ligaveruntque eum duobus novis funibus, et tulerunt
/eum/ de petra Ethan.

12 As thei diden to me, Y dide to hem. Thei
    seien, We comen to bynde thee, and to   55
    bitake *thee* in to the hondis of Filisteis.
    To whiche Sampson answeride, Swere ӡe,
    and biheete ӡe to me, that ӡe sle not me.
13 And thei seiden, We schulen not sle thee,
    but we schulen bitake *thee* boundun.   60
    And thei bounden him with twei newe
    cordis, and token fro the stoon of E-

54 deden F, dedin P; so I I; did E
55 seyn CaHaKMQX, seid E, seiden N; come EG; bind E; þe EF; to: om. G
56 bitak E, take I; *thee* AIK, om. cet.; to: om. E; hondes EF; h. of F.:
    philistees hondis I
57 which E, whom I, wiche K; answerde CaFGMPQUW, answerd DE,
    answerede L; ӡee OSU
58 bihete AcCCaDFHaKMMaQRW, bihote ELPU, bihoteþ I; ӡe (1°): ӡee
    GU; ӡe (2°): ӡee U; slee CaFKPQSU, sleen G; not me: me not I
59 seid E; schullen CaFMW, shul EILP; slee CaFGKPQSU; þe EFR
60 bot E; schullen CaFMW, schuln D, shul EILP; þe EF; bounden
    CaDEFGHaKLMMaPRSUW, b. *to hem* I
61 boundun BC, boonden X; tweye BCaFKMMaRW, two GIQ, tweine S;
    new EHa
62 coordis AcBCaDHaKLMMaPWX, cordes F; token him AcBCCaDFHa-
    LMMaQRSUW, tok him E, tooken him GKNOPX, þei tooken him I;
    from K; ston EILU

14 The which whanne was comen to the   65
place of the cheek boon, and Philistiens
criynge out weren aȝen comen to hym,
the spiryt of the Lord felle into him, and
as ben wont at the smelle of fier trees to
be waastid, so and the boondis, with the   70
whiche he was bounden, ben scaterid and
15 loosid. And takynge a foundun cheek
boon, that is, the cheeklap of an asse,
that lay, he slewȝ with it a thousand
16 men; and seith, In the cheek boon of   75
an asse, that is, in the iow of the colt
of assis, I haue doon hem awey, and

65 whiche *BCEHLoX*; whenn *BH*, whan *CLoWoX*, whann *F*; commen *BFWo*,
come *CX*, comyn *E*
66 the: om. *Lo*; cheke *CELoX*, chek *Wo*; bon *BCEHWoX*, boone *Lo*; and:
om. *X*
67 criende *CX*, crying *F*; oute *BLo*, ouȝte *H*; weryn *E*, om. *H*; aȝeyn *BFHWo*,
aȝeen *E*, a-ȝeyne *Lo*; commen *BFWo*, come *CX*, comyn *E*
68 spirite *BHLo*, sperit *X*; fell *BF*, fel *CEHWoX*
69 wonte *Lo*; smell *BFWo*, smel *CEHX*, hete *Lo* (on eras.); fijr *CE*, fire *Lo*,
fuyre *Wo*
70 ben *BEFHLoWoX*; wastid *CEFHWoX*, wastede *Lo*; bondis *BCEX*, bondes
Lo
71 which *FWo*; bounde *CFWo*, bowndyn *E*; scatered *BF*, scatered *CEHWoX*,
scateride *Lo*
72 lowsed *BFH*, lowsede *Lo*, lousid *Wo*, losid *X*; takende *CX*; founden
BCFHLoWoX, fowndyn *E*; cheke *CLoX*, cheeke *E*, chek *Wo*
73 bon *CEWoX*, boone *Lo*; the: in the *H*; chec *CE*, cheke *LoX*; lappe
BCEFHWoX, boon *Lo* (on eras., marg. 'jouwe')
74 sloȝ *CX*, slowȝ *EWo*, slewe *H*, slowȝe *Lo*; thousend *CX*, þousande *Lo*
75 seys *Lo*; cheke *CLoX*, cheeke *E*; bon *CEWoX*, bone *Lo*
76 iouwe *CX*, jowe *ELo*; coolte *Lo*
77 asses *LoX*; haþe *E*; done *BH*, do *CX*, don *EWo*; þem *CLoX*; aweye *BH*

14 Qui cum venisse/n/t ad locum maxillae, et Philistiim
vociferantes occurrissent ei, irruit spiritus Domini
in eum, et sicut solent ad odorem ignis ligna con-
sumi, ita et vincula, quibus ligatus erat, dissipata
sunt et soluta.

14 than. And whanne thei hadden come to
the place of cheke, and Filisteis criynge hadden runne to hym, the spirit of   65
the Lord felde in to hym, and as stikis
ben wont to be wastid at the odour of
fier, so and the bondis, with whiche he
was boundun, weren scaterid and vn-
15 boundun. And he took a cheke found-   70
un, that is, the lowere cheke boon of an
asse, that lay, and he killyde with it
16 a thousinde men; and seide, With the
cheke of an asse, that is, with the lowere
cheke of a colt of femal assis, Y dide   75
hem awey, and Y killide a thousynde

63 when E, whan GLP; þai E; haddin EP; com E
64 of: *þat is clepid* I; þe philistees I; criynge: comynge CaDGHaMNQX,
    criyng E, criynge hi ʒe I
65 hadde AcBDLPSU, had E; rune D, ronne R; spiritt K
66 fel CaEFLMPW, filde D, felle I; stickis BCCaDEGHaIKLMMaNOP-
    QRWX, stickes F
67 wond L, wonte R; be: ben E; wasted EF, wastide K, waastid MaOX;
    odoure DE, hoot tastyng I
68 fijr CaIMWX, fire D, fyr EFLP; and: om. EN; boondis AcBCDGLMMa-
    OPRWX, bondes CaF; which E, wiche K; he: sampson I
69 bounden CaDFGKMMaRW, bound E, bonden Ha, bounde LP; scatered
    LU, scatrid R; vnbounden CaDFGHaKMMaRW, vnbound E, lowsid I,
    vnbounde LP
70 tok E, toke IR, tooke Ha; chek E, cheek Ac, cheeke CG; founden
    CaDEFGHaKLMMaPRW; & whanne he had foundun a cheke I
71 lower BDHaLPRX, lawer E, neþer I; cheeke C; bon EHaILU; an: a E
72 þere lay I; and: om. I; killid D, killed E, killede FLP, toke it & killide I;
    with it: þerwiþ I
73 þousind CaIMW, þousand DEHaMaNQRX, þousend FGLP, þousande K;
    seid E, he seide I; wit E, whiþ S
74 chek E, cheeke G; with: om. O; lower DELMPRX, neþer I
75 chek E, cheeke G; colte ELP, coolt S; of (2°): om. E; female HaKORX,
    femele L, femel P, sche I; asse E, asses FR; did E, dede F, haue don I
76 hem awey: awey philistees I; killid D, killed E, haue killid þerwiþ I, killede
    LP; þousynd CaIMMaNW, þousand DEHaQRX, þousend FGL, þousande
    KS, þousende P

15 Inventamque maxillam, id est mandibulam asini, quae
iacebat, arripiens, interfecit in ea mille viros,
16 et ait: In maxilla asini, id est in mandibula pulli
asinarum, delevi eos, et percussi mille viros.

17 smyten a thousand men. And whanne
    thes wordis syngynge he hadde fulfillid,
    he threwe awey the iow fro the hoond;   80
    and he clepide the name of that place
    Ramathlei, that is to mene, the heuynge
18 vp of the cheek boon. And threstynge
    wel mych he cried to the Lord, and
    seith, Thou hast ȝeuen in the hoond of   85
    thi seruaunt this moost helthe and vic-
    torie; and loo! for threst I dye, and I
    shal falle into the hoondis of the vncir-

78 smytyn *E*; thousend *CX*, þousande *Lo*; whenn *B*, whan *CWoX*, whann *F*, whenne *H*
79 þese *BCEHX*; woordis *C*, woordes *E*, wordes *LoWo*, wrdus *X*; singende *CX*; had *BFLoWo*, fulfild *CEX*, fulfilled *Lo*
80 þrew *BCFH*, þrewȝ *E*, þreȝ *X*; aweye *BH*; jouwe *CX*, jowe *ELo*; hand *CE*, honde *LoWo*, hond *X*
81 clepid *BFHWo*, clepede *CX*, callid *Lo*
82 meenen *BFH*, menen *CLoWo*, meenyn *E*, meene *X*; heuyng *BCEX*
83 cheeke *BLo*, cheke *CEHX*, chek *Wo*; bon *CEWoX*, boone *Lo*; þristynge *BEFHLoWo*, þristende *C*, þrestende *X*
84 ful *CLoX*, wol *E*; myche *BCEHLoX*; cryed *BFHWo*; lorde *Lo*
85 seys *Lo*; haste *Lo*; ȝiuen *CLoWo*, ȝifyn *E*, ȝiue *X*; hond *CWoX*, hand *E*, hande *Lo*
86 seruaunte *Lo*; most *BFHWoX*, moste *CELo*; helþ *BFHWo*
87 lo *CEWoX*; þrist *BCEFHX*, þriste *Lo*, þirst *Wo*; dyȝe *Wo*
88 fallyn *E*, fall *F*; the: om. *Lo*; hondus *CX*, handis *E*, handes *Lo*, hondes *Wo*; vncircumcided *C*, vncircumcidide *Lo*, vncircumcisid *Wo*

17 Cumque haec canens verba complesset, proiecit mandi-
    bulam de manu, et vocavit nomen loci illius Ramath-
    le/h/i, quod interpretatur elevatio maxillae.
18 Sitiensque valde, clamavit ad Dominum, et ait: Tu
    dedisti in manu servi tui salutem hanc maximam at-
    que victoriam; et en siti morior, incidamque in
    manus incircumcisorum.

17 men. And whanne he songe these wordis,
and hadde fillid, he castide forth fro
the hond the lowere cheke; and he
clepide the name of that place Ramath   80
Lethi, which is interpretid, the reisyng
18 of a cheke. And he thristide greetly,
and criede to the Lord, and seide, Thou
hast ȝoue in the hond of thi seruaunt this
grettest helthe and victory; and lo! Y die   85
for thy[r]st, and Y schal falle in to the

77 when E, whan GHaLP; song AcBCaDEFGKLMMaNOPQSUWX, had
    hiȝe cried I; þes DE; wordes CaF
78 had E, om. I; filled EL, fully eendid hem I, fillide R; castid D, casted E,
    þrewe I, caste O, castede P; forþe E, om. GQ, awey I; from K
79 the (1°): is E, his I; lower DLPRX, lawer E, neþer I; chek E, cheeke G,
    cheke bon I; he: om. S
80 clepid D, cleped E, clepede F
81 whiche BGL, wiche K, þat I; interpretid: to say I; reisynge DGMaQUW,
    risyng Ha
82 a: om. L; chek E, cheeke G, cheke bon I; he: sampson I; þirstide
    AcBCCaIKMMaNOQU, þurstid D, þirsted E, þurstede F, þirstede LP,
    þurstide SWX; gretli AcILPSU, greteli EHa
83 cried DE, he criede I, cride W; þou lord I
84 ȝof E, ȝouen I, ȝofen K, ȝeue Ma; in: in to I; seruant E
85 grettiste AcBKMaOSU, gretteste CCaGMMaNQWX, grettist DIR;
    heelþe AcBIKMMaN, help W; victory ACE, victorie cet.; deie CaFMW,
    diȝe R
86 þurst DF, þrist HaU; Y schal: schal I DGHaIKNQX

19 cumcidid. And so the Lord opnede a
woong tooth in the cheek boon of the 90
asse, and watris wenten out of it, the
whiche drunkun he fedde the spiryt, and
strengthis took aʒen; and therfor is*
clepide the name of that place a Welle of
the inwardli clepynge fro the cheek boon 95
20 vnto this day that is nowe. And he
demyde Yrael in the dais of the Philistiens twenti ʒeer.

16. 1 He ʒede forsothe into Gazam, and there
he sawʒ a womman strompet, and wente

89 opned B, openede CELoX, opnyd F, opened H, openyd Wo
90 wonge BFHWo, wang CEX, wange Lo; toþ CX, toþe LoWo; in: of Wo;
cheeke BE, cheke CLoX, chek Wo; bon CEWoX, boone Lo
91 waters BH, watres Lo; wentyn E; oute BLo, ouʒte H
92 which Wo; dronken BFHLo, drunken CWoX, drunkyn E; spirite BFLo,
spiriʒte H
93 strenkthis E, strengþes Lo; toke BFHLoWo, toc CX; aʒeyn BFHWo,
aʒeen CEX, a-ʒeyne Lo; þerfore BCEFHWoX, þere-fore Lo; is: he A,
þis B
94 clepid BCEFHWoX, callid Lo; well BFH
95 inwardely Lo; clepende CX, callynge Lo; cheeke BE, cheke CHLoX; bon
CEWoX, boone Lo
96 now CEHWoX
97 demyd BFHWo, demede CX; daʒes CX, daies EFLoWo; the (2°): om. Lo
98 ʒere LoWo

16. 1 ʒide CX

19 Aperuit itaque Dominus molarem dentem in maxilla
asini, et egressae sunt ex eo aquae. Quibus haustis,
refocillavit spiritum, et vires recepit. Idcirco
vocatum est nomen loci illius, fons invocantis de
maxilla, usque in praesentem diem.
20 Iudicavitque Israel in diebus Philistiim viginti
annis.

16. 1 Abiit quoque in Gazam, et vidit ibi mulierem mere-
tricem, ingressusque est ad eam.

19 hondis of vncircumcidid men. Therfor the
Lord openyde a wang tooth in the cheke
boon of the asse, and watris ȝeden out
therof, bi whiche drunkun he refreischide   90
the spirit, and resseuede strengthis; therfor the name of that place was clepid the
Welle of the clepere of the cheke til in to
20 present dai. And he demyde Israel in
the daies of Filistiym twenti ȝeer.   95

16. 1 Also Sampson ȝede in to Gazam, and
he siȝ there a womman hoore, and he en-

---

87 hondes F, hoondis R; vncircumcisid E, vncircumcided L, vncircumcidide
W; þerfore BCaEGIKNQRUWX
88 openede BCaFKLMMaPX, opened DE, opnede I; wange HaKRX, woong
I; toþe E, toþ Q; cheek Ac, chek BE
89 bon EHaU, bone G; waters E, watres F; oute R
90 þeroff I, þere of R; which DEMaNR, wiche K; drunken BCaGIKLMPRW,
drink E, dronken FU, drinke Ma; bi wh. dr.: and whanne he hadde
drunken I; refreischid BD, refresshide CaFGLMPRSW, refressed E,
refreiȝsshede K
91 the: his I; spiritt K; resseyuede AcBCCaHaKLMMaNOPSWXU, resceyued
DE, resseiuyde G, receyuyde IRQ; þe strengþis D, strinȝt E, strengþes F,
strenkþis Ma; þerfore BCaEGIKMMaNQRWX
92 nam E; clepid: om. Ac
93 wel D; the (1°): om. D; ynwardly clepere I, cleper DR; clepere of the:
om. E; cheeke G, cheke boon I; til to: til in to AcBCCaDEFGKLMMa-
NORUX, vnto I
94 present: þis present IK[1]; he: sampson I; deemede MaX, demede
BCaFKLMPR, demyd D, demed E
95 dais P; ȝeris D, ȝere E, ȝer P; 94—95 in etc.: twenti ȝeer in þe dayes of
philistiym I

16. 1 Also Sampson: Sampson also I; ȝe[de] N

2 yn to hir. The which thing whanne
Philistiens hadden seen, and was pup-
plishid anentis hem, Sampson to haue   5
comen into the citee, thei segeden hym
about, kepers put in the ȝatis of the citee;
and there al nyȝt with silence abidynge,
that the morwetide comen him goynge

2 saȝ *CX*, sawe *Lo*; strompett *BFHWo*, strumpet *CEX*, strompette *Lo*; went
   BFHWo
3 hyre *BFLo*; whiche *BCEHLoX*; þinge *BLoWo*; whenn *B*, whan *CEFWoX*,
   whenne *H*
4 haddyn *E*, had(den) *Lo*, haden *Wo*; seeyn *BFH*, sene *Lo*, seȝen *Wo*;
   pupplisht *C*, pupplisched *E*, puplischede *Lo*, puplischid *Wo*, puplisht *X*
5 anentes *B*, anentus *C*, anent *X*; þem *CLo*; han *CEX*
6 commen *BFWo*, come *CX*, comyn *E*; cyte *BHLoWoX*; seegiden *BCH*,
   seegidyn *E*, segyden *FWo*, seegeden *Lo*
7 aboute *BCFLoX*, abowtyn *E*, abouȝte *H*; keperis *CELo*, keperes *X*; putt
   BF, putte *H*; ȝatus *C*, ȝates *LoX*; cyte *BCFHLoWoX*
8 þer *BWo*; alle *B*; nyȝte *Lo*; scilence *C*; abidende *CX*
9 morwtyde *BFH*, morntid *CX*, morewetid *E*, morowtide *Wo*; commen
   BFWo, comyn *E*; gooynge *BF*, goende *C*, goyng *E*

2 Quod cum vidissent Philistiim, et percreb/r/uisset apud
eos, intrasse urbem Samson, circumdederunt eum, pos-
itis in porta civitatis custodibus; et ibi tota
nocte cum silentio praestolantes, ut facto mane exeuntem occiderent.

2 tride to hir. And whanne Filisteis hadden seyn this, and it was pupplischid at
hem, that Sampson entride in to the   5
citee, thei cumpassiden hym, whanne
keperis weren set in the ȝate of the
citee; and thei abididen there al nyȝt
with silence, that in the morewtid thei

2 seiȝ CaFMW, seȝ E, sawȝe I, siȝe R; þer E; wumman CaFMW; hore
   BCF, strompet I, hoor R; he: om. Ma; entrid D, entred E, entrede P
3 her CaMW, here F, hire K; whan ELP; þe philistees I; had E; 3–4 hadden
   seyn: siȝen G
4 seyen BQ, seen DI, ysein E; puplischid CCaFHaMOPQRUWX, puplissid
   E, puppliȝsshed K, publischid L; at: among I
5 entrid D, entred E, had entrid I; the: þat O²
6 cite EFHaMPQW; & þei Ma; cumpaceden CaEFMPW, cumpasside U;
   when E, whan GLP, om. I
7 kepers DHaKLMMaRX, kepars E, keperes F, þe kepers I; were E, om. I;
   sette DK, setten E, sett IMaNR; ȝatis I
8 cite FHaMQW; thei: þe philistees I; abideden CaFKMNOW, abidden E,
   abidinge I, abiden LMa, abedin P; þer E; þe nyȝt B, þat nyȝt I
9 scilens D; with silence: priuely I; morntid BMa, morewetide CaMW,
   morwetide DM, morowtide EK, morewetid FGU, morowtid HaX,
   morewtijd I, morwetyd NQS, morwtide P, morewetide R

3 out thei my3ten slee. Forsothe Sampson   10
   slept vnto mydny3t; and thens rysynge
   he took both leeues of the 3ate(s), with her
   postes and lok; and put on the shuldres
   he beer to the cop of the hil that bihold-
4 ith Ebron. After thes thingis he louede   15
   a woman that dwellide in the valey of

10 oute *BLo*, ou3te *H*; my3te *C*, my3tyn *E*; slen *BCEFWoX*, sleen *HLo*;
    forsoþ *Lo*; Forsothe Sampson: S. f. *cet.*
11 slepte *CEHLo*, sleep *X*; myd ny3te *Lo*; þenns *B*, þennus *CX*, þennys *E*,
    þennes *Lo*; risende *CX*
12 toke *BFHLoWo*, toc *CX*; boþe *CEFHLoX*, boþe þe *Wo*; lefis *BCEH*,
    leeuys *F*, lefes *LoX*; þeir *BEFWo*, þer *CLoX*
13 postis *BEFHWo*, postus *C*; loke *Lo*; putt *BFH*, putte *Lo*; schulders
    BFHX, shuldris *CE*, scholdres *Lo*
14 bar *CEX*, bare *LoWo*; copp *BFHWo*, coppe *Lo*; hyll *BFH*, hille *LoWo*;
    beholdeþ *CE*, byholdeþ *Wo*
15 Aftyr *ELoX*; þese *CEWoX*; þinges *BLo*, thingus *CX*; loued *BFHWo*,
    loouede *CE*
16 womman *cet.*; dwellid *BFHWo*, dwelte *CX*, dwellede *E*; waley *Lo*

3 Dormivit autem Samson usque ad medium noctis; et
   inde consurgens apprehendit ambas portae fores cum
   postibus suis et sera, impositasque humeris portavit
   ad verticem montis, qui respicit Ebron.
4 Post haec amavit mulierem, quae habitabat in valle
   Soreth, et vocabatur Dalida.

3 schulden kille Sampson goynge out. For-   10
sothe Sampson slepte til to the myddis of
the nyȝt; and fro thennus he roos, and
took bothe (the) closyngis, *ethir leeues,*
of the ȝate, with hise postis and lok;
and he bar *tho leeues,* put on the schul-   15
dris, to the cop of the hil that biholdith
4 Ebron. After these thingis Sampson louyde
a womman that dwellide in the valey of

10 shulden AcBCFGIKLMaNOUX, scholden CaMW; goyng EFS; oute E;
    Forsothe: and I, forsoþ NX
11 slept E; til to: vnto E, to I; myddes F; 11—12 the myddis of the nyȝt:
    myd nyȝt I
12 nyȝte D; from K; þennes BCCaFHaMWX, þens DEMaQR, þennys GLN,
    þenis P, þenns IU; ros E; fro th. he roos: he roose up to go þenns I
13 tok E, toke HaR, he toke I; the: om. A²BCD¹W; closynges BCHa,
    cloosingis K; eþer AcBCDKNOSX, eiþer CaFGHaMMaQW, or EILP,
    eiþir R, oþer U; leues BCaFIMW, þe leues DE, leeuis GNQ, þe leeues I,
    leeues LP
14 his EFGLNPQW, þe I; postes F, poostis R; þe lok I
15 bare CDHaIR, baar KLNX; þoo R; leeuys AcGNQS, leues BCaDEFMW,
    ȝatis I, l_ _s Ma; putte BDHa, om. I, putt KMa; upon I; the: his I;
    shuldres ɼHaR, shuldrus O
16 coppe I; hille DHa, hul E; biholdeþ EFHaKL
17 aftir AcBCCaDGHaIKLNOPQRSWX; þes DKMX, þise U; þinges FHa;
    louede BCaFKLMMaPUWX, loued DE
18 wumman CaFMW; þise U; dwellid D, dwelled E, dwellede LP; valeie L

5 Soreth, and she was clepid Dalida. And
there camen to hyr princis of Philistiens,
and seiden, Bigijl hym, and lern of hym,
in what he hath so myche strength, and 20
in what maner wise hym we mowen
ouercome, and bounden tourmente; the
which thing if thou dost, we shulen ȝyue
to thee ech a thousand hundrid platis
6 of siluer. Thanne Dalyla spak to Samp- 25
son, Sey to me, I biseche, in what is
thi moost strength, and what thing (may) be
with the which boundun thou maist not

17 clepid: callid *Lo*
18 þer *CEHX*; coomen *BF*, camyn *E*, comen *HWo*, commen *Lo*; hyre *BFLo*;
    princes *LoX*
19 seidyn *E*; bygyle *BFHLoWoX*, begile *CE*; lerne *CEFLoWoX*; off *X*
20 hath: was *Lo*; mych *FWo*; strengþe *CEHWoX*, streyngþ *F*, of strengþe *Lo*
21 in: om. *cet.*; manere *Lo*; wee *CEX*; may *BFHLoWo*, moun *CEX*
22 ouercommen *BFWo*, ouercomyn *E*, ouercomen *HLoX*; bounde *CX*,
    bowndyn *E*; tourmenten *BFHLoWo*, tormente *CX*, tormentyn *E*
23 whiche *BCEHLoX*; þinge *BLoWo*; ȝif *BFHWo*, ȝife *Lo*; do *CX*, doist *E*,
    doost *F*; wee *CEX*; schuln *BEFH*, shul *CWoX*, schulle *Lo*; ȝeue *BFHLo*,
    ȝifyn *E*
24 þe *Wo*; eche *BCEFHLoX*; thousend *CEX*; hundreþ *BF*, hundride *Lo*,
    hundred *X*; platus *C*, plates *X*
25 þann *B*, þan *Wo*; spake *Wo*
26 say *BFHWo*, seye *Lo*; beseche *CEX*; is: be *cet.*
27 most *BFHWoX*, moste *CELo*; streyngþ *B*, strengþe *CELoWoX*, streyngþe
    F; þinge *BLoWo*
28 whiche *BCEHLoX*; bounden *BFLoWo*, bounde *CX*, bowndyn *E*; mayȝte
    Lo

5 Veneruntque ad eam principes Philistinorum, atque
dixerunt: Decipe eum, et disce ab illo, in quo hab-
e/a/t tantam fortitudinem, et quomodo eum superare
valeamus, et vinctum affligere. Quod si feceris,
dabimus tibi singuli mille /et/ centum argenteos.
6 Locuta est ergo Dalida ad Samson: Dic mihi, obsecro,
in quo sit tua maxima fortitudo, et quid sit quo
ligatus rumpere nequeas?

5 Soreth, and sche was clepid Dalida. And
the princes of Filisteis camen to hir, and   20
seiden, Disseyue thou hym, and lerne
thou of hym, in what thing he hath so
greet strengthe, and how we mowen ouercome hym, and turmente *hym* boundun;
that if thou doist, we schulen ȝyue to   25
thee ech man a thousynde and an hundrid
6 platis of siluer. Therfor Dalida spak to
Sampson, Y biseche, seie thou to me, wher
ynne is thi gretteste strengthe, and what
is that thing, with which thou boundun   30

19 chepid B, clepide HaOS
20 princis DGIKMaNPQSX; þe philistees I; comen E; her CaMW, here F,
    hire KS
21 deceiue EGHaLPQ; hym: Sampson I; lurne DQS; and ... (22) hym: om. R
23 grete DER, gret I; strengþ E, strenkþe MaR; moun AcBCCaDFGHaKM-
    MaNQW, mow ELPX, mowun OS, mowȝen R; ouercom E
24 turment E; bounden CaDEFGHaKLMMaPRUW, *whanne he is* b. I
25 that: þe whiche þing I; ȝif E; doste E, doost GMQW, dost HaILP;
    schullen CaMW, schuln DF, shul EILP; ȝeue BDGHaMaQRU, ȝife K,
    ȝiuen S
26 þe DEFR; eche KO; þousynd CaIMW, þousand DEHaMaNQRX,
    þousend FGLP, þousande K; hondred E, hundred Ha, hunderd LP
27 plates EFHa; seluer L, siluir Q; þerfore BCaGKMaNQRW, þanne I;
    spake IR
28 biseeche G, biseche þee I, bisiche S; say E, sey ILU; where BCaDR
29 in E, ynn R; þin G; grettiste AcBKMaR, grettist D, grettest EFGHaLPQ,
    moost I, greetiste O; stringþe E, strenkþe MaR; wat E
30 whiche AcDILPR, wiche K; thou: if þou were I; bounden
    CaDEFGHaIKLMMaPRUW; thou b.: b. þou B

7 breek? To whom answerde Sampson, If
with seuen senewy coordis not ȝit dried
and ȝit moyst Y were bounden, Y shal
8 be feble as other men. And the princis
of the Philistiens brouȝten to hir seuen
coordis, as she seide; with the whiche

30

29 breken *BFHLoWoX*, breke *C*, brekyn *E*; whome *BFHLo*; answerd *BWo*,
answeride *Lo*; ȝif *BFHWo*, ȝife *Lo*
30 seuene *CLoWoX*, sefne *E*; cordis *BCEX*, cordes *Wo*; ȝitt *BFH*; dryede *Lo*,
dryȝid *Wo*
31 ȝitt *FH*; moiste *CELoX*; bounde *CH*, bowndyn *E*
32 ben *ELo*; oþere *CX*, ooþere *E*; princes *LoX*
33 the: om. *WoX*; broȝten *CX*, broȝtyn *E*; hyre *BFLo*; seuene *CLoWo*, sefne
E, seuenn *X*
34 cordus *C*, cordis *E*, cordes *WoX*; which *FWo*

7 Cui respondit Samson: Si septem nerviceis funibus
necdum siccis et adhuc humentibus ligatus fuero,
infirmus ero ut ceteri homines.
8 Attuleruntque ad eam satrapae Philistinorum septem
funes, ut dixerat; quibus vinxit eum,

372

7 maist not breke? To whom Sampson answeride, If Y be boundun with seuene
coordis of senewis not ȝit drye and ȝit
moiste, Y schal be feble as othere men.

8 And the princis of Filisteis brouȝten to   35
hir seuene coordis, as he hadde seide;

31 maiȝt ELP, þou m. I; brek E; answerde CaFGMPQUW, answerid D,
    answerd E, answerede L
32 ȝif E; bounden CaDFHaIKLMMaPRUW, bounde EG; seuen EO
33 cordis CEGHaMaNQRU, cordes F; synewis DMaN, sinues ELP,
    senewes F, senowis HaL, moist senewis I; ȝitt Ma (2x); 33—34 and
    ȝit moiste: om. I
34 moist BDHaMaR; be: om. U; febil D, febul E, febele G, leþi I; oþer
    CaELRX, oþre FP
35 prynces AcBCCaFHaMORU; browten E; to: om. D; 35—36 to hir s. c.:
    s. c. to dalida I
36 her CaMW, here F, hire K; seuen CaDEMOW; cordis CEGLQRU,
    cordes F; had CEI; seide ADHaR, saide E, seid cet.

9 she bounde(n) hym, lurkynge anentis hir   35
   busshementis, and in the bed place abidynge the ende of the thing. And she
   criede to him, Philistien vpon thee,
   Sampson! The which brak the boondis, in
   what maner wise a man wold breeke the   40
   threed of a top of flexe, that is sponnen
   with spotel, whanne the smelle of fier it
   hath takun; and it is not knowun in
10 what thing his strength was. And Dalida seide to hym, Loo! thow hast bigilid   45
   me, and fals thou hast spokyn; namely
   nowe shewe to me, with what thing

35 bond *CEX*, bound( ) *Lo*, bonde *HWo*; lurkende *CX*; anentus *C*, anent *X*;
    hyre *BFLo*
36 busshementus *C*, buschmentis *FLoWo*, busshemens *X*; bedde *Lo*; abidende
    CX
37 eendynge *BF*, endynge *EWo*, ending *HLoX*; þinge *BFLoWo*
38 cryed *BFHWo*; uppon *Wo*; þe *LoWo*
39 whiche *BCEHLoX*; brake *LoWo*; bondus *C*, bondis *EX*, bondes *Wo*
40 manere *F*; wolde *CEFHLoWoX*; breke *BCFHLoWoX*, brekyn *E*
41 þreede *BFHLo*, þred *C*, þrede *Wo*; toppe *LoWo*; flaxe *BFHLo*, flax *CE*,
    flex *X*; spunne *CX*, spunnyn *E*, spunnen *BFH*
42 spotle *BCEFX*, spatil *Lo*; whenn *B*, whan *CEWoX*, whann *F*, when *H*;
    smell *BF*, smel *CEHWoX*; fyre *BLo*, fijr *CE*, þe fyre *H*, fuyre *Wo*
43 taken *BFHLoWoX*, take *C*, takyn *E*; knowen *BCFHLoWoX*, knowyn *E*
44 þinge *BFLoWo*; strengþe *CELoWoX*, streyngþ *F*
45 lo *CEX*; þu *B*; begilid *CE*, bygyled *FLoWo*
46 spoken *cet.*
47 now *CEWoX*; shew *CEX*; þinge *LoWo*

9 latentibus apud se insidiis, et in cubiculo finem
   rei expectantibus; clamavitque ad eum: Philistiim
   super te, Samson. Qui rupit vincula, quomodo /si/
   rumpat quis filum de stuppa tortum sputamine, cum
   odorem ignis acceperit; et non est cognitum, in quo
   esset fortitudo eius.
10 Dixitque ad eum Dalida: Ecce illusisti mihi, et
   falsum locutus es; saltem nunc indica mihi, quo
   ligari debeas.

9 with whiche sche boond him, while
buyschementis weren hid at hir, and
abididen in a closet the ende of the
thing. And sche criede to hym, Sampson, 40
Filisteis ben on thee! Which brak the
boondis, as if a man brekith a threed of
herdis, writhun with spotle, whanne it
hath take the odour of fier; and it was
not knowun wher ynne his strengthe 45
10 was. And Dalida seide to hym, Lo!
thou hast scorned me, and thou hast spok
fals; nameli now schewe thou to me,
with what thing thou schuldist be bound-

37 which E, þe whiche I, wiche K; bond CaFLQU, bonde I, bound E,
   bounde Ha; wil E, whil PR
38 boischementis B, busschementis CaDGM, busmentis E, busschementes F,
   bushmentes Ha, þe bushmentis of philistees I, boiȝsshementis K,
   buschmentis LPQW, boishmentis N; werin P; hidde K; at: anentis I; her
   CaMW, here F, hire K
39 abideden DKMNRW, abidden E, abiden FLU, þei abooden I, abedin P;
   closet: priuy place I; eende BGHaKMa, eend R; the (2°): þis I
40 cried DE, cride U
41 þe philistees I; been I; upon I; þe EFP; whiche GOR, and he I, wich K;
   brake DHaIR; the: þo I
42 bondes CaFHa, bondis EGIKNQUW; if: om. CaDGHaI¹KMMaOQSX;
   breeȝ E, brekeþ FHaLR; þrede CER
43 herdes F, heerdis KR, hirdis OX; wriþen CaFGKMMaR, wreþen ELU,
   þrowen I, wreþin P, wouen W; spotel AcL, spotil BDEIMaPR, spotele
   CaFGMOW, spotul Ha, spotile KN; whan EGHaLP
44 haþe E; tak E, touchid I, taken LR; odur EU, heete I; fijr CaIMW, fire
   DLP, fyr EF
45 not ȝit I; knowen BCaFGHaIKLMMaPRUW, know E; where BD; yn
   DE; strenkþe Ma, strenkþ R
46 saide E; hym: sampson I; loo K
47 haast R; scornyd GNQ, scornede Ha, scoorned KX; haast R; spok AE,
   spoken I, spoke cet.
48 false BHaR; nameli: neþeles I; now: om. Ma; sheu E; thou: om. G
49 schuldest CEFHaL, scholdist CaMW, schuldiste R; bounden
   CaDFGHaIKLMMaPRUW, boundon E

375

11 thow owist to be boundun. To whom
he answerde, If I were boundun with
newe coordis, the whiche weren not ȝit   50
[in] werk, I shal be feble, and of other
12 men lijk. With the which eft Dalida
boond him, and criede, Philistien vpon
thee, Sampson! in the bed place busshementis maad redi. The which so brak   55

48 owest *LoWoX*; ben *EX*; bounden *BFHLo*, bounde *CX*, bowndyn *E*,
bonden *Wo*; whome *BF*
49 answerd *B*, answeride *Lo*, answerid *Wo*; ȝif *BFHWo*, ȝife *Lo*; bounden
BFHLoWo, bounde *CX*, bowndyn *E*
50 cordis *CE*, cordes *WoX*; the whiche: þat *C*, þe which *FWo*; weryn *E*, were
Lo; ȝitt *BFH*
51 werke *HWo*; ben *E*; oþere *C*, ooþere *E*
52 lyke *BEFHLoWo*, lic *CX*; the: om. *C*; whiche *BCEHLoX*; efte *Lo*
53 bond *CEX*, boonde *H*, bonde *LoWo*; cried *BFHWo*; uppon *Wo*
54 þe *Wo*; bedde *Lo*; buschmentus *FWo*, busshemens *X*
55 made *FHLoWo*, mad *X*; whiche *BCEHLoX*; brake *BLoWo*

11 Cui ille respondit: Si ligatus fuero novis funibus,
qui numquam fuerunt in opere, infirmus ero, et aliorum hominum similis.
12 Quibus rursum Dalida vinxit eum, et clamavit: Philistiim super te, Samson; in cubiculo insidiis prae-
paratis. Qui ita rupit vincula quasi fila telarum.

11 un. To whom he answeride, If Y be 50
    boundun with newe coordis, that weren
    not ȝit in werk, I schal be feble, and lijk
12 othere men. With whiche Dalida boond
    him eft, and criede, Sampson, Filistees
    ben on thee! the while buyschementis 55
    weren maad redi in a closet. Which brak

50 answerde CaFGMPQUW, answerid D, answerede EL; ȝif E
51 bounden CaDFGHaIKLMMaPRUW, bounde E, booundun O; new E; cordis CEGINQRU, cordes F; were E
52 ȝut E, ȝitt Ma; werke PRX; febil DE, feeble GX, leþi I; like DELP, lyk FGHaQSU
53 oþer ELX, oþir DS; which ELS, þe whiche I, wiche K; boon Ac, bond CaDFGQU, bounde E, bonde HaIR
54 efte LR; cried E, sche criede I, cride U; þe philistees I
55 on: vpon I; þe DEFR; the: om. I; wile EHa, whil R; buschementis CCaDLMRW, busmentis E, busschementes F, þe busshementis G, bushmentes Ha, bushmentis IPQ, boiȝsshementis K, boyshmentis N
56 werin P, ben N, were U; made DEKR; reedy S, om. E; closett K, priuy place I; whiche CGOR, And S. I, wich K; brake DHaIR, braak K

377

13 the bondis as thredis of webbis. And
   Dalida eft seide to hym, Howe long shalt
   thow bigile me, and fals thow shalt speek?
   Shewe where with thou owist to be
   boundun. To whom answerde Sampson,   60
   he seith, If seuen heerys of myn heed
   with warp threed thow pla(i)ttist, and a
   nayl with hem about bounden to the
14 erthe thow ficchist, I shal be feble. The
   which thing whanne Dalida hadde doo,   65
   she seide to hym, Philistien vpon thee,
   Sampson! The which arysynge fro sleep,
   drow3 out the nayl, with heeris and warp.

56 boondis *BFHLo*, bondus *C*, bondes *Wo*; þreedis *BE*, þredes *Wo*; websters
    Lo, webbes *Wo*
57 efte *Lo*; how *cet.*; longe *cet.*
58 begile *C*, begilen *E*; speken *BFHWo*, speke *CLoX*, spekyn *E*
59 sheu *CEX*; wher *CEX*; owest *ELoX*; ben *EX*
60 bounden *BFHLoWoX*, bounde *C*, bowndyn *E*; whome *BFLo*; answerd *B*,
    answeride *Lo*
61 he seith if: /3/if he s. *cet.*; 3if *BFHWo*, 3ife *Lo*; seuene *CLoWoX*, sefne *E*;
    heris *BCEFHLoWo*, heres *X*; my *BEFHWo*; heued *BEFHWo*, hed *CX*,
    hede *Lo*
62 warpe *Lo*; þred *CX*, þreede *Lo*, þrede *Wo*; plattest *X*
63 nayle *BLo*, vayle *Wo*; þem *CELoX*; aboute *BCFLoX*, abowtyn *E*, a-bou3te
    H; bounde *CX*, boundyn *E*
64 erþ *B*; ficchest *ELoX*; ben *E*
65 whiche *BCEHLoWoX*; þinge *BLoWo*; whenn *BH*, whan *CEFLoWoX*;
    had *BFHLoWo*; doon *BFH*, do *CX*, don *EWo*, doone *Lo*
66 uppon *Wo*; þe *Wo*
67 whiche *CEHLoX*; risende *CX*; sleepe *BFHWo*, slep *CX*, sclepe *Lo*
68 dro3 *C*, drowe *Lo*, drow *X*; oute *BLo*, ou3te *H*; nayle *Lo*, vayles *Wo*;
    heris *BCEFHWo*, heres *X*; warpe *Lo*

13 Dixitque Dalida rursum ad eum: Usquequo decipies me,
   et falsum loqueris? ostende quo vinciri debeas. Cui
   respondit Samson: Si, inquit, septem crines capitits
   mei cum licio plexueris, et clavum his circumligatum
   terrae fixeris, infirmus ero.

13 so the boondis as thredis of webbis. And
   Dalida seide eft to hym, Hou long schalt
   thou disseyue me, and schalt speke fals?
   Schew thou to me, with what thing thou   60
   schalt be boundun. To whom Sampson
   answeryde, he seide, If thou plattist*
   seuene heeris of myn heed with a strong
   boond, and fastnest to the erthe a nail
   boundun a-boute with these, Y schal be   65
14 feble. And whanne Dalida hadde do this,
   sche seide to hym, Sampson, Filisteis
   ben on thee! And he roos fro sleep, and
   drow out the nail, with the heeris and

57 so: om. I; the: his I; bondes CaEFHa, bondis DGIKQU; þreedis AcGO,
   þe þredis D, þredes FHa; webbes FL
58 saide E; efte ELR, om. N; longe BCCaFGHaIKLMMaNOPQRUWX
59 descei[ue] E, desceyue GHaLPQ; schalt: om. I; spek E; false BR
60 shew AE, shewe cet.; whiþ S
61 bounden CaDEFGHaIKLMMaPRUW, booundun O
62 answerde CaFGMPQUW, answerid D, answerd E, answerede L; he seide:
   om. W; saide E; ȝif E; he seide if: If he seide I; plauntis A¹, plattest EFL,
   plattist togidre I, plattiste R
63 seuen EIM; heris BCaMW, heres EF; mine ER, mijn K; hede E; stronge
   HaR
64 bond CaEGLQUW, bonde R; fasteneste BR, fastneste C, fastened it E,
   fastnyst GLPQ, fastenist Ha, fastenest Ma; eerþe R; a: an R; nayle ER
65 bounden CaDEFGHaIKLMMaPRUW, booundun O; a-bout E; þes
   DKX, þese heeris I
66 febil D, febul E, feeble G, leþi I; whan EFGHaLPW; had ELW; y do
   CaM, doon W
67 said E; þe philistees I
68 been F; upon I; þe EF; rose E, roose I; from K; slepe E; and: om. W
69 drowȝ CaGHaKMMaNQWX, drowe D, he drewe I, drowȝe R; oute R;
   naile E, nailes Ha; heris CaMPW, heres EI, heeres Ha

14 Quod cum fecisset Dalida, dixit ad eum: Philistiim
   super te, Samson. Qui consurgens de somno extraxit
   clavum cum crinibus et licio.

15 And Dalida seide to hym, What maner
   wise thou seist, that thou louest me,   70
   whanne thin ynwit is not with me? Bi
   thre sithis thou hast lowen to me, and
   thow woldist not seye to me, in what
16 thing is thi moost strength. And
   whanne she was heuy to hym, and bi   75
   manye dais to hym bisili cleuede, space
   to reste(n) not ȝyuynge, hyre lijf failide,

70 thou seist: s. þ. *X*; seyest *Lo*; loouest *CE*
71 whenn *B*, whan *CEFLoWoX*; þi *E*, þine *Lo*; in-wytt *BFHWo*, inwitte *Lo*
72 þree *B*; siþes *CELoX*; þu *B*; lowyn *E*, lyed *Lo* (on eras.)
73 woldest *CLoWo*; seyn *BEFHLoWo*, sei *CX*
74 þinge *BLoWo*; is: be *cet.*; most *BFHWoX*, moste *CELo*; streyngþ *BE*,
   strengþe *CEHLoWoX*
75 whenn *BH*, whan *CELoWoX*, whann *F*
76 many *BFHLoWo*; daȝes *CX*, daies *EFLoWo*; besili *CE*; cleued *BFHWo*,
   cleuyde *E*; to hym bisili cleuede: b. to h. she cl. *X*
77 restyn *E*, reste *LoWo*, resten *cet.*; ȝeuynge *BH*, ȝiuende *CX*, ȝifynge *E*,
   ȝeuyng *F*; hir *CEHWoX*; lyf *BCEFHWoX*, life *Lo*; feylid *BFHWo*, failede
   CEX, fayled *Lo*

15 Dixitque ad eum Dalida: Quomodo dicis, quod amas me,
   cum animus tuus non sit mecum? Per tres vices menti-
   tus es mihi, et noluisti mihi dicere, in quo sit
   maxima fortitudo tua.
16 Cumque molesta ei esset, et per multos dies iugiter
   ei adhaereret, spatium ad quietem non tribuens, defecit anima eius, et ad mortem usque lassata est.

15 strong boond. And Dalida seide to hym,   70
   Hou seist thou, that thou louest me, sithen
   thi soule is not with me? Bi thre tymes
   thou liedist to me, and noldist seie to
   me, wher ynne is thi moost strengthe.
16 And whanne sche was diseseful to hym,   75
   and cleuyde to hym contynueli bi many
   daies, and ȝaf not space to reste, his lijf
   failide, and was maad wery til to deeth.

70 a strong I, stronge HaR; bond EFGHaLPQU, boond *tied þerto* I, bonde R,
    hond W; said E
71 saist E, seiest R; that thou: þattou E; that etc.: þou louest me þat þou W;
    louist GQ; siþþen CaMW, siþ I; s. ... me (73): om. Ha
72 thi soule: þin ynward affeccioun I; tymys GQ
73 liedest CFL, hast lied I, liȝedist R; noldest EFHaL, woldist not I, nooldist
    MaX; sey EI
74 where BDENRW; in DE; mooste BGNX, moste CaEP, most HaQ;
    strenkþe MaR
75 whan EHaLP; diseful Ac, disseseful D, disseful Ha, diseeseful KX,
    deseseful GLO
76 cleuede BCaFKLMMaPRU, cleuyd D, cleued E; contynuelly CaGIMW,
    continuli E; manye BGKMaQR
77 to him ȝaue I, ȝaue R; not: no I; rest EKR; lif EFGHaLPQU
78 failid D, failede EFKLPU; made D; weeri AcOS; til to: vnto EI; deþ
    AcCEFOPUX, þe deþ I, þe deeþ KW

381

17 and vnto the deeth is feblid. Thanne
openynge the trewth of the thing, he
seide to hir, Yren neuer wente vp on myn   80
heed, for thi Nazare, that is, sacrid to the
Lord, Y am fro the wombe of my moder;
if myn heed were shauen, my strength
shal goon awey fro me, and shal fayl,
18 and be as other men. And she seynge   85
that he hadde knowlechid to hir al his
inwit, she sente to the princis of Philistiens, and badde, Stye ȝe vp ȝyt oons, for
nowe to me he hath openyd his herte.
The whiche stieden vp, takun to the   90

78   deth *BCEFHWoX*; feeblid *E*, feblide *Lo*; þann *BFH*, þan *Wo*
79   opnynge *BF*, openende *CX*; trewþe *CEFHLoX*, truþe *Wo*; þinge *FLoWo*
80   hyre *BFLo*; neuere *LoX*; went *BFWo*; uppon *Wo*; my *BEFHLo*
81   heued *BFHWo*, hed *CX*, heuyd *E*, hede *Lo*; thi: þe *CELoX*; sacride *BFH*,
     sacrede *Lo*
82   modyr *EHX*, modre *Lo*
83   ȝif *BFHWo*, ȝife *Lo*; my *BEFHLoWo*; heued *BFHWo*, hed *CX*, heuyd *E*,
     heuede *Lo*; shaue *C*, schauyn *E*; 83 – 84 my strength shal goon awey:
     sh. g. aw. my str. *cet.*; streyngþ *BF*, strengþe *CEHLoWoX*
84   gon *CEWoX*, gone *Lo*; aweye *B*; fayle *BCFHLoWo*, failyn *E*, failen *X*
85   ben *CEX*; oþere *CX*, ooþere *E*; seeynge *BEFHLo*, seande *C*, seȝinge *Wo*,
     seende *X*
86   had *BFHLo*, om. *Wo*; knowlachid *BFHWo*, knowlechide *Lo*, shewed *X*;
     hyre *BFLo*; alle *B*
87   in-wytt *BFWo*, inwitte *Lo*; she: om. *C*; sent *BFWo*, sende *Lo*; princes
     LoWoX
88   bad *BCEFHX*, bade *LoWo*; steyȝe *BLoWo*, steȝe *CEX*, stey *F*, styȝe *H*;
     ȝe: om. *BHLoWo*, ȝee *CEX*; vpp *X*; ȝitt *BFHWo*; ones *CX*, onys *E*, oones
     Lo, oonys *Wo*
89   now *cet.*; hath: om. *Lo*; opnyd *BF*, opened *CHX*, openede *Lo*; hert *BFH*
90   which *FWo*; steyȝiden *BFWo*, steȝeden *CX*, steȝedyn *E*, styȝeden *H*,
     steyȝeden *Lo*; taken *BFHWoX*, take *CLo*, takyn *E*; þee *Lo*

17 Tunc aperiens rei veritatem, dixit ad eam: Ferrum
numquam ascendit super caput meum, quia nazareus,
id est consecratus Domino, sum de utero matris meae;
si rasum fuerit caput meum, recedet a me fortitudo
mea, et deficiam, eroque sicut ceteri homines.

17 Thanne he openyde the treuthe of the
thing, and seide to hir, Yrun stiede ne-   80
uere on myn heed, for Y am a Nazarei,
that is, halewid to the Lord, fro the wombe
of my modir; if myn heed be schauun,
my strengthe schal go awei fro me, and
Y schal faile, and Y schal be as othere   85
18 men. And sche si3 that he knowlechide
to hir al his wille, *ether herte*, and sche
sente to the princes of Filisteis, and comaundide, Stie 3e 3it onys, for now he
openyde his herte to me. Whiche sti-   90
eden, with the money takun which

79 þan EHa, þane R; openede BCaFKLMMaP, opened D, opnede I, opynede
U; truþe BGHaLMaNPQRX
80 said E; her CaM, here F, hire KL; yren CaEFIKLMMaPRW; stied DE,
steiede F, cam I, sti3ede MaNR; neuer DHaINR, n. 3it I
81 upon I; my KR; hede E, hed IL
82 halued EL, halowid HaKMa, halewide O, halwid PQ, halowed U; from
K; wom E; 82−83 the wombe of my modir: my modir wombe I
83 moder FHaLRU; myn: mijn K, myne R; heed: om. Ca, hede E, hed I;
schauen BCaEFGHaIKLMMaPRUW
84 strenkþe Ma; a-way EHa, aweie R; from K
85 faile *strengþe* I; oþer DELP, oþre R, oþir X
86 sche: dalida I; sei3 CaFMW, si3e DR, saw3 I; he: sampson I; knoulechid
D, knowleched E, had knowlechid I, knowlechede LOP
87 her CaMW, here F, hire K; alle R; wil EGHaIQU; eiþer CaFGHaMQRW,
of E, or LP, eiþir Ma, eþir O, oþer U; *ether herte*: om. AcB[1]I; and: om. I;
sche: om. NW
88 sent E, shente N; princis DGIKNPQSWX; comaundid DE, comaundide
hem I, comaundede LP, commaundide R
89 stie 3e: steie 3e FW, stie 3e up I, sti3e 3e MaNR, stie 3ee U; 3it: it L,
3itt Ma; oonys BDGHaIMaNPQX, oones KL
90 openede BCaFKLMMaPX, opened DE, haþ opned I, haþ openyd N;
hert E; which E, þe whiche I, wiche K; steieden F, wenten up I, sti3eden
MaNR
91 with: om. I; the: om. X; moneye CaL; taken BCaEFHaKLMMaQRUW,
taken wiþ hem I, takin P; whiche GHaLPR, þat I, wiche K

18 Vidensque illa quod confessus ei esset omnem animum
suum, misit ad principes Philistinorum, atque mandavit: Ascendite adhuc semel, quia nunc mihi aperuit
cor suum. Qui ascenderunt, assumpta pecunia quam
promiserant.

19 money that thei bihiȝten. And she made
hym sleep vpon hir knees, and in hir
bosum to leyn the heed; and she clepide
the barbour, and he shoofe seuen heeris
of hym; and she biganne to throwe hym   95
awey, and fro hir to putte; forsothe
20 anoon strength fro hym wente. And she
seide, Philistiens vpon thee, Sampson!
The which fro sleep rysynge, seide in his
inwit, I shal goo out, as I dide before,   100
and me I shal shaake out; vnknowynge
that the Lord was goon awey fro hym.

91   monee *BCEFHX*; behiȝten *C*, behiȝtyn *E*
92   sleepe *BF*, slepen *CX*, slepyn *E*, slepe *HLoWo*; uppon *Wo*; hyre *BFLo*;
     kneese *BF*, knes *C*, knese *Lo*; hyre *BFLo*, her *H*
93   bosome *LoWo*; lei *C*, leyne *Lo*; heued *BEFHWo*, hed *CX*, hede *Lo*; clepid
     BFHWo, clepede *CEX*, callid *Lo*
94   barboure *LoWo*; shoof *CEX*, schofe *Lo*, shooue *Wo*; sefne *F*, seuene
     LoWoX; heris *BCEFHWoX*
95   began *CE*, bygan *FHLoWoX*; þrowen *CX*, þrowyn *E*, þrow *FH*
96   aweye *BH*; hyre *BFLo*; puttyn *E*, putt *Wo*, putten *X*; forsoth *B*; 96–97
     forsothe anoon: an. f. *cet.*
97   anoone *Lo*, anon *Wo*, anoen *X*; streyngþ *B*, strengþe *CELoWoX*, streynþ
     F; went *BF*
98   uppon *Wo*; þe *Wo*
99   whiche *BCEHLoX*; slep *CX*, sleepe *FHWo*, sclepe *Lo*; risende *CX*
100 in-witt *BFHWo*, inwitte *Lo*; gon *CEX*, go *LoWo*; oute *BLo*, ouȝte *H*;
     byfore *BFHLoWo*, beforn *CE*, bifor *X*
101 schaken *cet.*; oute *BFLo*, ouȝte *H*; vnknowende *CX*
102 gon *CEWo*; a-weye *H*

19 At illa dormire eum fecit super genua sua, et in
sinu suo reclinare caput. Vocavitque tonsorem, et
rasit septem crines eius, et coepit abicere eum, et
a se repellere; statim enim ab eo recessit fortitudo.
20 Dixitque: Philistiim super te, Samson. Qui de somno
consurgens, dixit in animo suo: Egrediar, sicut /et/
ante feci, et me excutiam; nesciens, quod recess-
isset ab eo Dominus.

19 thei bihiȝten. And sche made hym slepe
on hir knees, and bowe the heed in hir
bosum; and sche clepide a barbour, and
schauede seuene heeris of hym; and sche   95
bigan to caste hym awei, and to put fro
hir; for anoon the strengthe ȝede awei
20 fro him. And sche seide, Sampson, Filisteis ben on thee! And he roos fro
sleep, and seide to his soule, Y schal go   100
out, as and Y dide bifore, and Y schal
schake me *fro boondis*; and he wiste not,
that the Lord hadde goon awei fro hym.

92 sleepe CGHaQ, sleep D, to slepe IL
93 upon I; hir (1°): her CaFLMW, hire K; and: om. S; bouwe B, bowede C,
    bowide Ha, to leie I, bowȝ R; the: his I; hede E; hir (2°): her CaFLMW
94 bosom R; clepid D, cleped E, clepede F
95 shauyde AcCGHaIOQRS, schaued DE, he schauyde I; seuen CaE; heres
    EF, heeres HaR, heris MUW
96 bigane R; cast E, schyue I; away Ha, aweie R; putte
    BCCaFGHaKLMMaNPQUWX, p. him I; from K
97 her CaMW, here F; anon EP; strengþe of him K, strenkþe MaR, streyngþe
    O; away EHa, aweie R
98 from K; said E; þe philistees I
99 upon I; þe E; ros E; from K
100 slepe EMaR, slep I; sayde E; to: in cet.; soule: ynwitt I
101 oute R; and: om. EHaIK¹LMaPR; did E, dede F
102 from K; bondis BEGHaQUX, boondes Ca, bondes F, þese b. I; wist E
103 had E; gon AcCFGHaILPQU, go BDN, gone ER, goen O; away EHa,
    a-weie R; from K

21 Whom whanne Philistiens hadden cauȝt,
anoon thei drewen out his eyen, and ladden hym boundun with cheyns to Ga- 105
zam, and closid in prisoun thei maden to
22 grynde. And nowe his heeris bigunnen
23 to growe aȝen; and the princis of Philistiens camen to gidre in oon, for to offre
oostis of greet worship to Dagon, her 110
god, and for to eete, seyinge, Oure god
hath takun oure enemye Sampson* into

103 whome *BF*; whenn *BH*, whan *CELoWoX*, whann *F*; Philistiens: þe filisteis
X; haden *B*, hadde *C*, haddyn *E*; caȝt *CX*, cauȝte *Lo*
104 anoone *Lo*, anoen *X*; drowen *CHLoWoX*, droowyn *E*; oute *BLo*, ouȝte *H*;
eyȝen *BFHLoWo*, eȝen *CEX*
105 hym: om. *cet.*; bounde *BFHLoWo*, bounden *CX*, bowndyn *E*; cheynes
CELoWoX
106 closed *BFH*, closide *Lo*; prisoune *Lo*; madyn *E*
107 grinden *C*, gryndyn *EX*; now *CEHLoX*; heris *BCEFHWo*, heres *X*; bygunn
B, begunne *C*, begunnyn *E*, bygunne *FHWo*, bygonne *Lo*
108 growen *CX*, growyn *E*; aȝeyn *BFHWo*, aȝeen *CX*, aȝeyne *Lo*; princes *LoX*
109 coomen *BFH*, camyn *E*, comen *LoWo*; to giþer *BF*, togidere *CEX*, to
gyder *HWo*; oone *H*, oen *X*; offren *BFHWo*, offryn *E*
110 hoostis *BFHWo*, ostus *C*, hostys *E*, oostes *Lo*, ostes *X*; grete *BFHLoWo*,
gret *CX*, grett *E*; wirschip *BFH*, worshipe *CELo*, wrshipe *X*; þeir *BCFWoX*,
þer *Lo*
111 for: om. *C*; eten *BFHLoWoX*, ete *C*, etyn *E*; seiende *CX*; our *B*
112 has *Lo*; taken *BCFHLoWoX*, takyn *E*; enmye *BFWo*, enemy *CEX*; Sompson
A

21 Quem cum apprehendissent Philistiim, statim eruerunt
oculos eius, et duxerunt Gazam vinctum catenis, et
clausum in carcere molere fecerunt.
22 Iamque capilli eius renasci coeperant;
23 et principes Philistinorum convenerunt in unum, ut
immolarent hostias magnificas Dagon, deo suo, et
epularentur, dicentes: Tradidit deus noster inimicum
nostrum Samson in manus nostras.

21 And whanne Filisteis hadden take hym,
anoon thei diden out hise iȝen, and led-   105
den *hym* boundun with chaynes to Gaza,
and maden *hym* closid in prisoun to
22 grynde. And now hise heeris bigunnen
23 to growe aȝen; and the princes of Filisteis camen togidere to offre grete sacrifices   110
to Dagon, her god, and to ete, seiynge,
Oure god hath bitake oure enemy Samp-

104 And: om. W; whan EGLP; þe philistees I; had E, hadde R; taken EU
105 anone E, anon PR; þai E; deden FU, putten I, dedin P; oute R; his
     AcEFGIPQSX; eiȝen CaFMW, ien E; ledde CR, led E, þei l. I, ladden K
106 bounden CaDFGHaKLMMaPQRUW, bound E, bounde I; cheynes
     AcDEFKMMaRX, cheynis IQ
107 made Ha, madin P; closed EKL; prison EK, presoun PQSU, þe pr. X;
     107−8 þei closiden him in prisoun & maden him to grinde I
108 now: þanne I; his EFHaILPQX; heris CaELMPW, heres FR, heeres HaS;
     bi-gunnun E, bigonne U
109 grow E; aȝein B; princis DGIKMaNPQSWX; þe F. GI
110 comen E; togidre DIR; offre S; greet D, greete GMaQ; sacrifisis
     CaDGMMaPQWX
111 here FGQR; eete GR; and to ete: *and þei maden festis* & eeten I; saying E
112 haþe E; enemye DMaR, enmy EI; oure enemy S.: S. oure enmy I

24 oure hoondis. The which also the puple
seynge preyseden her god, and the same
thing seiden, Oure god hath taken into
oure hoondis oure aduersarie, the which
hath doon a-wey oure loond, and slayn

25 many. And thei ioiynge bi feestis, nowe
taken meetis, thei comaundiden, that
Sampson shulde be clepid, and biforn

hem pleye; the which lad out fro the
prisoun pleyde beforn hem; and thei
maden hym stoond bitwen two pileers.

113 hondus *C*, handis *E*, hondes *LoWo*, hondis *X*; whiche *BCEHLoX*; peple
BFHLoWo
114 seeynge *BEFH*, seande *C*, seyinge *Lo*[1] *Wo*, seiende *X*; preysedyn *E*, preysiden
Wo, preisede *X*; þeir *BEFWo*, þer *CLoX*; god: lord *Wo*
115 þinge *BFLoWo*; seidyn *E*; our *B*; takyn *E*
116 our *F*; hondis *BCX*, handis *E*, hondes *LoWo*; our *BF*; the which: þe whiche
BEHLoX, þat *C*
117 don *CEWoX*, done *H*; aweye *H*; our *BF*; lond *CWoX*, land *E*, londe *Lo*;
sclayne *Lo*
118 manye *CELoX*; ioȝende *CX*, ioȝynge *E*; festis *BCEFH*, festes *X*; now
BCEFHWoX
119 take *C*, takyn *E*; metis *BEFHLoWo*, metus *C*, metes *X*; comaundeden *C*,
comawndidyn *E*, commaundiden *Lo*
120 schuld *BWo*; ben *ELo*; cleped *E*, callid *Lo*; befor *C*, beforn *E*, biforne *Lo*
121 þem *C*; pleyen *BEFLoWoX*, pleiȝen *C*, pleyn *H*; whiche *BCEHLoX*; ledde
Lo, ladde *Wo*; oute *BLo*, ouȝte *H*
122 prisone *Lo*; pleyȝid *BH*, pleiede *CELoX*, pleyed *FWo*; befor *C*, byforn
FHWoX, biforne *Lo*; þem *CLo*
123 madyn *E*; stonde *BHWo*, stonden *CLo*, stondyn *E*, stoonde *F*, to stonde *X*;
bytwene *BFHLoWo*, betwe *C*, between *E*, bitwe *X*; twey *Wo*; pilers *BFHWo*,
pileris *CELo*, pileres *X*

24 Quod etiam populus videns, laudaba/n/t deum suum,
eademque diceba/n/t: Tradidit deus noster in manus
nostras adversarium nostrum, qui delevit terram
nostram, et occidit plurimos.

24 son in to oure hondis. And the puple
seynge also this thing preiside her god,
and seide the same thingis, Our god hath   115
bitake oure aduersarie in to oure hondis,
which dide awey oure lond, and killide
25 ful many men. And thei weren glad bi
feestis, for thei hadden ete thanne; and
thei comaundiden, that Sampson schulde   120
be clepid, and schulde pleie bifor hem;
which was led out of prisoun, and pleiede
bifor hem; and thei maden hym stonde

113 hondes CaFL, hoondis O; peple CaFILMMaNPWX
114 seiyng E, seyinge F; preiseden DMaU, preised E, preisede KLP, preside O;
    here FGQ
115 seiden DFMaU, seid E; þinges FHa; our AF, oure cet.; haþe E
116 bitak E; hondes F
117 which: þat I, wiche K; end E, dede F; a-weie R; our L; killid D, killed E,
    killede FKLP
118 manye BGHaKMaQ; gladde K
119 festis ELMW, festes FHa, *making* of festis I, feestes R; haddin LP; eete
    GQ, eet R; þan Ha; for etc.: And þanne whanne þei hadden ete þei ... I
120 comaunded E, comaundide F, comaundeden LMPUWX; scholde CaFMW,
    shuld E
121 cleped F, om. D; and: om. D; schulde: om. CaDGHaIKMNOQSX,
    shuld E, scholde FW; plei E; bifore AcBCaEHaIKLMaNPQRWX; him L
122 þe whiche I, wich K, whiche LP; ledde DHa, ladd K, leed S; prison EK,
    presoun Q; pleide CaFIOSU, pleied D, plaied E
123 bifore AcBCaEGHaIKLMaNPQRWX; madin P

25 Laetantesque per convivia, sumptis iam epulis, praeceperunt, ut vocaretur Samson, et ante eos luderet.
Qui eductus de carcere ludebat ante eos; feceruntque eum stare inter duas columnas.

26 The whiche seide to the child gouern-
   ynge his goyngis, Leet me, that I towche   125
   the pileers on the whiche stoondith al
   the hows, that Y lene vpon hem, and a
27 litil while reste. Forsothe the hows was
   ful of men and of wymmen, and there
   weren the princis of Philistiens, and of   130
   the roof and soleer aboute three thowsand
   of either kynde, bidynge Sampson plei-
28 ynge. And he seith (to) the Lord inwardli
   clepid, Lord, my God, haue mynde of
   me, and ȝeeld to me nowe the fornhad   135
   strength, my God, that I wreche me on
   myn enemyes, and for the lesynge of two

124 which *FWo*; childe *LoWo*; gouernende *CX*
125 gooyngis *BF*, goingus *CX*, goynges *ELo*; lete *BFHWo*, let *CEX*, lette *Lo*
126 pylers *BFHWo*, pileris *CELo*, pyleres *X*; which *FWo*; stont *BFHWo*,
     stant *CEX*, stonde *Lo*; alle *BLo*
127 house *B*, houȝs *H*; uppon *Wo*; þem *ELo*
128 lytyll *BF*, lytel *Wo*; rest *FLoWo*; forsoþ *B*; Forsothe the hows: þe h. f.
     cet.; houȝs *H*
129 wymen *C*; þer *BCFHWoX*
130 weryn *E*; princes *LoX*
131 roofe *Lo*; soler *BCEFHWo*, solere *Lo*; abowten *BFLoWo*, abowtyn *E*,
     a-bouȝten *H*; þousant *B*, thousend *CEX*, þowsande *Lo*
132 bidende *CX*, abidynge *Lo*; pleying *BF*, pleiende *CX*, pleyenge *E*
133 inwardely *Lo*
134 callid *Lo*; hafe *E*
135 ȝeelde *BWo*, ȝeld *C*, ȝelde *Lo*; now *CEFHWoX*; former had *Lo*
136 streyngh *B*, strengþe *CEHLoWoX*, streyngþ *F*; wrek *B*, wreke *CEFHLoX*
137 my *EFWo*, myne *Lo*; enmyes *BFHWo*, enemys *CEX*; leesing *CEX*; twey
     BEFHWo, tweyne *Lo*

26 Qui dixit puero regenti gressus suos: Dimitte me,
   ut tangam columnas, quibus omnis imminet domus, ut
   recliner super eas, et paululum requiescam.
27 Domus autem erat plena virorum ac mulierum, et erant
   ibi /omnes/ principes Philistinorum, ac de tecto et
   solario circiter tria millia utriusque sexus /ex-/
   spectantes ludentem Samson.
28 At ille, invocato Domino, ait: Domine, Deus meus,
   memento mei, et redde mihi nunc pristinam forti-

26 bitwixe twei pileris. And he seide to
   the child gouernynge hise steppis, Suffre   125
   thou me, that Y touche the pilers on
   whiche al the hows stondith, that Y be
27 bowid on tho, and reste a litil. Sotheli
   the hows was ful of men and of wymmen,
   and the princes of the Filisteis weren   130
   there, and aboute thre thousynde of euer
   either kynde, biholdynge fro the roof and
28 the soler Sampson pleynge. And whanne
   the Lord was inwardli clepid, he seide,
   My Lord God, haue mynde on me, and,   135
   my God, ȝelde thou now to me the formere
   strengthe, that Y venge me of myn enemyes, and that Y resseyue o veniaunce

124   bitwix EFQ; tweie CaKMMaRW, two GIQ; pilers AcDFHaIKLMOQ-
        RSUX, pillers E, peleris G, pileers P; he: Sampson I; said E
125   chijld K, childe U; gouernyng E, þat gouernyde I; his EFGKLNPQX;
        steppes F; suffere S
126   pileris BCCaMaNQW, pillers E, pileres F, peleris G, pileers P, pelers U;
        on: om. IN
127   which AcCaEFMNPQSUW, þe whiche I, wiche K; stondeȝ E, stondeþ
        FHaKL, stondiþ upon I
128   bouwid B, bowed FL, bouȝid R; upon I; þoo R; rest ER; litel KL, litle R;
        soþli DFGLMMaPQUWX, And I
129   wommen BG
130   princis DGIKMaNPQSWX; the (2°): APUW, om. cet.; were O, werin P
131   and: om. GKX; about E; þree K; þousynd CaFMW, þousandis D,
        þousend EGP, þousand HaMaNQX, þousande K, þousende L; euere DG;
        131−32 of euer either kynde: of men & of wymmen I
132   eþer DE, eiþir PS; biholdyng CE, bihooldynge G; from K
133   the: om. BMa, fro þe I; solere E, soleer GQ; pleynge AM, plaiynge E,
        pleiynge cet.; whan EGHaLP; 133−34 And he clepide ynwardly þe lord &
        seide I
134   seide: om. E
135   on: of EK, upon I
136   mi lord god ER; ȝeelde CaR, ȝilde D; now to me: to me now D; former
        BDEFLMaPRX
137   strenkþe MaR; of: on ELP; myne CaEKMMaNQRW, my O; enmyes I
138   resseyue: take I; oo GHaKLPQR; vengeaunce KU

tudinem, Deus meus, ut ulciscar me de hostibus meis,
et pro amissione duorum luminum unam ultionem re-
cipiam.

29 liȝtis o veniaunce I take. And catch-
    ynge the twey pileers, to the whiche al
    the hows stood, and the tother of hem   140
    with the riȝt, and the tother with the left
30 holdynge, seith, Die my lijf with Philis-
    tien! And the pileers strongli smyten
    to gidre, the hows felle vpon alle the
    princis, and the tothir multitude, that   145
    there was; and many mo he slewȝ di-

138 liȝtus *CX*, liȝtes *Lo*; oo *BFHWo*, oon *E*; vengeaunce *ELo*; cacchende *CX*
139 two *CX*; pylers *BFHWo*, pileris *CELo*, pileres *X*; which *FWo*; alle *BLo*
140 houȝs *H*, house *Lo*; stode *BFHLoWo*, stod *X*; oþer *X*; þem *CELoX*
141 riȝte *Lo*; oþer *X*; lift *CHX*, lifte *LoWo*
142 holdende *CX*; dyȝe *H*; lyf *BCEFHWoX*, life *Lo*
143 pylers *BFHWo*, pileris *CELo*, pileres *X*; strongely *BFLo*; smyte *CX*,
    smytyn *E*
144 to giþer *BF*, togidere *CEX*, to gyder *HWo*; houȝs *H*, house *Lo*; fell *BH*,
    fel *CEFX*, fil *Wo*; uppon *Wo*; all *F*, al *H*, om. *X*
145 princes *X*; toþer *BCEFHLoWo*, oþer *X*
146 þer *BEFH*, om. *Wo*; manye *CEX*; slooȝ *C*, slowȝ *EHWo*, slowȝe *Lo*,
    slow *X*; diende *CX*, dyȝinge *H*, dyeinge *Lo*

29 Et apprehendens ambas columnas, quibus innitebatur
    domus, alteramque earum dextera, et alteram laeva
    tenens,
30 ait: Moriatur anima mea cum Philistiim. Concussis-
    que fortiter columnis, cecidit domus super omnes
    principes, et ceteram multitudinem, quae ibi erat;
    multoque plure interfecit moriens, quam ante vivus
    occiderat.

29 for the los of tweyne iȝen. And he took
  bothe pilers, on whiche the hows stood,   140
  and he helde the oon of tho in the riȝt-
  hond, and the tother in the left hond;
30 and seide, My lijf die with Filesteis!
  And whanne the pileris weren schakun
  togidere strongli, the hows felde on alle   145
  the princes, and on the tother multitude,
  that was there; and he diynge killide
  many moo, than he quyk hadde slayn

139 losse I, loss KMaN; twey C, two GHaQ, tweyn FLP, my two I; eiȝen
     CaFMW, iȝhen I; he: om. E; toke DEIR, tooke Ha
140 boþe þe BI, booþ R; pileris BCCaMaNW, peleris G; upon I; wiche EK,
     which FR, þe whiche I; al þe hous GQ¹; house E; stode DER, stoode I,
     stod U
141 held BF, heeld CaGLMMaNPX, heelde DQR, heuld K; the (1°): om.
     BFW; one E, toon K, on UW; the (2°): his I
142 hond (1°): honde IU; tother: oþer EM, tooþer L, toþir MaOPRS; the
     (2°): his I; lift BEFGKLMaOPW, lefte DIR; hond (2°): om. E, honde I,
     hoond LR
143 said E, he seide I; lif EFGHaLPQU; deie CaFMW, diȝe R; þe philistees I
144 whan EHaLP; pilers AcDEFHaIKLMMaRSUX, peleris G, pileers P;
     were M; schaken CaEFKLMMaRUW, schake I, schakin P
145 togidre DIR, togider E; fel CaEFILMPW, filde D; upon I
146 princis DGIKMaNPQSX; upon I; the: al þe I; tother: om. I, tooþer L,
     toþir MOR, toþere Ma
147 þer E; he: Samson I; deiynge CaFMW, dyenge L; killid D, kylled E,
     killede FKLP
148 manye BKMaQR; moo: AOSU, mo cet.; þanne CaDUW; quyk: alyue I,
     qwyke R; had EI; sleyn I, slayne R

393

31 ynge, than beforn he slewʒ on lyue. And
his bretheren comynge doun, and al his
kynrede, token hys bodi, and byrieden it
bitwix Saraa and Escahol, in the birielis   150
of his fader Manue; and he demyde
Yrael twenti ʒeer.

17. 1 A maner man there was in that tyme
of the hil of Effraym, Mychas bi name.
    2 The which seide to his moder, The thou-
sand hundryd platis of siluer, the whiche
thow seueredist to thee, and vpon the   5
whiche me herynge thou swore, loo! Y
haue, and anentis me ben. To whom she
answerde, Blessid my sone to the Lord.

147 þann B, þanne Lo; byforn BFHWoX, bi-forne Lo; sloʒ C, slowʒ EHWo,
    slowʒe Lo, slow X
148 breþer BWo, breþern EX, breþere F; commynge BFLo, comende CX;
    alle BLo
149 kynreden Lo; tookyn E; byryʒid BFH, biriedyn E, biryed Wo, birienden
    X
150 bytwene BFHLoWo, betwe C, betwen E, bitwen X; biryels BH, byrieles
    WoX
151 fadre BLo, fadyr EHX; demede CELoX, demyd FWo
152 ʒeere Lo, ʒere Wo

17. 1 þer BCEFHWoX
    2 of (1°): in C; hyll BF, hille HLoWo
    3 whiche BCEHLoWoX; modir BEH, modre Lo; þousant B, thousend CEX,
      þousande Lo
    4 hundreþ BF, hundred EWo, hundride Lo; platus C, plates WoX; the whiche:
      þe which F, þat XC¹
    5 seuerdist BFH, seueredest C, seueredest Lo, seruedist Wo; thee: þe Wo;
      vppon Wo; the: om. X
    6 which F; heerynge BEFH, herende CX; swoore CX; lo CEWoX
    7 hafe E; anentus C, anent X; whome BF
    8 answeride Lo; blyssed BC, blyssede F, blisside H, blissid X

31 Descendentes autem fratres eius et universa cogna-
tio tulerunt corpus eius, et sepelierunt inter
Saraa et Estahol in sepulchro patris sui Manue;
iudicavitque Israel viginti annis.

17. 1 Fuit eo tempore vir quidam de monte Effraim nomine
Michas;

31 bifore. Forsothe hise britheren and al
the kinrede camen doun, and token his   150
bodi, and birieden bitwixe Saraa and Escahol, in the sepulcre of his fadir Manue; and he demyde Israel twenti ȝeer.

17. 1 In that tyme was a man, Mycas bi
     2 name, of the hil of Effraym. And he
seide to his modir, Lo! Y haue a thousynde and an hundrid platis of siluer,
whiche thou departidist to thee, and on   5
whiche thou sworist, while Y herde, and
tho ben at me. To whom sche answeride,

149 bifor D; Forsothe: and I; his EFGILPX; breþren CaFMW, breþeren
       EHaILPUX, briþren G, briþern K; alle CD
150 the: his I; kinred E, kynreed R; comen E; tooken CGKLNOX, tookin P,
       tokun S
151 biriden E, þei birieden it I; bitwix DEQ
152 of: and of D; fader CaEFLPRU; his fadir M.: manue his f. I
153 he: sampson I; deemede BMaX, demede CaFKLMPR, demed DE, had
       demed I; ȝere E, ȝer I

17. 1 Mycas bi name: þat hiȝt mych(e)as I
     2 hille D
     3 said E; moder EFU; loo K; þousynd CaMOW, þousand DHaMaQRX,
        þousend EFGLNP, þousande K
     4 and an: om. GIKMaNQS¹X; honderde E, hundred Ha, hunderd LP;
        plates Ha; seluer L, siluir Q
     5 which EF, wiche K; departidest AcHa, departedist CaMNW, departedest
        EFLP, depardidist O, departedeste R; þe EF; vpon I
     6 which CEX, þe whiche K, wiche K; sworest EFHaL, swoorist NOX,
        sworeste R; whil EKLPR, while þat I
     7 þoo R; at: anentis I; sho E; answerde CaEFGMPQUW, answerid D,
        answerede L

2 qui dixit matri suae: Mille /et/ centum argenteos,
quos separaveras tibi, et super quibus me audiente
iuraveras, ecce ego habeo, et apud me sunt. Cui
illa respondit: Benedictus filius meus Domino.

3 Thanne he ȝeeldide hem to his moder;
the which seide to hym, I haue sacrid
and auowid this siluer to the Lord, that
of myn hoond my sone tak, and mak a
grauen thing and a ȝotun; and now I take
4 it to thee. Thanne he ȝeeld to his moder;
the which took two hundrid platis of siluer, and ȝaf hem to the siluer smith, that
he make of hem a grauen thing and
a ȝotun, the which was in the hows of

(right margin line numbers)
10

15

9 þann *BFH*, þan *Wo*; ȝeld *CEX*, ȝelde *Lo*, ȝelded *Wo*; þem *CLo*; modir *BEH*, modre *Lo*

10 whiche *BCEHLoWoX*; hafe *E*; sacride *BFHWo*, sacrede *Lo*

11 auowide *BFH*, avowed *LoWo*, auouwid *X*; seluer *C*, seluyr *E*

12 my *ELo*; hoonde *BF*, hond *CX*, hand *E*, hande *Lo*, honde *Wo*; take *cet.*; make *cet.*

13 graue *C*, grauyn *E*; þinge *BLoWo*; a: om. *X*; ȝoten *BCFHLoWoX*, ȝotyn *E*; nowe *BFHLo*

14 þe *Wo*; þann *BF*, þan *HWo*; ȝeelde *B*, ȝeld *CEFHX*, ȝelde *LoWo*; modir *BEH*, modre *Lo*

15 whiche *BCEHLoX*; toke *BFHLoWo*, toc *CX*; hundreþ *BFWo*, hundride *Lo*; plates *WoX*

16 ȝaue *BFHWo*, ȝafe *Lo*; þem *CELo*; smythe *Lo*

17 þem *CELo*; grauyn *E*, greuen *Wo*; þinge *BLoWo*

18 a: om. *Lo*; ȝoten *BCFHLoWoX*, ȝotyn *E*; whiche *BCEHLoWoX*; houȝs *H*

3 Reddidit ergo eos matri suae; quae dixerat ei: Con-
secravi et vovi hoc argentum Domino, ut de manu mea
suscipiat filius meus, et faciat sculptile atque
conflatile; et nunc trado illud tibi.
4 Reddiditque igitur matri suae; quae tulit ducentos
argenteos, et dedit eos argentario, ut faceret ex
eis sculptile atque conflatile, quod fuit in domo
Michae.

3 Blessid be my sone of the Lord. Therfor
he ʒeldide tho to his modir; and sche
seide to hym, Y halewide and avowide   10
this siluer to the Lord, that my sone resseyue of myn hond, and make a grauun
ymage and a ʒotun ymage; and now I
4 ʒyue it to thee. Therfor he ʒeldide to   15
his modir; and sche took twei hundryd
platis of siluer, and ʒaf tho to a werk man
of siluer, that he schulde make of tho a
grauun ymage and ʒotun, that was in

8 Blissed E, Blessed L; son E; þerfore BCaGKMMaNQRW, þanne I
9 ʒeeldide CaR, ʒildid D, ʒeldede EKP, bitoke I, ʒelde L; tho: om. Ha,
   þoo R; moder EFLU, modr X
10 saide E; to hym: om. D; halowid D, halowed E, haliwide G, halowide
   HaKMa, haue halewid I, halwide LQ, halwede P, halowede U; avowid D,
   vowed E, auouwede F, avowed I, avouwide MW, avowede PX, a-vouʒide R
11 siluur E, siluir QS; son E; resseyue: take it I, receyue X
12 mi E, mijn K; honde I; mak E, make þerof I; grauen CaEFGIKLMMa-
   PQUW, grauene R
13 ymage: om. I; and a ʒotun ymage: om. Ca; a: om. MMa; ʒoten
   EFIKLMMaPRW
14 ʒeue BDGHaMaQRX, ʒif E, take I, ʒife K; it: þis I; þe EF; þerfore
   BCaGKLMaNQRW, and I; ʒildid D, ʒeldede ELP, toke it ... aʒen I
15 moder EFGLMU; ʒhe S; toke DEIR, tooke Ha; two
   AcBCaFGIMMaNQW; hundride D, hundred E, hunderd LP
16 plates EFHa; siluir Q; ʒaue I; tho: hem N, þoo R; werke HaR; 16–17
   and ... siluer: om. D
17 siluir MaQ; scholde CaMW, shuld E; þoo R
18 grauen CaEFGIKLMMaPQUW, grauene R; ʒoten CaFIKLMMaPRUW,
   ʒotten E; ymage and ʒotun: & a ʒ. y. I

5 Mychee. The which a litil hows forsothe
in it to God seuerde; and made a coope,   20
and theraphyn, that is, the prestis clooth,
and mawmettis; and he fulfillid the hoond
of oon of his sones, and he is maad to
6 hym a preest. In tho dais was no kyng
in Irael, but echon, what semyd to hym   25
7 riȝt, that he dide. And there was another ȝonglynge of Bethlem of Juda, of
the kynrede of him, and he was a Le-

19 whiche *BCEHLoWoX*; lytel *BWo*; houȝs *H*, house *Lo*; 19—20 forsothe
in it: in it f. *Lo*
20 in it: om. *H*, & hit *Wo*; seuerede *CELoX*, serued *Wo*; made: om. *H*; cope
BCEFHLo, coppe *Wo*, coepe *X*
21 prestus *CX*, preestis *Lo*, prestes *Wo*; cloþ *BCEFHWoX*, cloþe *Lo*
22 maumetys *CELo*, maumetes *X*; fulfilde *CELoX*, fulfilled *Wo*; hond *BCHX*,
hand *E*, honde *LoWo*
23 one *HWo*, oen *X*; sonys *BEFH*, sonus *CX*; made *BFHLoWo*, mad *X*
24 prest *BCEFHWoX*; þase *B*, þoo *CLo*, þat *E*[1], þes *FWo*, þese *HX*; daȝes
CX, daies *EFHLoWo*; kynge *BLo*
25 bot *B*, bute *F*; echeon *BFHWo*, eche on *C*, eche one *E*, echone *Lo*, eche
X; semede *CELoX*, semed *Wo*
26 riȝte *Lo*; dydde *F*; þer *BCEFHWoX*; an ooþer *E*
27 ȝungling *CX*, ȝonglyng *E*, ȝongelynge *Lo*
28 kynreden *Lo*

5 Qui aediculam quoque in ea Deo separavit, et fecit
ephod, ac theraphim, id est vestem sacerdotalem, et
idola; implevitque unius filiorum suorum manum, et
factus est ei sacerdos.
6 In diebus illis non erat rex in Israel, sed unusquisque, quod sibi rectum videbatur, hoc faciebat.
7 Fuit quoque alter adolescens de Bethleem Iuda, ex
cognatione eius; eratque ipse levites, et habitabat
ibi.

5 the hows of Mycas. Which departide
also a litil hous ther ynne to God; and   20
made ephod, and theraphym, that is, a
preestis cloth, and ydols; and he fillide
the hond of oon of his sones, and he was
6 maad a preest to hym. In tho daies was
no kyng in Israel, but ech man dide this,   25
7 that semyde riȝtful to hym silf. Also
another ȝonge wexynge man was of Bethleem of Juda, of the kynrede therof, *that*
is, of Juda, and he was a dekene, and

19 the hous of M.: mycheis hous I; whiche D, and myche I, wiche K;
    departid D, departed E, departede LP; 19−20 departide also: also departide
    IW
20 litel FK, litle R; hou[s]e D, hous '*or an oratorie*' I; þere BR, in E
21 he made *in þat* I; ephot B, effod E, an ephot I, Ephoth Ma; therathym F,
    a theraphyn I
22 prestis AcBCCaGHaIKLMMaNPSUWX, prestes EF; clooþ AcCaKMMaW,
    cloþe R; ydoles FI, ydolis GLNQW; fillid D, filled E, fillede FLP, fulfillide
    wiþ richesse I
23 honde I; on EU; hise AcBCCaDHaKMMaNOUW; sonis GHaQRS; he:
    þat sone I
24 made DER, mad MaQ, om. BN¹RW; prest AcBCCaIKMNSUWX,
    preste E; a pr. to hym: to him a pr. I; þoo R
25 noo G; in: of U; eche DKLO, ich E; dud E, dede F; this: þat I, om. L
26 seemede BX, semede CaFKLMMaNPR, semed DE, symede O; riȝ[t]ful
    E; self CaEFKLMPRUW
27 an oþere Ac, anoþir BGMaORS; ȝong BCCaEFGHaKLMMaNOPQSWX,
    ȝung D, ȝunge I; waxinge BK, wexyng C
28 of: & of I; kinred E; therof: of him I; 28−29 *that is of Juda*: om. BIKW
29 dekne EFMPW

8 uyte, and dwellide there. And gon out
of the cytee of Bethlem pilgrimage he   30
wold, where euere he fonde profijt to
hym. And whanne he was comen in to
the hil of Effraym, and weye makynge
hadde bowid doun a litil in to the hows of
9 Myche, he is askid of hym, Whens comest   35
thou? The which answerde, A Leuyte
Y am of Bethlem of Juda, and I goo,
that I dwelle where I shal mowe, and

29 dwellid *BFHLo*, dwelte *CX*, dwelled *Wo*; þer *Wo*; goon *BFHLo*; oute *BLo*,
    ouȝte *H*
30 of (1°): fro *cet.*; cyte *cet.*; pilgrimagen *BCFHLoWoX*, pilgrimagyn *E*
31 wolde *cet.*; wher *CX*; euer *BWo*; founde *CX*, fond *E*, foonde *F*; profyte
    BFLoWo, profit *CEX*, profiȝte *H*
32 whann *B*, whan *CEFHLoWoX*; commen *BF*, comyn *E*, come *Lo*; in: om. *X*
33 hyll *BFH*, hille *LoWo*; wey *Lo*; makende *CX*
34 had *BFLoWo*; bowed *Lo*; lytyll *B*, litel *Wo*; house *B*, houȝs *H*
35 asked *EH*, askide *Lo*; whenns *B*, whennus *CWoX*, whennys *E*, whennes *Lo*;
    commyst *BF*, comyst *EH*, commest *Lo*
36 thou: -ow *Wo*; whiche *BCEHLoX*; answeride *Lo*, answared *Wo*
37 go *CELoWoX*
38 wher *C*; mowen *BFHLoWo*, moun *CEX*

8 Egressusque de civitate Bethleem, peregrinari voluit, ubicumque sibi commodum repperisset. Cumque
venisset in montem Effraim, iter faciens, et declinasset parumper in domum Michae,
9 interrogatus est ab eo: Unde venis? Qui respondit:
Levita sum de Bethleem Iuda, et vado, ut habitem
ubi potuero, et utile mihi esse perspexero.

8 dwellide there. And he ʒede out of the   30
citee of Bethleem, and wolde be a pilgrim,
where euere he foond profitable to hym
silf. And whanne he made iourney, and
hadde come in to the hil of Effraym, and
hadde bowid a litil in to the hows of   35
9 Mycha, he was axid of hym, Fro
whennus comest thou? Which answeride,
Y am a dekene of Bethleem of Juda, and
Y go, that Y dwelle where Y may, and

---

30 dwellid D, dwelled E, dwellede LP; þer E, in bethleem I; oute R
31 cite CaFHaLMPQUW; ben S; pilgryme DHa
32 wher ILP; euer BDEFIP; fond CaEFGLOQU, fonde HaIR; profitable
     þing I[1]
33 self CaEFIKLMPRUW; whan EGHaLP; had maad I, maade O; iurneye
     C, iurney EHaQ, iornei LP
34 had com E, came I; hul E
35 had EI; bowid: lowid AcEGPQRSU, lowed DL, bowed F, bowide Ha;
     a litil: a l. aside I, a litel K, om. W; house E; 35−36 the hows of Mycha:
     mycheis hous I
36 axed EG, axide Ha; he was axid of hym: mychee axide him I; from K
37 whennes CCaFHaMW, whens DEIMaQR, whennis GLNSX, whenis P,
     whenns U; comes E, comist GILOQS, commest R; þe which I, wiche K;
     answerde CaFGMPQUW, answerd D, answered E, answerede L
38 a: om. E; dekne CaFLMPW, deken ER
39 where euere M; and: & *where* I I

10 biholde to be profitable to me. Dwel, he
    seith, anentis me, and be to me fader and   40
    preest; and I shal ȝyue to thee bi eche
    ȝeer ten platis of siluer, and dowble cloth-
    inge, and what thingis ben necessarye to
11 lijflod. And he asentide, and dwellyde
    anentis the man; and was to hym as oon   45
12 of the sones. And Mycha fulfillid the
    hoond of hym, and hadde a child preest
13 anentis hym, seiynge, Nowe I woot, that
    God wol doo wel to me, hauynge a preest
    of Leuytis kynde.   50

39 byholden *BFHLoWoX*, beholden *C*, beholdyn *E*; ben *BEHLo*; profiȝtable
    H; me: om. *H*; dwell *B*, dwelle *FLoWo*
40 anentus *C*, anent *X*; fadyr *EH*, fadre *FLo*
41 prest *BCFHWoX*; ȝeue *BFHLo*, ȝifyn *E*; þe *Wo*; ech *Wo*
42 ȝer *CX*, ȝeere *Lo*, ȝere *Wo*; tenn *B*; platus *C*, plates *WoX*; seluer *C*,
    siluyr *E*; cloþing *CEHX*
43 thingus *CX*, þinges *LoWo*
44 lyfelode *BF*, liflode *CEHLoWoX*; assentide *CEFHLo*, assentid *Wo*, assentede
    X; dwellyd *BFHLoWo*, dwelte *CX*
45 anent *X*; one *BFHWo*, oone *Lo*, oen *X*
46 the: his *X*; sonys *BEFH*, sonus *CX*; fulfilde *CEX*, fulfilled *LoWo*
47 hond *CX*, hand *E*, honde *Lo*; had *BFLoWo*; childe *Lo*; prest *BFHWoX*
48 anentus *C*, anent *X*; seiende *CX*; now *BCEHWoX*; wote *BFHLo*, wot
    CEWoX
49 woll *B*, wile *C*, wil *EX*, wolle *F*, wole *HLo*; do *BCHWoX*, don *E*, doon *Lo*;
    wele *BFH*, weel *E*; hauende *CX*, hafynge *E*; prest *BCFHWoX*

10 Mane, inquit, apud me, et esto mihi parens ac sacer-
    dos; daboque tibi per annos singulos decem argent-
    eos, ac vestem duplicem, et quae ad victum sunt
    necessaria.
11 Acquievit, et mansit apud hominem, fuitque illi
    quasi unus de filiis.

10 se that it is profitable to me. Micha 40
 seide, Dwelle thou at me, and be thou
 fadir and preest to me; and Y schal ȝyue
 to thee bi ech ȝeer ten platis of siluer, and
 double cloth, and tho thingis that ben
11 nedeful to lijflode. He assentide, and 45
 dwellide at the man; and he was to the
12 man as oon of sones. And Mycha fillide
 his hond, and hadde the child preest at
13 hym, and seide, Now Y woot, that God
 schal do wel to me, hauynge a preest of 50
 the kyn of Leuy.

40 see CaFHaMWX; it: om. CaFGMaR; profitabil G; Micha: And myche I
41 saide E; dwel U; at: wiþ I
42 fader FLU; prest AcBCGHaIKLMNPSUX, preste E; f. & pr. to me: to
    me a f. & p. I; ȝeue BDGHaMaQR, ȝif E, ȝife K
43 þe E; eche FK; ȝere E, ȝer LP; plates EFHa; siluir LMaQS
44 a double I, dubble E; clooþ AcCaDKMMaRW, cloþe E, cloþing I; þoo
    R; þingus E, þinges FHa; beth E
45 needeful G, necessarie I, nedful LPSU; liuelode E, liflode FGHaILNPQSU,
    lijfloode X; assentid D, assented EP
46 dwellid D, dwelled E, dwellede LP, dwelde U; at the: atte E, wiþ þat I;
    the (2°): þat I; 46−47 as oon of sones he was to þe man W
47 one E, on U; sonis GHaLQ, his sones I; fillid D, filled E, fillede FKLP;
    47−48 fulfillide his hoonde wiþ goodis I
48 hoond R; had E, he hadde I; prest AcBCDEHaKMNOPSUWX; þe ch.
    pr.: þe pr. ch. G; at: wiþ I
49 he seide I; wote EIR, wott K, wot LPU
50 welle E, weel Ma; hauyng E; prest AcBCCaDEGIKMNOPSUWX
51 kynrede F

12 Implevitque Micha manum eius, et habuit puerum
 sacerdotem apud se.
13 Nunc scio, dicens, quod bene faciet mihi Deus, hab-
 enti levitici generis sacerdotem.

18. 1 In tho days was no kyng in Yrael;
and the lynage of Dan souȝte possessioun
to hym, that he myȝte dwelle in it; forsothe vnto that day amonge othere ly-
2 nagis he hadde takun no lot. Thanne   5
senten the sones of Dannys stok, and of
his meyne, fyue moost stronge men fro
Saraa and Escahol, that thei aspien the
loond, and bisily biholden. And thei
seiden to hem, Gooth, and biholdith the   10
loond. The whiche, whanne goynge thei
weren comen into the hil of Effraym,
and weren goon into the hows of Myche,

18. 1 þose BFWo, þoo C, þat ELo, þese HX; daȝes CX, dayes FLoWo; kynge
BLo
2 souȝt BFHWo, soȝte CX, sowte E
3 myȝt BFHWo; dwellyn E, dwellen FHLoWo; forsoþ B
4 forsothe vnto that day: vnto þ. d. f. cet.; among CEHX; oþer BHLoWo,
ooþere E; lynages LoWoX
5 had BFLoWo; taken BFHLoWo, take CX, takyn E; lott BFHWo, lotte
Lo; þan BFWo, þann H
6 sentyn E; sonys BEFH, sonus CX
7 meynee BFH; most BCEFHWo, moste LoX; strong C
8 aspie CX; 8–9 that thei aspien the loond and bisily biholden: þat þei
biholde bisili & aspie þe lond X
9 lond BCWoX, land E, londe Lo; besili CE; beholde C, beholdyn E,
biholde X
10 seydyn E; þem CLoX; goþ CELoWoX; beholdeþ CE, biholdeþ LoWoX
11 lond CX, land E, londe LoWo; which F; whann BFH, whan CLoWoX;
gooynge BF, goende CX
12 wer C, weryn E, were Wo; commen BFLo, comyn E, come X; hyll BFH,
hille LoWo
13 wer C, weryn E; gon CEWoX; houȝs H, house Lo

18. 1 In diebus illis non erat rex in Israel, et tribus
Dan quaerebat possessionem sibi, ut habitaret in ea;
usque ad illum enim diem inter ceteras tribus sortem
non acceperat.
2 Miserunt igitur filii Dan stirpis et familiae suae

404

18. 1 In tho daies was no kyng in Israel;
      and the lynage of Dan souȝte possessioun
      to it silf, to dwelle ther ynne; for til to
      that dai it hadde not take eritage among
   2 other lynagis. Therfor the sones of Dan   5
      senten fyue the strongeste men of her
      generacioun and meynee fro Saraa and
      Escahol, that thei schulden aspie the lond,
      and biholde diligentli. And thei seiden
      to hem, Go ȝe, and biholde the lond. And   10
      whanne thei goynge hadden come in to
      the hil of Effraym, and hadden entrid in
      to the hows of Mycha, thei restiden there.

18. 1 þoo R; days E; No kyng was in þo daies in I. I
     2 souȝt D; possession K
     3 it: hym D; self CaEFKLMPRUW; to (1°): forto I; þere BR; in E; til to:
        vnto EI
     4 it: dan I; had E; heritage MaR; amonge IR
     5 oþere AcBCCaDGHaIKMMaNQRW, oþur E, oþir FS; lynages CaHaRU;
        þerfore CaGKLMaNQRW, þanne I; sons E, sonys GLQ
     6 sente AcCILMaPU, sent E; fyfe K; the: of þe G; strongiste BMa, strongist
        D, strongest ELP, mooste stronge I, strengeste KX; here QR
     7 generacioun: lynage I, generacion KP; meine EFHaLMPQUW, of her
        meynee I; from K
     8 þai E; scholden CaFMW, shuldon E; londe I
     9 biholde it I, aspie W; diligentli: bisily I; thei seiden: dan seide I
    10 ȝe: om. L, ȝee U; biholde ȝe B, bihold D, biholdeȝee G
    11 whan EGLP; goyng E, goynge forþ I; had I, haddin ELP, hadde RU;
        com CE, comen I
    12 hul E, hille Ha; haddin ELP; yentred E, entride Ha
    13 þai E; resteden CaEFMPW

quinque viros fortissimos de Saraa et Estahol, ut
explorarent terram et diligenter inspicerent. Dixeruntque eis: Ite, et considerate terram. Qui cum
pergentes venissent in montem Effraim, et intrassent
domum Michae, requieverunt ibi.

3 thei restiden there. And knowynge the
  voys of the ȝonglynge Leuyte, and vsynge   15
  the restynge place of hym, thei seiden to
  hym, Who brouȝte the hidir? What here
  dost thow? For what cause hidir come
4 thou woldist? The which answerde to
  hem, Thes thingis and thes thingis My-   20
  chas hath ȝeuen to me, and me bi meed
  hath hyrid, that I be to hym a preest.
5 And thei preiden hym, that he shulde
  counseyl the Lord, and wite thei myȝten,
  whethir welsum weye thei shulden goo,   25

14 thei: om. *X*; resteden *CLoX*, restydyn *E*; þer *Wo*; knowende *CX*, knowyng
    E
15 voyce *BEFHLoWo*; ȝungling *CX*, ȝonglyng *EH*; vsende *CX*, vsyng *E*
16 resting *CX*; seidyn *E*
17 brouȝt *BFHWo*, broȝte *CEX*; þee *BCEFHLoX*; hyþer *BF*, hider *CEHWoX*,
    hidre *Lo*; heer *CEX*, heere *F*
18 doost *Lo*; hiþer *BF*, hider *CEHWoX*, hidre *Lo*; commen *BF*, comen
    CHLoWoX, comyn *E*
19 þu *B*; woldest *CLoWo*; whiche *BCEHWoX*; answerd *B*, answeride *Lo*,
    answered *Wo*
20 þem *CLoX*; þese (2x) *CEX*; þinges *B*(1°)*LoWo*, thingus *X* (2x)
21 ȝiue *CWo*, ȝifyn *E*, ȝyuen *Lo*, ȝoue *X*; meede *CF*, mede *ELoWoX*
22 hyride *BFH*, hired *ELoX*, huyred *Wo*; prest *BCFHWoX*
23 preȝeden *C*, preyedyn *E*, preyeden *HLoX*, prayden *Wo*; scholde *Lo*
24 counseyle *BCFHWoX*, cownseilyn *E*, counseylen *Lo*; lorde *Wo*; wyten
    BFHLoX, wityn *E*, weten *Wo*; myȝtyn *E*
25 wheþer *cet.*; welsomme *Lo*, welsome *Wo*; wey *Lo*; schuldyn *E*; go *CWoX*,
    gon *E*, goon *Lo*

3 Et agnoscentes vocem adolescentis levitae, utentesque illius diversorio, dixerunt ad eum: Quis te huc
  adduxit? quid hic agis? quam ob causam huc venire
  voluisti?
4 Qui respondit eis: Haec et haec praestitit mihi
  Michas, et me mercede conduxit, ut sim ei sacerdos.
5 Rogaverunt autem eum, ut consuleret Dominum, et
  scire possent, an prospero itinere pergerent, et
  res haberet effectum.

3 And thei knewen the voys of the ȝong
wexynge dekene; and thei restiden in the   15
yn of hym, and seiden to hym, Who
brouȝte thee hidur? What doist thou here?
For what cause woldist thou come hidur?

4 Which answeride to hem, Mychas ȝaf
to me these and these thingis, and hiride   20
me for meede, that Y be preest to hym.

5 Forsothe thei preieden hym, that he
schulde counsele the Lord, and thei
myȝten wite whether thei ȝeden in weie
of prosperite, and the thing schulde haue   25

14   voice DI; ȝonge AcCaFGHaKLMaRWX, ȝunge D, ȝoung I
15   wexing E, waxing K; dekne CaFLMPW, deken EIQ; resteden CaEFMW;
    in: om. ELPU
16   inne EHaN; 15–16 the yn of hym: his place I; sayden E
17   thee: om. E, þe FLPRX; hidir DGIMMaPQRUX, hider FL, hidere K;
    doist thou: dostow E, dost þou GI, doost þou LMPQW; heere GKHaI²-
    KMaP, heer R, hire U
18   woldist thou: woldest þou CFHaL, woldestou E, woldiste R; cum E;
    hidir DEGMaQUX, hidere IK, hider L, hedir P, hiþir R
19   þe whiche I, wiche K, whiche L; answerde CaFGMPQUW, answerid D,
    ansuered E, answerede L; to hem: to hym Ac, om. I; haþ ȝoue I, ȝaue R
20   þes DKNX (2x); þinges FHa; these and these thingis: þese þingis & þese
    I; hirid D, hired E, hirede FLOPU, he haþ hirid I
21   mede CaEFHaIKMQRW; prest AcCCaDEHaIKMNOSUWX
22   Forsothe: and I, forsoþ X; þai E; praiden E, preiden W
23   scholde CaMW; counceile BFGHaLMMaPQRUWX, consele C, om. Ca,
    counceil D, consaile E, counseile wiþ I; lorde E; and: & þat I, þat N
24   miȝtin P; wete U; where DEI, wher cet.; ȝede D; wey DEMaU, þe wey I,
    þe weie CRWX
25   prosperitee K; and: & þat I; the: om. E; þing of her purpos I; scholde
    CaMW, schuld D

6 and the thing shulde han effecte. The
which answerde to hem, Gooth with pees,
the Lord hath biholden ȝoure weye, and
7 the gaat that ȝe goon. And so goynge
the fyue men camen to Lachis; and thei 30
seen the puple dwellynge in it withouten
eny drede, after the vsage of Sydonyes,
sikir and in rest, no man to hem vtterli
withstondynge, and of greet ritchessis,
and fer fro Sidon, and fro alle men se- 35
8 uerd. And thei turneden aȝen to her
britheren in Saraa and Eschahol; and
what thei hadden doo to hem askynge

26 þinge LoWo; schuld B, schul Wo; haue HLo; efect C, effect ELoX
27 whiche BCEHLoWoX; answerd B, answeride Lo, answered Wo; þem
CLoX; goo B, goþ CELoWoX; pese BE, pes CWoX
28 beholde C, beholdyn E; ȝour BCFH; wey Lo
29 gate BCEFLoWoX, weye H; ȝee CELoX; gon CEWoX; so: om. X;
gooynge BF, goende CX, goyng H
30 camyn E, comen Wo
31 seeȝen BCFH, seeȝyn E, sawen Lo, seiȝen Wo, seȝen X; peple BFHLoWo;
dwellende CX, dwellyng E; with oute CX, wiþ outyn E, wiþ ouȝten H
32 any CEX; dreed B, dreede FH; aftyr ELoX
33 syker cet.; reste BCELoX; to hem: om. H; þem CELoX; outirli CE,
outerly X
34 withstondende CX; of: om. X; grete cet.; richesses CLoX, richessys EWo
35 ferre BF, ferr X; all F, al Lo; seuered BCEFHWoX, seuerede Lo
36 tornyd B, turned CWoX, turnyd E, turnyde F, tornyde H, turnede Lo;
aȝeyn BFWo, aȝeen CX, a-ȝeyne Lo; þeir BEFWo, þer CLoX
37 breþeren BEFHLoWo, breþern CX
38 hadde C, haddyn E; do CHWo, don EX, doon Lo; þem CLoX; askende CX

6 Qui respondit eis: Ite cum pace; Dominus respicit
viam vestram, et iter quo pergitis.
7 Euntes itaque quinque viri venerunt La/ch/is; vide-
runtque populum habitantem in ea absque ullo timore,
iuxta consuetudinem Sidoniorum, securum et quietum,
nullo eis penitus resistente, magnarumque opum, et
procul a Sidone atque a cunctis hominibus separatum.
8 Reversique /sunt/ ad fratres suos in Saraa et Estahol, et quid egissent sciscitantibus, responderunt:

6 effect. Which answeride to hem, Go ʒe
with pees, the Lord biholdith ʒoure weie,
7 and the iourney whidur ʒe goon. Therfor
the fyue men ʒeden, and camen to La-
chys; and thei siʒen the puple dwellynge 30
ther ynne with outen ony drede, bi the
custom of Sidonyis, sikur and resteful, for
no man outirli aʒenstood hem, and of
grete richessis, and fer fro Sidon, and
8 departid fro alle men. And thei turn- 35
eden aʒen to her britheren in Saraa and
Escahol; and thei answeriden *to britheren*

26 effecte R; whiche Ha, þe whiche dekene I, wiche K; answerde CaFMPQUW,
answerid D, answede E, answerede L; ʒee GOU
27 with: in Ac; þese E, pes I; biholdeþ FHaKLMa; ʒour KM; wey DEIMaU
28 iurney EGQS, iorney LP, iourneie R; whidir DGMaPQX, whider FU,
whidere I, whidire K, which LM, whiþir R; ʒee GOU; gon
AcCGHaILPQUX, goen BDNORS, gone E; þerfore BCaGKLMaNQRWX,
þanne I
29 the: þo I; fyfe K; ʒeden forþ I, ʒeoden K; camen E
30 sien AcBEGLPQS, seiʒen CaM, seien FW, sawʒen I; peple
CaEFILMMaNPWX; dwelling E
31 þere BR; wiþoutyn S; eni EHa, any K; dreede BG
32 custum BCaDEGHaIMMaQWX, costom L, custoum O; sykir BCaDG-
ILMMaNPQRWX, siker EFKU; restful AcBCaDEIKLMaRSWX
33 non OS; outerli AcCFISU, vttirli DGHaKMaPQX, utterli ELN, outtirli R;
no man outirli: outerli no man AcMa; aʒenstode DEHaIR, aʒenstod U;
33—34 & þei weren ful riche I
34 greet D, greete GMaOQX; richesses FLR, ricchessis KMa; and fer: &
dwelliden fer I; from K
35 departide HaKR, weren departid I; from K; An[d] E; thei: *þese fyue* I;
turnyden G
36 aʒein E, aʒeen F; here FGQR, hire L; breþren CaFMW, breþeren
EHaLPUX, briþren G, breþern K
37 answerden CaDEFGMPQUW, asweriden Ha, answereden L; breþren
CaFMW, breþeren EHaLPUX, briþren G, hem I, briþern K

409

9 thei answerden, Rysith, and stie we vp
  to hem; forsothe we han seen the loond   40
  ful riche and plenteuous; wolith not
  leeue, woleth not ceese, goo we, and weeld
10 we it; no traueyle it shal be; we shulen
  goo in to the sikyr, in to the regyoun
  moost brood; and the Lord shal taak to   45
  vs the place, in which is scarsnesse of no
  thing of hem that ben goten in the erthe.
11 Thanne wenten of the kynrede of Dan,
  that is, of Saraa and Escahol, six hundrid

39 answerdyn *E*, answereden *Lo*; riseþ *CELoWoX*; steyȝe *BFLo*, steȝe *CEX*,
    styȝe *H*, steiȝ *Wo*; wee *CEX*
40 þem *CELoX*; forsoþ *B*; forsothe we han seen: we h. s. f. *cet.*; wee *CEX*;
    seeȝen *BFH*, sene *Lo*; lond *CHX*, land *E*, londe *LoWo*
41 full *BF*; plenteuose *B*, plenteuouse *F*, plenteouse *H*; wolliþ *BF*, wileþ *CEX*,
    willeþ *Lo*, wolleþ *Wo*
42 leuen *BCFHLoWo*, lefyn *E*, lefen *X*; wolliþ *B*, wileþ *CEX*, wolleþ *EWo*,
    woliþ *H*, willeþ *Lo*; cesen *BCFWoX*, cesyn *E*, cessen *HLo*; go *CELoWoX*;
    wee *CEX*; welde *cet.*
43 wee *CEX*; hit *Wo*; no: to *B*; trauaile *CELoX*, traueyl *Wo*; ben *BEFHLoWo*;
    wee *CEX*; schuln *BFWo*, shul *CELoX*, schullen *H*
44 go *CWoX*, gon *E*, goon *Lo*; syker *BFHLoWoX*, sikere *CE*; regyon *Wo*
45 most *BCEFHWoX*, mooste *Lo*; brode *BFHWo*, brod *CEX*, broode *Lo*;
    take *BCFHWoX*, takyn *E*, taken *Lo*
46 whiche *BCEHLoWo*, þe whiche *X*; scarnesse *BCE*, scarnes *F*, scarsnes *Wo*
47 þinge *BLoWo*; þem *CLo*; gotyn *E*; erþ *BF*
48 þann *B*, þan *FWo*; wentyn *E*; kynreden *Lo*
49 sex *BLo*, sixe *CEHWoX*, sexe *F*; hundreþ *BF*, hundride *Lo*, hundred *X*

9 Surgite, et ascendamus ad eos; vidimus enim terram
  valde opulentam et uberem; nolite negligere, nolite
  cessare; eamus, et possideamus eam, nullus erit
  labor.
10 Intrabimus ad securos, in regionem latissimam, trad-
  etque nobis Dominus locum, in quo nullius rei est
  penuria eorum, quae gignuntur in terra.

9 axynge what thei hadden do, Rise ȝe,
and stie we to hem, for we siȝen the
lond ful riche and plenteuous; nyle ȝe be   40
necgligent, nil ȝe ceesse, go we, and haue
10 it in possessioun; no trauel schal be; we
schulen entre to sikir men, in to a largeste
cuntrey; and the Lord schal bitake to vs
a place, wher ynne is not pouert of ony   45
thing of tho that ben brouȝt forth in
11 erthe. Therfor sixe hundrid men gird
with armeris of batel ȝeden forth of the
kynrede of Dan, that is, fro Saraa and

38 axing E, enqueringe I; had I, haddin P; don N, do & *seiden* I; ȝee U
39 stie we: steie we F, stie we up I, stiȝe we NR; hem: hem *of lachis* I; sien
    AcBLPQX, seien CaFW, seiȝen M, han seen I
40 plenteuouse AcORS, plenteouse CU, plentyuous DF; nil E, nele FU; ȝee U
41 necligent AcBCFHaIMMaPQRX, neccligent D; nil ACaE, nele FU, nyle
    cet.; ȝee SU; cese EFLX, ceese HaIKPR; go we forþ I; haue we GI;
    41 nil ... (44) cuntrey: om. Ca
42 in to I; possession IKP; traueil DHaLX, traueile FGMaR, trauail MQ,
    trauayle UW; be *to us* I
43 schuln DF, shul EILP, schullen MW; in to K; sikur CHa, sickir E, siker
    FLMOSUW, sikire I (+ *men*), sikere K; men: placis DGHaKMaNQSX,
    places MOW; a: om. D; largiste D, largest EGHaPQ, ful large I, largist
    LMa
44 contrey C, cuntre ELP, countrey G; be-tak E, betake LP; to: om. C
45 where G; in E; no Ha; pouerte Ca; eny Ha
46 tho: þo þingis I, þoo R; bene E; brouȝte KR; foorþ D
47 eerþe R; þerfore BCaGKLMaNQRWX, þanne I; six I; hundrede E,
    hundred Ha, hunderd LP; girt EP, girde K; 47–49 of þe kynrede of dan
    six hundrid men gird wiþ armeres of batel ȝeden forþ I
48 armers DKLMR, armis E, armeres FI, armuris Ma, armes X; bateil
    DKRX, batil E, bateile Ma, bataile U; foorþ D, forþe E
49 kynred E

11 Profecti igtur sunt de cognatione Dan, id est de
Saraa et Estahol, sexcenti viri accincti armis bell-
icis;

12 men gird with armes of werre. And thei   50
   stiynge vp dwelliden in Cariathiarym of
   Jude, the which place fro that tyme took
   name of the Tentis of Dan, and is bihynde
13 the bak of Kyriathiarym. Thens thei
   passiden into the hil of Effraym; and   55
   whanne thei weren comen to the hows
14 of Myche, seiden the fyue men, that before hoond weren sent to the loond of
   Lachis to ben biholden, to her other britheren, Knowe ȝe, that in thes howsis   60
   be ephot, and theraphyn, and grauen thing
   and ȝoten; seeth what plesith to ȝou.

50 gyrde *Lo*; aarmys *BF*, armys *CEH*; werr *BFWo*
51 steyinge *B*, steȝende *CX*, steeȝynge *E*, steiȝynge *FLoWo*, styȝinge *H*;
    dwelten *CX*, dwellydyn *E*
52 whiche *BCEHLoWoX*; toke *BFHWo*, toc *CX*, tooke *Lo*
53 tentus *C*, tentes *WoX*; behinde *CE*
54 þennus *CX*, þennys *E*, þennes *LoWo*
55 passeden *BCFHLoWoX*, passedyn *E*; hyll *BFH*, hille *LoWo*
56 whann *B*, whan *CEFWoX*; weryn *E*, were *Wo*; commen *BF*, come *CX*,
    comyn *E*; houȝs *H*, house *Lo*
57 seidyn *E*; byfore *BFHWo*, befor *C*, before *E*, bi-forne *Lo*, biforn *X*
58 hond *CHX*, hand *E*, hoonde *F*, hande *Lo*, honde *Wo*; weryn *E*; sende *Lo*;
    lond *BCHX*, land *E*, londe *LoWo*
59 beholden *C*, beholdyn *E*; þeir *BFWo*, þer *CELoX*; oþere *CEX*; breþeren
    BEFHLoWo, breþern *CX*
60 ȝee *CELo*(+*not*)*X*; þese *CEWoX*; houses *BLoWoX*
61 grauyn *E*, graue *X*; þinge *BLoWo*
62 ȝotyn *E*; seeȝip *BFH*; pleseþ *CEX*

12 ascendentesque manserunt in Cariathiarim Iudae, qui
   locus ex eo tempore castrorum Dan nomen accepit, et
   est post tergum Cariathiarim.
13 Inde transierunt in montem Effraim. Cumque venissent
   ad domum Michae,

12 Escahol. And thei stieden, and dwell-   50
iden in Cariathiarym of Juda, which
place took fro that tyme the name of
Castels of Dan, and is bihyndis the bak
13 of Cariathiarym. Fro thennus thei passiden in to the hil of Effraym; and whanne   55
thei hadden come to the hows of Mychas,
14 the fyue men, that weren sent bifore to
biholde the lond of Lachis, seiden to her
other britheren, 3e knowen, that ephod,
and theraphyn, and a grauun ymage and   60
3otun is in these housis; se 3e what

50 steieden F, stieden up I, sti3eden MaNR; dwelleden CaEFLMPW, dwelden
     U
51 wich EK, þe whiche I, whiche P
52 toke EHaIR; from K; fro þat tyme toke I; name of: om. GQ
53 castellis E, tentis I, castelis S; it is I; bihynde BIN, byhyndes FHaO;
     back R
54 from BK; þennes CaFHaIMW, þens DMaQR, þennis EGNX, þenns LU,
     þenis P; thei: dan I; passeden CaEFKMPW, passide forþ I
55 hille D, hul E; whan EGLP
56 haddin EP; com C, cum E, comen S; in to CM
57 the: þo Ma; sente KRU
58 londe E; sayden E; here FQR
59 oþere AcBCCaGHaIKMMaNOQRSW, oþre F; breþren CaFMW, breþeren
     EHaLPUX, briþren G, breþern K; 3e knowun D, knowe 3e IW, knowen
     3e KMaNX, 3ee knowen U; ephod: a coope I, þe ephod O
60 theraphyn: a prestis cloþ I; a: om. E; grauen CaEFGIKLMMaPQUW,
     grauene R; ymage: ydole I
61 a 3otun B, 3oten CaEFKLMMaPRUW, a 3oten ymage I; þes DKLX;
     houses CaFHaLMP; see CaFMW; 3ee U; wat E

14 dixerunt quinque viri, qui prius missi fuerant ad
considerandam terram La/ch/is, ceteris fratribus
suis: Nostis, quod in domibus istis sit ephod, et
theraphim, et sculptile, atque conflatile; videte
quid vobis placeat.

413

15 And whanne a litil thei hadden bowid
doun, thei wenten into the hows of the
ʒonglynge Leuyte, that was in the hows   65
of Myche, and thei salutiden hym with
16 pesible wordis. Forsothe sixe hundrid
men, so as thei weren armed, stoden be-
17 fore the dore. And thei, the whiche
weren goon into the hous of the ʒong   70
man, the grauen thing and ʒoten, and
ephot, and theraphyn thei enforsiden to
taake; and the preest stood before the dore,
the sixe hundrid men moost stronge not

63   whann *B*, whan *CFLoWoX*; lytell *B*, lytyll *F*, lytel *Wo*; haddyn *E*, had *FWo*;
bowed *EWo*, bowide *Lo*
64   wentyn *E*; house *BLo*, houʒse *H*
65   ʒungling *CX*, ʒonglyng *E*, ʒongelynge *Lo*, ʒonlynge *Wo*; houʒs *H*, house
Lo
66   saluteden *CX*, salutydyn *E*, saluted *Wo*
67   peesible *Lo*; woordus *C*, woordis *E*, wordes *LoWo*, wrdis *X*; forsoþ *B*;
Forsothe sixe hundrid: s. h. f. *cet.*; sexe *BF*, sex *Lo*; hundreþ *BF*, hundride
Lo
68   weryn *E*, were *H*; aarmyd *BF*, armyd *EHWo*, armede *Lo*; stoodyn *E*,
stode *FWo*; byfore *BFHLoWoX*, befor *C*, beforn *E*
69   the whiche: þe which *BF*, þat *CX*
70   weryn *E*; gon *CEWoX*; house *BLo*, houʒs *H*; ʒonge *BEFHLoWo*, ʒunge
CX
71   grauyn *E*; þinge *BLoWo*; ʒotyn *E*
72   thei: þes *H*; enforseden *BCFHLoX*, enforsedyn *E*, enforsed *Wo*
73   take *BCFHWo*, takyn *E*, taken *LoX*; prest *BCFHWoX*; stoden *BFHX*,
stod *C*, stoode *Lo*, stode *Wo*; byfore *BFHWo*, befor *C*, beforn *E*, bi-forne
Lo, bifor *X*
74   sex *BLo*, sexe *F*; hundreþ *BF*, hundride *Lo*; most *BCEFHWoX*, moste *Lo*;
strong *CE*

15 Et cum paululum declinassent, ingressi sunt domum
adolescentis levitae, qui erat in domo Michae, salu-
taveruntque eum verbis pacificis.
16 Sexcenti autem viri, ita ut erant armati, stabant
ante ostium.

15 plesith ʒou. And whanne thei hadden
bowid a litil, thei entriden in to the hows
of the ʒong dekene, that was in the hows
of Mychas, and thei gretten hym with 65
16 pesible wordis. Forsothe sixe hundrid
men stoden bifore the dore, so as thei
weren armed. And thei, that entriden in
to the hows of the ʒong man, enforsiden
to take awey the grauun ymage, and the 70
ephod, and theraphin, and the ʒotun
ymage; and the preest stood bifore the
17 dore, while sixe hundrid strongeste men

62 pleses E, pleseþ FHaKL, pleesiþ GQ; to ʒou I; whan EGLP; haddyn EP
63 bouwid BW, bowide Ha, bowid a litil *aside* I, bowed L, bouʒid R; litel
KL, litle R; entreden CaFMPW, entred E
64 ʒonge AcGHaKMaRS, ʒunge D, ʒoung I; dekne CaFLMPQW, deken EI
65 grettin P
66 peesible GPQ; wordes CaFO; Forsothe: Soþeli D, and I, forsoþ X; six I,
seuene N; hundred EHa, hundride K, hunderd LP
67 stooden LNX; dor E; as thei: astey E
68 armyd GQ; aarmid Ha, aarmed N; entreden CaEFMPW
69 ʒonge AcCaFGHaKMMaR, ʒounge I; þe ʒounge mannes hous I;
enforceden CaFLMPW, enfoorsiden D, enforseten E, enforsiden hem I
70 away Ha; the: a Ha; grauen CaEFGIKLMMaPQRUW; ymage: ydole I;
the (2°): a I
71 ephod: cope I; theraphin: þe t. G, þe prestis cloþ I; the: a I; ʒoten
IKLMMaRW, grauen Ca
72 ymage: mawmet I; prest BCCaDHaIKMNPSUW, preste E; stode EHaI;
bifor AcMO; 70−72 to take awei þe cope & þe prestis cloþ & þe grauen
ydole & a ʒoten mawmet I; and the preest stood: and preesthode R
73 doore S; whil EKPR; þe vi G, six I; hondred E, hundred Ha, hunderd LP;
strongiste BK, strongist DMa, strongest EFHaLP, om. G, ful stronge I

17 At illi, qui ingressi fuerant domum iuvenis, sculptile, et ephod, et theraphim, atque conflatile
tollere nitebantur; et sacerdos stabat ante ostium,
sexcentis viris fortissimis haud procul expectantibus.

18 ferre abidynge. Thanne tho ilk that 75
entriden token the grauen thing, ephot,
and the mawmettis, and the ʒoten; to
whom seide the preest, What doon ʒe?

19 To whom thei answerden, Whist, and
put fynger vpon thi mouth, and com 80
with vs, that we han the[e] fader and
preest. Whether is it beter to thee, that
thou be a preest in the hows of o man,
other in o lynage and meyne in Yrael?

20 The which thing whanne he hadde herd, 85
he assentyde to the wordis of hem, and
took ephot, and the grauen thing, and

75 ferr C, fer *ELoX*; abidende *CX*; þann *BF*, þan *Wo*; þoo C, þoe E; ilk:
om. *CX*, ilke *EHLo*; tho ilk: þilk *B*

76 entreden *CLo*, entridyn E; tookyn E, tooken *Lo*; grauyn E; þinge *BLoWo*

77 maumetus *CX*, mawmetis *ELo*; ʒotyne E

78 whome *BF*; prest *BCFHWoX*; done *BH*, do *CX*, don *EWo*; ʒee *BCEFLoX*

79 whome *BF*; answerdyn E, answeriden *Wo*; whisht *CE¹LoX*

80 putt *BFH*; fyngyr E, fyngre *Lo*; vpon: in *Wo*; mowþe *LoWo*; comme *BF*,
cum *CEX*, come *HLoWo*

81 wee *BEX*; ha B, haue X; þe *LoWo*; fadir *BEH*, fadre *Lo*

82 prest *BCFHWoX*; betere *CEX*, betir F, betre *Lo*, better *Wo*; þe *Wo*

83 prest *BCEFHWoX*; houʒs H, house *Lo*; oo *BFH*, oon E

84 or *CLoX*, ouþer E; oo *BFHWo*, oon E; meynee *FH*

85 whiche *BCEHLoWoX*; þinge *BFLoWo*; whenn B, whan *CEFHLoWoX*;
had *BFLoWo*; herde *LoWo*

86 assentyd *BFHWo*, assentede *CX*; woordus C, woordis E, wordes *LoWo*,
wrdis X; þem *CELo*

87 toke *BFHLoWo*, toc *CX*; grauyn E; þinge *BFLoWo*

18 Tulerunt igitur qui intraverant, sculptile, ephod,
et idola, atque conflatile. Quibus dixit sacerdos:
Quid facitis?

19 Cui responderunt: Tace, et pone digitum super os
tuum; venique nobiscum, ut habeamus te patrem et
sacerdotem. Quid tibi melius est, ut sis sacerdos

18 abideden not fer. Therfor thei that
   entriden token the grauun ymage, ephod,   75
   and idols, and the ʒotun ymage; to whiche
19 the preest seide, What doen ʒe? To whom
   thei answeriden, Be thou stille, and putte
   the fyngur on thi mouth, and come with
   vs, that we haue thee fadir and preest.   80
   What is betere to thee, that thou be preest
   in the hows of o man, whether in o
20 lynage and meynee in Israel? And
   whanne he hadde herd this, he assentide
   to the wordis of hem, and he took the   85
   ephod, and ydols, and the grauun ymage,

74 abididen AcBCDGMaNOQSUX, abidden E, abiden FHaL, aboden I,
   abedin P; feer GS, f. þenns I; þerfore BCaEGKLMaNQRWX, þanne I
75 entreden CaEFHaMP; tokun AcS, tooken GKLOPX; grauen CaEF-
   GIKLMMaPQUW, grauene R; ephod: þe cope I
76 ydolis CaDIQW, ydoles F; ʒoten CaFILMMaRW; to: om. C; which
   DEMa, whom I, wiche K
77 prest AcBCCaHaKMMaNOSUWX, preste E; said E; don AcCDGHa-
   ILPQX, doon CaFKMMaW, done ER, do U; ʒee CaIX
78 answerden CaDEFGMPQUW, answereden L; put E, putt R
79 the: þi C¹EIKRX; fyngir AcCaDEGMMaNPQWX, fynger FKRU,
   fyngre I; upon I; mouþe E; cum E
80 þe EFGLS; fader EFLU; prest AcBCCaEHaIKNOSUX
81 is: is it I; bettir DR, better E, bettere KMaN, beter Ha; þe EF; that thou:
   þattou E, þan þou S; preest ADFQR, preste E, prest cet.; 81−82 that ...
   the: om. G
82 o (1°): oo GHaKLPQR; wher BG, wheþir MaORS, eþir EP, eþer L,
   oþer I; o (2°): oo GHaKLPQR, a I
83 and (1°): of N; meyne CaEFHaLMMaPQRUW; in: of CI
84 wan R, whan GHaLP; had EI; herde HaORSU; assentid DE, assentede LP
85 wordes F; the wordis of hem: her wordis I; toke EIR, tooke GHa, tok U
86 ephod: cope I; idolis DQW, ydoles FI; grauen CaEFIKLMMaPUW,
   grauene R

   in domo unius viri, an in una tribu et familia in
   Israel?
20 Quod cum audisset, acquievit sermonibus eorum, et
   tulit ephod, et idola, ac sculptile, et cum eis
   profectus est.

21 mawmettis, and with hem wente. The
whiche whanne weren goon, and before
hem hadden maad children and beestis   90
22 to goon, and al that was precious, and
now whanne fro the hows of Myche thei
weren ferre, the men that dwelliden in
the howses of Myche, to gidre criynge
23 folweden, and after the bak bigunne to   95
crien. The whiche whanne thei hadden
24 beholdun, thei seiden to Myche, What to
thee wolt thow? whi criest thow? The
which answerde, My goddis that I
made to me, ȝe han takun, and a preest,   100
and alle thingis that I haue; and ȝe seyn,

88 maumetus C, mawmetis ELo, maumetes X; þem CELo; went BFHWo
89 which FWo; whann B, whan CEFLoWoX, whenn H; weryn E, þei were
Wo; gon CEWoX; befor C, beforn E, byfore FWo, bi-forn LoX
90 þem CELo; haddyn E, had Lo; made BFHLoWo; childer C, childryn E,
childre Wo; bestes BWoX, bestus C, bestis EFH
91 go C, gon EWoX; all BFX, alle Lo
92 nowe FLo; whann BH, whan CFWoX; house B, houȝs H
93 wer C, weryn E; ferr CX, fer E; dwelten CX, dwellydyn E
94 housis CE, houȝses H, hous X; to giþer BF, togidere CEX, to gyder HWo;
criende CX, crienge E
95 foloweden BFHWo, foleweden CX, folewedyn E; aftyr ELo; bygunnen
BFHWo, begunne C, begunnyn E, by-gonnen Lo, bigunnen X
96 which F; whan CEFLoWoX, whann H; haddyn E
97 byholden BFHLoWo, beholden CX, beholdyn E; seidyn E
98 þe EWo; wilt CEX
99 which AWo, whiche cet.; answerd B, answeride Lo, answered Wo; goddes
LoWo, godis CX
100 maade Lo; ȝee CELoX; taken BCFHLoWoX, takyn E; prest BCFHWoX
101 all F; þinges BLo, thingus CX; hafe E; ȝee CELoX; seyne Lo

21 Qui cum pergerent, et ante se ire fecissent parvulos ac iumenta, et omne quod erat pretiosum,
22 cumque iam a domo Michae essent procul, viri qui
habitabant in aedibus Michae conclamantes secuti
sunt,
23 et post tergum clamare coeperunt. Qui cum respex-

21 and ȝede forth with hem. And whanne
   thei ȝeden, and hadden maad the litle
   children, and werk beestis, and al thing
22 that was preciouse, to go bifor hem; and   90
   whanne thei weren now fer fro the hows
   of Mychas, men that dwelliden in the
   housis of Mychas, crieden togidere, and
23 sueden, and bigunnun to crye aftir the
   bak. Whiche whanne thei hadden bi-   95
   holde, seiden to Mychas, What wolt thou
24 to thee? whi criest thou? Which answeride, Ȝe han take awey my goddis
   whiche Y made to me, and the preest,
   and alle thingis whiche Y haue; and   100

87 foorþ D; whan ELP
88 ȝeden forþ I; had E, haddin P; made DEHaR; the: her I; litil AcBDEX,
   litile I, little K, litele U
89 werke BHaR, wherk E, her werke I, weerk S²; bestis EFILPU
90 precious CaDEFGHaILMMaNOPQSUWX; bifore BCaDEGHaIKMa-
   QRUWX
91 whan EHaLP; now: not AcE; feer G; from K; hows: hoondis R; 91–92
   the hows of M.: mycheis hous I
92 dwelten Ca, dwelled E, dwelleden FLMPW, dwelden U
93 hows BEIKMaX, houses CaLPW; criden F; to gidre DIR, to gyder E
94 suweden CaFMW, suede U; bigunnun AAcHaS, bigunnen cet.; after EFU,
   bihinde I; the: her I
95 back RU; whic E, whom I, wiche K, which L; whanne: om. C, whan ELP;
   handen E, haddin P; bihoolde F, biholden G
96 seyde B, saiden E, þei seiden I; wolt thou: woltow B, wolte þou D, wiltow
   E, wilt þou LPW
97 to thee: to þe F, *be do* to þee I; wy E, what GQ; cries E; tow E; whiche B,
   þe whiche I, wiche K; answerde CaFGMPQU, answerd DE, answerede L,
   answerden W
98 ȝee U; haue R; taken ELPS; away Ha; goddes F
99 which DE, þat I, wiche K; mad E, maade G; the: my I; prest
   AcBCCaDHaIKMNOPSUWX, preste E
100 þinges FHa; whiche: þat B¹I, which DE, wiche K; & ȝit I

issent, dixerunt ad Micham: Quid tibi vis? cur
clamas?
24 Qui respondit: Deos meos, quos mihi feci, tulistis,
   et sacerdotem, et omnia quae habeo; et dicitis:
   Quid tibi est?

25 What is to thee? And the sones of Dan
   seiden to hym, Be war, lest eny more
   thou speke to vs, and men styred with
   corage comen to thee, and thou thi silf   105
26 with al thin hows perishe. And so the
   bigunne weie thei wenten. Forsothe Mycha seynge, that thei weren strenger than
   him self, he turnyde aȝen into his hows.
27 Forsothe sixe hundrid men token the   110
   preest and that we aboue seiden, and
   camen into Lachis to the puple restynge
   and siker; and thei smyten hem in
   mouth of swerd, and the cite with bren-

102 thee: þe *Wo*; sonys *BEFHWo*, sonus *CX*
103 seidyn *E*; warre *BF*; leste *Lo*; any *CX*, ony *E*
104 sterid *E*, stirede *Lo*
105 commen *BFWo*, comyn *E*; self *cet.*
106 all *B*, alle *Lo*; þi *BEFHLoWo*; houȝs *H*, house *Lo*; pershe *CEX*, perysch
    FWo
107 bygunnen *BFHWoX*, begunne *C*, bygunnyn *E*, bigonnen *Lo*; wey *LoWoX*;
    wentyn *E*; Forsothe Mycha: M. f. *cet.*
108 seeȝinge *BFH*, seande *C*, seeynge *ELo*, seȝinge *Wo*, seende *X*; weryn *E*,
    were *Lo*; strengre *B*, strengere *CEX*; þann *B*, þanne *Lo*
109 selue *E*, seluen *Lo*; tornyd *B*, turnede *CELoX*, turned *FWo*, torned *H*;
    aȝeyn *BFWo*, aȝeen *CEX*, a-ȝeyne *Lo*; houȝs *H*
110 Forsothe sixe hundrid: s. h. f. *cet.*; sex *BLo*, sexe *F*; hundreþ *BF*, hundrede
    Lo, hundred *WoX*; tookyn *E*, toke *FWo*
111 prest *BCFHWoX*; wee *CEX*; abowen *BFHWo*, abouyn *E*, a-bouen *Lo*;
    seydyn *E*
112 comyn *E*, comen *Lo*; peple *BFHLoWo*; restende *CX*
113 and: in *C*; smytyn *E*; þem *CELo*
114 mowþe *LoWo*; swerde *BFHLoWo*; brennyng *BCEX*

25 Dixeruntque ei filii Dan: Cave, ne ultra loquaris
   ad nos, et veniant ad te viri animo concitati, et
   ipse cum omni domo tua pereas.
26 Et sic coepto itinere perrexerunt. Videns autem
   Micha/s/, quod fortiores se essent, reversus est in
   domum suam.

25 ʒe seien, What is to thee? And the sones
of Dan seiden to hym, Be war, lest thou
speke more to vs, and men styrid in soule
come to thee, and thou perische with al

26 thin hows. And so thei ʒeden forth in   105
the iourney bigunnun. Forsothe Mychas
siʒ, that thei weren strongere than he,

27 and turnede aʒen in to his hows. Forsothe sixe hundrid men token the preest,
and the thingis whiche we bifor seiden,   110
and camen in to Lachis to the puple
restynge and sikur; and thei smytiden
hem bi the scharpnesse of swerd, and bi-

---

101 ʒee GU; seyn CaFHaIKMMaQWX, sayen E; is to: is þat to E; thee: þe
    EFR; sonys GQ
102 sayden E; ware D; leste BK
103 spek E, speke þus I; moore B; stirrid E, sterid GHaQU, stired KL, stiride
    R; soule: corage I
104 cum E; þe EFR; peresche B, pershe ELP, periʒsshe K, perisch R
105 þi K; þe[i] E, dan I; ʒeden: wente I; foorþ D
106 iurney EGLPQ; bigunnen BCaDEFGHaKLMMaPQRW, bigunne CIN;
    Forsothe: and I, forsoþ X
107 seiʒ CaFMW, seʒ E, sawʒe I; stronger DFHaMaRX, strongar E, strenger
    I, strengere LP; þanne D; hee S
108 turned DE, turnyde GHaQR; a-ʒein BE; in: om. CN; Forsothe: And I,
    Forsoþ X
109 þe six I, six N; hondred E, hundred Ha, hunderd LP; men: om. Ca; tooken
    CNPX, tookin L, taken OU; prest AcBCCaHaIKMNOSUWX, preste E
110 the: þo Ma; þinges FHa; wiche EK; bifore CaEGHaIKMaNQRWX;
    saiden E
111 comyn E, þei camen I; in: om. F; peple CaEFILMMaNPWX
112 resting E, þat restiden þere I; and: in Ma; sikur AAcHa, siker FL, weren
    sikire I, sikir cet.; smyteden CaKMW, smitten E, smyten F, slewen I,
    smeten L, smetin P
113 bi: in I; sharpnes E, scharpnesse R; bitooken CGKLOX, þei bitoken I,
    bitookin P

---

27 Sexcenti autem viri tulerunt sacerdotem, et quae
supra diximus, veneruntque in La/ch/is ad populum
quiescentem atque securum; et percusserunt eos in
ore gladii, urbemque incendio tradiderunt,

28 nynge thei token, no man vtterly berynge
sokour, forthi that ferre thei dwelten fro
Sydon, and with noon of men thei hadden eny thing of felawship and of erand.
Forsothe the citee was set in the regioun
of Roob; the which eft makynge out

29 dwelliden in it; the name of the citee is
clepid Dan after the name of his fader,
whom Irael gat, the which before La-

30 chis was seid. And thei putten to hem
a grauen thing, and Jonathan, the sone
of Gerson, sone of Moysy, and the sones
of hym, prestis in the lynage of Dan,

115 tookyn *E*; outirli *CEX*; berende *CX*
116 socoure *LoWo*; ferr *CLoWo*, fer *EX*; dwellydyn *E*, dwelliden *Lo*
117 noen *X*; haddyn *E*
118 any *CE*; þinge *BLoWo*; felawschipe *BLo*, felashipe *CX*, felaweschipe *E*; erande *CE*, erende *LoX*
119 Forsothe the citee: þe c. f. *cet.*; cyte *cet.*; sett *BCEFH*, sette *LoWo*; regioun: cite *X*
120 whiche *BCEHLoWo*; efte *LoWo*; makende *CX*; oute *BLo*, ouȝte *H*
121 dwelten *CX*, dwellydyn *E*; cyte *cet.*; is: om. *cet.*
122 callid *Lo*, cleped *Wo*; aftyr *ELo*; fadre *BFLo*, fadyr *EH*
123 whome *BF*; gatt *BEFHWo*, gate *Lo*; the which: þe whiche *BEHLoX*, þat *C*; byfore *BFHWo*, beforn *CE*, bi-forne *Lo*, biforn *X*
124 seide *BFHLoWo*; putte *C*, puttyn *E*; þem *CELoX*
125 grauyn *E*; þinge *BLoWo*
126 sonys *BEFH*, sonus *CX*
127 preestis *Lo*, prestes *WoX*

28 nullo penitus ferente praesidium, eo quod procul
habitarent a Sidone, et cum nullo hominum haberent
quidquam societatis ac negotii. Erat autem civitas
sita in regione Roob; quam rursum exstruentes habitaverunt in ea,

29 vocato nomine civitatis Dan, iuxta vocabulum patris
sui, quem genuerat Israel, quae prius La/ch/is dic-
ebatur.

30 Posueruntque /s/ibi sculptile, et Ionathan, filium
Gersan, filii Moysi, ac filios eius, sacerdotes in
tribu Dan, usque ad diem captivitatis suae.

28 token the citee to brennyng, while no
man outirli ȝaf help, for thei dwelliden   115
fer fro Sydon, and hadden not ony thing
of felouschipe and cause with ony of
men. Forsothe the citee was set in the
cuntrei of Roob; which citee thei bild-

29 iden eft, and dwelliden ther ynne; while   120
the name of the citee was clepid Dan, bi
the name of her fadir, whom Israel hadde
gendrid, which citee was seid Lachis

30 bifore. And thei settiden there the
grauun ymage, and Jonathas, sone of   125
Jerson, sone of Moises, and Jonathas
sones, preestis in the lynage of Dan, til

114 the: her I; cite CaFHaMPQW, brennynge DGHaMaNQRU; whil EPR
115 vttirli DEGHaKPQX, outerly IU, vtterli LMaN; ȝaue IR; helpe GQR,
     help *to hem* I; dwelleden CaEFLMPW, dwelden U
116 feer G; from K; haddin EP, þei h. I; eny Ha, to do ony I
117 felauschipe CaFMW, felouschip DEHaINR, feloschipe Ma; cause: of nede
     I; ony of: out E, ony B¹GHaKM²Ma²NOQSX, eny Ha, ony *manere* I
118 Forsothe: and I, forsoþ I; þe: *þat* I; cite CaEFHaLMPQW; sette ER,
     sett IKMaN, seet S
119 cuntre ELPQ, countre G, cuntreie R; þe whiche I, wiche K, whiche P;
     cite CaFHaLMQW; thei: þai E, *dan* I; bildeden CaEFKLMPW, beeldiden
     R
120 efte R; dwelleden CaEFLMPW, dwelden U; þere BR; in E, yne N;
     while: om. CaMO, whil ELPR, & DGHaIKMNQSX
121 the: þat I; cite CaFHaLMPQW; cleped S
122 here FGQ; fader EFLMU; wham E; had E; 122−23 hadde gendrid:
     bigaate I
123 gendride Ha, gendred L, genderid U; þe whiche I, wiche K; cite
     CaFHaLMPQW; seide DR, clepid I
124 thei: dan I; setteden CaELMPW, setten F, settide I
125 grauen BCaEFGIKLMMaPQRUW; þe sone EIR; 125 sone ... (126)
     Jonathas: om. Ha
126 sones FS; 126−27 Jonathas sones: þe sones of ionathas I
127 sonys GHaLQ; prestis AcBCCaDHaKMMaNOPSUWX, prestes E, *to
     be* prestis I; 127 til ... dai (128): om. R

31 vnto the day of his chetifte. And there
dwellide anentis hem the mawmet of
Myche, al the tyme that the hows of   130
God was in Sylo. In tho days was no
kyng in Yrael.

19. 1 A maner man Leuyte was dwellinge
in the side of the hil of Effraym, the
which took a wijf of* Bethlem Juda.
2 The which lafte hym, and is turned aȝen
into hir fader hows of Bethlem, and she   5
dwellide anentis hym foure monethis.

128 cheytyfte *BFH*, caitifte *CWoX*, cheytiftee *E*, chaytifte *Lo*; þer *BCEH*
129 dwelte *C*, dwellid *Lo*, dwelled *Wo*, dwelten *X*; anentus *C*, anent *X*; þem
CELo; mawmett *BFH*, maumete *CELo*
130 alle *BLo*; houȝs *H*
131 þos *BF*, þese *CWoX*, þat *E¹*, þes *H*, þoo *Lo*; daȝes *CX*, daies *EFLoWo*
132 kynge *BLo*

19. 1 man: om. *X*; dwellende *CX*, dwellyng *FH*
2 hyll *BFH*, hille *LoWo*
3 the which: þe whiche *BEHLo*, þat *CX*; toke *BFHLoWo*, toc *CX*; wyf
BCEFHWoX, wyfe *Lo*; of: in *A*
4 whiche *BCEHLoX*; laft *BFH*; torned *BH*, turnyd *E*, turnyde *F*, turnede
Lo; aȝeyn *BFWo*, aȝeen *CEX*, a-ȝeyne *Lo*
5 hyre *BLo*; fadris *C*, fadyr *EH*, fadre *Lo*; houȝs *H*
6 dwellyd *BFHLo*, dwelte *CX*, dwelled *Wo*; anentus *C*, anent *X*; four *H*;
moneþes *ELo*

31 Mansitque apud eos idolum Michae omni tempore, quo
fuit domus Dei in Silo. In diebus illis non erat
rex in Israel.

19. 1 Fuit quidam vir levites, habitans in latere montis
Effraim, qui accepit uxorem de Bethleem Iuda;
2 quae reliquit eum, et reversa est in domum patris
sui /in/ Bethleem, mansitque apud eum quattuor
mensibus.

424

31 in to the dai of her caitifte. And the
idol of Mychas dwellide at hem, in al
the tyme in which the hows of God 130
was in Silo. In tho daies was no kyng in
Israel.

19. 1 A man was a dekene dwellinge in the
side of the hil of Effraym, which dekene
2 took a wijf of Bethleem of Juda. And
sche lefte hym, and turnede aʒen in to
the hows of hir fadir in Bethleem, and 5
sche dwellide at hym foure monethis.

128 in: om. AcMa; to: om. O; here EGPQR; caitif[t]e E, caitiftee I, catifte X
129 ydole FGIQW; dwellid D, dwelled E, dwellede LP, dwelde U; at: wiþ I
130 the (1°): om. I; in which: in whiche GO, þat I, in wich K
131 þoo R

19. 1 dekne CaEFLMPQW, deken R; dwelling EKL
     2 the hil of: om. N; whic E, þe whiche I, wich K; dekenene Ac, dekne
        CaEFLMPQW, om. I, deken R
     3 toke EHaIR, tok F; wif EFGHaLPQU
     4 lafte K, lefte 'at' S; turned DE, turnyde GHaQ; a-ʒein E
     5 her EFMUW; fader FLM
     6 dwellid D, dwelled E, dwellede LP, dwelde U; hym: hir fadir I; moneʒ E,
        moneþes FP, monþis GQ

3 And hir man folwede hyr, wolnynge to
be recounseild to hir, and to softli treten,
and to brynge aȝen with hym; hauynge
in ledynge a child, and two assis. The   10
which took hym, and brouȝte hym into
the hows of hyr fader; that whanne his
fader in lawe hadde herd him, and seen,
glad he aȝens cam to hym, and clepide
4 the man. And the sone in lawe dwellide   15
in the hows of the fader in lawe thre
days, etynge and drynkynge with hym

7 hyre *BFLo*; folowide *BH*, folewide *CEX*, folowyd *FWo*, folwide *Lo*; hyre
BFLo; wylnynge *BFHWo*, willende *C*, wilynge *E*, willynge *Lo*, wilnende *X*
8 ben *ELo*; recounseylid *BFH*, recouncilid *CEX*, reconseylide *Lo*, reconseyled
Wo; hyre *BFLo*; softely *BCEFLoWoX*; tretyn *E*
9 bryngyn *BE*, bryngen *EHLoWo*; aȝeyn *BFWo*, aȝeen *CEX*, aȝeyne *Lo*;
hauende *CX*, hafynge *E*
10 ledende *C*, leding *X*; chylde *BLoWo*; asses *LoWoX*
11 whiche *BCEHLoX*; toke *BFHLoWo*, toc *CX*; brouȝt *BFHWo*, broȝte *CEX*
12 house *B*, houȝse *H*; hyre *BFLo*; fadir *B*, fadre *Lo*; whann *BH*, whan
CEFWoX
13 fadyr *EH*, fadre *Lo*; had *BFLoWo*; herde *HLoWo*; seeȝen *BF*, sene *Lo*,
seȝen *Wo*
14 glade *Lo*; aȝeynst *BF*, aȝen *CX*, aȝenst *EHWo*, ageynes *Lo*; came
BFHLoWo; clippede *BCEFWo*, collid *Lo*, clepede *X*
15 dwellede *BF*, dwelte *CX*, dwellid *H*, dwelliden *Lo*, dwelled *Wo*
16 houȝs *H*; fadir *BEH*, fadre *Lo*
17 daȝes *CX*, daies *EFLoWo*; etende *CX*; drinkende *CX*, drynkyng *FH*

3 Secutusque est eam vir suus, volens ei reconciliari,
atque blandiri, et secum reducere, habens in comitatu puerum et duos asinos; quae suscepit eum, et
introduxit /eum/ in domum patris sui. Quod cum
audisset socer eius, eumque vidisset, occurrit ei
laetus,
4 et amplexatus est hominem. Mansitque gener in domo
soceri tribus diebus, comedens et bibens cum eo
familiariter.

3 And hir hosebonde suede hir, and wolde
be recounselid to hir, and speke faire,
and lede *hir* a ʒen with him; and he
hadde in cumpany a child, and tweyne   10
assis. And sche resseyuede hym, and brou ʒte
him in to the hows of hir fadir; and
whanne hise wyues fadir hadde herd this,
and hadde seyn hym, he ran gladli to
4 hym, and kisside the man. And the   15
hosebonde of the dou ʒtir dwellide in the
hows of his wyues fadir in three daies,
and eet and drank hoomli with hym.

7   hir (1°): her CaEMW, here F, hire S; husbond DR, hosbond E,
    housbonde G, husbonde ILMaPQ; suwide CaMW, sued DE, suwede FN,
    suide Q; her CaMW, here F, hire K; wold E, he wolde I
8   recounselide AcO, recounsilid BKMaQ, reconselide C, recounceilid
    DGIPR, reconceiled EL, reconsiled F, recounseilide HaS, reconselid U;
    her CaMW, here F; spak EMa, to speke I; faire *wiþ hir* I
9   leede BG, to lede I; *hir*: AI, om. cet.; a-ʒein B
10   had E; cumpeny AcCFOS, cumpanye CaEHaLMPUW, cumpenye DK,
    his cumpanye I; chijld K; tweyn ELP, twey HaN, two I, tweie Ma
11   asses F; sche: he Ha; resceyued DE, resseyuyde GQR, receyuyde I,
    receiuede LX; broʒte C, brouʒt E
12   her CaLMW, here F; fader FL; the hous of hir fadir: hir fadir hous I
13   whan EHaLP; hise AN, his cet.; wifes K, wyuis Q; fader EFLMaPQU;
    had DEI; herd: om. E, herde R; hadde herd: herde Ha
14   had E; seyen BGQ, seen DMa, seyne E; hadde seyn: sawʒe I; rane R
15   kissid D, kissed E, kissede FLP, biclippide I
16   husbond DR, housbond E, housbonde G, husbonde ILMaPQ; douʒter
    CCaFKLMNSU, douʒtur E; dwellid D, dwelled E, dwellede LP, dwelde
    U; 16—17 the hows of his wyues fadir: his wyues fadris hous I
17   wifes K, wyuis Q; fader FLMPUW; in: om. CaDFGHaIKMMaNOPQSX;
    þre AcBCCaGIMMaNQWX
18   he eet AcKMa, ete EHaR, he eete I; dranke HaIRU; homeli AcBCDHaI-
    KNO, homly EFGLQU

5 homeli. Forsothe the ferthe day fro nyȝt
rysynge wold goo forth; whom with-
heelde the fader in lawe, and seith to   20
hym, Tast rather a litil of breed, and
comfort the stomak, and so thow shalt
6 goo. And thei seten, and eten to gidir,
and dronken. And the fader of the wom-
man seide to his sone in lawe, I biseche   25
thee, that this day here thou dwelle, and
7 to gider we gladen. And he rysyn[ge by]ganne
to wiln to goo forth; and neuerthelater
the fader in lawe bisily heelde hym aȝen,
and anentis hym he made hym to dwelle.   30

18 homli *CEWoX*; Forsothe the ferthe: þe ferþ/e/ fors. *cet.*; ferþ *BF*; nyȝte *Lo*
19 risende *CX*; wolde *BCEFHLoWo*, he wolde *X*; goon *BFHLo*, go *C*, gon
    EWoX; forþe *Lo*; whome *B*
20 heeld *BCEFX*, held *H*, helde *LoWo*; fadir *BEH*, fadre *Lo*
21 taste *CELoX*; raþere *CLoX*; lytyll *BF*, lytel *Wo*; brede *BHWo*, bred *CEX*,
    breede *Lo*
22 counfort *BH*, counforte *CE*, comforte *F*, conforte *Lo*, counforte *X*; stomake
    BFH; schal *Lo*
23 go *CWo*, gon *EX*, goon *Lo*; setyn *E*, setten *Lo*; and eten to gidir: tog. & e.
    cet.; eeten *CX*, eetyn *E*; to giþer *BF*, togidere *CEX*, to gyder *HWo*, to
    gidre *Lo*
24 drunken *CWoX*, drunkyn *E*; fadir *BEHX*, fadre *Lo*; woman *Lo*
25 his: þe *X*; beseche *CEX*
26 þe *Wo*; heer *CE*, heere *FLoX*
27 to giþer *BF*, togidere *CEX*, to gidre *Lo*; wee *CE*; glade *C*, gladyn *E*;
    rysynge *BFHLo*, risende *CX*, risyng *E*, rysynge *Wo*; bygann *B*, began *CE*,
    bygan *FHWoX*, biganne *Lo*
28 wilne *CLoWo*; go *CWoX*, gon *E*, goon *Lo*; nerþelatere *CX*, neuer þe
    latere *E*, neuere þe later *HLo*, neuer þe latter *Wo*
29 fadir *BEH*, fadre *Lo*; in: y *Lo*; besili *CE*; heeld *BCEFX*, helde *HLoWo*;
    aȝeyn *BEFHWo*, aȝeen *CX*, aȝeyne *Lo*
30 anentus *C*, anent *X*; hym: om. *C*; dwell *B*, dwellyn *E*, dwellen *Lo*

5 Die autem quarto de nocte consurgens, proficisci
voluit. Quem tenuit socer, et ait ad eum: Gusta
prius pauxillum panis, et conforta stomachum, et
sic proficisceris.
6 Sederuntque simul et comederunt ac biberunt. Dixit-

5 Sotheli in the fourthe dai he roos bi
ny ʒt, and wolde go forth; whom the 20
fadir of his wijf helde, and seide to hym,
Taaste thou first a litil of breed, and
counforte thi stomak, and so thou schalt
6 go forth. And thei saten togidere, and
eeten, and drunkun. And the fadir of the 25
damysele seide to the hosebonde of his
douʒter, Y biseche thee, that thou dwelle
here to dai, and that we be glad togidere.
7 And he roos, and bigan to wilne to go;
and neuertheles the fadir of his wijf 30
helde hym mekeli, and made to dwelle

19 sooþli D, soþli FGLMMaPQUWX, And I; in: om. I; ferþe E; he: þe
   deken I; rose E, roose I
20 nyʒte CaDEFKLMMaPW; gon G, haue gon I; foorþ D, forþe E; wom
   Ha, whon L; 20–21 the fadir of his wijf: his wyfs fadir I
21 fader FLPU; wif EFGHaLPQU; heeld CaDFGKLMMaNPQWX, heelde
   Ha, hilde U; seid E
22 Taaste thou: taste þou CaDFHaIMMaNQSUW, Tastou E; firste R;
   litel FK, litle R; of: om. GHaIKQ; bred EIL; and: to X
23 coũforte AcIMMaN, comfort B, comforte CF, cõforte CaLWX, counforte
   D, confort E, conforte KP, cũforte Q; þin G; shal Ac, shult E
24 foorþ D, forþe E; saaten KNX, satin LP; togidre DIR, to gyder E
25 eten CaDEFLMOUW, eetin P; drunken AcCCaDGIKMMaOPQSWX,
   dronken EFLRU, dranken N; fader EFILMaRU; the: om. L
26 damesele AcBCU, damysel DEHaLNPR, damesel IMa, damysele O;
   saide E; husbonde BLMaPQR, husbond D, housbond E, housbonde G;
   26–27 the hosebonde of his douʒter: his douʒtris husbonde I
27 douʒtir AcBDGHaMaNOPQRX; biseeche G; þee: om. D, þe EF
28 heere KX; glade C; togidre DIR, to gidir E
29 rose E, ros Ha, roose I; bigane R; willen E; to: om. E; goo GX
30 neuerþelees B, neuerþelesse CDNOUX, nerþeles ELP, neþeles GIKMaQ,
   neuerlesse S; fader FLU; wif EFGHaLPQU; the fadir of his wijf: his
   wyues fadir I
31 heeld CaFGLMMaNPX, heelde HaQR, heuld K, hilde U, bigan to holde
   W; hym: h. aʒen I; meekely G, meekli X; made: m. him BGI

que pater puellae ad generum suum: Quaeso te, ut
hodie hic maneas, pariterque laetemur.
7 At ille consurgens, coepit velle proficisci. Et
nihilominus obnixe eum tenuit socer, et apud se
fecit manere.

8 Forsothe erely bigunne the Leuyte made
redi the weye; to whom the fader in lawe
eft, I biseche, he seith, that a litil of
meet thou take, and strengthis nomen to
the tyme that ful sprynge the day, and 35
after go thow forth. Thei eten thanne to
9 gider. And the ʒonglynge roos for to
goo with his wijf and child; to whom eft
spak the fader in lawe, Behoold, that the
day is more bowid to the sunne goynge 40
doun, and neiʒeth to the euen; dwel
anentis me also this day, and lede a
myrye day, and to morwe thow shalt goo

---

31 Forsothe erely: e. f. *cet.*; erly *cet.*; bygunnen *BFHWo*, begunne *C*, begunnyn
E, bi-gonnen *Lo*
32 wey *LoWo*; whome *BF*; fadir *BE*, fadre *Lo*; in: y *Lo*
33 efte *LoWo*; beseche *CEX*; lytyll *BF*, lytel *Wo*
34 mete *cet.*; þu *B*; streyngþis *F*, strengþes *Lo*; nomyn *E*, nommen *Lo*
35 full *BF*
36 aftyr *ELo*; goo *BFH*; forth: forsoþe *H*, forþe *Lo*; eeten *CX*, etyn *E*;
þann *B*, þan *FHWo*; to giþer *BF*, togidere *CEX*, to gidre *Lo*
37 ʒungling *CX*, ʒonglyng *E*, ʒongelynge *Lo*; rose *BFLo*, ros *CEWoX*; for:
om. *C*
38 go *CELoWoX*; wyf *BCEFHWoX*, wyfe *Lo*; childe *LoWo*; whome *BF*;
efte *LoWo*
39 spake *BFHWo*; fadir *BE*, fadre *Lo*; in: y *Lo*; byholde *BFHLo*, behold *CE*,
beholde *Wo*, bihold *X*
40 bowide *BLo*; sonne *Lo*; going *CEX*
41 neyʒith *BFH*, neʒheþ *CX*, nyʒeþ *Lo*; the: om. *X*; euyn *E*, euene *LoWo*;
dwell *BH*, dwelle *FLoWo*
42 anentus *C*, anent *X*; also: om. *H*; leed *C*
43 myre *Lo*, merie *X*; morn *CX*, morewe *E*, morow *Wo*; go *CWoX*, gon *E*,
goon *Lo*

---

8 Mane autem facto, parabat levites iter. Cui socer
rursum: Obsecro, inquit, ut paululum cibi capias,
et assumptis viribus, donec increscat dies, postea
proficiscaris. Comederunt ergo simul.
9 Surrexitque adolescens, ut pergeret cum uxore sua
et puero. Cui rursum locutus est socer: Considera,

8 at hym. Forsothe whanne the morewtid
was maad, the dekene made redi weie;
to whom the fadir of his wijf seide eft,
Y biseche, that thow take a litil of mete, 35
and make thee strong til the dai encreesse,
and aftirward go forth. Therfor thei
9 eten togidere. And the ȝong man roos to
go with his wijf and child; to whom the
fadir of his wijf spak eft, Biholde thou, 40
that the dai is lowere to the goynge doun,
and it neiȝeth to euentid; dwelle thou at
me also to dai, and lede a glad dai, and to
morewe thou schalt go forth, that thou go

32 at: wiþ I; Forsothe: But I; whan EHaLP; þe: om. C; morntid BMa,
morewetide CaMW, morwetide D, morwtid E, morewetid FG, morowtid
Ha, morewetijd I, morowtide K, morwetid LNPU, morwetijd Q, morewtide
R, morowtijd X
33 made DE; dekne CaFLMQW, deken EI; made: m. him I; reedi K; wey
DU, way E, to go his wey I
34 wham E; fadur E, fader FLU; wijf: om. EU, wif FGHaLPQ; the fadir of
his wijf: his wyues fadir I; sayd E; efte ELR
35 biseeche GL, biseche þee I; litel EKL, litle R; of: om. I; meete AcGQ
36 thee: þe CEFGLMaOPRSU; stronge HaR, stroong S; til: to E, vnto I;
encreese DGK, encrese EFHaLPRX, encresse IU
37 afterward EU; go þou BK, þat þou go W; þerfore BCaFGKNQRWX,
þanne I
38 eeten AcBCGIKMaNOQRSX, ete E, eetin LP; togidre DR, to gyders E,
togider LP; ȝonge CaMaW, ȝounge I; aros E, ros Ha, roose I
39 go forþ I; wif EFGHaLPQU; wiþ þe child I, chijld K
40 fader EFLMRU, om. S; wif EFGHaLPQU; spake HaIR; efte ER;
Bihold LP
41 lower DEHaLMPRX, fer forþ gon I, lowȝere W; to: toward I; goyng
BCEHaIKLNPX; doune E
42 neiȝiþ AcBCIOPU, neiȝȝiþ CaMW, nyȝeþ D, neiȝit E; euentide
CaEKMW, euentijd GQ, þe euentijd I, euenetide R; 42—43 at me also:
also wiþ me I
43 leede BG, lede þou *wiþ me* I; to: t- E
44 morowe BKMaX, morwe DGLNPQU, morow EHa; foorþ D; that thou:
þattou E

quod dies ad occasum declivior sit, et propinquat
ad vesperum; mane apud me etiam hodie, et duc laet-
um diem, et cras proficisceris, ut vadas in domum
tuam.

10 forth, that thou goo into thin hows. The
   sone in lawe wolde not assente to his   45
   wordis; but anoon wente, and cam aȝens
   Jebuse, that bi another name is clepid
   Jerusalem, (and) ledynge with hym two assis
11 chargid, and a secoundarie wijf. And
   nowe thei camen nyȝ biside Jebus, and   50
   the day was turned into nyȝt. And the
   child seide to his lord, Com, I biseche,
   and bowe we down to the citee of Jebu-
12 sees, and dwelle we in it. To whom answerde the lord, I shal not goo into the   55
   burgh toun of an alien folk, that is not
   of the sones of Yrael, but I shal passe to

44 forþe *Lo*; go *CELoWoX*; þi *ELo*; house *B*, houȝs *H*
45 in: y *Lo*; in lawe: om. *B*; assentyn *E*, assent *Wo*; hise *E*, his fader *X*
46 woordus *C*, woordis *E*, wordes *LoWo*, wrdis *X*; bot *B*, bute *F*; anoone *Lo*,
   anon *WoX*; went *FWo*; came *BFHWo*, come *Lo*; aȝeynst *BF*, aȝen *CX*,
   aȝenst *EHWo*, aȝeynes *Lo*
47 an ooþer *E*; callid *Lo*
48 ledyng *BE*, ledende *CX*; twey *Wo*; asses *LoWoX*
49 chargede *Lo*, charged *Wo*; a: om. *H*; secundarie *CX*; wyf *BCEFHWoX*,
   wyfe *Lo*
50 now *CEHWoX*; camyn *E*; neeȝ *CE*, nyȝe *H*, neiȝ *Wo*; bysyden *BFHLo*,
   beside *C*, besydyn *E*, bisides *Wo*
51 tornyd *B*, turnyd *EF*, torned *HWo*, turnede *Lo*; nyȝte *Lo*
52 chylde *BLoWo*; comme *BF*, cum *CEX*, come *HLoWo*; besche *CEX*
53 wee *E*; to: in to *C*; cyte *BCEHLoWoX*
54 wee *EX*; whomoe *B*, whome *F*, whōm *H*; answeride *Lo*, answerd *Wo*
55 noȝt *Lo*; go *CLoWoX*, gon *E*
56 burȝ *CX*, bourgh *FH*, bourghe *Lo*; aliene *CE*; folke *HLo*
57 sonys *BEFHWo*, sonus *CX*; bot *B*, bute *F*; passyn *E*, passen *Lo*

10 Noluit gener acquiescere sermonibus eius; sed statim perrexit, et venit contra Iebus, quae altero
   nomine vocatur Ierusalem, ducens secum duos asinos
   onustos, et concubinam.
11 Iamque aderant iuxta Iebus, et dies mutabatur in
   noctem. Dixitque puer ad dominum suum: Veni, ob-

10 in to thin hows. The hosebonde of the 45
dou3tir nolde assente to hise wordis; but he
3ede forth anoon, and cam a3ens Jebus,
which bi another name is clepid Jerusalem; and he ledde with hym twei assis

11 chargid, and the wijf. And now thei weren 50
bisidis Jebus, and the day was chaungid
in to ny3t. And the child seide to his lord,
Come thou, Y biseche, bowe we to the
citee of Jebus, and dwelle we therynne.

12 To whom the lord answeride, Y schal not 55
entre in to the citee of an alien folc, which
is not of the sones of Israel, but Y schal

45 þine E, þi O; husbonde DLMaPQR, hosbond E, housbonde G; the:
þi L; 45—46 The hosebonde of the dou3tir: þe dou3ters husbonde I
46 dou3ter BCEFKLMMaUWX; nold E, wolde not I, noolde MaX; assent E,
asente R; his EGIKLPQX; wordes F; bot E
47 3eed R; foorþ D; anone E, anon P; com E, he came I, came R; a3enus
AcCNO
48 which: þat I, wiche K; an oþere Ac, anoþir MaNPRS
49 ladde K; two BDEGHaIQ, tweie CaMMaW; asses FU
50 charged L; the: his I; wyf EFGHaLPQU; þai E
51 bisides HaK; chaunged F
52 chijld K; said E
53 cum E; biseeche GL, biseche þee I; bow E, bouwe FW, bow3 R; we: om. G
54 cite FHaLMPQW; þere ynne BR, þer in E
55 the: his I; answerde CaFGMPQUW, answerid D, answerd E, answerede L
56 the: a E; cite FHaMQW; aliene HaR; whiche G, þe whiche I, wich K
57 sonys GQ; bot E

secro, declinemus ad urbem Iebuseorum, et maneamus
in ea.

12 Cui respondit dominus: Non ingrediar oppidum gentis
alienae, quae non est de filiis Israel, sed trans-
ibo usque Gabaa;

13 Gaba; and whanne thider I shal come,
we shulen dwelle in it, othir certeyn in

14 the citee of Rama. Thanne thei passiden   60
Jebus, and the bigunnen weie thei wenten.
And the sunne wente doun to hem biside
Gaba, that is in the lynage of Beniamyn;

15 and thei turneden biside to it, tbat thei
myȝten dwelle there. Whider whanne thei   65
entreden, thei seeten in the strete of the
cytee, and no man hem* wold resseyue in

---

58 whann *BH*, whan *CFWoX*, whenne *E*; þydre *BFLo*; commen *BF*, comen
CHWo, comyn *E*

59 wee *CEX*; schul *BCEFHWoX*, schulle *Lo*; dwellen *BFHLoWo*, dwellyn *E*;
oþer *BFHWo*, or *CX*, ouþer *ELo*; certeyne *Lo*

60 cyte *cet.*; þann *BF*, þan *Wo*; passeden *BCHLoX*, passedyn *E*

61 begunne *C*, begunnyn *E*, begonnen *Lo*, bigunne *X*; wey *BCHLoWo*; thei:
om. *X*; wentyn *E*

62 sonne *Lo*; went *FWo*; þem *CLoX*; bysyden *BFHLoWo*, beside *C*, besidyn *E*

64 torneden *BFHLo*, turnedyn *E*; bysyden *BFHLoWo*, beside *C*, besidyn *E*

65 myȝte *C*, myȝtyn *E*; dwellen *BFHLoWo*, dwellyn *E*; whydre *F*; whann
BH, whan *CFWoX*, when *E*

66 entrydyn *E*, entriden *Wo*; seten *CFWoX*, setyn *E*

67 cyte *BCFLoWoX*; hym *A*, þem *CLo*; wolde *BCEFHWoX*, wolden *Lo*;
receyuen *BFHLoWoX*, resceyuyn *E*

---

13 et cum illuc pervenero, manebimus in ea, aut certe
in urbe Rama.

14 Transierunt ergo Iebus, et coeptum carpebant iter;
occubuitque eis sol iuxta Gabaa, quae est in tribu
Beniamin;

15 diverteruntque ad eam, ut manerent ibi. Quo cum intrassent, sedebant in platea civitatis, et nullus
eos recipere voluit hospitio.

13 passe til to Gabaa; and whanne Y schal
   come thidur, we schulen dwelle therynne,
14 ether certis in the citee of Rama. Ther-   60
   for thei passiden Jebus, and token the
   weie bigunnun. And the sunne ʒede doun
   to hem bisidis Gabaa, which is in the
15 lynage of Beniamyn; and thei turneden
   to it, that thei schulden dwelle there.   65
   Whidur whanne thei hadden entrid, thei
   saten in the street of the citee, and no

58 passe forþ I, passa S; til to: vn to E, in to I, to S; whann D, whan EHaLP,
   whane N
59 cum E; þidir DGMaOQRX, þider EFLU, þidere IK, þedir P; schullen
   CaFMW, schuln D, shul ELP, schal I; þere ynne BR, þeryne D, þer in E
60 eiþer CaFGHaMQRW, or I, eþir LO, eiþir Ma, oþer U; certes F, ellis I;
   cite CaFHaLMPQRW; þerfore BCaEGKLMaQRWX, þanne I
61 passeden CaEFLMPW; tooken CLNPX, tokun HaS
62 wey DEILU; bigunnen AcBCCaDEFGHaKLMMaPQRUW, þat þei
   bigunnen I; doune E
63 bisides HaLU, besidis Q; which: þat I, wiche K
64 of B.: of þe sones of B. I; turnyden GIQ
65 it: gabaa I; scholden CaMW, wolden I
66 whidir DGIKMaNQX, whider EFLPU, whiþir R; þanne Ac, whan ELP;
   thei (1°): þai E; hadde O, haddin P; entride Ha; thei (2°): þai E
67 satin LP, saaten X; the (1°): om. O; strete EHaKPRW, streete GLQ;
   cite CaFHaLMQW

435

16 hows. And, loo! an oold man aperyde
to hem turnynge aȝen fro the feeld, and
fro his werk at euen, the which and he   70
was of the hil of Effraym, and a pil-
grime dwellide in Gaba. Forsothe the
men of that regioun weren the sones of
17 Gemyny. And areryd vp the eyen, the
oold man sawȝ a man sittynge with his   75
litil chargis in the strete of the cytee,
and seide to hym, Whens comest thow?

68 houȝs *H*; lo *ELoWoX*; olde *BFHLoWo*, old *CEX*; apeerid *BF*, aperede
    CEX, aperid *H*, apperid *Lo*, appered *Wo*
69 þem *CLoX*; turnende *C*, comende *X*; aȝeyn *BF*, aȝeen *CEX*, a-ȝeyne *Lo*;
    felde *BFWo*, feld *C*, feelde *Lo*; and: om. *H*
70 fro: of *H*; werke *BHWo*; euyn *E*, euene *LoWo*; whiche *BCEHLoX*
71 hyll *BFH*, hylle *LoWo*; pilgrim *CEX*
72 dwellid *BFHLo*, dwelte *C*, dwelled *Wo*; forsoth *B*; 72–73 Forsothe the
    men: þe men f. *cet.*
73 weryn *E*; sonys *BEFH*, sonus *X*
74 arered *BH*, rerid *C*, reysede *Lo*, rered *X*; eyȝen *BFHLoWo*, eȝen *CX*,
    eȝyn *E*
75 olde *cet.*; saȝ *CX*, sawe *H*, sawȝe *Lo*; sittende *CX*
76 lytyll *BFH*, litle *CE*, litel *Wo*; charges *X*; of the cytee: om. *H*; off *X*; cyte
    cet. (-*H*)
77 whenns *B*, whenus *C*, whennys *E*, whennes *LoWo*, whennus *X*; commyst *B*,
    comys *E*, comyst *FH*, comes *Lo*

16 Et ecce, apparuit eis homo senex, revertens de agro
et de opere suo vespere, qui et ipse erat de monte
Effraim, et peregrinus habitabat in Gabaa. Homines
autem regionis illius erant filii Iemini.
17 Elevatisque oculis, vidit senex sedentem hominem
cum sarcinulis suis in platea civitatis; et dixit
ad eum: Unde venis? et quo vadis?

16 man wolde resseyue hem to herbore. And
lo! an eld man turnede aȝen fro the feeld,
and fro his werk in the euentid, and ap-   70
peride to hem, which also hym silf was
of the hil of Effraym, and he dwellide a
pilgrym in Gabaa. Therfor men of that
17 cuntrey weren the sones of Gemyny. And
whanne the eld man reiside his iȝen, he   75
siȝ a man sittynge with hise fardels in the
street of the citee; and he seide to that
man, Fro whennus comest thou? and

68 wold E; receiue LNX; herborewe B, herborw Ca, herborwe DELP,
herberwe GQU, herburghe Ha, herborouȝ I, herborowe MaR, herborow X
69 loo K, so E; eeld AcCCaFGHaMMaNORWX, eelde B, elde D, holde E,
oolde I, oold KLP, eld Q; turned DE, turnyde GHaQ, turneden R; aȝein
B; from K; felde E, feld HaS
70 from K; werke R; euentide CaDEMMaPW, euentijd GIKQ, euenetide R;
apperid D, appered E, he appeeride I, apperede LP, aperede U
71 to hem: om. B; þe whiche I, wich K; self CaEFIKLMPRUW
72 hille D; dwellid D, dwelled E, dwellede LP, dwelde U
73 pilgryme D; Therfor: and I, þerfore N, forsoþ X, forsoþe cet.
74 contre E, countrey G, cuntre LP; wheren E; of þe I; sonys GNQ, sonus I
75 whan CaGHaLP, when E, whane N; elde AcGW, eeld CDMMaRX,
eelde CaHaQ, holde E, olde I, oold KLP; reisid D, reised E, reisede
FKLP, reiside up I; hise AcBCCaDHaKMMaNORSUW; eiȝen CaFMW,
iȝhen I; 75—76 whanne he reiside hise iȝen þe eld man siȝ etc. B
76 seiȝ CaFMW, sawȝe I, siȝe R; sitting E; his EFGILPQX; fardeles F,
fardelis GKLPS
77 strete EHaIKPQRW, streete LX; cite CaFHaLMPQW; and: om. BELP;
saide E; that man: him I
78 from KP; whennes CCaEFHaKMUW, whens DGIMaQR, whennis NX,
whenis P; comyst DGIQ, cumes E, commest R; thou: tow E

18 and whidre gost thow? The whych answerde to hym, We ben comen fro Beth-
lem Juda, and we goon to oure place,   80
that is in the side of the hil of Effraim,
fro whennus we ӡeden to Bethlem; and
nowe we goon to the hows of God, and

19 no man vndur his roof wol resseyue vs, hauynge chaf and hay into the fodre of assis,   85
and breed and wyn into myn, and of thin
hand maydenys vsis, and of the child that
is with me; no thing we neden, but

20 hows. To whom answerde the oold man,
Pees be with thee; I shal make redi alle   90
thingis, that ben necessarye; oonlı, I bi-

78 whyþer BF, whider CEHWo, whidir X; goost Lo; whiche BCFHLoX;
    answeride Lo, answered Wo
79 wee CEX; beþ Wo, be X; commen BF, come CX, comyn E
80 wee EX; go C, gon EWoX; our F
81 hyll BF, hille LoWo; the hil of: om. H
82 whenns BH, whenne E, whens F, whennes LoWo; wee CEX; ӡiden CX,
    ӡidyn E
83 now CEHLoWoX; wee CEX; go C, gon ELoWoX; house B, houӡs H
84 vndir BEFH, vnder CWoX, vndre Lo; roofe Lo; wylle B, wile CEX, wyl F,
    wole Lo; resseyue vs: vs r. cet.; resceyuyn E, resceyuen LoX; hauende CX,
    hafynge E
85 chaff BFH, chaffe Lo; hei CEX, heey Lo; fodder CWoX, foddyr E; asses CX
86 brede BHLoWo, bred CEX; wyne BFHLo; myne Lo; þi ELo[1]
87 hond B, hoond FWo, honde H, hande Lo; meydyns B, maidenes CLoX,
    maydynys E, maydyns FWo, meydens H; vses CLoX; chylde BLoWo
88 þinge BFLoWo; wee CEX; nedyn E; bot B, bute F
89 house BFH; whome BF; answeride Lo; olde cet.
90 pese B, pes CEWoX; þe Wo; makyn E, maken Lo; al ELo, all F
91 thingus CX, þinges LoWo; onli CX, oneli EH; beseche BCE

18 Qui respondit ei: Profecti sumus de Bethleem Iuda,
   et pergimus ad locum nostrum, qui est in latere
   montis Effraim, unde ieramus /in/ Bethleem; et nunc
   vadimus ad domum Dei, nullusque sub tectum suum nos
   vult recipere,

19 habentes paleas et faenum in asinorum pabulum, et
   panem ac vinum in meos et ancillae tuae usus, et
   pueri, qui mecum est; nulla re indigemus nisi hospitio.

18 whidur goist thou? Which answeride
    to hym, We ȝeden forth fro Bethleem of   80
    Juda, and we gon to oure place, which
    is in the side of the hil of Effraym, fro
    whennus we ȝeden to Bethleem; and now
    we gon to the hows of God, and no man
19 wole resseyue vs vndur his roof, and we   85
    han prouendre and hey in to mete of
    assis, and breed and wyn in to myn vsis,
    and of thin handmayde, and of the child
    which is with me; we han no nede to
20 ony thing, no but to herbore. To whom   90
    the eld man answeride, Pees be with thee;
    Y schal ȝyue alle thingis, that ben nede-
    ful; oneli, Y biseche, dwelle thou not in

79 whidir DGIKQSX, wider E, whider FLMaU, whedir P, whiþer R; goist
    thou: goost CaLMPW, gostow E, gost þou GHaQ, gooste I; þe whiche I,
    wiche K, whiche P; answerde CaFMPQUW, answerd DE, answerede L
80 foorþ D; from K
81 goen BDN, goon CaGKMMaW, gone ER; our E; which: þat I, wich K
82 the side of: om. G; hille D; the hil: om. E; from K
83 whennes BCaFHaKMW, whens DEGMaQR, whenns IU, whom N,
    whenis P, whennis X; ȝede E; nowe I
84 goen BDNR, goon CaGKMMaW, go E; to: into Ma
85 wolde CO, wol EL, wil P; receiue LX; vs: om. P; vndir
    BDGHaIKMaNPQRSUX, vnder FL
86 haue R; mete ABINR, þe meete GPQ, þe mete cet.
87 oure assis I, asses F; bred EHaIL; wiyn BKMaN, wyne DER; myne
    EHaMRW; vses F
88 þijn K; hond mayde BO, handemayde Ha, handmayden S; childe E,
    chiȝld K
89 which: þat I, wich K, whiche L; me: þee D; haue R; not Ha; neede G
90 eny Ha; no: om. I; herborwe DEPU, herberwe GQ, herburghe Ha,
    herborewe K¹R, hir borwe L, herborowe Ma, herborw X
91 elde AcBDFOW, eeld CGNQ, eelde CaHaMMaSX, holde E, olde IU,
    oolde KLP, oold R; answerde CaFGMPQUW, answerid D, onswerd E,
    answerede L; pes I; with: to G; þe EF
92 ȝeue BDGHaMaQR, ȝif E, ȝiue to þee I, ȝife K; þinges FHa; beþ E;
    needful R, nedful U; thingis that ben nedeful: nedeful þingis I
93 oonli BCaDGHaIKLMMaNPRWX, onli QU; biseeche GL, biseche þee I,
    beseche Q; dwel U

20 Cui respondit senex: Pax tecum sit, ego praebebo
    omnia, quae necessaria sunt; tantum, quaeso, ne in
    platea maneas.

21 seche, ne bide thow in the strete. And
   he brouȝte hym into his hows, and fodre
   to assis he ȝaf; and after that thei
   wesshen her feet, he took hem into met-   95
22 ship. Hem etynge, and after the traueyl
   of the weye with meet and drynke fillynge the bodies, camen men of that cytee,
   the sones of Belial, that is, with outen
   ȝok, and enuyrownynge the hows of the   100
   oold man thei bigunnen to knoke the
   ȝatis; criynge to the lord of the hows,
   and seiynge, Bryng out the man that is
   goon into thin hows, that we mys-vsen

 92 abyde *BEFHLoWo*, abijde *C*, biyde *X*
 93 brouȝt *BFWo*, broȝte *CEX*; house *B*, houȝs *H*; fodder *CX*, foddyr *E*,
    foddre *LoWo*
 94 asses *X*; ȝaue *BFH*, ȝafe *Lo*; aftyr *ELo*
 95 wesshe *C*, wesschyn *E*, weeschen *Lo*; þeir *BEFWo*, þer *CLoX*; fete *Lo*,
    feete *Wo*; take *BFHLoWo*, toc *CX*; meteschip *BFHWo*, meteshipe *CELoX*
 96 þem *Lo*; etende *CX*; aftir *CELoX*; traueyle *BFHWo*, trauaile *CELoX*
 97 mete *cet*.; drink *CEWoX*; fillende *CX*
 98 camyn *E*; men: om. *X*; cyte *cet*.
 99 sonys *BEFH*, sonus *CX*; wiþ oute *BCEFX*, wiþ ouȝte *H*, wiþ out *Wo*
100 ȝocke *Lo*; enuyrounende *CX*, enuyrounnynge *FHLo*; houȝs *H*
101 olde *cet*.; begunnen *BC*, begunnyn *E*, bigonnen *Lo*, bigunne *X*; knockyn
    BEF, knocke *C*, knocken *HLoWoX*
102 ȝatus *C*, ȝates *LoX*; criende *CX*, crynge *Wo*; lorde *Wo*; houȝs *H*
103 seiende *CX*; brynge *BFHLoWo*; ouȝte *H*, oute *BLo*
104 gon *CEWoX*; þy *BEFWo*, þine *Lo*; houȝs *H*, house *Lo*; wee *CEX*; mys-vse
    C, mys-vsyn *E*

21 Introduxitque eum in domum suam, et pabulum asinis
   praebuit; ac postquam laverunt pedes suos, recepit
   eos in convivium.
22 Illis epulantibus, et post laborem itineris, cibo
   et potu reficientibus corpora, venerunt viri civitatis illius, filii Belial, id est absque iugo, et
   circumdantes domum senis, fores pulsare coeperunt,
   clamantes ad dominum domus, atque dicentes: Educ
   virum, qui ingressus est /in/ domum tuam, ut abuta-
   mur eo.

21 the street. And he brouȝte hym in to his
hows, and ȝaf mete to the assis; and after 95
that thei waischiden her feet, he ressey-
22 uede hem in to feeste. While thei eeten,
and refreischiden the bodies with mete
and drynk after the trauel of weie, men
of that citee camen, the sones of Belial, 100
that is, with out ȝok, and thei cumpassiden
the hows of the elde man, and bigunnun
to knocke the doris; and thei crieden to
the lord of the hows, and seiden, Lede out
the man that entride in to thin hows, that 105

94 strete DEHaIKPQRX, streete GL; brouȝt AcDR, brouth E; in: om. D
95 ȝaf him E, ȝaue IR; meete GHaQ; the: his EI; asses EF; mete to the assis:
his assis mete I; after AELOU, aftir cet.
96 thei: he* O; wasscheden CaEFLMPW, waischeden D, waschiden HaRSU,
'had' weishen I, waiȝssheden K, hadde* waischide(n) O; here FGQ; fete E;
resceyued DE, resseyuide GQ, toke I, receyuede X
97 him E; in: om. I; feest DK, feste EMUW, mete I, feestis R; wile E,
whil KLPR; eten CaDEFMUW, eetin LP
98 refresscheden CaEFLMPW, refreischeden D, refreschiden HaRS,
refreiȝsshiden K; the: her I; meete GHaOQ
99 drynke AcBCaDFHaILMMaPRUWX; after AEFIU, aftir cet.; traueil
DWX, trauayle GQU, trauele K, traueile Ma; of: & Ma; her wey I,
wei U
100 cite CaFHaMPQW; comen E; sonis GN, sonus I
101 wiþoute CaFHaIKMMaNRSUWX, withouten EGLPQ; ȝock R;
cumpaceden CaEFLMPW
102 eelde CaGHaMS, hold E, olde I, oolde K, oold LP, eeld MaORX, eld N;
the hows of the elde man: þe olde mannes hous I; bigunnen
AcBCCaDEGHaIKLMMaNOPQSUWX, bigonnen FR
103 knoc E, kn. on I; dores CaFHaLPR, dorres E; criden Ca
104 leede GK; oute ER
105 entred E, entrede PU; þijn K

23 hym. And the oold man wente oute to   105

hem, and seith, Wolith not, bretheren,
wolith not doon this yuel; for a man is
goo into myn hows; and cees ӡe fro this

24 foly. I haue a douӡter mayden, and this
man hath a secoundarie wijf; I shal   110
brynge hem out to ӡow, that ӡe lowen*
hem, and ӡoure lust ӡe fulfil; oonli, I
byseche, ne this hidows gilt aӡens kynde

105 olde *cet.*; went *FWo*; out *CEFWoX*, ouӡte *H*
106 þem *CELoX*; wolliþ *BFH*, wileþ *CEX*, willeþ *Lo*, wolleþ *Wo*; noӡt *Lo*; breþern *CX*
107 wolliþ *BF*, wileþ *CEX*, wylleþ *Lo*, wolleþ *Wo*; noӡt *Lo*; do *CX*, don *EWo*; euel *CWoX*, euyl *E*, yuele *Lo*; a: þe *X*
108 goon *BFHLo*, gon *CEWoX*; my *BEFHLoWo*; house *B*, houӡs *H*; cese *BCEFWoX*, cesse *HLo*; ӡee *CEHLoX*
109 fooly *B*, folie *CLoX*; hafe *E*; doӡter *CX*, doӡtyr *E*; meyden *BFH*, maydyn *E*
110 secundarie *CX*, secondarye *Wo*; wyf *BCEFHWoX*, wiffe *Lo*
111 bryngyn *E*, bringen *Lo*; þem *CELoX*; oute *BLo*, ouӡte *H*; ӡee *CELoX*; lowe *CX*, lowyn *ELo*, louen *cet.*
112 þem *CEX*; ӡour *BCFHWo*; luste *Lo*; ӡee *CELo*; fulfylle *BCHWoX*, fulfillyn *E*, fulfyll *F*, fulfillen *Lo*; onli *CWoX*, onely *E*
113 beseche *CEX*, bisech *Wo*; hidouse *E*, hydouӡs *H*; gilte *CELoX*; aӡeynst *BFH*, aӡen *CX*, aӡenst *E*, aӡeynes *Lo*, aӡeynus *Wo*

23 Egressusque est ad eos senex, et ait: Nolite,
fratres, nolite facere malum hoc; quia ingressus
est homo hospitium meum, et cessate ab hac stultitia.

24 Habeo filiam virginem et hic homo habet concubinam;
educam eas ad vos, ut humilietis eas, et vestram
libidinem compleatis; tantum, obsecro, ne scelus hoc
contra naturam operemini in virum.

442

23 we mysuse him. And the elde man ȝede
out to hem, and seide, Nyle ȝe, britheren,
nyle ȝe do this yuel; for the man entride
in to myn herbore; and ceesse ȝe of this
24 foli. Y haue a douȝter virgyn, and this   110
man hath a wijf; Y schal lede out hem
to ȝou, that ȝe make lowe hem, and fille
ȝoure lust; oneli, Y biseche, that ȝe worche
not this cursidnesse aȝens kynde aȝens the

106 mysvsen I, missuse K; eelde CCaGHaMQSX, olde EI, oolde K, oold LP,
eeld O, eld R
107 oute R; sayde E; Nil E, nele F; ȝee U; breþren CaFMW, breþeren
EHaILPUX, briþren G, breþern K
108 nil E, nele F; ȝee U; yuele Ac, euel E, euyl GLPQ; the: om. S; entrid D,
entred E, haþ entrid I, entrede P
109 myne R; herborwe DELP, herberwe GQU, herburghe Ha, herborowe MaR,
herborw X; cese EFHaX, ceese KLPR; ȝee U
110 folye CaEGKLMMaRUW; douȝtir AcCCaDGHaMMaNOPQRX,
douȝtere I; virgyne CaGHaIMQRW, vergyn U
111 wyf EFGHaLPQU; Y: & I I; leede BGK, brynge I; oute R; out hem:
hem out CaI
112 ȝee U; low BEP, lowȝ CaMNW; make lowe hem: make hem lowe I;
fulfille I
113 ȝour CaKL; oonly BCaDGHaIKLMMaNPRWX, onli EFQSU; biseche
ȝou I; ȝee U; wurche CaFMW, wirche EILR, werche P
114 cursidnessis B, cursednes E, cursednesse U; aȝens (1°): aȝenus AcCNO,
aȝeins E, aȝen I; kynd HaR; aȝens (2°): aȝenus AcCNO, anentis I; the:
þis BIX

25 ȝe worchen in the man. Thei wolden
not assente to his wordis; the which
thing biholdynge the man broute out to
hem his secoundarie wijf, and to hem
he took hir to be scorned. The which
whanne al nyȝt thei hadden mysvsid,

26 thei laften hir eerly. And the womman,
goynge aweie the derknessis, came(n) to
the dore of the hows, where dwellide hir

---

114 ȝee *CELoX*; wirchen *BFWo*, werche *CX*, werchyn *E*; woldyn *E*
115 assenten *BFHLoWoX*, assentyn *E*; hise *E*; woordus *C*, woordis *E*, wordes
LoWo, wrdis *X*; whiche *BCEHLoX*
116 þinge *BLoWo*; beholdende *CX*, beholdyng *E*; brouȝte *BFHLo*, broȝte *CEX*,
brouȝt *Wo*; oute *BFLo*, ouȝte *H*
117 þem (1°) *CEX*; secundarie *CHLoX*; wyf *BCEFHWoX*, wyfe *Lo*; þem (2°)
CX
118 toke *BFHLoWo*, toc *CX*; hyre *BFLo*; ben *ELo*; scornede *BLo*, scornyd *E*;
whiche *BCEHLoX*; whanne al nyȝt: al n. wh. *Lo*[1]
119 whenn *B*, whan *CEFLoWoX*, whann *H*; all *BF*; nyȝte *Lo*; haddyn *E*, had
Lo; mysused *BFHLoWo*
120 laftyn *E*, leften *X*; hyre *BFLo*; erly *cet.*
121 goende *CX*, goyng *E*; awei *CELoWoX*; dercnesses *CEHLoX*; camen *BFH*,
cam *CEX*, come *Lo*
122 house *B*, houȝs *H*; wher *C*; dwellid *BFHLo*, dwelte *CX*, dwelled *Wo*;
hire *BFLo*

25 Nolebant acquiescere sermonibus eius. Quod cernens
homo, eduxit ad eos concubinam suam, et eis tradidit
illudendam. Qua cum tota nocte abusi essent, dimiserunt eam mane.

26 At mulier, recedentibus tenebris, venit ad ostium
domus, ubi manebat dominus suus, et ibi corruit.

25 man. Thei nolden assente to hise wordis; 115
which thing the man siȝ, and ledde out
his wijf to hem, and bitook to hem hir
to be defoulid. And whanne thei hadden
misusid hir al niȝt, thei leften hir in the
26 morewtid. And whanne the derknessis 120
departiden, the womman cam to the dore
of the hows, where hir lord dwellide, and

115 nolde ELOR, nolden not Ha, wolden not I, noolden MaX; assent E; his
EFGILPQX; wordes F
116 þe whiche I, wiche K; seiȝ CaFMW, seȝ E, seynge I, siȝe R; and: he I;
led E, ladde K; oute R
117 wif EFGHaLNPQU; to hem (1°): om. R; bi-toke EHaR, bitok F, he
bitoke I; her CaMW, here F, hire K; to hem hir: hir to hem GHaINQ
118 defoulede E, defouled LPU; whan EFGHaLP, whane N; þai E; had E,
haddin P
119 mysused EKPU; her BCaMW (2x), here F (2x), hire K (2x); þai E; leftin P
120 morntid BMa, morewetide CaMW, morwetide DL, morowtide EK,
morewetid FG, morowtid Ha, morewtijd I, morwetyd N, morwtide P,
morwetijd Q, morewtide R, morowetid U, morowtijd X; whan EGHaLP;
the: om. N; derknesses F, derkenessis of niȝt I, derkenessis R,
derkenesses U
121 departeden CaEFMPW; wumman CaFMW, woman E; com E, came IR;
doore S
122 wher GSU; her CaEMW, here F, hire KL; dwellid D, dwelled E, dwellede
LP, dwelde U

27 lord, and there she felle down. The
   morwe tide doon, the man roos, and
   openede the dore for to fulfil the bigunne   125
   weye; and, loo! his secoundarie wijf lay
   at the dore, spred the hoondis in the
28 threswold. To whom he wenynge hir
   to reste spak, Ryse, and goo we. The
   which no thing answerynge, vndurstond-   130
   ynge that she was deed, took hir, and
   putte on the asse; and he is turnyd aȝen

123 þer *HWo*; fell *BFH*, fel *CEWoX*
124 morwtyde *BFH*, morntid *CX*, morewtid *E*, morowtide *Wo*; done *BFH*,
     don *CEWoX*; rose *BF*, ros *CEWoX*, roose *Lo*
125 opnede *BF*, opened *Wo*; fulfillen *BCFH*, fulfillyn *E*, fulfille *WoX*; bygun *B*,
     begunne *C*, begunnyn *E*, by-gonnen *Lo*
126 wey *Lo*; lo *CEFWoX*; secundarie *CX*, secoundary *Wo*; wyf *BCEFHWoX*,
     wife *Lo*; ley *Lo*
127 spredde *BFHWo*, sprede *Lo*; hondis *BX*, hondus *C*, handys *E*, hondes *LoWo*
128 þreschwolde *BFWo*, þreshold *CEX*, þreschfolde *H*, threschefolde *Lo*;
     whome *BFLo*; weenende *C*, wenyng *E*, wenende *X*; hyre *BFLo*
129 resten *BCFHLoWoX*, restyn *E*; spake *FWo*; ris *CEX*; go *CELoWoX*; wee
     CEX
130 whiche *BCEHLoX*; þinge *BLoWo*; answerende *CX*; vndirstondynge *BE*,
     vnderstondende *CX*, vnderstondynge *FH*, vndrestondynge *Lo*,
131 dead *BCE*, dede *LoWo*, ded *X*; toke *BFHLoWo*, toc *CX*; hyre *BFLo*
132 put *Lo*(+hire)*Wo*; tornede *BFH*, turned *CWoX*, turnede *Lo*; aȝeyn *BFWo*,
     aȝeen *CEX*, aȝeyne *Lo*

27 Mane facto surrexit homo, et aperuit ostium, ut
   coeptam expleret viam; et ecce, concubina eius iacebat ante ostium, sparsis in limine manibus.
28 Cui ille, putans eam quiescere, loquebatur: Surge,
   et ambulemus. Qua nihil respondente, intelligens
   quod erat mortua, tulit eam, et imposuit asino, re-
   versusque est in domum suam.

446

27 there sche felde doun. Whanne the morewtid was maad, the man roos, and
openyde the dore, that he schulde fille   125
the weie bigunnun; and lo! his wijf lay
bifor the dore, with hondis spred in
28 the threischfold. And he gesside hir to
reste, and spak to hir, Rise thou, and
go we. And whanne sche answeride no   130
thing, he vndirstode that sche was deed;
and he took hir, and puttide on the
asse, and turnede aȝen in to his hows.

123 þer E; fel CaEFIKLMPW, filde D, felle R; whan EHaLP, and whanne I;
     morntid BMa, morewetid CFU, morewetide CaMW, morwetid D,
     morowtide EK, morewetijd G, morowtid HaX, morewtijd I, morwtide LP,
     morwetijd NQ, morewtide R
124 made DR; ros EHa, rose I
125 openede BCaKLMMaP, opened DE, opnyde I, opynede O; scholde
     CaFMW, shuld E; 125−26 that he schulde fille the weie bigunnun:
     forto go forþ his iourney I
126 wei LU; bigunnen AcBCaDEFGHaKLMMaPQRUW; wif EFGHaLPQU
127 bifore BCaGHaKLMMaNPQRUWX, at I; with: hir I; hondes CaF;
     spredde C, sprad Ha, spred abrod I; in: on X
128 þreisfold AcHaOSU, þreischefoold B, þresfold C, þres/s/chfold CaFIMRW,
     þreshold ELP, þreiȝshfoold K, þreischold Ma, þreishfoold X; gessid D,
     ghessed E, gessede LP, gisside O; her CaMW, here F, hire S; 128−29
     And ... thou: To whom he spake gessynge þat sche had restid hir rise I
129 rest ER; spake DHaR; her CaMW, here F, hire K
130 whan EGHaLP, whane N; answerde CaEFGMPUW, answerid D,
     answerede L; And etc.: þe whiche no þing answeringe I
131 vndurstood AcCCaMOW, vndirstood BDFGKMaPQX, vndirstode E,
     vnderstood LS, vndirstod N, vnderstod U; dede E, dead Q
132 toke EIR, tok FU, tooke Ha; her CaMW, here F, om. I, hire K; puttid D,
     putted E, putte FM, hir puttide G, putte hir I, puttede LP; the: an I
133 turned DE, turnyde GHaNQ, he turnede I; aȝein E; in: om. ELP

29 into his hows. The which whanne he
was goon yn, he cauȝte a swerd, and the
careyn of the wijf with hir bonys in   135
twelue parties and gobetis hewynge, he
30 sente into alle the teermys of Yrael. The
which thing whanne alle thei hadden
seen, thei crieden to gidre, Neuer siche
thing is don in Israel, fro that dai that   140
oure faders stieden vp fro Egipt vnto the
tyme that is nowe; ȝyueth sentens, and
in comoun deme ȝe, what is nede to the
deed.

---

133   house *B*, houȝs *H*; whiche *BCEHLoX*; whann *B*, whan *CFHLoWoX*
134   gon *CEWoX*; inne *Lo*; cauȝt *BHWo*, caȝte *CX*; swerde *BFHLoWo*
135   careyne *ELo*; wyf *BCEFHWoX*, wyfe *Lo*; hyre *BFLo*; bones *CEWoX*,
     boones *Lo*
136   partus *C*, partes *X*; gobetus *C*, gobyttes *Lo*, gobettis *Wo*, gobetes *X*;
     hewende *CX*, hewyng *E*
137   sent *FH*, sende *Lo*; all *F*, al *H*; termys *BEFHWo*, termes *CLoX*
138   whiche *BCEHLoWoX*; þinge *BFLoWo*; whann *B*, whan *CEFWoX*; all *F*;
     haddyn *E*
139   sene *Lo*; criedyn *E*; to giþer *BF*, togidere *CEX*, to gyder *HWo*; neuere *LoX*;
     such *CEX*, sich *FWo*, suche *Lo*
140   þinge *BFWo*; done *BH*, doon *F*, doone *Lo*
141   our *F*; fadris *CEWoX*, fadres *HLo*; steyȝiden *BWo*, steȝeden *CX*, steȝedyn
     E, steyȝieden *F*, steiȝeden *Lo*
142   now *CEWoX*; ȝifiþ *BFH*, ȝifeþ *E*; sentence *CEHLoWoX*
143   comun *CEX*, comyn *Wo*; ȝee *CELoX*; neede *B*
144   deede *BCEFHWoX*, dede *Lo*

---

29 Quam cum esset ingressus, arripuit gladium, et cadaver uxoris cum ossibus suis in duodecim partes ac
frusta concidens, misit in omnes terminos Israel.
30 Quod cum vidissent singuli, conclamabant: Numquam
res talis facta est in Israel ex eo die, quo ascenderunt patres nostri de Aegypto, usque in praesens
tempus; ferte sententiam, et in commune decernite,
quid facto opus sit.

29 And whanne he entride in to that hows,
he took a swerd, and departide in to   135
twelue partis and gobetis the deed body
of the wijf, and sente in to alle the
30 termes of Israel. And whanne alle men
hadden herd this, thei crieden, Neuere
siche a thing was don in Israel, fro that   140
dai in which oure fadris stieden fro
Egipt til in to present tyme; seie ʒe
sentence, and deme ʒe in comyn, what is
nede to be doon.

134   whan EGHaLP; entrid AcD, entred E, was entrid I, entrede P; to that
      hows: om. I
135   toke ER, tooke Ha, cauʒte I; departid DE, he hewide I, departede LP
136   twelfe K; partise E, parties S; gobettis DS; dede E, deede G, deade Q;
      body: careyn I
137   the: his I; wif EFGHaLPQ; 135–37 in to ... wijf: þe deed careyn of his
      wijf wiþ hir boones in to xii parties & gobetis I; sent E, he sente þese I;
      al U; the: om. F
138   teermes DMaNRX, termis EGQ, coostis I; whcn E, whan FGLP; alle men:
      þei alle I
139   hadyn E, haddin LP; herde HaU; 138–39 And ... this: þe whiche þing
      whanne þei alle vndirstoden I; criden U, seiden togidre wiþ hiʒe voice I;
      neuer CaDEHaI
140   sich AcBCFIKMaSUX, such CaGHaLMNPQRW, suche D, shuc E; a:
      om. I; doen B, doon CaKMMaQSW, done ER, doun Ha; from K
141   in which: þat I, in wiche K, in whiche R; our E; faders E, fadres FHa;
      steieden F, st. up I, stiʒeden MaNR; from K; 139–42 Neuere etc.: fro
      þat dai þat oure fadris stieden up fro egipt vnto þe tyme þat is now was
      neuer sich þing don in I. I
142   til in to: vnto EI; present tyme: þe tyme þat is now I, þis present t. K¹;
      seie: ʒiue I; ʒee GU
143   þe sentence AcMa, sentens DE; deeme BGMaX; ʒee U; in comyn: in
      comoun doom G, herof in comoun I, in comune Ma, in comun X
144   neede P; don AcDHaNSUX, done ER, don *for þis dede* I

20. 1 And the sones of Yrael wenten out,
and to gidre gedreden as o man, fro Dan
vnto Bersabee, and fro the loond of Ga-
2 laad to the hows of Maspha; and alle
the corneres of puplis, and alle the ly-   5
nages of Yrael camen to gidre into the
chirche of the puple of God, foure hundryd thowsandis of foot men fiȝters.
3 And it was not vnknowun to the sones
of Beniamyn, that the sones of Yrael   10
hadden stied vp into Maspha. And a
Leuyte, the housboond of the slayn womman, askid, what maner wyse so myche

20. 1 sonys *BEFH*, sonus *CX*; wentyn *E*; oute *BFLo*, ouȝt *H*
  2 to giþer *BF*, togidere *CEX*, to gyder *HWo*; to gidre gedreden: g. tog. *Lo*;
    geþerd *BF*, gadered *C*, gaderid *E*, gederd *H*, gaderide *Lo*, gidered *Wo*,
    gedered *X*; oon *BEF*, one *H*, on *Wo*
  3 lond *CWoX*, land *E*, londe *Lo*
  4 vn to *X*; houȝs *H*, house *Lo*
  5 corners *BFHWo*, corneris *ELo*; peplis *BFHLoWo*, puples *X*; all *F*, al *H*;
    lynagis *BCEFH*
  6 camyn *E*, comen *Lo*; to giþer *BF*, togidere *CEX*, to gyder *HWo*
  7 chirch *Wo*; peple *BFHLoWo*; four *B*; hundreth *BF*, hundride *Lo*, hundred
    Wo
  8 thousend *CX*, thousendis *E*, þousandes *LoWo*; fote *BFHLoWo*, foote *E*;
    fiȝteres *CLoX*, fiȝteris *E*
  9 noȝt *Lo*; vnknowen *BCFHLoWoX*, vnknowyn *E*; sonus *CX*, sonys *EFH*
 10 sonus *CX*, sonys *F*
 11 haden *B*, haddyn *E*; steȝid *BC*, steȝed *EX*, steyȝid *FWo*, styȝid *H*,
    steiȝede *Lo*
 12 hosbonde *BF*, husbonde *CEX*, houȝsebonde *H*, housebonde *Lo*, husbond
    Wo; sleyn *BFH*, slaine *CE*, sclayne *Lo*
 13 asked *EWo*, askide *Lo*; moche *Lo*

20. 1 Egressi itaque sunt omnes filii Israel, et pariter
congregati, quasi vir unus, de Dan usque Bersabee,
et terra Galaad ad Dominum in Maspha;
  2 omnesque anguli populorum, et cunctae tribus Israel
in ecclesiam populi Dei convenerunt, quadringenta
millia peditum pugnatorum.

20. 1 Therfor alle the sones of Israel ʒeden [out],
and weren gaderid togidere as o man,
fro Dan til to Bersabee, and fro the lond
of Galaad to the Lord in Maspha; and
2 alle the corneris of puplis; and alle the   5
lynagis of Israel camen to gidere in to the
chirche of the puple of God, foure hun-
3 drid thousynde of foot men fiʒters. And
it was not hid fro the sones of Benia-
myn, that the sones of Israel hadden stied   10
in to Maspha. And the dekene, hosebonde
of the wijf *that was* slayn, was axid,

20. 1 þerfore BCaGKLMaNQRUWX, Therefore F, And I; alle: om. I; sonys
GNQ; ʒeden: wenten out I, ʒeden oute R, ʒeden out cet.
2 weren: om. I; gederid CKN, gadered EL, gadrid FGR, gedride hem I;
to gidre DFINR, to gyder E, to gidir U; oo GHaKLPQR
3 from K (2x); til to: vnto EI, al to X
4 Lord: lond Ha; 1−4 And fro dan vnto B. & fro þe lond of G. to þe lord
in M. þe sones of I. wenten out & gedride hem to gidre as o man I
5 corners DEHaIKLMPRX, corneres F; peplis CaEIMMaNPWX, peples F;
alle... puplis: þe peplis in alle corners *of þe lond* I
6 lynages FR; comen E; to gidre DINR, to gyder E, to gidir U
7 cherche CaFLM; peple CaEFILMMaNPWX; the puple of God: goddis
peple I; hundred EHa, hunderd LP
8 þousynd CaIMW; þousand DEHaMaNQRX, þousend FGLP, þousande
K; fote ER; fiʒteris AcBCCaEFGNOPQSW; foot men fiʒters: fiʒtinge
foot men I
9 hid: vnknowen I; fro: to I, from K; sonis GHaQ
10 sonis GQ; haddin EP; steied F, stiede HaO, stied up I, stiʒed MaNR
11 to: om. GHaQ; the: whanne þe I; dekne CaEFLMPQW; husbond DER,
housbonde G, husbonde IMaQ, hosbonde LP
12 wijf: wumman CaFMW, woman E, womman cet.; *that was*: om. cet.;
sleyn I, slayne R; wijf ... slayn: sleyn womman I; axed E

3 Nec latuit filios Beniamin, quod ascendissent filii
Israel in Maspha. Interrogatusque levita, maritus
mulieris interfectae, quomodo tantum scelus per-
petratum esset,

4 hidows gilt were doon, he answerde, I
cam into Gabaa of Beniamyn with my 15
5 wijf, and thidre I turnede. And loo! the
men of that cytee enuyrounden at ny3t
the hows, in the which Y dwelte, willynge to slee me, and my wijf traueyl-
ynge with vntrowable woodnes of lust, 20
6 and therfor she is deed. The which
taken Y hew3 into gobetis, and I sente
partis into alle the teermys of 3oure possessioun; for neuer so myche felony and
so myche trespas worthi to be punysshid 25

14 hidouse *ELo*, hydou3s *H*; gilte *CELoX*; done *BFH*, do *CX*, don *EWo*,
doone *Lo*; answeride *Lo*, answered *Wo*
15 came *BFHWo*, come *Lo*
16 wyf *BCEFHWoX*, wife *Lo*; þider *CEHWoX*; tornede *BFH*, torned *Wo*;
lo *CELoWoX*
17 that: þe *Lo*; cyte *BCFHLoWoX*; enuyrounende *C*, enuyrownydyn *E*,
environeuden *LoX*, enuyrounde *Wo*; ny3te *Lo*
18 hou3s *H*, house *Lo*; the: om. *C*; whiche *BCEHLoX*; dwellide *ELo*, dwelled
Wo; wilnende *C*, wilynge *E*, willende *X*
19 slea *B*, sle *CWo*, slen *EX*; wyfe *BLo*, wif *CEFHWoX*; trauailende *CX*,
trauailynge *E*
20 vntrowhable *E*, vntroweable *Lo*; wodnesse *BCFHX*, woodnesse *E*, wodenesse
LoWo; luste *Lo*
21 þerfore *BCEFHWoX*, þerefore *Lo*; dead *BCE*, dede *LoWo*, ded *X*; whiche
BCELoX, wyche *H*
22 takyn *E*; heew3 *E*, hewe *LoWo*, heew *X*; gobytis *BF*, gobetus *C*, gobyttes *Lo*,
gobetes *X*; I: om. *X*; sent *FHWo*, sende *Lo*
23 partyes *Lo*, partes *X*; all *F*, al *H*; termys *BEFHWo*, termes *CX*, tentis *Lo*;
3our *BCFH*
24 neuere *EHLoX*; mych *F*; felonye *CLo*, felownye *EX*
25 myche: grete *BFHLoWo*, gret *CX*, grett *E*; trespasse *BFH*, trispas *Lo*;
wrþi *X*; ben *ELo*; punshid *CX*, punshed *E*, punyschede *Lo*

4 respondit: Veni in Gabaa Beniamin cum uxore mea,
illucque diverti.
5 Et ecce, homines civitatis illius circumdederunt
nocte domum, in qua manebam, volentes me occidere,
et uxorem meam incredibili furore libidinis vex-
antes, denique mortua est.

4 how so greet felonye was doon; and he
answeride, Y cam with my wijf in to Gabaa of Beniamyn, and Y turnede thidur. 15
5 And lo! men of that citee cumpassiden in
nyʒt the hows, in which Y dwellide,
and thei wolden sle me, and thei bitra-
ueliden my wijf with vnbileueful woodnesse of letcherie; at the last sche was 20
6 deed. And Y took, and Y kittide hir
in to gobetis, and Y sente partis in to alle
the termes of ʒoure possessioun; for so
greet felonye and so greuouse synne was

13 how: in what manere wise I; grete ER, myche I, gret L; felony AcHa, an
hidous gilt I; were I; don AcCDGHaINPUX, doen B, done E; and: om.
CaDGHaIKMNOQX
14 answerde CaFGMPQUW, answerd D, answered E, answerede L; com E,
came IR; wif EFGHaLPQU; 14−15 cam … Beniamyn: came in to G. of
B. wiþ my wijf I
15 Y: om. I; turnyde AcGHaQW, turned D; þidir DGMaQRX, þider ELU,
þydere IK, þedir P
16 loo K; cite CaEFHaMNQW; cumpaceden CaEFLMPW, cumpasiden D,
cumpaaseden M
17 þe niʒt I; the: þat K; in: om. AcCaDEFHa¹IKLMMaNOPQSUX; þat I,
wich K; dwellid D, dwelled E, dwellide ynne IK, dwellede P, dwelde U
18 wolde E; slee CaFGKPQU, haue slawe I; traueliden AcBCKNOS,
trauaileden CaFMUW, traueileden D, traueleden ELP, traueyliden
GHaMaRX, han traueilid I, trauailiden Q
19 wif EFGHaLPQU; with: in B; vnbileful AcDQR, vnbileeful B, vnbilefful
ELP, vnleful GMa, vnbileeueful HaK, vncredible I, unbileefful N, vnbileuful
SU; wodnesse EILOP, wodenesse R
20 lecherie CaFLM; at the: & at þe I, atte E; last ADR, laste cet.
21 dede E, ded Ha, dead Q; tok EF, tooke Ha, toke IR; Y (2°): om.
GHaIMMaNQRWX; kittid D, kitted E, kutte F, kitte I, kittede LMP;
her CaMW, here F, hire K
22 gobettis BDES; Y: om. KRX; sent E; part Ca, partes F, þo partes of hir I
23 termys GHaQ, teermes MaNRX; ʒour EIKM; possessions G, possession K
24 gret EILP, grete R; greuous CaDEFGHaKLMMaNQX, gret I

6 Quam arreptam in frusta concidi, misique partes in
omnes terminos possessionis vestrae; quia numquam
tantum nefas, et tam grande piaculum factum est in
Israel.

7 is doon in Irael. ȝe ben nyȝ to alle the
   sones of Yrael; demeth, what ȝe owen
8 to doon. And stondynge al the puple as
   with word of o man answerd, We shulen
   not goon aȝen into oure tabernaclis, ne
9 eny man shal goo into his hows; but
   this aȝens Gabaa in comoun we shulen

26 done *BFHWo*, don *CEX*; ȝee *CELoX*; neeȝ *CE*, neiȝ *Wo*; all *F*
27 sonys *BEFH*, sonus *CX*; deemiþ *B*, demiþ *FH*; ȝee *CELoX*; owe *C*, owyn
   E, owiþ *H*
28 do *CX*, don *E*, done *HWo*; stondende *CX*; alle *BLoWo*, all *F*; peple
   BFHLoWo
29 woord *CE*, worde *LoWo*, wrd *X*; oo *BFH*, oon *E*; answerde *BCEFHX*,
   answeride *Lo*, answered *Wo*; wee *CEX*; schul *cet.*
30 go *CX*, gon *EHWo*; aȝeyn *BFWo*, aȝeen *CX*, aȝeyne *Lo*; tabernacles *EX*
31 any *CE*; goon *BF*, go *CX*, gon *EHWo*, gan *Lo*; house *B*, houȝs *H*; bot
   BFH
32 aȝeyn *BFHWo*, aȝen *CEX*, aȝeyne *Lo*; comun *CEX*, comyn *Wo*; wee *CEX*;
   schul *BCEHLoWoX*, schuln *F*

7 Adestis omnes filii Israel; decernite, quid facere
   debeatis.
8 Stansque omnis populus, quasi unius hominis sermone
   respondit: Non recedemus in tabernacula nostra, nec
   suam quisquam intrabit domum;
9 sed hoc contra Gabaa in commune faciemus.

7 neuere doon in Israel. Alle ȝe sones of   25
  Israel ben present; deme ȝe, what ȝe owen
8 do. And al the puple stood, and answeride as bi word of o man, *that is acord-*
  yngli, with out aȝenseiyng and with out
  delay, We schulen not go awei in to   30
  oure tabernaclis, nethir ony man schal
9 entre in to his hows; but we schulen do

25 neuer DEHaILPR; don AcCDGHaINQUX, doen B, do ELP, done R;
    now alle I; ȝe: þe CFNO, ȝee U; sonys GQ
26 bene E; deeme BGMaX; ȝee U (2x)
27 to do DEIKMMaOR²S²; alle EMa, all U; the: om. E; peple
    CaFILMMaNPWX; stode EIR, stoode Ha, stod U; answerde CaFGMP-
    QUW, answerd D, answered E, answerede L, answeriden Ma
28 worde E, þe word I, woord P, o word X; oo GHaKLPQR; acoordingly B,
    accordingli K
29 with out (1°): wiþouten CaDEGHaQ, wiþoute FKLMNPRUWX, and
    wiþout AcMa; aȝenseiynge AcCaFGHaMMaQRW, aȝeinseiyng B, ony
    aȝenseiynge DLP, eni aȝenseiyng E, aȝen-seinge U; with out (2°): wiþoute
    CaEFKLMMaNPRUWX, wiþouten GHaQ; 28−30 gloss om. I
30 dilay B, dalai P; schullen CaMW, schuln DF, shul EILP; awai EHa,
    aweie R, henns I, aȝen W
31 our E; tabernacles FR; neþer AcBCDKLNPSUX, neiþer CaFGHaIMQRW;
    eni EHa, ani LP; man: of us I
32 schullen CaMW, schuln DF, shul EILP; 32−33 do this in comyn: in
    comoun do þis þing I

10 doo. Ten men ben chosun of an hundrid,
of alle the lynagis of Yrael, and an hundrid of a thowsand, and a thousand of
ten thowsandis, that thei beren to the
oost metis, and we fiȝtynge mowen aȝens
Gabaa of Beniamyn ȝeelden to hym for

11 the hidows gilt, that he deserueth. And
al Yrael cam to gidre to the citee, as
o man, in the same thouȝt and with o

12 counseil. And thei senten messageris to
al the linage of Beniamyn, the whiche
shulden seye, Whi so myche felonye is

33 done *BFHWo*, do *CX*, don *E*, doon *Lo*; tenn *BH*; be *CLoX*; chosen
BCFHLoWo, chosyn *E*; an: a *Lo*; hundreth *BF*, hundride *Lo*
34 all *F*, al *H*; lynages *Lo*, men *X*; an: a *Lo*; hundreþ *BF*, hundride *Lo*
35 a: an *BF* (2°); þousand *BF* (2°), thousend *C*(2x)*X*, þousande *Lo* (2x);
and a thousand: om. *X*
36 tenn *BH*; thousend *CX*, þowsendys *E*, þousandes *LoWo*; bere *CX*, bern *E*;
36—37 to the oost metis: m. to þe o. *C*
37 ost *CWoX*, host *E*; metus *C*, metes *LoWoX*; wee *CEX*; fiȝtende *CX*,
fiȝtenge *F*; moun *CEX*; aȝeyn *B*, aȝen *CX*, aȝenst *EHWo*, aȝeynst *F*,
aȝeynes *Lo*
38 ȝeelde *CX*, ȝeeldyn *E*, ȝelden *HLoWo*
39 hidowse *ELo*, hydouȝs *H*; gilte *CELoX*; deseruyþ *BFH*
40 alle *BLo*; came *BFHWo*, comen *Lo*, camen *X*; to giþer *BF*, togidere *CEX*,
to gyder *HWo*; cyte *BFHLoWoX*
41 o (1°): oon *BEFWo*, one *H*, a *Lo*; thoȝt *CEX*, þouȝte *Lo*; o (2°): oo *BFH*,
oon *E*
42 counseyle *LoWo*; sente *C*, sentyn *E*; messagers *BFH*, messageres *CWoX*
43 alle *B*, all *F*, all(e) *Lo*; the whiche: þe which *FWo*, þat *C¹*
44 schuldyn *E*; seyn *BEFLoWoX*, sei *C*, seyen *H*; mych *BF*; felownye *EX*,
felony *Wo*

10 Decem viri eligantur e centum ex omnibus tribubus
Israel, et centum de mille, et mille de decem millibus, ut comportent exercitui cibaria, et possimus
pugnantes contra Gabaa Beniamin reddere ei pro
scelere, quod meretur.
11 Convenitque universus Israel ad civitatem, quasi
homo unus, eadem mente unoque consilio.
12 Et miserunt nuntios ad omnem tribum Beniamin, qui
dicerent: Cur tantum nefas in vobis reppertum est?

10 this in comyn aȝens Gabaa. Ten men
    be chosun of an hundrid, of alle the ly-
    nagis of Israel, and an hundrid of a thou-   35
    synde, and a thousynde of ten thousynde,
    that thei bere metis to the oost, and that
    we, fiȝtynge aȝens Gabaa of Beniamyn,
    moun ȝelde to it for the trespas that
11 that it deserueth. And al the puple, as   40
    o man, cam togidere to the citee bi the
12 same thouȝt and o counsel. And thei
    senten messangeris to al the lynage of
    Beniamyn, whiche messangeris seiden,
    Whi so greet felony is foundun in ȝou?   45

33 comoun GI, comune Ma; aȝenus AcCNO; 33—34 Ten men be: Be þer ten
    men I
34 be: ben B¹D¹Ma; chosen CaFHaILMMaPRUW, chosin E, chosene K;
    hundred EHa, hunderd LP; al Ma; linages EFRU; lynage Ma
35 hundred EHa, hundrid men I, hunderd LP; a: an E; þousynd CaIMW,
    þousand DEHaKMaNQRX, þousend FGLP
36 þousynd (2x) CaI(2°)MW, þousand (2x) DEHaKMaNQRX, þousend (2x)
    FGLP, þousynd men I (1°)
37 beere HaQ, beire R; metes EF, meetis GHaQ; host E; that (2°): om. CI
38 fiȝting E; aȝenus AcCNO
39 moun ELP, mowen IU; ȝeelde Ca, ȝilde D; trispas D; the: þis I; that:
    þat þing I; 39—40 to it þat þing þat it haþ disserued for þis trespas I
40 that: at E; disserueþ AcBCCaDFKMaNOSU, haþ deserued E, deseruiþ G,
    haþ disserued I, disseruiþ Q; alle EMa; peple CaEFILMMaNPWX;
    40—41 as o man: om. I
41 oo GHaKLPQR; com E, came IR, camen Ma; to gidre DIR, to gydur E;
    cite CaFHaMPQW
42 and: & bi I; o: om. CCaDM, oo GHaKLPQR; consel C, counceil
    CaDFGHaIMMaNQSWX, counsaile E, counceile R; thei: israel I
43 sente I; messangers DMX, messagers EK, messangeres FHaR,
    messengeris G, messengers LP; alle ER; lynages R
44 whiche m.: which m. EF, & þei I, wiche m. K; messangers DFMX,
    messagers EK, messengeris G, messangeres HaR, messengers LP,
    massangerus O; sayden E
45 grete ER, gret LP; felonye CCaEFKMMaPQRWX, a felonye I, filonie L;
    whi is so gret a f. I; founden CaDEFGHaLMMaPRUW

13 foundun in ʒou? Takith the men of Ga- 45
baa, that this trespasse han doo, that thei
dyen, and yuel be doo awey fro Yrael.
The whiche wolden not here the mawnde-
ment of the sones of Yrael, her britheren,

14 but of alle the cytees, that weren of her 50
lot, camen togidre in Gabaa, that to hem
thei myʒten bere helpe, and aʒens al the

15 puple of Yrael fiʒten. And there ben
founden fyue and twenti thowsandis of
Beniamyn, of men drawynge out swerd, 55

45 fonden *B*, founden *CFHLoWoX*, fowndyn *E*; takeþ *CEWoX*
46 trespas *CEWoX*, trispas *Lo*; done *BHWo*, do *C*, don *EX*, doon *FLo*
47 die *C*, deyen *H*; euel *CWoX*, euyl *E*, yuele *Lo*; don *BCELoWoX*, doon *F*, done *HWo*; aweye *BH*
48 which *FWo*; woldyn *E*; heren *BHLoX*, heeryn *E*, heere *F*
49 sonys *BEFH*, sonus *CX*; þeir *BEFWo*, þer *CLoX*; breþeren *BEFHLoWo*, breþern *CX*
50 bot *B*, bute *F*; cytese *B*, cites *CE*; þeir *BEFX*, þer *CLo*, þe *Wo*
51 lott *FHWo*, lotte *Lo*; camyn *E*, comen *Lo*; to giþer *BF*, togidere *CEX*, to gyder *HWo*; þem *CEX*
52 myʒte *C*, myʒtyn *E*; beren *BFHLoWo*, bern *CEX*; and aʒens: aʒ. & *C*; aʒeynst *BF*, aʒen *CX*, aʒenst *EHWo*, aʒeynes *Lo*; alle *BFLo*
53 peple *BFHLoWo*; fiʒte *C*, fiʒtyn *E*; þer *BCEFHWoX*; beþ *Wo*
54 founde *CX*, foundyn *E*; thousend *CX*, þousendis *E*, þowsandes *LoWo*
55 drawende *CX*, drawyng *ELo*; oute *BLo*, ouʒt *H*; swerde *BFHLoWo*

13 Tradite homines de Gabaa, qui hoc flagitium per-
petrarunt, ut moriantur, et auferatur malum de Israel. Qui noluerunt fratrum suorum filiorum Israel
audire mandatum;

14 sed ex cunctis urbibus, quae sortis suae erant,
convenerunt in Gabaa, ut illis ferrent auxilium, et
contra universum populum Israel dimicarent.

15 Inventique sunt viginti quinque millia de Beniamin
educentium gladium, praeter habitatores Gabaa,

13 Bitake ȝe the men of Gabaa, that diden
 this wickidnesse, that thei die, and yuel
 be doon awey fro Israel. Whiche nolden
 here the comaundement of her britheren,

14 the sones of Israel, but of alle the citees,
 that weren of her part, thei camen togidere in to Gabaa, to helpe hem, and to

15 fiȝte aȝens al the puple of Israel. And fyue
 and twenti thousynde weren foundun of
 Beniamyn, of men drawynge out swerd,

50

55

46 ȝee GU; diden: han do I, dedin P
47 wickednesse E; þai E; deie CaFMW, diȝe R; euil EFGPQ, þe yuel I,
 euel L; 47—48 be þe yuel don away I
48 bi U; don AcCDFGHaIUX, doen B, done E; away Ha; from K;
 wiche K, But Beniamin I; nolde C, wolde not I, noolden MaX
49 heere GHaKMaNSX, hire U; cummaundement E, heest I, commaundement
 R; hire L, here QR; breþren CaFMW, breþeren EHaILNPUX, briþren G,
 breþern K
50 sonis GQ; of: men of I; cites L
51 her part: here p. FQ, þe p. of beniamyn I, here parte R; thei: om. I;
 comen E; togidre DEIR, togider P
52 help DE
53 fiȝt E; aȝenus AcCNO; alle E; peple CaEFILMMaNPWX; And: om. O
54 þousynd CaIMW, þousand EHaKMaNQRX, þousend FGLP; wheren E,
 were CaMW; founden AcCaDFGHaKMMaQRUW, founde EILP;
 53—55 And of þe lynage of beniamyn weren founde fyue & twenti þousynd
 of men I
55 drawyng EP

459

16 biside the dwellers of Gabaa, that weren
  seuen hundryd moost myȝti men, so with
  the lift as with the riȝt fiȝtynge, and so
  with slyngis stones at certeyn throw-
  ynge, that an heer forsothe thei myȝten   60
  smyte, and in to noon other partie the
  strook of the stoon shulde be born aweye.
17 Forsothe of the men of Yrael, with outen
  the sones of Beniamyn, ben foundun foure
  hundrid thowsandis of men drawynge out   65

56 bysydes *BFLoWo*, beside *C*, besydys *E*, bysydis *H*; dwelleris *CELoX*;
   weryn *E*
57 sefne *E*, seuene *LoWo*; hundreþ *BF*, hundride *Lo*, hundred *X*; most
   BCEFHWoX, moste *Lo*
58 lifte *LoWo*, left *X*; riȝte *Lo*; fiȝtende *CX*
59 slingus *CX*, slengis *Lo*, slynges *Wo*; stoones *Lo*; certeyne *Lo*; þrowende *CX*
60 here *BFHWo*, her *CEX*, heere *Lo*; forsoþ *BH*; myȝte *C*, myȝtyn *E*
61 smyten *BFHLoWo*, smytyn *E*; non *Wo*, noen *X*; ooþer *E*; part *CX*, party
   Wo
62 stroke *BFHWo*, stroc *CX*, strooke *Lo*; stone *BFHWo*, ston *CEX*, stoone
   Lo; schuld *Lo*; ben *ELo*; borne *BFHLo*; awei *CELoWoX*
63 Forsothe of the men: of þe m. f. *cet.*; wiþ oute *BCEFX*, wiþ ouȝte *H*,
   wiþ out *Wo*
64 sonys *BFH*, sonus *CX*; founden *BFHLoWo*, founde *CX*, foundyn *E*
65 hundreth *BF*, hundride *Lo*; thousend *CX*, thousendis *E*, þousandes *Lo*;
   drawende *CX*, drawyng *E*; oute *BLo*, ouȝte *H*

16 qui septingenti erant viri fortissimi, ita sinistra
  ut dextra proeliantes, et sic fundis lapides ad
  certum iacientes, ut capillum quoque possent per-
  cutere, et nequaquam in alteram partem ictus lapidis
  deferretur.
17 Virorum quoque Israel, absque filiis Beniamin, in-
  venta sunt quadringenta millia educentium gladium,
  et paratorum ad pugnam.

16 outakun the dwelleris of Gabaa, whiche
weren seuen hundrid strongeste men,
fiȝtynge so with the lefthond as with the
riȝthond, and castynge so stoonus with
slyngis at a certeyn thing, that thei myȝten   60
smyte also an heer, and the strook of the
stoon schulde not be borun in to the
17 tother part. Also of the men of Israel,
with out the sones of Beniamyn, weren
foundun foure hundrid thousynd of men   65

---

56 out taken CaFMW, outaken BEGHaKLMaPQRU, wiþoute I, outtakun
OSX; dwellers DEHaKLMPUX, dwelleres F, men dwellinge I; of: in I;
which EF, þe whiche I, wiche K
57 weren: om. E; seuene BNW, vi CFGHaOQRSU, sixe AcCaEKPX, six L;
hundred EHa, hunderd LP; strongiste BO, strengeste Ca, strongist DLMa,
strongest EHaP, ful stronge I
58 fiȝting E; lift hond BEGKLMaQW, lifte hond HaP, lefte hond IK
59 casting E; so: of K²; c. so: so c. I; stoonys AcGMaNOQS, stoones BPX,
stonys CU, stones CaDFHaIKNRW, stonus E
60 slynges CaFHa; at: as at M; a: om. W; certayn E, certeyne R; þng E;
miȝtin EP; 60–61 þat þei also þei (exp. & cr. out) myȝten smyte an heer I
61 smyten O; here E, her LN; strok EGIOU, stroke R; the: a E
62 ston EHaIU; scholde CaFMW; born CaDFGKLMMaNPWX, borne ER,
born awei I; the: noon I
63 toþir BGOPRX, oþer I; partie *or asijde* I, parte R
64 wiþoute CaDFIKLMMaNPRUWX, wiþouten EGQ; sonis GHaNQ;
were AcMW, wher E
65 founden CaDFGHaIKLMMaPRUW, funden E; hundred EHa, hunderd
LP; þousynde AcBCOSU, þousand DEHaKMaNQRX, þousend G,
þousende LP; of men: om. I

18 the swerd and redi to the fiȝt. The
whiche rysynge camen into the hows of
God, that is in Silo; and thei counseyl-
den hym, and seiden, Who shal be in
oure oost prince of the strijf aȝens Ben-   70
iamyn? To whom the Lord answerde,
19 Judas be he ȝoure duyk. And anoon the
sones of Yrael rysynge eerly setten tentis
20 aȝens Gabaa. And thens goynge forth to
the fiȝt aȝens Beniamyn, thei bigunnen to   75
21 fiȝt aȝens the cytee. And the sones of
Beniamyn goon out fro Gabaa, slowen of
the sones of Irael that day two and

66 the (1°): om. *X*; swerde *BFLoWo*; the (2°): om. *FLo¹WoX*; fiȝte *Lo*
67 which *FWo*; risende *CX*; camyn *E*, comen *Lo*; houȝs *H*
68 counseileden *CLoWoX*, cownseiledyn *E*
69 hym: þe lord *Lo²*; seidyn *E*; ben *BCEFHLoWo*
70 ost *CWoX*, host *E*, hoost *H*; stryfe *BHLo*, strif *CEFWoX*; aȝeynst *BF*,
aȝen *CX*, aȝenst *EHWo*, a-ȝeynes *Lo*
71 whome *BFLo*; the Lord answerde: answ. þe l. *cet.*; answerd *BF*, answeride
Lo; answered *Wo*
72 ȝour *BCFH*; duyke *BFH*, duke *CELoWo*, duk *X*; And: om. *Lo*; Anone *Lo*,
anoen *X*
73 sonys *BFH*, sonus *C*; risende *CX*; erly *cet.*; sette *C*, settyn *E*; tentus *C*,
tentes *X*
74 aȝeyns *BF*, aȝen *C*, aȝenst *EX*, a-ȝeynes *Lo*, aȝenes *Wo*; þennus *CWo*,
þennys *C*, þenns *H*, þennes *LoX*; gooynge *B*, goende *CX*; fo[r]þ *H*, forþe
Lo
75 fiȝte *Lo*; aȝeyns *BF*, aȝen *CX*, aȝenst *E*, a-ȝeynes *Lo*; begunne *C*, begunnyn
E, bigonnen *Lo*
76 fiȝten *BCFHLoWoX*, fiȝtyn *E*; aȝeynst *BF*, aȝen *CX*, aȝenst *EH*, a-ȝeynes
Lo; cyte *BCFHLoWoX*; sonys *BEFH*, sonus *CX*
77 gone *BFWo*, gon *CEX*; oute *BFLoX*, ouȝte *H*; fro: of *BH*; slowyn *E*
78 sonys *BEFH*, sonus *CX*

18 Qui surgentes venerunt in domum Dei, hoc est in Silo;
consulueruntque /D/eum, atque dixerunt: Quis erit in
exercitu nostro princeps certaminis contra filios
Beniamin? Quibus respondit Dominus: Iudas sit dux
vester.
19 Statimque filii Israel surgentes mane, castrametati
sunt contra Gabaa.

18 drawynge swerd and redi to batel. Whiche
riseden and camen in to the hows of
God, that is in Silo; and thei counceliden
God, and seiden, Who schal be prince in
oure oost of the batel aȝens the sones of 70
Beniamyn? To whiche the Lord an-
19 sweride, Judas be ȝoure duyk. And anoon
the sones of Israel risiden eerli, and set-
20 tiden tentis aȝens Gabaa. And fro thennus
thei ȝeden forth to batel aȝens Beniamyn, 75
and bigunnen to fiȝte aȝens the citee.
21 And the sones of Beniamyn ȝeden out of
Gabaa, and killiden of the sones of Israel
in that dai two and twenti thousynde of

66 drawyng E, dr. out GIK; sweerd D, swerde E; reedi K²; bateil DK,
bateile MaR, bataile U, bateil X; which E, þe whiche I, wiche K
67 risiden BCGHaQRX, ros E, risen FM, arisen up I, resen L, reisiden MaO,
resin P, reiseden S, reseden U¹; com E
68 counceliden BGHaKMaQRX, conceliden C, counceileden CaDFLMPW,
conseileden E, counseilidin with I
69 seid E, seide U
70 ost E; the (1°): þis E; bateil K, bateile MaR, bateil QX, bataile U;
aȝenus AcCNO; sonys GHaQ
71 which E, whom I, wiche K; answerde CaFGMPQUW, answerd DE,
answerede L
72 J. be: Be J. I; ȝour EFK; duk E, duke LP; anone E, anon HaP
73 sonys GQ, soones S; riseden CaDKNRUW, risen EFLM, arisen up I,
resin P; erli CEGI; setteden CaLMP, setten EF, þei settiden I
74 tentes F; aȝenus AcCNO, aȝeines E, aȝenis P; And: om. W; from K;
þennes CCaFHaKMW, þens DEGMaQR, þennys NSX, þenis P, þenns U
75 ȝedyn S; foorþ D, out I; bateil DIQRX, bateile KMa, bataile U;
aȝenus AcCNO, aȝains E, aȝenis P
76 bigunnun CE, israel biganne I, bigonnen R, bigunnyn S; fiȝt ER;
aȝenus AcCNO, aȝans E; þe cite FHaLMPQW, gabaa I
77 sonis GQ; oute E; of: aȝens GQ
78 killeden CaFKLMNPW, killed E, þei k. I; of (1°): om. O; sonis G
79 þousynd CaIM, þousand DEHaMaNQRWX, þousend FG, þousande K,
þousende LP; of: om. GI

20 Et inde procedentes ad pugnam contra Beniamin, urbem
oppugnare coeperunt.
21 Egressique filii Beniamin de Gabaa, occiderunt de
filiis Israel die illo viginti duo millia virorum.

22 twenti thowsandis of men. And eft the
   sones of Yrael and in strength and in   80
   noumbre trustynge, in the same place in
   which rather thei stryuen, thei dresseden
23 the sheltron; so neuerthelater that before thei stieden, and wepten before the
   Lord vnto the nyȝt, and counseilden hym,   85
   and seiden, Shal I more goon forth to
   fiȝten aȝens the sones of Beniamyn, my
   bretheren, or nay? To whom he answerde, Stieth vp to hem, and goth into
24 the strijf. And whanne the sones of   90
   Yrael the tother day aȝens Beniamyn to

79 thousend *CX*, þowsendys *E*, þousandes *Lo*; efte *LoWo*
80 sonys *BEFHWo*, sonus *CX*; streyngþ *BF*, strengþe *CELoWoX*
81 trostende *CX*, trestynge *Lo*, tristynge *Wo*
82 whiche *BCEHX*, (þe) whiche *Lo*; raþere *CELoX*; thei: om. *X*; dressedyn *E*, dressiden *Lo*
83 scheltrone *BFWo*, sheltrun *C*, scheltrome *ELo*, scheltrū *HX*; neuer þe latere *CE*, neuere þe later *HLo*, nerþelatere *X*; beforn *CE*, byfore *FWo*, biforne *Lo*, biforn *X*
84 steyȝeden *BF*, steȝeden *CX*(+vp), steȝedyn *E*, styȝeden *H*, steiȝiden *Wo*; weptyn *E*; befor *C*, beforn *ELo*, byfore *FWoX*
85 counseileden *CLoX*, cownseiledyn *E*
86 seydyn *E*; goone *B*, go *CX*, gon *EWo*; forþe *Lo*
87 fiȝtyn *E*, fiȝte *LoX*; aȝeynst *BF*, aȝen *CX*, aȝenst *EHWo*; sonys *BFH*, sonus *X*
88 breþern *CX*; whome *BF*; answeride *Lo*, answered *Wo*
89 steyȝiȝ *BF*, steȝeþ *CEX*, stiȝiþ *H*, steyȝep *LoWo*; þem *CEX*
90 stryfe *BFLo*, strif *CEHWoX*; whann *BH*, whan *CEFLoWoX*; sonys *BEFH*, sonus *CX*
91 the tother: þᵗ oþer *Wo*, þe oþer *X*; aȝeynst *BFH*, aȝen *CX*, aȝenst *EWo*, a-ȝeynes *Lo*

22 Rursumque filii Israel et fortitudine et numero con-
   fidentes, in eodem loco in quo prius certaverant,
   aciem direxerunt;
23 ita tamen, ut prius ascenderent et flerent coram
   Domino usque ad noctem, consulerentque eum, et dic-

22 men. And eft the sones of Israel tristiden   80
   in strengthe and noumbre, and dress-
   iden schiltrun, in the same place in which
23 thei fouȝten bifore; so netheles that thei
   stieden bifore, and wepten bifor the
   Lord til to nyȝt, and counseliden hym,   85
   and seiden, Owe Y go forth more to fiȝte
   aȝens the sones of Beniamyn, my britheren,
   ether nay? To whiche he answeride, Stie
24 ȝe to hem, and bigynne ȝe batel. And
   whanne the sones of Israel hadden go   90
   forth to batel in the tother dai aȝens

80 men: om. G; efte DER; sonis GQ; tristeden CaEFMPW
81 þe strengþe BC, her owne strengþe I, strenkþe MaR; and: & in I, of N;
   noumbre of peple I; and (2°): om. R; dresseden CaEFLMPW, þei dr. I,
   drissiden U
82 scheltrum Ha, sheltrom K, scheltron R, sheltrū cet.; whiche DGILO,
   wich K
83 fauȝten I; bifore: om. L; naþelees B, neles EP
84 steieden F, st. up I, stiȝeden MaNR; bifore: b. 'to þe hous' I; weptin ELP,
   þei w. I; bifore BCCaDEGHaKMMaNPQRWX, tofore I
85 til to: vn to EI; counceiliden BGMaQRSX, conseliden C, counceileden
   CaDEFLMPW, conseiliden Ha, þei counseileden wiþ I
86 saiden E; owe: schal I, ow R, ouwe W; to go BX; foorþ D, bifore Ha¹,
   forþe R; moore B, om. E; to: & D; fiȝt E
87 aȝenus AcCNO; sonys GQ; breþren CaFMW, breþerin E, briþren G,
   breþeren HaILPUX, breþern K
88 eiþer CaFGHaMQW, or ELP, eiþir MaR, eþir OS; which D, wiche EK,
   whom I; answerde CaFGMPQUW, answerid D, answerd E, answerede KL;
   steie F, stiȝe MaNR
89 ȝee U; bigunne E; ȝee U; bateil DQX, þe b. EI, bateile GKMaR, bataile U
90 whan EGHaMP; sonis GQ; hadin E, haddin P, hadde U; gon I
91 foorþ D; bateil DRX, bateile KMa, bataile U; toþir BOPRS; aȝenus
   AcCKNO, aȝeins E

   erent: Debeo ultra procedere ad dimicandum contra
   filios Beniamin, fratres meos, an non? Quibus ille
   respondit: Ascendite ad eos, et inite certamen.
24 Cumque filii Israel altero die contra Beniamin ad
   proelium processissent,

25 the batayl weren goon, the sones of Beniamyn breken out fro the ȝatis of Gabaa, and aȝen comynge to hem, [in] so mych
slauȝter thei mich wexen wood in hem,   95
that eiȝt and twenti thousandis of men
drawynge out swerdis thei threwen doun.
26 For what thing alle the sones of Yrael
camen into the hows of God, and sittynge thei wepten before the Lord, and   100
thei fastiden that day vnto euen; and
thei offreden to him* brent sacrifices and
27 pesible sleyn sacrificis, and vpon her
staat thei askiden. That tyme was there
the arke of the boond of pees of God in   105

92 bateyle *BFHWo*, bataile *CELoX*; weryn *E*, were *H*; goone *B*, go *C*, gon
    EWoX; sonys *BEFH*, sonus *CX*
93 breeken *BCFX*, brekyn *E*, braken *Lo*; oute *BLo*, ouȝte *H*; ȝatus *CX*,
    ȝates *Lo*
94 aȝeyn *BFHWo*, a-ȝeyne *Lo*; commynge *BF*, comende *CX*; þem *CEX*;
    [in] so: 'in' so *Lo*; myche *BCEX*, moche *Lo*
95 slaȝter *CX*, slawtyr *E*; myche *CEH*, moche *Lo*, miȝty *X*; wexe *C*, wexyn *E*;
    wexinge *Lo*; wode *BHLoWo*, woode *CEFX*
96 eiȝte *CELoX*; thousend *CX*, þousandes *Lo*
97 drawende *CX*, drawyng *E*; oute *BLo*, ouȝte *H*; swerdes *BLoWo*, swerd *X*;
    þrewe *CX*, þrewyn *E*
98 þinge *BFLoWo*; sonys *BEFHWo*, sonus *CX*; of: om. *Lo*
99 camyn *E*, comen *Lo*; into: to *H*; house *B*, houȝse *H*; sittende *CX*
100 thei: om. *X*; weptyn *E*; byforen *B*, befor *C*, beforn *E*, byforn *FH*, bifore
    LoWo, bifor *X*
101 fasteden *CLoWo*, fastedyn *E*; vn too *X*; euen: þe euen *C*, þe euyn *E*, euene
    Lo
102 offriden *CWo*, offredyn *E*; hem *A*; brente *BELo*; sacrificis *BFH*, sacrefises
    Wo; 102−3 and ... sacrifisis: om. *Wo*
103 peysyble *FH*, peesible *Lo*; slain *CF*, slayne *ELo*; sacrifises *CELoX*; þeir
    BEF, þer *CLoX*
104 state *Wo*; askeden *CWoX*, askedyn *E*
105 bonde *BHLoWo*, bond *CEX*; pese *B*, pes *CEX*

25 eruperunt filii Beniamin de portis Gabaa, et oc-
currentes eis tanta in illos caede baccati sunt, ut
/x/x et viii millia virorum educentium gladium prosternerent.
26 Quamobrem omnes filii Israel venerunt in domum Dei,

25 Beniamyn, the sones of Beniamyn braken
out of the ȝates of Gabaa, and camen to
hem; and *the sones of Beniamyn* weren
wood aȝens hem bi so greet sleyng, that   95
thei castiden doun eiȝtene thousynde of
26 men drawynge swerd. Wherfor alle the
sones of Israel camen in to the hows of
God, and saten, and wepten bifore the
Lord, and thei fastiden in that dai til to   100
euentid; and thei offeriden to the Lord
27 brent sacrifices and pesible sacrifices, and
axiden of her staat. In that tyme the
arke of boond of pees of God was there

92 sonis GQ; brakin EP
93 oute R; of (1°): fro I; ȝates AF, ȝatis cet.; and: om. RS; comen E,
    came R
94 hem: israel I; sonis GQ; wheren E
95 woode AcCDNOUX, maad wode Ca, wode BEFGIKLMMaPQRSW;
    aȝenus AcCNO; hem: israel I; gret EILP, grete R; sleynge AcDGMa-
    PQRUW, fers sleyng I
96 þai E; casteden CaFLMPW, castede E, þrewen I; eiȝtetene N; þousynd
    CaIMW, þousand DEHaMaNQRX, þousend FGP, þousande K,
    þousende L; of: om. I
97 men of israel I; drawyng EK, dr. out I; swerde E: wherfore
    BCaEGIKLMaNQRWX
98 sonis GHaQ; comen E
99 satin ELP, þei s. I, saaten X; weptin LP; bifor AcCFLMOPSU
100 thei: om. D; fasteden CaEFLMPW; til to: vn to EI
101 þe euentid B, euentide CaDEMMaW, euentijd IQ, þe euentijd K, euenetide
    R; offreden CaFMPUW, offe[?]den E, offriden cet.
102 brente KR; sacrifisis CaDGMMaPQWX, sacrifice E; peesible GQ;
    sacrifisis CaGMMaPQWX, sacrifice E
103 axeden CaEFMPW, þei axiden *þe lord* I; here FQR; state DEGQR
104 ark DL; bond CaEGHaLPQU, þe boonde I, bonde R; God: þe lord I,
    þe *lord* god Ma

et sedentes flebant coram Domino; ieiunaveruntque
die illo usque ad vesperam, et obtulerunt ei holocausta et pacificas victimas,
27 et super statu suo interrogaverunt. Eo tempore ibi
erat arca foederis Dei in Silo;

28 Sylo; and Phynees, the sone of Eliazar,
sone of Aaron, was prouost of the hows.
Thei than counseilden the Lord, and
seiden, Shulen we more goon out to the
fi3t a3ens the sones of Beniamyn oure   110
bretheren, othir resten? To whom seith
the Lord, Stieth vp, forsothe to morwe
29 I shal taak hem into 3oure hoondis. And
the sones of Yrael putten busshementis
bi the enuyroun of the cytee of Gabaa;   115
30 and the thridde sithe as oons and twyes
a3ens Beniamyn the oost brou3te forth.

107   sone: þe s. *E¹FLo¹Wo*; house *BF*, hou3s *H*
108   þann *BF*, þan *HWo*, þanne *cet.*; counseileden *CWoX*, cownseiledyn *E*,
      counseiliden *H*, counseyleyden *Lo*; lorde *Lo*
109   seydyn *E*; schuln *BEFHWo*, shul *CLoX*; wee *CELoX*; mor *C*; gone *B*,
      gon *CEWoX*; oute *BFLo*, ou3te *H*
110   fi3te *Lo*; a3eynst *BF*, a3en *CX*, a3enst *EHWo*; the sones: om. *X*; sonys
      BEFHWo, sonus *C*
111   breþern *C*, briþern *X*; oþer *BFHWo*, or *CLoX*, ouþer *E*; restyn *E*; whome
      BF; seyde *H*
112   stey3iþ *BFWo*, ste3eþ *CEX*, sti3iþ *H*, stei3eþ *Lo*; forsothe to morwe: to
      m. f. *cet.*; morn *CX*, morewe *E*, morwen *Lo*, morowe *Wo*
113   take *BCFHWoX*, takyn *E*, taken *Lo*; þem *CEX*; 3our *CFH*; hondis *BX*,
      hondus *C*, handis *E*, hondes *LoWo*
114   sonys *BEFH*, sonus *X*; puttyn *E*; busshementus *C*, buschmentis *FWo*,
      busshemens *X*
115   the (1°): om. *C*; cyte *BCEFLoWoX*
116   þredde *E*; ones *CLoX*, oonys *E*, onys *Wo*; twyse *BF*
117   a3eynst *BF*, a3en *CX*, a3enst *EHWo*, a3eynes *Lo*; ost *CWoX*, host *E*,
      hoost *H*; brou3ten *BFHLoWo*, bro3ten *C*, bro3tyn *E*, bro3te *X*; forþe *Lo*

28 et Phinees, filius Eleazari, filii Aaron, erat prae-
positus domus. Consuluerunt igitur Dominum, atque
dixerunt: Exire ultra debemus ad pugnam contra
filios Beniamin, fratres nostros, an quiescere?
Quibus ait Dominus: Ascendite, cras enim tradam eos
in manus vestras.

28 in Silo; and Fynees, the sone of Elea- 105
zar, sone of Aaron, was souereyn of the
hows. Therfor thei counseliden the Lord,
and seiden, Owen we go out more to
batel aȝens the sones of Beniamyn, oure
britheren, ethir reste? To whiche the 110
Lord seide, Stie ȝe, for to morewe Y schal
29 bytake hem in to ȝoure hondis. And the
sones of Israel settiden buyschementis bi
30 the cumpas of the citee of Gabaa; and the
thridde tyme as onys and twies thei 115

105 the: om. B
106 þe sone I; aaron *prest* B; souerain E, soueryn O, souereyne R
107 *lordis* hous I; þerfore BCaGKLMaNQRWX, þanne I; counceiliden BGHaMaOQRX, conseliden C, counceileden CaDEFLMPUW, counseiliden wiþ I
108 owen: schul I; to go DGHaMaQ; out: om. Ma, oute R; moore B; go out m.: m. gon out I
109 bateil DRX, batail I, bateile KMa, bataile U; aȝenus AcCNO; sonys GHaQ
110 breþren CaFMW, breþerin E, briþren G, breþeren HaILPUX, breþern K; eþer AcBCDKNSX, eiþer CaFGHaIMQRW, or ELP, eiþir Ma, oþer U; reste: nai Ac, schul we reste I, rest R; which DE, whom I, wiche K
111 steie ȝe F, st. ȝe up aȝens hem I, stiȝe ȝe MaNR, st. ȝee U; to morowe BHaKMaRUX, to morwe DLNPQ, tmorow E
112 hem: beniamyn I; in: om. R; ȝour K; hondes CaF
113 sonys GQ; settide C, setteden CaELMPW, setten F; busschementis CaDEFGHaILMOQR, boiȝsshementis K, boishmentis N, bushmentis PW
114 the: om. I; cumpace E; cite FHaLMPQW; of (2°): om. GHaQ
115 þirdde E; oonys BDGHaKMaNQX, ones CaR, oones ILP; tweies FHa, tweis O, tw. bifore I

29 Posueruntque filii Israel insidias per circuitum
urbis Gabaa;
30 et tertia vice, sicut semel et bis, contra Beniamin
exercitum produxerunt.

31 But and the sones of Beniamyn hardili
breken out of the cytee, and the aduersaryes fleynge lenger thei pursueden, so   120
that thei woundiden of hem, as the first
day and the secounde, and slowen bi two
pathis the turnynge backis; of the whiche
oon beer into Bethel, and the tothir into
Gabaa. And thei threwen doun aboute   125
32 thretti men; forsothe thei wenden in the
wont maner to sleen hem; the whiche
feynynge fliȝt at the bigynnynge, wenten
in counseil for to drawe hem awey fro the
cytee, and as fleynge to bryngen to the   130

118 bot *B*, bute *F*; sonys *BEFHWo*, sonus *C*; hardly *H*
119 breeken *BCX*, brekyn *E*, kreken *H*, braken *Lo*; oute *BFLo*, ouȝte *H*; cyte
BCFHLoWoX
120 fleeȝinge *BFH*, fleande *C*, fleȝinge *Wo*, fleende *X*; lengre *BFH*, lengere
CEX; pursuedyn *E*, pursweden *Lo*
121 woundeden *CLoX*, wowndidyn *E*, woundyd *F*, wounded *Wo*; þem *CE*;
firste *CEHX*
122 sloowen *C*, slowyn *E*
123 paþes *ELo*; turnende *CX*, turnyng *Lo*; backes *WoX*; which *FWo*
124 oone *HLo*, one *Wo*, oen *X*; bar *CEX*, bare *Lo*, bere *Wo*; into: in *Lo*; the
tothir: þe toþer *BCEFHLoX*, that oþer *Wo*
125 þrewe *C*, þrewyn *E*; abowtyn *E*, abouȝte *H*, about *Wo*
126 þrytty *BFHLoWo*; wendyn *E*, wende *Wo*
127 wonte *Lo*; slen *BEHX*, sle *C*; þem *CE*; which *FWo*
128 feynede *C*, feynende *X*; fliȝte *Lo*; begynnyng *CE*, bigynnyng *X*; wentyn *E*
129 conseil *C*, counseyle *LoWo*; for: om. *H*; drawen *BFHLoWo*, drawyn *E*;
þem *CX*; aweye *BH*
130 cyte *cet.*; fleeynge *BF*, fleende *CX*; bringe *CX*, bryngyn *E*

31 Sed et filii Beniamin audacter eruperunt de civitate,
et fugientes adversarios longius persecuti sunt, ita
ut vulnerarent ex eis, sicut primo die et secundo,
et caederent per duas semitas vertentes terga, qua-
rum una ferebat/ur/ in Bethel, /et/ altera in Gabaa,
atque prosternerent triginta circiter viros.
32 Putaverunt enim solito eos more caedere. Qui fugam
arte simulantes, inierunt consilium, ut abstraherent
eos de civitate et quasi fugientes ad supradictas
semitas perducerent.

31 brou3ten forth oost a3ens Beniamyn. But
also the sones of Beniamyn braken out
of the citee booldli, and pursueden fer-
there the aduersaryes fleynge, so that thei
woundiden of hem, as in the firste dai   120
and the secounde, and killiden bi twey
paththis *the aduersaries* turnynge backis;
of whiche paththis oon was borun in to
Bethel, the tother in to Gabaa. And thei
32 castiden doun aboute thretti men; for   125
thei gessiden to sle hem bi customable
maner; whiche feyneden fli3t bi craft,
and token counsel, that thei schulden
drawe hem fro the citee, and that thei
as fleynge schulden brynge to the for-   130

116 foorþ D, out Ma; ost E, þe oost I; a3enus AcCNO; a3ens *þe sones of* B. B
117 also *þanne* I; sonis GQ; brakin ELP; oute R
118 of: fro I; cite CaFHaLMPQW; booldely BFIO, boldly CaGQW,
    boldely ERU; of the c. booldli: boldely fro þe citee I; pursuweden CaFMW,
    pursued D, þei p. I, pursuiden Q; firþer B, ferþer CER, furþer D
119 fleyng E; thei: om. E
120 woundeden CaEFLMPW, wondriden Ma; hem: israel I; as: as þei diden I;
    first EHaIR
121 the: om. AcDMa, in þe INW; secunde BEMaNQR, seconde K; killide C,
    killeden CaELMPW, þei k. I; twie Ca, tweie FMQ, two IMa
122 paþis CaEFGIKLMMaPUX; *the aduersaries*: israel I; turnyng E; backes
    FR, here b. I
123 which DF, þe whiche I, wiche K; paþis AcCaEIKLMMaOPRSU, paþes F;
    one E; born CaDEFGKLMMaPWX, strei3t out I, borne R; in: om. MW
124 & þe toþer IW, þe tooþer L, þe toþir MaO; thei: beniamyn I
125 casteden CaEFMPW, þrewe I; a-bout E, abou3te LU; þritti
    AcBCaDIMN; men: m. *of istael* I
126 gesseden CaFLMPW, ghesseden E; slee CaFGHaKQ, destrie I; hem:
    israel I; custumable CCaEGHaLMMaQWX; 126—27 bi c. maner: as þei
    diden bifore I
127 manere CaFGLMQW; which ES, wiche K; fayneden E, feyniden GQ;
    crafte IKR; 127—28 And bi crafte isrl token counseil feynynge hem to fle I
128 tokin E, tookin LP, tooken NX; consel C, counceil CaDFGHaIMMaNQ-
    RWX, counseile E; scholden CaFMW, schulde Ma
129 hem: beniamyn I; from K; cite FHaLMPQW; þai E
130 fleiynge C, fliyng E; scholden CaFMW; bring E, br. forþ beniamyn I;
    forsaid E, forseide FGKPR

471

33 forseide pathis. And so alle the sones of
Yrael rysynge fro her seetis tiȝten shiltron in the place that is clepid Baalthamar. Forsothe the busshementis, that (weren)
about the cytee weren, litil melome hem   135
34 seluen bigunnen to opne, and fro the
west parti of the citee to goon forth.
But and othere ten thousandis of men
of Yrael dwellers of the cytee terreden
to stryues; and the bateil is agreggid   140
aȝens the sones of Beniamyn, and thei
vndurstoden not, that on alle sidis to hem

131 fore seyde *BH*, fornseide *E*, forseid *X*; paþes *BELo*; sonys *BEFH*, sonus *CX*
132 risende *CX*; þer *BCLoX*, þeir *EFWo*; setis *C*, seetes *X*; tiȝtyn *E*; sheltrone
BFWo, sheltrun *C*, sheltrome *ELo*, sheltrū *H*, shell-[trū]*X*
134 forsoþ *X*; Forsothe the busshementis: þe b. f. *cet.*; buschmentis *BFWo*,
busshementus *C*, busshemens *X*
135 abouten *BFLoWo*, aboute *CX*, abowtyn *E*, abouȝten *H*; cyte *BCFLoWoX*,
cytees *H*; weryn *E*; litil melum *CX*, alitil & alitil *H*, litil melom *Lo*,
litel-melome *Wo*; þem *CEX*
136 self *CX*, selue *E*; begunnen *C*, begunnyn *E*, by-gonnen *Lo*; openyn *BEFH*,
openen *CLoX*, open *Wo*
137 weste *Lo*; part *CX*, partie *EFHLoWo*; cyte *cet.*; gon *BEWo*, go *CX*;
forþe *Lo*
138 bot *B*, bute *F*; oþer *BFHLoWo*, ooþer *E*; tenn *BH*; thousend *CX*, þowsendes
E, þowsandes *LoWo*
139 yrael: al I. *CE*, alle i. *Lo*; dwelleris *CELoX*; cyte *cet.*; terredyn *E*
140 strifes *E*, stryuys *BFH*; bateyle *BF*, bataile *CELoWoX*; agreggide *Lo*
141 aȝeynst *BFH*, aȝen *CX*, aȝenst *EWo*, a-ȝeynes *Lo*; sonys *BEFHWo*, sonus
CX
142 vndrestoden *BLo*, vnderstoden *CFHWoX*, vndyrstoodyn *E*; all *F*; sides
CEFLoWoX; þem *CX*

33 Omnes itaque filii Israel surgentes de sedibus suis,
tetenderunt aciem in loco, qui vocatur Baalthamar.
Insidiae quoque, quae circa urbem erant, paulatim se
aperire coeperunt,
34 et ab occidentali urbis parte procedere. Sed et alia
decem millia virorum de universo Israel, habitatores
urbis ad certamina provocabant. Ingravatumque est
bellum contra filios Beniamin, et non intellexerunt,
quod ex omni parte illis instaret interitus.

33 seid paththis. Therfor alle the sones of
Israel risiden of her seetis, and settiden
schiltrun in the place which is clepid
Baalthamar. And the buschementis, that
weren aboute the citee, bigunnen to opene   135
34 hem silf litil and litil, and to go forth
fro the west part of the citee. But also
othere ten thousynde of men of al Israel
excitiden the dwelleris of the cite to
batels; and the batel was maad greuous   140
aȝens the sones of Beniamyn, and thei
vndurstoden not, that perisching neiȝede

131 paþis EGIKMMaPX, paþes F; þerfore BCaGKMMaNQRX, þanne I,
     þerfore whanne W; sonis GQ
132 riseden CaDKMNRWX, resin EP, risen FL, risynge up I; of: fro IX;
     here FGQR; setis CaEIMQ, setes F; and: om. I; setteden CaELMP,
     setten F
133 sheltrom K, scheltrum Ma, scheltron R, shel trū cet.; whiche G, þat I,
     wiche K
134 buyschementis AcBCMaSUX, busschementes F, bushmentis HaIP,
     boiȝsshementis K, boyshmentis N, buyschmentis R
135 about E, abouȝte LU; cite FHaILMPQW; bi-gunne EHa, bygonnen FR;
     open E, opyne N
136 self CaFKLMPRUW, selue E; a litil (2x) I, litel (2x) K; and (1°): om. O
137 from K; weest Ha; cite FHaLMPQW
138 oþer ELX; þousynd CaIMW, þousand DEHaMaQR, þousend G, þousande
     K, þousende LP, þousant N; of (1°): om. GI; al: om. I
139 exciteden CaDEFKLMPW, stiriden beniamyn I, exitiden U; dwellers
     DEHaIKLRU, dwellers F, men M; the (2°): þat IR; citee AcBDEGIK-
     MaNRSUX, citte O
140 batels: batel E, bateilis G, batelis Q, bateils RX, batailes U; batel: bateil
     KRX, bateile Ma, bataile U; made DE, mad GMa; greuouse AcBCOS
141 aȝenus AcCNO; sone E, sonis GQ, sonus Ma
142 vndirstoden BDFGIKMaNQR, vndurstodun C, vndurstode E, vnderstooden
     L, vndirstooden PX, vndirstondin S, vnderstoden HaU; pereschynge B,
     perischynge DGMaQU, pershing EHa, periȝsshing K, pershinge LP;
     neiȝide AcBOQSU, neȝide C, neiȝȝide CaMW, nyȝed D, neiȝȝede F;
     142—43 on eche part neiȝede to hem I

35 stood yn deeth. And the Lord smoot
hem in the si3t of the sones of Yrael,
and thei slowen of hem in that day   145
fyue and twenti thowsandis and an hun-
drid men, alle fi3ters and drawinge out
36 swerd. Forsothe the sones of Beniamyn,
whanne thei hadden seen hem self to be
the nethermore, thei bigunne to flee.   150
The which thing biholdynge the sones
of Yrael, 3euen to hem place to flee, that
thei mi3ten come to the maad redi
busshementis, the whiche bisyde the

143 stoden *BFHWo*, stod *C*, stode *Lo*; deþ *BCEFHWoX*; smote *BFHLoWo*,
   smot *CX*
144 þem *C*; si3te *CELoX*; sonys *BFH*, sonus *CX*
145 slewen *B*, slowyn *E*
146 thousend *CX*, þowsendis *E*, þousandes *LoWo*; an: a *Lo*; hundreth *BF*,
   hundrith *Lo*
147 al *Lo*; fi3teres *CWoX*, fi3teris *ELo*; drawende *CX*; oute *BLo*, ou3te *H*
148 swerde *BFHLoWo*; Forsothe the sones: þe s. f. *cet.*; sonys *BEFH*, sonus
   CX
149 whann *BH*, whan *CFWoX*, when *E*; hadde *C*, haddyn *E*, had *Lo*; seey3en
   B, sey3en *H*, sene *LoWo*; þem *CEX*; selfen *B*, selue *E*, seluen *FHWo*;
   ben *BCEFHLoWo*
150 neþermor *CX*; bygunnyn *BF*, begunne *C*, begunnyn *E*, bygunnen *HWoX*,
   by-gonnen *Lo*; flee3e *BF*, fle *LoWo*
151 whiche *BCEHLoX*; þinge *BHLo*; beholdende *C*, beholdyng *E*, biholdende
   X; sonys *BFH*, sonus *CX*; 151–2 The ... flee: om. *Wo*
152 3efyn *E*, 3yuen *Lo*; þem *CEX*; flee3e *BF*, fleen *X*
153 my3te *C*, my3tyn *E*; commen *BF*, comyn *E*, comen *HLoWo*; made
   BEFHLoWo
154 busshementus *C*, buschmentis *F*, buschmentes *Wo*, busshemens *X*; the
   whiche: þat *C*, þe which *FWo*; bysydis *BFH*, besides *C*, besidys *E*, bisides
   LoWo

35 Percussitque eos Dominus in conspectu filiorum Israel, et interfecerunt ex eis in illo die viginti
quinque millia et centum viros, omnes bellatores et
educentes gladium.
36 Filii autem Beniamin, cum se inferiores esse vid-

35 to hem on eche part. And the Lord smoot
hem in the siȝt of the sones of Israel, and
thei killiden of hem in that dai fyue and   145
twenti thousynde and an hundrid men,
alle the werryours and drawynge swerd.
36 Sotheli the sones of Beniamyn bigunnen
to fle, whanne thei sien, that thei weren
the lowere. And the sones of Israel sien   150
this, and ȝauen to hem place to fle, that
thei schulden come to the buyschementis
maad redi, whiche thei hadden set bi-

143 ech AcBCCaDGHaLMMaNOPQRSUWX, uche E; smot EU, smote HaIR
144 hem: beniamyn I; siȝte DGU; sonys GQ
145 thei: israel I; killeden CaEFKLMPW, killide I; da[i] C
146 þousynd CaFIMW, þousand DEHaMaNQRX, þousend G, þousande K,
     þousende LP; hundred EHa, hunderd LP; of men C
147 alle the: and alle þese weren I; werriouris BDGMaNQW, weriours ER,
     werrioures FI, worriours O; and: om. AcMa; drawing L, men dr. out I;
     swerde E, sweerd R
148 soþli EFGLMMaPQUWX, And I; sonys GQ; bigunnun AcES, bygonnen
     FR, bigunne Q
149 flee CaFGP; whan EGLP; seien CaEFW, siȝen GHaKMaNQRX, hadden
     seen I, seiȝen M
150 lower DEHaMaRX, lowere part I; sonys GQ; seien CaFW, siȝen
     DGHaKMaNQRX, sawȝen I, seiȝen M; 148—50 And whanne þe sones
     of beniamyn hadden seen hem silf to be þe lowere part þei bigunnen to fle I
151 ȝaf E, þei ȝauen I, ȝafen K; to: om. I; flee CaFGLMaPRX
152 þai E; scholden CaMW; busschementis CaDEIMOQR, busschementes F,
     bushmentis GHaMaPW, boiȝsshementis K, boyshmentis N
153 made DEK; reedi GS, reedie K; which DEFP, þe whiche I, wiche K;
     thei: israel I; haddin EP, had I; sette CIR, sett KMaNU; bi-side E,
     bisides FHaKU

issent, coeperunt fugere. Quod cernentes filii Israel, dederunt eis ad fugiendum locum, ut ad prae-
paratas insidias devenirent, quas iuxta urbem
posuerant.

37 cytee thei setten. The whiche whanne
hadden ryse sodeynly fro the hidilis,
and Beniamyn ȝaf backis to the sleers,
thei wenten into the cytee, and smyten
38 it in mouth of swerd. Forsothe the sones
of Yrael hadden ȝeuen a tokne to hem
that weren sett in busshementis, that
after that thei hadden take the cytee,
fier thei shulden teend, and the smook
stiynge vp into heiȝt, thei shulden shewe

155 cyte *cet.*; settyn *E*; which *F*; whann *BFH*, whan *CELoWoX*
156 hadde *BF*, haddyn *E*, had *Wo*; rysen *BCFHLoWoX*, risyn *E*; hydyls *BF*,
   hidelis *CELoX*, hydels *Wo*; 156—7 fro ... B.: om. *H*
157 ȝaue *BFHWo*, ȝafe *Lo*; backes *EX*, backe *Lo*; slears *BFHWo*, slearis *CE*,
   sleeris *Lo*, sleeres *X*
158 wentyn *E*; cyte *BCHLoWoX*; smytyn *E*
159 it: om. *C*; mowþe *LoWo*; swerde *FLoWo*; forsoþ *H*; Forsothe the sones:
   þe s. f. *cet.*; sonys *BFH*, sonus *CX*
160 off *E*; haddyn *E*, hadde *X*; ȝiuen *CLoWo*, ȝifyn *E*, ȝouen *X*; token
   BFHWo; þem *CEX*
161 wer *C*; sette *Lo*, set *X*; buschmentis *BFH*, busshementus *C*, busshemens *X*
162 aftyr *ELoX*; haddyn *E*; taken *BCHLoX*, takyn *E*; cite *CFLoWoX*
163 fijr *CE*, fuyre *LoWo*; schuldyn *E*; teenden *BFH*, teende *CX*, teendyn *E*,
   tenden *LoWo*; smoke *BCEFHWoX*, smeke *Lo*
164 steyȝinge *BFLoWo*, steȝende *CX*, steȝynge *E*, styȝinge *H*; heyȝte *BCEFH*,
   þe heghet *Lo*, heuene *X*; shulde *C*, schuldyn *E*; schewen *BFHLoWo*,
   schewyn *E*

37 Qui cum repente de latibulis surrexissent, et Beniamin terga caedentibus daret, ingressi sunt civitatem, et percusserunt eam in ore gladii.
38 Signum autem dederant filii Israel his, quos in insidiis collocaverant, ut postquam urbem cepissent,
ignem accenderent, et ascendente in altum fumo,
captam urbem demonstrarent.

37 sidis the citee. And whanne thei hadden
rise sudenli fro hid places, and Beniamyn 155
ȝaf backis to the sleeris, thei entriden in
to the citee, and smytiden it by the
38 scharpnesse of swerd. Sotheli the sones
of Israel hadden ȝoue a signe to hem
whiche thei hadden set in buyschementis, 160
that aftir that thei hadden take the citee,
thei schulden kyndle fier, and that bi
smook stiynge an hiȝ, thei schulden

154 cite CaEFHaLMPQRW; whan ELP; thei: þese bushementis I; hadde Ac,
     haddin EP
155 risun D, risen up I; sodeynli BCaEFGILMPQW, sudeynli DMaRX,
     sodenli HaK; from K; hidde DK; placis DGHaIKLMaPQSWX, place E
156 ȝaue I, ȝafe R; backes FR; sleers DEHaIKLMX, fleeres F, fleers R,
     fleeris U; entreden CaEFMPW
157 cite FHaLMQW; smyteden CaMOW, smiten EF, þei smoten I, smeten L,
     smetin P; the (2°): om. EI
158 sharpnes EMa; swerde ER; soþli EFGLMMaPQUWX, And I; sonis GQ
159 had E, haddin P, hadde R; ȝof E, ȝofen K, ȝeue Ma; sing E, token I
160 which CaEFLM, þat I, wiche K; had E, haddin LP; sette CDR, sett
     IKMaU; busschementis CaDLQ, bushmentis EGHaMPW, buschementes F,
     þe bushementis I, boiȝsshementis K, buyschementis Ma, þe boishmentis N;
     160 set ... hadden (161): om. S
161 after BEFU; that (2°): om. GHaIQR; had E, haddin LP; tak E; cite
     EFHaLMPQW
162 scholden CaMW, shuld E; kyndele BGHa, kindel E, kendle U; fijr
     CaIMW, fire DE, fyr FLP, þerynne fijr I; 162–63 & þat þei schulden
     schewe þe citee to be taken bi smoke stiynge up an hiȝ I
163 smok E, smooke GOP, smoke cet.; stiyng E, steiynge FW, stiynge up I,
     stiȝinge MaNR; on E; heiȝ CaFMW, hiȝe D, hiy E; scholden CaFMW,
     shuld E

39 the cytee takun. The which thing
    whanne the sones of Yrael put in that
    strijf shulden biholde, forsothe the sones
    of Beniamyn wenden hem to fleen, and
    more bisily folweden, sleyn of the oost
40 of hem thretti men; and thei seen as a
    piler of smook fro the citee to stien vp;
    forsothe Beniamyn biholdynge bihynde,
    whanne he saw3 the cytee takun, and the

165 cyte *cet.*; taken *BCFHLoWoX*, takyn *E*; whiche *BCEHLoX*; þinge *BFLoWo*
166 whann *B*, whan *CEWoX*; sonys *BEFHWo*, sonus *CX*; putt *BFHWo*
167 stryfe *BFLo*, strif *CEHWoX*; schuldyn *E*; byholden *BFHLoWoX*, beholden
      C, beholdyn *E*; sonys *BEFHWo*, sonus *CX*
168 wendyn *E*; þem *C*; flee3en *BF*, flee *CX*
169 besili *C*, beseli *E*; foloweden *BFH* (þe[i] f.)*Wo*, foleweden *CX*, folewedyn
      E; slayn *BCEFHWoX*, sclayne *Lo*; ost *CWoX*, host *E*, hoost *H*
170 þem *CE*; þritty *BFHLoWoX*; see3en *BCFH*, see3yn *E*, sawen *Lo*, sei3en
      Wo, se3en *X*
171 pileer *CE*; smoke *BCEFHWoX*, smeke *Lo*; cyte *BCFHLoWoX*; stey3en
      BFLoWo, ste3en *CX*, stee3yn *E*, sty3en *H*
172 forsothe Beniamyn: B. f. *cet.*; beholdende *C*, beholdyng *E*, biholdende *X*;
      behinde *CE*
173 whann *BF*, whan *CEHLoWoX*; sa3 *CX*, sawe *Lo*; cyte *BCFHLoWoX*;
      taken *BCFHLoWoX*, takyn *E*

39 Quod cum cernerent filii Israel in ipso certamine
    positi, putaverunt enim filii Beniamin eos fugere,
    et instantius /per/sequebantur, caesis de exercitu
    eorum triginta viris,
40 et viderunt quasi columnam fumi de civitate con-
    scendere. Beniamin quoque aspiciens retro, cum cap-
    tam cerneret civitatem, et flammas in sublime ferri,

39 schewe the citee takun. And whanne
the sones of Israel set in thilke batel   165
sien this, for the sones of Beniamyn
gessiden hem to fle, and thei sueden bi-
siliere, whanne thretti men of her oost
40 weren slayn; and the sones of Israel
sien as a piler of smoke stie fro the   170
citee; also Beniamyn bihelde bihynde,
whanne he siȝ the citee takun, and

164 shew E; cite CaEFHaLMPQW; taken BCaEFGKMMaQRW, to be taken
     I, takin LP; when E, whan GLP, þat I, om. S
165 the: om. U; sonys GQ; sette DK, sett IMaRU, om. W; þilk BEHaR,
     þat I; bateil DRX, bateile KMa, batal N, bataile U
166 seien CaFW, siȝen EGHaKLMaNPQRX, schulden se I, seiȝen M; this:
     þat I; sonis GQ
167 gesseden CaFLMP, ghesseden E; hem: israel I; flee CaGLMaPR; and:
     om. G; suweden CaFMW, suiden GQ, pursueden hem I; bisilier
     BDKLMaPRX, bissilier E, bisiloker I
168 whan LP; þritti AcCaIMMaNOWX; hir E, here FGQS, israels I; ost EI
169 wheren E, were FM; sleyn I, slayne KR; and: om. W; sonys GQ; the s.
     of I.: þei I
170 seien CaFG¹W, siȝen G²HaKLMaNPQRX, sawȝen I, seiȝen M; smok E;
     steie F, st. up I, stiȝe MaNQ, stiȝ R; from K
171 cite CaFHaLMPQW; And also I; biheeld CaGMMaOPQWX, biheld ELN,
     biholdinge I, biheuld K; bi-hind E
172 whan AcEGHaLP; seiȝ CaFMW, siȝe DR, sawȝe I; the: his I; cite
     CaEFHaLMPQW; taken BCaEFHaIKMMaQRUW, taaken G, takin LP

41 flawm(b)is to be born into hei3t, the whiche
beforehoond feyneden fli3t, turnede the   175
face strongly withstoden. The which
thing whanne the sones of Beniamyn
hadden seen, thei ben turned in fli3t,

42 and to the weye of deseert thei bigunne
to goon; forsothe thider hem aduersaryes   180
pursuynge, but and thes, that setten the

43 toun on fier, a3en comyn(ge) to hem. And
so it is doon, that on either parti thei
ben slayn of enemyes, ne there was eny
reste of men dyynge; and thei fellen, and   185
ben throwen down at the eest coost of

174 flawmbis *BFWo*, flaumes *CLoX*; ben *BCEFHLoWo*; borne *Lo*; hei3te *CEX*,
heghet *Lo*; which *FWo*
175 byfore honde *BHWo*, beforhand *C*, befornhande *E*, byfore hoonde *F*,
biforne hande *Lo*, bifornhond *X*; feynyden *BFH*, feynedyn *E*; fli3te *Lo*;
torneden *BFHWo*, turned *CLoX*, turnyd *E*
176 strengrely *BFWo*, strengereli *CE*, strengerly *HLoX*; wiþstoodyn *E*; whiche
BCEHLoX
177 þinge *BFLoWo*; whann *BFH*, whan *CLoWoX*; sonys *BFHWo*, sonus *CX*
178 haddyn *E*; see3en *BF*, sene *Lo*; turnyd *B*, torned *FHWo*, turnede *Lo*; in:
in to *C*; fli3te *Lo*
179 wey *LoWo*; deserte *BHLo*, desert *CEFWoX*; begunne *C*, begunnyn *E*,
bygunnen *H*, by-gonnen *Lo*
180 go *C*, gon *EWoX*; forsothe thider: þ. f. *cet.*; þidre *BFLo*; þem *CEX*
181 pursuende *CX*; bot *B*, bute *F*; þeis *BFWo*, þese *CEX*; settyn *E*
182 toune *Lo*; on fijre *C*; on fire *EX*, a fier *H*, of fyre *Lo*, on fuyre
Wo; a3eyn *BFHWo*, a3en *CEX*, a-3eyne *Lo*; commynge *BF*, camen *C*,
comyn *E*, come *Lo*, comende *X*; þem *CEX*
183 done *BFHLo*, do *CX*, don *EWo*; partye *BEFHLoWo*, part *CX*
184 slawen *B*, sclayne *Lo*; enmyes *BFHWo*, enemys *CEX*; þer *BCEFHWoX*;
any *CEX*
185 rest *LoWo*; diende *CX*, dy3inge *H*, dyeinge *Lo*; fellyn *E*
186 þrowe *CX*; este *B*, est *CEFHWoX*; cost *CEWo*, coest *X*

41 qui prius simulaverant fugam, versa facie fortius
resistebant. Quod cum vidissent filii Beniamin, in
fugam versi sunt,

42 et ad viam deserti ire coeperunt; illuc quoque eos
adversariis persequentibus, sed et hi, qui urbem
succenderant, occurrerunt eis.

41 flawmes borun an hiȝe, thei that feyn-
    eden fliȝt bifore, aȝenstoden strongliere
    with face turned. And whanne the sones   175
    of Beniamyn hadden seyn this, thei weren
42 turned in to fliȝt, and thei bigunnen to go
    to the weie of deseert; while also aduer-
    saries pursueden hem there, but also thei,
    that hadden brent the citee, camen aȝens   180
43 hem. And so it was doon, that thei
    weren slayn of enemyes on ech part, ne-
    ther ony reste of men diynge was; and
    thei felden, and weren cast doun at the

173 flawmys GQ, þe fl. I; born CaDEFGLMMaPWX, be born I, borne KR;
     on E; hiȝ AcBCGHaKLMaNOPQUX, heiȝ CaFMW; fayneden E, feynyden
     GQR
174 fliȝt: to fle I; aȝeinstoden BE, aȝenstooden GLNX; stronglier
     BCDEKRX, strongli Ha, more strongli I
175 turnyd GQ, turnide Ha, turnede R; And: om. C; when E, whan GLP;
     sonus E, sonys GQ; 174—75 turneden her face to beniamyn & wiþstoden
     him more strongly I
176 had E, haddin LP; seyen BEGHaLS, seie Q, seen DIMa; þis þing I; were
     EMS
177 turnyd GHaQ, turnede KR; to: om. S; fliȝte D; bigunnun E, bigunne G,
     bigonnen R
178 to: om. CI; wey EIMaU; desert AcCCaDEFGHaIKMNOPQRU, deserd
     SWX; whil ELPR
179 pursuweden CaFMW, pursuiden Q
180 had E, haddin LP; brente Ha; the: her I; cite CaEFHaLMPQW; comen
     E; aȝenus AcCNO
181 don AcCDGHaINPUX, done ER; þai E, beniamyn I
182 was I, were Q; sleyn I, slayne KR; enemys E, enmyes I; ich E, eche IK;
     neiþer CaFGHaIMQ, neiþir MaRW, neþir OPX; 182—83 neiþer þer was
     ony rest of men diynge I
183 eni EHa; rest EIKR; deiynge CaFMW, diyng E, diȝynge R
184 fellen CaEFILMW, filden D, fellin P; weie BQ, werin P; caste DGHaKQR

43 Atque ita factum est, ut ex utraque parte ab hosti-
    bus caederentur, nec erat ulla requies morientium.
    Cecideruntque, atque prostrati sunt ad orientalem
    plagam urbis Gabaa.

44 the cytee of Gabaa. Forsothe there weren,
    that in the same place ben slayn, eiȝteen
    thousandis of men, al moost stronge fiȝters.
45 The which thing whanne hadden seen   190
    that leften of Beniamyn, thei flowen
    into wildernes, and wenten to the stoon,
    whos name is Remmon. Forsothe in that
    fliȝt opynli hidir and thider rennynge
    and into dyuerse placis goynge thei   195
    slowen fyue thowsandis of men; and
    whanne ferther thei wenten, thei pur-
    sueden hem, and slewen also othere two

187 cyte *cet.*; Forsothe there weren: þ. w. f. *cet.*; forsoþ *B*; þer *BCEFHWoX*;
      weryn *E*
188 sclayne *Lo*, slayne *X*; eyȝtene *BFHLoWo*, eiȝtetene *CE*
189 thousend *CX*, þowsandes *ELo*; of: om. *X*; al moost: al most *BFHWo*,
      alle most *CEX*, al moste *Lo*; strong *CE*; fiȝteris *ELo*, fyȝteres *HX*
190 whiche *BCEHLoX*; þinge *BFLoWo*; whann *BH*, whan *CLoWoX*; haddyn
      E; seeȝen *BH*, sene *LoWo*
191 leftyn *E*; floun *CX*, flowyn *E*
192 wyldrenesse *BF*, wildernesse *CEHLoWoX*; wente *C*, wentyn *E*; stone
      BFHWo, ston *CEX*
193 whose *BF*, whois *E*; forsoth *B*; Forsothe in that: in þ. f. *cet.*
194 fliȝte *Lo*; openli *CLoWoX*, opely *E*; hiþer *BF*, hider *CHLoWoX*; þidre
      BFLo; rennende *CX*
195 dyuers *BFX*; places *LoWoX*; goende *CX*
196 sloowe *C*, slowyn *E*; thousend *CX*, thowsendis *E*, þousandes *LoWo*
197 whann *BFH*, whan *CLoWoX*, whenne *E*; ferþere *CEX*, forþere *Lo*; wentyn
      BE; pursuedyn *E*
198 þem *CE*; sloowen *C*, slowyn *E*, slowen *HLoWoX*; oþer *BFHLoWoX*,
      ooþere *E*

44 Fuerunt autem, qui in eodem loco interfecti sunt,
    decem et octo millia virorum, omnes robustissimi
    pugnatores.
45 Quod cum vidissent, qui remanserant de Beniamin,
    fugerunt in solitudinem, et pergebant ad petram,

44 eest coost of the citee of Gabaa. Forsothe thei, that weren slayn in the same
place, weren eiȝtene thousynde of men,

45 alle strongeste fiȝteris. And whanne thei
that leften of Beniamyn hadden seyn
this, thei fledden in to wildirnesse, and
thei ȝeden to the stoon, whos name is
Remmon. And in that fliȝt *the sones of*
Israel ȝeden opynli, and ȝeden in to
dyuerse places, and killiden fyue thousynde men; and whanne thei ȝeden fer-
ther, thei pursueden hem, and killiden

190

195

185 est EOQR; coste E, cost Q, cooste X; cite CaFLMPQW; forsoþ ENX, And
I
186 werin P, were R; slein I, slayne KR
187 was C; eiȝteene N; þousynd CaIMW, þousand DHaMaNQRX, þousend
EGLP, þousande KS; men: om. I
188 alle: om. I; strongiste BO, strongist DMa, strongest EL, stronge G, ful
stronge I; fiȝters DEHaKLMRUX, fiȝteres F, fiȝtinge men I; whan EGLP
189 laften EKL, l. *alijue* I; hadde E, hedden L, haddin P; seyen BHaQS, sei E,
seie G, seen IMa
190 þai E; fled E, fleddin P; in: om. W; wildirness D, wildurnesse Ha,
wildernisse L, wildernesse U
191 stone E, ston IU; wose E
192 sonis GQ; children Ma[1]
193 openli AcCaEFGLMMaNPQW, opunli Ha, o. *aftir* I; and ȝeden: om. EI
194 dyuers DFMa; placis DGHaIKLMaNPQSX; killeden CaFLMPW, killed
E, þei k. of hem I, killide U; fife K, also E (cr. out); þousand
DHaMaNQRX, þousend EFGLP, þousynd IMW, þousande K
195 of men K[2]Ma; whan ELP; thei: beniamyn I; ȝeden: fledde forþ I;
ferþere BW, forþ þere AcCCaFGHaKMMaNOQSUX, furþer D, forþe E,
forþer LR, forþere P
196 pursuweden CaFMW, pursuiden Q; killide C, killeden CaFKLMPW,
killed E

cuius vocabulum est Remmon. In illa quoque fuga
palantes, et in diversa tendentes, occiderunt quinque millia virorum. Et cum ultra tenderent, persecuti sunt eos, et interfecerunt etiam alia duo
millia.

46 thowsandis. And so is doo, that alle
that fellen of Beniamyn in dyuerse placis,   200
weren fyue and twenti thowsandis, fiȝters
47 at batayls moost redy. And so there
laften of al the noumbre of Beniamyn,
that myȝten scape, and fleen into wilder-
nesse, sixe hundred men; and thei setten   205
in the stoon of Remmon foure monethis.
48 Forsothe the sones of Yrael goon out,
smyten with swerd al the relif of the
cyte, fro man vnto beest; and alle the
citees and lytil touns of Beniamyn de-   210
uowrynge flawm waastide.

199 thousend *CX*, thowsendis *E*, þousandes *Lo*; do *BCEHWoX*; all *B*, al *H*
200 that: om. *FWo*; fellyn *EF*; diuers *FLoWoX*; places *LoX*
201 were *C*, weryn *E*; thousend *CX*, þousandes *LoWo*; fiȝteres *CX*, fiȝteris *ELo*
202 bateyls *BFWo*, batailis *CX*, batailes *ELo*, bateylis *H*; most *BCEFHWoX*, moste *Lo*; þer *BCEFHWoX*
203 laftyn *E*; alle *BFLoWo*; noumber *B*
204 myȝtyn *E*; ascapen *BFHLoWo*, scapen *CX*, ascapyn *E*; fleeȝen *BF*
205 sexe *BF*, sex *Lo*; hundreþ *BF*, hundrid *CEHWo*, hundride *Lo*; seeten *BCFHWo*, setyn *E*, seten *X*
206 stone *BFHLo*, ston *CEWoX*; four *BF*, moneþes *ELo*
207 forsoþ *B*; Forsothe the sones: þe s. f. *cet.*; sonys *BFHWo*, sonus *CX*; gon *CEWoX*, gone *Lo*; oute *BEF*, ouȝte *H*
208 smytyn *E*; swerde *BFLoWo*; alle *BF*; relef *BEFX*, relife *Lo*
209 cytee *BH*; men *CE²Lo*; beste *BFHX*, bestus *C*, bestis *E*, beestis *Lo*, best *Wo*
210 cites *CX*; lytyll *B*, litle *CE*, lytel *Wo*; townys *BEFH*, tounes *CLoX*, tounnus *Wo*; deuourende *CX*
211 flawme *cet.*; waastyd *B*, wastide *CEH*, wastede *LoX*, wastid *Wo*

46 Et sic factum est, ut omnes, qui ceciderant de Beniamin in diversis locis, essent viginti quinque
millia, pugnatores ad bella promptissimi.
47 Remanserunt itaque de omni numero Beniamin, qui e-
vadere et fugere in solitudinem potuerunt, sexcenti
viri; sederuntque in petra Remmon mensibus quattuor.

46 also othere twei thousynde. And so it was
   doon, that alle [that] felden doun of Beniamyn in diuerse places, weren fyue and
   twenti thousynde, fiȝterys moost redi to   200
47 batels. And so sixe hundrid men leften
   of al the noumbre of Beniamyn, that
   myȝten ascape, and fle in to wildirnesse;
   and thei saten in the stoon of Remmon
48 foure monethis. Forsothe the sones of   205
   Israel ȝeden out, and smytiden with
   swerd alle the remenauntis of the citee,
   fro men til to werk beestis; and de-
   uourynge flawme wastide alle the citees
   and townes of Beniamyn.   210

197 also of hem I; o. tw.: tw. o. K; oþer ELX, oþre R; two AcBGIKQRWX,
    tweie CaM; þousynd CaFIMW, þousand DEHaMaNQRX, þousend GP,
    þousynd men I, þousande K, þousende L
198 don AcCDEGHaINPUX, done R; al E, alle þe men I; fellen CaEFLMW,
    filden D, felleden G, fellin P; doun slayn I
199 dyuers DEMaS; placis DGHaIKMaNPQSX; fife K
200 þousynd CaFIMW, þousand DEHaMaNQRX, þousend GLP, þousande
    K; fiȝters DEHaKLMaX, of f. G, men I, fiȝteres U; most
    CCaEFHaLQU, ful I; reedie K
201 batelis EP, bateils RX, batailes U; six I; hundred Ha, hunderd LP;
    laften K, leftin P
202 al: om. E
203 flee CaLP; wildernesse ELU, wildurnesse Ha
204 thei: þese I; satin LP, saaten X; ston EIU
205 moneþs EL, moneþes FP, monþis GHaQ; forsoþ EX, And I; sonys GQ
206 oute R; smyteden CaW, smytten E, smyten FM, þei smoten I, smetin LP
207 swerde R; the (1°): om. E; remainants E, remenauntes F, remnauntis R;
    cite CaFHaLMPQW
208 from K; til to: to E, vnto I; werke HaIR; bestis EI, bestes F, beestes R;
    deuouring EP, brennynge I
209 wastid D, wasted E, wastede L, waastide MaX
210 townis GHaQ, þe litle t. I

48 Egressi autem filii Israel, omnes reliquias civitatis a viris usque ad iumenta gladio percusserunt,
   cunctasque urbes et viculos Beniamin vorax flamma
   consumpsit.

21. 1 The sones forsothe of Yrael hadden
sworn in Maspha, and seiden, Noon of vs
shal ȝyue to the sones of Beniamyn of
2 his douȝtris a wijf. And alle thei camen
to the hows of God in Sylo, and in the
siȝt of hym sittynge vnto euen thei rereden a voys, and with greet ȝeelynge bi-
3 gunnen to wepe, seiynge, Whi, Lord God
of Yrael, this yuel ys doo in thi puple,
that this day o lynage be doon awei fro
4 vs? Forsothe the tothir day eerli rysynge
thei maden vp an auter, and offreden
there brent sacrificis and pesible sleyn

21. 1 sonys *BFHWo*, sonus *CX*; hadde *C*, haddyn *E*
2 sworne *Lo*; seidyn *E*; non *Wo*, noen *X*
3 ȝeuen *BFH*, ȝifyn *E*, ȝyuen *Lo*; sonus *CX*, sonys *EFH*
4 douȝters *BH*, doȝtris *CX*; wyf *BCEFHWoX*, wife *Lo*; camyn *E*, comen *Lo*
5 house *B*, houȝs *H*
6 siȝte *CELoX*; sittende *CX*; euyn *E*, euene *LoWo*; reredyn *E*, reyseden *Lo*
7 voice *BEFHLoWo*; grete *BFHLoWo*, gret *CX*, grett *E*; ȝellynge *BEFHLoWo*, ȝelling *CX*; begunne *C*, begunnyn *E*, by-gonnen *Lo*
8 wepen *BCFHLoWoX*, weepyn *E*; seiende *CX*
9 euel *CWoX*, euyl *E*, yuele *Lo*; done *BFHWo*, do *C*, don *EX*, doon *Lo*; peple *BFHLoWo*
10 oon *BEF*, one *H*, on *Wo*; ben *BFH*; done *BFH*, don *CEWoX*, doon *Lo*; aweye *BH*
11 forsoth *B*; Forsothe the tothir: þe t. f. *cet.*; toþer *cet.*; erly *cet*; risende *CX*
12 madyn *E*; autre *B*, auteer *E*; m. vp an a.: m. an a. vp *X*; offredyn *E*, offriden *Wo*
13 þer *Lo*; brente *ELo*; sacrifises *CELoX*, sacrefices *Wo*; peysyble *BF*, peesible *Lo*; slayn *BCFHWoX*, slayne *E*, sclayne *Lo*

21. 1 Iuraverant quoque filii Israel in Maspha, et dixerunt: Nullus nostrum dabit filiis Beniamin de filiabus suis uxorem.
2 Veneruntque omnes ad domum Dei in Silo, et in conspectu eius sedentes usque ad vesperam, levaverunt
vocem, et magno ululatu coeperunt flere, dicentes:

21. 1 Also the sones of Israel sworen in Maspha, and seiden, Noon of vs schal ȝyue to
the sones of Beniamyn a wijf of hise douȝ-
2 tris. And alle camen to the hows of God
in Silo, and thei saten in the siȝt of hym
til to euentid, and thei reisiden the
vois, and bigunnen to wepe with greet
3 ȝellyng, and seiden, Lord God of Israel,
whi is this yuel don in thi puple, that
to dai o lynage be takun awey of vs?
4 Sotheli in the tother day thei risiden
eerli, and bildyden an auter, and offriden
there brent sacrifices and pesible sacri-

5

10

21. 1 Also: Certis I; sonis GQ; sworun B, swooren OX
2 saiden E; None E; ȝeue BDGHaLMaR, ȝife K
3 sonis GHaQ, sone U; wif EFGHaLPQU; his EFILPQSX; douȝtres F
4 alle: al israel I; comen E, came I; into G
5 satyn ELPS, saaten X; siȝte CaMaU; s. of hym: lordis s. I
6 til to: vn to EI; euentide CaDEMaW, þe euen tijd I, euentijd K,
euenetide R; reisiden CaDEFKLMPW, reriden up I, reseiden S; the: her I
7 uoice ELP; bigunne G, þei b. I, bigonnen R, bigunnyn S; grete EPR,
gret I
8 ȝellynge DFGLMaQRU; saiden E
9 euel ELP, euyl FGQ; doon BCaKMMaQW, done R; peple CaEFIL-
MMaNPWX
10 oo GHaIKLMaPQR, oon S; be: bi D; taken BCCaDFKMMaQRUW,
takin ELP, take I; away Ha; of: fro CG
11 soþli FGILMMaPQSUWX; ooþer I, toþir ORSX; riseden AcCaDIKMNRW,
risen EFL, resin P
12 erly CEINQ; bildeden CaFLMPW, biledden E, beldiden R; auteer G;
offreden CaFLMPUW, offered E
13 there: her B, þer CE; brente R; sacrifisis (2x) CaDGK(2°)LMMaPQWX;
peesible GPQ

3 Quare, Domine Deus Israel, factum est hoc malum in
populo tuo, ut hodie una tribus auferetur ex nobis?
4 Altera autem die diluculo consurgentes, exstruxerunt
altare; obtuleruntque ibi holocausta et pacificas
victimas, et dixerunt:

5 offryngis, and seiden, Who stiede not vp
in the oost of the Lord of alle the lynagis 15
of Yrael? Forsothe with greet ooth thei
bounden hem seluen, whanne thei weren
in Maspha, hem to be slayn that thennus
6 weren. And lad by othenkynge the sones
of Yrael vpon her brother Beniamyn, thei 20
bigunnen to seyn, There is doon awey
7 o lynage fro Irael; whens shulen thei
taake wyues? forsothe alle in comyn we*
han sworn vs not to ȝyue oure douȝtres

14 offringus *CX*, offrynges *E*, offerynges *Lo*; saidyn *E*; steyȝid *BFWo*, steȝede
CEX, styȝid *H*, steiȝede *Lo*
15 ost *CWoX*, host *E*; al *Lo*; lynage *Lo*
16 forsoth *B*; Forsothe with greet: w. gr. f. *cet.*; grete *BFHLoWo*, gret *CX*,
grett *E*; ooþe *BF*, oþ *CWoX*, oþþe *H*, oþe *Lo*
17 boundyn *E*; þemself *CX*, þemselue *E*, hem self *Lo*; whann *B*, whan
CEFHLoWoX; weryn *E*
18 ben *cet.*; sclayne *Lo*, slayne *X*; þenns *BF*, þennys *E*, þens *H*, þennes *LoWo*
19 weryn *E*; oþinkynge *BEFH*, othenking *CX*; sonys *FH*
20 off *E*; vppon *Wo*; þeir *BEF*, þer *CLoX*
21 begunne *C*, begunnyn *E*, bi-gonnen *Lo*; þer *BCEFHLoX*; done *BFH*, don
CEWoX; aweye *BH*
22 oon *BEF*, one *H*, on *Wo*; whenns *BFH*, whennus *CX*, whennes *LoWo*;
schul *BCEFWoX*, schull *H*, schulle *Lo*
23 taken *BFLoWo*, take *CHX*, takyn *E*; wyfis *BH*, wifes *E*; forsothe alle:
a. f. *cet.*; comoun *BFHLo*, comun *CEX*; wee *CEX*, þei *AFHWo*
24 sworne *Lo*, swore *X*; ȝeuen *BFH*, ȝiuen *CLoWo*, ȝifyn *E*; our *F*; douȝtren
BFHWo, doȝtris *CX*, dowȝtris *E*

5 Quis non ascendit in exercitu Domini de universis
tribubus Israel? Grandi enim iuramento se constrinx-
erant, cum essent in Maspha, interfici eos, qui defuissent.
6 Ductique paenitentia filii Israel super fratre suo
Beniamin, coeperunt dicere: Ablata est una tribus
de Israel;
7 unde uxores accipient? omnes enim in commune iura-
vimus, non daturos nos filias nostras his.

5 fices, and seiden, Who of alle the lynagis
of Israel stiede not in to the oost of the   15
Lord? For whanne thei weren in Mas-
pha, thei hadden bounde hem silf with
a greuouse ooth, that thei that failiden

6 schulden be slayn. And the sones of Israel
weren led bi penaunce on her brother Ben-   20
iamyn, and bigunnen to seie, O lynage of

7 Israel is takun awey; wherof schulen thei
take wyues? for alle we sworen in comyn,
that we schulen not ȝyue oure douȝtris to

14 al R; linage E, lynages FOR
15 stied DE, steiede F, stiȝede GMaNQR; in to: in AcBCaDEFGKLNOP-
    QRSU, to CMa, up into I; oste E
16 wan E, whan LP; þai E; werin P
17 þai E; had E, om. GKMa²QX, haddin LP, hadde OU; bound E, bounden
    GHaKQSUX; self CaEFKLMPRW
18 an D; greuous BCaDEFGHaKMMaNPQRSUWX, ful gret I; oþ G;
    faileden CaDEFKLMNPUW, f. þenns I
19 scholden CaMW, shuld E; slay E, deed I, slayne KR; sonis GQ
20 werin S; ladde K; upon I; here GQ; broþir MaOSX
21 bygonne F, þei b. I; sei EI; oo GHaKLMaPQR
22 taken CaEFGHaIKLMMaQUW, takin PR; aweie R; where of ER;
    schullen CaM, schuln DF, shul EILP, scholden W
23 taken EU, takun S; wifes K, wyuis Q; for: certis I; al O; alle we: we alle I;
    sworun B, sworn E, swooren GNOX, han sworn I; comen E, comoun GI,
    comune Ma, comyne N, comun X
24 schullen CaFM, schulden DMa, shul EILP, scholden W; ȝeue
    BDGHaLMaQR, ȝife K; douȝtres EF, doutris L, doȝtris X

8 to hem. And therfor thei seiden, Who 25
is of alle the lynagis of Irael, that stiede
not vp to the Lord in to Maspha? And
loo! there ben foundun dwellers of Jabis
9 Galaad not haue ben in that oost. Forsothe that tyme, whanne thei weren in 30
10 Sylo, noon of hem is foundun there. And
so thei senten ten thousand moost stronge
men, and comaundiden to hem, Goth, and
smitith the dwellers of Jabis Galaad in
mouth of swerd, as wel wymmen as the 35

25 þem *CEX*; þerfore *BCEFHWoX*, þere fore *Lo*; seidyn *E*
26 all *BH*; lynages *X*; stey ʒid *BFWo*, ste ʒeþ *CE*, sty ʒid *H*, stey ʒes *Lo*,
   ste ʒede *X*
27 no ʒt *Lo*; in M. *X*
28 lo *CEWoX*; þer *BCEFHWoX*; beþ *Wo*; founden *BCFHLoWoX*, fowndyn
   E; dwelleris *CELoX*
29 to not *X*; han *CX*, hafe *E*; ost *CX*, host *E*, hoost *H*; forsoþ *H*; 29—30
   Forsothe that: þat f. *cet.*
30 whann *BH*, whan *CWoX*
31 noone *Lo*, noen *X*; þem *CX*; founde *BEFHWo*, founden *CLoX*
32 sentyn *E*; tenn *BH*; thousend *CEX*, þousande *Lo*; most *BCEFHWoX*,
   moste *Lo*; strong *E*
33 comaundeden *C*, comawndidyn *E*; þem *CEX*; gooþ *F*
34 smyteþ *CELoWoX*; dwelleris *CEX*
35 mowþe *LoWo*; swerde *BFLoWo*; wele *BFWo*, weel *E*; the: om. *C*

8 Idcirco dixerunt: Quis est de universis tribubus
Israel, qui non ascendit ad Dominum in Maspha? Et
ecce, inventi sunt habitatores Iabis Galaad in illo
exercitu non fuisse.
9 Eo quoque tempore, cum essent in Silo, nullus ex
eis ibi repertus est.
10 Miserunt itaque decem millia viros robustissimos,
et praeceperunt eis: Ite, et percutite habitatores
Iabis Galaad in ore gladii, tam uxores quam parvulos
eorum.

490

8 hem. Therfor thei seiden, Who is of alle   25
   the lynagis of Israel, that stiede not to
   the Lord in Maspha? And lo! the dwelleris of Jabes of Galaad weren foundun,
9 that thei weren not in the oost. Also
   in that tyme, whanne thei weren in Silo,   30
10 noon of hem was foundun there. Therfor thei senten ten thousynde strongeste men, and comaundiden to hem, Go
   ȝe, and smyte the dwelleris of Jabes of
   Galaad bi the scharpnesse of swerd, as   35
   wel the wyues as the litle children of

25 þerfore CaGKLMaNQRWX, þanne I; is: is it I
26 the: om. O; lynages FHaRU, lynage Ma; stied DE, steiede F, stieden L, stiȝeden N, stiȝede MaR; to: up to I
27 dwellers DEHaIKLMPRUX
28 werun D, were MQW; founden CaDEFGIKLMMaOPRUW
29 þai E; wer E; the: ADHaI, þat cet.; oste E, lordis oost I
30 when E, whan LP; thei: israel I; weren: was I, werin P
31 non E; hem: iabes meynee I; founde AcCCaDFHaMNORS, founden EGIKLMaPUW; þer E; þerfore BCaEFGKLMaNQRWX, þanne I
32 thei: þe sones of israel I; þousynd CaFIMW, þousand DHaMaNQRX, þousend EG, þousande K, þousende LP; strongiste B, strongist D, strongest E, ful stronge I, strengist Ma
33 comaundeden EFLMPW, þei c. I, commaundiden R
34 ȝee U; smyte ȝe I; dwellers DEHaIKLMRUX; of (2°): & of I
35 the: om. I; sharpnes EMa
36 wele E, weel Ma, wil U; the: her I; wyues of hem D, wyfes K, wyuis Q; as the: aste E, as Ma; litil AcBDEMaX, litel K; 36–37 her ȝounge children I

11 litil children of hem. And this shal ben,
that ȝe shulen kepe wel, alle of maal
kynde and wymmen, that han knowun

12 men, sleeth; maydens kepe ȝe. And
there ben foundun of Jabis Galaad foure   40
hundryd maydens, that knewen not the
bed of man; and thei brouȝten hem to
the tentis in Silo, in to the loond of Cha-

13 naan. And thei senten messagers to the
sones of Beniamyn, that weren in the   45
stoon of Remmon; and thei comaundiden
to hem, that thei shulden take hem in

36 lytyll *B*, litle *CE*, litel *Wo*; childryn *E*, childer *CX*; þem *CE*; be *C*
37 ȝee *CELoX*; schuln *BEFWoX*, shul *CLo*, schullen *H*; kepen *BFHLoWo*,
   kepyn *E*; wele *BFWo*, weel *CE*; al *HLo*; male *BEHLoWoX*, mal *C*, maale *F*
38 knowen *BFHLoWoX*, knowe *C*, knowyn *E*
39 sleaþ *BF*, sleþ *CEX*, scleeþ *Lo*; meydens *BH*, maidenes *CLoX*, maidenys
   EWo; ȝee *CELoX*
40 þer *CEHWo*; founden *BFHLoWoX*, founde *C*, foundyn *E*
41 hundreþ *BFWo*, hundrithe *Lo*; meydens *BH*, maidenes *CLoX*, maydenys
   EWo; knewe *CLo*, knewyn *E*
42 bedde *LoWo*; broȝten *CX*, broȝtyn *E*; þem *CE*
43 tentus *C*; lond *CWoX*, land *E*, londe *Lo*
44 sentyn *E*, senden *Lo*; messageres *CX*, messageris *ELo*
45 sonys *BFH*, sonus *CX*; weryn *E*
46 ston *CEWoX*, stone *Lo*; comaundeden *C*, commaundiden *Lo*
47 hem (1°): þem *CX*; schuldyn *E*, shulde *X*; taken *BFHLo*, takyn *E*; hem
   (2°): þem *CX*

11 Et hoc erit, quod observare debetis: omne generis
   masculini et mulieres, quae cognoverunt viros, inter-
   ficite; virgines reservate.

12 Inventaeque sunt de Iabis Galaad quadringentae virgines, quae nescierunt viri torum, et adduxerunt eas
   ad castra in Silo, in terram Chanaan.

13 Miseruntque nuntios ad filios Beniamin, qui erant
   in petra Remmon, et praeceperunt eis, ut eas suscip-
   erent in pace.

11 hem. And this thing schal be, which
  ȝe owen to kepe, sle ȝe alle of male
  kynde, and the wymmen, that knewen
  men fleischli; reserue ȝe the virgyns.   40
12 And foure hundrid virgyns, that knewen
  not the bed of man, weren foundun of
  Jabes of Galaad; and thei brouȝten hem
  to the castels in Silo, in to the lond of
13 Chanaan. And thei senten messangeris   45
  to the sones of Beniamyn, that weren in
  the stoon of Remmon; and thei comaundiden to hem, that thei schulden resseyue

37 be: be to ȝou I; which: þat I, wich K, whiche GR
38 ȝee U; owen to: schul I; keepe G, kepen S; slee CaGHaKQ; ȝee U; al E;
   maale K
39 kind E; wommen BGQ; knew E², han knowe I, knowen L
40 fleischely B, fleisly C, fleschly CaEFLMPQRUW, fleiȝssli K; resserue Ac,
   kepe EL, but kepe I, keepe P; ȝee U; virgynes CaDFHaRW, virgynis GQ,
   maidens I, vergyns U
41 And foure hundrid virgyns: om. E; four K; hundred Ha, hunderd LP;
   virgynes CaHaMW, virgynis GQ, vergyns U; knewe L
42 were EMQW; founden CaDEFGHaIKLMMaPRUW; of: in CHa
43 of: & of I; broȝten E
44 to: into L; castels: tentis I, castelis PS; in: of L
45 thei: israel I; messangers DFIMX, messagers EK, messangeres Ha,
   messengers LP, massangeris O
46 sonys GHaQ
47 ston I; comaundeden CaEFLPW
48 scholden CaMW, shuld E, schulde O; resseiue LX

493

14 pees. And the sones of Beniamyn camen
in that tyme, and ben ȝeuen to hem
wyues of the douȝtres of Jabes Galaad;   50
forsothe other thei founden, the whiche
15 lijk maner thei shulden take. And al
Yrael greetli sorowide, and dide othenkynge vpon the slauȝter of o lynage of
16 Yrael. And the more thurȝh* birth seiden,   55
What shulen we doo to the tother, that
han take no wyues? Alle the wymmen in
17 Beniamyn fellen togidre, and with greet
bisynes to vs and myche stodye it is to
puruey, lest o lynage be doon awey fro   60

48   pese *B*, pes *CEWoX*; sonys *BFH*, sonus *CX*; camyn *E*, comen *Lo*
49   ȝiuen *CLoWo*, ȝifyn *E*, ȝoue *X*; þem *CEX*
50   wyfis *BH*, wifes *EX*; douȝtren *BFHWo*, doȝtris *CX*, douȝtris *E*
51   forsothe other: o. f. *cet.*; oþere *CX*, ooþere *E*; fowndyn *E*; the whiche:
þe which *FWo*, þat *C¹*
52   lyke *BEFHLoWo*, lic *CX*; schuldyn *E*; taken *cet.*
53   gretely *BF*, gretli *CEHWoX*, grete *Lo*; sorewide *CE*, sorowid *Wo*, sorewede
X; oþinkynge *BEFHWo*, othinking *C*, othenking *X*
54   slaȝter *CX*, slaȝtyr *E*; oon *BEF*, one *H*, on *Wo*
55   thurth *A*, þorȝ *B*, þurȝ *CWoX*, þurgh *E*, þoruȝ *FLo*, þoru *H*; birþe
CEHLoX; seidyn *E*
56   schul *BCEFHWoX*, schulle *Lo*; wee *CEX*; done *BHLoWo*, do *CX*, don *E*,
doon *F*; toþere *CE*, oþere *X*
57   taken *BFHLoWoX*, takyn *E*; wyfis *BH*, wifes *EX*; al *BH*; in: of *X*
58   felle *C*, fellyn *E*; to giþer *BF*, togidere *CE*, to gyder *HWo*, togiþere *X*;
grete *BFHLoWo*, gret *CEX*
59   besinesse *CE*, bisynesse *X*; mych *FWo*, moche *Lo*; studie *CELoWoX*,
stody *F*
60   purueie *CHWo*, purueyn *ELo*, purueyen *X*; oon *BEF*, one *H*, on *Wo*;
done *BFH*, don *CEWoX*; aweye *B*
61   douȝters *BHLo*, doȝtris *CX*, dowȝtris *E*; wee *CEX*; moun *CEX*, mowe *Wo*

14 Veneruntque filii Beniamin in illo tempore, et datae
sunt eis uxores de filiabus Iabis Galaad; alias
autem non reppererunt, quas simili modo traderent.
15 Universusque Israel valde doluit, et egit paeniten-
tiam super interfectione unius tribus ex Israel.

14 tho wymmen in pees. And the sones of
Beniamyn camen in that tyme, and the   50
dou3tris of Jabes of Galaad weren 3ouun
to hem to wyues; forsothe thei founden
not othere wymmen, whiche thei schulden
15 3yue in lijk maner. And al Israel sorewide
greetly, and dide penaunce on the sleyng   55
16 of o lynage of Israel. And the g[r]ettere
men in birthe seiden, What schulen we
do to the othere men, that han not take
wyues? Alle the wymmen in Beniamyn
17 felden doun, and it is to vs to puruey   60
with greet cure and greet studie, that o

49 tho: þe GHaQRS; wommen BGQ; sonys GQ
50 comin E; tyme: t. *to israel* I
51 dou3tres F, dou3ters U; of (2°): in C, & of I; were MQW; 3ouen
    CaEFGILMaPRW, 3ofene K, 3owen U
52 to (1°): om. I; wifes K, wyuis Q; forsoþ ENX, for I; foundun B, fonden D,
    fondun O
53 not: none I; oþer EFLP; wommen BGQ; which DEFP, wiche K; scholden
    CaF; 53−54 in lijk manere þei schulden 3iue *to hem* I
54 3eue BDGHaMaOQR, 3. *to hem* I, 3ife K, 3yuen S; like DELP, lyk
    FGHaNQU; manere AcCaFGHaLMPQSW; alle E; sorowide
    BHaKMaX, sorwide DN, sorowed E, sorowiden IO, sorwede LP,
    sorowede U
55 gretli AcIPQS, greteli ER; dede F, diden IK; on: of I; sleynge
    AcCaDFHaLMMaOPRU, sleeynge GQ, sleeing K
56 oo GHaKLPQR, þat o I; grettir Ac, gretere CU, gretter CaDEFHaPX
57 schullen CaMSW, shul EILP, schuln F, shule X
58 the: om. N; oþer CaEX, toþere K, oþre R; that: þan S; haue R; taken
    EU, takun S
59 wifes K, wyuis Q, viues S; al O; wommen BGQ; in þe lynage of B. I
60 fellen CaFLMW, filden D, fellin EP, han falle I; to (2°): om. F; purueye
    BCCaDEFG; 60−61 and wiþ gret charge it falliþ us to studie I
61 greet (2x): gret EP, grete R; cure and greet: om. Ca; stodie EGLPU; oo
    GHaKLPQR

16 Dixeruntque maiores natu: Quid faciemus reliquis,
qui non acceperunt uxores? omnes in Beniamin feminae
conciderunt,
17 et magna nobis cura ingentique studio providendum
est, ne una tribus deleatur ex Israel.

18 Yrael. Oure douȝtres we mowen not
   ȝyue to hem, bounden bi ooth and cursynge, in the which we han seide, Cursid
   that shal ȝyue of his douȝtris a wijf to
19 Beniamyn. And thei token counseil, and   65
   seiden, Loo, the solempnete of the Lord
   is in Silo, torn[ed] aboute bi the ȝeer, that
   is set at the north of the cytee of Bethel,
   and at the eest coost of the weye that
   goth fro Bethel to Siccymam, and to the   70
20 south of the burȝ toun of Lebona. And
   thei comaundiden to the sones of Beniamyn, and seiden, Goth, and lurkith in

62 ȝeuen *BFH*, ȝifyn *E*, ȝyuen *Lo*; þem *CEX*; bounde *C*, boundyn *E*; oþe
   BFLo, oþ *CWoX*, oþþe *H*; cursing *CLoX*
63 the: om. *X*; whiche *BCEHLoX*; wee *CEX*; seid *CEX*; cursede *BFHLo*
64 ȝeuen *BFH*, ȝifyn *E*, ȝyuen *Wo*; hise *E*; douȝters *BH*, doȝtris *CX*,
   douȝtres *Lo*; wyf *BCEFHWoX*, wyfe *Lo*
65 tookyn *E*, tokon *Lo*; counseyle *LoWo*
66 seidyn *E*; lo *CELoWoX*; solempnyte *LoWo*
67 turned *CEX*, turnede *Lo*, turne *Wo*; a-bouȝte *H*, about *Wo*; ȝer *CX*, ȝere
   LoWo
68 sett *BCEFHWo*, sette *Lo*; northe *Lo*; cyte *BCFHLoWoX*
69 este *BF*, est *CEHWoX*; cost *CEWo*, coest *X*; wey *LoWo*
70 gooþ *F*
71 southe *Lo*; bourȝ *BFH*, burgh *E*, bourghe *Lo*
72 þe[i] *X*; comaundeden *C*, comawndidyn *E*, commaunden *Lo*; sonys *BFHWo*,
   sonus *CX*
73 seidyn *E*; gooþ *F*; lurkeþ *CELoWoX*

18 Filias nostras eis dare non possumus, constricti
   iuramento et maledictione, qua diximus: Maledictus
   qui dederit de filiabus suis uxorem Beniamin.
19 Ceperuntque consilium, atque dixerunt: Ecce sollem-
   nitas Domini est in Silo anniversaria, quae sita est
   ad septentrionem urbis Bethel, et ad orientalem
   plagam viae, quae de Bethel tendit ad Siccimam, et
   ad meridiem oppidi Lebona.
20 Praeceperuntque filiis Beniamin, atque dixerunt:
   Ite, /et/ latitate in vineis.

18 lynage be not don awey fro Israel. We
moun not ȝyue oure douȝtris to hem, for
we ben boundun with an ooth and cursynge, bi which we seiden, Be he cursid 65
that ȝyueth of hise douȝtris a wijf to Ben-
19 iamyn. And thei token a counsel, and
seiden, Lo! annyuersarie solempnyte of
the Lord is in Silo, whych is set at the
north of the citee of Bethel, and at the 70
eest coost of the weie that goith from
Bethel to Siccyma, and at the south of
20 the citee of Lebona. And thei comaundiden to the sones of Beniamyn, and
seiden, Go ȝe, be ȝe hid in the vyneris; 75

62 doon BCaKLMMaQW, doun O, done R; away Ha; from K
63 mowen I, mowe U; ȝeue BDHaMaQR, ȝif E, ȝife K; douȝt[r]is C,
    douȝtres F, douȝters IU; hem: beniamyn I
64 be E; bounden CaDFHaKMMaRUW, bound E, bounde GLP; oþe E,
    oof S; and: & wiþ I; cursynge DGMaQU
65 bi: om. GQ; whiche BGNQR, þe whiche I, wich K; we: þei C, he U;
    saiden E; Be he: He be Ma[1]; cursed EKL
66 ȝeueþ BDHaLMaQ, ȝifeþ K; his EFGILPQSX; douȝters IU; wif
    EFGHaKLNPQU; to B. of his douȝtris a wijf I
67 tookin L, tooken NPX, tokun S; a: om. IKX; counceil CaDFGHaIKM-
    MaNQWX, consail E, counceile R
68 saiden E; an vniuersarie Ma; solempnete AcLP, solennite E, solēnete F,
    solempnytee I, solēnyte N, solemnite U; 68–69 þe solempnytee of þe lord
    is in S. þe ȝeris turnyng aboute I
69 is: om. M; whiche G, þat I, wich K; sett IKMaNR; at the: atte E
70 norþ coost I; cite FHaMPQW; of: om. X; and at the: & atte E, and þe S
71 est EGQ; coste E, cost QU; wey EIMa; gooþ CaMW, goþ EFGHaIPQ;
    from AKL, fro cet.
72 at the: atte E; souþe D, suþ S; of: to W; 70 and ... (72) B.: om. L
73 cite CaEFHaLMPQW, c. eþer burgh toun X[2]; of: om. M; thei: þe E,
    Israel I; comaundeden CaEFLMPW, comaundide I
74 sonys GHaQ
75 saiden E, seide O; ȝe (1°): ȝee GSU; & be GI; ȝe (2°): ȝee GU; hidde
    EK; the: om. S; vyners DEHaIKLMPRUX, vyneres F

21 the vynes; and whan ȝe seen the douȝ-
tris of Sylo at the dauncis to be lad aftir   75
the maner to goo forth, goth out so-
deynly out of the vines, and takith hem,
eche sondry wyues, and goth into the
22 loond of Beniamyn. And whanne the
faders of hem and britheren comen, and   80
aȝens ȝou bigynnen to pleyne and chiden,
we shulen seye to hem, Hath mercy on
hem; forsothe thei rauysheden not hem
bi lawe of fiȝters and of ouercomers; but
to hem preyinge, that thei myȝten take,   85
ȝe han not ȝeuen; and on ȝoure parti is

---

74 vynys *H*; whann *B*; ȝee *CELoX*; douȝters *BH*, doȝtris *CX*, douȝtres *LoWo*
75 daunces *LoX*; ben *BEFHLoWoX*; ledde *Lo*; after *BCFWo*
76 go *CELoWoX*; forþe *Lo*; goo *B*; oute *BF*, ouȝte *HLo*
77 oute *BLo*, ouȝte *H*; the: om. *H*; vynys *BH*; takeþ *BCEFLoX*; þem *CE*;
77—8 and ... wyues: om. *Wo*
78 sondre *BEFH*, sunder *CX*, sondrye *Lo*; wyfis *BH*, wifes *EX*
79 lond *CHWoX*, land *E*, londe *Lo*; whann *BH*, whan *CEFLoX*
80 fadris *ELoWoX*; þem *C*; breþeren *BEFHLoWo*, breþern *CX*; commen
BFWo, comyn *E*
81 aȝeyn *BFHWo*, aȝen *CELoX*; bygynnyn *BFH*, begynnen *C*, begynnyn *E*,
by-gynnynge *Lo*; pleynen *BFHLoWoX*, pleynyn *E*; chidyn *E*
82 wee *CEX*; schuln *BFWo*, shul *CELoX*, schullen *H*; seyn *BEFHLoWoX*,
sei *C*; þem *CEX*; hafeþ *E*, haueþ *Lo*; mercye *Wo*; on: of *cet.*
83 þem *CE*; forsoþ *B*; raueshiden *C*, raueschedyn *E*, rauychiden *Wo*,
rauesheden *X*; not hem: þem not *C*, not þem *E*
84 fiȝteres *CX*, fiȝteris *ELo*; ouercommers *BFLo*, ouercomeres *C*,
ouercomeris *E*, ouercome[re]s *X*; bot *B*, bute *F*
85 þem *CX*; preyȝinge *BFH*, preȝende *CX*, prayinge *Wo*; myȝte *C*,
myȝtyn *E*, myȝt *Wo*; taken *BFLoWo*, takyn *E*
86 ȝee *CELoX*; ȝiue *C*, ȝifyn *E*, ȝyuen *LoWo*, ȝoue *X*; ȝour *BFH*; partye
BEFHLoWo, part *CX*

---

21 Cumque videritis filias Silo ad ducendos choros ex
more procedere, exite repente de vineis, et rapite
eas, singuli uxores singulas, et pergite in terram
Beniamin.
22 Cumque venerint patres earum ac fratres, et adversum

21 and whanne ȝe seen douȝtris of Silo go
   forth bi custom to lede daunsis, go ȝe out
   of the vyneris sudeynli, and rauysche ȝe
   hem, eche man o wijf, and go ȝe in to the
22 lond of Beniamyn. And whanne the fa-   80
   dris and britheren of hem schulen come,
   and bigynne to pleyne and plete aȝens
   ȝou, we schulen seie to hem, Haue ȝe
   mercy of hem; for thei rauyschiden not
   hem bi riȝt of fiȝteris and ouercomeris,   85
   but ȝe ȝauen not to hem preiynge that
   thei schulden take; and the synne is of

76 whan ELP; ȝee CaU; se E, seyn U; douȝtres EF, þe douȝters IU; to go I,
   gon LP
77 foorþ D; custum BCaDGHaMMaQW; leede G; daunces CaEF; goo P;
   ȝee U; þanne out I, oute R
78 the: om. EI; vyners DEHaIKLMPRX; sudenli AcCNOSU, sodeynli
   BCaEFGILMPQW, sodenli HaK; rauesche BLP, rauish E, rauiȝsshe K;
   ȝee U
79 eche AK, ech cet.; o: oo GHaKLPQR, a I; wif EFGHaLNPQU; ȝee GU
80 whan EGLP; fadres EF
81 breþren CaFMW, breþeren EHaLPRU, briþren G, breþern K; hem: þo
   wymmen I; schullen CaMSW, schuln DF, shul EILP; com E
82 schul bigynne I; playne AcBCDFHaIKLNOPQSUWX; pleete GKMaQ,
   to pl. I; aȝenus AcCNO, ayens E
83 schullen CaMW, schuln DF, shul EILP; say E, sey I; ȝe: ȝee BU, om. I
84 mercie R; of: on G; of hem: om. R; raueschiden BGQ, rauyschide C,
   rauyscheden CaDMW, rauesheden EFLP, han [not] rauyshed I, rauiȝshiden
   K, rauischen R
85 hem: þo wymmen I; riȝte K; fiȝters DHaIKLMRX, fiȝtars E, fiȝteres U;
   ouercomers DEHaIKLMRSX, ouircomeris G
86 but forþi þat ȝe I; ȝee U; han not ȝouen ȝoure douȝters I, ȝafen n. K;
   praying EHa, preiyng W
87 þai E; scholden CaFMW, shuld E, shulen O; take hem to wyues I

vos queri coeperint atque iurgari, dicemus eis:
Miseremini eorum; non enim rapuerunt eas iure bel-
lantium atque victorum, sed rogantibus, ut acciperent, non dedistis; et a vestra parte peccatum est.

23 the synne. And the sones of Beniamyn
   diden as to hem was comaundid, and
   after her noumbre thei rauyssheden to
   hem, of hem that ladden dauncis, sondry   90
   wyues, And thei wenten into her possessioun, bildynge vp cytees, and dwell-
24 ynge in hem. Forsothe the sones of
   Yrael turneden aȝen, bi lynagis and meynees, into her tabernaclis. In tho days   95
   was no kyng in Yrael, but ech on that
   to hym semyde ryȝt, that dide he.

87 synn *B*; sonys *BEFHWo*, sonus *CX*
88 deden *C*, didyn *E*; þem *CEX*; comaundyde *BFH*, comaunded *C*,
    commaundide *Lo*
89 aftyr *EX*; þeir *BEFWo*, þer *CLoX*; rauesheden *CX*, raueschedyn *E*,
    rauyschydyn *FWo*
90 hem (1°): þem *CEX*; hem (2°): þem *E*; laddyn *E*, ledden *Lo*; daunces
    LoX; sondre *BEFHLo*, sunder *C*, sundre *X*
91 wyfys *BH*, wifes *EX*; wentyn *E*; þeir *BEFWo*, þer *CLoX*
92 bildende *CX*; cites *CFX*; dwellende *CX*
93 þem *CE*; forsoþ *B*; Forsothe the sones: þe s. f. *cet.*; sonys *BFH*, sonus *CX*
94 tornyden *BFH*, turnedyn *E*; aȝeyn *BF*, aȝeen *CEX*, a-ȝeyne *Lo*; lynages
    LoX; meyneese *B*, meines *CELoX*
95 þer *BCELoX*, þeir *FWo*; tabernacles *ELoX*; þoo *CLo*; daȝes *CX*, daies
    EFLoWo
96 kynge *BLo*; bot *B*, bute *F*; echone *BFHLo*, eche *CX*, eche one *E*
97 semede *CELoX*, semyd *Wo*; riȝte *Lo*; dydde *BFH*; he: om. *cet.*

23 Feceruntque filii Beniamin, ut sibi fuerat impera-
   tum, et iuxta numerum suum rapuerunt sibi de his,
   quae ducebant choros, uxores singulas. Abieruntque
   in possessionem suam, aedificantes urbes, et habi-
   tantes in eis.
24 Filii quoque Israel reversi sunt, per tribus et
   familias, in tabernacula sua. In diebus illis non
   erat rex in Israel, sed unusquisque, quod sibi rectum videbatur, hoc faciebat.

23 ȝoure part. And the sones of Beniamyn
diden as it was comaundid to hem, and bi
her noumbre thei rauyschiden wyues to   90
hem, ech man o wijf, of hem that ledden
daunsis. And thei ȝeden in to her possessioun, and bildiden citees, and dwellyden
24 in tho. And the sones of Israel turneden
aȝen, bi lynagis and meynees, in to her   95
tabernaclis. In tho dayes was no kyng in
Israel, but ech man dide this, that semyde
ryȝtful to hym silf.

88 ȝour KL, ȝore S; parte R; the: om. U; sonis GHaQ, sonus Ma
89 dedin EP, deden L; comaundide DHaOS, comaunded ELP
90 here GQS; noumber E; raueschiden BQ, rauescheden CaEFP,
    rauyscheden DNW; wifes K, wyuis Q
91 eche K; oo GHaKLPQR; wif EFGHaLPQU; ladden K, leddin P
92 daunses CaEFPR; here GQ, hir L; possessione E, posession KP
93 bildeden EFLMPUW, þei b. I, beeldiden R; dwelleden CaFLMPW,
    duelled E, dwellen U
94 in tho: om. D, in hem N, in þoo RX; sonis GQ, sonus Ma; turniden GHaQ
95 aȝein B; lynages CaERU, her l. I; meynes EU; here QR
96 tabernacles FR; þoo R
97 bot E; eche KL; this: þat þing I, om. Ma; semede BCaFKLMaPRX,
    semyd D, semed E
98 self CaFIKMPRUW, selue E

III. Abbreviations

General

acc. = according; accusative
Atlas = McIntosh etc. (see *Titles*)
AN = Anglo-Norman
cet. = ceteri
comp. = comparative
cr. out = crossed out
dem. = demonstrative
E = East
EM = East Midland
ELV = Early & Later Version
EV = Early Version; EV I = -Bar. 3.20
exp. = expunged
FM = Forshall & Madden (see *Titles*)
gen. = genitive
GP = General Prologue
IV = Interlinear Version
inst. = instance(s)
LV = Later Version
M = Midland
ME = Middle English
MEB = Middle English Bible
N = Northern
obl. = oblique
OE = Old English
OF = Old French
ON = Old Norse
om. = omitted
ONT = Old & New Testament
OT = Old Testament
OV = Original Version
pl. = plural
pos. = positive
pt. = past, preterite
ptc. = participle
pt.p. = past participle

502

S = South
SE = South East
SM = South Midland
SW = South West
sup. = superlative
var. = variant, Var. = Vulgate variant
voc. = vocative
vs. = versus
W = West
WB = Wyclif Bible
WS = West Saxon
x = instance(s)

Manuscripts

A = Corpus Christi College Oxford 4
A = B.L. Royal I.C.VIII
Ac = formerly Acland; now Scheide 12, Princeton
B = Bodley Douce 370
B = B.L. Royal I.C.IX
C = Bodley Douce 369 (1st part)
C = B.L. Cotton Claudius E.II
Ca = Cambridge Univ. Libr. Additional 6680
D = Lambeth Palace 25 (1st part)
D = B.L. Lansdowne 454
E = Bodley 959
E = B.L. Arundel 104
F = Trinity College Dublin 66 (A.I.9)
F = Sion College London ARC L 40.2/E.1
G = B.L. Egerton 617
G = Lincoln College Oxford Latin 119
H = Cambridge Univ. Libr. Additional 6681
H = Corpus Christi College Oxford 20
Ha = B.L. Harley 2249
I = Bodley Fairfax 2
I = Bodley 277
K = Bodley Douce 369 (2nd part)
K = Bodley Fairfax 2

L = Bodley 296
Lo = Longleat 3 (Marquis of Bath)
M = Queen's College Oxford 388
Ma = Magdalene College Cambridge (Pepys) 1603
N = St. John's College Oxford 7
O = New College Oxford 66
P = Emmanuel College Cambridge 21
Q = Cambridge Univ. Libr. Mm. 2.15
R = Cambridge Univ. Libr. Dd. 1.27
Ry = Rylands (Manchester) Eng. 91
S = Corpus Christi College Cambridge 147
U = Lambeth Palace 25 (2nd part)
V = Lambeth Palace 1033
W = City Library Norwich Ih 20
Wo = Ducal Libr. Wolfenbüttel Aug.A.2
X = Christ Church Oxford 145
X = Hereford Cathedral Libr. O.VII.1
Y = B.L. Additional 15.580
Y = Trinity College Dublin 67 (A.I.5)
Z = Cambridge Univ. Libr. Ee.I.10

Titles

Brunner, Abriss der mittelenglischen Grammatik
Deanesly, The Lollard Bible
Forshall & Madden, The Holy Bible etc. (Oxford 1850)
Fowler, John Trevisa and the English Bible (Modern Philology 1960 : 2)
Fristedt, The Wycliffe Bible I—III (Stockholm Studies in English IV, XXI, XXVIII)
Fristedt, Articles in Stockholm Studies in Modern Philology 1956, 1960, 1964, 1968, 1972, 1976
Heyse-Tischendorf, Biblia Sacra Latina
Hudson, Selections from English Wycliffite Writings
Jordan, Handbuch der mittelenglischen Grammatik
Lindberg, MS Bodley 959 1—5 (Stockholm Studies in English VI, VIII, X, XIII, XX)
Lindberg, MS Christ Church 145 (Stockholm Studies in English XXIX)

504

Lindberg, The Manuscripts and Versions of the Wycliffite Bible (Studia Neophilologica 1970 : 2)

Lindberg, The Break at Baruch 3.20 in the Middle English Bible (English Studies 1979 : 2)

Lindberg, Who Wrote Wyclif's Bible? (Stockholm Studies in Modern Philology 1984)

Lindberg, The Vocabulary of Wyclif's Bible (Studia Neophilologica 1985 : 1)

Lindberg, The Language of Wyclif's Bible (Bamberger Beiträge zur Englischen Sprachwissenschaft 15)

Lindberg, Reconstructing the Lollard Versions of the Bible (Neuphilologische Mitteilungen; 1989 : 1)

McIntosh, Samuels, & Benskin, A Linguistic Atlas of Late Mediaeval English (Aberdeen Univ. Press)

505